The Little Lark Still Sings

the little LARK STILL SINGS

A True Story of Love, Change
& an Old Tuscan Farmhouse

VICTORIA SMITH

NEW YORK

LONDON • NASHVILLE • MELBOURNE • VANCOUVER

The Little Lark Still Sings

A True Story of Love, Change & an Old Tuscan Farmhouse

Published in New York, New York, by Morgan James Publishing. Morgan James is a trademark of Morgan James, LLC. www.MorganJamesPublishing.com

ISBN 9781631952197 paperback
ISBN 9781631952203 eBook
Library of Congress Control Number: 2020938582

Cover Design:
Rachel Lopez
www.r2cdesign.com

Interior Design:
Chris Treccani
www.3dogcreative.net

Cover and Author Photos:
Mikael Melbye

Lark Drawing:
Barry Svigals

Morgan James is a proud partner of Habitat for Humanity Peninsula and Greater Williamsburg. Partners in building since 2006.

Get involved today! Visit
MorganJamesPublishing.com/giving-back

For Larry

Love of my life and finest man I know.
Thank you for caring about my dreams
and making our marriage
a bold and romantic adventure.

"Nothing can be compared to the new life that the
discovery of another country provides for a thoughtful person.
Although I am still the same
I believe to have changed to the bones."

Johann Wolfgang van Goethe
THE ITALIAN JOURNEY, 1816

June 2006

When I turned sixty, I intended to throw away all my underwear, empty the drawers of my life, and start over with La Perla. I never bought the fancy lingerie, but we did buy an old stone farmhouse on a hillside of olive trees where I learned more about Italy, marriage, and myself than I ever imagined. Moving to a foreign country was far more revealing than La Perla ever would have been.

Dreams Can Be Unsettling

We have landed in Italy, but this is not vacation. On vacation we would collect our well-packed bags, breeze through airport exit doors, claim our rental car, don our sunglasses, and drive south to relax in our favorite Tuscan hilltown, Cortona. But this morning we claim two luggage carts and pile them high with four maximum weight suitcases, three bulging carry-ons, a bubble-wrapped antique sconce I insisted on safeguarding during the flight, and a cardboard box Larry locates in oversized baggage.

As of today, Italy is home.

For three years my husband and I have worked to make this move. Year one, we chose a town, bought an uninhabited farmhouse surrounded by abandoned olive trees, and hired an Italian architect. Year two, we collaborated with the architect on restoration plans, then waited months for township approvals. During year three, we visited as often as possible, watching with curious anticipation as our Tuscan home grew out of a near-ruin.

Back in Chicago, we took Italian lessons and did our homework. We sold our city condo overlooking Lake Michigan and sorted through belongings, putting each item in one of four piles: sea-container for Italy, long-term storage, giveaway, trash. We assembled documents required by Italian immigration law including proof of financial resources, fingerprinted FBI clearance, and international health insurance. After long applications and personal interviews, the Chicago Italian Consulate approved our visas to stay in Italy more than ninety days. Lastly, we said goodbye to three parents, five grown children and their families including five grandchildren, and thirty years of Chicago friends. Larry and I had retired and were reaching for our dream.

But dreams realized can be unsettling. Even now, in the Florence airport with luggage collected, our move to Italy feels like something in the future. Perhaps it's like this for everyone who yearns to live abroad, this disorientation when the day finally comes. I stand motionless in baggage claim, wondering what to do next.

"Let's go handle this box," Larry says, pushing his cart toward the sign for *Dogana*, Customs.

Trailing him with the second cart, I press the handlebar down with my right hand to unlock the brakes and hold my left hand atop the unstable stack. As I struggle to steer and keep up, my handbag slips off my right shoulder and lands on my bent elbow. I lose my grip, the handlebar pops up, and the cart jolts to a stop. Do I look as clumsy and conspicuous as I feel?

Larry is waiting at the customs counter. The stylish officer in his fitted blue uniform looks at Larry, then at me, and then at our luggage. He seems baffled. Larry gestures to the cardboard box and explains he wants to *pago la tassa*, pay the tax. The officer confers with his buddy nearby, then goes into an office partly visible through Venetian blinds and talks with a different agent inside. They rifle through a tall metal cabinet and our officer returns with a faded form.

Larry and I glance at one another. Can we be the first-ever foreigners to choose the Goods to Declare lane in the airport exit? We still need in-country approval for residency so would not even consider trying to sneak through with our brand new, high-tech sound system. Electronics are restricted imports in Italy, require customs tax even for personal use, and our box is not only big and new, the well-known American maker's logo is proudly printed on every panel.

Larry writes the details on the form: name, address, description of goods and cost. The officer does a quick calculation and scribbles our tax on the bottom line.

"*Cinquecentocinquanta euro,*" he says, five hundred fifty euros. I do the exchange in my head. Seven hundred dollars? Almost half the value?

Seeing my dismay, the officer strikes through "550" and writes "500".

"*Sconto,*" discount, he whispers, leaning toward me as though it's a personal favor. Larry steps between us, hands him the cash and takes our signed copy of the form, proof we complied with Italian law.

"I hope the cash goes to the right place," I murmur as we exit with our carts.

Larry frowns and looks down. "Shhh...."

We push our precarious cargo out of the air-conditioned terminal into the sun, across the bumpy pavement to the car rental kiosk, then down the cracked sidewalk to the gravel lot where we find our silver-gray Volvo SUV, and organize to fit our belongings inside. Larry does the loading. I open the doors to let out some heat, perch sideways on the front passenger seat, and think about what we're doing. This move to a foreign country is the boldest adventure of our married life and, though we expect it to be a dream come true, we cannot predict how it will turn out.

As we drive south on the A1 *autostrada* with cool air on full blast, I mentally retrace the evolution of this yearning. Our Italian honeymoon nineteen years ago exceeded our expectations. We're both romantics. We enjoy superb yet simple food, fine wines, Renaissance and religious art, opera, history, and adventure. We returned to Chicago exclaiming, "Italy has the best of everything we love!" For the next sixteen years, before each vacation, one of us would ask, "Should we go back to Italy or try somewhere new?" At least once each year, Italy won our votes. When we were visiting three times a year, Italy had won our hearts.

We decided to try living there for six months. For one long winter, Larry and I rented an apartment inside the walls of Cortona, a small medieval town where we had vacationed with friends years earlier, and had returned again and again.

That winter, we braved bitter winds whistling between ancient stone buildings, climbed steep stone streets, cooked in dented pans on a toy-sized gas stove, ate amazing dinners in barely-heated restaurants, and laughed out loud when our freshly-laundered garments froze on the pulley clothesline outside our kitchen window. In thirty Chicago winters, I had never felt so cold.

But there were sunny days, misty and atmospheric days, leisurely car trips to Siena, Orvieto and Assisi, all within an hour's drive, and easy train rides to Florence and Rome. Cortona had been eerily beautiful that winter, with church domes peeking through dense fog. Life moved more slowly. Conversations were completed. I stopped rushing.

New Year's Eve, held in *Piazza Signorelli*, one of Cortona's two main squares, was a family affair. The *Comune*, town government, provided endless bottles of Prosecco, Italian sparkling wine, and hilarious live entertainment. A few *Cortonesi* adopted us so warmly we forgot the cold. In all my life, I had never felt so alive.

Our decision to move to Italy was not running away. We had not lost jobs, split with a spouse or hoped to escape children or parents. Larry and I had met twenty-one years earlier and built a good marriage. He was and still is the most interesting man I've ever known. His penetrating eyes, pale blue with darker rims, disquieted me in our early conversations. He's six feet two, lean and blonde, with gorgeous long legs. His upper body is narrow, as if his Creator had held his shoulders and stretched his torso upward when he was being formed. He carries his left shoulder ever so slightly higher than his right. Except for an aquiline nose, his features are delicate, like English aristocracy. When he smiles, the corners of his eyes crinkle and his chin turns up, forming a shallow dimple in his chin. My heart had quickened when he smiled that way, especially when he smiled at me.

It was impossible for us not to meet. His oldest child, Angela, and my youngest, Amber, were best friends in fifth grade, so I knew him as Angela's dad long before I knew his name. One afternoon when Angela's dad came to pick her up, he told me a mutual friend, Joe, had suggested he talk with me about being a single parent. He was getting divorced and would have custody of his three children. I had been a single mom for thirteen years and quite liked it. The girls were playing in Amber's room, so I invited him in to chat right then and there. That afternoon, sitting on my living room sofa, I learned his name was Larry and that he was intense, smart, sensitive, and fascinatingly attractive.

Soon after, also thanks to Joe but unbeknownst to either of us, Larry and I were assigned to the same project for Kraft Foods. Larry, a Vice President at The Boston Consulting Group, was responsible for advising Kraft on business strategy. I worked for Needham, Harper & Steers advertising agency and led the team responsible for creating consumer demand. Before I knew Larry was on the project, our team had given it a code name to protect confidentiality: *Project Romance*. It was a market test of imported European cheeses, often called romance cheeses, under the Kraft brand.

Early in our work on *Project Romance*, Larry invited me for a sail on his boat, ostensibly to discuss advertising strategy. He brought a lovely plate of cheeses for us to sample as we sailed. About a mile off Chicago's shore, a gale kicked up, Larry sat on the cheese plate and I got seasick. He still insists he was impressed with the way I hung over the hull and heaved my guts into Lake Michigan. He says he fell in love with me that very afternoon, which he now claims was our first date. The market test failed, but our romance flourished.

Larry was and is a deep thinker. From the beginning, I admired the way he engaged new challenges, analyzing every detail. Only thirty-two years old when we met, he was already a partner in his consulting firm. He loved to study history, art and theology. Every morning, he got up at five-thirty to read. He compiled excerpts and quotes, reflections and observations in a growing document he labeled his *florilegium*, Latin for gathered flowers. Though an introvert, he had no fear of new experiences and encouraged me to seize the unknown, asking about my dreams, stretching and supporting me in ways that were new to me.

Like most women, even more than how he looked or acted, I loved how I felt about myself when I was with him. For the first time in years, I felt pretty, smart and playful. I charmed him, he said, insisting I was "the funniest girl," even though I'm not very humorous. He loved my voice and wouldn't hang up the phone when our conversations ended, lingering and listening to me breathe, and then murmuring more goodbyes until one of us finally broke the connection. He looked at me in a tender but searing way that made me feel desirable and desired. My blood raced when we were together and my heart became wax. He was cute, competent and committed, and not the least bit intimidated by my success or independence. He said I was the best thing that ever happened to him and I felt it was true. I loved feeling known, more deeply than anyone had ever known me, respected and valued.

When we married two years later, we were blissfully blind. We merged our families of five teenagers — four daughters and a son — a dog, two cats, a hamster and a fifty-gallon tank of fish. The pets were from my side, as Larry and his kids were allergic. We both had full custody with no relief, even for weekends. My former husband had remarried and moved to Florida; Larry's former wife took only one teen at a time. The early years were incredibly more difficult than we expected, but the kids endeavored to get along and the dog wooed Larry by curling up on his feet while he worked. By the time we considered retirement abroad, our kids were adults, some with kids of their own, and the pets were long gone.

Many of our reasons for moving to Italy were shared. We both wanted to experience living in a different culture while we were still healthy and energetic. But we had different dreams.

Larry thrives on the challenge of anything new and complicated. Living in a foreign country, learning a new language, restoring an ancient farmhouse with unfamiliar building techniques, materials and codes, and relying on a confusing and archaic banking system, would create a complex and compelling life for him. Once restored, our farmhouse on a hillside of olive trees would be an idyllic setting for reflection, contemplation and writing. He hoped to study, read and write without interruption. When we sent our belongings to the cargo ship, he announced he was not retiring, simply "shifting focus from clients to study – like a sabbatical." A natural scholar with many subjects on his list to explore, I doubted he would ever go back to gainful employment.

I longed to live closer to the land. My parents were from farm families. My father was a university professor, but his passions were growing and building things. Dad designed and built my childhood homes, one in Statesboro, Georgia, not far from Savannah, and one in Carbondale, Illinois, near the foothills of the Ozark Mountains. In both places we had land. In Statesboro, Dad grafted different colored camellia varieties onto the same bush. In Carbondale, he specialized in chrysanthemums and roses. He named his new chrysanthemum with straw-colored flowers Krista, after my very blond little sister. His favorite rose, Peace, was creamy yellow with pink-blushed petal edges, ironically cultivated in France just before World War II. Dad raised corn, tomatoes, eggplants, green peppers, melons, pears, strawberries, raspberries, honeybees, hunting dogs, barn cats, chickens, ducks, geese, and horses. He built a downsized, hip-roofed barn to shelter our horses, store the hay he grew and bailed, and protect his aging miniature John Deere tractor. Next to the barn was a pond with a white wooden dock he built for fishing. As an adolescent, I sat on that dock for hours, reading *The World Book Encyclopedia*, writing lovelorn poetry, and catching bluegill on a bamboo pole with a red and white bobber.

Mom was a homemaker in the best sense, turning Dad's houses into homes. She cooked, canned, pickled and froze Dad's produce and prepared the comfort foods he liked best. His favorites were chicken-fried round steak and coconut cream pie. I preferred her deep-fried eggplant, home-caught catfish, and hushpuppies. When my girlfriends spent the night, Mom insisted on fixing their favorite foods. She made my clothes and taught me to sew. She hung the laundry on a retractable clothesline in our back yard. Mom's giant white irises with yellow beards and exotic perfume were from her mother's beds, carefully cultivated to preserve the legacy. She loved caring for our family.

I was the oldest. Jim was born two years after me and Krista came seven years later. I adored my family, the land, and our gentle, rural yet intellectual life. At age eleven, I decided I must be the luckiest girl alive.

Now in Italy, nearly five decades later, I am still a farmgirl at heart. I dream of picking olives and pressing our own oil. I will cook in-season vegetables from local markets or my garden, and shop daily for fresh bread unless I decide to bake it. I'll make *marmellata* from the wild cherries, figs and plums on our land. And I will grow flowers and herbs that evoke aromas simply by their names: lavender, rose, jasmine, sage, rosemary, thyme, oregano, bay leaf, lemon verbena and mint.

In my mind, I can see the gardens at our Tuscan home. There, I'll write, play the piano, and learn to speak Italian by living life rather than studying a book.

While Larry continues to drive, I close my eyes, lean back in my seat, and take a long breath. Yesterday, my life was predictable. Today, I can't even imagine what tomorrow will bring.

First Glimpse

"What are you thinking about, my love, as you stare out that window instead of paying attention to me," Larry teases, pulling me back from my reverie. He looks across at me with a grin that lights up his face.

"Oh… just imagining life in Cortona," I say, smiling back.

Suddenly he grips the wheel and jerks his head left. Our SUV swerves as a black Mercedes sedan zooms past too fast and too close. Larry glares ahead as the car gets smaller and disappears.

"I hate the A1," he scowls. "It's a battleground. Seriously. Drivers are so aggressive it takes concentration not to get blown off the road."

He continues to grip the wheel and grimace. I think he may be over-reacting, but choose not to break the magic of our first day living in Italy. After an appropriate pause, I restart the conversation.

"How 'bout you?" I ask. "What were *you* thinking about while I was not paying enough attention to you?"

"Not much, just driving… wondering about the house, what life'll be like. Same as you, I suppose."

"Remember all those towns we tried?" I start to chatter nostalgically, loosening my seatbelt and turning toward him. "And the house we bought *four* times?"

Choosing the town had been a serious project for Larry. Ever the analyst, he studied the map, identified which Tuscan hilltowns had easy train access to Florence and Rome, were big enough to have good museums, restaurants and cultural events, and yet small enough to offer a simpler Italian lifestyle. He wanted our town to feel Italian and be run by Italians. Choices narrowed, we stayed in several towns for at least a week, looking at houses with agents and imagining life there. Only Volterra, with its rich history, excellent museums and wildly rugged landscape, rivaled Cortona.

I had endeavored to give Larry my open-minded participation. For me, the choice seemed obvious from the beginning. Since we'd made friends in Cortona and had returned again and again, I thought it was already our town in Italy.

Describing our dream house was easy, finding the right one was not. We wanted to live on a hillside with olive trees — secluded, yet close enough to walk to town. The house, preferably ancient and stone, could be small, but needed space for a good kitchen, guests and a piano.

Early in our search, we had been intrigued by a house near Cortona with a worn date of 15-something carved on an interior keystone. It had been a refuge for Franciscan monks as they walked from town to town, the representative had said. Excited, we agreed on a price and both parties signed the deal, sealed with an escrow check. Back in Chicago, we received word that they wanted more money. Each time we made yet-another agreement, usually for a higher price, we celebrated with a bottle of Prosecco. Not long after the fourth deal and fourth bottle, Mama accepted a handful of cash from a foreigner who came to her door with a lesser but immediate offer. Our deal was dead.

Our first lesson in Italian real estate was that it does not follow American rules. The more important lesson, we now know, was how naïve we were.

I'll never forget our first visit to the house we bought. A Cortona real estate agent, Lorenzo, had emailed photos of a stone farmhouse within walking distance of town. He was certain it was perfect for us. We looked at the photos, but concluded it was too small. Lorenzo urged us to reconsider. When we said our decision was final, he sold it to a couple from Rome.

When we visited four months later, Lorenzo, a native *Cortonese*, said he knew hundreds of properties and still believed this was our perfect home.

In his charming, lilting English, he said, "The owners think to make a few improvements, only to look better… then to sell. They improve nothing yet. I have the keys." He smiled impishly and dangled the keys. We agreed to go.

We took Lorenzo's car because, as he said, the house was impossible to find. After a hidden turnoff under a gigantic umbrella pine, the winding uphill lane seemed nearly impassable. From the long driveway, I peered ahead expectantly, but the house that emerged looked like a boring, single-story ranch.

Lorenzo rolled the car to a stop where the driveway petered out into a patch of weeds. By then, I could see the house had two stories, with a lower level built directly against the hill.

The main door was upstairs in the back. Cracked terracotta pots with dead geraniums flanked the door and the entry terrace was cheap industrial terracotta tiles. It was October. Crimson Virginia creeper dangled from the gutters, the only pretty thing about the place. A burned-out garage was on the terrace above.

Lorenzo unlocked the door, pushed it open, and motioned for us to enter. Once inside, I was even more disheartened. Everything, including the stone perimeter walls, had been slathered with whitewash. Whitewashed electrical cords, stapled to whitewashed plywood interior walls, ran up to bare bulbs and down to protruding outlet boxes — clearly not installed by professionals.

In contrast, the high ceilings with huge wood beams and terracotta tiles were nearly black, probably from centuries of smoke. A massive fireplace, the centerpiece of the main upstairs room, sat directly on the floor. The wood-beam mantle was held up by chiseled stone side pieces. One was broken, propped up with a wood stake.

"Let's look in here," Lorenzo said as he walked through a low doorway near the fireplace. We entered a modest-sized, corner room with two windows — we guessed a bedroom. It too had been whitewashed. Beyond this room was a long, narrow space containing a rusted shower stall, white enamel washtub on bent legs, and toilet with dirty standing water. I flushed the toilet to see if it worked.

Lorenzo led us back across the fireplace room to a smaller room on the opposite side. We guessed it was a second bedroom, but without a bathroom.

"This is a total gut," Larry said conclusively, standing in the central room and looking around. "The only thing worth saving is this fireplace."

No kidding, I thought silently.

"It is like a camp, but not a house," Lorenzo replied, "You will make it a home."

"Making *this* a home would be an enormous undertaking," I resisted. "And I'm not sure it would be worth it. It's even smaller than I thought and there are no closets."

"At least we won't pay for someone else's bad renovation," Larry said, already imagining the project and ignoring my obvious lack of enthusiasm.

"Ready to go downstairs?" Lorenzo asked, moving us along.

At a hole in the floor, he stopped and looked down.

"Is that the stairway?" I asked, stunned.

Lorenzo nodded and smiled, offering his hand to help me. My eyes narrowed in disbelief. I took his hand.

The ladder had planks, not rungs, and each plank had a half-circle cutout on alternating sides. If someone started on the correct foot, they could climb down more like stairs, pulling alternating feet through the cutouts. I went down backward, gripping the sides, but started on the wrong foot and had to switch. The cutouts helped.

Downstairs, Larry could barely stand.

"The ceiling is low because this was for animals, not people. In Tuscan farmhouses, the family lived upstairs and the animals below," Lorenzo explained.

"They must've had pigs and sheep, not cows or horses," Larry mused, ducking under low beams.

The floor was covered with tiles, but I could imagine dirt and dung under my feet. It smelled moldy and felt damp. Every wall was whitewashed stone. The central room had no natural light, only a solid wood door to the outside. A bare bulb hung from a beam.

Larry and I followed Lorenzo through a low, wide opening to another room we guessed was a living room. Whitewashed stone benches lined the back wall. Lorenzo explained they were originally mangers for feed, filled in and bricked over to use for seating or counters. In this room, a small high window and a side door with filthy glass panels let in some daylight.

On the other side of the central ladder room was a heavy curtain. Following Lorenzo, I held the dingy fabric back and stepped down into the worst kitchen I had ever seen or smelled. Putrid odors of decayed food, kerosene and mold made me turn my head and suck air through pursed lips, avoiding the full impact of the stench. The only window was small, with glass panels clouded by grime. Below the window, a stained enamel sink leaned on uneven legs. An under-counter refrigerator door hung open and a coffee pot sat on the warped wood counter above, frayed cord dangling to the floor. Across the back wall were more mangers, filled in, whitewashed and gray with soot. A potbellied stove next to the door was likely the source. I tried to discern if this cave-like room could become a modern kitchen and could not imagine it. As I retreated back past the curtain, I touched the whitewashed stone wall and a chunk fell off, exposing black mold beneath.

Larry and Lorenzo had already escaped to the front yard and were looking up at the front of the house when I joined them. I turned and saw it: two stories of gray-brown fieldstones. Not grand, yet stately. Three windows were evenly spaced on the upper floor, two doors and a small window on the ground floor, all with gray stone frames. Its simplicity was surprisingly elegant and inviting.

Like the back yard above, the front yard was dirt and weeds. Along the entire front edge, less than twenty feet from the house, was a tall, dense hedge of dark ivy enfolding the house and obscuring any view of the valley. I wondered what happened in that hidden yard that required such privacy.

Despite the small size and crumbling condition of the house, we were enchanted. The *posizione,* position, was *squisita,* exquisite, Lorenzo said. *Posizione* in Italy is as important as location, location, location in America. He assured us we could walk to Cortona in under thirty minutes, rare for country houses. The property was steep and terraced with over a hundred olive trees, two streams and dense forests. The land, long abandoned, could be reclaimed into productive olive groves, and landscaping would transform the house.

"The house's name is *La Lodolina*," Lorenzo explained as we walked back to his car. He said that in pre-postal times, before houses had numbers, even the most modest Tuscan houses had names. How egalitarian, I thought. Tenant farmers lived in homes with names.

"A *lodola* is a lark, so *lodolina* means little lark," he continued, opening the car door for me. "This hillside is known for songbirds, especially larks."

That evening Lorenzo sent me an internet link to the song of the *lodola*. I listened over and over, imagining waking up to those melodious warbles, trills, and chirps. In Romeo and Juliet, Shakespeare calls the lark the "herald of the morn," because its song marks the new day. Francis of Assisi felt a special kinship to the lark because of its plain brown cape and hood, humble manner, and love for singing. Then I read that male and female larks have no real color differences and are monogamous. I was smitten.

We went for a second visit, accompanied by Francesco, an Italian architect who spoke English, and learned what *La Lodolina* could become. He believed the burned-out garage could be converted into a guesthouse. Tuscan law does not allow any increase in cubic meters of old structures, so the garage volume was *molto importante*. Upstairs in the main house, Francesco suggested combining the fireplace room with the smaller bedroom to make a large, open study-library-sitting area, adjacent to a single bedroom and bath. Upstairs would become our private space for working, reading, watching television and sleeping, warmed by glowing fires in winter.

Using modern building techniques to control humidity, Francesco said we could enlarge the downstairs rooms by incorporating into the house the *scannafosso*, the air passage between the house and the hill, traditionally used to control dampness. That meant the kitchen could be larger, we could have a small laundry area and powder room, and there would be space in the living room for my piano.

Importantly, he was confident we could get permission to lower the ground floor by digging into the hillside to create sufficient ceiling height.

"To feel more free," Francesco had said, taking an expansive breath and opening his arms toward the ceiling. Two inches taller than Larry, Francesco could not extend his arms upward because the overhead beams were too low.

Larry and I immediately went back to Lorenzo.

"You were right," Larry told him, "The house is perfect for us. We should have listened to you months ago."

We then learned our second lesson in Italian real estate: listen to local experts. The new owners increased the price by one hundred thousand euros without making one improvement except the whitewash. They would not budge. We paid.

The purchase was not difficult. There were no restrictions against foreigners owning property. After a local lawyer reviewed the contract, we went to the formal closing accompanied only by our agent, Lorenzo. Stefano, the *Notaio*, a combination lawyer-accountant-notary representing both parties, handled the proceedings flawlessly. Ilena, a caramel-voiced Canadian, read the contract aloud, translating the twelve pages of small type into English. Oral reading was a legal requirement to be certain both parties understood what they were signing, a law to protect anyone illiterate or foreign.

The sale was concluded with multiple signatures, a flurry of rubber stamps pounded onto the pages, vigorous handshakes and lots of kisses. It was a uniquely Italian experience, lasting hours and followed by a long, celebratory dinner.

Step by step over nineteen years, from honeymooners to homeowners, we were taking root in a foreign country. Once we owned the property, we fantasized about the house and our future Italian life. We worked diligently with Francesco on plans for renovation, *ristrutturazione,* which he reviewed with the *Comune* and submitted for approvals. After very few modifications, building permits were issued and demolition began. Scaffolding surrounded the exterior, the roof was removed, and the interior nearly gutted, saving only the fireplace, some interior stone walls, and the three-foot-thick exterior walls.

"We have opened the heart," Francesco warned when the roof came off. "Now we must do the surgery."

It was an enormous project. Every fragment that could be reused was saved. For anything new, we went on fieldtrips with Francesco to Tuscan artisan workshops. We relished every minute and every mile.

"There it is!" Larry says, lifting his chin toward a distant hill and again drawing me back to the present. One of us always says, "There it is!" when we first see Cortona.

Dusty yellow stucco and gray-brown stone houses with faded tile roofs nestle against the hillside, spreading like a bird's wing across the lush green slope. As we get closer, domes, bell towers, and a lone umbrella pine create a jagged silhouette against a cobalt sky. At the summit, a bell tower and corner ruin of an ancient fortress stand guard. Bathed in sunlight, Cortona looks like one of those storybook towns vacationers wistfully observe from the window of a speeding train.

Snaking up Cortona's hill, we pass *Santa Maria della Grazie al Calcinaio*, a landmark cathedral, active for nearly five hundred years. As we curve up and around the ancient gray stone structure, I open my window to breathe fresh hillside air, truly different than Chicago air, and admire the church's perfect Renaissance symmetry and weathered gray metal dome.

Nearing the city walls, bells ring from the *centro*, city center, calling the faithful to Sunday morning *Messa*, Mass. I so hope we hear church bells at Lodolina.

We skirt the city walls with their massive Etruscan stone foundations from as early as 700BC, and take a single-lane blacktop road along the ridge overlooking the vast Chiana Valley. The road was once a Roman road, we have been told. During the Middle Ages, the valley below was a malaria-infested swamp, but today it's the most fertile farmland in Tuscany. Looking south we see part of *Lago Trasimeno*, Lake Trasimeno, mostly hidden by the hill where Hannibal defeated the Romans in 217BC.

"To think… this will be our drive to town. Every day. So much history," I marvel.

Larry inhales slowly, deeply. "Less than ten minutes and we're home. Are you ready for our new life?"

My eyes open extra wide at such a big question. I guess it is a new life, certainly a new *way* of life. I wonder if Larry was reading my mind earlier when I felt disoriented, or if he has similar mixed feelings of apprehension and excitement. Life is funny that way, giving us opposing feelings and letting us wonder which will become true.

Though I can't predict how, so early in our adventure, I sense our move to a foreign country, without friends or family, will change us — individually and as a couple. I expect our new life to be fascinating and our marriage to deepen, but this is an adventure. There are no guarantees on adventures.

The Hidden Door

Am I ready for our new life?

"Wow, that's a big question," I reply, catching my breath. This is not something to take lightly. "Yes… I think so. Are *you*?"

Larry nods; his eager schoolboy expression charms me.

His query makes me thankful our marriage is solid. A new life is a serious undertaking, and marriages, like these old buildings, need diligent tending. If it has a solid foundation plus loving upkeep, the structure stays strong and can support new endeavors. If crevices are ignored, the structure deteriorates. It's a major project to restore anything left untended — houses and relationships.

I'm curious to see how we have changed *La Lodolina*, but I'm even more curious to see how *La Lodolina* will change us.

Larry eases the Volvo SUV down a steep, cypress-lined curve above *Il Palazzone*, literally the big palace. Its massive stone tower has dominated and defined our side of the Cortona hill since the Renaissance. Crowned with a double row of swallowtail crenellations, cutouts allowing marksmen to shoot but not be shot, this majestic tower's true function was to impress. Its construction was started around 1520, long after noble families needed watch towers for protection from invaders.

Cardinal Silvio Passerini built *Il Palazzone* as a summer palace — with twelve decorative-only fireplaces — to proclaim his noble position. Appointed by his life-long friend, Giovanni di Medici (Pope Leo X), Silvio became governor of Florence, Bishop of Cortona, papal finance commissioner, and a Cardinal. Mostly due to the wealth Silvio accrued, the palace remained a Passerini family residence for four hundred fifty years, until 1974 when

Count Lorenzo Passerini and his wife Lyndall donated the palace and its contents to the *Scuola Normale Superiore di Pisa* for use as a conference center.

Immediately below *Il Palazzone*, Larry turns onto a country lane nearly hidden between a soaring umbrella pine on the right and an ancient stone wall as tall as our SUV on the left. On the top corner of the wall stands a tiny shrine encasing a blue-and-white glazed tile of the Virgin Mary and Child. A cluster of wilting wildflowers is tucked inside.

His side mirror brushes blackberry brambles, iris blades, ferns, ivy, and red poppies, all clinging to the ancient wall. To our right are a dozen rows of well-tended grape vines, a farmer's family vineyard. Down the hill, as far as I can see, are terrace after terrace of silvery olive trees. And at the bottom of the hill is *La Pieve di San Michele Arcangelo*, my favorite neighborhood church. Lombard Christians built it in the seventh century on the ruins of a Roman temple. It was renovated around 1000 and declared a *Monumento Nazionale* in 1907. A parish church for over a thousand years, services are still held most Sundays and the exquisitely unadorned sanctuary has become a frequent choice for weddings.

"Larry… listen," I say in a hushed tone.

Frowning, he whispers, "To what?"

"Except for the birds and our car, there's *no* sound."

Larry chuckles and steadies the wheels. We know this bad road all too well, having driven it dozens of times in the past three years, but we've never attempted it with such a big car or heavy load. He accelerates and skids around the first uphill turn. A dust cloud rises from tires spinning on loose gravel over dirt. This *strada bianca*, white road, as these country lanes are called, is a rutted, rocky trail, more like the set for a Jeep commercial than a proper road. Spring rains have left gullies and heavy construction vehicles have not helped. Larry presses up the hill and rounds the top curve cautiously, our car bouncing from side to side as it crawls over bedrock jutting into the road. I brace one hand against the dashboard and hold the door grip with the other.

At the top is an ancient lichen-splotched stone wall and, above the wall, a hunter's stone cottage. The trunks of three cypress trees, planted too close to the tiny structure decades ago, encase the edges of flat roof stones in a row of toothless grins.

"This is worse than ever!" Larry says, now squinting. "Once Lodolina is done, the builders must work on this road. We've got to get it back to pre-construction condition, which was bad enough. This is absurd."

After a flat stretch of another hundred yards, we turn right and slightly downhill onto a newly-graveled lane through a small forest. Our driveway.

Overhead, tree branches create a sparse canopy. Since I was a girl in Georgia, I've dreamed of having a driveway with a leafy canopy like Tara in *Gone with the Wind*. I'm sitting tall now, barely breathing. My earlier apprehension has vanished and I feel only joy and wonder. Flowering wild *ginestra* bushes, broom in English, grace the edge of the lane with bright yellow bouquets, welcoming summer and, I want to believe, Lodolina's new residents. I take it all in like it's my first visit instead of my hundredth. I hope it's always new for me. Our car crawls in slow motion, my eagerness stretching time like a child waiting for Christmas morning.

Larry and I have visited every couple of months since construction began. The last visit was February, four months ago, our longest lapse. Francesco sent weekly email reports with photos to keep us up to date, but absorbing the real thing with my own eyes will be different than viewing parts and angles on a laptop screen. I stare ahead, but cannot see the house.

Where a trickle of water from a spring uphill makes a little ditch across our driveway, the forest opens to a vista of terraced olive trees and the blue haze of the distant valley. Here our driveway widens and the house starts to emerge. Yet my eyes are drawn, not to views of the valley or to Lodolina's restored rooftop, but to piles of building materials lining both sides of the driveway for at least thirty yards. Half-used pallets of roof tiles, terracotta blocks, small wood beams, bright blue and red plastic conduit, flat roof stones, stacks of field rocks and heaps of rubbish have been here since construction began, but we assumed they'd be removed by today. Disappointments always come from unmet expectations, and this one takes us by surprise.

"What a mess!" Larry blurts, as he slows the SUV. "Did you expect *this*?"

"Of course not. It's awful." I'm not sure if he's upset with the situation or with me. His tone says I should have warned him. Though he thrives on adventure, Larry does not do well with disorder.

For a fleeting instant, I wonder if we've made a mistake. Our life in Chicago was calm, organized and interesting; our home finished and furnished. I recall the day Larry suggested we try living in a foreign country. We'd relocated to the city only seven months earlier from a pristine northern suburb along Lake Michigan. Larry had wanted to move to the city for years. We designed our ideal urban home in a new, mid-rise condominium overlooking Lincoln Park and Lake Michigan. I thought moving to the city would satisfy his need for diversity and stimulation. But soon he was itching to move on. I, like most women, need my nest.

"Tell me where you most want to live," I had pleaded. "You can choose the location. We'll build our dream house and I'll make it home. Just tell me where."

He paused for a long, pensive moment and said, "Wherever we're not."

It was supposed to be a joke, but in every bit of teasing is a little bit of truth.

"Wherever we're not" has become one of those iconic phrases we replay as we try to explain to friends and family why we're moving so far away. Larry loves change and the challenge of wherever we're not.

My sincerest dream for our new life in Italy is that Larry is happy here. If he is, I can be. But if he is not, it will be a long summer and a costly experiment. In a real marriage, unless each spouse is happy, neither can be. We're still in the car and he's already agitated.

"Let's hope it's not this bad inside," he adds with more than a hint of sarcasm as he turns off the engine. We pause for a few moments.

Francesco is standing at the end of the driveway, grinning and waving with his wife, Rita, and architect-associate, Gabriele. Francesco had insisted we call when we landed in Florence. He said he wanted to guide our first inspection of Lodolina and, I suspect, explain a few things. Since he was kind enough to come on a Sunday morning, we suggested his wife join him. Gabriele, who has managed every phase of our project, wouldn't miss today either.

When we first met Francesco three years ago, we had been impressed with his creativity and knowledge, thankful for his good English, delighted by his humor, and valued his desire to listen, consider our concerns and ideas and, without ego, design a better solution. I thought he was strikingly handsome, unusually tall for an Italian with broad shoulders, thick wavy black hair, searching dark eyes and a winsome smile. When I asked him why we should hire him, he said, playfully but not in jest, "Because I am clever." Indeed, in addition to many other qualities, he has been very clever. It has been a charmed alliance, one Larry and I hope will blossom into a lasting friendship.

"Francesco should have been clever enough to hide these piles," I say to commiserate, "or tell us to expect a mess."

Looking at the bigger picture, Larry softens, "It's his only transgression in three years. I'll bet it's all gone in a couple of weeks, at least before we move in."

I silently disagree about the piles being gone soon, but this is not a time for voicing doubt. Larry looks at me, smiles, squeezes my hand in solidarity, opens his car door and says, "Let's go see our new home."

The materials unmentioned, we greet our welcoming party warmly, lightly gripping right hands as we lean forward to brush-kiss both cheeks, Italian style.

"*Piacere*," I say to Rita, who I have never met. A pleasure.

Turning to Francesco for reassurance, I ask, "So! Lodolina is ready for us?"

"Yes, but of course. You will see," he replies, assured but modest, and gestures toward the house with his open hand, inviting me to go first.

I walk in anticipation, almost dancing down the driveway. Larry reaches to take my hand, probably to slow me down. I want to run ahead, but restrain my exuberance to remain part of the group. Stopped by the chain-link and orange plastic safety fence still surrounding the construction area, I peer inside. What I see makes me lower my expectations even more. Francesco unlocks the padlock and pulls the metal gate open enough for us to enter one by one.

The back yard is uneven dirt littered with rocks, broken roof tiles, a flattened cardboard box, bits of wire, pieces of conduit, wood scraps, and cigarette butts. There is a deep excavation surrounding the half-built guesthouse. Orange safety fences are everywhere. I glance at Larry, whose eyes have widened.

Toward the valley, a rusty corrugated-metal tool shed leans right. When I tilt my head in the same direction, Francesco explains. "It blew over in a strong wind in March, after you were here. The workers needed a place to protect their tools, so they pushed it back up. It is still a little… leaning."

"Like in Pisa," he adds, an ironic reference to the elegant Leaning Tower.

We step gingerly through the rubble to a narrow concrete slab along the back of the house. Originally this entry terrace was covered with broken tiles; now it's newly poured concrete. My imagination starts to compensate. One must hold fast to dreams when reality is unpleasant. I imagine handmade terracotta tiles on the slab and, against the wall, three pots of waxy-leafed lemon trees with sweet white blossoms and ripening yellow fruit. I envision a grassy lawn, roses in bloom, jasmine climbing the stone walls, and an herb garden. Looking at the current scene, I wonder how long it will be before Lodolina has a level backyard without debris, to say nothing of a lawn or landscaping. I may need my imaginary gardens for a while.

Francesco's voice reminds me of the reason we are here. "For the first opening of the hidden door," he says in his endearing way. He puts his hand in his pocket like reaching for a treasure and ceremoniously offers Larry the key.

The hidden door, upstairs and on the back of the house, is tucked into a vestibule that, before our renovation, had been a family's wood-burning oven. An outside oven, *forno*, was typical in Tuscan homes before electricity or indoor gas. Francesco suggested we move the back door there for privacy and create a small vestibule with a roof.

"I am so curious to see your face," he whispers to me.

Before inserting the key, Larry pauses to run his hand over the thick chestnut planks in the new-but-traditional double door and admire the hand-chiseled ribbing on the new-but-traditional doorframe of *pietra serena*. This dove-gray sandstone is ubiquitous throughout Italy as church columns, streets and sidewalks, as well as window and door frames in grand palaces and modest farmhouses.

Gabriele snaps photos as he has throughout *la ristrutturazione*. Francesco's firm must have thousands of Lodolina photographs. Someday I'll put the best in an album, but today I'm focused on what's behind that door.

As Larry inserts the key, I place my hand over his to share the significance. He looks down with that smile I love, his chin dimpled in delight. Every marriage is made richer by creating iconic moments to cherish. I sense this "first opening of the hidden door" will become one of our moments, like "wherever we're not." Simple, meaningless phrases in the abstract, they represent milestones in our union.

I wish Larry held a big iron *chiave* of centuries past, instead of a small stainless-steel key. He turns it several times, rolling back interior bolts to release the door's modern, secure locking system. He gently pushes both doors open wide, then moves aside for me to enter first. I have the sense of stepping into our future — elated, but tentative, unable to predict what life at Lodolina will bring.

For the first time, I see the walls of pale peach hand-troweled plaster called *grassello di calce*, the ceiling with massive axe-hewn chestnut beams, floors of handmade rose terracotta tiles, all one soothing earth-toned palette. I take in the overall effect, then walk forward so others can follow.

"It is perfect… just perfect," I whisper to Francesco, who is grinning broadly. We have seen all the elements arranged on a table in his studio, but not installed. They integrate better than I had imagined.

An elegant arch soars overhead in the center of the main upstairs room. We didn't want an arch; Lodolina is too rustic. But the *Comune,* township, said they would not issue building permits unless we added an arch as a "reading key" to show that what we now call the sitting room had been two separate rooms. It will be Larry's office, a library, our television room, and an overflow sleeping area for grandchildren.

"I'm so glad the *Comune* insisted on the arch. Look at it!" Larry says. The curve draws our eyes upward to the chestnut beams and bestows this simple farmhouse with unexpected grace.

I open a window, pulling both sides toward me like little doors, and push the solid chestnut shutters outward, flat against the exterior stone. Light floods in, magnifying the textures. The walls look like flesh-colored suede.

I glance at Rita and wonder if she interprets our body language and voice tone even though she doesn't understand our words. She silently walks to a different window and opens it. By her clothing, manner and direct gaze, I surmise she has a curious mind, a strong sense of style, and some interesting opinions. But today she stays respectfully in the background. I wish I knew what she is thinking.

Lodolina's transformation is remarkable. After one year of planning, three months for permissions, and thirteen months of construction, this space — once inhabited by a farmer, his family and their livestock — has new life, ready for our new life. It is rebuilt, re-wired, re-plumbed, re-walled, re-poured, re-roofed, re-plastered, re-trimmed and re-finished. The foundation has been reinforced and every crevice mended. It even smells new.

"They buy a pod and make a butterfly," the geologist said when he came to inspect for seismic regulations to insure Lodolina can withstand an earthquake. He told Francesco that he had known this house for much of his life. We were touched when he described our renovation as the metamorphosis from cocoon to butterfly.

"Larry, look at the fireplace. It's clean… and fixed," I say.

The original *pietra serena* surround has been cleaned just enough. I love its chips and worn places that indicate age, more apparent since the grimy soot is gone.

Larry turns every iron latch on every window and shutter, pushing each wide open. A gentle breeze comes from the valley, surprising me on this still, scorching day. I lean out of a window to look all directions. Each vista is a postcard of Tuscan landscape. Larry squeezes in beside me, turning sideways since the window is not wide enough for two. I hear a tractor in the distance.

"The views are breathtaking," I murmur, as though seeing them for the first time.

To the left, at the top of Cortona's hill, stands a fragment of the stone *fortezza*, a Renaissance fortress with Etruscan foundations. About a third of the way down, a line of cypress trees encircles the hill. Six hundred *cipressi* were planted, one for each *Cortonese* soldier killed in World War I. Imagine, a town of less than five thousand residents losing six hundred men and boys in their prime. Most of a generation. The cypress-lined road is officially *Viale Passerini,* named for the noble family that built *Il Palazzone,* but townspeople call it *Via della Rimembranza,* Road of Remembrance. The cypress trees stand like soldiers, fifty feet tall, resolutely guarding their beloved town.

Near the *fortezza,* but beyond our view, reigns *La Basilica di Santa Margherita,* the church dedicated to Cortona's patron saint. At the front altar, Margherita's eight-hundred-year-old shriveled body is on display in a glass and silver case. In a side chapel, the names of the six hundred fallen soldiers are hand-painted, grouped by neighborhood. It is haunting to recognize surnames of people we know: Ghezzi, a local realtor and friend; Nocentini, owner of the town's bookstore; Magini, the family from whom we rented our apartment that first winter in Cortona; Lovari, our builder-friend who keeps local monasteries and churches in good repair; and Rossi, a Cortona artist who carves exquisite sculptures in exotic woods.

Only one generation after the losses of The Great War, we've been told that occupying Nazis during World War II imposed a brutal retaliation: ten locals for each German killed. When a German soldier was killed near Cortona, Nazi soldiers lined up ten schoolboys before a firing squad. A local priest stood in front of them, saying, "If them, first me." The firing squad backed down.

Larry and I see elderly priests in town and wonder who was the hero. When I asked an Italian friend which priest saved the boys, she said tenderly, "Many Fathers did that. I do not know which one you mean." The wars are not only a part of Cortona's history; they inhabit *Cortonesi* hearts today.

Still leaning out the window, but alone because everyone else has vanished, I look to my right, directly into two cypress trees — the same size as those along the road — and wonder if they were planted in memory of farmers' sons lost in the war.

Beyond our *cipressi* is a long valley bordered by the foothills of *San Egidio,* one of the tallest mountains in Tuscany. The forested foothills fade one into the other, each more mysteriously hazy than the one before.

Across the stream, yet with intimate closeness, is a hillside of meticulously tended olive trees. Some terraces still have stone retaining walls. Three widely-spaced stone farmhouses are partially hidden by trees and shrubbery. Rising above the crest is the sagging roofline of a long-abandoned *casa padronale*, landowner's house. Once important but deteriorating for decades, it'll be a monumental project to restore. Near the bottom of this hill is a stone arch, perhaps once a small chapel, now mostly a pile of rocks overgrown with bushes.

High on a more distant hill stands a grand hunting lodge, a three-story, yellow stucco villa, built in the Renaissance by five leading families of Cortona. Locals say those families were so wealthy they could ride their horses from that lodge to Florence, seventy miles, and never leave their own properties.

I am struck by the sheer beauty of this land and want to linger at the window taking in every leaf and stone, but the others have gone outside.

"Aren't you ready?" Larry urges, calling me from the hidden door.

"Sure..." I say reluctantly, glad we'll move in soon and I can take my time.

"We must go downstairs by the outside," Francesco says when I join them. "You will see why."

Larry, Francesco, Rita, Gabriele and I step back through the debris and walk in single file down a dirt construction ramp at the side of the house. The front yard is like the back: dust and rubble. The old ladder, once the only stairs, is on the ground half-covering an empty cement bag. I make a mental note to rescue it.

From the lower level, Lodolina's façade looks renewed, yet still stately. Scaffolding, surrounding the house for a year, is finally gone. Cleaning the stones, repairing patches, re-grouting and tuck-pointing was a *grande lavoro*, a big work, workmen told us.

By law, exteriors in our area must not change. We were not allowed to add openings, enlarge doors or windows, change the stonework, or alter any positions. Fortunately, there is great care to preserve the authenticity of Tuscan farmhouses, especially in Cortona's *Belle Arti* area that includes our hillside.

Turning the same stainless-steel key, Larry unlocks the downstairs front door, now our main door for guests. This time I simply watch, standing close.

"Shall I carry you across the threshold?" Larry whispers as he looks up, his twinkling blue eyes and boyish smile tempting me.

"You missed your opportunity upstairs," I purr. It would not be pretty to have him try to lift me, especially with an audience. Since he's not serious, neither of us is at risk.

Downstairs, like upstairs, Francesco has attended to every detail and the quality of the workmanship is superb. We remove our shoes and step on sheets of styrofoam, strategically placed across freshly waxed rose terracotta tiles.

The ceiling height feels expansive with the floor lowered a meter, roughly forty inches, giving us the breathing space Francesco promised. We were told workers burned out two jackhammers on the *pietra serena* bedrock under our home. I reach for, but can no longer touch, the beams.

The new stairway is missing three bottom steps. Francesco explains he left it unfinished so the workmen's boots would not ruin the chestnut planks.

"We install the day you move in, no sooner," he assures us. Now I understand why we walked down the outside ramp.

In my new kitchen, now on the same level as the other rooms, I turn slowly and blissfully dream of the stirring and peeling and slicing and dicing and spicing and chopping and cooking and baking and tasting and chatting and adjusting flavors that will come. I will prepare celebratory dinners for friends, cheerful family lunches, and romantic evenings for two. The room is empty except for a new corner fireplace awaiting a fire and pan of roasting chestnuts. The mantle is a former ceiling beam, and the hearth and surround are re-claimed *pietra serena* doorframes. Next week, modern Italian cherry cabinets, lighter than American cherry but characteristically reddish, will arrive and *pietra serena* counter-tops come soon after. Then, appliances can be installed. Empty, my new kitchen looks enormous.

"Wow, so different. I still remember the stench," I say, wrinkling my nose.

"It is a miracle the workers have done so much so fast, without loss in quality," Francesco replies, pleased that after only thirteen months of construction, even with the surprises that always happen in old farmhouses, Lodolina is ready for us.

Lodolina's biggest surprise was the collapse of a thick interior stone wall we wanted to highlight as an architectural feature. When the workers started to clean it, instead of a solid wall they discovered two thin stone walls stacked directly on the earth, the middle filled with mud. No wonder Lodolina had seemed dank and moldy. That wall had been soaking up ground water for centuries.

Despite the wall collapse and a few minor setbacks, the entire project was on time and on budget, a remarkable feat. Francesco has good reason to feel pleased.

Eleven days from today, ten working days and a Sunday, our sea-bound belongings arrive and we move in. Francesco says it's enough time to finish.

He reviews the *programma*, a dizzying list. He knows every step and seems confident. I am less so, but take him at his word. As long as our furniture and boxes can be delivered, we'll be okay with whatever small things need to be finished while we settle in. I anticipate the chaos will be challenging, especially for Larry. Rebuilding Lodolina has been a joy so far, but we have not been living in it. I'm so eager to move in, I wouldn't consider putting it off one day more than essential.

"We know we may be camping for a while," I try to reassure Francesco. He nods, but does not smile. He knows us well by now and may doubt our ability to cope comfortably with what lies ahead.

After a three-hour tour, our welcoming party leaves us to explore privately. Larry and I stand in every room again, imagining our furniture and our future. We hold hands or lean together arm-in-arm, chat, and take it all in.

We arrange and rearrange belongings in our imaginations and mostly agree on where things should go. Then, we walk our property. We own, *possediamo* — a word I never expected in my Italian vocabulary — three hectares, almost seven acres. The terraced hillside is buzzing with life, in contrast to the dry dirt and debris around the house. Insects float up from the tall grass as we disturb their rest with our strides. Grasshoppers arc away from us, like an unsynchronized modern dance, and smaller bugs flit around our legs, then settle as we pass.

Our olive trees are covered with tiny flower buds like clusters of seed pearls ready to burst open. Scarlet poppies, tiny white daisies, deep purple alpines and hyacinths, golden *ginestra* and countless other wildflowers decorate the olive terraces. We walk slowly, luxuriating in the chirping of crickets, trills and warbles of songbirds, and the earthy perfume of the land.

As we climb back up the hill, the Tuscan sun drops behind the ridge above the house. Together we close and latch the windows, leaving the shutters open. Workers will be here at eight in the morning and there's nothing inside to steal.

My excitement is greater now than when we arrived. It's hard to lock the door behind us, but we must drive to the hotel, check in, unpack our bags, clean up and then go into Cortona, our new hometown, for dinner. Without anything to eat since breakfast on the plane, I'm suddenly starving.

Cleaned up, parked and climbing up *Via Guelfa* into Cortona, Larry stops to let me catch up. He's eager to say hello to Marco, our friend and the eldest son in the family that owns *Molesini Enoteca*. The stone street is steep and I struggle to breathe.

"Go ahead," I say, panting. "I'll meet you. I just can't climb it without stopping."

Larry, the triathlete, swiftly makes it to the top. As I join the boys in the wine shop, Marco teases me about my shortness of breath. "She will improve," he says.

Dinner is at *Pane e Vino*, our favorite *taverna*, specializing in natural wines from smaller vineyards and local foods, especially dried meats and cheeses. Greeting us warmly, Arnaldo, the owner, declares, "Today you become *Cortonesi*. From now, we speak only Italian." Good to his word, there is no more English from him for the entire meal.

We devour wild boar sausages and vegetables under oil, including thin, green ones called *barba dei frate*, monk's beard. Arnaldo chooses a superb wine. The warm peach tart makes me long for a completed kitchen where I can bake.

"Did you like the chocolate truffles I left for you," I ask. When he doesn't react, I add, "In February? For Valentine's?" Arnaldo lights up, remembering.

"Especially Deborah," he says, "She likes very much the chocolate." Ah, a lapse into English for the compliment.

Last February, when we were in Cortona, I brought homemade chocolate truffles to give to people who had been especially kind to us, including Arnaldo and Deborah. They were on holiday, so I had left my small gift at the restaurant.

Leaving *Pane e Vino* about midnight, we're surprised to see a crowd watching big screen television outside the bar next door. Bystanders in the piazza crane to see through pots of tall, pink-flowering oleander surrounding the bar's outdoor seating. Everyone cheers wildly, stomping and yelling. We wonder what could provoke such energy so late, but we're too tired to stick around to figure it out.

"*Buona notte*, my love," Larry says as we fall into bed. "This was a good day. I like our house. I like the choices we made, the quality of the work, the beauty of the land, the history of our valley, our new hometown... everything about it."

"Me, too. I like our new life, at least the first day of it. Mostly, I like you and that we're doing this together. *Sogni d'oro*," dreams of gold, I murmur, wishing him the Italian equivalent of sweet dreams.

Exhaustion compounded by excitement precludes sleep, so I lie awake, look out of the hotel window at the distant lights of Cortona on the hilltop, and think about our unfolding dream. We're surrounded by history, more than ever in our lives. Our new home is hundreds of years old, built of hillside stone by a tenant farmer whose family slept above their livestock and gave half of everything they produced to the landowners. Our new hometown, a community for three-thousand years, still provides its families a haven of protection where children grow, learn and are safe. We drive on Roman roads, now blacktopped, and look at Hannibal's hill.

In addition to the land's history, into our new life Larry and I each bring our personal histories: childhood memories, successes and failures in school and career, failed prior marriages, relationships with parents, children, grandchildren and friends, our marital exchanges over nineteen years, and our individual passions, hopes and dreams. These histories will shape our future, even more than the history that surrounds us.

We like to think we start new experiences with clean slates, but slates are never clean — and wherever we go we drag ourselves along. Larry and I cannot predict this new chapter, but we do know that life here will be different than the one we left in America. This is a bold move, reaching for a dream, and it started today. No wonder my mind is churning and I am sleepless.

I recall a poem I wrote when I was sixteen, about searching for perfect love. I now know it was about more than romance.

> *Ecstasy is reaching out again and again*
> *with no fear of letting go,*
> *for it's the only way I'll ever know*
> *when I'm holding it in my hand.*

I still want to reach for ecstasy, realistic but unafraid to take on the unpredictable.

It's been a monumental day, our first day living on foreign soil. Larry inhales rhythmically, peacefully. I'm glad he's resting; tomorrow will be demanding. I count backwards from one-hundred in Italian to focus my brain and stop the inner chatter. *Cento, novantanove, novantotto, novantasette…*

The Art of Slowing Down

Thanks to jet lag, we awaken early and have time for a leisurely *Il Falconiere* breakfast. The hotel terrace is like a movie set, the service impeccable yet personal, and the breakfast feast exceeds my most-excellent food imagination. It's the perfect way to begin the second morning our new Italian life.

First to arrive, we choose a table on the terrace overlooking a nearby vineyard, the vast Chiana Valley, and distant purple mountains silhouetted against the horizon. Iron chairs with thick cushions and wide arms are perfect for slow dining and long lingering. White-linen draped tables are set with daintily-flowered china. Waiters glide from table to table. I feel more like a princess being wooed by her prince charming than a jet-lagged American wife on her way to a construction site.

We enjoy our first cappuccino. For me, the thick creaminess of steamed milk, dense and velvety but never stiff, gently poured into intense, rounded, never bitter espresso is one of life's most restorative morning pleasures. We've spent years perfecting our at-home *cappuccini*. Almost in unison, we push aside packets of *zucchero* left beside our cups.

At *Il Falconiere, la colazione* is a grand buffet served in the *limonaia*, a glass room for wintering potted lemon trees. Food is arranged on multiple, linen-draped levels on an oval table in the center of the room. Irresistible for me are the savory dried meats and cheeses, including tiny balls of creamy *mozzarella di bufala*, *Parmigiano Reggiano*, fresh ricotta, and local pecorino. With my meats and cheeses, I'll have one flaky croissant and a sample of crusty breads. I'll skip the obligatory stewed prunes, dry cereals with toppings of raisins, walnuts and dried figs, various fruit and plain yogurts, fancy sweet pastries, and freshly chopped fruit salad called *Macedonia*.

After strolling around the table, I take one of the larger plates.

At a side table, an aproned chef stands ready to make omelets in little skillets on his portable gas burner. Small bowls offer fillings of Italian bacon called *pancetta*, chopped red onion, various grated cheeses, diced sweet red pepper, and minced fresh herbs.

Seeing me eye his ingredients, the chef asks, "*Ne posso farne uno per Lei?*" May I make one for you? I understand his question more from context than from his words.

"*No, grazie... domani,*" no thank you... tomorrow, I reply, smiling and nodding. I wish I knew how to say, "I'm sure they are delicious," but my Italian includes only basic phrases. Most staff and merchants in Cortona speak some English, so it's possible to get along in our new town without Italian. But I long for the day I can speak in full sentences and have meaningful conversations. For now, I must rely on common nouns, verbs in the infinitive, courtesy phrases, hand gestures, nods and smiles.

So much of a culture resides in its food and language. To experience a culture one must savor its foods, but to understand a culture one needs to know the language. I *must* learn Italian.

At another side table the same chef operates a contraption that squeezes fresh orange juice. I ask for some by pointing. *"Poco, per favore."* A little, please. I use my thumb and index finger to indicate how much. He chooses an extra-large orange from the wicker basket and juices the perfect amount.

Each day I'll try a few foods until I've sampled everything. This morning I start with meats and cheeses, cherry tomatoes to compliment the tiny *bufala* mozzarella balls, a buttery croissant Italians call a *cornetto*, and a thin slice of dark walnut bread. We'll be here eleven mornings, including our checkout day — plenty of mornings for omelets.

My sampler plate full, I return to our table. Larry is waiting for me. I sip my cappuccino, now lukewarm since I took so long at the buffet, and decide to wake up my taste buds with a crimson cherry tomato, *pomodoro ciliegino*, literally tomato cherry. In Italian, the adjective follows the noun.

I normally don't like tomatoes, but summer and sunshine burst onto my tongue when I bite into this one. The flavor — intense, rich, red — startles my taste buds. It is acidic and sweet at the same time, juicy with a surprisingly thin skin. With this organoleptic experience, it's easy to comprehend that this is a fruit, not a vegetable.

I cut a second tomato, add part of a tiny *bufala* mozzarella ball and a fragment of basil leaf, then place them on my tongue. The creamy, rich-yet-delicate cheese compliments the sharp, succulent tomato and aromatic basil perfectly. I will choose this combination all eleven mornings.

My second cappuccino arrives in time to sip with my *cornetto* and a few chunks of aged pecorino. Tuscany is famous for this sheep's milk cheese. *Pecorino fresco*, fresh pecorino, is almost spreadable. As it matures, pecorino becomes denser and firmer, subtly flavored by whatever it's aged with, from peppercorns to walnut leaves. Sometimes red pepper flakes or black truffles are worked into the cheese before aging. I share bites with my Prince Charming, gently placing in his eager, open mouth a sliver of semi-aged pecorino on a bit of moist walnut bread.

Larry doesn't have a second cappuccino, insisting Italians would never put milk over so much food. Indeed, Italians don't have a cappuccino after meals, only espresso or *macchiato*, espresso stained with a touch of steamed milk.

We order omelets after all, small ones knowing we'll run out of appetite before we run out of time. This is the breakfast of my dreams.

In Chicago we don't eat much breakfast — a few spoonfuls of plain oatmeal with plain yogurt and freshly-squeezed grapefruit juice. But here on the terrace of *Il Falconiere*, under a cloudless cerulean sky and overlooking the far-reaching valley, savoring a luxurious breakfast seems an essential element of our Italian experience.

Breakfast feasts are not typical for Italians either. They *fanno una colazione*, do a breakfast rather than eat breakfast, and *prendono il caffè*, take the coffee rather than drink coffee. Italy may be famous for long meals and Slow Food, but Italians also do fast food faster than McDonald's. Pastry and *espresso* for breakfast at the coffee bar, or a *panino* and *espresso* at the same bar for lunch, take less than five minutes to order and enjoy. The word *espresso*, rapid, says it all.

I lose myself in the pleasures of aromas, tastes, textures, and of time that seems suspended. Larry reads the Italian newspaper and tells me Italy may make it to the World Cup soccer championship. I realize that if I concentrate on food while he reads Italian newspapers, he'll be speaking Italian long before I do.

Reluctantly taking my last bite, I think about the art of savoring. In Cortona, food, wine, concerts, evening strolls, and impromptu conversations all seem meant for savoring. It requires slowing down enough to hear, see, touch, smell, feel and taste all that is around — to focus on each detail and engage in the present. Heightened senses and a slower pace have drawn us back to Italy again and again, and were part of our decision to live here.

But to really slow down requires a decision and then dedication to stay the course. We cannot expect to reflect and grow — to live more deeply, as I hope to live here — unless we slow down.

"Larry... as we make Cortona home, let's slow down. We live fast in America. I don't want to live like that here. Part of our new life. What do you think?"

"I think we'd better get going or we're going to be late," he chuckles, enjoying his own joke as he looks at his watch and hurries me along.

I long to sit in the sunshine, gaze over the countryside, and chat with my handsome husband until noon, except we must handle our Italian residency today. And Prince Larry has little tolerance for wasting time or being late.

Our first task of the day is to meet Lorenzo, our real estate agent, who offered to help us apply for residency. We told him we'd meet him at eight, which gives us nine minutes to drive to town, park and walk up the steep hill to his office. I grab my handbag, Larry scoops up our papers, and we half-run to our SUV in the hotel *parcheggio,* parking area.

So much for slowing down.

What About the Women?

Rushing to Lorenzo's office, Larry zigs and zags our still-loaded SUV up the Cortona hill. I breathe deeply and stare out the open window, determined to really *see* this hillside. Mist envelops the silvery olive trees and the still-dewy field grass looks like an emerald velvet carpet. Near the entrance to the old *cimitero,* cemetery, we pass a grove of olive trees I've never noticed. On this side of Cortona's hill, olive buds have already opened into masses of tiny ivory flowers, making the treetops seem slightly out of focus.

Slowly, I tell myself, slowly… absorb every detail. It is in the lingering that one finds time for wonder. I turn to look behind me, hoping for a last glimpse as we round the final bend into town.

Walking up *Via Guelfa,* I stop to catch my breath and tell myself again to slow down. Better to be five minutes late than to miss this new day unfolding. Sunlight streams through humidity between the ancient stone buildings, creating bands of ethereal haze. I pinch myself, thinking I *live* here.

Near the top, a miniature street cleaner whisks past me and then encircles *Piazza della Repubblica.* It floats around delivery vans, benches and planters as if in a ballet. The perfume of coffee and sweet pastries fills the air. People stop to greet friends and acquaintances, chatting warmly as they come and go from coffee bars.

Larry motions for me to hurry.

Lorenzo's office is on the second floor, overlooking the main piazza. We greet with a kiss on each cheek. I ask about his wife and son. Lorenzo asks about our flight and if everything is good at Lodolina. Long ago he offered to help us obtain residency when we arrived. Since he understands the process and can interpret if we run into trouble, we gratefully accepted.

After our warm exchange, he walks with us across the piazza to a glass-fronted *ufficio*, office, and introduces us to Franco, the town official responsible for residency. Franco, speaking only Italian, informs us that the laws have changed with the new government. He can process our Cortona residency, but cannot help us apply for Italian approvals. For that, we must go to Arezzo, the provincial capital. Lorenzo translates to make sure we understand and then leaves us, certain we can handle local residency on our own. Franco gestures toward two chairs facing his desk and we sit down.

Did he really say the laws just changed?

Franco asks Larry question after question in carefully articulated Italian and types Larry's answers into the computer: date and place of birth, passport number, Cortona address, local phone number, *codice fiscale* (like a social security number), and *Permesso* status, which Franco insists we apply for *subito*, right away.

Not all expatriates (what a strange word) want residency, but we think the advantages are worth the trouble to pursue it. As residents we can remain in Italy more than ninety days, are eligible for national health care, and can own and insure a car. Importantly, we need to be residents before our household goods arrive at Italian Customs to avoid a twenty percent import tax. Although every item is personal and used, the tax could be thousands of dollars.

Franco explains in Italian that someone from the *Comune* will arrive at our home without warning to confirm we are *in residenza*. We both nod. I doubt they'll find Lodolina without a guide.

On ceremoniously long paper, Franco prints Larry's life details. He hands it to Larry to review and sign. Then he pounds the document with five official stamps, striking first the inkpad, then the paper. Bam-bam... bam-bam... bam-bam... bam-bam... bam-bam! Finally, he stands and extends his hand across his desk.

"*Benvenuto, Signor Smeet*," he says, welcome, vigorously shaking Larry's hand.

I'm ready for my turn, thinking in advance how to answer in Italian.

"*Arrivederci, buona giornata.*" Franco ushers us on our way, saying goodbye and good day. Larry stands to leave.

"What about me? Don't *I* need to register?" I ask, confused and somewhat insulted. I stay seated, ready to respond about *my* life.

"*Non importa,*" Franco replies, catching my gist even in English. "*È la moglie di Larry.*" Never mind. You are the wife of Larry.

Never mind? The wife of Larry? Larry looks at me and light-heartedly tries to explain that if the husband is a resident, the wife enjoys the benefits without being registered.

"I understand. But I *want* to be registered!" I protest, not budging.

Franco smiles and says, "*Questa è Italia.*" This is Italy. As if that explains everything.

And this is 2006, I scream silently as I rise to leave. I do not like legally existing only as a man's wife. I'm not sure I want to live in a country that still recognizes married women as extensions of their husbands. I thought I had out-lived such nonsense.

This chauvinism is a throwback for me. In 1972 at Procter & Gamble, I was one of two women in marketing who were not secretaries. The male executives were unaccustomed to female colleagues. I would walk into meetings and the room would become hushed. It seemed I had interrupted some off-color joke or chitchat about me — or both. I recall a male colleague admiring my "toe cleavage" in my high heel office shoes. I'm sure it was fun to tease me because I was young, naïve and modest. I'd been embarrassed, yes, but honestly, I had rather liked the attention.

I decided early in my career that the best way to be taken seriously was to work as hard or harder than my male associates, but still be feminine. I won colleagues' and superiors' confidence and was promoted as rapidly as many male associates with Harvard MBAs, despite my bachelor degree in Home Economics and master in design from a non-prestigious state university. I'd been hired based on aptitude tests at a time P&G wanted to start developing women executives. Nine years later, when I left as a mid-level executive to take a better-paying job in Chicago, nearly one-third of the brand management and marketing staff, hundreds of professionals, were women. Mine was a transitional era, one I do not wish to re-live thirty years later, retired and starting my new life in Italy.

I know chauvinism and bravado are accepted in Italian culture, even admired, but residency is an issue of *legal* status.

Back in Lorenzo's office, I tell him I'm disappointed not to need to personally register, expressing but minimizing my concern. He shrugs his shoulders and gestures with open hands, as if to say, "What can I do?"

He phones the immigration office in Arezzo and confirms we must go there to apply for our permission to stay in Italy. The *Questura*, the government branch that processes immigration requests, is open Tuesday, Wednesday and Friday mornings, eight-thirty to one o'clock.

"We will go Wednesday morning. I will take you," Lorenzo offers.

Larry quickly accepts. "Thank you for being so helpful... and flexible. This is not your problem, but we really value your help. *Molto gentile.*" Very kind.

"Of course," Lorenzo smiles. He must have better things to do than to help clients who have already bought their house manage their Italian immigration, but his warm voice and quick smile seem genuine.

"I hope I get my own card," I quip, a little too cynically.

Lorenzo tells us the document we need is a *Permesso di Soggiorno*, permission to stay more than ninety days without returning to the USA. Before this new law, he says, *Permesso* applications could be submitted in nearby Camucia.

Laws and regulations frequently change in Italy. They have had sixty new national governments since 1946, when Italians voted to eliminate the monarchy and become a republic — a new one almost every year. Each new government passes its own regulations and changes old ones, resulting in confusing systems, burgeoning bureaucracy, and mountainous paperwork.

I remind Lorenzo we need our Italian residency before our belongings arrive in ten days. "We will do what we can," he assures me. I doubt local residency and "what we can" will suffice.

"Can I get a *codice fiscale* in Cortona?" I ask. "The shipment is in my name and we just learned we can't use Larry's code for delivery."

"You can do it here, but in a different office. I will show you."

How could anyone figure all this out on their own?

Lorenzo escorts us to another *Comune* office nearby and introduces us to two women. One speaks English, so Lorenzo again leaves us on our own. The low-ceilinged utilitarian office has two desks with computers, no guest chairs, a few filing cabinets, and stacks of paper covering every horizontal surface.

Larry explains our dilemma. The woman confirms she can process a *codice fiscale*, but not a *permesso*. She asks me questions — *me*, directly — and types *my* answers into a computer. I stand a little taller, having regained some individual value and dignity.

She looks up and says, "You already have a *codice fiscale*."

Larry and I are baffled. She prints an official copy of both our fiscal codes, stamps and signs them, then hands one to each of us.

We thank her, walk outside and decide to relax with another cappuccino on the piazza, having done what we can for this morning. Larry orders one despite his huge breakfast. I smile, but say nothing.

"Lorenzo must have applied for my number when he applied for yours," I say. "The house is in both of our names, so he probably needed both numbers. Wonder why he never gave me mine." Secretly, I wonder if it's because I'm a girl.

Sitting in the piazza with our *cappuccini*, I call Maryte, our Italian contact in Milan for the moving company, hoping to give her my *codice fiscale* and tell her we have local residency, but can't apply for Italian residency until Wednesday. The phone rings and rings. I leave a message and pull out my camera.

"What're you doing?" Larry asks.

"Taking photos," I answer.

"I can see that. But *why*? You live here now." He seems annoyed that I act like a giddy tourist when he has become an official *Cortonese*.

"I want to send some to the kids and Mom. This morning light is magical."

"Put the camera away, please," he says, taking another sip.

It is a not request, but a command. I take one more shot, then comply to keep peace.

Larry calls BNL, our bank in Arezzo, regarding funds he wired ten days ago. Our contact, Paola, is the only agent in the bank who speaks English. She confirms the money has been in Florence at the main branch for a week, but it has not been transferred to Arezzo so we cannot access it. Larry is astounded.

We walk to Lorenzo's office once again, this time to ask about local banks. Larry's certain there must be a better option.

"The Italian banking system is always a problem for foreigners," Lorenzo says. "A Cortona bank will not help. They are the same, only smaller."

"There are two *Cortonese* proverbs," he muses. "*If you need money, dig in the piazza.* Under this piazza for many years was a bank vault, but now is filled in. Impossible to get anything out, no matter how much digging."

When Larry chuckles, Lorenzo continues, "*If you are waiting for money, you can get it from the hands of Pietro Berrettini.*" Lorenzo points to a statue above an arched opening over a street. The bust of the famous *Cortonese* artist has no arms.

Lorenzo is entertained by our predictable complaints about Italian banks and reactions to the Cortona proverbs. Larry seems amused by the jokes, but not by our banking experience.

Back in the piazza, I call Francesco to tell him we're free for the rest of the morning, hoping he can meet us early. He has appointments, but says it will be a pleasure to meet us at Lodolina at four o'clock as planned. With six hours free and my resolve to live more slowly, we decide to take a *passeggiata*, stroll, through the park and check out the new public swimming pool and amphitheater.

Walking along *Via Nazionale*, the main shopping and only flat street in Cortona, we're surprised to see Veronica sitting in front of a favorite antique shop.

"Why are you here," I ask, "and not at your restaurant?"

"It was too much work for too little money," she says. "After two years, I decided to sell the pizzeria and return to antiques."

"But you worked so hard to get it going," I say, recalling her enthusiasm.

"I was not like most chefs who get fat at their job. I worked every minute and weighed five kilograms less when I stopped."

"That's eleven pounds!" I gasp. Veronica is a lovely woman and looks more svelte than ever. I'm a bit jealous.

Reaching the *Parterre*, Cortona's public park, we pause at the tall bronze statue of an angel holding up a dying soldier, dedicated to *"seicento caduti nella Guerra,"* six hundred fallen in the War. It honors the same soldiers for whom the cypress trees were planted around the Cortona hill.

In the fountain nearby, sunlight dances on a circle of water-stream arcs in the shape of a huge donut. In the center, reflections flicker on verdigris dolphins and youths, twisted together in play. The mist feels refreshing. It's still morning, but already a scorching day.

Beyond the fountain is a wide, gravel lane lined with sycamore, chestnut, linden and redbud trees. It reminds me of the Tuileries in Paris, and for good reason. Legend is that the lane was built when Napoleon's troops needed a level, smooth kilometer to exercise their horses. When I first heard the story, I was doubtful, but history supports the possibility. In 1799, Napoleon's troops attacked but did not take Cortona. Then, in 1809, Elisa Bonaparte, Napoleon's sister and the Grand Duchess of Tuscany, spent some of August here.

Near a children's playground, Italian mothers and grandmothers sit on benches or stand in twos and threes. Even in conversations with one another, they watch the children. The *bambini* kick balls, climb, swing or slide, always under that guardian eye. A little ahead of us on the gravel lane, a tiny tot grips his *nonna's* extended finger as he waddles, missteps and lands with a thud. His grandmother picks him up, dusts off his bottom, turns him around, extends her finger and urges him to walk again. He reaches for her finger and confidently waddles back toward the other children, acting very grown up.

Several women greet us with a nod and smile as we pass.

If I were a painter, this is the Cortona scene I would capture: women with their children and grandchildren in the *Parterre*.

Women like these are the glue of Italian society. In fact, women are the glue of most societies. They hold the families together, raise the children, feed the fathers and grandfathers, and teach everyone in the family to be respectful, hardworking, clean and honest. They instill in their loved ones the importance of family, school and faith. Italian women go to Mass and pray, calling on the Blessed Virgin for the wellbeing of their families and the families of their friends. These women, dedicated to raising the little ones, are the overseers of Cortona's present and architects of Cortona's future.

Italian boys adore their mothers, who feed and fawn them into adulthood. The men love their wives, too, but not always as much as they love their mothers. Their wives have sons for that.

This morning's interaction with Franco continues to disturb me. Perhaps the more influential women are in a society, the more the men need to appear to be in charge. Women in Italy seem so vital, strong and industrious. Could Italian bravado be a counter-balance to the strength and competence of its women?

Goethe said he saw "no idle Italian women" on his *Italian Journey* two centuries ago, and it seems true today. It is the women, hard-working and strong-minded, who hold Italy in their hands and nurture its greatness and uniqueness, while Italian men change the laws, call the shots, run the businesses, and appear to be in charge.

These women are role models, guiding the development of their children's characters and influencing the behavior of their men. They make the decisions that affect their families and know those are the most important decisions of all. Family is the core of Italian society, for centuries past and for the foreseeable future, and women lead the families.

Watching these women and mulling over this morning's incident, I conclude that Italy is a matriarchal society with a patriarchal veneer.

"Aren't these women extraordinary?" I whisper to Larry. "Women like these make Italy great. I wonder why Italian women don't demand more respect. Like this morning at Franco's office... or that wine dinner at Arnaldo's. It's the same stupid chauvinism."

Larry chuckles, recalling a wine tasting at *Pane e Vino* the winter we rented the apartment in Cortona. Enjoying some of the finest wines of Italy, there were a dozen men around the table — and me.

"When you asked the guy sitting next to you why you were the only woman, he said the evening was way too expensive to bring wives and girlfriends. You were shocked."

"Only in Italy! Do you think that'd happen today?"

"Probably not. It was quite a few years ago," Larry says, trying to appease me.

"But look at this morning. You're a Cortona resident and I count only as your wife. That's insulting," I say.

"Maybe for Italian women it's not such a big deal… Maybe the wives didn't want to go to the wine tasting. Or, maybe they see advantages in being the weaker sex," Larry teases. "You could, too. You can't always choose your circumstance, but you can choose your attitude toward your circumstance. That's what you always say."

"It's different. Residency is a *legal* status," I insist, justifying my indignation.

I don't understand why Italian women tolerate the chauvinism and bravado. Perhaps the dramatic maleness makes women feel more feminine, protected and provided for by their men. Or, perhaps chauvinism and bravado are simply accepted as a deeply ingrained part of Italian culture, never to change and not to be taken too seriously.

"Okay. Maybe there are advantages…" I say, deciding to let go of being upset about something I'm not going to change. "Maybe I should work this dependency thing. Let you protect me, buy me gifts… wine and dine me."

"Does that mean you want me to take you to dinner?" he laughs.

"Well, I'd love to cook for you, but my kitchen isn't ready," I reply coyly.

Larry makes a little pout of neglect. "Since you can't cook for me," he says, "guess I'll take you out. Where would you like to go?

"How about *La Bucaccia*?" he adds, before I have a chance to consider choices.

"Perfect. But let's celebrate *my* dependency rather than *your* residency. If I must be your dependent, I might as well make the most of it!"

"Enough! Back to the hotel," Larry says. "We need to unpack. But we sure don't need lunch… with that big breakfast and a huge dinner ahead."

Larry always wants to skip lunch before a big dinner. I like three meals.

Back at the hotel, we share a perfect peach from the fruit bowl in our room. Not lunch, but at least it's something. While Larry reads, I make notes about the women we saw today: Gilda, Enza, Veronica, the mothers and grandmothers in the *Parterre*, the office workers and shopkeepers. Yes, *questa è Italia*, this is Italy, the land of competent, dignified, industrious, and faith-filled women.

Perhaps bravado is in the *doing*; strength is in the *being*.

I treasure strong women and miss my girlfriends, so far away. I hope to make some Italian girlfriends. I will ask them why they don't seem offended by the chauvinism. They must know something I do not. I hope living here will give me insights into my new culture that will enrich who I am and my empathy for the women I meet. Perhaps I'd be less offended by this morning's incident if I saw it through Italian eyes.

I can't expect people of another culture to treat me in the same way I'm treated in my own culture — just one of many things to learn.

And now, my loving, without-bravado husband and I must meet Francesco, make house decisions, and eventually have dinner. My stomach has started to rumble.

One Bite at a Time

When we arrive at Lodolina mid-afternoon, five worker's vans are lined-up in the driveway. Yesterday, Sunday, the property was silent. Today it's buzzing. Sawing, pounding, scraping and male voices emanate from the guesthouse construction. Francesco and the painter are inside the main house waiting for us.

Francesco explains we must decide the color, height and accent stripe for the *battiscopa*, baseboard, to be painted while Lodolina is empty. In Italian homes, baseboards are painted rather than made of tile or wood as in America. Larry and I agree with Francesco that the *battiscopa* should be the traditional gray, matching the *pietra serena* doorframes and thresholds, but which gray and what height must be decided. How hard can this be?

We begin in the living room. Alessandro paints a range of grays at the base of the wall. They are almost the same color, yet different.

"Can you mix something a little warmer and darker?" I ask. "These all seem bluish and bright to me. Perhaps a hint more brown?" I only want to make this choice once.

Alessandro mixes three additional grays. We choose a medium-warm gray, a hint browner than our *pietra serena* doorframes. Francesco says that *pietra serena* becomes browner with age, so our choice is good.

We agree the *battiscopa* will be twelve centimeters high, about five inches. Francesco suggests a contrasting red line above an open space where the peach *grassello*, plaster, will show through. We like his idea, but then deliberate far too long over the height of the open space.

In a private moment while Francesco confers with Alessandro, I whisper to Larry, "Finishing Lodolina will take months if every decision takes this long."

"And it'll be a difficult summer," he adds. "You may have to handle most of the decisions with Francesco or I'll never get any work done." Larry's already protecting his sabbatical. I wonder about *my* projects, but now's not the time to mention it.

I do love discussing the design, artistry and finishes of Lodolina. If we were not working against a moving-day deadline, I would relish every minute of our conversations. Larry has less patience with it, but is good at assessing issues and creating solutions, and has strong design opinions, so I don't want to make important decisions without him.

When Alessandro finishes a sample and we all agree it's perfect, we walk up the dirt construction ramp to check our *battiscopa* choices upstairs, "where the light is different," Francesco says.

Larry pushes open the upstairs hidden door, as he did ceremoniously just yesterday morning. Inside, a dark spot is moving across the floor. I bend to pick up a large iridescent turquoise and lime beetle, cupping it in the palm of my hand.

"It's a scarab! Aren't scarabs good luck?" I ask, delighted that Lodolina's first visitor is a royal scarab.

Alessandro lets it crawl on his paint-speckled hand while I take photos. To me it looks exactly like the beetles of the Egyptian pharaoh's carvings, but the men seem unimpressed.

In Italian, Alessandro tells Francesco that, as a child, he and his friends would tie a string to one leg of these and fly them like kites. Francesco translates. I'm appalled. I let our visitor fly freely out of the window. No tethered leg for Lodolina's honored guest. (After my gardens are planted, I will learn these beetles destroy roses and no insecticide controls them. I will loathe each one, huge black females and smaller iridescent males, and will cut them in half as I deadhead my roses. But today, in my ignorance, this gorgeous scarab-looking beetle has been my revered first visitor.)

Baseboard confirmed, we turn to colors for the exterior stucco corner. The oldest houses in the valley are fieldstone. Later, bricks were used, sometimes mixed with stone. More important villas were covered with stucco and painted. Our bedroom corner, the final addition to Lodolina, was brick. I wanted to retain the exposed brick, but Larry insisted we should stucco it. Francesco agreed because of the bad condition of the brick. He suggested painting the stucco a brick color, since valley neighbors are used to seeing brick. But dark stucco colors are not attractive to me.

Larry, Francesco and I concur, conceptually, on a happy, buttery yellow, like most of the houses in the valley. Alessandro prepares small buckets of yellows and has little bottles of pigment to adjust the shade, drop by drop. When it looks right, he paints a large swatch on the wall. Then he brushes a half-shade deeper next to it. They both look too bright to me. I try to explain that I hope for a yellow that doesn't call attention to itself. I want Lodolina to look like a stone house, not a stucco house.

Larry tires of my obsessing. I explain to Francesco that I wrote my master's degree thesis on *Color Combination Preferences Related to Selected Aspects of Personality,* and tell him color is of great interest to me.

"That was forty years ago," I add more modestly.

"But a fascinating subject," Francesco protests my dismissal. "We will let you choose the colors for Lodolina. Someday you will tell me more about your study."

Encouraged, I wax on. "The yellow must be subtle, happy but receding, and blend with the new grout. I don't like the grout color right now. Looks like baby poop. But you said it will change?"

Francesco nods. "The grout will become more, how do you call it… the color for hiding?"

"Khaki, like camouflage?" I say.

He nods. "You will like it. It will be soft. Now is strong."

"How long will it take?" I ask.

"For the stucco or the grout?" he asks.

"Both," I reply.

"You have time, depending on conditions."

I don't like his response; it suggests longer than I hoped on both.

Since we arrived, we've been listening to the rhythmic tap-tap-tap of stones being shaped for the guesthouse walls. The masons are building a wall high enough to support the *pietra serena architrave*, the supporting stone beam over the widest door. With the *architrave* in place, walls can be finished and the roof added. Francesco hopes the guesthouse will be finished by August, when our children and grandchildren arrive, about six weeks from now.

To me, that means daily workers until August.

I hope we also have grass and a few plants by then. The yard is so barren it doesn't even have weeds. I imagine lavender bushes lining the walk to the guesthouse and have chosen a sunny, well-drained area where roses will thrive.

We leave Alessandro and go outside to discuss with Francesco how to direct guests to come to the main house front door — one level down, facing the valley, and unseen from the driveway — instead of walking directly to our private back door, the first entry everyone sees. A solution has eluded us all.

One idea is a wide stairway from the driveway down into the olive grove and then a landscaped path through the trees.

"That's a great idea!" Larry says. "Think about it... A wide stairway at the prettiest part of the view, then a garden walk through the olive trees to the house. It would be beautiful."

Beautiful, but I can't imagine lugging groceries down so many steps and through the olive grove to the kitchen door.

This discussion is only starting, so I don't divulge my opposition. I trust the boys will come to their senses soon enough. It seems obvious to me: the path needs to be a gradual incline near the house rather than a remote grand stairway. For this particular design problem, though not my tendency, I prefer function over form.

While the boys talk of diggers and new stone walls, stairs and walkways, I dream of lavender, white hydrangea, purple iris, golden *ginestra*, trailing cotoneaster with red berries, and, of course, roses and herbs.

Francesco leaves around eight o'clock. It's still light, but the sun is red-bronze and heavy, poised to drop behind the hill. This is our first pre-move workday. We made one choice: the color and configuration of the baseboard. We have hundreds more decisions and only nine more working days.

My head is spinning. In any large project there is a moment when the scope and details seem overwhelming. At that point, one must let go of the whole and break the project into manageable pieces. As Desmond Tutu famously said: "There is only one way to eat an elephant: a bite at a time."

Timing will also be important. If one tradesman falls behind — or if we do not make one decision on time — all the workers and deliveries must be rescheduled. I'm relieved that Francesco will manage the schedule, the workers, and us.

Making decisions on time will be more complicated if, or when, Larry and I don't agree. We are strong individuals, become fully immersed in the creative process, and like our own ideas. Everyone does. Larry thinks my opinions typically prevail, but I believe his do. I give in when he feels strongly, like I did about stucco over the brick, because he has good judgment. However, when I feel strongly, I can be stubborn. I was unwavering about the railing on the staircase, and Francesco and Larry finally gave in. Fortunately, we admire each other's creativity, have similar tastes, and usually concur.

When Larry and I do not agree on house decisions, we use a method that always works: we ask the architect. Francesco listens carefully, honoring both our perspectives, gives his opinion clearly and honestly, and shares his reasons. Sometimes he agrees with one of us, but more often he offers a different solution that is better than either of ours.

We tease Francesco that part of the job of an architect is marriage counseling. Everyone knows the admonition: renovate and separate. Decisions that must be made in the midst of chaos can be volatile, especially when irreversible and with high costs. I fear we'll face some tricky deliberations in coming days and am thankful today went well.

I take a deep breath, knowing I must concentrate on one day and one decision at a time, trusting the expert management of Francesco. To me, it seems impossible that Lodolina will be ready for our belongings in nine work days, but he still says it can be.

Impeccable Ingredients

Romano's face lights up when we walk into *La Bucaccia*. Francesca, his nine-year-old daughter, runs to jump into my arms. She is so big! Soon she won't leap into my arms but will brush-kiss my cheeks like an adult. Agostina, Romano's wife, is in the kitchen, so I go back to say hello. I wish we could chat in Italian. She's one of the loveliest women I've met and an exceptional chef. Her food is unsurpassed, *secondo me*, in my opinion, literally seconded by me.

That first winter in Cortona, *La Bucaccia* was near our apartment and became our hangout. Since it was bitterly cold and windy, few Italians ventured from their fireplaces, but we spent long evenings talking with Romano about food, wine and family. One night, Larry left his credit card. The next day Romano watched for him and chased him down to return it, increasing our bond. We love their food and their family. It's nice to be back.

To celebrate my dependency, Larry orders an exceptional vintage of my favorite local wine, *Il Bosco* from d'Alessandro. Then he asks if I really care that I wasn't personally registered, as if I shouldn't.

"Well. How'd you like it if you didn't count except as my husband?"

"I'd like it if you were the official resident. Then you'd have to take care of me. If we are really equal, it shouldn't matter who gets registered, right?"

"I already take care of you! And I don't think you'd like it if only I had been registered. Men just expect to be the important one. And in Italy, it isn't even a question."

Studying the menu, I ponder why I find this morning's experience with Franco upsetting. Is it the years struggling to be treated as an equal in my profession? Or is it because I honestly do feel more secure when Larry is around, but don't want to admit it?

Perhaps my upset is heightened because everything seems to matter more here. Rather than on vacation conversing with strangers we'll never see again, we're building relationships, attempting to become part of an already-cohesive community. Not being registered seems more like I don't belong.

I wonder if I should confess my new sense of insecurity to Larry, but choose to say nothing and, for now, focus on the food.

Though we share every course, we order way too much — all favorites we can't resist after months away. For *antipasti*, appetizers, Larry wants local cured meats from three types of Tuscan pork: farm-raised pigs, wild boar, and *Cinta Senese*, an ancient breed raised near Siena. Our *primo*, first course, will be two homemade pastas: *mezzalune*, half-moons made with chestnut flour, filled with sheep's milk cheese and served in braised artichoke leaves; plus my favorite, *gnudi*, spinach and ricotta dumplings, like ravioli without pasta jackets — nudes. Agostina spoons slow-roasted tomatoes, sweetly caramelized, over the *gnudi* and sprinkles them with grated *Parmigiano Reggiano*, the finest of parmesans. The plate is green, red and white, like the Italian flag, and scrumptious. I can't wait to try to make *gnudi* at home.

Romano urges us to order *bistecca*, steak, because the cow is *femminile*, female, so extra tender. *Chianina*, the preferred beef in Tuscany, is the largest and perhaps oldest extant cattle breed in the world, mentioned in poetry by Virgil and Dante. The dense, lean meat is seared over flames, sliced into strips, drizzled with warm olive oil infused with rosemary, and served rare.

"A small portion, please, *uno per due*," one for two, Larry insists.

To first awaken our palates, the waitress brings freshly homemade ricotta cheese finished with a drizzle of surprisingly green and spicy olive oil and black pepper. We toast Lodolina, thanking God for each other, Francesco who still surprises us with his cleverness, the culinary skill of Agostina, the food knowledge and kindness of Romano, and our new Italian life.

While we savor the ricotta, Romano talks about olive oil. Larry brags a little, "Ours is amazing… green and peppery."

"We only tasted it once, in February," I confess, using my finger to lift to my lips a drop from the tiny green puddle on my plate. "It's being stored in a cellar, but we hope to get it soon."

"I will buy your production!" Romano declares. "I buy from many farms in Tuscany. I choose only the best."

"We only pressed sixty-five liters," Larry says. "I think Victoria will need every drop, but we will bring you a bottle so you can try it."

"Our hills produce the finest oil in the world," Romano continues. "With pure Tuscan oil, it takes only the smallest amount to get the flavor. Some foreign producers mix Tuscan oil with oil from Spain or Greece, claiming it is Tuscan. But it is not the same. I will be happy to have even one bottle of the famous Lodolina oil."

He leaves us to seat a large party at the long center table. Romano's restaurant is an intimate room with beamed ceilings, stone walls and floors, about a dozen tables and a modern, stainless steel kitchen in the back. He personally restored the building, a small twelfth-century palazzo. Their family home is above the restaurant. Tonight the room is bustling and we're delighted to see their business doing well.

Even with constant foot traffic, food, and wine, the restaurant is spotless. "*Igiene*," hygiene, Romano declares, "is the first job of a restaurateur." He certainly follows his conviction; we could eat off his stone floors.

He carries a platter of gorgeous *tagliata* to a corner table. "*Femminile*," Larry whispers. I smile and try not to stare.

When Romano arrives with our first pasta, we ask about his health. It was not good when we last saw him. "Better since winter. But I have not had the surgery. Maybe I will have the baby first," he jokes, patting his round and seemingly growing belly.

"*Mangi, mangi*," he says to us, eat, eat, urging us to start. Pasta must be enjoyed immediately and never allowed to get cold, which would insult the cook. In Italy, if the food is hot, each person starts when served rather than waiting for others to be served.

Romano never rests, but rushes about making certain each guest is cared for, well informed, and happy.

After the best steak I can remember, Larry and I share one dessert and agree it's time to say goodnight. Romano insists we stay, pouring *Vin Santo* dessert wine and setting homemade warm *biscotti* on our table.

"*Vin Santo*," Romano says, sharing one last lesson, "means holy wine. It started as the wine for Mass. The grapes are harvested late, dried, then pressed and aged, so takes a long time to produce." We both nod, having seen *Vin Santo* drying rooms. Of all we've tasted, this may be the smoothest.

"In Tuscany for many years," Romano continues, "*Vin Santo* was made at home and served only to friends and family, mostly at Christmas. Now, it's served to everyone, but there is a big difference in the quality. This *Vin Santo* is so excellent, I buy the barrel."

It has been a delicious and educational night. Agostina created an exquisite meal and Romano taught us about the ingredients. Of course, Romano knows I love to cook, so he has an appreciative audience.

"I think I'll try making *gnudi* as my first experiment in my new kitchen," I tell Larry. "But I doubt they could be as good as Agostina's."

"I love your experiments… most of them," he says, always honest.

One of my favorite games is to taste something and attempt to replicate it, although not always with success. In Italy my ingredients will be fresh, in season, perfectly ripe and carefully chosen, like Romano's. The odds of making good *gnudi* are pretty high.

Every great Tuscan meal — or *any* great meal — requires impeccable ingredients. Italians cook so well because they are passionate about the ingredients, preparation, presentation, and the people for whom they prepare it.

Larry is certain Tuscans have figured out food better than any other culture. Italians know what foods they like and like the foods they know. They're proud of their cuisine and, in fact, don't like foreign foods much at all. Except in large cities like Rome or Florence, we rarely see Thai, Mexican, French, Japanese, or Chinese restaurants. For Tuscans, foods from Sicily, Milan and Naples are foreign enough. Globalization may change that but, for now, Tuscans want Tuscan foods.

The value of ingredients and simplicity of preparation is honored by the way Tuscan food is served. Typically, each dish is presented on a separate plate, unlike American plates piled high with a variety of flavors.

Italians delight in the seasons, because each new season brings new tastes and textures. In spring, they exclaim over wild asparagus thin as twigs, glistening green peas, purple artichokes that can be eaten raw, and pale green fava beans in their cushioned pods. When summer arrives, markets are a brilliant array of crimson tomatoes, green zucchini with golden flowers still attached, majestic purple eggplants, and red peppers tossed in the same bin with yellow, orange, and green ones. By July, velvety apricots and delicate yellow and white peaches are plentiful, followed in August by lime-green and purple-black figs. Then fall rolls in with brown porcini mushrooms, dark green kale, golden squashes and vibrant green olive oil. All naturally matured, picked ripe, and intensely fragrant and flavorful.

To celebrate local ingredients, Italian towns hold festivals. Hundreds, even thousands of visitors feast on one ingredient, often cooked numerous ways. In August, Cortona holds a *Sagra di Bistecca* featuring slabs of grilled Chianina beef, and a couple weeks later, a *Sagra di Funghi Porcini,* offering porcini mushrooms as appetizers, pasta sauce, and over meat. Truffles, snails, chestnuts, ostrich, and wild boar are just a few of the foods honored by a *sagra* somewhere in Tuscany.

For his restaurant, Romano says he buys only from local farms, only the best and only in season. He usually finds something unique on each buying excursion, such as tonight's ultra-tender female cow and exquisite *Vin Santo.* Tuscan flavors seem to carry a heaven-designed alliance from sharing the same earth: basil and tomatoes, cheeses and local honey, olive oil and crusty bread. The list is long.

Larry and I are never concerned about chemical preservatives or hormones in Tuscany, as foods are preserved without artificial chemicals. Meats are dried with salt in open air. Cheeses are coagulated with natural enzymes and microbes. *Marmellata* is preserved with sugar and natural pectin. Wines are grown without poisonous pesticides, or even irrigation, aged in wood barrels, all preserved naturally.

One Italian neighbor says the Tuscan secret to great food is removing the water. Strong espresso, thick ragù, dried meats, aged cheeses, gooey *marmellata,* dense tapenades, pungent vinegars, rich wines and liquors all qualify.

Food is like life… its quality reflects the care put into it. Never truer than in Tuscany.

When we go to the bar to pay, Romano insists we share a little grappa. I'm not keen on this high-alcohol after-dinner drink, made by distilling fermented, pulp, stems and skins of wine grapes. But how can we resist Romano's generosity? His grappa will be the smoothest, most flavorful we've sipped.

Larry happily agrees. I hesitate, then nod, *"Un po,"* a little. As always, Romano fills both tiny glasses way too full.

We drive back to our hotel satiated with the tastes of our evening, new insights about food, and the pleasure of time spent with people we enjoy, especially each other. For me, superb food is one of life's greatest pleasures, and to share it with loved ones is even better. I fall asleep happy, despite persisting jet lag and over-indulging at dinner.

I've all but forgotten my upset at not being registered as a Cortona resident, only as Larry's wife. Perhaps chauvinism is simply part of the rich complexity in our new Italian life.

Remembering the Remarkable

Today is our nineteenth wedding anniversary. The bathroom mirror reflects a swollen face with a red patch under each eye. What could have provoked such unattractive blotches on a day I want to look especially lovely? I try cold compresses, but the puffy redness remains.

We down *cappuccini*, rush through a one-plate Falconiere breakfast, and hurry to Francesco's office in Castiglion Fiorentino, twenty minutes away, to make more decisions. We hope to finish quickly, having set today aside to relax at the hotel pool and celebrate our years together.

Sitting in Francesco's swivel guest chairs, my first task is to choose kitchen garbage containers from countless configurations. Francesco has marked a few options in a thick catalog. I select a pullout system with three bins, having not a clue.

"Stainless steel or plastic?" he asks.

I raise my eyebrows and say, "Stainless steel?" Surely stainless-steel bins will be easier to keep clean and odorless, therefore worth an extra cost. I don't know how much extra.

Garbage seems important here. In our Chicago condo, I never thought about it. I had a kitchen sink disposal and a nearby garbage shoot. In rural Italy, I won't have either. For country dwellers like us, garbage bags must be deposited in public bins along roads and in parking lots. Italians are serious about recycling. Gray bins are for regular trash, green for glass and plastic, yellow for paper, with a few marked for botanical and agricultural wastes. Someday I'll compost fruit and vegetable scraps. Until then, we'll collect all wastes in my separated stainless bins and carry our bags to public receptacles.

Francesco, Larry, Carlo, Gabriele and I rehash a solution for leading guests to our front door. After more indecision, Francesco says for now he will draw a stone path on the current construction ramp. Larry agrees, but hopes for a more creative solution like the *belvedere*. To me, the construction ramp is the only practical option.

We discuss Lodolina construction for three hours. Francesco's guest chairs are upholstered the aqua color of a swimming pool, but swiveling is not the same as swimming. The list of workers for this week includes every trade.

Francesco asks if we'd like an espresso, sensing our fading energy. Larry declines, saying he wants to finish so we can go back to the hotel. I would have said yes, but Larry's intent on moving on.

I remain pleased that our architects and builders are willing to deliberate every decision, and I enjoy our creative discussions. But today I want to finish.

"Now, we must go to Lodolina," Francesco declares. "We must decide the way to bring guests to your front door because excavation begins tomorrow."

Larry and I look at one another. Didn't we just agree on a stone path down the ramp?

"This is a decision for all time and must be confirmed on site," he adds, seeing our unspoken exchange.

Lodolina is a powerful magnet against which I have no resistance, not even today. I rise and go willingly, happily.

Standing in the front yard, Francesco, Larry and I review the challenge. There is no perfect resolution. I cannot think any more. "I don't know. You boys decide." Larry shakes his head and frowns at me, knowing that if we don't all decide, the decision is not made.

"You must agree now, before tomorrow," Francesco says with the first hint of impatience I've seen in the three years we've worked together.

After we conclude the ramp is the reasonable solution, Francesco motions toward the facade of the house and changes the subject, asking reverently, "Do you see the three hands in your home?"

Larry and I have looked at the front of Lodolina hundreds of times, in person and in photos. Can it be that we have never really *seen* it? Sure enough, there are clearly three sections, all with the same brown and gray fieldstones, but different stonework.

"The first hand was the farmer who built a two-story lean-to, probably with a slanted stone roof like that little tower." Francesco points to an abandoned ruin on the adjacent property, taller than it is wide. "The first walls needed to support a stone roof, so were very thick. Of course, we leave everything the original way, so the walls in the oldest section are three feet thick. Later roofs became tile, so walls could be thinner. When you bought, the roof was tiles, but we dug up many roof stones in your excavation. We will use them for tops on your new stone walls."

He continues, "Probably, a different generation built Lodolina's second section for more animals below and more comfort above. The third hand is your living room, downstairs only. Your bedroom was added much later, in the last century. But brick does not show the maker's hand. Pierangelo and Luciano have matched each hand perfectly. We call the repairs *cuci scuci*, the same as sewing a patch on cloth. Lodolina's patches, mostly under upstairs windows, were *bruttissimo*, very ugly. Now are not noticeable."

He pronounces ugly "oogly" and makes the motion of sewing as he talks. I laugh out loud because Francesco's mending motion is charmingly accurate. He even makes a twist of his wrist, so authentic I would trust him with a button. He enjoys being funny and is very funny, just as he is very clever.

"The guesthouse will be a fourth hand," he concludes philosophically. "Adding to the story of Lodolina, but made by you."

"Actually, made by Luciano and Pierangelo." Larry corrects. "It will be *their* hands."

"It is important each wall has one mason or it looks confused. Pierangelo and Luciano can match any hand, even each other."

"They are masters and we are fortunate," Larry agrees.

"It is not so easy now to find anyone skilled at stone," Francesco says. "Young people are not interested in becoming *muratori*. Many old and important arts are fading, soon will be gone."

With Francesco, we climb to town for a late lunch at *Fufluns* where we hear local gossip. The *Comune* plans to install an outdoor escalator from *Piazza Garibaldi* to a new parking lot below the walls and townspeople are not happy. An escalator does seem offensively modern for such a small and historic hilltown. Other towns with escalators to their *centro*, city center, like Perugia and Siena, are much larger. I love Cortona's steep hills and small-town life. Fortunately, township leaders have restricted bus parking to three spaces, so busloads of day-tourists do not take over. As more visitor conveniences are added, I wonder if Cortona will lose the authenticity that drew us here.

I feel a bit hypocritical, a tourist myself only three days ago.

After lunch, Francesco offers to drive us over the mountain to an antique center in *Città di Castello* where our newly restored *armadio*, Italian armoire, and kitchen china cabinet, chosen in February, are ready to be approved for delivery. And, he says, we can look for other furniture we need.

Giving up on our anniversary respite, we make the one-hour journey. The furniture we had restored is beautiful and will be delivered before our moving day, but we don't find bedroom dressers, dining chairs, desks or a credenza.

On the long drive back, I tease Francesco about being like Frank Lloyd Wright, designing every aspect of a property, including the furniture and wife's clothing.

"I do not want to choose your clothing," he shakes his head, "But I do like to help with the furniture. Only we do not design it, just find it."

When challenged about designing Larry's desk since we can't seem to find one, Francesco confesses he's been thinking about a desk of old chestnut beams, cut into thick planks, with iron at the base. Larry grins and nods.

I get queasy on the winding mountain roads and open the window for air. With a blotchy face and nausea, how can I look extra nice at our anniversary dinner in less than an hour? At the hotel, I'm relieved to plant my feet on solid ground.

"Sabina! You're back! We've missed you," I hear Larry say when he goes to the reception cottage for our key. (In Italy, as in most places in Europe, we leave our key at the front desk when we leave the hotel.) The flame-haired Sabina has become one of our favorites over years of staying here, so I join them. She greets me warmly, kissing each cheek.

As we chat, I mention today is our wedding anniversary.

"We have remembered you," she says mysteriously.

Larry explains that we need to extend our stay until next Thursday.

"Until next Thursday, we are happy that you stay with us. Then the hotel is full, so will be impossible to extend again. I am sorry we must say this to you."

"We'll be fine," I assure her. "Thursday's our delivery day, confirmed and double-confirmed. I can't imagine a problem."

In our room, we're greeted by a bottle of chilled Prosecco and a handwritten note regarding our *anniversario*. We both have failed to write our cards and we want to think about what to say rather than writing a quick "*Ti amo,*" I love you, so we agree to exchange cards in Naples. Since it's nearly time for dinner, we'll save the Prosecco for our first night at Lodolina.

Il Falconiere may be the most romantic dinner setting in Tuscany. We stroll into a large courtyard enclosed by castle-high stone walls and are seated at the perfect spot. Candles flicker on the tables and flames dance in terracotta pots atop the walls. At the far end, water trickles into an ancient cistern. The weather is perfect, so the umbrellas are open only for the intimacy they create. Purple wisteria clusters among dark green leaves cover the building like an enormous bouquet.

With moist eyes and a wobble in his voice, Larry toasts our marriage. "Thank you for agreeing to be my wife all those years ago. The best years of my life."

I am touched. Ours is a good marriage. I lift my glass, choked up myself. "To you…. It is an honor to be your wife," I say, echoing my answer to his proposal.

"Ron's wedding toast is truer now than ever," I whisper, now teary and nostalgic.

Ron, Larry's son, then only twelve, took his role as best man seriously, including the best man's toast. Though he fainted during the ceremony, bashed his chin and was still a bit dazed at dinner, he looked us each in the eye, raised his glass and with the dignity of a boy becoming a man, and said, "May you have many remarkable years." We have had nineteen remarkable years.

Before Larry proposed, we had written our life-promises on a single page, employing the discipline of one-page documents from our business training. We were committed to one another but, coming from failed marriages, I preferred the creative tension of two strong, successful adults choosing to make a life together rather than a legally binding contract. On the night we completed those promises, Larry, on one knee, proposed. He was fairly certain I would not accept. Caught by surprise and melted by his risky tenderness, I heard myself say, "I would be honored to be your wife."

Each anniversary we get out that dog-eared page to re-read our promises, assess how we have done and decide if there is anything we want to change. In twenty years, we made two minor changes, and then changed them back the following year, preferring the original.

Our dream of living in Italy may bring the most remarkable years yet, if the past few days are any indication. For the richest life possible, we try to never overlook and always celebrate that which is remarkable.

Strolling back to our room, I quote from "our song," chosen before we married. "Show me your smile and I'll fill it with laughter… As long as we believe, the best is yet to come."

"You are just so lovely," Larry sighs. "Thank you for being my wife."

I put my arm through his. He squeezes it, drawing me closer.

"I remember the first time you did that," he smiles down at me. "It was a thrill. I felt chosen. I was amazed and honored that you'd choose me. It still thrills me."

As I get ready for bed, I check the mirror. Thankfully, my face is no longer blotchy or swollen. I look relaxed and happy, just like I feel.

Accurate, Honest, Honoring

Due to jet lag, we're up before five. Larry puts on a plush hotel robe, makes us each coffee in his travel espresso maker, kisses my forehead as he sets mine beside the bed, and settles into the overstuffed armchair, feet propped on a suitcase. With computer in his lap and a book on the arm of the chair, he could study this way for hours. I sit in bed, leaning back on two pillows with another under each arm and type away.

I feel ultra-alive and ultra-aware, like someone flipped a switch I didn't know I had. I'm shocked by how much has happened in only three days. I was certain yesterday could not be as eventful as the day before. Then the day unfolded, astonished me with surprise after surprise, and now I type as fast as I can, trying to capture it all.

As I finish recording our anniversary dinner, deep in thought and fingers flying, I look up and say, "Do you want breakfast?" As much as I adore Falconiere breakfasts, this morning I'd like to stay right here, swept away.

"Nope, not a bit," he says, eyes glued to his book. "You?"

"No, dinner last night was plenty. I've been thinking about something I want to capture, before it flies from my head."

He half-nods and I turn back to my journal with an exhilarating, yet disquieting sense that I may be developing the mind of an immature writer. I have started noticing details more than ever and long to preserve them. I find myself internally rehearsing the most precise words to describe each facet of every event. I want to render my experience so vividly that a future reader might experience it.

I like imagining how my words might sound in my reader's ears. Perhaps every writer imagines a reader, whether for an email or an epic, as I imagine mine right now. I long to ask my reader, "Can you tell your presence is felt?"

Taking another sip of espresso, I reflect on this emerging obsession. There is so much in our new life to observe and record. Our new home. Each unique person. The land and culture. The foods and wine. Every plant. My feelings about it all.

I confess I like the sound of my voice in my head, surely another danger sign. I imagine a phrase, reshaping it until the perfect image is conjured in my mind. But I lose the words if I don't write them down immediately. I have never kept a journal, though every good writer I know has insisted I must. Now, when I can't get to my computer to capture something, I replay it again and again to etch it into my memory so I can record it later. I carry a small notebook to register immediately what I see and feel, but it's not always polite to scribble away.

I may enjoy too much my imagined ability to manipulate my reader's experience of my experience. Moments ago I typed:

> *Lying motionless in the luxurious hotel bed, silky sheets wrinkled from last night's tenderness, I watch the dawn sky slowly transform from inky indigo to lavender-gray with golden clouds floating above a tangerine horizon. A competition of songbirds and roosters serenade us as we awaken. The scent of jasmine wafts through an open window. Larry reaches to touch my thigh. He rises to make us each a bracing espresso in his travel Bialetti, coffee we sip from stemmed champagne glasses left yesterday by hotel management on the tray with a bottle of Prosecco and a note complimenting us on our anniversario. I linger in bed, capturing my deepest thoughts as my beloved studies.*

True, but too flowery and contrived for believable reading.

With heightened senses but without excess or drama, I want to record colors, smells, lines and shapes, sounds, textures, movements, thoughts and expressions. I want to tell my story simply, truthfully and vividly, without overstatement. I become more fully aware of my experience as I struggle to be precise in my description.

I glance at the bedside clock. Soon we'll start our fourth day in Italy. But I'm on a roll and don't want to stop. How do I understand this new thing that's consuming me — this need to describe and attach meaning to my new world so that I might share it?

The phone rings. I get up to answer. An urgent fax has been received and hotel management wants to make sure we don't leave without collecting it. Larry offers to go to the front desk. He shaves, showers and hurries out, reminding me that we must leave in an hour.

I feel compelled to continue while my thoughts are fresh. Yet in capturing moments passed, I wonder if I risk missing the moment I am living. It is not possible, I conclude, to live and write simultaneously without altering either the living or the writing. The same has been said of research, that it's not possible to measure something without changing it. Being new at this, I want to be cautious. Yet I succumb, enjoying the sensation of writing in the same way a young woman enjoys giving herself to her first lover... innocently, clumsily, passionately.

I get up to brush my teeth, but am drawn back to my computer for a few final thoughts.

I decide on three rules for my writing — principles I also try to apply to my life. It must be accurate, honest, and honoring. I've long dreamed of writing a book. If this summer gives me a story, as I am beginning to feel it will, I want to do it justice. I shift my position, fingers flying again, pondering my three principles, three promises to my readers.

Accuracy is a challenge for me, I confess. After thirty years in marketing and advertising, it's too tempting to embellish. My intention is not to tell an untruth, but to make the truth more interesting. Innocent additions are not such a big deal, are they? When I forget a detail, why not simply make it up? Yet, even minor fabrications would render the whole untrue, if accuracy has been promised. My reader must feel my story's truth; I do not want to risk their trust. Truth is perceived most naturally if the telling is unadorned. "Just the facts, Jack," my friend Susan, a brilliant author of non-fiction, demanded of herself.

To be accurate, I will record details without exaggeration or alteration. A pink dress will not become scarlet and a colorless sunset will remain so. An unpleasant odor will not be wretched; irritation will not be portrayed as rage. Of course, memory is imperfect and perceptions vary, but I will strive for accuracy. I will force myself to backspace when my mind and fingers get carried away with a fascinating, but inaccurate, retelling.

Secondly, I will be honest. Honesty is different than accuracy; it requires courage and vulnerability. I'll try to see others and their actions with insight and grace, but without excuses. I'll capture the way their words lift my spirits or sting my heart, but I will also try to comprehend and respect their point of view. I must not try to persuade readers of my point of view to make an ally, but present the facts and trust my reader's ability to apply their own judgment. When speaking from my heart, I must be willing to be transparent, so readers see my true self, not the better one I wish to present. It can be risky, being honest.

To write with honesty I must, without pride or justification, expose myself. For example, I am too old and seasoned to be intimidated, but I already feel intimidated by my new Italian life. I am baffled in the grocery store when the women wear clear plastic gloves to touch the produce and I don't know where to find the gloves, let alone how to weigh my apples and print my own price stickers. I'm embarrassed that I can't count coins quickly, ask for directions, or even make small talk about the weather.

Honesty begins within; it requires introspection. I must not try to fool my readers or myself. For example, I deeply dislike being dependent, but in Italy I already depend on Larry to drive and to speak for me. When someone asks a question, I stare blankly, not even courageous enough to say, "*Non capisco,*" I do not understand. In turn, when I try to speak Italian, the person often stares at me, unable to discern what I said. They remain silent, giving me time to say it better. That silence after the stare paralyzes me. I smile and nod, like I mostly understood, and hope Larry will tell me later what they said. I don't want to admit that learning a new language feels too hard, especially at my age, but it does.

Lastly, my writing will be honoring — not elevating, but honoring. Being cynical is as seductive as embellishing. It's too easy to entertain, enrapture or amuse, or make myself seem superior and clever by diminishing someone else. All cultures and creatures have anomalies and idiosyncrasies. But prejudices and generalizations are too often disguised as insights. Cynicism masquerades as wit. People are fascinating, as much for their variety as for their similarities. I want to understand, rather than to judge those I meet, and never to ridicule. I want to honor my reader by honoring those about whom I write.

My laptop warns that its battery is low, so I move to the desk to plug it in. I want just ten more minutes while I'm in this groove.

I do love words, the sound and shape of words, the cadence of phrases, the unfolding of characters, actions and thoughts through words. I take pleasure in the letters lining up as I type, forming clusters that create meaning. Substance from squiggles; meaning from putting them in a row. Perhaps that is why "a line," the theatrical term for a phrase, is called "a line." A line of letters; words lined up. Images, places, people or emotions emerge from the letters I line up. Painting with words requires deliberation. Each word must be chosen, each phrase applied to the page with clarity and simplicity. Ernest Hemingway said, "My aim is to put down on paper what I see and what I feel in the best and simplest way." To do that, he lined up letters, spaces and punctuation marks.

It must be similar for all who create. Painters surely see colors more vividly, the relationship between colors more strikingly, and the lines and voids separating one color from another more distinctly than the rest of us. They put down in colors, voids, lines and shadows what they see or imagine.

For sculptors, forms are surely imagined within an unworked mass and felt beneath their fingers. Shape must be seen in their mind's eye before it can be seen in the resulting work. The sculptor's touch must be more sensitive, their fingers able to create what exists in their minds, delighted or disappointed as the form emerges.

Musicians, I believe, hear volume, pitch and rhythm in everything. They must discern tones, chords and discords, harmony and disharmony, and tempo more clearly than I do. This mastery can result in the disciplined composition of a symphony or the freedom to adhere mostly to tempo and key, creating what we admire as jazz.

Once in a while, the thing being created takes on a life of its own, pulling along the one creating it. The writer lines up letters to form words and discovers they are imbued with unexpected meaning. The sculptor taps the chisel or pushes the substance with his fingers beyond conscious thought and likes what happened. The painter makes the perfect brush mark before imagining it, or the musician plays an unintended riff. The creator sighs and acquiesces, eager to see where this new creation will go. It is joyful to feel the thing being created exert its own velocity and energy. It is the ride of a lifetime to serve one's creation. It happens with offspring. We create them and then we serve their energetic formation, only partly in our hands.

I must stop and get dressed. But there are two lingering thoughts I long to capture.

If this new life of ours becomes a book, or just a record for family, I'll experience it many times, not only twice as Anaïs Nin famously observed when she wrote, "We write to taste life twice, in the moment and in retrospect." Rather, I'll experience it first in the living, again imagining the words to best capture it, yet again writing it down, and countless times more in the editing. If the resulting prose is worth pulling out again, I'll re-live it, perhaps decades later, in the re-reading. Each word must be as carefully chosen as a musical note or a chisel's strike. It will become part of Larry's and my indelible history, perhaps affect our future, and become a stranger's knowledge if shared.

I look at my watch. Larry will be upset if I'm not ready, but there's one last thought I don't want to lose.

Whatever arises in our marriage because of our move to Italy, I'm going to report it honestly, even if our story becomes exposed to people we don't know. There will be moments when we are not our best, moments we would prefer were not remembered or shared. Everyone has such times. But challenges in a marriage are not only our story; they are every couple's story. If there are hurdles in this new experience of ours, old crevices we haven't tended or new conflicts, as there surely will be, I hope and pray working together to resolve them will take us to a stronger place. Perhaps our story will help others to a stronger place, too.

And now I *must* stop. The most important skill in writing may be to know when to stop. Mastery in any art is to perceive when the words, colors, forms, texture or sound represent such unity that one word, brush stroke, chisel tap or grace note would render the finished work less complete. Michelangelo reportedly said, "Carving is easy, you simply go down to the skin and stop." In my endeavor to record our first summer in Italy, I want to tell our story in the clearest and simplest way. I hope to occasionally feel the exhilaration of words that carry me along, as they did this morning. And I hope to know when to stop.

In fact, one of *life's* most useful tools is to know when to stop.

I breathe a long sigh and gently close the lid of my computer. For today, I must stop *now*. I promised Larry I'd be ready when he came back and I still need to shower. He hates being late, and if I type one more word, I'll make us late.

Italy Teaches Patience

Larry walks in carrying a tray with two *cappuccini* as I emerge from the bathroom ready for the day. He says the mysterious fax was the contract to sell our Chicago condo. The closing is in ninety days, early September, but our agent says we must sign and return the contract immediately. She says the buyers may want to close early. I think she just wants to seal the deal.

"Sorry I was so long. Sabina was there and she gave me the scoop on Naples… says there's an increase in crime because mafia families are fighting again. She says it's serious, but they're always fighting. And, she insisted I bring you a cappuccino."

"Thank you, Sabina," I say, raising my cup in a toast. "Does this make you want to reconsider this weekend?"

"No… I want to get away for a few days, don't you? We can't go inside Lodolina while the floors are drying. If we're going to Naples, now is the time."

"Besides," he adds with a dreamy smile, "once we move in, we won't want to leave."

"Let's talk while we walk. Lorenzo's probably waiting for us," I say, taking a gulp of cappuccino, grabbing my handbag and heading toward the door.

"Oh! We're late!" Larry downs the rest of his coffee, picks up his book in case we have to wait, and slips a memory stick with documents into his pocket. For once, being late is not my fault.

Lorenzo is waiting in the parking area, ready to lead us to the immigration office in Arezzo, about forty minutes away. Today we hope to get our *Permessi*, our permission to stay longer than ninety days. We'll take two cars so Lorenzo can leave if the wait is long. He shows us where to park and walks with us to the *Questura*, Police Headquarters, which includes the immigration office. We're starting early because Lorenzo says it's important to be among the first to arrive.

A white plastic tent has been erected in front of the small building. Lorenzo says it's a temporary location for the *Questura* while the real one is being renovated. About fifty people are standing in a queue. We take our place just as the *Questura* door opens. The tent, meant for shade from the blistering sun, is already a kiln.

Larry says it's impossible to read. I try to write in my journal, but my pen is too slippery. The line barely moves. After nearly an hour, Larry urges Lorenzo to leave.

"I go for to see how long," Lorenzo says, then speaks with the policeman guarding the door.

Lorenzo motions us to join him. Inside he murmurs, "I tell to the officer, where is the line for residency without work? My friends do not want to pass over anyone, but do not want to stand in the wrong line. He says to me that no one ever tell to him, 'I do not want pass over anyone,' and that we must go inside and wait for window three."

I feel guilty passing all the people in line, but am relieved to follow Lorenzo to a bench inside. The building is not air-conditioned, but at least we're sitting. Guessing from their ages, most must be seeking work permits as well as residency, so I don't feel so badly moving ahead.

It's soon our turn at *sportello tre*, window three, applications without work permits. Larry tells the agent that the *Consolato* in Chicago said our documents were all approved so we would need only our passports with our Italian visas to be approved.

"*No. Impossibile*," the agent states curtly.

He informs us, in rapid Italian, that only the *Questura* can check documents and send them to Rome, and only Rome has the authority to grant permission to stay. We take deep breaths, knowing there is no use arguing. In fact, there's risk in arguing.

The agent pushes a list of essential documents under the glass in the *sportello*. Most are the same ones we submitted to the Chicago *Consolato* and, fortunately, they are on the memory stick in Larry's pocket. In addition, the list says we each need four passport photos, a completed application, and a *marche di bollo*, stamp proving we paid for processing — none of which we have.

Larry tells the agent he has the documents on a memory stick, but needs a computer and printer. He asks respectfully, in Italian, if it is possible to use a computer, printer and copier here, pointing to the one in the hallway. Lorenzo hovers, in case we need help.

The agent shakes his head. "*No, non qui*," no, not here. He motions to the next person in line, dismissing us.

Lorenzo assures us he knows where to get what we need, so we pile in his car. In central Arezzo, he points to a *tabacchi*, a small store that sells cigarettes, candy, batteries, postcards and bus tickets — and official items like postage, payment stamps, and lottery tickets. He drives around the corner and points to a camera shop, "Here photos should be printed immediately."

Then he takes us to a STOP shop and introduces us to the owner who can help us print documents and make copies. Lorenzo also seems surprised by the long list, perhaps to show sympathy. We're dismayed but determined, and thankful Lorenzo knows his way around Arezzo.

"*Questa è Italia*," Lorenzo teases. I recall my upset just two days ago. Yes, *this is Italy*, complicated, exasperating and wonderful.

"Thank you. We would've been lost, quite literally, without you," Larry says as Lorenzo leaves us to return to Cortona.

"It was nothing, truly a pleasure. *In bocca al lupo!*" Lorenzo says, a phrase to say good luck that literally means "in the mouth of the wolf," like "break a leg" in English. It's bad luck to wish someone good luck.

Lorenzo, already high in my estimation, leaps toward sainthood with today's kindness. Larry and I print, copy and assemble documents with the help of Lorenzo's friend, buy payment stamps at the *tabacchi*, have not-so-flattering photos made at the camera shop, and walk back to the *Questura* five blocks away.

Fortunately, the agent had scribbled "*ritorna*" on our application, so we don't have to stand under the tent again. Nearing noon, the tent feels more unbearable than ever. My guess is one hundred degrees and one hundred people. Everyone can't possibly get in before the *Questura* closes in one hour.

After a short wait inside, the same agent goes through our documents and nods at each page, declaring all is in order. He writes our name at the top of each page, staples photos onto two pages and hands us the spares. We're instructed to sign every page of every document. Proudly, I sign my own. The agent actually smiles, then pounds the pages with three official stamps, puts everything in two large envelopes — one to send to Rome, one to give to us.

He explains what will happen after our documents are, hopefully, approved by Rome. "*Tornate in un mese, se il nome è sulla lista accanto alla porta ... lì ... allora il documento è pronto. Andrà bene per un anno, poi deve essere rinnovato.*"

I listen for key words: *un mese,* one month; *nome sulla lista... alla porta,* name on list... at the door; *documento è pronto,* document is ready... *Un anno... deve rinnovato,* one year... must renew. Larry assures him we understand.

The moment we're out the door, I turn to Larry, as if he doesn't already know the problem, and exclaim, "A month! We can't wait a month! What about our shipment? We need Italian residency *now.*"

"There's nothing we can do," he says calmly. "*Questa è Italia.*" I am not amused.

I call Maryte, our moving agent in Milan. "I must inform *Dogana* immediately," she says. "Your shipment arrived at Naples yesterday, is at *Dogana* now and will be released for transport to Cortona tomorrow. The tax must be their discretion. I will explain to them. It should be the full amount by law. Sometimes they feel generous."

"Larry has Cortona residency," I offer.

"Only the *Permesso di Soggiorno* matters," she says. "It is national law, not local."

"Let's hope for generosity," I say, feeling helpless.

Larry's right, there's nothing we can do. I'm disturbed that after all we researched and the number of officials we talked with in the past three years, no one told us it would take a month after we applied in Italy — if we are approved. We could have applied for *Permessi* when we visited Cortona in February, had we known.

Today has been steeped in bureaucracy. But it has also been touched by kindness: Lorenzo's willing assistance, the *Questura* officer letting us enter ahead of those wanting work permits, and the STOP owner's helpfulness. We're now at the mercy of the Italian *Dogana,* Customs. We hope for their kindness as well. Based on our experience in the Florence airport with our big box, we know *Dogana* officers have some discretion about how much to charge.

For years, we will tell stories about dealing with what seems to us to be unreasonable, illogical and complicated Italian bureaucracy. We'll learn to follow the rules without resistance, whether they make sense or not. This is Italy and we must do as Italians do. It is part of the experience. Enza, Marco's wife, warned us when we first talked of moving to Cortona. "Italy will teach you patience," she said. She was right.

We will need patience, perseverance, plus good humor, if our new life is to be happy and exciting rather than exasperating. Accept and enjoy the differences in cultures and in people, a worthy guide for us all.

My Imaginary Friend

Permesso application and lunch completed, we hurry to Francesco's office for more deliberations and decisions, too many to describe, and then on to Lodolina with Francesco in the car with us. Below Palazzone at our turnoff, a long concrete pole is lying near the roadside.

"A Lodolina birthday gift!" laughs Francesco. "Your *Enel* pole, I believe… A birthday gift because it is exactly one year we have been asking *Enel* to remove it."

Sure enough, when we get to Lodolina, the concrete pole is missing. Underground wiring for electricity and phone was installed when our renovation began and we paid *Enel* twelve hundred euros for pole removal, but the unsightly obstacle remained like an upright dinosaur bone in the middle of the back yard throughout the construction.

Inside, I check the floors. Francesco says more coats of liquid bees wax will be needed to seal the terracotta.

"We must walk only on the styrofoam," he warns. "After this dries, Marcello will add more hands, more layers. If treated in the correct way, the floors will gleam but not shine. But cannot be rushed."

After stepping on styrofoam through all the rooms to approve the *battiscopa*, baseboards, we stand outside in the dirt yard to discuss schedule. Francesco still thinks the house can be ready on time, but the floors are drying more slowly than expected. It's Wednesday. Nothing but floor treatments can be done this week, he says. Next week, Monday through Wednesday we'll have painters, tile layers, cabinetmakers, stonemasons, electricians, plumbers and ironworkers, plus himself, Gabriele and us.

Thursday morning the movers will arrive with our belongings.

"Now, we must decide about how to make the front door call your guests," Francesco says, knowing that yesterday we agreed, but were not convinced. "While you are in Naples, we will pour concrete for your terrace."

After another ten minutes of back and forth getting nowhere discussing the ramp or *Belvedere*, we put off deciding until the terrace is poured.

Larry and I also disagree about terrace size. He wants a large grassy lawn to soften the stone house and for grandchildren to play. I want a large stone terrace to the edge of the front yard to make the entrance more important and for a long table for dinner parties. We both feel strongly.

"You need to be our counselor again," I tell Francesco.

Francesco climbs onto the seat of the *scavatore*, a small yellow bulldozer, and starts to sketch. We stand and watch, curious to see what will unfold.

"The front terrace," Francesco explains as he draws, "must be at least as wide as the oldest section of the house and extend forward to the line of the first *cipresso*.

I love to watch him create. Soon, he gets down and we pace off his plan including a separate outdoor dining table area and breakfast corner. More terrace than Larry wants and less than I want, but it meets our needs. I imagine over-sized terracotta urns with blue hydrangea to mark each side of the front door.

Suddenly, a black squirrel scampers across the ivy hedge at the front edge of the lawn and scurries up one of the cypress trees.

"Hey!! Did you see the squirrel? He was black!"

Pierangelo, our foreman, had told us a family of *scoiattoli* was living in the ivy hedge, but we hadn't seen one in all our visits. I never imagined they would be black. This little guy has a skinny black body, furry tufts on his very tall ears, the scraggliest tail I've ever seen, and a white chest. It's as if he dressed up in a tuxedo just for me. I wonder if he'll eat raw almonds if I leave some. I wonder if he is a *he*. I wonder where his family will go when we cut down the ivy hedge blocking our view. In fact, I now wonder if we should cut down the hedge at all.

Somehow this little black squirrel, vulnerable and surely frightened by all the activity and noise, seems like a new friend to me. He must feel as disoriented as I do.

Francesco continues to sketch outdoor spaces for us, walkways, walls, stairs, and an outdoor grill. We won't be surprised to be presented with watercolor sketches for the walls and walkways, as he did with the house.

Larry says quietly, "We could spend a fortune on stone walls and terraces. It seems the outside of the house is as important as the inside. We need to take this step by step."

It's a seductive undertaking, restoring an ancient farmhouse on a Tuscan hillside, and we're deliriously happy victims. But we hope to finish and still afford to live here.

I'm beginning to realize this won't be the tranquil summer we anticipated. Francesco tells us workers will be here daily until at least August to finish the guesthouse. They'll start every morning at eight o'clock, six days a week. Saturday will be half-days, unless they fall behind and need to stay longer. Sunday will be quiet. He adds, like a postscript, that the materials along the driveway must stay until the guesthouse is finished.

Suddenly it's nearly seven o'clock. I long for a brief nap before dinner, but Francesco says we must visit the glassmaker before we leave for Naples. Like every artisan he chooses, the glassmaker is in Tuscany. But Tuscany is large. We drive thirty minutes into the valley.

Once there, Larry paces while the rest of us discuss the problem of opening the bathroom glass door against the stone trim. He loses patience and retreats to the car to read while we continue discussing the color and thickness of the glass, how to create the semi-opaque look we want, plus hinges and handles.

It's almost ten o'clock when we drop Francesco and Carlo at their studio. I check off today's accomplishments to make myself feel better. We applied for Italian residency, approved the floors, agreed to the dimensions of the front terrace, started a hardscape layout, ordered glass for bathroom walls, and met the little black squirrel.

Not only did I not get my nap, we didn't get dinner. It's the end of our fourth day in Italy, our third day of construction decisions. Yesterday I was tired; today I'm exhausted.

Finally back at the hotel, we still must handle emails and pack for Naples.

"Do we really need to go so early?" I ask. "We could have a nice breakfast and stick around in case Francesco needs us. Maybe leave at noon?"

"If we're going to Naples, this is the time," Larry says, nixing my idea. "We can't get into Lodolina until Monday. Next weekend we'll have boxes to unpack. Besides, we've wanted to look for Rossi paintings for years. The only fast train leaves at seven. We'll be there by noon. If we wait, it could take the full day."

I acquiesce. I could use a break from construction decisions and a romantic getaway with my husband.

While Larry finishes his emails, I look on the internet for locations of Nunzio Rossi paintings and fold a few garments so I'll be quicker in the morning. By midnight, I put my head on my pillow, serenaded by the rumble of my empty stomach and feeling like this new life is moving very fast. Larry's still on his computer.

As I drift off, my last thought is about my new friend, the little black squirrel. I smile. Even an imaginary friend can be comforting. Perhaps that's why the elderly and lonely talk to themselves, for the comfort of a like-minded companion.

Some say pretend friends are only for children, but being childlike may be the most natural defense when you're feeling strangely alone and disoriented.

Undone in Naples

We leave *Il Falconiere* at six-fifteen to catch the train to Naples. Larry talks with the agent for a long time and looks upset when he turns around.

"The direct train's sold out. We're on the *regionale*. It doesn't leave for another hour. Two trains plus a layover in Rome. What a waste... We should've reserved."

"Who'd guess such an early train to Naples would sell out?" I try to be supportive despite getting up at five-thirty, rushing to pack, skipping breakfast after no dinner last night, and now with an hour to wait.

"Really, sweetheart, it's okay," I add when he doesn't respond. "We'll get there, just a few hours later. Let's get a cappuccino and a croissant. I'm starving." He seems on edge and I'd like to reduce the tension before spending hours on a train together.

On the *regionale*, stopping at every station no matter how small, I read, sleep, write and watch Tuscany become Umbria, and then Lazio, the region of Rome. Larry reads his books and the documents for selling our Chicago condo.

The train glides through fields of young sunflowers, full of hope. *Girasole*, what a perfect name: *gira*, it turns; *sole*, sun.

We wait three hours to change trains in Rome and finally pull into central Naples late afternoon. It feels good to stretch my legs. Exiting the once-grand Naples train station, I look around in stunned disbelief, instantly comprehending *la scena di Napoli*, the scene of Naples, a phrase some Italians use to describe utter chaos. While Larry searches for the taxi line, I stand aghast, shaking my head in disbelief.

Trash is everywhere. Flattened cardboard boxes are stacked two feet high on the sidewalk in front of the station, as if a modern art installation. Heaps of discarded plastic water bottles have collected against the station's front wall. Near the curb, twisted bicycle parts are locked to the metal racks like rusty old bones, their frames stolen long ago. People walk around the rubbish mindlessly, as if this is normal.

The noise is deafening. Buses, taxis and limos zoom around the front circle without observing lanes. Mopeds and motorcycles weave in and out at dangerous speeds. Revving motors compete with a car alarms and police sirens. Horns blare, warning people to watch out, but the warnings come from all directions so no one pays attention. To be heard over the vehicle roar, people must lean toward each other and shout.

Fumes from gasoline and garbage foul the air. Nearby dumpsters overflow with sour garbage. Behind them is a weedy lot strewn with newspapers, clothing, empty liquor bottles, disposable diapers, and piles of animal feces. I hold my breath without thinking and hurry to join Larry in the limo line.

"The taxi line is impossible," he yells. "I want to get out of here fast. We'll take a limo." I don't even ask him what a limo to our hotel costs. It has to be worth it.

To me, each Italian city has its defining verb: Venice enchants, Florence inspires, Rome impresses, and Naples assaults. This is the loudest, most disorderly, in-your-face place I've ever been. Naples may excite the adventurous, but it is not for the meek or timid.

At the Hotel Excelsior, consistent with our sold-out train experience, the receptionist says we do not have a reservation. He checks his computer again and, nodding, informs us that our agent booked a room at a sister hotel by the same name, but in Sorrento on the Amalfi Coast. It's nearly dinnertime. We're hungry and tired and want to be in Naples, not Sorrento, though I wonder why.

"*Non è un problema,*" he says, not a problem, then quotes the daily rate for "*una camera bella,*" a pretty room. We look at each other, eyebrows lifted.

"Of course, Naples is more expensive than Sorrento," he adds in flawless English.

Larry calls our travel agent in Chicago to ask her to cancel the room in Sorrento and check on Naples hotel rates. She says the best rate at this hotel is half what the receptionist quoted. He agrees to the lower rate without skipping a beat.

As we leave for dinner, the concierge warns us not to wear jewelry outside the hotel. When I say we're going just around the corner, he raises his eyebrow. I turn my wedding ring to close the stones inside my fist and we take off our watches, tucking them into a zippered pocket inside Larry's jacket. I leave my small diamond stud earrings in, hoping I'm not jeopardizing my earlobes.

At *Ristorante Luciano* we share every course, as we often do. First, an assortment of seafood and fresh *mozzarella di bufala*. The Naples area produces the world's finest *mozzarella di bufala*, so tender it melts onto the plate as I cut into it. Then we share *pasta con vongole* with succulent clams — Larry's favorite — and, lastly, a whole *branzino* in *acqua pazzo*, sea bass in crazy water with stewed fresh tomato and spices. The restaurant is fragrant and cozy and the friendly service is calming after our experiences at the station and hotel.

"Why are you eating so fast? Slow down," Larry says in an irritated, hushed tone.

I frown at him, taken aback, and look down at my plate, then his. He has less food left than I do and we were served equal amounts. I'm nearly sixty, surely I can decide how quickly I want to eat.

"Please don't micro-manage me. I have more left than you do," I answer sweetly, trying to hide my ire.

We have been together twenty-four hours per day for five days and today has been extra stressful. Some tension can be expected. I don't think Larry meant to insult me, but I feel corrected and hurt.

After a few moments of silence, I say, "I think you owe me an apology. I wasn't eating so fast. Besides, shouldn't I decide how fast to eat?"

Under his breath he says, "You were gobbling. You've been gobbling since we got to Italy.

"That's not true... or kind," I say flatly.

Dinner, delicious as it is, has become not so enjoyable. After several more minutes of silence, I decide to move on and change the subject. This is not a good start to our anniversary weekend. Despite a more pleasant conversation through dessert, I feel on guard. I wonder what's up with him.

About midnight, the hotel phone rings, waking us both. It's our Chicago realtor. Larry gave her our Naples information in case there was a problem with the documents.

He talks for a few minutes, hangs up and turns toward me. "Our buyers want to close and move in next week. Can we do it?"

"Next week?" I gulp. "We're supposed to close in September. We still have furniture in all the rooms, art on the walls, and the boxes for storage aren't even marked. What about the cars? It's the weekend and we're on vacation."

My voice and heart rate rise as I think of each new hurdle.

Larry suggests Dale might handle finishing the move with professional help. I say it's a lot to ask of a friend, but if she's willing there is no one more organized or trustworthy.

After a heated back and forth with me recounting all the obstacles and Larry saying we should at least try because it saves a great deal of money, he gets up and makes a list of everything that would need to happen and who might handle it. It does seem possible, though I feel overwhelmed and reluctant to agree this fast to something this big. He keeps pushing until I give in. We will accept the buyer's request.

At one in the morning, mid-day in Chicago, Larry exchanges a flurry of emails, phone calls and faxes with our realtor, lawyer and Dale. It's almost two when he turns off the lights, crawls in, and falls asleep immediately. I lie awake thinking *I do not like this.*

* * *

The next morning, I write emails and Larry makes phone calls. I confirm that Dale will arrange for and supervise the movers. Larry connects our agent with our lawyer, asking them to work together to cover the closing. By late morning, when the biggest challenges are handled, I feel exhausted.

After a quick breakfast at what looks like a fantastic buffet if we had more time, we ask the concierge about Nunzio Rossi paintings. He says *Chiesa San Pietro a Maiella,* the location of Rossi's major fresco, closes at noon, in ten minutes. It's too late for today.

"Let's walk to the church this afternoon, just to be sure we know where it is," Larry says, energized by the Chicago successes.

The concierge warns, "Don't walk in Naples. It's not safe. Take a taxi."

Larry nods, but I'll be surprised if he does it. A frugal athlete, he likes to walk everywhere. We leave our jewelry in the hotel safe, including my earrings and our wedding rings.

After finalizing and faxing documents, we venture out of the hotel into the sunshine. In the distance across the glistening bay, Mount Vesuvius is belching a trail of white smoke. Larry summons a taxi, much to my relief, and we head into the heart of Naples.

Our taxi driver darts onto trolley tracks to avoid a motorcycle and veers back only when we're nearly nose-to-nose with an oncoming trolley.

He stops near a church and points out the rest of the way, saying we must continue on foot. On the bay, where our hotel is located, Naples seems serene. In stark contrast, the city center is more frenetic than the train station.

Aggressive street vendors, lining both sides of the sidewalks, hawk their wares from wobbly tables and dirty blankets. Pedestrians must pass in single file, because the sidewalk is crowded with books, handbags, toys, bras, clothes, shoes, games, sunglasses, wallets, rugs, jewelry, statues, dishes, calendars, pots and pans, sandwiches, lemon ice and gelato. Vendors with fake designer wares scoop up their blankets when they hear a siren, then lay them out as soon as the police car passes. The ground is littered with trash and animal droppings and the air reeks of gasoline, cigarettes, garbage, and excrement.

I love Saturday market in Cortona, but this is a different planet.

From overhead windows in dilapidated post-war apartments nearby, we hear couples argue, televisions blare and babies cry. Someone who needs the practice pounds relentlessly on an out-of-tune piano. I take a photo of a grandmother, young mother and little girl in a frilly party dress clinging to each other on one scooter — all without helmets — easing into speedy, snarling traffic.

We escape to a side street lined with music shops and stumble upon the *Conservatoria San Pietro*. Classical music drifts from the doorway and we're greeted warmly by the ticket agent. Alas, we are still in Naples: inside the gate cars are parked haphazardly, a broom in a big metal trash can blocks the walkway and weeds fill the courtyard. In the center, a greater-than-life bronze statue of Beethoven transcends the setting. The plaque says "Ludwig van Beethoven, Francesco Jerace, 1895." Staring up at the imposing statue with classical music soothing our ears, I sense an eerie calm.

"I think the statue's the only attraction," Larry says, eager to move along. Around the corner we find the church with the Rossi paintings. As expected, it's closed. At least we know where it is, Larry says.

Despite the warning not to walk, we follow our map up a very long, very steep hill beside a major thoroughfare to the *Museo Archeologico Nazionale di Napoli*. Its art, amassed over centuries by generations of the powerful Farnese family, is considered the largest private art collection in Italy and includes paintings by Titian and other masters, priceless sculptures and other treasures. The *Museo* also claims the largest archeological collection in Italy, with treasures from Pompeii, Herculaneum and Stabiae, three cities buried by the massive eruption of Mount Vesuvius in 79CE.

The large museum is almost empty. We stroll through endless galleries of artifacts. I'm taken by a graceful bronze fawn from the House of the Faun in Pompeii, circa 200BC. Another room has a stone bust that looks like Larry's father. I snap photos; no one seems to care.

At the gallery of ancient erotic art, signs enticingly say "By Appointment Only" and "Children Are Not Allowed." Actually, it's open for anyone to walk in at will. Unlike the nearly vacant museum, these rooms are crowded.

I feel a bit squirmy standing close to strangers in a darkened gallery staring at over-sized phalluses, sex toys of antiquity, and vases decorated with scenes of copulation. Preoccupation with sex, it seems, is not a modern phenomenon at all.

"We still have time to see the *Pinacoteca*," Larry says as we exit the dark museum into the blinding sun. He pulls out the map to find the best way to walk.

"We've been walking for four hours," I say. "I'm ready for a taxi back to the hotel. Can't we go to the *Pinacoteca* tomorrow, after the Rossi church?"

"What are you going to do at the hotel… more emails? We came to see Naples, not the hotel," he replies energetically.

"We need to confirm arrangements for our Monday closing," I remind him. "And the concierge warned not to walk in Naples."

Larry reluctantly agrees to take a taxi to the hotel. We stand at a taxi sign, but none arrive. We give up and follow a hotel sign up a narrow street, hoping for taxis at the hotel. After several minutes' walking uphill, we're in a residential area with no hotel. A taxi is parked on the street with the driver inside, just sitting. When Larry asks if he is *libero*, free, he says in Italian he's waiting for a rider who called. Larry explains we need to go to the Hotel Excelsior. The driver says he'll wait one more minute and then take us.

When no one shows up, he motions us to get in. He drives like a drugged Mario Andretti, swerving across lanes at a ferocious speed. He follows a truck so closely we breathe its exhaust and then he honks angrily as our front bumper nearly touches the truck's tail pipe. He zooms past the truck at the first tiny opening. Rather than going down the hill toward the bay and our hotel, he drives away from the bay toward the *autostrada* around Naples.

"Our hotel is on the bay," Larry reminds him.

"*Si, lo so,*" he quips; yes, I know.

Larry grits his teeth. Soon he says, "Turn around." When the driver ignores him, Larry repeats, "*Gira. Nostro albergo è alla baia.*" Turn. Our hotel is at the bay.

Larry's Italian is clear but basic; the driver's is lightning fast with curses and rude gestures. Larry is sure we're being taken for a ride, literally and figuratively. At the hotel, Larry pays him the full fare but no tip, believing he had added significantly to the cost by taking a long way around. Both men are upset.

We spend several more hours on our closing. Dale has arranged to supervise the packing on Tuesday, the only day movers can come. The buyers agree to give us until Wednesday to get the condo cleaned. Our lawyer says the documents, except for our signatures, are in order. He advises to sign a Power of Attorney, just in case. We don't have storage for our cars and the buyers say they need both parking spaces immediately.

As we head to dinner, the concierge reminds us not to wear jewelry. I turn my wedding ring around again, reclaimed from the hotel vault, and put my watch in my handbag, tucked tightly under my arm with the shoulder strap wrapped around my wrist twice. Surely, it'll be okay. We're only walking across the street to a restaurant on the well-lit wharf.

Ristorante Transatlantico sits in the shadow of *Castel dell'Ovo*, Castle of the Egg. According to the hotel concierge, the medieval castle was named for Dante's description of the strength of an egg, but according to our waiter the name traces to a medieval legend that Virgil hid a magical egg inside the foundation to empower the fortifications.

We sip local white wine from grapes grown in volcanic soil, and chat in hushed tones about the challenges of the mafia and the surprising aggressiveness of the *Napolitani*. I wonder if it stems from a culture of passion, since even the calmest, kindest people seem intense.

At the next table an American couple and their pretty college-age daughter are ordering. The mom asks the waiter "What's mel-an-san-y."

He answers "Aubergine."

"Yes, I see that word on the menu," the mom replies, "but what *is* it?"

The waiter looks perplexed, as if he wishes he could help, but is stumped. Waiters in tourist locations must face this constantly, the variety of names for one food. To him, this woman speaks English, so aubergine, the English word for *melanzane*, should be enough. He probably knows the German, French, Spanish, even Russian or Japanese word for *melanzane*, just not the American one.

The woman appears gracious, but frustrated. "Mom… just order something else," her daughter pleads. Her husband looks down and remains silent.

"Eggplant," I offer quietly.

The woman nods with an appreciative smile.

She turns back to the waiter. "I'd like the mel-an-san-y."

I'm amused that every human must believe his or her mother tongue is the correct one. If I know a vegetable as eggplant, then it is eggplant and no other word will create the elongated, purple-globe vegetable in my mind.

After we order, Larry and I talk about the museum's exceptional collections, our favorite pieces, and how surprised we are that, except for the gallery of erotic artifacts, this important museum was empty.

Lit by reflections from spotlights on the castle, the water in the bay twinkles and dances. I look out to the sea and am reminded that my Uncle Herbert, my dad's younger brother, was shot down over the Bay of Naples in 1944. He was twenty. It seems ironic that my uncle, an young American farm boy I never met, was killed liberating this foreign land I now call home.

His marker is in the American Cemetery near Florence, where over five thousand American dead are honored.

Larry and I finish dinner, finally relaxed and ready for sleep. Tomorrow we'll go Rossi-hunting. Years ago, we bought a late-Renaissance painting attributed to Nunzio Rossi, an artist who lived in Naples in the mid-1600s. However, the few photos we've seen of Rossi's work make us question the attribution, so we hope to see other paintings and decide if we think Rossi really painted ours.

*   *   *

Early the next morning in the hotel room, I pull back the drapes and gaze at our view of the castle and bay saturated with sunlight. Sailboats and yachts fill the inner harbor. Outside the breakwater, a dozen fishing boats bob among shallow-water buoys. Fifty feet beyond is an open cargo ship, like the one carrying our belongings. The wood crates, stacked precariously high and exposed to weather, make me glad we bought the insurance.

It's Saturday. There should be no condo business for two days so we take off early for sightseeing. Walking, despite the concierge's warning not to, we stumble upon the Sansevero Chapel, *Capella Sansevero de' Sangri*, with illusionary sculptures carved in the 1750s by Giuseppe Sammartino. *The Veiled Christ* lies under seemingly transparent gauze sculpted of crystalline white marble. As we circle the masterpiece, Christ's expression mysteriously changes from troubled to peaceful. Another figure entitled *Despair* struggles under a stone net that looks flexible, yet the entire statue is carved from a single piece of marble. We wonder how stone could be appear so transparent, fluid and alive. These statues alone are worth a trip to Naples and we found them by accident while walking, against hotel advice.

Back on the streets, we search again for *Chiesa San Pietro a Maiella*, the church with the most important Nunzio Rossi fresco. When we find it, that part of the church is blocked off for no apparent reason and we cannot see anything.

Next on our list is a museum complex with several Rossi paintings, *Certosa di San Martino*. We think it's not far, but up the steep mountain, so

Larry finds a taxi. The driver drives toward *Capodimonte*, the mountaintop museum, going as out of the way as yesterday's driver. Larry explains to him in Italian that we only want to go to the *Certosa di San Martino*, which is close, not to the museum at the top. The driver says, "*Lo so*," I know.

"But this road goes around the city," Larry insists, "*away* from *San Martino*.

The driver acts like he doesn't understand English, so Larry repeats himself slowly in clear, slow, Italian.

"*Si, lo so*," the driver says, continuing in the same direction.

Larry pulls out our map, confirms we're headed away from the museum and starts to get angry, which seems to please the driver.

"*Gira!*" Larry instructs. Turn. "*Adesso!*" Now, he adds emphatically.

"I refuse to repeat the fiasco of yesterday," Larry says, turning to me. "Taxi drivers here make a sport of gouging foreigners."

The driver overhears, scowls, whips the car around into on-coming traffic and says in English, "You are not from Naples. You do not know."

Within moments we're at *Certosa San Martino*, escaping the taxi with relief. Our driver says he should wait for us because of the neighborhood, but we're so glad to be rid of him we say in unison, "*No, grazie*," and send him off.

In the museum we find a painting with the technique, color, texture and sensibility of ours, but the artist is unknown. "After Caravaggio," the sign says.

We wander into a room of paintings depicting the plague. The write-up says forty percent of Naples' population died from the epidemic in 1656, around the time our painting was completed. I wonder what kind of man Nunzio Rossi was. Was Antonio Rossi, an artist with paintings in this room from a later period, his son? Since the name Rossi is as common as Smith, they're probably unrelated.

We walk the entire museum and give up finding any Nunzio Rossi paintings. Outside, we see spectacular views of the city, bay, isle of Capri and Mt. Vesuvius, but no taxis.

Trudging down the hill to find a taxi or a coffee shop, we agree to go into whichever comes first. Neither appear. My feet are beginning to hurt.

Eventually we find two city buses. A bus in Naples feels risky to me, but we're desperate. As he boards, Larry shows the driver a map and where we want to go. The driver says, *"boos metro,"* pointing to the other bus.

"Alle quattro," he adds. We guess it leaves at four, in twenty minutes.

"Biglietti?" Larry asks, tickets?

The driver points to a café bar farther down the street. For one euro each Larry buys tickets. A bus may be a bad idea, but it seems to be our only choice. I would love a coffee, but now there is no time.

When Larry gets on what we think is the right bus, the driver points to a different bus leaving first. *"Grazie,"* Larry says and we head toward a third bus.

Larry stops to check our pocket dictionary so he can say, "Please tell us where to get off." We climb on and take the front seat, close to the driver. Larry shows him our map and says his practiced phrase. The driver laughs. "Sure. I'll tell you where to get off!" he teases in perfect English. We join him, chuckling at the unintended joke.

"Okay, okay!" Larry grins, then adds *"Grazie."*

On the ride down the hill, the bus driver philosophizes. "I don't care where you are from, you are my brother. That is my identification, my point of view."

Larry smiles, "That is a kind point of view, a kind identification. You must be a good man."

"Oh no!!!" the driver blurts, "Where will you watch *la partita?"*

I'm not sure what he means, but Larry remembers that tonight's soccer game is Italy versus USA. *La partita*, the match. Important for us, but even more for Italians who are crazy about soccer.

"Wherever we are, we will see it. It'll be unavoidable," Larry says.

"Ah, but of course," the driver sighs with a big, dreamy grin.

After about a mile, he stops the bus and tells us, "You must get out here." He points to the Metro entrance.

"You must take the Metro to the bay for your hotel." So much for being afraid to take a bus. This ride has been a delight.

The subway station is surprisingly clean and modern. It's easy to find our track and the train comes right away. The car is packed with people standing and leaning into one another. Most people get off at the next stop and we find seats. The top of my left foot hurts from all the walking, which is not good.

For two months before we moved, I wore a walking boot for a small fracture in my left foot. The orthopedist gave me the okay to stop wearing it the week we left for Italy. Now, I feel a small pinch where the fracture was.

A few minutes rest on the subway helps. We get off at *Piazza Dante*, a landmark that became almost too familiar as we walked in circles around it yesterday. The *Duomo*, or main cathedral of Naples, is a half-kilometer away and Larry wants to go there first. It's two o'clock. I suggest we stop for lunch first, but Larry wants to keep going and eat later.

We exit the subway behind a girl of about twenty. As she walks, Larry whispers, "She deserves a mention in your journal." She wears skintight white jeans, a red halter-top dotted with small white flowers, and a red leather belt hung with masses of silver chains and crosses. The back strap of her red bra has worked its way up, above the edge of her halter-top. Her shoes have four-inch stiletto heels and four-inch pointed toes.

But what she wears is not what drew Larry's attention — it is how she moves.

"Wow," I say with admiration and a hint of jealousy, "Can she *sashay*!"

"I can't even *do* that," I add, trying to swing my hips in the same way. Growing up in southern Georgia, I used to think I had a pretty good sashay myself.

"This *is* the south of Italy," Larry replies, as if that explains everything.

Her boyfriend studiously does not respond to her sexy moves, provoking even more gyrations from the girl. He walks in front of her, then turns to go a different direction. She follows, giving up the sashay for balance and speed. They soon move out of sight with her trying to sprint in stilettos.

I wonder about men who play hard to get and the women who desire them. If she didn't follow, would he be so quick to walk ahead? If he slowed down and made it easier for them to be together, would she lose interest? Sometimes, women and men are very much alike, striving all the more for what is out of reach.

For me, right now, what's out of reach is food and a place to sit. I'm hungry and my foot hurts with every step. I love to walk, but this marathon is beyond my comfort. On a side street I notice a *pizzeria* with a wood-burning *forno*, oven. I remind him Naples is the city for pizza. Larry protests, saying he wanted a more elegant lunch for us. I insist, so we go in.

The chef is mesmerizing. He grabs a pre-measured mound of dough, kneads and whacks it a few times, tosses the ever-expanding disc in the air, then flops it onto the counter, ready for toppings. He makes another, then another. I time him — under two minutes to form the perfect pizza crust. A woman who looks like his mother adds toppings. Our *pizza capricciosa* is on our table in less than ten minutes, piping hot. It's superb, one of the best I've ever eaten, even without the promised artichokes.

At the table nearest us, two plump women order a large pizza each. At another table, two fashionable men speak French in low, intimate tones and share one pizza. This tiny *pizzeria* is the perfect afternoon respite, complete with entertainment.

Larry is eager to continue our Rossi search, so we finish and leave. After a few minutes, we pass *Chiesa Santa Chiara*. Following our vacation rule of never-pass-an-open-church-because-it-will-be-closed-when-you-return, we go inside.

The sanctuary is enormous. Larry starts walking the perimeter to examine the art. Every step has become uncomfortable for me. The top of my left foot pinches and both soles burn. Since morning we have walked miles on stone streets, museum floors and concrete sidewalks. I sit in a pew, take off my shoes and rest my feet on the cool marble floor while Larry explores.

"Let's go to the *Battistero*. It's just around the corner," he says when he's done.

"Please, let's go back to the hotel," I say. "I don't think I can make it any farther. My broken foot has started to hurt and the bottoms of both feet burn."

"These streets *are* difficult, it's not just you," he reassures me. I don't think he understands. I am not confessing weakness; I'm requesting compassion and to stop walking.

"Can't we just find a taxi?" I plead.

"Let's look at the baptistry first. We're here," he says, heading for the door.

I'm not sure why he is so determined. I don't want to ruin our anniversary weekend with an argument, so follow him. Surely, he'll see I'm not exaggerating, since I'm limping and can't keep up.

Inside the baptistry, we're alone. I sit on the steps with my bare feet on the cool stone. I whisper a prayer for babies who are dedicated here and must grow up in Naples, for our Chicago closing, for my feet, and for our marriage. Larry still wants to see the *Duomo*, saying it's next door. Even next door seems a long way to walk, especially since once inside he'll walk every aisle and stop at every chapel.

There, he discovers an exceptional annunciation, unmarked. In most Italian cities, including Naples, important paintings still hang where they were originally placed. But in Naples they seem to be without signatures or attribution. After the unmarked annunciation, I wait in a pew.

"How about a coffee? It's been a long day," Larry suggests when he's done.

"Great idea. I'm worn out, really," I sigh, massively relieved.

We find a charming bar-gelateria with sea-foam green onyx floors. I want to put my bare feet on the glassy onyx, but there are too many customers, and the floor, upon closer inspection, is not so clean.

Instead of coffee, since it's late afternoon, Larry suggests we order Campari, a bitter alcoholic aperitif. He even agrees to sit at a table, though it costs more than standing at the bar. Plates of gherkins, peanuts, small pizzas, and corn nuts come with the price of sitting down and I enjoy them all. As we get ready to leave, I dread each step to the taxi stand.

Larry helps me stand, then says, "I'm sort of fascinated with the Metro. I think it's close. Let's walk back to *Piazza Dante* and catch it to the hotel."

"Larry, please, I don't want to walk *anywhere*, especially if we don't know where or how far it is. The taxi stand is right outside."

He asks the cashier where the closest Metro stop is. She says it's in *Piazza Cavour*, up the street to the left. Not far, she says. My eyes brim with tears.

Outside, I point toward the taxi stand and say, "It can't cost that much and my feet really, truly hurt. Can't we just go back?"

"If we get a taxi like yesterday, we'll end up half-way to Rome."

I take a deep breath, shudder and clinch my jaw. I'd refuse, but don't want to make him mad and think he should show some sympathy.

"I'll walk to the Metro if you insist… but I am in pain, not happy and will not be good company. In fact, I may get in the taxi alone," I say.

"Don't do that, Victoria. Don't threaten me," he retorts.

"Are you serious? I'm not threatening you. I'm begging to take a taxi to the hotel."

"We still have lots of time before dinner. How else will we get to know how normal people live in Naples?"

After a couple more back and forths, I give in, but add, "You really don't know how far the Metro stop is and this is a bad idea."

I walk slowly, painfully, still hoping Larry will acquiesce and take a taxi. He walks past the taxi stand. Neither of us speak. Too often, he presses until I give in. We've done it for twenty years.

At the first intersection, we look left and right. No "M" for Metro. We walk another block. Again, no "M." I ask to turn back.

"Let's go one more block. The road ahead looks big enough for a Metro stop," Larry says, starting across the street.

We walk the long block to a wide boulevard with four lanes of traffic. An "M" sign is about two blocks to the left on the opposite side of the street. I look both directions for a crosswalk, but don't see one.

"Let's cross here," I say. "I can't take an extra step." We wait for an opening in traffic and run across all four lanes, nearly clipped by a motorcycle driver who refuses to slow down.

In the Metro station, the ticket machine won't work. Finally, an attendant appears, reeking of cigarettes, goes into her booth and hits a button. Our tickets pop out. We climb down three flights. My feet hurt with every step. Larry looks for a metro wall map to figure out which direction to go in the confusing underground walkways. I follow him through a convoluted maze to the correct track. There are no benches, so we stand.

Our train is old, with filthy, cracked plastic upholstery. I don't care. Now that I'm seated, I take deep breaths, willing myself to get over my upset. It does not help to be angry, but I'm fuming. I wish I had gotten into the taxi.

We sit silently until our stop approaches. The area looks like a suburb, not the bay. Larry gets off and I start to step down.

"Let's go one more stop, this isn't the bay," Larry says and hops back on.

The next stop looks like central Naples, but Larry sees a taxi stand so we get off.

Before opening the door, Larry asks the driver how far to the Hotel Excelsior. Surely, he isn't considering walking, I think.

"Five kilometers, more or less," the driver answers and I crawl in. Larry follows.

As the driver pulls into traffic, Larry asks him, "Where should we have gotten off the Metro?"

He shrugs, "With the Metro, is impossible to reach your hotel."

I glare at Larry, who smiles sheepishly. We both have to laugh.

The driver talks non-stop about his beloved *Napoli*. He speeds through a tunnel, swerves from lane to lane, waxes on continuously, waves his arms, clasps his heart to show his intense adoration of his city and slows down only when another driver comes within an inch of his door. His passion is so genuine I begin to wonder what I've missed.

As we walk up the front steps at the Excelsior Hotel, Larry gently takes my elbow and whispers, "That didn't work so well. I just want you to know I know."

His acknowledgement is not enough, though it's nice to hear.

In the room he takes a quick shower while I lay on the bed trying to forget I have feet.

"May I draw a bath for you?" he offers.

He knows I'm not a bath girl. We lived in our Lake Forest home for thirteen years and I never once took a bath. In the Chicago condo, we had a Jacuzzi in our guest bathroom, but I never used it. Tonight, a bath sounds divine.

"Yes. Thank you," I answer, somewhat coolly.

I soak in the water with my eyes closed, concentrating all my energy on restoring my feet. No book. No music. Only warm, soothing water on my soles and gently enveloping my entire aching body.

"I don't think I've had a solo bath since we've been married," I say as I emerge, wrapped in a huge terrycloth hotel robe and feeling more agreeable.

"What would you like to do right now," he asks. "Read? Relax? Get dressed for dinner? I was not a very good husband this afternoon. I'm sorry. Really. Can I make it up to you?"

It's already eight o'clock and, though I'm not hungry and can read Larry's desires between his lines, I ask him to call the concierge for a dinner reservation — soon and nearby.

"Something close, please," I hear Larry say. At least he's trying to be more kind and respect my requests.

The concierge books at *Ristorante La Scialuppa*, on the same wharf as last night. He reminds us to put our jewelry out of sight. Feet soaked and in different shoes, caressed by a sea breeze and Larry's warm and conciliatory affection, I almost enjoy the stroll. We sit on a romantic terrace on the water. I'm surprised this restaurant is not busier on a Saturday night.

The waiter brings menus and offers drinks. Larry is distracted by something over my shoulder. I turn, expecting to see a voluptuous woman. Instead, it's a television set on a makeshift stand. Every man is seated facing the television while every woman is seated with her back to the screen. Ah, *la partita!* No wonder so few diners are here. Most Italian men will be at their favorite bar or at home. And, I suspect, wives taken to dinner tonight will be largely ignored.

"Will you pay attention to me this evening?" I ask, "Or should we change places, so *I* face the TV?"

"You are the very center of my existence and attention," Larry insists, but he does not offer to switch.

As the American national anthem plays, we sing along. The game begins. Conversations cease. This is the World Cup play-offs, Italy against America. I move my plate to Larry's side to watch together. Every person on the wharf cheers wildly when Italy scores the first goal, even us.

When the Italian center elbows a USA star and bloodies his nose, the crowd is hushed but not disapproving. I frown; it looked aggressive to me.

"This will require retaliation," Larry predicts.

As the game progresses, he explains important plays, but says the Americans seem a little off their game.

We watch through three courses, *antipasti... primi... secondi...* then linger for *dolci... caffè...* and finally *limoncello*. Four hours later, the bill arrives only after the game clock stops. The final score is one to one. It's after midnight, but everyone on the wharf is wide awake.

* * *

The next morning, finally enjoying the hotel's grand buffet breakfast, Larry reads the Sunday sports page. He tells me the American team played one man short, which explains why they seemed out of sync. He says there isn't much about the head-butt.

We finally exchange our anniversary cards, written with tender sentiments. I also give Larry a Father's Day card. Tears well, making his eyes even bluer. Today isn't Father's Day in Italy. Larry says he'd forgotten. I suspect the card feels more significant because I brought it from Chicago.

"You deserve to be remembered. You're a wonderful father. I'm sure the kids will send you messages today, but they're sleeping now."

For the first time since that day one Falconiere feast, we enjoy a leisurely breakfast. The buffet is not as elegant as Falconiere's, but it is even more abundant. Larry says he's confident everything is in order for our Chicago closing. I still do not understand what happened yesterday. I don't want to carry my upset into our new day, but my feet and my feelings are still tender.

We go back to our room unhurried, enjoy some relaxed anniversary getaway-time together, take a second shower, and pack our bags.

Our taxi driver to the station becomes animated when he sees we are Americans. He explains that the Italian's elbow to the face of the American player was wrong. He loves his team, he says, but cannot tolerate such disgrace. His team played "*senza sportivo*," without sport.

"*Non giusto*," not right, he insists, making wild gestures as he drives. "It is like war, but without dignity!"

He apologizes as though the international reputation of Italy's soccer team rests on his shoulders. He chatters away, taking a breath only to apologize again as he races to the station, ignoring all traffic laws.

Yes, Naples assaults. I'm glad we came and glad to be leaving, though I'm sad Larry and I had so much discord on what should've been a romantic holiday.

I will come back. This city has a curious draw. Italians say, *Vedi Napoli e poi muori!* See Naples and then die, as if one cannot have truly lived without visiting Naples. Finally, I understand. The majestic beauty of the once-grand, historical city, rising out of the sea and up the mountainside, the tranquil bay carved from the rugged shoreline, a medieval castle seeming to float on water, Vesuvius smoking and the island of Capri in the distance, and an aquamarine Mediterranean as far as one can see are, indeed, captivating.

There also is a fervor for life in Naples like nowhere else I've been. Perhaps where existence is chaotic and unpredictable, never knowing what tomorrow will bring, people develop a unique passion for living.

Two centuries ago, Goethe penned in his *Italian Journey:* "Naples is a paradise; everyone lives in a state of intoxicated self-forgetfulness, myself included. I seem to be a completely different person whom I hardly recognize. Yesterday I thought to myself: Either you were mad before, or you are mad now.... People know nothing whatever about each other.... In the midst of so many people and all their commotion, I feel peaceful and alone for the first time. The louder the uproar of the streets, the quieter I become." He describes the *Napolitani* as "so natural that one might even become natural oneself."

Naples was a liberating experience for that well-heeled, highly-educated Enlightenment male taking his Grand Tour in the late 1700s. But I did not feel peaceful, safe or liberated. Now that I have survived my first experience of Naples, I long to return with a local, a *Napolitano* who can lift the curtain of decay and corruption, like a corner on a circus tent, and allow me to see Naples through their eyes, to experience the glory of paradise beneath the din.

That, perhaps, is the only way to truly *see* Naples.

We arrive at the station barely in time to catch our train. From Naples to Rome I study the passengers and conclude we must be the only Americans. At the third stop, a lovely Italian woman, tall and statuesque, sits in front of us. A few pounds thinner and she'd qualify as willowy. I've wanted to be willowy my entire life. I think she and I are about the same height and I wonder if we're about the same weight. I've been on every diet imaginable since I was sixteen, working to lose those last five pounds. Maybe this summer, with climbs to town and healthy food made of the freshest ingredients, I'll lose the last five pounds for good. The almost-willowy woman has enviable posture. I wish I had straight posture, but I started stooping in junior high when I was taller than the boys. No matter how hard I work at it, I still stoop.

At *Roma Termini*, we run to catch the train to Cortona. Mostly Italians fill this car too. I love the sense of a private cocoon, speaking English amidst Italians, though some surely understand enough English to eavesdrop.

From Rome to Cortona I think about how this weekend could've been happier. When pressed beyond my limits, I need to simply say I cannot go farther, get in a taxi or find a place to rest, and let Larry do whatever he does. Setting reasonable boundaries without fear of his reaction is essential to take care of myself and our marriage. It is each individual's responsibility, a gift we give the other as well as ourselves, because we build less resentment. But my boundaries are up to me to say, not up to him to guess.

We're back in time for dinner at *Trattoria Dardano*, a favorite for us because of their *bruschetta pomodoro*, toasted bread with thinly sliced ripe tomatoes, oil and a hint of garlic, and roasted meats. I'm glad to be away from the hyper-stimulation of Naples and back in Cortona — our calm, civilized, clean, and unhurried town.

Reconnected and happy, Larry and I walk hand in hand back to the car. My feet are tender but no longer painful. I open the car window for some cool night air and lean back in my seat, letting the breeze soothe away my worries. Larry smiles contentedly. At least for tonight, we have relaxed. I pray all goes well with the Chicago closing tomorrow, the emptying of our condo on Tuesday, and our move into Lodolina on Thursday.

Truth Versus Grace

It's six o'clock Monday morning at *Il Falconiere*. I awaken, slightly disoriented about where I am, remembering workers will arrive at Lodolina in two hours where a zillion decisions will face us, and today is our Chicago closing. I lie still, longing for more sleep, but my mind is swirling.

For our closing, we must trust those in Chicago. Emotionally I'm not ready, but it looks as though we got the work done. Or, more accurately, Larry got it done.

I'm having second thoughts about Lodolina's floors. We dreamed of having smooth floors, obviously hand-made, but satiny and foot-friendly as if worn over centuries. Looking down before I step out of bed, I see the hotel's old tiles in shades of deep brown, straw yellow and brick red, all smooth as baby's skin.

When Larry stirs, I whisper, "These floors are what we wanted. Right?"

Larry walks toward the bathroom, seeming put off that I'm already asking questions about the house. "You should make sure you get exactly what you want," he murmurs.

I sense a coolness in his voice.

"It's not only what *I* want, Larry. We'll both live there. Please tell me what *you* want."

He makes his coffee without responding. The floors have become a tired subject. Francesco doesn't agree with me about smooth floors, saying ours look more handmade. I trust Francesco's judgment on almost everything, but am not so sure this time.

"If you want to change it, Victoria, now is the time. Don't be shy. It's *your* house," Larry says with finality, settling in to study.

"I'll look today when we're there," I say. "But I'd like your opinion. This is *our* house, not *my* house."

He doesn't answer. We finish reading and dressing without finishing the conversation.

On the way to another Falconiere breakfast, I find a four-leaf clover beside the gravel path. It's my first of this season. Every summer I wonder if

I'll find any, then find the first one. Before long, I find them everywhere. As next summer begins, I will wonder again.

I put the clover beside Larry's glass of freshly squeezed orange juice. He smiles at my gift, but barely looks up, deep in his Italian newspaper. This week's sports news is all about the World Cup. I'm pleased when he tells me that the Italian press is upset with their player for aggressively injuring the American star.

"For all their despair, Italy just might go to the World Cup," he concludes.

Breakfast is as delicious this morning, just not as magical. So accustomed to my clovers, Larry doesn't pick it up when he gathers his things to leave. I rescue it and, by tucking it into my journal, make it part of our summer story.

Six vehicles are in the driveway at Lodolina. Cabinetmakers have carried one section down the dirt ramp into the kitchen. Marcello, the tile-man, greets us saying he still needs to apply more coats of wax, so we must use the Styrofoam walkways to keep the floor clean. The electrician is waiting for me to place light fixtures.

I take off my shoes and test a dry area with my bare feet. The tiles seem foot-friendly enough and are a lovely color. I cannot decide, so say nothing to Francesco about my ambivalence.

Carlo has come with Francesco to help Larry hook up the *Telecom Italia* internet. Francesco vows he leaves office technology to Carlo. I suspect Larry will be helping Carlo connect the internet rather than helping me make decisions.

Francesco and I place light fixtures. Last Thursday, before we left for Naples, Gabriele and I put masking tape on ceiling tiles to mark locations for twenty-nine fixtures. Over the weekend, the tape drifted to the floor. Now we must do it again, but with a mark that stays.

I'm eager to unwrap the antique sconce I carried from Chicago. With eight curving, gold-gilded metal arms, each with a hand-carved, gilded-wood candleholder and tiny lampshade, it's unwieldy yet whimsical. We bought it in Florence for our Chicago condo and now it's back in Tuscany. I plan to hang it in the powder room.

To find the right placement, Francesco and I both try to fit in the powder room, the size of a small closet. He holds the sconce against the wall behind the toilet at his eye level.

"Perfect!" I say. "Here, let me hold it for you."

We turn, facing each other as if in a dance. This is not a two-person room. Francesco steps outside, looking in, and nods as I hold it in place. I'm not sure when it can be installed, but at least we know it fits.

"The room feels more elegant with such an important light," he says. "I did not know before seeing. I thought over the toilet to be an odd placement. But it is nice… a little fantasy."

On Thursday, when our shipment arrives, we'll add a tiny wood cabinet on tall thin legs, perfect for storing an extra roll of toilet paper. It'll be a tiny *Alice in Wonderland* powder room for guests.

Francesco hears the cabinetmakers deliberating about where to place the kitchen island, so hurries to help. The walls are not square, straight or even. Knowing this, the cabinetmakers wisely made all the wall cabinets a little narrower than the side walls, so they float. The remaining challenge is centering the island.

"We must decide for all time," Francesco reminds us. "Once placed, the stone top cannot be moved."

The *pietra serena* slab arrives tomorrow. Two inches thick, it'll take eight men using a special dolly to move the stone from the truck into the kitchen and lift it into place. My stone sink — so large that Larry and Francesco call it my *cucina piscina*, kitchen swimming pool — will be installed first and the countertop placed over it. For all time.

Stefano and his assistants adjust the island until it feels centered, even though it isn't. For such a critical decision, Larry and Carlo take a break from their internet hookup to participate. When it's right, we all instinctively sense it and nod.

Looking out from the kitchen doorway, Francesco says gently, "The light in your house is really beautiful, even on an overcast day. And the breeze is fresh. You have chosen in a good position."

Yes, there is much to appreciate about Lodolina. It's another blistering day, though cloudy, but the rooms inside are pleasant and the workers seem comfortable.

Larry announces the tech team's success. The internet works! I am glad they're done, as I have been waiting to ask his opinion about the floors. I lean down and rub them with my hand. They're obviously handmade, with wrinkles like old skin. If we grind them smooth, the texture will be lost. Perhaps better as they are.

"Carlo says the download speed is faster than in their office." Larry exclaims.

This is a big deal for me, too. With fast internet, I can stay connected to loved ones.

We've been in Italy one week and one day, but it feels longer. Time is curious that way. Though relentlessly regular, time seems to expand and contract depending on the situation. Engaged in normal activities with familiar people, a week passes quickly. Staying somewhere unfamiliar, interacting with new people and engaged in an unusual activity, time stretches. When we lived in Chicago, an afternoon sailing on Lake Michigan could make the weekend seem like a holiday. Likewise, after four days in Naples, a different place indeed, it feels like we were away much longer. Though we left only eight days ago, life in Chicago seems long, long ago.

Hardest was leaving people I love. Some Chicago friends felt abandoned, as if they weren't important enough to keep us there. We tried to explain our dream, but it seemed to make their sense of abandonment worse to know that we love where we were headed, as though we rejected the life they were choosing. One of our dearest friends mimicked our enthusiasm saying "Cortona, Cortona, blah, blah, blah, blah, blah." He was teasing *and* he was being truthful. Even surrounded by today's constant activity, I feel lonely, missing family and friends, especially girlfriends. I wonder if I'll make girlfriends in Cortona who become as important to me as those back home.

The most painful to leave were my daughters and grandson. Lara and Amber are the only two of our five children who, after college, returned to Chicago to live. We held Lara's wedding in our back yard in Lake Forest, and

Amber and Chad gave us our grandson, Aiden, in Chicago. Angela came back for a while, but eventually moved on.

This month Amber and family will move to Portland, Oregon. I feel sad for Lara. Her mom, sister, and nephew are all leaving in the span of one month. I recall how she stayed in Chicago after her divorce, even though she dreamed of moving to Los Angeles or New York. Lara has many friends, but I imagine how it would feel for me. She said she did okay with Amber's move until Aiden, only two, said "Bye, bye La-la... we go Por-lun now," then turned and waddled away. It broke her heart, she said. And when she told me, it broke mine.

The workers must think I'm crazy, standing in my new kitchen wiping away tears while Larry beams, thrilled that his internet is fast.

After nine hours of construction and decisions, we head back to *Il Falconiere*. I'm tired and a bit miffed. Once the internet worked, Larry spent most of the day on his computer reading his newspapers and catching up with correspondence while I handled house decisions. When I complained after everyone left, he declared flatly, "You're wrong," insisting that he was engaged in every conversation where he was needed. I said he didn't even know where he was needed. He disagreed. I decided not to press it, preferring a nice evening to an argument about a day that's nearly over.

On the ride, I can't shake feeling displaced. Our house in Italy is unfinished and our Chicago home is sold. No nest, no friends, and a husband who pays more attention to the internet than to me. There were many good people around today, so I shouldn't feel lonely. But we employ them.

Back at the hotel, Larry makes calls about our Chicago closing. Miraculously, everything has fallen into place. Dale will supervise the move of our remaining belongings into long-term storage. Kathleen arranged storage for our winter coats. Suzana (with one n) will make the condominium spotless for the new owners. The car dealer found storage for both cars. And Tedi will adopt my enormous spherical boxwood in its turquoise glazed pot, the only plant I could not bear to leave.

Strolling to the restaurant from our room, we stop to say hello to Riccardo, *Il Falconiere's* owner.

"This is my favorite hotel in Tuscany," I tell him, "And my favorite room is *numero due*."

He seems happy to see us. "When guests come again and again like you, they are no longer guests, but friends. We take extra care with friends." He may say that to everyone, but I want to believe him.

A large exotic bird with a pale orange chest, black and white wings and an orange tufted crown, lands in the grass nearby.

"What kind of bird is that?" I ask him, mystified that I've never seen one before.

"Upupa. Special, because is like a good guest," he continues with his flirtatious charm and, I suspect, practiced English lines. "After going away for the winter, it always returns."

"I'm sure you know there are pheasants along your road," Larry says, knowing Riccardo is an avid hunter. "They fly up every time we pass, always from the same area."

"I know the place," Riccardo nods with a big grin. "Pheasants are like dogs on a country road... they wait to ambush passing cars."

We take a seat on the terrace to enjoy the *aperitivo* Riccardo generously offers and to watch the sunset before dinner. A black smoke cloud is forming over Cortona.

"Like Vesuvius," our waiter notes. I chuckle; everyone is full of metaphors today.

Clinking glasses of bitter Campari, Larry toasts our condo sale. It's great that everything went well, but it feels so final... a door closed on our former life. I don't mention to Larry that I feel sad. I don't think he's in the mood for it, so euphoric over the Chicago sale, his internet hook-up, and our new life in Italy.

Without a blush, the sun drops below the mountains across the valley. This summer alone, our first Tuscan summer, we'll have one hundred and five sunsets to enchant us with fiery red, coral, violet and gold. Or, like this one, the sun can simply disappear. A colorless sunset matches my mood.

"Do you want to hear more about Abelard?" Larry asks. I nod with interest. He has been reading about Abelard and Heloise, among the most tragic love stories of European history. Peter Abelard was the tutor of brilliant and beautiful Heloise, and they were secret lovers. When she became pregnant, the couple married secretly, against Heloise's original wishes, then lived in different abbeys. Their lifetime separation and devotion are preserved in letters. One would write on wax, the other would read the message, then melt the wax and write over it. Heloise wrote hers on paper first, and copied Abelard's before melting it, thereby preserving their now-famous exchange.

Larry continues, "Abelard was tried for heresy because he questioned church doctrine in a time of near-absolute church authority. Remember, this was France, twelfth century. His work became a classic of Christian theology, but it did not keep him from being accused and tried."

"Was he hanged... or burned?" I ask, remembering how heretics were treated during the Middle Ages.

"Neither, he wasn't convicted. But his trial was widely known, even then."

Our table is ready. Standing, I brush away white flecks from my black silk pants and top. The mysterious smoke cloud has dropped ash on everything.

The courtyard at *Il Falconiere* feels tranquil, though it's bustling. Wisteria fills the air with sweet aroma and round-leafed plants with white flowers that look like passion fruit blossoms grow in crevices on the stone side wall. (Later, I'll learn they're caper plants. The buds are brined for capers, and the seedpods for caper berries.)

After a Prosecco toast, Larry tells me more about Abelard and his lifelong devotion to Heloise. We nibble *crostini foie gras*, then enjoy a cool, creamy soup of lobster, zucchini and tiny spring peas.

I try to concentrate on Larry's tales about Abelard and Heloise, but I'm distracted trying to figure out what went wrong today. Our tension started when I said he hadn't helped, leaving decisions to me while he read. He said it wasn't true, that I was wrong. But I believe it was true, and worse, that his dismissal of my concern lacked empathy and grace.

We often disagree about truth versus grace. Larry holds truth as his highest value. I believe grace is more important. He says facts simply are, they have no feelings and should not provoke feelings. Therefore, truth requires no grace. Yet truth, as he presents it, often feels hurtful. Not that anyone should tell or accept lies, but perspectives differ. He will never see through my eyes, nor I through his, though grace urges me to try. Why not say, "We see it differently," instead of a blunt and dismissive, "You're wrong"?

Perhaps the greatest strength is not in truth or grace, but in truth *and* grace. If we joined our perspectives instead of arguing about which is right, we would see that truth plus grace creates a better foundation for life and for marriage. And, it often leads to generosity.

Pondering truth versus grace, I fear I missed most of Abelard's trial. I think Larry could tell I wasn't concentrating on his story. We finish dinner without dessert or much personal connection.

Despite my upset with Larry, first for not helping and even more for declaring I was wrong, he can be deeply appreciative and sensitive, especially with others. Back in our hotel room, he says he wants to call the doormen in our Chicago building to explain our early move-out and thank each personally for their excellent care for the past five years. I'll email other condo owners, most of them now friends. Everyone in the building still believes we'll be back in September.

Our mid-rise building had only eleven families, a vertical neighborhood. I loved living there. I'm glad Larry is making the doorman calls, because I can't say aloud without tears that in two days, every trace of us will be gone forever. I hear him talking with Kirk, the morning doorman, saying, "Yes, Victoria always brings that out in people, doesn't she?" Because of the time difference, Larry tells Kirk he'll call Victor and Basil tomorrow.

As I'm falling asleep, Larry leans over, kisses my forehead and says softly, "Kirk sent you a message. He said that no matter what was going on in the building, you always smiled and then others smiled. He said to tell you he misses you." I imagine the twinkle in Kirk's kind eyes and feel tears rising again in mine

I awaken several times during the night thinking of things I must do before we move in. Dishes. We didn't pack any dishes and I have no idea where to buy them. We need appliances that run on Italian current: vacuum cleaner, coffee maker, toaster, iron. And we'll need groceries, staples and perishables. I make mental notes, hoping to remember everything in the morning.

Too soon, I'm aware of birds beginning their choruses. I need to sleep at least a couple more hours. The next two days will be filled with for-all-time decisions. I feel like a character in an unrehearsed play, swept into a dramatic vortex. I must stay alert and engaged. When Lodolina is ready for our belongings, I can sort out feeling ignored by Larry, unsettled and alone. Sometimes feelings must be put on the back burner for the sake of a more urgent goal. But I know they will creep back if I don't resolve them soon.

Six Angry Men and a Fairytale Castle

On moving day — can it be here so soon? — we check out of *Il Falconiere*, load our suitcases into the SUV and head for Lodolina. I'm so excited that one last Falconiere breakfast, perhaps my last forever, doesn't interest me.

Driving around the walls of Cortona, we pass a large flatbed truck struggling to turn a corner. Strapped to the center of the truck bed is an enormous wooden container, like those I saw stacked on the open ships in Naples.

"Maybe ours," I joke, surprised by such an enormous truck on the narrow road.

"Can't be," Larry says. "They're bringing our stuff in small trucks, right?"

"That's what Maryte said when we confirmed yesterday."

We arrive at Lodolina before eight. Movers are scheduled for eight-thirty. Five vans, a truck, and Francesco's car are lined up in our driveway, but they know to clear the drive once they've unloaded.

Inside, Francesco is talking with the plumber while the electrician and cabinetmakers are working away. The activity is dizzying and I don't know where I'm most useful, if at all. Larry retreats to the living room to read the Wall Street Journal and New York Times on his fast internet while I work with woodworkers to place the last cabinet in the kitchen.

At nine o'clock the piano technician arrives. Gabriele was hired by the moving company to reassemble and tune my newly rebuilt 1920 Baldwin. The movers still aren't here. The piano tuner says he can wait. There's no place to sit except the fireplace hearth, so Gabriele sits beside Larry who continues to read.

At nine-thirty, I dial Maryte to ask if she has heard from them or can reach them, but her phone just rings. At ten, I try again. No answer.

At ten-thirty, a van arrives. We hear a door slam, but no one comes to the house. Francesco goes up to speak in Italian with the movers. I linger in an open door, listening. Almost immediately their voices are raised. Even Francesco sounds angry, an emotion I've never observed in him. One of the movers is screaming. I wonder if Francesco needs help, but it's all Italian so I'd be useless. After several minutes of yelling and what sounds like cursing from the movers, the door slams again, but the engine doesn't start.

Francesco comes back down the ramp, obviously shaken, and explains. "Your movers first thought they could come up your road with a flatbed truck and unload the container here. They get a ticket at Cortona because such large trucks are not allowed, of course. Then they try to drive the truck up your road... impossible, and had to back out. They spent the last hours renting two vans, like they drive now. They will open the container this afternoon in a parking lot in Camucia. They have six men today, but can't bring any boxes until tomorrow. They are angry because of the ticket, because they lost a day, and because no one told them your road was so bad."

I feel my blood pressure rise. "I told Maryte exactly what to expect and even drew a map. She had an English-speaking dispatcher call from Milan to confirm details. I told him they did not need a tractor, a standard question, but they need vans with good clearance or very small trucks. There should've been *no* confusion."

"And *they* should know Italian traffic laws, not me," I add.

Now I'm angry. I cannot believe my careful directions could be so misinterpreted. Worse, we have no bed for tonight and the hotel is full.

Larry is exasperated, too. Last week Marco invited us to join a small group at the Antinori castle near Orvieto for an overnight, but Larry told him we couldn't because we were moving in today.

"Do you think it's too late call Marco?" I ask, reading Larry's mind.

"Great idea," he says. "Why don't you call him?"

"Why don't *you* call him?" I ask, now irritated because he's been on his computer while I've been dealing with movers and workers. "I need to finish with Francesco."

Larry flashes me a look that says I'm being uncooperative, but agrees to call. I hope it works. I'd love to spend an evening in a medieval castle sipping fine wine instead of searching for a hotel vacancy and worrying about hostile movers.

Marco says, of course we must come. He will call and increase the number. However, he warns Larry not to be late to the meeting place because we must drive in tandem. We have less than an hour to get there.

"If we go, I'm not rushing back," Larry insists. "Who knows when those jerks'll show up."

Larry asks Francesco to explain to the movers that they should deliver our belongings starting at eleven o'clock tomorrow morning. Francesco walks back up the ramp. We hear car doors slam, the engine rev and tires spin on the gravel, probably on purpose. My anxiety eases as the sound fades into the forest.

Francesco still looks rattled but assures us he's okay and offers to stay for the rest of today, handle construction questions, and make sure Lodolina is clean for tomorrow.

We arrive at the meeting point precisely on time. Marco is already fidgeting, but takes a moment to introduce us to the other couples. After about forty minutes driving south on the A1 *autostrada*, he exits and leads the caravan east through cultivated farmlands toward the foothills of the Umbrian Apennine mountains.

Suddenly, a castle on a wooded hill emerges like a page from a pop-up fairy tale. At a round stone watchtower, a massive gate opens mysteriously and we drive into a landscaped parking area. Walking single file, we follow Marco up a path through more gardens, then into a courtyard big enough to hold a small village. Long stone buildings flank all four sides, three stories high. Geranium-filled boxes hang from high windows and sweet baking aromas waft into the courtyard from arched openings at the ground floor. Inside, women in crisp white aprons are busy making something amazing.

Our hostess is a lovely woman of about thirty, the Director of Hospitality for *Castello della Sala*. She tells us this estate covers over twelve hundred acres, three hundred fifty planted with grapes and twenty with olive trees.

The estate produces eight wines, goat cheese and olive oil. It's one of seven Antinori vineyards in Tuscany and Umbria.

The winsome, dark-haired guide starts our tour in the dining room with the family story. The castle, a medieval fortress, was built around 1350 for a family whose ancestors came to Italy in the ninth century. She explains that the brothers battled each other for three generations to control Orvieto, the most important town in the area. Eventually, the family broke into four feuding clans, each taking a new surname. Angelo Monaldeschi, the most ferocious of them all, took *della Vipera*, of the snake, becoming Angelo Monaldeschi *della Vipera*. Angelo's grandson, Gentile, took the name *della Sala*, of the hall. He was dictator of Orvieto for a decade but lost his position in a war against the Venetian Cardinal Pietro Barbo, who eventually became Pope Pius I. The family called a truce in 1480 when Gentile's son, also named *della Sala*, married his cousin in an arranged union. As a symbol of family peace, the couple restored the castle and renamed it *Castello della Sala*.

Our guide points to a fresco depicting the family humbly presenting a large gold gift to Jesus, making amends for indiscretions of past generations. Luca Signorelli, an important Renaissance artist from Cortona, painted it in the early 1500s.

I feel silly writing everything down, but don't want to miss a word or forget a name.

On our tour, pausing in a corner watchtower for a panoramic view of the vineyards, our hostess explains that the machine in the distance is a fog-maker. So far inland, the grapes on this estate sometimes need a little man-made moisture.

Lastly, she leads us down a stone stairway to the wine cellar-library, an ancient labyrinth of underground caves where row upon row of dust-covered bottles representing decades of wines are stored.

"Please don't touch anything," she warns. Evidently, the undisturbed dust is part of the library's value.

We take a break to freshen up and meet in the courtyard. A table awaits with chilled sparkling wine, locally produced dried meats, and warm focaccia with green olives and walnuts baked into the crust — likely the enticing aroma I smelled earlier. I must learn to bake this bread, so delicate and flavorful.

The sky takes on a peach blush as our conversation intensifies. This unlikely collection of Marco's clients sits in a small circle and talks in cross conversations about where we're from, how we met our spouses, if we have children, why we bought homes in Italy, why Cortona, our favorite wines, and how long we've known Marco. Marco seems to want to say something, but our chatting persists. It's an interesting assemblage, different yet congenial. I wonder why Marco put us together, suspecting it was intentional.

When asked why we chose Cortona, I say we investigated several Tuscan towns, analyzing the best one for us. "But it was our friendship with Marco, which has deepened over many years, that made the difference. So... I guess Marco is the reason."

Turning to Marco, I add with sincerity, "Thank you."

Others nod, declaring that Marco was at least a part of the reason they chose Cortona. He seems embarrassed, but pleased.

Ginny, the only one not with us yet, leans out of an upstairs window and calls down in her loveliest Texan drawl, "Dahling, should I weah my hat?"

"I don't know, *carissima*," Giancarlo calls up. "You will be beautiful... with or without it. Will you be ready soon?" He smiles at us apologetically.

Giancarlo, handsome, white-haired, and aristocratic, is a Count of Montalcino. He doesn't claim his title openly, but Alex whispered it to me in the wine cellar. It seems his ancestors sold their properties generations ago, so he has no wealth or land, only a title he doesn't use. His wife, Ginny, is vivacious and very Texan. Ginny and Giancarlo have a home in Cortona and an antique store in Dallas. Giancarlo was born and raised in Rome and seems to be a trove of knowledge about this entire region. Alex said he's a sought-after guide, especially by wealthy Texans looking for top quality Italian antiques.

Giancarlo and Ginny seem quite infatuated with one other, perhaps from living apart much of the time since she manages the store in Dallas while he lives in Cortona. It's hard to believe they've been married sixteen years.

Alex and Tony live in Brighton, England. Alessandra is a dark-haired, dark-eyed Italian beauty, diminutive and shapely, soft-spoken and commandingly charming, who Tony nicknamed Alex when they met. She has a cultured northern Italian accent, since she grew up in Torino, and a lyrical English lilt from living in London since she was eighteen. Tony is a tall, dashing Englishman with a proper manner, captivating presence, self-effacing wit, and an undercurrent of perpetual dissatisfaction. Alex and Tony met in London when she moved there to improve her now-flawless English. They fell in love, married, had twin daughters, and she never returned to Italy except for vacations. Tony promised that, if she married him, he'd buy her an Italian villa. They own property not far from Cortona but haven't started the renovation. I feel an immediate bond with Alex, though Tony puts me a bit on guard.

Mike and Lynn, from New Jersey, seem gentle and unpretentious, preferring not to be the center of attention. Mike tells a short-people joke, poking fun at their smaller stature in this unusually tall group. He seems warm, generous and a good listener. Lynn is sunny and lively. I like them, especially Lynn, who has a feisty, playful edge, and I'm eager to know them better.

Linda and Michael are Ginny's friends, visiting from Dallas. Linda's lime green sandals match her lime green outfit perfectly. As usual, I'm wearing black sandals that match everything I own, since it's all black. If I still lived in the South, I wonder if I'd wear lime green and hot pink. Probably not, since I feel conspicuous in bright colors and would not have matured small and delicate in Georgia any more than I did in Illinois.

We continue sipping wine and enjoying new acquaintances as daylight fades. Coral clouds now streak the sky, washing everyone's face with a healthy glow.

Near our corner of the courtyard, a wisteria vine with a gnarled stem as thick as a tree trunk winds its way around the base of a stone staircase, up the bannister and across a second-floor balcony, creating a waterfall of purple clusters. The courtyard's long shadows have an aura of time suspended.

When the conversation slows, I ask Marco about Margherita, his three-year-old daughter. Last November, Marco and Enza took Margherita to a pediatric surgical center in Massa to close a congenital hole in her heart. We kept up with her progress via email while in Chicago, but haven't heard a full report since coming back.

The group becomes hushed; all want to hear. Marco suggests we move to the dining room where he'll share his story. We climb the wisteria-laden stairway back to the dining room and take our places around an enormous antique wood table, sinking into high-backed upholstered chairs that feel like thrones. Servers pour chilled Antinori Chardonnay, *Cervaro*, and Marco explains that this is the white wine always in his family's *frigo*, refrigerator. With one sip, I understand.

Marco starts again. "This has been the most difficult season of my life, and for my family. The friends around this table prayed and supported us. Of course, there were others. But you stood with me from the beginning. The reason I ask you here for this night is to say thank you." His voice deepens and cracks a little.

I remember their ordeal. Margherita was born with a hole in her heart, not immediately life-threatening but increasingly dangerous, and it required open-heart surgery. When she was eighteen months old, she was put on the waiting list. Early this year, she was given a two-week window at the pediatric heart surgery center in Massa, a three-hour drive northwest of Cortona. Marco and Enza abandoned all else, left their five-year-old son with Marco's parents, and went to Massa to wait. Priority is given to emergencies, but Margherita's case was not considered an emergency. Each day her surgery was postponed, their hopes diminished. After this window, she'd be back on a waiting list.

We had prayed that Margherita would stay healthy, her surgery would happen in that window, and that it would be successful. On the last possible day, we breathed a long sigh of relief when Marco emailed that the surgery was long, delicate and textbook perfect.

Marco pauses to regain his composure, then continues. "Last week, as you know, we went to Massa for Margherita's first check-up. I am happy I can say the surgeon's report was excellent. We do not need to return for another year. Our family is celebrating… You must know it. Of course, she will have annual reviews for many years."

While Marco is talking, fine Antinori wines are poured and beautiful food is served, but I have little awareness of drinking or eating.

"I have waited until now," Marco concludes, "when we are certain that Margherita is okay, to invite you here to say to you my deep appreciation. Your prayers and support were more important to me and to my family than I can explain. You are my friends in the most important time of my life." He swallows hard as his voice breaks again.

Every tear-filled eye is fixed on Marco. I'm honored to be here. This is the best of life, to share moments of significance with people we love. As tears trail down my cheeks, our delayed move seems like a divine gift.

Suddenly, I'm struggling to stay awake. To my right, I see Giancarlo lighting a cigar for Lynn. Alex is deep in conversation with Marco. Dessert has yet to be served. This evening is only beginning, I think.

"Are you ready?" I lean over and whisper to Larry. When he nods, I ask Marco if we might go to our room without disturbing the rest of their evening.

Marco nods and smiles. I put my hand on his shoulder in appreciation for his beautifully expressed thoughts and he reaches up to touch mine in reply.

Our castle bedroom is cozy and comfortable, with ancient furniture, pull-down mosquito screens, and twin beds. I only need a pillow and a toilet, though I would have preferred a bed for two. I fall asleep instantly and awaken disoriented about where I am.

After a typical Italian breakfast of pastries, juice and *cappuccini* in the courtyard, we reluctantly say good-bye to our new friends, promising to get together soon. I believe they will hold a special place in our hearts someday, as they do for Marco. I wonder if Marco knows he's given us far more than we've ever given him.

Marco's comments at dinner were genuine, with no bravado. Italian men seem better at expressing emotion than American men. In America, showing emotions can be interpreted as girlish or sappy. In Italy, it is part of being a man.

Italian expressiveness is also a mystery to me, as Italians also can be very private. They may be warm, generous, loving, authentic and able to articulate feelings and opinions openly, but it's often hard to really know them. Larry and I believe we know Marco and Francesco, but I suspect we do not know them as well as we think.

We reluctantly say goodbye to our new friends, who have decided to spend the day exploring Orvieto with Giancarlo as their guide.

The moment we drive out the gate, the spell of the castle is broken. We're running late and must hurry home on the A1 *autostrada*, rather than on scenic back roads as we had planned. Larry stiffens as he takes the toll ticket and, before he even gets settled in his lane, a minivan flies by.

"That idiot must be going a hundred miles per hour," Larry fumes, gripping the wheel to keep our massive Volvo steady. He clenches his jaw and frowns.

Fields of sunflowers blur as we pass. They may be the same fields we saw from the train to Naples last weekend. The slanted sun through delicate flower petals creates a luminescent sea of gold.

While Larry concentrates on driving, I reflect on last night. I was moved by Marco's comments. I'm certain many others prayed for Margherita and that Marco has found appropriate ways to thank them. For us, this get-away was the best possible gift. It not only provided a place to sleep when we had no bed, it offered us new friendships with genuine, caring, interesting, kind people.

Sometimes what we consider to be important turns out not to be so essential, and what seems like a frivolous activity is life changing. Yesterday was one of the most emotional days I've ever experienced — from the intense anger of the movers to deep emotions expressed among strangers whom I hope will become friends. I want the loving emotions to last, not the combative ones.

Moving Day Madness

My anxiety escalates as we drive up our access road. Thankfully, not one car is at Lodolina. I wonder what awaits us after yesterday's flurry of construction.

Larry reaches for my hand as we walk between the stacks of material. I think he can tell I'm apprehensive. When we left, tools, trash and materials were in every room. Yet this morning when we walk in, the house is empty, floors are swept and the Styrofoam walkways have disappeared. Francesco has managed another small miracle.

I take time to sweep again, knowing that once our rugs and furniture are in place the floor underneath will not be cleaned for months, perhaps years. I long for a vacuum, mop, and helper. Broom and dustpan still in my hands, I hear a vehicle pull into our drive.

I stiffen, preparing to meet six angry men.

They are in better moods today, even the foreman. The youngest speaks some English and seems eager to help translate. Perhaps this will go okay. I'm excited that our personal belongings, on a boat for three months, will finally make Lodolina our home.

My piano is first. It weighs one thousand pounds according to the piano restorer who built the wooden crate for its sea voyage. My wedding gift from Larry nineteen years ago, it recently has been stripped of black stain, refinished to its original mahogany, and rebuilt by a master who has been rebuilding pianos for forty years.

All six men wrestle the gigantic crate off the back of the van and gently place it on a too-small dolly. I hold my breath. They grip the box, trying to control the dolly as it rolls too quickly down the bumpy dirt ramp. I breath again when it's at the door. It takes thirty minutes to unscrew the sides and uncrate it. With the help of the piano technician, who kindly returned this morning, they bring the parts inside, attach the legs and stand it up. My tiny grand looks so happy here!

The challenge of exact piano placement takes another fifteen minutes. I imagined playing while I look out the window at the camellia bushes I will plant. But the technician says the lid should open into the room, which puts my back to the window. Since I can't decide, we place it as the technician advises, adjusting the exact distance from each wall until the movers run out of patience and go back to their trucks.

Standing at the van with my packing list from Chicago, I'm ready to check off items as the movers unload them. The foreman motions to the boy who gives me a different list. I ask why not use the original list. In halting English, the young mover explains they made a new list when they unpacked the crate yesterday and I should use their list. I shake my head, insisting I must use the original list or I won't know what's missing. The foreman scowls, turns red and threatens to leave. For the sake of getting anything done, I offer to make a third list as each item is taken out of the van. Then I'll compare all three lists. The foreman is not happy, but seems to understand I will not negotiate.

I write numbers as fast as I can. Some stickers have fallen off, so I note the box type and room. Six men can unload boxes quickly and I can't keep up. Larry, who is very organized, stays in the house and tells them where each box goes.

After the first load, they divide up to be more efficient. Three men unload the second van with me writing as fast as I can, while the other three go to the parking lot to reload the first van. With two vans going back and forth, there is no time for me to take a break.

By the time I go back in the house, Lodolina has been filled with boxes, plastic-wrapped furniture, rugs rolled in paper, crated art and various loose items, all deposited wherever Larry pointed or the movers found space.

La scena di Napoli in my own home!

The technician has reassembled my piano's innards and is playing — adding to the absurdity. He says the mechanics function perfectly, but suggests we wait until it has acclimated to its new home to tune it. Even un-tuned, the sound is rich and lively as it bounces off low ceilings, wood beams, tile floor and stone walls. I cannot wait to play it myself, but today I must focus on our move. Besides, I don't like an audience when I make mistakes, which I always do.

Between vans, I compare the three lists. They are not even close. I'm upset that I can't use the original list. The foreman is mad because it takes me so long to write the new one and I won't simply use his. He grumbles that they cannot turn the vans around in the driveway and must back out, about two hundred feet. He complains that they must carry everything down the long dirt ramp to get to the house. Everyone is tired, dirty, sweaty and frustrated, but we try to be cordial.

I offer them water. They have their own. They eat lunch on their ride to reload.

When the movers assemble our four-poster iron bed, one foot is bent. They cannot bend it back, so leave the bed tilted. It'll be strange to sleep on the slant and may bend the foot more. I quietly make a note of it. Larry helps them unwrap our king-sized mattress, which completes the unlevel bed.

At the end, when the last van is empty and there's nothing more in the parking lot, the foreman wants me to sign that all items have been delivered and are undamaged. I've tried to compare lists along the way, but many items seem missing. Further, I won't know the condition of the contents until the boxes are opened. It's obvious that some furniture is not in the same condition it was when it left Chicago.

I will not sign.

The foreman acts shocked. He insists. I refuse. He yells at the boy as if it's his fault. Veins on the foreman's neck bulge and his face is red from hard work, heat and anger. He jabs his finger at me and tells the boy what to say to me. I don't think the boy repeats it all, but the poor young man does explain they cannot leave without my signature. I call Maryte. No answer. It's late Friday afternoon.

I agree to sign, but with a disclaimer that only items on the new list have been delivered, and we do not know the condition or completeness until we have unpacked all the boxes, inspected the contents, and compared the new list to the original packing list. The boy translates. The foreman glares at me with slitted eyes and clinched jaw. I calmly write the disclaimer on a separate sheet, using a dictionary and Larry's help to translate it into Italian. I take my time to get it right. I read the Italian version to the foreman and the young man. Despite the foreman's protest, I write the disclaimer on all three lists in Italian and English, and sign each one.

I offer him the pen.

He fumes and stalls, but finally adds his *firma*, signature. We shake hands. The poor boy, covered with dust and dripping with sweat, is visibly flustered. I grasp his hand gently but firmly and thank him for his hard work, kind help, and good English. I, too, am covered with dust and sweat and long for a hot shower and a glass of wine. Larry gives them a nice tip, which I think should go mostly to the boy, but agree they all worked hard. As they drive away, I exhale with relief.

I'm glad I held my ground, not easy for me because I typically want to please everyone. But sometimes being respected is more important than being liked.

Lodolina is ours, silent and stacked with our belongings. The birds, which I suspect have chirped all day without attracting my ear, seem especially joyful, as though they're singing in celebration. We take leisurely showers in our elegant little bathroom with its rose terracotta floor, swirling *scabas* travertine counters, and modern Italian rain-head shower. I let warm water run over my body for a long, long time.

Truth is, I'm sad our move was so difficult. Perhaps the movers had good intentions and were simply misinformed, although trying to drive a flatbed truck around Cortona and up our narrow gravel access road was not smart. In all my communications I tried to be clear about what to expect, but what reached the movers may not have been what I said, drew or wrote. We'll find many occasions like today when our poor Italian will cause problems. Miscommunications can undermine even the best of intentions, and I'm thrilled this day is over.

Rather than fall into bed without dinner, more exhausted than hungry, we dress in the finest clothes we can locate in the wardrobe boxes and head to a fancy event where we will be Francesco's guests at the annual inauguration of Rotary Club officers. When Francesco invited us, we enthusiastically accepted with no idea it would be moving day or that moving day would be so stressful. What to wear baffles me, as nothing I find seems appropriate. Eventually I pull out cream linen pants, a wispy black silk top, and my standby black suede pumps.

The dinner is held at *Villa Il Sodo*, near the Etruscan burial excavations of *Sodo I* and *II*. It's not far from *Il Falconiere*, the hotel where we've stayed for the past two weeks. Following handmade signs, Larry parks in a grassy field among the olive trees. We walk the path to the villa and find Francesco in the garden among at least fifty guests. He says Rita must work tonight, so he is alone. It seems like a different world to be elegantly dressed, chatting in the garden of an historic villa, sipping Prosecco and being served *antipasti* by strolling waiters in formal black uniforms.

Francesco asks about the move. "I've been worried," he says.

Larry describes our day, ending with the story of how the foreman cursed when I wrote the disclaimer, but signed when I offered him the pen. We all laugh and I feel better, finding it funnier in retrospect. Laughter is often the only sane response to an insane experience.

After too many *antipasti* and too much Prosecco, we find our names on the chart. Tables are set with white linens, fresh flowers and flickering candles, arranged in a glass conservatory amidst lush potted plants. We're the first three at our table.

A woman walking toward us lights up when she sees Francesco.

"Ah, Ester!" he exclaims. Francesco has a warm, delighted exuberance when he sees someone he truly likes. His greeting has charmed me many times.

"May I present my friend, Ester, who said to me where to buy your Miele dishwasher… and this is Victoria."

I smile. "*Grazie. Miele molto importante. Sono Victoria,*" I extend my hand. Thank you. Miele very important. I am Victoria. My Italian allows a few words of courtesy and a small joke about the importance of a good dishwasher, but no real conversation. I'm a bit worried about how dinner may go.

Ester's calm, graceful, dignified yet warm manner mesmerizes me. I cannot help but be fascinated by her and hope I'm not staring. Her skin is finely textured, like delicate porcelain, with a sun-kissed olive color too rich and lively for fragility. She has sparkling dark eyes, no noticeable make-up, thick bobbed silver and black hair parted in the middle and framing her face, and those dense black eyebrows only Mediterranean women seem to possess. Her simple taupe and black beaded dress is adorned with unpretentious yet exquisite jewelry. There is nothing glitzy about Ester, only sophisticated grace and under-stated elegance.

Fortunately, Ester speaks English and happily translates for our table as others arrive. She and her husband, Fernando, own *La Calonica*, a successful local winery. Fernando has the confident, easy manner of a man who does not strive to impress.

What is most defining about Ester is not her appearance or grace, but how authentically interested she is in everyone at the table. It's as if seeing each person she knows, and meeting Larry and me, has been the most important element of her day.

Toward the end of our evening, Ester toasts us, saying, "Cortona is fortunate to have such lovely new residents."

Everyone joins, wishing us, "*Tanti auguri nella tua casa nuova*," all good wishes in your new home. At the insistence of our new Italian acquaintances, Larry is renamed Lorenzo.

Nearing home, I realize this move offers me a new beginning — a chance to redefine myself after sixty years. Just as this is *our* new life, it's *my* new life. As I choose my personal Italian style, I'm inspired by Ester to be natural, grace-filled and focused on others.

With such a joyful close of the day, the angry movers are all but forgotten.

Poetry at Dawn

In rare repose, Larry, who always wakes before I do, sleeps peacefully. This was the first night in our own bed in Italy. We were so exhausted after our day of moving and the fancy dinner that the slant from the bent leg didn't seem to matter.

Sunlight streams across my pillow. I lie propped on my elbow, gaze out of my window at our twisted almond tree and the distant foothills, and pinch my arm to make sure this is real. Soft coos from the pigeon farm across the valley provide low-pitched accompaniment to the melodies of larks, finches, sparrows, and countless songbirds I have yet to identify. It's a sweet first morning and I'm sure this little arched window was placed in exactly this position for the sun to awaken the farmer and his wife.

Larry kisses my back, stands and stretches, then grabs his robe to go downstairs. Lodolina is pure *tranquilità* on our first awakening here. I must not linger; the workers arrive at eight sharp.

"Victoria! Come quickly! There's a butterfly in the dining room."

As I hit the bottom step, a yellow and black swallowtail flutters back into the sunlight.

Windows in Tuscan homes typically don't have screens and we want to preserve that unbroken connection to nature. The obvious result is that hillside critters are at liberty to come and go. I hope for more butterflies and fully expect the little lizards to find their way into the cool shade of our living room.

I'd love a cappuccino, my morning indulgence since our honeymoon in Italy nineteen years ago, but we don't have the equipment yet. I make espresso in Larry's travel *Bialetti*, add some pan-warmed milk with no froth, have plain yogurt because it's all we have, take a shower and put on old clothes for a day of unpacking.

The plumber, electrician, painter and stonemason, plus Pierangelo the foreman, arrive and are immediately hard at work. Today the plumber will hook up the kitchen faucet and adjust the water softener. Francesco says the reason I like the taste of our well water is that it is *troppo dolce*, too sweet. I'm not so sure about *dolce*, as the water tastes slightly salty to me.

Unpacking for hours, Larry and I reposition furniture and place familiar items in unfamiliar places. Painters, electricians, and plumbers work around us and the stacks of boxes. A new level of confusion surpasses yesterday's. Decisions must be made regarding where to put each item, as well as answering tradesmen who seek our approval on the tiniest decision now that we're living here. The dream finally feels real, but more like a nightmare than a fantasy. May I please wake up when the house is done and all these boxes are unpacked?

The last worker leaves after five. Exhausted from unpacking and excited that our home is taking shape, we crawl into bed for an afternoon nap. Our tenderness is slow, luxurious, and calming. We declare work finished for the day and drift into a temporary twilight.

"It takes a heap o' livin' in a house t' make it home," Edgar Guest wrote ninety years ago and it's still true. We have put our furniture where we drew it on the plan, hung clothes in the recently delivered *armadio*, placed personal products in the bathroom, and put well-used kitchen tools in my brand-new kitchen drawers. Our house feels comfortable and comforting. But it'll take some livin' before Lodolina feels like home.

The heat is oppressive. Today's high was forty degrees Centigrade, one hundred and four Fahrenheit, even hotter than yesterday. Everyone loves cloudless sapphire skies, but there is no relief in a sapphire sky day. We're told this inferno is unusual. Italians typically close their shutters during the day to keep out the hot sun, but I leave all the windows open hoping for a breeze. Someday, we'll have a lawn and outdoor furniture, so won't be imprisoned. But now our yard is dirt clods and construction rubble, with no place to sit.

Everyone complains. Marco's father, Giuliano, says the Etruscans were smart. *"Vivevano sulle colline e sepolti i morti della valle."* They lived on the hillsides and buried their dead in the valley, referring to the famous Etruscan burial sites at the base of Cortona's hill. At least Lodolina is on the hillside.

We drive to the outlet mall thirty minutes away to look for dishes, towels, a drip coffee pot and an ironing board, and to be in an air-conditioned car and stores. Perhaps we made a mistake not installing it, but, like screens on windows, air conditioning is rare in Tuscan homes. We hope to do without.

After finding most of what we need at surprisingly good prices, we rush back to meet Oliver. He picked our olives last fall, has our oil, and we hope to hire him to care for the olive trees this year and, someday, for our landscaped gardens. We like Oliver, but we've been worn thin trying to contact him. Our appointment today was rescheduled from last week when he had a client emergency. I finally bought some olive oil at the market, unable to get any of the sixty-five liters Oliver has stored for us.

We roll into the driveway at precisely six o'clock, the time Oliver agreed to come. At six-thirty we have no word. We need to walk to town before stores close at eight. As I start to lock up, I hear a car. Looking out our bedroom window, I see Oliver hoist a huge shiny metal tank out of his trunk. I thought we were getting bottles. Larry runs out to help him carry the tank down the dirt ramp and into the kitchen.

"Ciao, Oliver. It's *great* to see you.... We almost gave up. And now we're in a rush. We expected you at six." I'm friendly, but don't hide my upset.

"We've been dying to taste our oil," I add, "but I thought you were bringing bottles."

"Sorry I'm late, really sorry. I had a big problem at another house and couldn't leave. For the oil, I can bottle it if you want, but the best way to store it is in the stainless tank," he says. "Do you have a cool place for the tank?"

Larry suggests the technical room, saying we'll have a cantina when the guesthouse is done.

"We really need to leave," I repeat. "The stores close in an hour and it takes thirty minutes to walk."

Larry motions for Oliver to follow him. They're back within seconds. Larry says there's no space; Oliver says it's too warm. He offers to fill a few bottles now and continue to store the tank in his *magazzino*, warehouse.

Rummaging in his trunk, Oliver finds five new bottles but only four caps. We want to take one bottle to Ginny tomorrow night as a hostess gift and have some for ourselves.

"Can you bottle the rest when you take it to your storage?" I ask.

"Due respect, you really should keep it in the tank to protect it from air, light and heat. And the oil rests on the sediment, which improves the flavor," he explains. "I'll bring you a few more bottles when you run out. Just tell me."

Larry looks at me for a decision. I agree reluctantly, wondering how long it'll take to get "a few more bottles."

To protect the counter from oil stains, I spread a large plastic packing bag on the new and extremely porous *pietra serena* stone. Larry and Oliver lift the stainless-steel tank, positioning the spout over the stone sink.

I taste it on my finger. "Wow! That's spicy!"

Oliver smiles and nods, telling us prized Tuscan oil is green, tastes of artichokes and grass, and is spicy enough to tickle your throat, like you need to cough, yet delicate and sweet, never bitter. He suggests I buy cheaper olive oil for cooking. New oil should never be heated, he says, or it loses its best properties.

He adds, "I was afraid since we picked so late, it wouldn't be *piccante*, but this is excellent. You are going to make brilliant oil."

After a hurried goodbye to Oliver, we climb the hill to town. Quickly surveying four ceramic shops, we find a charming Etruscan bird pattern at *l'Etruria*. Since Lodolina means little lark, bird dishes would be perfect. Today we bought cheap white dishes at the mall, but I want something nicer for guests. Unfortunately, there are only three small bird plates and they're outrageously expensive. Looking for a different pattern in the stacks on the floor, I find one more bird plate. I ask for the best price if we take all four. The shop owner offers a tiny discount, but not a close-out price, which is what I think we have. He says they are more important because these are the last ones, handmade in Cortona many years ago. To me, it means if I chip one, I'm down to three and can't serve guests. I tell him I'll think about it.

In Molesini Market, Etta, Marco's mother, is working behind the deli counter. She says something I don't understand. I think she's recommending the *farro* salad, made from cooked wheat grains, cucumber, tomatoes, onion and herbs. Larry doesn't like *farro*, but I buy some anyway to please Etta, and because I'm curious.

While Larry chats with Marco, I go to Roberto's *frutta e verdure*, fruit and vegetable shop, for a melon and cherry tomatoes. I love the small stores in Cortona and would rather shop daily, supporting local merchants, than to go to the big grocery stores in Camucia and stock up like I would at Costco in Chicago. Besides, my Italian *frigo*, refrigerator, is tiny. I can't buy much.

We stop at the hardware store a few feet away for a hairdryer with an Italian plug. The owner is locking up, but takes time to recommend his favorite. Since moving in, we have been drying *naturale*, even for our fancy dinner.

With the owner, who speaks only Italian, we ask about products to clean our white leather armchairs, dingy from twenty years of use and made worse on their ocean voyage. I'm grateful for words that are similar to English. He recommends *ammonica*, which I fear is too strong for leather. He insists he cleaned his white leather chairs with *ammonica* and they are *bellissima*. Based on his enthusiasm, I buy it. He locks the door behind us. I wish I'd purchased rubber gloves.

We have another delicious dinner at *Trattoria Dardano*. I've started to crave Paolo's *coniglio*, roasted rabbit, and a homemade bright green *digestivo*.

The first time I tasted it, the beautiful waitress, Lucia, made us guess what was in it. I finally came up with bay leaf, but only after guessing pine needles, pine nuts and basil.

"There's always room for gelato," Larry announces as we leave. Inspired by the slenderness of Ester, I don't get my own, but beg a couple of bites from Larry. I've also decided to curtail afternoon snacks as I start my new life in Italy. Not just no nuts, my snack of choice, but no snacks. I still hope for willowy.

Walking home in the dark after eleven and with heavy bags in tow, we're surprised to run into our realtor and friend, Lorenzo, making a *passegiata* in the city park with his wife, Rita, and their three-year old son. We excitedly tell them we moved into Lodolina yesterday. Larry thanks him again for finding our perfect house.

"So far, Cortona is even better than we hoped," I add. "There's so much going on!"

I doubt Rita understands much of our conversation and wish I could converse in Italian to include her.

"Do you know of the White Night?" Lorenzo asks. "*Notte Bianca*. It's tonight. Shops and restaurants are open all night with wine, music and food. It happens one night every summer. This year we celebrate also the opening of the pool."

"Sounds like fun... but I need sleep tonight," I say.

"As you prefer. If you wake up in time, you can go to the poetry reading in the new *anfiteatro* near the pool. It will happen at five, so the last poem should be at sunrise. The poet is very famous in Italy. After, the *Comune* will provide breakfast. Pastries and juice... Italian breakfast."

"By invitation... or can anyone go?" I ask.

"Everyone should go without invitation. It is for the whole town — the gift of the *Comune*. You should go," Lorenzo urges us.

After goodbyes and heading down the hill, Larry says, "Wouldn't you just *love* to go? Let's see if we wake up."

We miss our path and end up in someone else's yard. Finally at home, Larry uses our pre-paid phone card to make a few calls to ensure our Chicago condo is ready for the new owners to move in. When I crawl into bed after midnight, he's still talking.

* * *

Thanks to a buzzing mosquito, I wake up before dawn. Tucking all my body parts under the sheet, I try, unsuccessfully, to fall back to sleep.

Larry reaches for his watch. "It's four-twenty," he whispers, "Let's go."

I pull on the clothes I just took off. We climb up the rocky path we just climbed down. Lights at farmhouses across the valley look like big stars against a black void. How surreal, I think. On our second night in our new home, in the dark at four forty-five in the morning, we're climbing as fast as we can up a steep, rocky path to a poetry reading by a famous poet in a new amphitheater at the top of our hill, where we will comprehend almost nothing.

Near the top of the hill, I hear a man's voice, rich and expressive. The performance has started and we still need to walk up to the pool and across to the amphitheater. We turn off our flashlights and step carefully, trying not to make noise as we approach. There's barely enough moonlight to find the path.

In the amphitheater, silhouettes in tiers of semicircles sit motionless like Roman statues. A male form is moving back and forth against an expansive pre-dawn sky. His presence is that of actor, philosopher and statesman. The poems are clearly his own and he is in command of every syllable, phrase and pause. His movements, gestures, the cadence of his breath, his tone and intensity, all communicate. Without seeing his face or understanding his words, I sense the power of a gifted *poeta*.

We find seats near the back. Though I can't comprehend most of the poet's words, I identify subjects and experience his passion... a mother and father at the cemetery, then going about their daily life: "*la guerra, l'amore, la vita,*" the war, the love, the life. Another is about *dodici settembre*, September twelfth, the day after nine-eleven. Another poem light-heartedly describes love and its addiction.

As a piercing ray breaks over the ridge, suddenly illuminating the faces of mesmerized listeners, the poet's final work is about daybreak.

The stage's backdrop is the *Valdichiana*, Chiana Valley. I think about its long history. Inhabited since pre-historic times, the Villanovans were the first known civilization, followed by the Etruscans who date as far back as 800BC. By 200BC, ruling Romans had built stone roads for trade and taxation. In the Middle Ages, silt accumulated in the enormous valley, creating a vast malarial swamp. Around 1500CE, at the request of the Medici family, Leonardo da Vinci drew a map and a system of canals to drain the valley. His plan was implemented over two hundred years, completed long after his death. Today, in the fertile farmland, there are still towns called *Nave*, ship, and *Barco*, boat. Many of Leonardo's canals, according to archeologists, reclaimed canals the Etruscans had built two millennia before.

We don't stay for breakfast, but climb back down the hill to catch another hour of sleep before workers arrive. The panorama is spectacular at dawn. I can't imagine this view ever becoming boring, no matter how many times I walk up and down our hill. Magenta and coral streaks cut across the sky with a lavender dome overhead. The intense sun promises another beastly day.

We crawl back into bed, filled with a sense of wonder and timelessness. I hope this is more than one magical morning, but our foray into spontaneity. I'm typically cautious and Larry is a consummate planner. But spontaneity ignites a spark that can enrich one's life, both by the experience itself and the exhilarating liberation of being impulsive. I hope for more experiences like this morning's pre-dawn poetry.

Perhaps a small town in Tuscany will be the perfect setting for both of us to embrace spontaneity.

An Evening Escape

In Italy, as part of my new style, I will wear my black silk robe every morning. I feel more feminine and elegant in it than I did in the athletic clothes I put on daily in Chicago, hoping for a brisk walk along Lake Michigan or a half-hour on the stationary bike. In Italy, I want to be elegant.

Hearing me on the stairs, Larry calls cheerfully from his living room chair, "I made extra decaf. You're welcome to some, if you want." His preference is to start each day with a cappuccino and then a half-pot of decaf. Yesterday at the mall he found the perfect eight-cup drip pot.

"Thanks. I'll have my lousy cappuccino first. Then I might," I say, smiling as I walk to the kitchen. I love mornings in our new home.

I freeze, stunned. The entire pot of decaf has run across the island and over the edge, creating a small brown lake on the new terracotta tiles.

"Larry! Coffee's all over the floor!"

He bolts from his chair and rushes in to help.

We sop up as much as possible with paper towels and then wash the area with soap and water. The rose tiles that need two more hands of treatment are dark brown. Coffee is a natural dye, so the color may never come out. Equally upsetting, our new coffee pot must be taken back to the mall across the valley. Try as I might, the basket will not stay latched. After a few seconds, it eases open just enough for the coffee to miss the pot. Since it took a few minutes to start dripping through, Larry had no idea it was leaking.

Outside the front door, Pierangelo and Luciano are creating the front terrace. Their conversation warns of their proximity, but they're careful not to disturb us. I decide: not only will I wear my black silk robe every morning, I'll wear it until I am ready to shower and dress for the day, no matter who is working, what time it is, or if the doors are open or closed. It doesn't seem to faze them, why should it bother me?

With my predictably awful cappuccino, I sit in a dingy white leather armchair typing furiously about this morning's pre-dawn poetry reading and the coffee spill. Larry sits in the armchair next to me reading. The men outside are cutting bars of rebar, their shirts off and their torsos dripping. After a while, I stop to discreetly watch them work.

The terrace area is soon rebar-laced, ready for concrete. Each batch must be churned by hand in a small mixer, once painted turquoise but now dented and rusty. When the concrete is ready, they pour it down a wooden trough into a battered wheelbarrow, bump it down the construction ramp, then pour, level and trowel it by hand.

If we had a normal access road, concrete trucks would have poured the foundations for the house, guesthouse, exterior stone walls, terraces, and eventually the base layer for the roofs. But trucks so large cannot maneuver our road, so we must use slower and more costly on-site labor. At Lodolina, the entire concrete construction has been done by hand using that one small mixer.

In the guesthouse, I hear *muratori*, masons, working on the exterior stone walls. I love the predictable, rhythmic sounds. First the 'whack... whack' of a hammer against a stone, making it exactly the right size and shape. Then a whoomp as mortar is thrown into place, followed by tapping to adjust the stone's position, and then the scrapes of the trowel removing excess mortar. There is a longer pause while the next stone is found in the pile. Then whack, whack, whack... whoomp... tap, tap, tap... scrape, scrape... pause... over and over again.

All weekend we have stacked flattened empty boxes outside the hidden door, nearly filling the little vestibule. As each box is opened and investigated, I compare it to the three moving lists, checking off items that arrived in good condition and making three additional lists: damaged and missing items to submit for insurance, small appliances we need with Italian wiring, and groceries to stock the kitchen. Today Larry has agreed to go with me to Arezzo to find Euronics, a superstore for appliances, and Esselunga, the supermarket everyone raves about for groceries.

Finding Arezzo is easy, but even with Francesco's carefully-drawn map we cannot find Euronics. On our way to Esselunga, we pass Euronics by chance, park in a far-away lot and walk to the door. On the door a sign says they're closed Mondays until four o'clock. It's one o'clock. We decide to have lunch, get groceries, and come back after four for our vacuum, iron, food processor, toaster, mixer, and printer. Arezzo is forty minutes from Cortona and we don't want to drive back another day.

At Esselunga's lunch café, I have the best tuna salad I've ever eaten, with sweet corn, black olives and chunks of mozzarella. Italian tuna is packed in glass jars in olive oil, so different from tuna out of a can — sweeter and meatier, less salty and, well, not canned.

Inside Esselunga we can't find shopping carts, only carrying baskets. I suggest we each take two baskets and get only what we really need. But people are coming in with grocery carts, so Larry's determined to find one.

While he's gone, I stand in the produce section looking around, feeling lost and self-conscious. At least I now know touching the fruit and vegetables is not allowed. I watch other shoppers until I understand what to do. I follow one lady to the plastic gloves and bags, then choose and weigh one vegetable at a time so I can remember each code.

Larry comes back with a cart, saying they were locked in a corral in the parking lot. To get one, he put a euro into a box on the cart handle. The coin releases a chain. After shopping, he'll return the cart to the corral and re-hook the chain, which will return his euro.

Almost immediately, he's agitated that I'm so slow. He hates grocery shopping and wants to be done. He asks for items to find, but I'm afraid to show him the full list so only ask him to get water, coffee, and bread. After fruits and vegetables, I rush through the unfamiliar aisles, gathering essentials for a few days instead of the big stocking up I'd planned. I don't know where to find anything and feel overwhelmed by Esselunga and rushed by Larry. I'd love to spend time perusing the shelves, learning about the Italian products in this well-stocked megastore.

I hurry to the cash registers with the cart half full. Larry's waiting, arms loaded and with an impatient look on his face.

"Ready?" he asks, looking for the shortest check-out line.

"I have the essentials," I say, trying to sound normal.

He senses what I'm doing and says, "You're here, Victoria. Get what you need."

His response does not feel like support, it feels like instruction. He doesn't grasp all that *we*, not *I*, need to stock a new home. What *I* need will greatly exceed his patience. In fact, what I need *is* his patience.

I'm stuck. Should I stock the kitchen or get food only for this week? Larry loves to eat at home, saying home is the best restaurant of all. But no one can cook without ingredients.

"This is not working," I say to him. "Do you want me to stock up so I can cook, or do you want to leave more quickly? Stocking up will take more time. Your choice."

He says we should buy heavy items or those not available in Cortona, and everything else at Molesini Market. This could be fun if we were exploring, but Larry's not in a grocery-exploring mood, so we check-out and leave.

He loads the car and takes the cart back to the corral to get his euro. We drive back to Euronics in silence.

Euronics is more overwhelming than Esselunga. Larry says at least it's one location where we can buy everything we need and get out fast. He looks at my appliance list, raises his eyebrows, and looks for a clerk to help. She only speaks Italian — rapid Italian. When Larry tells her that we speak very little Italian, she talks more slowly and loudly, but I still don't understand.

I ask Larry to ask her which vacuum is good for terracotta tile floors, hoping he'll know the words in Italian, but he says curtly, "Ask her yourself."

"Even if I could ask in Italian, I need the answer in English," I say under my breath.

Larry finally tells her we must have help in English. She says only one clerk speaks English, but she's with a customer. There are not many clerks, several customers are waiting, and no one is smiling. Larry tells me I'll have to choose appliances without English. I look for pictures on the boxes. Like the grocery store, this could be fun, but it is not.

We choose a Miele vacuum, not the top of the line, but *"buono per terracotta pavimento e tappeto vecchio,"* good for terracotta floors and antique rugs. We find an inexpensive toaster and hand mixer. I'm surprised by the array of irons, some with separate water tanks, but choose something American-looking. There are no Cuisinart food processors like I have in Chicago, so I settle on a Moulinex with attachments for a blender, dough processer, spice grinder, and a variety of slicers, dicers, ricers and graters — most of which I'll never use. The Moulinex box is as big as the vacuum box and I fear the attachments will take an entire shelf of my limited cabinet space. Lastly, Larry finds the perfect Hewlett-Packard printer on sale.

"Do you want to get a different coffee pot? Some are really cheap," I ask him, thinking it'd be easier and faster than taking the other one back to the outlet mall. He says we'll get the other one replaced or fixed and we don't need two, as if I'm being frivolous.

We head home with our SUV loaded. Larry is quiet. I'm tense and disappointed. The trip could've been a little adventure, but it did not go well.

"This is like a wedding shower, getting all new appliances," I finally say, trying to reconnect and be cheerful. Truthfully, I don't feel like a bride. I feel intimidated by Esselunga and Euronics, and dependent on and disapproved of by Larry.

After my failed attempt at levity, we are silent. Larry unloads the car while I put away groceries. We need to dress quickly to go to Ginny and Giancarlo's for dinner with our new castle friends. It was kind of Ginny to invite us all, which she did in part because she knew Larry and I are camping amidst boxes and without a working kitchen.

It's been a tough day. We worked hard, but still have stacks of unopened boxes and now boxes of unopened appliances. We don't know where to shop and when we find a good store, I don't know how to choose. I'm embarrassed most of the time because I don't know the right thing to do or say. Language has become more stressful instead of less, because I think I should be getting better but am not. I'm afraid to speak for fear of making some humiliating mistake, and can't understand most of what is said because I feel so embarrassed it's hard to concentrate. I'm even too ashamed to say *non capisco*, I don't understand. Living in Italy is not like our honeymoon or any of our Italian vacations.

I think back to the poetry reading this morning and my hope for more spontaneity. Life switches pretty quickly from highs to lows, even without the complication of a new country. The challenge, it seems to me, is to let the lows pass without dwelling on them, and appreciate the highs. But already I am too often on edge, uneasy in my new culture, and sensing that Larry is upset with me. It's only our third day in the house.

This evening, at Ginny and Giancarlo's, I hope we can start afresh. I mentally decide to put away the difficulties of today, reconnect with Larry, and find joy in getting to know our new friends. We dress without much conversation.

"I look forward to tonight," I say as we drive down the access road. "We really should stay and unpack, but I don't want to. We need a change of pace…. Today has been tough. Are you still happy about this move?"

Larry reaches for my hand and gently squeezes it. I guess he wants the evening to be better, too. I give him my most hopeful smile.

Giancarlo and Ginny's home is new construction, but looks old because of antique doors, sconces, chandeliers, and other architectural artifacts built into the structure. Art and ancient treasures are everywhere. Not surprising, since they're antique dealers.

During the house tour, I'm intrigued by a basket of metal balls with textured surfaces, the size of grapefruits.

"What are those?" I ask Giancarlo.

"Pick one up," he says.

"Wow… That's heavy! They're too pretty for cannonballs."

"Antique bocce balls," he says, amused by my predictable reaction.

"I've seen elderly Italian men playing *bocce*," I say. "They're so graceful. I had no idea the balls weighed this much."

Ginny calls from outside in her Texan drawl, "Com'on out. We're rehdy 'n waitin'."

Giancarlo grins and motions us toward the back door. Larry takes my hand and I feel myself relax. In the presence of interesting people, especially those we're just getting to know, and away from construction and our conflicts of the day, Larry and I seem re-bonded, at least for now. He pats a cushion, inviting me to sit beside him on the Texan-style wrap-around back porch they call the veranda.

Ginny serves gorgeous, runny Gorgonzola on endive spears, braided *bufala mozzarella* with tiny crimson tomatoes — sweet, but not as sweet as Falconiere's — and ripe musky cantaloupe draped with delicate, paper-thin slices of *prosciutto*. It's a warm evening and I eat too many appetizers and drink too many flutes of Prosecco before we're ushered to the table.

The main course is a delicate *frittata*, a light egg dish served room temperature. Ginny planned our menu knowing Alex avoids gluten. The perfect summer meal is healthy, delicious and satisfying.

"When I was preparin' for ya'll," Ginny confesses, "Linda told me, 'I'd never spend so much time cookin' for *anybody*... 'specially folks I hardly know.' But I *love* to cook. And, I hope we'll be friends for a long, long time."

It was a lovely sentiment. Linda, her girlfriend from Dallas, says Ginny has been preparing for two days. I wonder if I'll have the courage to cook for Ginny.

After dessert, Giancarlo announces the best is now arriving. He brings out tiny frosty glasses and a bottle of icy *limoncello* — homemade by him. We've had plenty to drink, but the limoncello goes down smoothly, the night is gentle, and the conversation as sweet as a second dessert. Chatter and laughter have replaced the ooohs and ahhhs over Ginny's dinner.

Their long table is even more enchanting with the array of emptied glasses now collected at each place, reflecting the variety of wines we consumed. Their plates, from an old monastery, feature a different hand-painted funny monk on each one. Candles, flickering in a huge, ornate iron candelabra sitting in an old copper basin, throw light on guests and empty glasses. Candle wax from countless dinners has dripped down the candelabra and filled the bottom of the basin. I would love to find a similar candelabra for our terrace. I would love to have a terrace.

Giancarlo holds a flame to Lynn's thin cigar, like he did at the castle. It doesn't seem in keeping with her sweet and feminine persona, but I did sense some feistiness when we met. Her husband, Mike, is unruffled, so this must be normal Lynn behavior. Larry is laughing with Tony and Alex. It's been a charmed evening. I hope these budding friendships will not wither as couples return to their homelands.

"Can anyone do this?" Ginny stands on one leg and places the other ankle across her standing knee, surprising the group with her challenge. Then she lowers her elbow onto her ankle and rests her chin on her curled fist, like a standing Thinker. I study her position and feel confident that, after two years of yoga, I can do it. Perhaps the limoncello has affected my judgment, but I'm unable to resist.

I accept the dare, much to Ginny and Giancarlo's surprise. Larry knows I'd only accept if I think I can do it. I assume the tree pose, then pull my ankle across my knee and slowly lower my elbow, chin on my fist. I find a spot for visual focus.

Our friends start to count: "One... two...." I breathe deeply and slowly, in rhythm with their counting. "Nine... ten...." Ginny and I hold the pose. Our friends continue. "Eighteen, nineteen... twenty-five, twenty-six." I try not to hear the numbers, but breath slowly with the rhythm and maintain focus. Ginny starts to wobble at sixty-something. I try not to watch her sway. Focus. She regains composure... seventy-one... seventy-two... seventy-nine. At eighty-seven, she lowers her leg in defeat. The counting stops and applause begins.

I maintain the pose and taunt others to try. Larry grins, his chin dimples in that adorable way. Our new friends must be wiser or less intoxicated than I am, because no one accepts my dare. I lower my leg, having been awarded the title of new world champion. Ginny, grinning ear to ear, gives me a generous congratulatory hug.

It's past midnight when we thank Giancarlo and Ginny profusely, say goodnight to all and drive up our bumpy road. Their home is less than a mile down the hill from ours, but our bad road makes it seem much farther.

Finally resting my head on my pillow, Larry reaches for my hand, whispering, "This was a good day." I squeeze his hand. I don't want to correct him, but for me it was a difficult day with a lovely ending. I'm grateful for this moment and want to hold onto this warm affection and make it last. As I've noted before, when you can least afford a few hours off is often when you need it the most.

Fear Not

An apricot dawn has blossomed into another blazing sapphire-sky day. No time for lingering between the sheets. Workers are going strong and the temperature is climbing. This will be our fourth day living at Lodolina, hopefully our last day of major unpacking. I pull on my silk robe, make another wimpy cappuccino, and carry it upstairs to shower.

Outside our bathroom window, three workers are laying terracotta tiles on the narrow terrace leading to the hidden door. Close enough to touch the glass, all the men are bent down with their eyes averted.

For privacy, I lean out to pull the shutters closed, but tools are propped against one side. I can't go out, because there's adhesive on the concrete slab. Nor do I want to make it obvious that I'm about to shower. Trying to be discreet, I pull one shutter closed, close the glass window on the other side and drape Larry's towel over it. The towel doesn't quite cover, so I remove my robe and carefully place it over the gap.

I am acutely aware of standing stark naked next to an open, iffy-covered window where three Italian men are bobbing up and down as they work. I shower quickly, wrap myself in a towel, dart into the bedroom, and close the door.

I may brag about wearing my black silk robe until noon, but when it comes to showering with uncertain privacy, I'm not such a brazen girl.

My modesty may be heightened because Marcello, the tile foreman, is so attractive. Yesterday, when he, Francesco and I were talking about the finish on the floors, he let Francesco translate my English into Italian for the entire conversation. Then Marcello answered me directly, in English.

"Oh! You speak English," Francesco exclaimed. "Why you never tell me?"

Marcello smiled and looked at me for a reaction, rather than at Francesco. He's thirty years my junior and perfectly appropriate, but I sense he has a warm way with women.

Dressed and downstairs, I want to check emails but the internet is down again. So fast when first installed, now it's temperamental at best.

Last night's happy glow with our castle friends is dimmed by unpredicted tension with Larry. He seems preoccupied this morning, so I don't interrupt. I miss my friends and family. I miss my organized, predictable, easier American life. This Italian adventure is fascinating, but we're living in a house that feels like a stranger's even with our own belongings. The stress between Larry and me flares and dissolves without an obvious cause. There are a dozen decisions to make each day. Too often I must use my own judgment because he hates being interrupted, but I worry he won't agree with what I decide. Life is stimulating, but neither of us are having the relaxing Tuscan summer we imagined.

In her email yesterday, my friend Dale wrote, "You must feel like Cinderella!"

"Exactly," I replied, "when Cinderella has the broom in her hand and expects the toil and loneliness to last forever. Everything here is covered with dust. The plumbing is not hooked everywhere and, with only six interior lights connected, we bump around in the dark. Workers arrive at eight o'clock six mornings a week, so we have little privacy. Our yard is dirt, rocks and construction rubbish. I am terrified to drive our enormous SUV on the narrow roads, so can't leave the house unless my only companion, who has become as irascible as the stepsisters, will take me. Yes, I feel like Cinderella on her worst day, long before she goes to the ball."

While my reply sits in the outbox with four others, I decide to make the bed.

Each morning at Lodolina, I meticulously make the bed. I smooth the sheets, then the summer blanket, stretching each taut, and tuck the extra under the mattress. I want no wrinkles in any layer. I fluff the pillows, smooth the cases and put them in a line. The quilted ivory bedspread goes up over it all, and I crease it ever so slightly under the pillows. It requires several trips around the king-sized bed to get it right. When the bedspread is smooth, I lean three bronze-gold silk shantung cushions against the pillows so they look tossed casually, not placed. Perfectly imperfect.

My compulsiveness about bed making at Lodolina is opposite to my more casual approach in Chicago, where I simply pulled the covers up and tossed the cushions against the pillows. Here, the bed is the one thing I can control. Made tightly, it is protected from the construction dust that settles on everything else. And, workers don't need to disturb it to install fixtures or cabinetry.

I stand back and appreciate the contrast of the hand-hammered iron bed and the luminous quilted silk cover. Both made in Italy, they were shipped to Chicago for our condominium and now have come back home. Despite a bent leg, the bed is beautiful.

It reminds me of one of my life rules: only purchase exactly what you want; do not settle. I suspect most disciplined people don't buy things that are not perfect for them, but I do. I'm never sorry when I wait to find something that's just right — like our bed and the linens — but always sorry when I buy something that's just okay. Better to do without. I try to ask, "Is it perfect?" But too often, I simply want to check it off my list. We bought many appliances at Euronics yesterday. I hope they are not hasty mistakes.

I also hope my Etruscan bird pottery is not a mistake. The purchase felt extravagant. The shop owner found four plates, four bowls, and two serving pieces. When I bought them all, he did not give me a bigger discount, as I hoped. Instead, he gave me a mug. It's modern, not very interesting, but decorated with the same bird. I love the dishes, but feel remorse about the cost.

This morning, I took Larry a second cappuccino in the bird mug. He said he prefers his white mug from Tedi, our Chicago friend.

For my cappuccino, I always use my Tedi cup, white with a pewter trim, her early gift for my sixtieth birthday. Two days ago, unpacking a kitchen box, I was overjoyed when I found Larry's mug and my cup. Now thousands of miles away, I don't know if I miss Tedi less when I'm drinking from her gift, or more.

I sigh, my orderly life and deep friendships in Chicago were so different than the chaos and loneliness here. I know that peace can only come from accepting that life contains both order *and* chaos, companionship *and* loneliness, but sometimes the negative seems to take over.

Now I must put away my angst and get busy. Our first visitors arrive in less than an hour. Jay and Amy are the age of our children, a happy couple full of positive energy, curiosity and grace. It'll be fun to share our new hometown with familiar friends, even if they're not my longed-for girlfriends.

Larry wants to walk to town to meet them, saying he needs the exercise. My left foot — the one that had a small fracture before we moved — hurts again, probably from walking in Naples, climbing to the poetry reading, standing to unpack, and holding the pose at Ginny's last night.

"I don't think I can climb the hill with my foot," I say, surprised at his request since he commented earlier that I was limping.

"Then you can drive and I'll walk," he says.

I stare at him. He knows driving here is less comfortable for me than climbing with an injury.

"Just try, please Vic. We've barely walked to Cortona since we moved in. I think you'll be fine," he urges.

"Okay, but no promises. If my foot hurts, we need to drive. We'll be climbing all day with Jay and Amy, up and down Cortona hills. Not smart to injure it again."

After walking about a hundred yards on our flat driveway, I know I should not go on.

I stop. "Larry, please. Let's drive. It hurts."

He tightens his lips and shakes his head, then turns sharply and jogs back to the house to get car keys.

We get into the car without speaking. At the end of our driveway he announces, "Since you won't walk up, I'll drive up," and turns toward the trail.

Surely, he's teasing. The trail is steep, mostly gullies with big rocks and a sharp curve. Iffy for a tractor, but downright dangerous for a car, let alone a top-heavy SUV.

"Please don't. It's not a road…." I beg.

He keeps driving. Even if he's teasing, it feels unkind.

"Please turn around! You're scaring me."

He doesn't relent.

"If you try to drive up that trail, I'll get out of the car and stay home. You can meet Jay and Amy on your own. Is that what you'd prefer?"

"Why are you being so defiant? I'm obviously not serious! You are constantly difficult these days… on my case and difficult."

"I am not difficult, just honest. I *will* get out of this car," I declare, more upset since our problem is now my behavior.

"Don't threaten me! You're being ridiculous," he scowls.

I'm upset and hurt. He continues uphill. When I start to cry, he backs down… both his teasing and the SUV. We ride to town without speaking. Swallowing back tears, I'm relieved we'll be with other people today.

Jay and Amy are waiting in *Piazza della Repubblica* with broad smiles and vacation exuberance. After *cappuccini* and catching up, we go to the

Museo Diocesano, Cortona's tiny museum of fine art. With our friends, Larry seems to have overcome his irritation. He leads us to Cortona's greatest art treasure, *L'Annunciazione* by Fra Angelico, and stands in admiration before it. The annunciation depicts the moment the Archangel Gabriel announces to Mary that she will bear God's son, a favorite theme in Renaissance art.

Fra Angelico created five large annunciations, now in museums around the world. Cortona's, painted in 1433-34, is often deemed his finest. He lived in Cortona twice, from 1408-1418 in the Dominican monastery, when he decorated the interior of the church of San Domenico with frescoes, now mostly destroyed, and then again in 1433-34, after he took his vows as a Dominican friar. Then, he painted this masterpiece.

This annunciation was so admired by the Medici family, rulers of Florence, that they asked to borrow it. As a thank you for the loan, the Medici sent a larger, opulent, gold-leafed triptych to hang in its place. The thank you gift still hangs above the main altar in the *Chiesa di San Domenico*, while the priceless *L'Annunciazione* is held in the museum.

Despite standing before this painting dozens of times, its tenderness still moves me. A Florentine art historian told us that Fra Angelico was such a gentle man that he could not bear to paint evil or tragedy. Rather, he would ask an apprentice to paint that part.

Larry asks Jay and Amy what they see and listens closely to their observations. I love to watch him teach, so connected and respectful, and feel myself softening toward him.

Together, they identify symbols typical of Renaissance annunciations: the undisturbed bed signifying Mary's virginity, Gabriel's opulent heavenly robe and Mary's plain earthly one, Mary's book indicating her intelligence, and the dove representing the Holy Spirit. Larry points to the golden lines of Latin words flowing between Gabriel and Mary, an unusual element of this painting, and translates their exchange. Mary's words are upside down, as though she could be directing her thoughts to God. Her reaction does not seem to be shock, as it is in many annunciation paintings, but pensive obedience. Though I point out that she did drop her book.

Gabriel lifts his finger to his lips and I imagine him first saying, "Fear not, Mary." Throughout the Bible, angels typically say, "fear not" when approaching humans. If an angel approached me, especially today when I'm feeling insecure, "fear not" would be most appreciated.

Despite Larry's warm teaching, he's giving me a cold shoulder. In a private moment when I ask him what's wrong, he says I've been on his case since we moved in and he's tired of it. I try to think of what I've done or said, and conclude he's being critical and feeling criticized without cause.

But feelings are feelings, and he clearly feels mistreated. I hope our tension isn't apparent to our guests. It's not fair that our discord would diminish their joy.

After a picnic lunch of Molesini deli food spread out on a lichen-covered stone bench in the *Parterre*, with us all perched around the edge, Jay and Amy say they're eager to explore more. They're energizing and fun, so I decide to go along despite my now-puffy foot.

As we climb the hill past *Chiesa di San Francesco*, we're surprised to see the door open. This church has been closed for renovation for years. Brother Elia, a Franciscan monk living in Cortona and the leader of the order after Francis died, designed the building in 1245. Originally a plain Franciscan structure, the interior is now decorated with Renaissance side chapels and ornately carved Baroque pews. We're the only visitors.

Inside, a beam of light through a tiny stained-glass window over the front door creates a scarlet beam on the wall. About ten feet tall, it seems animated, moving with us as Amy and I walk from chapel to chapel. We agree, the scarlet light feels supernatural, reassuring, and alone is worth the visit. I make a note of the time, so I might revisit another day.

This church's relics include Saint Francis' personal artifacts — his pillow, tattered brown robe, and small worn Gospel book recounting the life and teachings of Jesus — conserved in a glass case at the front, and a fragment of the True Cross over the main alter. The ivory Byzantine cross reliquary was brought to Cortona by Brother Elia, Francis' chosen successor, when Elia visited the East on a papal mission. So, if Constantine's mother Helen found the true cross when she traveled to Jerusalem in 326 to search for Jesus's relics, the authenticity of Cortona's fragment is plausible. The ornate silver Baroque frame was added centuries later.

Our final destination is *Le Celle,* the monastery three miles outside Cortona where Saint Francis lived briefly and wrote his last testimony. The honeycomb of beige stone rooms clinging to the hillside astounds our friends as it always astounds me. Following Francis' death in 1226, Brother Elia added five small rooms — cells — and a refectory, and the monastery grew from there. At its peak, as many as two hundred monks lived at *Le Celle.* It was all but abandoned for two centuries. Then, in 1537, it was granted to the Capuchins, the order of *friars* who adhere most closely to Francis' teachings of service and simplicity. We understand only nine brothers live here now, consistent with the Capuchin's covenant to live in small groups of no more than twelve.

At the bottom of a zigzag descent, we cross a bridge over a small stone gorge. Today the rock-bed is dry and *Le Celle* is silent, but we've seen torrents rushing down after a rainstorm. Francis was drawn to dramatic natural formations like this. Dense oak and cypress forests still surround *Le Celle,* like they did when he was living here.

Francis' room is little more than a cave and his bed a worn wooden plank about five feet long and a foot wide.

"He must've been a very small man," Jay whispers as he turns from looking into the room, "and not worried about comfort."

"That pretty much defines him," Larry says. "Small in stature, enormous in faith, without concern for personal comfort. His simple approach reformed much of the Catholic Church and he's still among the most influential people in Christianity."

"Did he die here?" Amy asks.

"No," I say, explaining that he wrote his last testimony here, but Franciscan brothers came with soldiers from Assisi to escort him to his hometown. Relics, body parts or belongings of saints, were a big trade in the time of Francis and his followers were afraid that a gang from Perugia might steal his body to cut it up for relics. They wanted to bury him in Assisi, whole.

"He was sainted within two years, a record," Larry adds.

Many *Cortonese* believe Saint Francis and *Le Celle* are the soul of Cortona today, and I agree. I breathe in the peacefulness and re-read the small wooden sign that says, in Italian, "Stop yourself. In the silence before God, rediscover who you are." I wonder if our new life in Italy might help me rediscover who I am. So far, I'm feeling more lost than rediscovered.

As we start up the hill toward our car, Jay and Amy walk slowly and solemnly, hand in hand, seemingly moved by this exceptional place. A brown-robed monk in the vegetable garden gathers lettuce as we pass, perhaps for this evening's supper for the brothers.

Over pizza, we chat about their Chicago lives and our Tuscan adventure. I wonder if any of us are fully honest. Life is rarely all good, but I want only good news to travel home with them.

My foot is still swollen when Larry and I get home. Surely ice, elevation and ibuprofen will make it better by morning. The important injury to worry about is hurting one another. This morning's argument still stings, but time with friends helped us reconnect. I wonder what tomorrow will bring.

I drift to sleep thinking of the angel's "fear not," whispered to a young girl who did not know what her future held, only that her life was changing. Our future in Italy is unknown. We have taken a different course and, as life changes, we'll change. I'd love for an angel to show up and say "fear not," then tell me how to better handle our difficulties.

Perhaps this summer, I'll discover something new about being unafraid.

Expectations, Hope, and Singing Angels

In the two days since Jay and Amy left, life has been nonstop construction. Larry and I seem more in sync, settling into our new Tuscan home. My foot has recovered enough that I'm comfortable climbing the hill to town. Importantly, we are slowly giving up the expectation that this summer will be anything like our dreams.

We expected an idyllic summer with time to explore Italy and work on personal projects. So far, it is the opposite. Perhaps we set ourselves up to fail by thinking we had it figured out. In fact, any disappointment is even greater when we think we know what to expect. We'd lived in Cortona for a winter, vacationed here a dozen times, and done our homework. We knew living in Italy would be different than a vacation, but we were shockingly naïve about how different.

We thought residency was handled in Chicago, but weeks later we still don't have *Permessi*. I never imagined choosing small appliances in Italian would be so confusing or that the manuals would be in every language except English. I didn't anticipate that driving narrow roads would unnerve me or that I would be too embarrassed to speak. I've been a single mom and a successful executive, but here, when I expected a summer of joy, I'm beginning to wonder if something is wrong with me. I am so easily discombobulated.

Mostly, I did not expect this tension between Larry and me. Nor was I prepared for loneliness, intimidation and dependency, also not normal for me. But I am not ready to give up. Building a new life in Italy may require each of us digging into our deeper selves, looking for greater strength and new ways to interact.

In fact, being naïve is probably part of any true adventure. If we really knew what to expect, the anticipation would be less exhilarating, learning less edifying when reality strikes, and we might not do it at all. For the fullest life, we must remain willing to be naïve, reach for bold dreams, embrace disappointment as instructional, and never lose hope. But this is easier to say than to live.

And while neither of us fathomed we'd be living in a construction site for so long, I definitely would rather be living at Lodolina than staying at a hotel. There is a magic about Lodolina and daily life on our hillside that will keep me forging ahead for a long time. This move may seem like a disaster so far, but I still have hope.

After a morning of trying not to disturb Larry, and of him grimacing whenever I stand beside him waiting to ask a question, he comes into the kitchen and says, "How about if I take you out for lunch? I'm not getting anything done. Let's turn this day around." Perhaps he feels the magic, too.

"Let's pretend to be on vacation, just for one hour?" I say, surprised and grateful. Larry suggests lunch on the piazza, knowing it's one of my very favorite things to do.

Sipping crisp white wine in the sunshine at *Pane e Vino*, Larry tells me about the deaths of Abelard and Heloise, the twelfth century lovers whose story he has been reading and recounting to me. Larry reminds me that when she became pregnant, Abelard proposed marriage but she resisted because it might harm his career. Thugs, likely hired by Heloise's protective uncle, broke into Abelard's room in the night and castrated him. Completely devoted to each other, they secretly married, then went to separate abbeys and never saw one another again. When Abelard died, his abbey sent his body to Heloise for burial. When Heloise died years later, she was buried at Abelard's side.

Larry sighs respectfully as he concludes their story and tells me Will Durant gave Abelard a full chapter in his eleven-volume masterpiece, *The Story of Civilization*, a lifetime pursuit for which Durant and his wife won a Pulitzer Prize. "That," Larry says, "is an honor Durant did not even grant the great Thomas Aquinas!"

As he finishes Abelard's story, Larry gets choked up. He pats his chest and clears his throat. In a raspy voice and with glistening eyes, he says, "Sorry, didn't expect that."

I love that Larry can get choked up over the death of a man who lived nine hundred years ago. He is tender, this husband of mine, deep and touchable. I sometimes need to be reminded of that, especially during these confusing days.

After a quiet afternoon of construction without questions, Larry and I climb back up the hill for a sacred music concert at the *Cattedrale*, led by a famous composer-conductor from the Vatican.

In the *Parterre*, we see a familiar shape sitting alone on a park bench. It's Marco, unusual for him to be out of the shops and even more rare for him to be sitting.

"*Buonasera*," Larry and I say in unison, good evening.

"*Buonasera, amici. Fate una passeggiata?*" Good evening, friends. Taking a stroll?

"Well, climbing up our hill isn't exactly a *passeggiata*, but we like it. You're off work early. Did you get fired?" I tease.

"Today is my mother's birthday," Marco says. "We're going to *Il Cacciatore* for a family dinner, so I must go back soon. I never sit in the park. I needed a break."

"How late's the store open?" I ask, remembering we're out of milk.

"What do you need?" Marco asks. "I have the keys. It is closed, but tell me what you need... I go in and get it. You pay me later. This is easy."

I refuse his kindness, though we won't be able to enjoy even sub-standard *cappuccini* tomorrow morning without milk. It seems like an imposition when he's stealing a moment's rest.

Leaning toward Larry as we walk, I whisper, "Can you believe someone would open a grocery store for us? That'd never happen in Chicago."

We decide to have a simple dinner and people-watch from a table on *Via Nazionale*, the street where everyone strolls. Tonight the town is packed.

An elderly woman saunters past. I try not to stare, but she's wearing a clingy white spandex dress, metallic gold athletic shoes, and a large lime green straw hat. Though she isn't fat, gravity has lowered and plumped her curves and the white spandex is ultra-revealing. I lift my chin in her direction, so Larry won't miss the spectacle. Since she's dressed to be noticed, I probably don't need to be so discreet.

A curious fashion mélange passes before us. Musicians dressed in black carry black-cased instruments. *Stranieri*, foreigners, wear short shorts and tank tops, even the men. Adult Italian men dress casually and comfortably, but their shorts cover their knees and their shirts have sleeves. A bevy of Italian teenage girls parade by in micro skirts, bare midriffs, and low-cut tops with push-up bras that create extra-rounded cleavages. Surely, their mothers did not see them leave the house that way.

Mike and Lynn, friends from the castle, stop to chat as Larry and I finish our *insalatone*, big salads. I'm delighted to see them and thankful for our budding friendship. We invite them to join us for coffee and the concert, but they have plans.

At the *Cattedrale* early, we watch the sunset from the overlook. The cloud-streaked sky is on fire and the valley floor is illuminated with a copper-gold glow. I wish I had my camera.

Music spills into the piazza each time the cathedral door opens, enticing people inside even though it's an hour before the concert. The sound is enormous and we, too, are drawn inside to listen to the final minutes of rehearsal. After instructions from the maestro, the musicians re-arrange their chairs and leave.

Six nuns in pure white habits slide into the pew in front of us.

Larry asks, "If something happened to me, would you become a nun?"

"I think it's a little late for that. Besides, who'd write our story if I dedicated my life to God? As a nun, I'd have to leave out all the juicy parts."

"Your passion for writing is wonderful… but I'm not getting enough attention," he whispers, pursing his lips in a little-boy pout. I wonder if he's just revealed the underlying cause of his recent unpredictable crabbiness.

As we wait, Larry notes that the paintings in the sanctuary, though interesting, aren't as important as the church. Built in the eleventh century on the ruins of a pagan Roman temple, with medieval elements still visible in today's stone façade, this church has been a center for religious life in Cortona for nine centuries.

High on the altar are gilded *putti*, cherubs, and massive silver candleholders. I wonder how God views the extravagance. Church defenders say the opulence was to give worshipers, most of whom were paupers, a glimpse of heaven. But I wonder if it would have been better to invest in education to help raise paupers out of serfdom.

Actually, I don't believe God focuses on what we humans view as excess. Instead, I think he sees the hearts of those who built this cathedral, those who appreciate it, and those who worship in it — not the extravagance itself. I want to believe the artists, artisans and laborers who created this splendor hundreds of years ago did so with loving, true, and faithful hearts. I hope when God looks at me, he finds my heart loving, true, and faithful.

Suddenly, over fifty singers dressed in black with long burgundy scarves file onto the platform. The conductor's introductions are in Italian, then, to my surprise, he repeats his welcome in English. This concert is not a performance, Father Frisina tells us, but a time for spiritual reflection. Monsignor Marco Frisina is the primary priest-composer in Italy and was the papal conductor and composer for Pope John Paul II. He says tonight's concert will begin with his original composition about Santa Margherita, Cortona's patron saint.

Father Frisina shares Margherita's story in Italian and then in English. A beautiful, vivacious but poor girl fell in love with a young lord who promised to marry her. She lived with him for ten years and bore his son, but they never married because of their differing social classes. The nobleman was mysteriously murdered, leaving Margherita and her son penniless. Kicked out by his family, then rejected by her father and stepmother, Margherita walked with her son to Cortona. Here, they were welcomed by a family of Francis-followers. She dedicated her life to service after she had a vision of Jesus reaching out from a crucifix, saying *"mia figlia,"* my daughter. She cared for the sick and the poor of Cortona, made accurate prophecies, admonished the local bishop for his personal excess, and founded Cortona's first hospital.

Suddenly, glorious voices — a cappella — lift me to another realm. A soloist, introduced as "tenor for the Pope," sings effortlessly, ethereally.

Father Frisina explains that the purpose of sacred music is to help man encounter God. The danger, he says, is that a sacred concert could become a show. "We hope this music changes people, that their faith might become stronger. In 2004, Pope John Paul II asked God to bless him with a stronger faith. Though God became real for many people because of the example of Pope John Paul, even *he* prayed for stronger faith."

Two *Capuchin* monks on my left are wearing rough brown robes with rope belts, the three knots reminding them of their vows of poverty, chastity, and obedience. They surely live at *Le Celle*, the monastery we visited with Jay and Amy.

The church, packed with people standing in the back and sides, has become an oven. Men remove their jackets and women fan themselves with whatever they can find. After a while, I feel like I'm sitting in a puddle of perspiration and wonder if my black linen pants are truly wet. The performers in their formal black attire and monks in those long robes must be miserable.

A dark-haired soprano, set apart as a soloist by her burnt orange shawl, walks to the front. Her first note fills the sanctuary, reverberating into the beams. Her voice is arresting, intense, soothing and haunting. If a human can make this sound, what must be the sounds of angels?

People sit motionless; women stop fanning.

Father Frisina turns to address us again, this time very quietly, saying "The bigness of our faith is in loving God."

He announces the next song is dedicated to *San Francesco d'Assisi.* I recall the prayer of Saint Francis: *Make me an instrument of your peace. Where there is hatred, let me sow love… sadness, joy…* and wish I could remember the rest.

Father Frisina says Francis thanked God ultimately for "the gift he received in his hands and feet." Every Italian in the sanctuary knows "the gift" means the stigmata, the wounds made by the nails in Jesus's hands and feet. When Francis received "the gift," the monk with him recorded the phenomenon in detail. Though others have reported receiving the stigmata, Francis was the first.

I sit, feeling deeply grateful to live near a monastery where Francis lived, wrote and prayed. Faith is a treasure to me, a gift not everyone experiences but can, simply by accepting it.

After the long applause ends, the monk on my left introduces himself as Brother Andrea. In flawless English, he asks our names and where we are from. His dark eyes connect affirmingly, intensely, as though he can see my thoughts. I hope we meet again.

Outside the cathedral, the night breeze lifts the white habits of the sisters ahead of us and, as if in unison, they reach down to hold their skirts in place.

Back home, filled with serenity, disappointments all but forgotten, I lay my head on the pillow and think about the sounds of angels. Through the open window beside my bed, the dense Milky Way arcs across the night sky like a handful of diamonds strewn against black velvet. I feel simultaneously humbled and enlarged, pondering the sights and imagining the silence and sounds of distant realms. Larry breathes peacefully, his lips parted, almost in a smile. Tonight, he looks like a sleeping angel himself.

July

The Roundabout

A new month has arrived, but life at Lodolina feels the same. After breakfast, Larry seems agitated and distant and I don't know why. We were so happy last night at the concert and earlier this morning. When I ask if we can talk about it, he mutters, "Later."

I attempt to write about Father Frisina and the concert but am too distracted by the tension to concentrate. I'm glad I carry a small journal, so I can turn to my notes later. I sit in an armchair in the living room, my mind whirling. Larry's in a wicker chair outside on the new cement slab. He seems to prefer to be away from me.

Larry's my only friend in Italy and my twenty-four-hour companion. We've been in Cortona three weeks and living in the house nine days. We were so excited to be here, ready for our retirement dream. How could it fall apart this quickly?

I try to analyze our lives here versus Chicago, hoping for a clue. In Chicago, Larry worked full time, including frequent travel to clients, and handled our finances with the help of a bookkeeper. He had time to study and write, exercise and take on volunteer teaching. I was retired and had time to care for our home, spend with my daughters and girlfriends, volunteer as I wanted, and do my own projects. After retirement, I viewed my job as caring for Larry while he worked to fill our retirement coffers.

For Chicago building projects, we both worked with the architect. Then I found materials, presented them to Larry and he approved or didn't approve my choices. In my teens, I dreamed of becoming an architect, so I enjoyed the creative process and the hunt. Larry has excellent taste and thinks of out-of-the-box solutions, which I value. It was a partnership that worked, though I did most of the legwork.

For Lodolina, we did everything together. We found the house together, bought it together, and went together to every meeting and fieldtrip with Francesco. When we came to Italy to work on the house, it was a vacation with a purpose. I assumed we'd continue to work on Lodolina together. But now that we live here, I seem to be responsible for most of it.

The morning passes quietly. I make the bed and do mindless household chores since I can't concentrate. Larry moves to a living room chair after I leave. I endeavor to stay out of his way. It's not easy to stay out of someone's way in a house this small, open and full of moving boxes.

I hate this tension. I hate what is happening to us. Only three weeks ago, *three weeks*, we were starting our happy new life. Now I'm constantly on guard. I choose my battles, try not to escalate, and feel lonelier and more confused each time he gets upset. We haven't spoken since breakfast.

I hate what is happening to me. My typically strong self-confidence has been undermined by feeling out of place and, too often, stupid. I thought I would feel exhilarated by living in Italy, not discombobulated and dependent.

Francesco and Gabriele come at noon to check progress and make decisions about the bookcase wall. Gabriele brings boxes of Bose speakers to be installed eventually, which he stacks in the living room beside the wardrobe boxes.

Francesco, Gabriele and I stand around the kitchen island, where everyone always gathers, and discuss the schedule for this week. The plumber and electrician will come most days, and the washer and dryer may arrive Thursday. Progress is steady, but the list is long. I smile and nod, but my heart is not dancing like it was before we moved in.

I ask Francesco for his help with the oven. The LED display is in German and I cannot change it to English. I spread six manuals on the island. None, of course, in English. Francesco laughs and follows the Italian manual to change the language, but it doesn't work.

"We must call the Siemens man," he says, amused that it has confounded us both.

"I guess I can manage a little longer with an oven that speaks German," I sigh. "At least the numbers are the same."

Francesco's humor lightens my mood. I wish I could shake this feeling of being overwhelmed and sad.

Larry joins us upstairs to discuss the bookshelves for his library. They'll be cut from the solid chestnut salvaged from Lodolina's original ceiling beams. Larry is warm and cheerful. Francesco recommends a traditional system of saw-toothed shelf frames called *dente di cane*, teeth of the dog, so individual shelves can be adjusted. He draws a sketch for Larry.

"It's perfect. An ancient system with old Lodolina wood." Larry smiles.

Francesco unveils a design for Larry's desk, also to be made of old beams. It's an adaptation of a seventeenth-century desk we saw at an antique store in Florence. We considered buying it until we learned the price was twenty-five thousand dollars. I took a photo instead.

The desk can be finished in two weeks, but the bookcases will take a month. Until then, books must stay in boxes stacked behind the upstairs sofas.

With Francesco, Larry acts as though nothing's wrong. With me, I feel his iciness.

After they leave, he says, "Let's go look for a chair. I'll need one in two weeks and we'll probably have to order it. Francesco says there's a good office furniture store in Arezzo. You need milk, so we can stop in Cortona for lunch and your milk."

I remind him we have been invited to a dinner north of Siena, a long drive, and shouldn't be late. Larry assures me we can do it all, if we leave right away.

"I need five minutes," I say, unconvinced about having time, but hurry to change shoes and put on a little make-up.

His characterization of *your* milk annoys me. We both use it. It's *our*, not *my* milk. Am I being too sensitive?

When we get to Cortona, Molesini Market is closed for the midday break. When will we learn? I thought we might have a nice lunch and try to resolve our differences, but Larry insists on a fast lunch since we're tight for time. We get *panini* and *espressi* at a bar near the main piazza.

Larry would rather stand at the bar, but I ask if we can please sit. Sitting at a table costs more and takes longer, but seems more civilized to me for lunch. I still hope to talk about what's wrong. We take a table near the window. The sandwiches are small but tasty. We finish without speaking.

The *conto*, bill, surprises us both. Larry says under his breath, but loudly enough to be heard, "What a rip-off! Sixteen euros for two tiny sandwiches and *espressi*?"

He pays, but leaves no tip.

As I follow him out the door, he grumbles, "We should *not* have sat down. It took an extra fifteen minutes." Unspoken is the extra cost. I can't keep up with him, so follow several steps behind.

Larry's chair is another sore subject. We intended to move my desk chair for him. It's an ergonomic Aeron chair and I love it, but at Lodolina my desk will be in the kitchen and a modern black mesh chair on rollers would look out of place. So we agreed Larry would use my chair at his desk upstairs. Unfortunately, when the movers put the last of our Chicago belongings into the crate, I was sitting at my desk reviewing documents and failed to give my chair to the packers. It became my fault that Larry does not have a desk chair. I feel badly, but can't change it now.

We ride in silence for twenty minutes, half way to Arezzo. I hesitate to bring up our discord, fearing it will make things worse.

"So… can we talk?" I finally say. At least the air conditioner has cooled the car to a tolerable temperature.

"What about?" he asks.

I turn toward him. "I want to know what's upsetting you?" I say, trying to keep my tone even. "You were fine last night, but not now. What changed?"

He looks straight ahead and doesn't answer. I try to read his expression. Nothing.

"Larry, you're not happy. I don't know how to make you happy," I add.

Still, he does not respond.

After waiting a while for him to say something, I decide to explain my perspective and see if I can unearth the problem.

"You seem so easily irritated. One day you tell me I'm your Heloise and the next I get a cold shoulder and sarcasm. At least tell me what I'm doing wrong. You seemed to like me better in Chicago. Is it because I was independent there, but in Italy I'm a burden?"

Larry's jaw muscles flex. He must be gritting his teeth.

When he says nothing, I add a couple of examples of when he got irritated and I felt it was without much provocation. He looks exasperated.

After a pause, he says sternly. "Do you want to know why I'm upset, or do you just want to keep telling me I'm treating you badly?"

I answer, perhaps too quickly. "I really want to know. I want to understand what's happening to us." My voice quivers.

He hesitates. "Okay. You asked…. This morning you teased me about going off 'to do my thing', as you put it, before the breakfast dishes were done. I was miffed. I do plenty. If you want me to do more, ask me, but don't act like I don't do my share. And don't act like you're teasing when you're not. You're on my case constantly."

I'm baffled, but respond cautiously, trying to show I understand his perspective and to share mine. "I know you want to read and study… and I want you to be able to. But you get to do what you want most of the time… read your books or newspaper, study Italian, go for runs. But you don't seem the least bit concerned if I get to do *anything* I want to do. *All* I do is clean, cook, wash laundry by hand, deal with the construction, and tiptoe around you. I know I did more of the construction work in Chicago, but here it isn't fair. You're retired and I'm buried."

He squints, but says nothing. Silent, be silent, I tell myself. Let him tell his side.

When he glares ahead and doesn't talk for a couple more minutes, I feel compelled to defend myself again. I explain that in Chicago things were finished and organized. I had help with laundry and cleaning. I drove on familiar, flat, wide streets. I knew where to buy whatever we needed. I could communicate with everyone in English.

"*Everything* here is harder," I say. "The kitchen isn't finished, so it's harder to cook. We don't have a washing machine, so I wash what we need by hand. I'm afraid to tell you when we need groceries. And, when we're in the grocery store, I rush because you're waiting, so I only get the essentials and never stock up. You only want to take time to talk with me at meals. I feel like your house slave while you study."

"Don't be ridiculous!" he scoffs, eyes slits and jaw clinched.

This is not going well. We ride silently for several minutes.

"Can we start again?" I ask. Simply listen this time, I tell myself. Seek first to understand, then to be understood, like sages through history including Saint Francis have advised. Why is it so difficult?

Larry takes another deep breath, slowly shakes his head side-to-side, and continues to drive without comment. I stay quiet to see what he will do.

"Is there *more* you want to say?" he asks, with a detached, disciplined tone.

His expression is unchanged, but this time he asked, so maybe he wants to listen. I begin again. Better to get it all out.

"I'm overwhelmed. Lodolina is impossible to keep clean and I have no help. Construction dust is everywhere. Plus, the workers leave piles of trash, especially the electrician. So, in addition to answering questions, I clean up after they leave every day. We're totally disorganized and neither of us do well with chaos."

"Hire some help," Larry says coldly.

The corners of my mouth turn downward. "I don't know how," I say.

After another mile, he asks, "Are you finished? Do you truly want to know how it is for me or do you just want to criticize me? You said you wanted to understand why I'm upset, but since we started this conversation you haven't stopped talking about how awful life is for you and how I'm not helping."

I'm on the verge of tears but don't want to cry. He'll think I'm trying to provoke sympathy.

"I think I understand," I say softly.

"No, you don't," Larry says flatly. I sense intense frustration under his controlled façade.

He continues. "Nothing this summer is working for me. *Nothing...* I started my first full-time job when I was seventeen and never stopped. For the first time in my life, I should have time to do what I want to do. But every day, not just some days, *every day* is filled with distractions. Each distraction is understandable, important and fine, but all together they are *not* fine. You want my help, which I give you, yet you are constantly on my case that I'm not doing enough. You won't even try to drive a car that's fully automatic."

He inhales and continues. "I have not been able to read, study or write for *one* full day yet. And now, you complain that everything is more difficult, like this was all my idea. This was your dream too. It's harder than we expected, so you want me to help with everything that's difficult. Why can't you do *anything* without me?"

We sit in silence for the next few minutes, both looking straight ahead. I shift in my seat. There's a knot in my chest. I do not know what to say. I do not want to be in this car. I do not want to look at desk chairs. I want to go home. Not home to Lodolina. I want to go home to Chicago and wait until Lodolina is finished and start all over again. I roll down the window for fresh air, but the outside air is suffocating.

After a long silence where I do not disagree or defend myself, Larry continues in a gentler voice. "I had no idea we'd live in such chaos. I thought we'd move in... maybe with a few days of workers still around, and then settle into the main house while they finished the guesthouse. I expected that we'd read, work on our projects, enjoy our new hometown, explore and make friends. Instead, I have all the administrative responsibility for the sale of the condo, bills for the move, the purchase of everything for this house, and invoices for the construction. I'm dealing in two currencies with two banks. BNL doesn't even have email. We need to get a different car because our month is about over. I suppose that'll be up to me too. Plus, I have to answer every question you ask me about the house immediately, because someone's waiting. If I don't agree with your decision, you argue and I give in. Why not just do what you want in the first place?"

He takes another deep breath and his tension seems to escalate. "You won't even *try* to drive or to speak, so I am stuck with every errand you want to run. I go with you to the grocery store, hardware store, post office, pharmacy, appliance store and dry cleaner. I drive, translate and carry packages. And you are *my* slave?"

There is a bit of a pause, but I don't think he's finished.

"After you retired, you had years of being able to do whatever you wanted. You volunteered, worked on your projects, had lunch with girlfriends. I thought this summer would be my turn. So, this morning, when you complained that I went back to reading while you were doing breakfast dishes, it felt like piling on."

I sit quietly, trying to absorb what he has said. It's not that I can't understand or don't care. It's not that I don't see his side, though my instinct is to defend myself. The problem is that I do not know what to do.

When it seems he's ready for me to answer, I start with where I agree. Agreement can shift a battle into a discussion, an opponent into an ally. It's important to try.

"You're right... I wanted to move here. And I don't like being dependent any more than you like it. I don't know if everyone who moves to another country feels so out of place at first, but I did not expect this. And what I *really* didn't expect is that it would hurt our relationship. You and I are together all day every day, but I *feel* lonely."

I don't say anything about wanting to go back to Chicago or that I don't want to learn to drive a stick shift or speak another language or hunt for desk chairs.

He doesn't answer.

This SUV is claustrophobic. I roll the window down again and immediately roll it back up because the outside air is even hotter.

Perhaps it would be good to go home. Only for a week or two. I could stay with Tedi. It would be an expensive trip and I would not like traveling so far on my own. But it would give me a couple weeks to find myself and Larry would learn how many things I handle without him. I could escape this constant tension and allow some tenderness to grow again.

Larry takes a deep breath. I take a deep breath.

He speaks first. "Maybe it's just the mess and chaos. As soon as the construction is done, we can organize. With the house in order, we can have a more tranquil life, more like we expected."

He's trying to blame it on the chaos, but he seems mad at me, not the chaos.

"Larry, that would help... but it's not just the chaos. What would make you happy... *with me?*" I ask. "I'm glad to know what you want from this summer and why, but I also want to know what you want from *me?* I can't and don't want to change who I am... but I can try to change what I *do.*"

He thinks for a few moments. This is a question he can answer. Larry, like most men, is better at finding solutions than sympathy.

"I'd like for you to drive. I know you're not happy depending on me so much, but until you drive it won't change. You're the most competent woman I know. I don't understand why you are so afraid."

I'm not surprised that his first request is for me to drive so I can be independent. Part of what first attracted Larry to me was that I was self-sufficient. I had a successful career, owned a nice home, drove a company-issued Mercedes, and was raising two daughters. I suspect he thought he would never have to take care of me. Now, at a time he expected to be happily absorbed in study, he must take care of me for almost everything.

He looks at me, as if to make sure I'm listening. I raise my eyebrows and nod. "Go on," I say.

"I would like to have the morning for my study and exercise. I get up at five-thirty. I have that time to study and reflect. But I am bombarded with questions from the minute you get up. I'd like for you to save your questions for when I'm taking a break, we're having breakfast or lunch, or for the afternoon. If it's essential, then ask, but I would like my mornings to study."

Okay, he's made two requests: protect his mornings and drive. Those, I can try to do. I wonder if that's all.

Suddenly, we're in Arezzo entering the first roundabout and should look for the store.

"Do you know which exit we should take?" Larry asks.

"No, but I think it's the same as for OBI. We passed the OBI sign, so we need to go around again," I say. We both watch for signs for Mondo Office but don't see any. After another circle, he finally takes an exit saying he hopes it works.

How like an argument, I think, wondering which roundabout exit we'll take in our discussion. One of us must choose to exit, or we'll keep going in circles. We know the options: hold fast to being right and maintain status quo; defend ourselves and become the victim; give in to keep the peace but resolve nothing; or, forgive and find a mutually beneficial solution. I want to forgive and find a lasting solution, and hope he does too. Unless we both choose the same exit, the distance between us will grow. I collect my thoughts, wondering how we might get out of this argument.

"I love you and want us both to be happy," I start. "I wanted to make this move too, and am willing to work to make it work. I want you to have a great summer, and I believe you want me to have one too. So far, it hasn't been what we expected and I'm also disappointed. What you ask is reasonable and it helps to understand some background, but I can only promise what I can really do."

He waits. Now he seems to be listening.

Continuing, I promise to protect his mornings by saving questions until breakfast, lunch, or when he takes a break. Regarding driving, I promise to try though confess I'm unsure I'll ever be comfortable with such a big car on narrow roads.

I wait, but he doesn't react. He still has not asked what I want for the summer or made any offers of what he might do.

"In exchange," I finally say, deciding to make a request, "I'd like for you to go to Saturday market with me — willingly. I love your company and need your help."

"And, if you're good company," I add, trying a bit of romantic levity, "I'll buy you a cappuccino on the piazza."

I pause and look closely at my husband. His shoulders seem a little more relaxed and his face less drawn, but he hasn't agreed. For me, it feels good to make promises to someone I love and want to be happy — promises that are specific and possible to keep. I wish he'd lighten up and not be so tense. I cannot relax until he does.

"Larry, we need to cut each other some slack. The construction and chaos are not my fault. The move's been a bigger deal than we thought and, yes, I need more of your help. But we both need to adjust our expectations."

"Mostly," I add without thinking, "I'd like to feel like I'm being a good wife and that you love me. I'd like for us to be friends again."

My voice is less steady than I intend, "We're together constantly, but I'm lonely. I miss you."

Larry reaches across the console and puts his hand on mine. I smile cautiously. He glances at me, then smiles, too. We've exited the roundabout together and made progress in the same direction, but I still feel unsettled.

When he doesn't speak again, I change subjects, I'm sure to his relief.

Couples seem to have their toughest discussions in the car. It's intimate, private, and neither can walk away.

Got Your Courage Back?

We're still in the car searching for Mondo Office. I shift positions, my legs sticky with perspiration though the air-conditioning is on high. It seems our discussion is over and we can focus on the chair, at least for now.

I ask Larry what kind of chair he wants.

"Something like yours," he says. "Probably mesh if every summer is this hot. Surely in Italy, with the best furniture designers in the world, we can find a decent desk chair."

When we pass Jumbo Office, not Mondo Office, the third time, Larry parks. Perhaps it was a problem with translation, he says.

Their metal warehouse showroom is hotter than the parking lot. A quick glance around says none of the chairs are Aeron chairs, copies, or even attractive. Larry, ever the analyst, wants to sit in every chair. When he's finished without finding one he likes, the salesman says *"piu di sopra"*, which I fear means more upstairs. I want to wait in the air-conditioned car, but it's important to show support. We ride upstairs in a creaky freight elevator that's a kiln. The chairs upstairs look the same as downstairs to me, only ten degrees hotter, thankfully too hot for Larry to try.

He glances at every chair, then we ride back down in the same elevator. I hope gravity helps it go faster, but it creaks down as slowly as it creaked up. When the doors finally open, we all rush out to breathe.

Larry asks the salesman, in Italian, if he knows where to find Mondo Office. The man chuckles, goes to his desk and comes out with a catalog. "*Solo dal catalogo,*" he says, only from the catalog. There is nothing to do but laugh. Fortunately, Larry laughs, too. We look at every page of chairs, but there is not a perfect one in the Mondo Office catalog either.

We head home engaged in cordial, chair-focused conversation. When we pass Techno-Office, Larry turns around. I think we should concentrate on getting to our dinner on time, but say nothing.

He finds two chairs he likes, both black leather. It's hard to consider black leather in this heat.

"I wonder how much it'd cost to order a chair like yours and have it shipped," Larry says as we near home. I wish it wasn't my fault he doesn't have a chair.

We hurry to dress and head off to the birthday dinner. Friends of friends invited us to join them at an estate they're renting in Chianti. We've never met them, but our mutual friends say we'll love the hosts and the estate alone is worth the drive. Larry thinks it's about an hour away, but when we enter the town, Anqua, into the GPS, it shows the drive is over three hours. It's five o'clock and we're supposed to arrive around six-thirty.

Larry calls to say we'll be terribly late. Should we still come? Our host insists, saying their children are also late, just heading back from a day in Siena at the *Palio*, the famous horse race.

I dread three more hours in the car, despite softened hearts. But with a common enemy of the long road and late hour, and having had a somewhat satisfying discussion, the tension between us feels mostly dissolved. We listen to the radio, change channels constantly because the music is awful, and talk about designs for bookcases, his desk, and our disappointment with the chairs. Farm fields and vineyards roll past. Silence has become comfortable again.

"Shall we forget this day and have a great night?" Larry asks. "This dinner could be fun. In fact, let's *make* tonight fun."

"Good idea," I say, knowing we have more to discuss, especially if I'm going back to Chicago for a break, but that topic will wait.

He reaches to take my hand again, this time lifting it to his lips to kiss it. I feel my whole body unwind, as though I no longer need to be on guard. A wordless, gentle touch is often the most effective remedy. I settle into my seat, smooth my linen blouse under the seat belt so it won't get too wrinkled, lean my head back on the headrest, and squeeze his hand in return.

We cleared some air today, each expressing our deeper dream for this summer and why it isn't working. I've never thought about Larry having no time of his own since he was seventeen. His first child was born when he was nineteen, and he and his wife had two more children in rapid succession. As a dad and husband working full-time, he put himself through college and Harvard Business School. Years later, when he was a young Boston Consulting Group partner and vice president, he became a single dad of teenagers. After we were married, he made the bulk of our income, working long hours even after I retired. And it is true that I've had some years of my own time and freedom. This is the first time — perhaps in his life — when time has been truly his. I want him to feel fulfilled working on what matters to him, which now means study and writing.

We discuss how to better organize Lodolina and agree that simply buying a bedroom dresser would help, so we're not living out of suitcases. He offers to look at the antique shops in Cortona with me, despite disliking to shop.

The estate is two hours away, but thankfully not three. The first hour is on the A1. Then we drive winding narrow roads, one with a roadblock and confusing detours. Larry decides we must be lost. When he stops to ask directions from two teenage girls, they point ahead and giggle. We look up and see a sign to turn right for *Villa Anqua*. After a gravel road through a forest, we come to a collapsed bridge and call our hosts.

"You're at the bridge?" Lee says with admiration. "No one makes it to the bridge without us guiding them! Just drive across the riverbed and stay on that road. You're almost here. We haven't started cooking, so you're not late at all."

We're at the estate in ten minutes. It's truly in the *mezzo di niente*, middle of nothing, as Italians say. Larry and I laugh about the roadblock, detours, and fording a dry stream. We're relieved to arrive before dinner. And, we're grateful to be reunited. Before we get out of the car, Larry leans over and gives me a long, passionate kiss. I smile, feeling some of that joy and appreciation I crave.

"I love your smile," he says. "Let's go find our hosts."

Lee welcomes us and, after pouring glasses of much-appreciated chilled white wine, offers a tour of the estate and gardens. *Villa Anqua* is a castle built on a castle. First constructed in the 1200s, it became mostly a ruin. In the 1500s a branch of the Hapsburg family built another castle on its remains. Overlooking Chianti vineyards, it's now a rambling estate with a chapel, workers' cottages, barns and a winery, all connected by meandering walkways, courtyards and low stone walls. White wisteria clusters hang from a long, covered walkway, making me long for gardens at Lodolina.

Our guide, a charming elderly caretaker, hurries us along, saying we must finish in the daylight because many castle rooms have no electricity. He tells us he has lived and worked here since he was nine. In the entrance courtyard between two main buildings, he points to a lead box riddled with bullet holes. During the war, he says, the family and workers hid in a tunnel under the main house. They could hear the Germans shooting rounds of bullets into the building above. *Villa Anqua* is a rare property in Italy, he says proudly, still owned by descendants of the original family, one of the oldest in Siena. He does not divulge their name.

We enter a stone cottage built around the largest wood-burning oven I've ever seen. The blaze is immense. For centuries, Tuscan *forni*, ovens, were separated from the house, and this one served a village-sized estate.

"What're you making?" Larry asks the charming young adults we meet inside.

"Breadsticks," Lee's son replies. "We don't have a recipe, but how hard can it be?"

He pulls back a wet towel covering a huge mound of rising dough. "We're about to make this glob into sticks. Hope it works!"

"Looks like we're in for a treat!" I say, suddenly starving from the aroma of fermenting yeast.

Dinner is beyond spectacular. *Prosciutto* and *melone*, *radicchio* and lettuce salad, grilled meats, and roasted potatoes, zucchini and yellow peppers with wedges of lemon, and the famous bread-sticks now dubbed "Italian French fries" because they're so irresistible. The grand finale is a chocolate birthday cake covered with chocolate-lavender ganache. The kids prepared all the food to honor their father's sixtieth birthday.

Our celebration is held in the largest of four dining rooms, seventeen of us at a table that seats twenty-four. Lee's friends are warm, accomplished, and interesting, all staying at the villa. The conversation flows easily. We don't feel one bit out of place partaking in this intimate celebration. Rather, we feel honored.

The dialogue continues into the wee hours. Our hosts insist we spend the night, promising airline toothbrushes and a fabulous breakfast. We explain that workers and our architect will arrive at our home in only a few hours.

After warm goodbyes, we retrace the drive along country roads. The forests are alive with nocturnal animals: wild boar with spotted piglets, black and white striped porcupines, and tiny deer we later learn are called *cervi*.

Soon we're back on the A1. Larry stops at an all-night *Autogrill*, remembering we need milk. I'm impressed and grateful.

As he drives the *autostrada*, now empty except for an occasional truck, I close my eyes and reflect on our earlier exchange, searching for what I can learn. I'm sad we've been so testy with one another and glad we talked openly, but arguments are always hard for me. I avoid confrontation until I cannot maintain peace any other way.

I was glad to understand the significance of Larry's study time and will try to honor it. I also observed again how quickly my heart softens with the slightest bit of tenderness from him, perhaps too quickly. I'm disappointed that he didn't make promises, but that may come later. Perhaps we'll be more aligned with some distance from our dispute.

As I lean back on the headrest, my eyes fly open wide, physically and mentally. I sit straight up in my seat, thinking of two key factors I've failed to see.

Larry is more committed to living in Italy than I am. People who are committed to making something work find solutions to problems; people less committed want to run away. He urges me to learn to drive and to speak Italian to feel more comfortable here; I want to go home to Chicago.

When we were first married, I was jealous of the way he argued. Larry disagreed from within a commitment, insisting we find a solution. I, on the other hand, was less secure and argued with one foot out the door. His question was how to resolve our issue; mine was whether or not to stay.

For Larry, Italy has been declared home. He's studying the language, reading Italian literature, and buying a desk chair. For me, it's an experiment. If it doesn't work, we can sell the property and move back to Chicago. In fact, if our experiment fails and we move back, I'll no longer need to learn Italian or drive on narrow roads.

His way is better. In fact, the key to making any big change in life work is the decision that it is a new life, not an experiment. Commitment gives us the courage to conquer. It's time I got serious that Italy is my new home, not an extended vacation or an experiment.

Secondly, and this is harder for me to acknowledge, my dilemma is not only with Larry or with my commitment, but with my own insecurities. Perhaps I fear I'm not so competent or smart after all. My recurring childhood dream was going to church in my pajamas. Even after I'd achieved career success, I dreamed I was in the wrong place for a client meeting or forgot my presentation notes. I know such dreams are common, but I hate being unprepared and fear looking incompetent or stupid. Often, the most crippling conflict we have is not with others; it is with ourselves.

There is no way to be truly prepared to live in a foreign country. Even when the culture has similar roots — Italy and America are Western — everything about daily life is different: language, currency, traditions, customs, attitudes, foods, appliances… *everything*. When stumbling with language or counting coins, I feel conspicuous and stupid, the emotions I most fear.

In fact, it's naïve to believe we aren't naïve in someone else's culture. I feel less and less assured and don't like it. Perhaps I want to go home because I'm afraid that I might not be the competent woman I think I am.

In the dark cocoon of the car I smile, recalling my daughter Lara's lesson on courage. She was seven, her sister was three, and I was a single mom.

A friend of mine had called to talk to me. Lara, ever the concerned little helper and advanced talker, had told my friend that I wasn't home and she had a babysitter, but she could talk. My friend, amused, told Lara her problem. Lara listened and asked my friend what thought she should do. After my friend shared possible solutions, Lara asked, "So, you got your courage back?" My friend said she realized what she needed most was her own courage.

I feel better simply by making the commitment to stay, re-claiming my courage, and examining my ways. It's only when we see our own shortcomings and our own contributions to a situation that we have any power to change it.

With these insights, I feel less like escaping and more determined to stay here and work to assure our new life — our Tuscan dream — is fulfilling for both of us. We do love Lodolina and Cortona, even more than we expected. We only need to rekindle and strengthen our love for one another.

I'm suddenly awake and thankful we're nearing home. I stretch my neck and roll my shoulders. I wonder what Larry has been pondering since he stopped at the *Autogrill* for milk. I'll ask tomorrow. Workers arrive in four hours and we both need sleep.

Always an American

I awaken to the cacophony of electric saws cutting through stone and concrete, the loudest construction yet. Usually the workers are quiet in the early morning. The racket is excruciating, especially since we got home less than five hours ago from Lee's birthday celebration at *Villa Anqua*.

As my foot hits the bottom stair, the noise stops.

"The electricity just went off," Larry says, not happy. I give him a kiss and ease into a living room armchair across from him.

"That was nice," he says.

"Guess you don't mind being interrupted for some attention," I tease. "What happened to the power?"

"Don't know, but it's precisely nine o'clock," Larry looks at his computer clock.

"Uh, oh," I say. "Remember those *Enel* signs near Palazzone. They said *mercoledi* and *venerdi*, Wednesday and Friday, right? We thought they weren't for us."

Larry nods. "Pierangelo must have known so was going full guns this morning. You'd think *Enel* could make repairs at night."

"I was looking forward to a cappuccino with the milk you remembered last night."

"You're welcome to some of mine," he offers.

"Thank you, that's so kind," I say, truly grateful.

Without power, we won't have water, so no showers and no internet. With some of Larry's cappuccino in my cup, I sit in the chair next to him and type until my battery runs out. I wish I'd charged it last night. I get up to make oatmeal, if I can find a match to light a gas burner.

The rooster on the hilltop becomes exceedingly vocal, as if sensing the hush and believing the world is now his stage.

Today is the Fourth of July. It seems strange not to be in America. For the past nine years, our friends Tedi and Dick have held a huge cookout. Their celebration was our granddaughter Sydney's favorite Chicago event. When she was five, she flew unescorted from San Antonio to Chicago to visit us and go to Tedi's party. That year, one of our friends had asked her, "Did you fly to Chicago all by yourself?"

"No... I came on an airplane," she had replied, looking baffled by the silly adult question.

Every Fourth of July since, the story is retold and we remember how hard we all laughed.

"You know what today is, right?" I ask Larry.

"Yes, Fourth of July. Seems strange not to be in Chicago with Sydney," he says.

"I was just thinking the same thing. She won't be flying 'all by herself' this year."

I love America and have greater appreciation for the ease of living there than I did a month ago. I feel grateful for democracy and the people who upheld our principles and fought our wars so my loved ones and I can enjoy freedom. As Churchill said, "Democracy is the worst form of government, except for all the other forms that have been tried from time to time." Today is a day for remembering the heroes and heroines of democracy.

July Fourth is also the day my father died. He was only seventy-five, but had battled leukemia for two years. The night of July third, I stayed in the hospital so I could have a last few hours with him, sitting quietly, holding his hand through the night. He had slipped in and out of consciousness and seemed at peace. Dad's vital signs were strong and his doctor said he might hang on for a while. So the next evening, Larry and I went back to Chicago so we could return to work. While we were on the train watching fireworks explode over small towns in Illinois, my father died. Every year I think of him as I watch some majestic display. This year, there will be no fireworks for me.

Late morning, Francesco comes to check on us since he knows we are without power, and to talk about what will happen this week.

"The power will arrive at noon. I have confirmed this by calling *Enel*," he tells us. "You can call the green number the next time, if you do not see the postings. The recording is in Italian, of course." He gives us the number and then reviews the myriad of workers who will come and go this week.

Sure enough, at noon sharp the electricity returns, just as Francesco leaves.

Late-afternoon, with Larry still studying, I decide to take a nap. Workers, forced into manual labor this morning, have made a deafening racket with saws and drills all afternoon. Now only Pierangelo and Luigi are here, turning the cement mixer, tapping stones into place, and talking in hushed tones. Larry comes upstairs to lie next to me and strokes my shoulder. The workers have become so familiar that afternoon naps aren't one bit awkward. The men don't even notice.

Back downstairs, Larry asks, "How about if I take you to town to get the ingredients for pesto, so you can get some joy from cooking? That's what you want, right?" I know he's been longing for his favorite pasta sauce now that I have a food processor.

"We'll need fresh pasta, too, and maybe sausage to go with it. Oil and pine nuts. And sun-dried tomatoes."

"For you to make pesto for me? Just give me the list."

In Cortona we find big bunches of fresh basil at Roberto's. Then we walk up *Via Dardano* to *Pasta Fresca* for *cavatelli*. It's like thin penne, slightly longer, with ruffled sides that Larry says should hold plenty of pesto.

He wants to find some less precious olive oil than ours to use for cooking, so he takes me to the Coop in Camucia, at the bottom of the Cortona hill. I find the Coop overwhelming and prefer small Cortona shops and the Saturday market. But we're meeting Gabriele in the Coop parking lot today so it's not an extra stop.

"I'll watch for Gabriele. You only need oil and pine nuts, right?"

The Coop is big and confusing. I don't know where anything is and, if I can't find something, I don't know how to ask. I wish he'd offered to go in with me. But I muster that courage I promised myself and go in alone.

With a little searching I find my items. The checkout lines are long. When it's my turn, I remember to ask for *una busta*, a bag. The bags are thin, lousy plastic, hardly worth reusing even for garbage, so it annoys me to have to buy it. I count out the money without awkwardness and quickly bag my purchases. That wasn't so bad, I think, walking out head held high.

To leave, I push open an exit door and start through. A siren blares. My heart stops. I close the door quickly. Every head in the store turns to stare at me. I see a larger open door nearby and hurry out. I'm in tears when I get to the car.

"What happened? Are you okay?" Larry asks.

"No. I opened the wrong door and set off the alarm. The sign over the door said *uscita*, so I thought it was the exit. There was something else written on the door, but I couldn't read it.... Everyone in the entire store stared at me. I felt so stupid."

"I'm sorry. Really, it's okay. No one'll remember you," Larry says to comfort me. He also seems amused.

"I hate the Coop," I persist. "There're so many olive oils I couldn't figure out what to buy. And the pine nuts cost five euros for a tiny packet, not even enough for one batch of pesto. At Costco, I get an enormous bag for thirteen dollars. Then the line took forever. And they don't even have an express lane"

After a few calming breaths, I add, "Besides, it smells bad. Like old frying oil. They really need to renovate that place."

"Sweetheart, forget it. Everyone else will. You never go to the Coop anyway."

"Less now," I declare.

Gabriele pulls up at the appointed time, gets in the back seat, and directs us to the Bose store in Castiglione del Lago, a town on the lake we see from Cortona. Gabriele will help us make arrangements with the Bose expert to install our sound system and we can look at TVs, still on our list.

At the small shop, we choose a well-priced, big-screen TV from the four on display and are surprised to learn it must be ordered. In Chicago, it would go home with us. Mr. Rochetti, the store owner, says our television should arrive in about six weeks. Six weeks?

Importantly, he says he can come next week to install the sound system we brought from Chicago, the big box on which we paid the customs tax at the Florence airport.

We get home too late to make pesto, so decide to walk to town for dinner. I wrap the basil in wet paper, as Roberto suggested, but it looks sadly wilted from baking in the hot car all afternoon.

We'd forgotten tonight is the big game between Italy and Germany in the World Cup semi-finals. Cortona is full of energetic fans wearing red, green and white flags, hats, and scarves, and official Italian soccer shirts.

Trattoria Dardano is packed. Fortunately, Larry had called and Paolo saved a table for us. The *bruschetta* is especially good, thin slices of ripe tomatoes on toasted, oiled and salted bread, rubbed with a hint of garlic. I wince, hearing Americans at the next table order "bru-sheta," but resist correcting them. In Italian 'ch' is pronounced 'k' so the word is "brus-keh-ta." Larry tries their pesto at the urging of Lucia. He whispers to me that it's good, but mine is still the best. He says he's dreaming of eating it tomorrow. It'll be the first real meal I've cooked at Lodolina, so I want it to be all of Larry's favorites.

By game time, *Dardano* is empty and *Piazza Signorelli* is jammed, most straining to see the big screen TV at the Lion's Well Pub, the same place with a crowd a few nights ago. We walk down *Via Nazionale* searching for a less packed venue, but most bars and restaurants with big screens are full so we head back to the Pub. The night air feels chilly, a relief after three scorching weeks.

A loud gasp erupts from every direction. Larry stops someone and learns the referee called a foul against an Italian player and Italian fans disagreed. Everyone seems so passionate, as if Cortona is one big family with sons on the Italian team.

In *Piazza Signorelli*, about a dozen school boys, too short to see over the oleander wall, kick a soccer ball around as though the cheers are for them.

Italy and Germany each make several goal attempts and the crowd goes crazy each time, cheering or booing with gusto. A foghorn blares nearby and fans start pounding on the tables. I can't see a thing either, but listening to these fans cheer wildly for their country's team makes me glad we're here, even on America's Independence Day.

The game ends zero to zero. Larry explains that first there will be overtime, and then, if necessary, a shoot-out between one kicker and the goalie representing each team. Unlike the normal season's games that can end in a tie, the World Cup finals must have a winner. I ask if he wants to stay until the end, but he says, "We'll learn the score in the morning."

Our walk home is magical. The sky is dense with brilliant, glittering stars, as though God has given us heavenly fireworks for the Fourth of July. I think of Dad, thankful he was my dad. I'm also thankful for Larry. We've been in sync today — considerate, respectful and having fun. It gives me renewed hope for a happier rest of the summer and for my new life in Italy.

Twenty-five days down, eighty-one days to go before we return to Chicago for a month. I'll stick it out until our scheduled departure mid-September, with commitment and courage. After time in Chicago, we'll return to Cortona until Christmas. We'll have many Tuscan adventures and I'm eager for them to unfold, but we will always be Americans. No matter where we choose to live, where we were born is always a part of who we are. I suspect I will learn even more about being American by living in a foreign land.

Yes, we are *stranieri*, foreigners. Strangers, like the word sounds. Guests.

My resolve for commitment to make Italy home, courage, and our recent more tender interactions have improved my outlook. I wonder if courage, commitment and positive outlook always go hand in hand.

Match Point

The surreal dawn horizon glows fiery coral under an indigo sky. Cool breezes drift across my bed. Every sunrise since we arrived has resulted in a sparkling blue sky and not a drop of rain. This one feels different.

In the early morning light, Larry and I sit silently in the living room, studying and writing. The *be-blunk* from Larry's computer means the internet is down. I'm protecting his mornings, so don't comment. I'm also mentally gearing up to drive at the first opportunity, but only because I promised. It's useless to write more emails that won't send, so I finish my journal entry about the Fourth of July.

Eager to make Larry's pesto, I head to the kitchen to uncrate and assemble my new food processor. Like our other new appliances, the manuals are in Italian, French, German, Spanish, Eastern European languages I don't recognize, and Arabic — but not English. I intuitively put the parts together and test it on chunks of *Reggiano Parmigiano*, the cheese I grate for pesto. It works.

The basil is on the counter, wrapped in damp paper. A little limp when we got home last night, this morning about half the bright green, leafy bunches are nearly black. I salvage as much as possible, gently pat dry each good leaf, and pile them into the food processor. I add pine nuts, garlic cloves, salt and a few black peppercorns that, since I don't have a pepper grinder, I crush under the blade of my butcher knife. Lastly, I add my secret ingredients: a pinch of cayenne and pat of butter.

The blade grinds slowly. I increase the speed and watch basil leaves ripped to dark bits rather than emulsified into a bright green paste as they were by my razor-sharp Cuisinart. I pour our personal olive oil into the lid opening, not realizing a clear plastic pusher is blocking the opening. Oil runs down the side of the machine, making a puddle on the counter. I cringe. Trying not to waste a drop, I now have squandered several tablespoons. With the pusher removed, I add oil in a fine stream. It begins to look like pesto. I taste it, add a little more salt and another garlic clove and taste again, add the ground parmesan and process it just enough to mix. It's surprisingly good. I pour enough for dinner into a bowl, drizzle extra oil on top to keep it from oxidizing, and then put the rest in a plastic bag to freeze. I wish I had small plastic containers to freeze dinner-sized portions, but don't know where to buy them.

For years, Larry has said I'm not allowed to die unless there is plenty of pesto in the freezer. He's tasted others, but insists he prefers mine. This batch only made enough for tonight and two more dinners. Guess I can't die yet.

After reviewing with Francesco the punch list which is way too long to be a punch list, I try to call Mom, my daughters and two girlfriends using our pre-paid calling card. The seven-hour time difference is awkward. Mom's line is busy and Lara will be off to work. I talk with Tedi and Kathleen, who tell me their news and ask about ours. It's too early to call Amber in Portland. Each conversation makes me wish I was home.

I finally reach Mom. She was talking with Joyce, her best friend for forty years. Joyce just learned she has an inoperable mass on her pancreas. Mom says Joyce seems to be taking it pretty well, but the sadness in Mom's voice breaks my heart. Life will be lonelier for Mom when Joyce is gone.

I then reach Lara, who has a new friend. He's a bit younger than she, but sounds interesting. She says Jason hung out with Amber and Aiden, Amber's two-year-old son, the day before they moved to Portland. She said it was hard to say goodbye to her sister and she was glad she wasn't alone. I feel sad and far away. It's late. I must cook dinner. Tomorrow I'll try to reach Amber.

My first home-cooked dinner at Lodolina raises my spirits. We sip local wine and nibble on crunchy slices of fennel dipped in our olive oil, then enjoy *cavetelli* and pesto, and lastly grilled sausage and a salad. Larry thinks the fresh *cavetelli* is the best pasta he's ever eaten. The pesto is acceptable, not the best ever, but better than I feared. He insists it's delicious.

It's still light so we decide to climb the hill to town and watch *Match Point*, Woody Allen's new film. Movies in English are shown at the *Parterre's* amphitheater on Wednesday evenings during the summer, but we've never been.

Larry says the poster said nine-fifteen, so we should leave by eight-thirty.

I rush to wash dishes and clean the kitchen while Larry closes windows. This will be a rare spontaneous outing for us and I'm excited. He has to wait for me to finish getting ready, and seems miffed when we leave a few minutes after eight-thirty. We'll still get there by nine, fifteen minutes early, so I'm not worried.

Walking up the construction ramp, I stop, saying, "We forgot the trash and it smells awful. We should take it to the dumpster by the tennis courts. Can you get it?"

Larry frowns, turns to run back and returns with two bags of trash. We're convinced it's important to take the trash every time we go anywhere. Food scraps in this heat quickly putrefy and stink.

At the end of the driveway, I realize we forgot flashlights for our walk home. There's no choice but to go back again.

"This time I'll go," I say.

Larry shakes his head, obviously more annoyed. "Keep walking. I'm faster. I'll catch you." He turns and runs, sacks of garbage swinging with every step.

I'm irritated that he's irritated. He could've thought of the garbage and flashlights while he waited for me to clean the kitchen.

Climbing the steep hillside alone, I relish my solitude. I take in the landscape, which I could not do if Larry were trekking to the top as fast as possible. It's restorative to simply move at your own pace. At the peak of the hill, the ruins of the fort form a dramatic silhouette against the evening sky. Below the fort, tall cypress trees ring the Cortona hillside like a necklace of dark feathers. Looking down the hill toward the village of Pergo, I'm reminded of our introduction to Cortona.

My friend Cynthia had invited us to vacation with them. They had a tiny cottage near Pergo and suggested we stay in Cortona at Hotel San Michele. During that visit, we had the quintessential Italian afternoon, one I've tried to repeat many times but have never matched. Sitting around an old wooden table under a sprawling horse chestnut tree, we lingered in the shade for hours, savoring old and new friendships, local produce from the market, meats from a nearby butcher, and bottle after bottle of local red wine. Across a patchwork of farmers' fields, we could see Cortona perched on the hillside a few kilometers away. The majestic tower of *Il Palazzone* dominated the scene, the most important landmark on the Pergo side of Cortona's hill. Who'd have guessed Cortona would become our home and we would pass that tower every time we drive to town?

The sound of Larry's footsteps brings me back to the present. I step up my pace so he doesn't think I've been dawdling. He passes me and walks ahead to toss the garbage into the bin. I look at my watch. We can still make it to the movies with at least five minutes to spare. He waits for me at the dumpsters.

Then he walks so briskly through the *Parterre* I cannot keep up.

"Please slow down… We have time."

I reach to take his arm, but he continues walking ahead, faster than is possible for me. It feels purposeful.

"Why are you walking so fast?" I ask. "Are you upset with me? We aren't late and it doesn't seem necessary to ruin our evening just because I wasn't quite ready when you wanted to leave, especially since I was washing dishes after I cooked your favorite dinner. Our very first dinner at Lodolina."

He slows a bit and says, "You agreed to leave at eight thirty, but at eight forty you were still getting ready. I always have to wait for you, even when you agree to a time."

"If the exact time was so important, you could've offered to help," I retort. "And, *you* could've remembered the garbage and flashlights. You should be grateful, not mad. We're going to be there on time; I didn't make us late. I want a nice evening together. This is *not* fair."

Larry stops in his tracks, turns around to face me and says, "You're right. When you're right, you're right. Let's have fun tonight." He smiles. I laugh. How easily he disarms me.

The truth is I'm hurt and don't want his charm, I want an apology and a change in behavior. I reflexively clench my jaw.

"May I?" Larry offers his hand to hold while we walk, as though all is forgiven.

"I am much too easy," I say, putting my hand in his. "I want an apology," I add lightly. He curls his fingers through mine and walks at a reasonable pace, but without an apology. I still feel wronged, but choose not to escalate it into an argument.

At the end of the park, an elderly man is putting up a table to sell movie tickets. The poster, surely the same poster Larry saw, says *Match Point*, nine forty-five. Not nine-fifteen. We're forty minutes early.

Larry looks at me with a sheepish half-smile, "Would you like a *passeggiata* with me, darling? We have more time than I thought."

"Guess you *really* didn't need to be upset with me, did you?" I answer, raising my eyebrows to make the point. "I'll happily walk with you — *after* I get an apology." I speak with all the playful charm I can muster, but I am dead serious.

Larry wisely says, "I'm sorry, really. Sorry. If you walk with me through town, I'll buy you a gelato."

We stroll the length of *Via Nazionale* and linger in *Piazza della Repubblica* to watch graceful *rondini*, swallows, swirl against the darkening indigo sky. Larry gets a three-flavor gelato, insisting I choose flavors. I pick his favorites, mint and chocolate, and melon for me. Back at the park, we take center seats in the nearly empty stone amphitheater. The movie starts, then people file in. Eventually, about a hundred people join us. It's like an old-fashioned drive-in movie: under the stars with a long intermission for concessions and a bathroom break.

The movie is strange, but it makes me think. The tennis match feels too much like our own back and forth. Though we're not dealing with murder or affairs, I do wish Larry and I were not in a competition. Today I feel as though I made the match point with his apology, but that will not be the final contest. Constant competition is tiring, especially between spouses who are together twenty-four by seven. And competition is the opposite of partnership — cooperation begins where competition ends.

As we walk downhill, shining our flashlights on the rocky trail, I add "do not compete with Larry" to my list of summer goals. If I stop competing, will he? While it feels natural to respond to provocation, it takes two to keep a game in play.

Friends in Sight

The electricity will be off today, noon until four o'clock, according to the *Enel* signs. We never ignore a posting now.

At noon, we drive to Francesco's studio to use the internet and, at three, return followed by the washer and dryer delivery men. It's impossible to find Lodolina without a guide, even for these delivery guys who know the back roads. Francesco says they'll set up my appliances, but I can't use them until the Miele technician checks them next week. I don't understand why, but I'll gladly hand wash essentials for one more week knowing it's the last.

As they trolley in the appliances, I realize these will be the first automatic washer and dryer at Lodolina — ever.

It takes two men over an hour. My laundry area is wide and shallow, like a closet. They set the machines side-by-side in the middle, but I insist they be stacked against one wall like the plan, so I can have space for shelves and a hanging rod. They gesture that the doors are not correct for stacking. I gesture please stack them anyway, which they reluctantly do. The installer tells me how to use the machine, but I don't understand. Then he hands me a manual — in English! — and tells me they are *pronti*, ready. I could kiss him!

I confirm, in Italian, that I can use the appliances before the Miele technician approves his installation. He grins and says, in Italian, to read the manual first.

The men leave after five, just as Oliver arrives with a budget for an annual olive grove program. It's more work than we imagined — annual pruning and fertilizing, mowing the terraces and banks three times per year, treating for insects and disease if needed — and it doesn't include picking, pressing or bottling any oil. It'll be expensive and we're not guaranteed a crop.

Larry tells me we are curators. If we think like farmers who need to make our land profitable, we'll be unable to enjoy our Tuscan life or oil. As curators, caring for the hillside and making oil from our olives will be a joy.

We agree to immediately mowing the grass that's knee high and probably a fire hazard, and say we want to think about the grand plan. Oliver also suggests clearing two more terraces toward the stream, leaving only olives and oaks, which the *Comune* allows to restore the old olive groves.

A phone rings, shocking us because it never rings. Larry rushes to the coat closet, where our only home phone is temporarily installed. I hear him speaking English. My heart stops. I listen hard, praying everything is okay back home.

"That was David," Larry says, grinning broadly as he comes out of the closet. "They miss us. They can't wait until September to see us, so will arrive in ten days and stay ten days... They think we could use some help unpacking."

He answers my unspoken question. "Yes, they know they'll sleep on sofas."

I'm overjoyed. David and Dale are dear friends who share our love for art, opera, theater, food, wine and life. David, Larry's doctor since Larry was twenty-five, is also his closest friend. They both love running, biking and intellectual conversations, discussing subjects most people find difficult, especially since their views differ. David is politically liberal, Jewish by heritage and a self-proclaimed atheist, although he's curious about ideas of faith and religion. Larry is politically and economically conservative, a Christian who studies daily and teaches Bible courses. But they share concerns for honesty and justice, fairness and equality, the downtrodden, and each has a deep respect for tradition. Dale and I are also well matched in our love of cooking and gardening, and we care deeply about family, friends, and the importance of character. We also have different political and religious views. Our fascinating, respectful conversations and our friendship have enriched my life immensely.

"We've got work to do!" I say. "We should at least get all these boxes out of the living room."

"You funny girl. They want to help unpack and you're worried about unpacking before they arrive."

"Always good to have a deadline," I say, grinning. "This is great!"

Even more than helping us unpack, maybe they can help Larry and me get back on track with each other. After twenty years together, Larry is still the most interesting man I know. I admire and love him, but we are testing our limits as each other's only friend. With David and Dale, we'll get a break from each other and two fresh voices. Dale is willing to see and say the truth and I value her perspective. With girlfriend counsel and some fun with friends who love us and love one other, I hope the dynamic between Larry and me will recalibrate.

Suddenly, I feel better about everything. Among the gifts of friendship, perhaps the greatest is the hope friends offer us. Less than two weeks until our friends arrive. It cannot come soon enough.

Crisis that Connects

Lightning zigzags across the night sky. With each burst of light, the illuminated valley floor seems frozen, and then is dark again. Wind blows into the open window, chilling my bare skin. I pull the covers up. This breeze has a wicked bite.

"Listen…" I whisper, "Can you hear it?

"Hear what?" Larry asks sleepily.

"Rain."

"You're dreaming," he murmurs, pulling me into his arms.

"Hey, you're wet! Guess there is rain," he says, now awake. We lay nestled like spoons, silent while our first summer storm at Lodolina rages.

We both love storms. When we were first married, we lived in a house with a copper roof and soaring glass walls. Storms in that house were exhilarating. Years later, when we moved to the city, we were delighted by the panoramic drama of storms over Lake Michigan, but we missed that cacophonous copper roof. Lodolina, with its insulated tile roof, will not have that pingity-pingity-ping of rain pummeling metal. But in the early morning light, staring into our long valley brought to life by lightning flashes, thunder bolts and a deluge of water, this storm is magnificent.

Raindrops thud like acorns on the tile. I close the window because the bed is getting seriously wet. The dawn sky has become a steely gray. I hug my pillow and consider getting up. Larry, already up, announces from downstairs, "Stay in bed. I'm bringing you half a cappuccino".

"Half?" I yell.

"We forgot to buy milk, so I made one to share."

He sets the cup down next to me and stands there. His posture seems strange.

"What's wrong?" I ask.

"My computer's a mess. I fear it may be serious."

"What happened?"

"I started reading. It was okay until I tried to connect to the internet. First it froze, then the screen went blank. I can't get it to start again. And, I can't find my reading glasses to figure out how to start a recovery program."

Larry's computer is his lifeline. A passionate student, he's added thoughts and quotes to his florilegium for twenty years. He cannot lose that work. His computer is also his connection to former clients, family and friends, on-line newspapers and web research. And it's my connection to my mother, daughters and friends. Our ability to live here successfully requires computers and internet. I wonder if it was the storm.

I help him search for his glasses. In this small house with very little furniture they can't be far. I search every horizontal surface including the tops of moving boxes. I empty my purse because sometimes he asks me to carry them for him. He thinks he had them earlier this morning. He has just started needing reading glasses, so only has two pairs and he left one at Francesco's office yesterday.

After no luck, he decides to look for them in the car, so pulls a rain jacket over his bathrobe. He comes back with the robe bottom drenched and without glasses.

"Found them," he soon hollers from the living room. "In the pocket of my robe. Guess I put them there when my computer froze."

He starts his computer in a recovery program. It churns slowly. We're hopeful. I'm afraid to connect to the internet to download my emails. Larry asks if my summer journal is backed up, and I tell him I don't think it is.

"You need to handle that," Larry says. "You can't be writing every morning and lose it all." He seems irritated with me, but I think he's simply upset.

I nod and tell him he's right, imagining how devastating it would be to lose my work.

After a quick shower, I strip the bed, put the towels I washed yesterday into the dryer and our sheets into the washer. It's a relief to be doing domestic chores the twenty-first century way, rather than by hand.

I notice piles of plaster dust in several places where the electrician worked. How could he grind so much plaster into the floor in one day? I clean it all up with a stiff brush, vacuum and wet rags.

Larry says we must get the workers to clean up their messes now that Lodolina is our home, not a construction site. I'm uncomfortable delivering criticism to anyone and now must do it in kindergarten Italian. We're not sure when Francesco is coming and need to stop the messes today. Also, we believe the tile layers have put the last coats of wax over construction dirt and think the floors need to be cleaned and redone, so they look like the original sample. I offer to speak to Marcello. He knows I like him and he speaks English, so it'll be easy to be warm but candid. The electrician speaks only Italian and makes the biggest messes, so I'm relieved when Larry says he'll talk with him.

Larry's computer continues to churn in recovery mode. He is understandably preoccupied.

When Marcello arrives to work in the guest house, I tell him in Italian and English, gestures and an occasional smile, that we think the floor in the main house must be cleaned and re-waxed, pointing out the worst areas. He responds well and says he'll bring a special cleaner that's natural. I think he means for me to use, not him, but I'm reluctant to say, "Surely you don't expect me to scrub the floors, since you put the wax over the dirt?" Marcello is a good man and a talented professional. He wants the floors to be beautiful. Who will clean them is left unresolved.

Larry talks with the electrician. In addition to better Italian, Larry has a firmer disposition than I have. He explains that it's necessary to put down plastic before starting and clean up after his work, period. Since I didn't have the courage to ask Marcello to do the cleaning, Larry also talks with Marcello. They agree the floor should look like the tile sample and that Marcello will clean and then re-wax.

The computer is still processing, which Larry says is a good sign.

It's late morning and I decide to cook a real breakfast. I love cooking at Lodolina. Even with a nearly bare refrigerator, we devour golden scrambled eggs with crispy *prosciutto*, toast with fig jam, cantaloupe and nectarine chunks tossed with a squeeze of lemon. Have eggs ever tasted this... eggy? Do all Tuscan eggs have such golden-orange yolks?

Larry's computer recovery continues. No changes, but he's still hopeful.

My first load of laundry is finally dry. Not fluffy dry like in America, but damp dry. I throw the towels over the living room chairs to finish. This European system takes forever. A cotton wash cycle takes two hours nineteen minutes. The dryer is not vented, but has a water collection tube, and after three hours of tumbling, the towels were not dry enough to fold.

Now I understand why Italians hang laundry on a line, even in city centers. If they have a dryer, they probably use a clothesline because things don't get dry and fuel is expensive. When we lived in Cortona during the frigid winter three years ago, I did laundry every morning, hung everything on the pulley line outside the kitchen window during the day, then brought them in at night to thaw and finish drying. For months, we lived with towels, socks, jeans, shirts and underwear draped over the chairs and sofa. Consequently, for Lodolina we ordered the largest capacity appliances available, but they are small by American standards.

Draping sheets over the chairs, I find only one pillowcase. How could I wash only two loads and already lose a pillowcase? I'm afraid to wash Larry's socks.

The computer recovery program has finished. We stare at the screen as the report cycles through thousands of numbers. Larry's not sure what the report means or what to do next. There's a long list of errors and the system has not rebooted. Feeling helpless, he decides to wait another hour until our tech in Chicago is awake and call him.

While he's attending to his computer like a critically ill child — checking vital signs, hovering and praying — I start another load of laundry.

Dark clouds roll in again. I hope it rains enough to break the heat wave, keep the dust down, and water the suffering olive trees.

Larry can't reach our Chicago tech, so finds a computer repair shop in the phone book and we head to Camucia. The sign on their locked door says they reopen at four-thirty, in one hour.

To spend the time productively, we drive up the hill to Cortona to make a reservation for Sunday night dinner with Lilli, the restaurant on *Teatro Signorelli's* terrace. Marco says the *Comune* plans to put up a three-story screen in *Piazza Signorelli* for the World Cup championship, Italy versus France, and Lilli's café will have the best view. In Italian, it's much easier for us to reserve in person than on the telephone.

We're the first Lilli says and asks which table we want. Of course, we want to sit near the rail looking directly at the screen.

Back in Camucia at the computer store, a new sign says they're away on a service call. Larry calls the number but can't understand except the man says he will be back *subito*, right away. We decide to look at espresso machines at a shop nearby.

Suddenly, the rain comes… *with a vengeance.*

No one is inside the kitchen store, though lights are on. We stand in the downpour, knocking loudly. A woman comes from an adjacent shop where she's washing the inside of the front display window. We're all drenched. She unlocks the door quickly to let us in.

After considering all options: push-button, pod, semi-automatic, fully-automatic with LED display, and traditional, we buy a traditional Pavoni with a pull-down handle. It's beautiful, like sculpture. The rain is still torrential, so we run to the car with Larry lugging the big box.

Thankfully, the computer store is open. There is no place to park, so Larry leaves me in the car and tells me to drive around the block. This will be my first time driving the SUV, in fact, my first time driving in Italy — ever.

I protest because of the rain. He tells me there's no choice, unless I want to take the computer to the store and explain the problem. I ask if I can sit in the driver's seat and let cars go around me. He says no.

"Just drive around the block until you find a place to park. You'll be fine." He shuts the door, splashes through puddles, and leaves me in the car in the middle of the street. I climb across the huge console to the driver's seat.

A small car pulls up behind me. My windshield wipers can't keep up. Although it is afternoon, it's so dark that it's hard for me to see. Sheets of water distort my view. My heart pounds. The car pulls around me.

A larger car pulls up and honks. I take a deep breath, start the car and slowly follow one-way signs to the end of the street, around the corner, down another street to the train station, up a side street, through a parking lot, and back down the street to the computer shop. I lean forward and squint as I drive, praying not to hit anything. There is no ordinary block to just drive around. When I get back to the store, Larry is not to be seen.

Breathe, I think, breathe and drive. I make the circuitous route again. I pray for Larry to appear each time I pass the store. On the third pass, I see him. My knuckles are pale from gripping the steering wheel and every muscle feels taut.

Larry waves goodbye to the computer repairman and runs toward the car.

"They have to keep it overnight," he says, jumping into the passenger side. "They think it has a virus and need to run some cleaning programs."

He seems elated.

"Are you okay to drive?" he asks when he looks at me.

"No. How about tomorrow, when it isn't raining?" I reply, getting out of the car in the rain to exchange seats. He gets out, too, holds the door for me and runs to the driver's side.

Both soaked, we seem to be friends again. Larry's grateful for my help getting his computer repaired and we're both excited about the Pavoni. I am eager to get up tomorrow morning and make a proper cappuccino.

Nearing home, we must drive around a stone wall that collapsed into the road. The passage is narrow and the downpour is relentless. I'm grateful Larry is driving.

At home, he helps me make the bed with clean sheets. It's good to have two weeks of summer body odor washed away.

As we drift to sleep, the stress of Larry's computer crash and driving in the storm behind us, I relax. Larry reaches to take my hand. His computer allowed us to bond over a shared threat, rather than seeing each other as the problem. Relationships work better when the enemy is on the outside, rather than within.

We Rarely Fool Those We Love

In the hazy, iridescent dawn light, I watch fog filling the valley, creating a lake of frothy milk. I'm excited about making a real cappuccino with our new Pavoni. It's early July, but after yesterday's downpour it feels like fall. Larry whispers, "Stay here," and soon comes back upstairs with a cappuccino for each of us to sip in bed.

"The new machine makes excellent espresso," he says, "but I can't figure out the steamer. The milk is lousy."

"I'm sure it's fantastic compared to what we've been having. We just need practice. Look at the fog… it's creeping up our hill on little cat feet, like in Sandburg's poem."

"It's even coming into the house," he says as wisps drift in, tiny ghosts that disappear as soon as they hit the warmer air.

Soon, Lodolina is enveloped in a cloud. All is silent. Even the birds have stopped singing.

Larry decides to go for a run, certain the fog will burn off. He loves the landscape when church domes float above the fog. He suggests that while he's gone I backup my journal on the memory stick he bought for me at the computer store. Each day I'm still surprised there is anything of significance to write about, then I can't type fast enough to capture it all. I wouldn't want to lose Larry's computer crisis, my solo drive in the rainstorm, our rather disappointing first Pavoni *cappuccini*, or this mysterious fog.

It's Saturday. I wonder if he'll offer to take me to market. With newly washed-out areas along the road, I'm even more fearful of driving on my own. Besides, I like his company even when I don't need it.

By the time he comes back, the sun has dispelled the fog and warmed the hills, producing a crystalline, near-perfect day.

"What a great run!" Larry says, perspiring and happy. "If you'll let me, I'd like to take you to market. It's gorgeous out."

He's not teasing. He wants to take me and I didn't have to ask.

"How fast can you be ready?" he adds, turning to go upstairs.

I have a sense something else is on his agenda.

"Are you hurrying me?" I ask, meaning to be playful but hearing unintended agitation in my voice.

"I'm just trying to do something you want," he says, returning my agitation. "Why are you mad?"

I immediately wish I could do a rerun. He's trying to do something nice and I'm reacting out of a past upset. I know we all do that, but I should've simply accepted his offer with gratitude rather than questioning his motive.

I start again with a more even tone.

"I'm not mad, but I still have laundry and dishes to do and it feels like you're rushing me. Half hour? Is that okay?"

"No problem," he replies sweetly. "Take as much time you need. I've got my book."

I clean the kitchen and put wet clothes in the dryer, trying to stay calm but feeling upset. I resent being rushed when his total responsibility this morning was to run, get dressed, and read his book. I compose myself and decide to address the issue of fairness head on. But my honesty provokes another rebuttal about how he does plenty and I'm always on his case. He says he told me to take my time and asks what he should've said. I say he could've offered to help. When the back and forth gets us nowhere, I decide to finish getting ready rather than to waste more time on a discussion that seems pointless. I simply tell him I'll hurry.

How easily we fall into old patterns.

Almost ready, I go to the back door to retrieve my sandals. Last evening, I left them outside the hidden door because they were caked with mud. As I lift one, I see the strap is torn. In fact, it looks chewed. What animal would come to our back door, chew a strap, and leave the sandal? We've seen porcupine quills on the driveway, but they're too shy to come to the door. Surely not a cat. Maybe a puppy... or a fox?

Pierangelo told us about a small, blond *volpe* that peered through a hole and watched them work when construction started, but we've never seen her. He said she probably lived in the old garage before we tore it down. It seems we have a feisty blond fox with a shoe fetish. I name her Imelda.

When I show Larry what Imelda did, he laughs, "Can't you just imagine a fox at the back door, gnawing on your shoe to teach us who really owns the place?"

"I think there's a shoe repair on *Via Dardano*," he adds when he sees my lower lip.

"Hope it's open this morning. These are new... and my favorites."

Larry's raised eyebrows suggest a visit to the repair shop is not on his list for this morning. I hope he doesn't rush me through the market like he rushes through a grocery store. Rather than create any upset, I cross shoe repair off today's list.

Finally on the road, Larry says he wants to stop by the computer store in Camucia first. Now I know why he was so willing to take me to market and why he was hurrying me. This time he finds parking near the store. I wait in the car.

He looks jubilant coming out of the store, despite empty hands. "It's going to be okay," he says, "But we have to come back at seven to get it."

"I'm so glad it's okay," I say, genuinely happy for him.

"I didn't think it was fatal, but it could've been. Without good backup, it could've been a disaster," he notes.

The Saturday market is as wonderful as I remember. This is our first market day since we arrived. Earlier tension between Larry and me has been melted by the fox's prank, relief over Larry's computer repair, and the pleasure of market day in the sunshine.

Cortona's market offers everything from food to clothes to household goods. Clothing blows in the breeze like colorful banners. People mill about, trying on items over what they wear. Larry finds drawstring linen shorts he likes for five euros, but he doesn't want to try them on, so puts them back. I wonder about the quality of the linen skirts that look so lovely.

The fishmonger has varieties of fresh fish, clams and mussels, eel, shrimp, squid and a whole octopus draped across a heap of shaved ice. About a dozen people are waiting in line to buy brown-paper cones of freshly fried shrimp, calamari, and tiny whole fish that look like smelt. The enticing aroma of the marketplace is enough to make anyone hungry, especially as lunchtime approaches.

After buying cheeses, I'm eager to find the vegetable stand. When we lived here that first winter, we had a favorite vendor, a family offering jewel-colored, in-season produce piled high in crates covering long display tables. I was especially drawn to the beautiful daughter who seemed to be in charge. We exchanged a few recipes back then and it'll be fun to see her again.

We find their stand downhill toward the cathedral. Her smile radiates with recognition and she exclaims, *"Bentornati!"* Welcome back! I try to tell her we live here now. She seems delighted, but I'm not sure she understands me. I point to the assortment of tomatoes, asking *"Quale più dolci?"* Which is sweeter? She lifts plump cherry tomatoes, still on the vine. When I nod, she puts some in a bag and holds it up for my second nod on the amount.

I carefully pronounce the word on each sign as I make choices, hoping to learn the Italian names. The pretty woman takes her time with me, though many people are waiting for help. Three other family members also wait on customers. I buy way too much, dreaming of all the lunches and dinners I can make this week. She stuffs in an extra head of red romaine lettuce, saying *"Regalo,"* a gift.

Then she asks me a question. I'm stumped, so shrug, *"Non capisco."* I don't understand. She repeats it. When it's clear I don't get it, she says, *"Un momento,"* and turns to the crates behind her. She holds up a huge handful of flat-leafed parsley and basil. I smile and nod. She's offering me a collection of herbs, carrot and celery, typically added gratis, the starter for soup or pasta sauce. She repeats the word: *odori.*

"Si, grazie," yes, thank you, I reply.

As we walk to the car carrying our bags, I contemplate trying to drive again. Larry heads toward the driver's door. Buoyed by the joy of market day and perfect weather, I say, "I was going to drive today, remember?" My stomach tightens a little.

Larry grins and hands me the keys. I really don't want to do this, but know our life in Tuscany will be much happier if I can drive. I tell myself it cannot be so hard. After all, the SUV is automatic and millions of Italians drive, surely not all of them are smarter than me.

I buckle in, back out of the parking space and cautiously pull out onto the street, leaning forward to see better. Our SUV seems bigger than any other vehicle on the road. I sigh with relief when we're safely all the way around the city walls.

Turning up the ridge road, I feel nervous again. This is a one-lane, two-way road. The right edge drops five feet to olive groves below; the left side is a stone wall with a ditch at the base. The wall, twice as tall as the SUV, creates blind spots at the curves. Small cars can pass at a few places, but one driver usually has to back up to a wider spot. With our big SUV, we must back up far enough to pull into a driveway. There are few driveways. I pray I don't meet anyone.

We meet one car. It's a tiny Fiat Panda and the driver backs into a driveway so I can pass. I wave gratefully. Larry is quiet. He looks intense.

I turn onto our access road, relieved to be this far. At the sharp uphill curve, I slow down to approach it cautiously.

"Don't slow down!" Larry blurts. "You need speed to make the turn!"

My anxiety increases. I back down the hill to get speed to take the turn. When the wheels skid on the gravel, I jam on the brakes, and then stop, knowing it was the wrong thing to do. I back down again to make another run at it. I really want to turn this car over to Larry, who is now clinching his jaw and, I suspect, trying hard not to give more instructions. I make it around the first curve and remember to build speed as I approach the second uphill turn.

I over-correct coming out of it, swerve too close to the ditch, then grip the wheel to go straight and steady. I'm thankful the rest is fairly straight and level. When we're in our driveway, I relax my grip and release a long, audible sigh, grateful to have completed the ordeal. I pull the car as close as possible to the construction gate so we don't have to carry the heavy vegetable and cheese bags too far.

As I pull the key out of the ignition, Larry says, "Nice job. It'll get easier with practice."

Trying to fit a week's worth of vegetables and fruit into my tiny refrigerator is impossible. I need a better way of organizing such a small space. A couple of baskets for inside the *frigo* would help. I leave out whatever doesn't need refrigeration. The kitchen smells earthy and sweet.

While Larry drives to Camucia for his computer, I call Amber. She left a cheerful message earlier so I think Portland is going well, but Amber's defining characteristic is cheerfulness. She's also thoughtful, steady, tolerant and a better mother than I was. I was a good mom, although single, and love seeing our children being great parents. I'm glad Amber and Chad followed their dream to live in a more tranquil, woodsy setting than Chicago.

The nine-hour difference means it's early morning for her. When we finally connect, I smile, hearing her happy voice. I beg for all the details about their new life, delaying questions about Italy.

I try to sound equally happy. I tell her we spent the morning at the market and now I'm doing laundry in my new washing machine. She asks about my piano and kitchen. I confess that I'm not playing yet and have only cooked a couple of meals. I tell her about Larry's computer virus and our sculptural espresso maker. No, we haven't made friends, but David and Dale are coming to visit.

Amber has endless questions and I put the best possible face on our experience so far. I wonder if she's doing the same about Portland.

It's hard to know how honest to be. For the kids and Mom, I tell the good parts so I don't worry them. For my girlfriends, I tell them it's harder than we expected. So far, I haven't told anyone that Larry and I are arguing way too much.

We all put a good face on things, especially when we're trying to prove that what we've chosen is a good idea. If I were telling the truth, I'd call this experiment a failure so far. I love the house, town, culture, and new experiences, but I don't like daily life as a foreigner who doesn't know how to speak, drive, or find anything. I enjoy conversations with Francesco, but not what living in construction is doing to our marriage or to me. I feel insecure, intimidated and lonely most of the time. I tiptoe around Larry, yet am totally dependent on him. The more I ask him for help, the more irritated he becomes and the more helpless I feel. Driving yesterday and today was progress, but we have not settled in and Lodolina does not feel like home. I choose not to tell Amber much of this.

I hang up wondering if I sounded falsely enthusiastic. My daughters know me well. I don't think I fooled Amber. In fact, we usually don't fool those who know and love us. Perhaps that's why David and Dale decided to visit. It's late, I'll call Mom and Lara tomorrow.

Campioni del Mondo!

Tonight is a big night. After an ordinary Sunday, we climb the hill and stroll hand-in-hand through the *Parterre*, basking in the goldish-apricot light of dusk. Except for our long shadows, Larry and I are alone. Usually at this time the park is filled with people taking an evening *passeggiata*. Ancient stone benches, their edges rounded by decades of derrières, are empty. Everyone must be in town.

This is our second walk to town today. The first was for church. We're not Roman Catholic and our Italian isn't adequate to understand the homily, but we enjoy worshipping with a community. This morning when the *Eucarestia* was offered, a young mother sitting in front of us took her daughter, about five, forward to stand in line. As they stood to leave, the father started whisper-singing, "Ain't no sunshine when she's gone...." The little girl glanced back frequently to make sure her *babbo*, daddy, was still singing. Her smile radiated. He stopped singing only when she climbed back onto his lap and hugged his neck.

This evening, we're in town for Italy's second religion — *Calcio*, Soccer. Tonight is the 2006 World Cup Championship between France and Italy.

Cortona is abuzz. Banners hang over the streets. Throngs of fans carry Italian flags or wear them as capes, scarves or headcovers. Men in bright blue soccer shirts with bold Italian logos are hyper-animated — laughing, high-fiving, hugging, kissing, chatting, gesturing, grinning, and slapping friends on the back. This is the most crowded we've ever seen our town, a *molto energico* mass of happy humanity.

Working our way up the main street, we stop to talk with Veronica, standing in front of the antique store where she works. It's still open at seven on Sunday evening.

"*I love calcio!*" she exclaims. "I don't know why, but I *adore* it. From a child, I have such a passion. This is the first time in twenty-four years we have a chance for the World Cup. For every game all season, I stay inside by myself to watch. Friends call and say, 'Please, may we watch with you?'

I tell them, 'Fine, come watch. But do not say *anything*. Do not make noise. Do not move around in my house. Only sit and watch. I do *not* want distractions.'"

In *Piazza Signorelli*, a crew is erecting a three-story screen in front of the building where Marco lives. People mill around looking for places to sit, though it's over an hour before kick-off. The wide stone stairway in front of *Teatro Signorelli* is already packed like bleachers.

Marco stands in the center of the piazza with several men who are installing the projection tower. He grins when he sees us. "I must be here... they need my signal. If the game goes well, I leave it connected. If it starts to go to France, I pull the plug."

We thank him for suggesting dinner at Lilli's.

"This is wonderful," Marco gestures around the piazza, elated. "You have *nothing* like this. Your country is so big that the contests are with other cities or schools. This is *nation* against *nation*."

"For us, the Olympics can be like this," Larry assures him. "Country against country."

Marco scoffs. "We have that, too. *This* is different."

We go to Lilli's long before game time to be sure she remembers our reservation. When we booked, she didn't ask our name or write anything down. We think she knows us, but maybe not. She greets us with her typical warmth and a twinkle in her eyes, and shows us to a perfect table for two. Lilli, perpetually kind, already looks frazzled.

The only table that might block our view is set for ten. We wonder if it's for Mike, Lynn and family. We told them about the big screen and suggested they reserve.

The screen is up. No image, but people are already vying for position in the piazza and hanging out of windows in surrounding buildings.

An older, dignified Italian man sitting next to us asks Lilli if he can move their table forward. She helps him. They're almost but not quite in our way. We nod our okay.

An American woman at the table next to us exclaims, "I've been in Cortona only forty-five minutes and here I am watching the World Cup with the best view in town! I can't believe it." Her friend, a photographer for the University of Georgia, is shooting the spectacle. She shows us a chart she made with the games in this year's contest and informs us that this could be the third World Cup win for Italy.

"If a country wins three, they keep the cup," she explains. "Then a new trophy is made. It's stunning… eighteen-carat gold and malachite. Italy won in 1938 and 1982. Tonight could be three." (Later, I learn Italy also won in 1934.)

A faint image appears on the screen. The crowd murmurs. When it disappears, they sigh. Cheers go up as a full image emerges and stays. It's still daylight.

The Italian national anthem blares from loud speakers and everyone stands and sings with pride. Some raise their fist skyhigh; others put a hand over their hearts. Marco is right: this is a *national* event. I feel proud too, as if I were Italian.

Official pre-game chitchat commences in Italian. We get permission from Lilli to move our table away from a pillar that blocks Larry's view. I insist he takes my seat, as he understands both soccer and Italian better than I do. But he refuses, promising to explain the plays.

People arrive for the table in front of us. Indeed, it's our friends from the castle night and their family visiting from America. Fortunately, even with ten, they don't obstruct our view.

Viewers are frozen for the kickoff. Within seconds a key Italian player is injured. The crowd groans in one disapproving voice, especially since it looks like a purposeful French infraction. The instant replay proves the offense was unintentional. There's still hope for a clean game.

A few seconds later, the referee makes a bad call against Italy and the American woman next to us fumes. "The game is fixed!" she declares. "Just like the Portugal game. The ref made a bad call early and, from that moment, the game was lost."

Almost immediately, France makes the first goal. The crowd groans again.

Lilli and Isabella, Lilli's daughter, lose track of orders as they try to serve tables and catch some of the game. Thirty minutes ago, before the game started, we ordered Campari, a bitter Italian before-dinner drink, and our entire meal. But we have nothing yet, not even napkins. The American woman and her photographer friend have been served salad, a fabulous-looking pizza and drinks.

Lilli comes to us, saying the lasagna is excellent. We remind her of our order, including lasagna, and she smiles, tapping her head as she remembers. She's a sweetheart and this is a tough night. Fortunately, we're not very hungry.

Our Campari arrives. We sip to make them last, unsure when we'll get anything else. We see Mike order something and point to our table. We raise our glasses and everyone at their table nods, grins, and gives us a thumbs up.

I pinch my arm like I did on our first morning at Lodolina. On this perfect summer evening, we are in a historic hilltown in Italy, sitting on the terrace of a neoclassical opera theater, having dinner and watching the World Cup Championship — a match our new homeland could win. I haven't experienced anything like this in my life. I scribble furiously without looking down, hoping I can read my journal tomorrow.

The Italians get into position to take a goal kick from the corner. Larry whispers, "Watch closely. This could be a *great* play." The ball arcs high across the field, descending toward the goal opening, and an Italian player head-butts it into the net.

The crowd goes wild — clapping and stomping, waving flags, blowing bullhorns, screaming, whistling, hugging, and leaping in the air. Larry leans in to see the re-play. I lean in to see the stuffed zucchini that has been served to the table in front of us. Now, I'm hungry.

Suddenly it's half time. One to one. From the third-floor windows of Marco's apartment, barely above the screen, people take photos of the crowd. Larry guesses two thousand people are packed into this small piazza.

Commentators chatter in Italian. I catch a word here and there but have little idea of meaning. Once in a while I hear "*Italiano*" or "*Francese.*" That's the essence of this match, isn't it? Italy *or* France. One winner.

Not understanding the halftime show, my eyes wander to the architectural contrasts surrounding us. Medieval and Renaissance buildings line two sides of the sloping, wedge-shaped piazza. *Teatro Signorelli*, where we sit on the terrace, regularly stages opera, dance, movies, and concerts. Built in 1854, when new local opera houses were opening throughout Italy, it presented Verdi to bejeweled audiences. At street level on the lower end of the piazza, artisans offer jewelry, linen, and soaps from spaces that were historically an open market for chickens, lambs, and pigs. Above those shops is Cortona's ancient town hall.

People on the piazza seem connected to one another. Elderly men lean on canes and chat with other elderly men, perhaps recalling *calcio* matches from their youth. Older women stroll arm in arm. Lovers hold hands. Teens stand in clusters, giggle, roughhouse and smoke. Boys of various ages kick soccer balls against the walls and little girls hold their daddies' hands.

This crowd is ignited, waiting for the contest to begin again.

Isabella brings our *antipasto* as halftime ends. I savor bites of prosciutto and melon very slowly hoping our lasagna will arrive before the game is over.

Italy makes another goal! We leap to our feet. The roar is deafening. Almost immediately the goal is reversed because of an offside foul. Viewers scream curses and make rude gestures. Larry tells me it was an arguable call.

The French coach, in his formal black suit, looks more like a conductor directing an orchestra than a coach managing a tough, rugged soccer team. I wonder if he always dresses so formally for games.

The lasagna, which arrives steaming hot, is as delicious as Lilli promised.

Every eye is riveted on the screen.

Official game time ends in a tie, one to one. There's a short time-out. Overtime starts. Each play seems like slow motion.

Suddenly, a French player turns and head-butts an Italian player in the chest, knocking him to the ground. The French star is thrown out of the game.

Larry says the Italians seem to be playing an individual game while the French are playing as a team. I have no clue. I only know I have never witnessed a sporting event like this one.

Overtime produces no winner. The shoot-out begins. Five Italians and five French alternate kicks with only the goalie defending... one-on-one. Each has a chance to score or not to score. Incredible pressure for the goalies and the kickers, moments of a lifetime. Someone in the stadium starts to chant. Soon, thousands on screen and in the piazza are chanting and clapping in unison.

One goal is scored for Italy... One for France. A second for Italy. Soon it's four Italy, three France.

The Italian goalie deflects a French kick. The crowd goes ballistic. I can't hear the commentators over the roar. The next shot could take the game. I hold my breath.

...*ITALY SCORES!!!!*

Bedlam erupts. Fans scream, cry, clap, stomp, hug, kiss, wave flags, blare horns, dance, and leap into the air. I take photos from Lilli's terrace, knowing I'll never capture the frenzy of this unbridled national euphoria.

After a half hour of craziness in the piazza, silent talking heads on the screen, and re-runs of the heat-butt and the last goal, a caravan of cars starts to crawl diagonally across the piazza. Riders in open convertibles stand and cheer wildly, sing and chant, and toss flares into the crowd. Men are stripped to the waist with war paint slathered on their torsos. The caravan continues into *Piazza della Repubblica* and on through town. Cars are typically forbidden to drive on *Via Nazionale*, but tonight anything goes.

We pay our *conto*. Lilli added one euro per item as an up-charge for the best seats in Cortona. We thank her profusely, leave an extra big tip, then work our way down the stairs into the piazza to be swept into the rapturous celebration.

For this suspended moment, *I am Italian*.

After a half-hour with revelers in *Piazza Signorelli*, we work our way to *Piazza della Repubblica*, where we run into Lorenzo, our realtor-friend, and his wife Rita. Beaming, they tell us they watched from the windows of their friend's apartment.

"Tonight no one will sleep," Lorenzo says. "Tomorrow many will not work, only will celebrate. Studies show the economy will go up half a percent just because of winning the World Cup. The new Prime Minister is a fortunate man; he does *nothing* and the economy improves. I was seventeen the last time we won. My father bought a newspaper to save the headline. I still have it. Tomorrow I will buy a newspaper to save for my son."

Beside the endless parade of cars with blaring horns and delirious riders, we work our way to *Piazza Garibaldi* at the other end of town, also jammed with exuberant fans.

From the piazza, we gaze across the valley. Long lines of car headlights like lava-snakes wind between clusters of bright lights in the villages. On a normal night, there'd be a few houses lit and an occasional car, but tonight the valley seems ablaze. Every hamlet, village, town and city in Italy must be celebrating.

We reach the end of the park and start downhill, our flashlights guiding us on the rocky path. The cacophony of blaring horns and cheering fans begins to sound like buzzing bees. By the time we reach our driveway, all we hear are nightingales.

There may never be another night like this in Italy, at least not in our lifetimes. I feel *leggera, euforica...* light, euphoric — and wide-awake. Tonight, I may not sleep either.

To truly engage in another culture is to celebrate their wins and mourn their losses. Tonight, I felt closer to our Italian friends than ever. Tonight, we celebrated a monumental Italian victory.

When Workmen Danced

One month ago today, we left Chicago. It feels much longer.

After the big World Cup win last night, workers roll in a little late. They're all smiles, as are we. Gabriele arrives to help Mr. Rochetti, the Bose man, install our sound system. The television we ordered should arrive late July, he assures us. Seems strange to wait so long, but if we have music we can do without television. As everyone works, all conversation is about the game.

The rooster at the top of the hill is in a contest with another across our valley. I love their languid back and forth. Songbirds have been our music since we moved in. The little black squirrel quietly dines in his tree, dropping cypress-cone cores that clatter to the ground, providing percussion. White clouds rest above the horizon, hardly moving.

This morning I decide to make *fegatini*, chicken liver spread, another of Larry's favorite Tuscan foods. I can't find my favorite recipe so improvise.

First, I chop *odori*: the onion, celery, carrot and parsley the vegetable lady tucked into my bag. With oil and heat, the parsley turns emerald, celery bright limey green, carrot deep tangerine, and the onion a reddish purple. My kitchen smells heavenly. As the *odori* begins to caramelize, I add the livers, rinsed and patted dry so they'll brown nicely. They are plump, firm, burgundy, and enormous.

Everything sizzles. The *fegatini* should be sweet and rich with all this browning. I add a splash of red wine and let the mixture reduce, merging flavors. I taste it and add some capers, then mash it with a fork. The mixture is balanced, rich, succulent, moist and delicately perfumed.

We're out of bread, so I put mounds of warm *fegatini* on silver-dollar-sized slices of raw zucchini for everyone to taste, including the construction crew. Gabriele teases me about opening a restaurant. I'll cook for him any day, he's such an appreciative audience.

When everyone is back to work, Larry offers to make an espresso for me, then calls me "Sweetie" as he hands me the cup. He seems surprised when I frown and asks my preferred term of endearment. "Anything but Sweetie," I reply. He promises to call me only what I want, as long as he knows. After suggesting "my love," "darling," or "sweetheart," I ask him the same question.

"Milord," he declares, easing into the wicker chair, "spoken affectionately, compliantly, and often."

"Affectionately I get. But do you really mean compliantly or subserviently?"

"I'll go for simple compliance. Truthfully, I don't have much hope for either."

Aha, that bit of truth in the teasing. Larry does crave my attention, affection, and compliance.

"I like Spike better than Milord," I say. Spike is the endearment he has requested in the past, a joke from a cartoon he saw years earlier.

The coffee is not as good as the one I made myself earlier, but I don't want to break the spell of our gentle playfulness, so just say, "Thank you, Milord."

Playfulness seems a useful tool for managing relationships. It disarms tension, provokes a smile, and even causes a healthy laugh at one's self.

Especially with Larry, I appreciate some playfulness — we're serious so much of the time.

While Mr. Rochetti and Gabriele are inside working on the sound system, Larry and I sit in the wicker chairs on the concrete slab in the shade of the cypress trees. Pierangelo is digging holes in the front yard toward the almond tree, skillfully operating the *scavatore*, a tiny yellow bulldozer. He sees us watching, grins broadly, gets off the *scavatore* and comes to talk to us, first apologizing for interrupting us. Pierangelo rarely stops to chat with us, but today he seems eager to talk about the game. He asks where we watched and tells us where he watched. He asks if we saw the last goal. Every Italian will remember where they were when Italy kicked the winning goal in 2006. So will we.

Music! Suddenly, I hear music. Mr. Rochetti and Gabriele – both quiet, reserved men – are clapping and dancing in the living room. Larry and I applaud. What an amazing difference. Music gives soul to Lodolina.

"*Bravi! Bravi!*" I yell as loudly as I can. Well done... everyone!

Mr. Rochetti and Gabriele come outside, beaming and obviously pleased. We offer coffee again, and this time they accept.

As we thank them and say goodbye, Mr. Rochetti gently insists, "*Chiamami Carlo, per favore.*" Call me Carlo, please. We interpret this invitation to use his first name as a sign of being accepted. Italians are somewhat formal in their use of names and language. Not long ago, Ivan, the owner of *Il Pozzo*, our favorite artisan gallery in Cortona, explained the "gift of *te*," as he put it. Many foreigners use the informal forms in Italian, even with strangers. To Italians, this informal form of you, *te*, like the informal greeting *ciao*, is reserved for family and good friends.

I'm brought to tears by this moment of joy. How could it get any better: *Campioni del Mondo,* music enriching our home, warm acceptance from a new friend, and a husband trying to be patient, helpful, and playful? These are the remarkable times — big and small — that I always want to celebrate.

On Hands and Knees Together

We awaken before dawn and decide to scrub the floors so Marcello can apply treatment. I put on the same old shorts and dirty tee shirt I wore yesterday when, after Gabriele and Carlo left, we scrubbed the white leather chairs. It felt great to do physical work, and even better because we did it together.

Marcello kindly agreed to do the cleaning, but we figure it'll save a day and be nicer for Marcello if we tackle the scrubbing. Hot July days have returned, so early morning is best for physical labor.

First, Larry and I discuss process. It seems obvious to me: loosen ground-in construction dirt with a brush, then vacuum, and then scrub with Marcello's special natural cleaner, rinse and dry. Larry says Marcello's treatment is an emulsion of beeswax in water, so we don't need to dry. I tell him surely the wax treatment will soak in better if the floors are not already saturated, but I stop short of creating an argument over something so trivial. We had fun working together yesterday, laughing and being silly, and I hope today will be the same.

He wants to finish reading, so I start in the kitchen. On my hands and knees, I brush hard in small sections, vacuum, wash with Marcello's special cleaner and a sponge, rinse with an old wet towel since we don't have a mop, and dry with another towel. If a spot remains, I spray it with a spot-lifter for fabrics called *Via Va*, which literally means it goes away.

I wish I had known when we moved into Lodolina what I know today about terracotta floors. Francesco assures me it's pointless to try to keep them looking new; better to let spots appear at random and, over time, be absorbed into the terracotta to create an aged patina. But we're determined to start fresh and let the patina develop over time instead of waxing over construction grime. There's a difference between patina and dirt.

The brown stain from the defective coffee pot lightens with my scrubbing, but not much.

Larry says he's ready and asks if my process is working. Still on my hands and knees, I twist my neck to look at him standing over me. I have to laugh. Milord, indeed.

"If the drying towel gets dirty, I rinse the floor again," I say, hoping he'll reconsider drying. "This floor is awful, so I usually have to rinse twice."

Larry heads upstairs with his arms full. He starts in our bathroom, second dirtiest after the kitchen. I hear the brush, the vacuum, swoosh of the scrub brush going back and forth, and then quiet while he rinses. Finally, a scrape as he drags the equipment to a new area. His work is steady and unceasing, but I don't think he is drying.

"Can I use the mop to rinse?" he hollers down the stairs.

"You could if we had one. Do you need more towels to dry? I'll bring some up." I need an excuse to get off my knees for a moment and want to see what he has done.

When I tell him again that I think he should be drying, he insists it's okay… it'll air dry. He adds that it's so hot upstairs, everything dries quickly.

I stifle my objection, since he's working so hard. After a while, I hear his footsteps on the stairs.

"The bathroom's much better. Bedroom, too. At least we're giving it a clean start. All that's left upstairs is the sitting room."

Larry offers to help me finish downstairs. A bee buzzes in through the kitchen door and out a window. I'm amazed at how filthy the rinse water becomes. Our old white towels, brought from Chicago to use until we bought new ones, have become as tan as our dirt yard. Thank goodness I have a washing machine.

"What happened to letting Marcello do the scrubbing?" I ask, half in jest as I towel-dry the dining room floor. "He's going to be surprised."

"This work's not so hard. We'll be done soon and I'm sure we saved a day," Larry answers.

I like investing our own physical labor in Lodolina and hear my father's voice from years ago saying a little honest labor never hurt anyone.

Upstairs in the sitting room, we stack everything on one side, where the floor is still clean. The pile includes four overstuffed sofa sections, several unopened boxes of light fixtures, four suitcases functioning as clothing drawers, three bicycles, the antique kitchen table that is Larry's temporary desk, eight boxes of books, rugs rolled and wrapped in paper, an antique chest, two nightstands that did not fit in the bedroom as well as they did on the plans, two boxes of leftover Bose parts, a stack of winter blankets, and armloads of shoes.

I marvel anew at what a diligent and thorough worker Larry is. We brush up the worst of the grit. As he starts to vacuum, the lights flicker.

"Hmm. Not good," I murmur.

"But there weren't any signs," Larry protests.

It's nine o'clock sharp, so must be *Enel*.

Without electricity, there's no pump for the well, so no clean water. Construction sounds have stopped. Pierangelo shrugs his shoulders when Larry asks what's happened.

Our house phone doesn't work without power, so I walk up the driveway to get a signal on Larry's mobile phone to call Francesco. We've been scrubbing floors for two hours and I need a shower.

Francesco says he didn't see any *Enel* signs either. He warns that if they're doing emergency work, rather than maintenance, it could be hours, and offers to call them for us.

Marcello arrives and is delighted by our cleaning. We tell him there's no electricity, so no water. He shrugs, like Pierangelo. "We cannot wait. We must do everything by hand."

"Does it matter if the floors are dry?" I ask him.

"As long as the dirt is gone, the water can stay," he says. Guess I was wrong. But drying does ensure the dirt is gone. Marcello says he'll start in the kitchen.

"I can finish upstairs on my own," Larry offers. "Without water or electricity, there isn't much we can do except brush and sweep…. And use the dirty water in the buckets to wash."

Larry's kind to finish and I don't want to insist, but I fully intend to dry upstairs once he's done. It's even more important now that we can't use clean water to rinse.

I want a shower. I also want a drink of water. But the faucets are dry since the pump is out and, by the time I think of it, Marcello has covered the kitchen floor with treatment, so our bottled water is out of reach.

I ask how long we must stay out of the kitchen, my thirst intensifying since I can't get to water.

"I can put down Styrofoam in an hour. But no sooner," he says.

Marcello whistles while he works, like Pierangelo. His tune is the same refrain over and over and I don't recognize it, but his whistling makes this ridiculous situation almost charming.

I dry the upstairs sitting room floor while Larry reads on the terrace, put clean clothes on my dirty body and work quietly on my computer. About eleven-thirty, the screen flickers and brightens.

Francesco arrives with the power. He says he tried to call our mobile phone, but the signal must be too weak inside the stone walls. He drove twenty minutes to explain that the *Enel* green number said the power would return at noon.

With a touch of humor, he adds, "Today they turn it on *before* they say. A gift. Not usually before the promise."

"Thank you for bringing electricity, Francesco," I tease. "We're not used to this. Power rarely goes out in Chicago, unless something catastrophic happens."

"Here, happens often. But usually you know before," he assures us.

"Larry and I want to ask you about an alarm system," I say, changing the subject. "We've heard that thieves are around and several homes have been robbed. We asked, but Pierangelo hasn't heard about any."

"An *allarme* could be good," Francesco answers. "But you don't sleep with windows open?"

Larry and I look at each other. Of course, we do. It's been one hundred degrees and our hillside seems like the safest place on earth.

"We lock the windows and doors downstairs, but not upstairs," Larry says. "We like to sleep with fresh air."

Francesco shakes his head. "They like that best. The upstairs windows are usually bigger and easier to get in. They sneak up a ladder without a sound. Climb in. Spray you. You wake up the next day with all your belongings gone. Even an *allarme* will not protect you with open windows."

"You're not serious?" I ask. "At your home, you close and lock all your windows at night?"

"Certainly. There is no reason to invite them to join us in the bed! And we are safer than you... We live in the town."

I find this hard to believe. I can understand closing windows to keep out mosquitoes, but surely not for thieves.

After Francesco leaves, I shower quickly, grateful for warm water. We must arrive in Arezzo before our bank closes at one o'clock. Our most recent transfer was finally processed after being held two weeks in the main branch in Florence. Larry called yesterday and Paola, the only English-speaker in the Arezzo branch, assured him it would take "five minutes" once we arrive.

In Arezzo with only minutes to spare, Larry gives up looking for free street parking and parks in the nearby underground lot. By Chicago standards, one euro eighty per hour is a bargain, around two dollars. But here, because street parking is usually easy to find and free, parking in the lot seems indulgent.

For bank security, we each must pass through double sliding glass doors. I push the green button and the first door slides open. I step inside. The first door closes and I stand, being scanned for weapons. The second door opens and I walk into the bank. Larry's behind me. It's two minutes before one o'clock.

Paola is watching for us and motions us to her half-walled cubical office.

"It will take a moment for the cash to be organized," she explains. "While you wait, we can arrange for a BNL credit card and fill out forms for *Telecom Italia* and *Enel* to be paid directly from the bank. It is the best way."

"We don't need the credit card," Larry explains. "We have USA cards without transaction or exchange fees that work fine here. But automatic payment for utilities is a good idea."

Larry fills out what seems like endless paperwork for two auto-payments: phone and power. There is also a form to put our name in the local phone book, which Larry doesn't want to sign because he wants to find a better service than *Telecom Italia*. But Paola says that not putting our name in the phone book may prevent us from making automatic payments. Larry shakes his head in disbelief, fills out the form, and signs multiple places on the stack of necessary applications.

Paola is concerned our *Telecom Italia* bill is three days overdue and warns it may be a "*grande problema.*"

"Is there no grace period? We just moved in and the bills were sent to our architect. We just got them yesterday," Larry says, stunned.

"No, no grace period. A two percent fee for only one day late. You must go to the post office in person immediately or your phone service could be cancelled. Very difficult to get it back. You must also know the post office will not accept checks or credit cards, only Italian debit cards or cash. May I ask why this bill is so high?"

Larry explains it's for installation of underground wiring and three month's service.

"Could be another problem…" she says, squinting her eyes a little. "The post office limit on paying by debit card is seven hundred and your bill is twice that."

"I guess we'll pay seven hundred by debit card and the rest in cash," Larry says, a bit exasperated. Paola says there is not time to get more cash today. "But we try," she adds, and picks up the phone to make the request.

"The next bill, in September, should be paid by automatic bank payment," she explains. "But you must call the bank in August to make sure the paperwork went through because the first payment is not always smooth. Once the first payment is made correctly, then will happen automatically."

Because we are three days late, she insists we go immediately to the post office in Arezzo, since Cortona's post office is only open mornings and closed for today.

"Or… I suppose tomorrow morning in Cortona is the same," she adds, making a characteristic circular gesture with her hand.

Larry tells her today we must go to the *Questura* immigration office before it closes in twenty minutes to get our *Permessi*, so we will pay the phone bill tomorrow morning in Cortona. Paola gets a call from the front counter that our cash is ready — but without the extra to cover the phone bill.

At the *Questura*, we're delighted to see our name on the list, so we get in line. After waiting over twenty minutes in the miserably hot tent, we're allowed in. The agent at *sportello* three retrieves our file and informs us that we cannot pick up our *permessi* until we have been fingerprinted. Larry tells him we were fingerprinted in Chicago for our FBI clearance, and that it was in our file the *Questura* sent to Rome. The agent insists Italian police in Arezzo must take our fingerprints in person, in Italy.

We don't have time to do it today, Larry explains in his best Italian. The agent says they are not open today for fingerprints anyway, only on Fridays.

"That makes no sense!" Larry declares in English. The agent doesn't react.

He turns to me. "That means we come back Friday, when David and Dale are here."

I frown and feel my lower lip protrude. This isn't what we had in mind for our friends, or for my sixtieth birthday.

I'm exhausted by our lack of progress. We have been in Cortona thirty-three days, still live in the midst of construction and disarray, and without official permission to stay. Thankfully, Larry and I have been getting along better, especially since David and Dale said they're coming. I'm working to keep the peace and he seems on best behavior, too.

After finishing our Arezzo business, we come home to Styrofoam walkways and working electricity. But it's hard to do anything except computer work while the floors dry.

After I turn out the lights, Larry suggests opening the windows.

"You're not afraid of robbers?" I tease.

"I'm only afraid of making my wife unhappy," he says tenderly as he pulls the sheet back for me to get in.

The full moon hangs low in the sky, like a child's lighted globe floating motionless above the ridge. Moonlight streams across our bed, giving our bedroom a silvery glow. My knees are sore from this morning's work. Larry's must be sore too, but he hasn't complained.

Soon he's sleeping peacefully. I too feel peaceful. All day Larry and I worked together. It has been good for my mind and emotions, as well as for my body. Working as a team is a matter of choice, and today we chose to be partners.

Drifting off, I hear the night sounds of frogs and nightingales near the stream, but not of thieves.

Where Have All the Good Feelings Gone?

The instant the sun creeps over the ridge, the temperature begins to climb. I've been lying in bed for thirty minutes, gearing up to face another day. It was good to work together yesterday, but my muscles ache and this heat is oppressive. Feelings come and go, often without reason, and this morning I feel a strange sadness.

I wonder about other women who watched the sunrise through this window, especially the one whose husband planted our cypress trees. I imagine those trees were in memory of sons lost in the Great War, like the cypress along the road around Cortona. Life was harder then and my predecessor would have been up to do chores long before me. I wonder if her husband was gentle or rough, and if she faced her days with joy, sorrow, worry… or nothingness.

For me, today could be an exciting day. Marco's mother arranged for a helper to clean for me. The big hitch is that she needs a ride to and from the bus stop at *Piazza Garibaldi*. Larry will not want to take the time and I'm terrified to drive it on my own.

I'm also nervous since she doesn't speak any English. This afternoon, I want her to concentrate on cleaning and ironing, so looked up words to practice. Since I washed our clothes in advance, I think I can point rather than try to explain in Italian.

After breakfast, Larry announces that he wants to walk to town to pay the overdue *Telecom Italia* bill and asks if I want to go. Our frigo is empty so I agree, warning him that I'd like to pick up some groceries. I dress less modestly than normal for me, and ask Larry if I'm decent enough to go to town. He laughs, saying everyone wears as little as possible in this heat, so I should not be self-conscious in a tank top and shorts.

By the time we reach the top of the hill, I'm dripping wet. We divide tasks since it's almost noon. Larry heads to the post office; I go for food.

At the vegetable store, two tourists ahead of me are confused by signs that say *non toccare*, do not touch. I explain that touching produce is prohibited by Italian law, suggesting they point to the item they want and hold up fingers for how many.

They smile and nod appreciatively. George introduces himself and his wife, Wendy.

"How long will you be in Cortona?" I ask.

"Just arrived. We'll stay a week. How 'bout you?" George asks.

"We moved here a month ago. From Chicago." Somehow, I feel different, voicing our shift from tourists to residents.

"Why Cortona? What do you like here?" Wendy asks.

"We love *everything*… the art, food, music, history. So much is going on all the time, but life still seems more tranquil, slower." I chatter about our new hometown, based on my dream rather than on our reality of unfinished construction and marital distress.

Wendy asks if they can buy fresh pasta in Cortona and I offer to walk with them, since that's where I'm going next. In the noonday sun, we trudge up *Via Dardano*. The stones radiate heat.

I tell them *Via Dardano* is named for the mythological god Dardano, son of Zeus and Electra. According to the ancient poet Virgil, Dardano was born in Cortona and founded Troy. Then his descendent founded Rome, which makes Cortona the mother of Troy and grandmother of Rome. As we pass *Trattoria Dardano*, I say it's a favorite restaurant for us and the whole legend is on their menu.

In *Pasta Fresca* we both buy fresh *pici*, the local hand-rolled pasta like thick spaghetti. George says his friend's favorite bread shop is just down the hill, so we stop on the way back. I ask for "*pane scuro*," hoping I said bread dark and hoping for something grainy. Someone in Cortona must make multigrain breads, but I don't know how to ask. I also buy two scones, one olive and one walnut, treats for Larry and me. I leave feeling happy.

My new acquaintances say they're curious about local wines, so we walk back to the wine shop where I introduce them to Marco so they can arrange a tasting, say goodbye and walk outside to look for Larry. I'm surprised he's not in the piazza, since it's been over an hour. Something must have gone wrong in the post office.

Soon he strides down the hill, obviously unhappy.

"Where've you been?" he asks. "You were supposed to meet me in the piazza a long time ago."

"I'm in the piazza now, but you weren't here when I got here. Why are you mad?"

"I looked all over for you, including walking up to the pasta store, but Lilliana Angelica said you already left. What took you so long?"

"We stopped to get bread," I say.

"Bread wasn't on the list and we don't need it."

Wendy and George come out of the enoteca and I introduce everyone. Larry is barely cordial and seems not at all charmed that I was playing tour guide while he waited. Truly, I should have paid more attention to time. We walk all the way home without speaking.

Back at Lodolina, Francesco is with the plumber, who will hook up the toilet and sink in our second bathroom so David and Dale have some privacy, but not the shower. I'm happy to see Francesco to break the tension, and for the plumbing.

It's soon time to pick up Rita. Larry is talking with Francesco about his desk so I wave to Larry who waves back, and walk up the hill to the car. It'll be my first solo drive to town. I pray not to meet another car, barely breathe all the way to town, and fortunately have the entire road to myself.

At *Piazza Garibaldi*, I recognize Rita right away. She's short and sturdy with dark hair, like we were told. I wave. She sees me and waves. She's been told we drive an SUV and look American. She climbs into the front seat head first, pulling herself up because the seat is so high. With her seat belt fastened, her feet don't reach the floor. As I drive, she looks straight ahead, wide-eyed and quiet. She knows I don't speak Italian and is quickly learning I can't drive.

I grip the wheel and choose the lower, longer road because it's wider, then head up a dirt-road shortcut by Palazzone. As we bounce over the ruts, I wonder if Rita is breathing. On our steep S-curve, she braces herself against the dashboard. I don't look directly at her until I turn the engine off in our driveway. Her pale face makes me more nervous about trying to speak Italian, but I must say something.

"*Mi dispiace... per la strada, per guido non buono, il mio Italiano brutto.*" I am sorry... for the road, for my not good driving, for my ugly Italian. She shrugs and half-smiles, nodding. I wonder what her nod means, but am pretty sure she agrees the trip was awful and she's glad to be on solid ground.

Once we're in the house, Rita seems to know what to do without instruction. I introduce her to Larry, show her the broom, vacuum and supplies, but don't give her any requests except that after cleaning, *dopo pulire*, I'd like for her *stirare*, to iron, and point to a stack of Larry's shirts. Two weeks ago, I ironed fourteen shirts and it took me all afternoon. He likes them ironed, even the knit ones. I hate ironing. Rita looks like she doesn't like it either.

Rita works hard without complaining, despite the house being filthy and disorderly. The scrubbed floors with Marcello's new hands of wax are clean, but all else is not despite my best efforts. She spends four hours washing windows, wiping off shutters, and dusting furniture in our one-bedroom house and another hour ironing. Even though she leaves the windows streaked, I don't mention it. They were so crusted that, by comparison, they sparkle. It'll take weeks to get this place really clean. For now, I'm mostly worried not to offend Rita. I like her and I need her.

When it's time for Rita to go back to Cortona to catch the bus, I ask Larry to please take her.

"She's not comfortable with me. I can't talk with her and she feels unsafe. She was stiff as a board the whole way here."

In a low, stern voice, he says, "You *must* learn to drive, Victoria."

I don't want to argue in front of our new helper, so I grab my handbag and trek up the hill again, trying not to show my upset. Rita follows me a few steps behind. I'm sure she's as uncomfortable as I am. We ride in silence.

Larry and I stay home for dinner, a simple pasta and salad, but we are not talkative. We agree to skip the concert we planned to attend in order to get some sleep.

Neither of us are screamers. But silent tension can have as much sharpness as a yelling match, and cut just as deep.

A strong, hot wind blows all night. The orange plastic construction fence flaps against the chain-link fence and the metal shed door creaks open and bangs shut. The full moon shines on the swaying, rustling trees. I cannot sleep.

Days have come and gone since we moved. Each has been filled with essential work and exciting events. This could be fun, even with the construction and my fear of driving, if Larry and I were happier with one another. We have made a truce. I try not to bother him in the mornings and am learning to drive. He has tried to be more kind and helpful. Though we have moments of levity, even playfulness, we are not friends. Today felt sad and unrelentingly heavy. I am eager for David and Dale to arrive.

UFO and Celestial Soprano

The next day passes with no construction questions and only a short visit from Francesco. All afternoon Larry and I rearrange the upstairs furniture, re-stack remaining boxes, and sweat so much Larry announces we deserve a night out. After a quick shower and dinner at home, we head toward *Le Celle*, the idyllic, thirteenth century Franciscan monastery near Cortona. We missed last night's concert in this week's Sacred Music Festival, but we expect tonight's concert at *Le Celle* to be uplifting and a welcome distraction from our chores.

What we couldn't possibly expect is what happens next.

Midway along our driveway we see a black object flying slowly down the center of the road toward us, about four feet off the ground. Larry stops the car. We both stare, fixated. The creature, about four inches long with a thick body, glides up and over the SUV, nearly grazing the windshield, then down the rear window and continues along the center of the driveway.

Its languid flight reminds me of the cicadas that buzzed drunkenly around our home in Lake Forest many summers ago. But this is too large to be a cicada.

Larry backs up slowly, hoping to get another look.

The black being curves back toward us in a steady arc, flies beside Larry's window until it's in front of the car, and then abruptly turns left and flies into the woods. We can't tell if it's insect, bird, bat... or something else.

Larry inches the car forward, wanting to see it again. It hovers in a clearing in the forest, then disappears as suddenly as it appeared.

"That was strange," he murmurs as if in a trance.

"What was it?" I whisper, equally astonished.

"I don't know, but I'm glad we *both* saw it," he replies and looks at me.

I search my memory. Rhinoceros beetle? Black hummingbird? It flew too low and slowly to be a bat and didn't have bat wings. It's still daylight; bats are sleeping.

Stunned, we drive on to *Le Celle*. At least the mysterious creature has given us something to talk about instead of how we're not getting along.

Turning onto the mountain road to the monastery, I pray this evening lifts my doldrums. Just to be at *Le Celle* is simultaneously calming and inspiring.

Larry stops to offer two nuns a ride.

"*No grazie. Abbiamo una macchina, ma preferiamo camminare,*" one sister says sweetly. We have a car, but prefer to walk. I admire their vigor. They must have walked from their convent in Cortona, at least two miles.

Around a curve, police stop us to say we must park and walk. We're still at least fifteen minutes by foot to *Le Celle*, so will cut it close. Larry pulls in beside the only other car in the small graveled area. He sets a brisk pace and I try to keep up.

Looking into the distance, Cortona and the Chiana Valley are washed with a pink-gold glow. The sun soon drops behind the distant mountaintops and the horizon is inflamed with streaks of vermillion and violet. Savoring the beauty, I understand why the sisters wanted their sunset walk.

At *Le Celle*, parking areas are jammed and cars line both sides of the narrow road. There will be gridlock after the concert, so we're glad we were forced to walk. As we pass under the stone arch entry, *Le Celle* suddenly appears. A honeycomb of blond stone rooms clings to the opposing hillside, as spiritually serene as ever.

It's precisely nine o'clock, starting time. Rows of dark green plastic chairs fill the upper stone ramp; we guess enough for three hundred people. A makeshift stage is at the lower end, created by marine blue carpet and pots of raspberry-colored petunias. One microphone is center front. Sadly, most of the chairs are empty. We sit immediately behind the reserved section, also empty. I'm surprised the concert is so poorly attended, especially with all those cars.

Within minutes, a big group comes up from *Le Celle* and fills the reserved section. Everyone seems to know everyone, kissing and hugging like family. The other sections are filling, too. There must have been a pre-concert event at the monastery.

One woman breaks away from her admirers, walks to the front, and turns to face the audience. In the spotlight, her earrings glitter like diamond waterfalls. She has a regal presence and is clearly esteemed by this crowd.

A monk introduces her and explains the concert in Italian. I catch a few words, mostly *Gesu Cristo* and *Signore*, Jesus Christ and Lord, to whom he refers without hesitation. Speaking and singing about spiritual subjects in a public concert is not taboo in Cortona, especially not at *Le Celle* or during the Sacred Music Festival.

The singer pauses, lifts her face as if to heaven. Her voice, rich and haunting, fills the gorge and reverberates against the stone buildings. After her first song, the front section leaps to their feet yelling *"Brava! Brava! Bravissima!!"* Each song is worth an ovation, but after that first outburst, spectators are restrained, sitting on the edge of their plastic chairs, spellbound.

She explains each selection in a soothing spoken voice. Then she sings. Even the birds are silent, as though listening reverently.

Spires of tall cypress grace the hilltop behind *Le Celle* and stars are so low they mingle with the trees. I turn and see every seat filled and every face fixed on her face. Her voice, complex and warm, is God's gift to her and to us. After over an hour, she concludes with Hebrew songs, as did the choir directed by Father Frisina on Sunday. "Shamai Israel," is the oldest prayer in Judaism, she explains before she sings.

The crowd, including us, jumps to its feet with a lengthy and loud ovation. *Brava! Bravissima!!* punctuates the deafening applause. Her encore is "Adonai."

Strolling to our car, I'm thankful for walkers with flashlights and for every car that passes. With no moon, the mountain road is dark. At the gravel area where we parked, other cars block ours and we must wait until their owners arrive. Surely, the nuns will be home before we are.

Larry seems calm. I can't tell if he's happy or only less tense, but I'm thankful for our evening, even more uplifting than I had hoped. I take deep, meditative breaths on the ride home, still enraptured by the purity of the singer's voice, the serenity of *Le Celle*, and the mystery of the black flying creature. With events like these that force me to be in the moment rather worrying about the past or future, the stress of past days seems softer, as though it could fade away. Distractions often help in difficult times, because they draw our minds to something beyond ourselves.

During the night I dream that our woods are full of black flying squirrels. They glide through the air and play in the branches. One baby lands on our car antenna and slides down to the car hood. It looks directly at me through the windshield and scampers off into the forest. I believe it has carried my sadness away with it, at least for that moment.

Declaring a Reset

I know the day is off to a bad start when Larry wakes me for the third time before dawn.

"Vic-TOR-i-a!" he grumbles, "You have *got* to be quiet. You've been snoring all night. It's almost five and I haven't had *any* sleep."

I don't think I've been snoring. I've been lying wide awake and quiet since he woke me the first time. Now he's up, brushing his teeth and *not* happy. I want to stay in bed and re-awaken with no one mad at me.

I have too much to do today to worry about irritating Larry. David and Dale arrive tomorrow and I need to wash the new sheets and towels, do our personal laundry, and organize everything we've stored in the big fireplace upstairs — an assignment Larry gave me yesterday when I suggested he organize the fireplace contents before our friends arrive. It's mostly his stuff, but he says if I want it done before they arrive, I need to do it myself. I also must wash the dishes we left last night when we rushed off to the concert and iron two of his shirts that weren't dry when Rita was here. And, I want to write about the flying object, the concert and my black squirrel dream.

Mostly, I don't want another day of being on-guard, afraid I'll do something wrong. Last night was wonderful, but we're back to tension this morning, simply because I snored. He snores, too.

I pull on my black silk robe and walk downstairs, feeling misunderstood, defensive and sad again.

Larry looks up from his reading. "You look upset. Are you okay?"

Tears fill my eyes.

"So, what did I do now?" he asks, a bit too sarcastically.

I stand there for a moment, decide his question is a non-starter, and turn to go to the kitchen to make my coffee.

"Sit down. Talk to me," he insists. His words are fine, but the tone sounds like a command. I comply. I've interrupted his study, so we might as well get this over with. I sit in the white leather chair next to him, slouched and silent.

He starts. "What's wrong?"

"I'm just not happy. It's not your fault. This whole move is just too hard."

Tears well up again. I don't know what else to say, so sit silently as tears drop on my robe making big dark spots.

After a pause, he asks without much warmth, "Are you going to tell me what's wrong? Or are you going to cry and not talk?"

I say again that it's not his fault. I'm just tired and exhausted.

"They're the same thing," he corrects.

That's enough, I think.

"Of course, they are," I say, standing up. "Sorry I interrupted your study. It's nothing. I'll get over it. I've got too much to do today to sit and talk. I'll be fine."

"Do whatever you want," he says. "But don't expect me to know what I've done if you won't tell me."

"You're just so easily irritated." I say, exasperated that it's my fault again. "And you were furious because I was snoring. But I don't think I was and if I was, it wasn't on purpose."

After more accusations and defenses back and forth, Larry abruptly goes back to his reading. I sit back down, unwilling to let it end like this.

I begin again, telling myself not to accuse, instead to use "I" statements.

"Larry, please just listen and don't tell me why I'm wrong. This move is not what I expected and I don't know if I'm strong enough. I feel lonely and inadequate most of the time. I feel like I'm losing myself… and losing you."

He listens. Thankfully, I didn't launch into what he did wrong, though I can think of a few things. After a few moments that seem endless, he leans across and takes my hand.

"Come sit with me…." He pulls me toward his lap.

"Larry, I don't want to sit on your lap," I say, baffled that he thinks all is resolved or that sitting on his lap would be a solution for anything. "I just want you to *understand*. And right now, I want some coffee."

He just doesn't get it and this is going nowhere. I stand up again and start toward the kitchen.

"Don't complain and then walk away from me," he snaps in an icy tone.

I turn back, more upset than ever, and sit down again... waiting. Moments pass. I clinch my jaw. At first, he continues to read. When I don't move, he looks up and stares at me as though he's thinking. Finally, he starts with a warmer voice.

"Okay," he says, "We're both upset, I get it. Let's review the facts. We both want this move to work. We both want this summer to work. I want you to be happy. You are gentle and lovely. You need for me to be gentle with you. These first weeks have not been easy for either of us, and we'll have other times when our new life is not easy. Maybe we need to establish a reset. No arguing about who was right, or what happened, simply request a reset. Is it a deal?"

No, it's not a deal, I think, narrowing my eyes and shaking my head. A reset is too easy. A reset means he doesn't have to acknowledge what's happened and there will be no change. He'll get irritated, I'll feel hurt, and he'll say we need a reset. A reset means I swallow my feelings without an apology. It'll drive the pain deeper and I'll end up resenting him.

But I don't want to continue to argue, especially not today. Slowly, I breathe in and nod. Perhaps he doesn't have the capacity to understand how it is for me. He sees things intellectually, not emotionally. Just now, he wanted to review the facts when I wanted to scream. It's often this way between men and women, the logical sex and the emotional sex, though I refuse to reduce our struggles this summer to gender stereotypes.

"Okay, I'll try it," I say. "It's an idea."

Then I add, "But we also need to be able to point out what caused the problem, not like criticism, but like information. Otherwise we'll keep repeating the same pattern. A reset, then a talk?"

"Does that mean you want to keep beating me up?" He asks, but this time with teasing eyes and a hint of a smile.

"I'm not being funny, Larry. I'm not beating you up. I'm worn out."

"Can we have a reset?" he repeats softly. "A reset... and a hug?"

He stands, looks at me with an apologetic expression, and holds out his hand to help me stand. I hesitate, rise, and then am folded into his embrace.

"May I make you a cappuccino?" he asks, smoothing back my damp hair.

"I'd like that…. Poof, you're a cappuccino," I tease. He grins at our old joke, relieved that I seem happier.

"Sit and rest," he says, meaning to be kind, but still telling me what to do. He goes to the kitchen and I hear the hiss of the Pavoni. I don't want to sit. I want to go into the kitchen and wash last night's dishes. I don't like being told what to do and I don't have time to waste. But I sit, avoiding another quarrel.

When did I start doing what he tells me to do?

I do have a choice here. I can agree to a reset and have a chance for a turnaround, or I can hold onto my upset and keep the argument going. I think I have good reason to be upset and hold my ground, but this may be the moment to let it go. Simply knowing it's my decision — to stay upset or let it go… to choose my attitude and my response — makes me feel stronger and softer-hearted. Declaring a reset is another way of saying our relationship is more important than being right.

I'm reminded of an incident years ago when Larry and I were on vacation. I don't remember why, but I went to bed angry and determined that it was in *his* best interest to make sure *he* learned a lesson. I lay awake, replaying what happened and why I was right to be upset, what I should say, and how he should change. I had prayed for a softer heart then, but my self-righteousness had overpowered my best intentions. Mentally rehashing our dispute, I had prayed, "Father God, it's not good for him to think this is okay. Please tell me what to do."

My next impression had been the strong sense of someone saying, "Victoria, I give you a new day every day and you insist on dragging yesterday into it."

That was not an idea I'd have come up with on my own. That instant, I decided to approach Larry without accusation, just a fresh start, reminding myself that he really is a good man and we have a good marriage. Then, I had slept.

That morning, I had told Larry about my prayer and impression of God's admonition. My anger had dissolved, leaving a desire to be the person I chose to be rather than someone driven by anger or disappointment. Anger too often prevents us from making the right choice. We had a straightforward and sensitive exchange, better than the lesson I was determined he should learn. Perhaps I was the one who learned the lesson. Perhaps I'm learning it again today.

Larry, back from the kitchen with a cappuccino for me, looks down at me smiling, "So, how 'bout that reset? I promise to help you with the house this afternoon, if you want my help."

"Okay. I agree. Let's start over for today," I say looking into his eyes, hopeful but not quite convinced.

"Nothing more to say?" he asks.

"Nope. *I'm* good as long as *we're* good."

He returns to his reading. I sip my coffee, skim emails and do the dishes, feeling happier, but still subdued.

In town, Mass is poorly attended. I sing a few choruses and make notes in my journal about last night's concert, since I can't understand a word of the homily.

As we *andate in pace*, go in peace, Larry says he'd like to take me to lunch, promising again he'll help get ready for David and Dale's arrival tomorrow. We relax in the courtyard at *Ristorante La Grotta* with a bottle of wine and an excellent meal. When we get home, good to his word, Larry helps without complaint, even clearing his things out of the fireplace.

Toward evening, Larry asks if I have time to discuss financial projections. I'm wary. Finances are typically tense conversations for us, but his voice is gentle. Together we make a list of what is needed to complete the house and guesthouse, build exterior walls and landscape the gardens. We guess at costs. We want to make sure this dream of living in Italy does not deplete the funds we need for thirty years of retirement.

The discussion goes well, despite my reluctance. So much of getting along well is deciding to get along well.

As I fall asleep, I think about a reset. With a reset, we can simply agree to put being partners ahead of being right. Larry may have initiated a valuable new tool for our marriage, a new tool for a better life.

A Little Help from Our Friends

I'm excited about David and Dale's arrival, relieved the house is ready, and calmed emotionally, knowing I can request a reset whenever needed. I've been given a fresh new day and I certainly don't want to drag our difficulties into our time with friends.

Again, I try to email my story and photos about Italy's World Cup championship to friends and family, but it will not upload. The signal is intermittent at best. In Chicago, I'd call our computer tech. Who do we call here?

Oliver arrives at nine o'clock sharp, the time "reset" from yesterday's missed appointment when he had to handle a client emergency. Larry's still out running, probably expecting Oliver to be late. Today could be a day of new beginnings for everyone. To pass the time, I ask Oliver about his family and his dog, Marcello. He asks about our family and is shocked to learn we have five children and five grandchildren. He says he doesn't want children, too much responsibility to bring new lives into our crazy world. Larry gets back, sweaty but ready to talk. We agree on an annual budget and plan. Everyone seems happy.

When Oliver offers me a ride to Cortona, I'm grateful and disappointed. I hoped Larry would take me and help with pre-guest shopping. Now he's off the hook and I can buy only what I can carry home. As Oliver and I leave, Larry looks up from his online newspapers and blows me a kiss. Oliver delivers me to *Via Guelfa* and I trudge up the hill, feeling put-upon.

Halfway up, I stop at the internet café to send my World Cup story. Lugging my four-pound laptop makes the climb all the harder. A scribbled sign says the owner will be back at sixteen hundred. That's four o'clock, so I carried the computer for nothing. David and Dale arrive at one-thirty.

In town at the small, densely stocked hardware store that carries all sorts of bric-a-brac, I search for coffee cups. I feel conspicuous because it takes me so long for such a simple, inexpensive decision. Since I have to carry them home, I buy only two cappuccino and two espresso cups for David and Dale to have coffee with us.

After finishing a few more errands, I run into Rita, our new helper, who greets me warmly, asking questions in rapid Italian. I'm too embarrassed to say I don't understand, so nod and smile. I think she's asking if her cleaning was okay.

"*Tutto bene*," I say, all is well. I want her to feel good about what she did against such filthy odds. She nods and smiles, too.

"*Ciao, molto grazie*," I say. Goodbye, thank you very much.

"*Ciao, grazie*," she repeats, kiss-kissing me again.

I cannot think of any more Italian words, so breathe easier when she says, "*Arrivederci*."

"*Arrivederci, ciao e grazie*," I respond with gratitude and more kisses.

At the antique store, I stop to talk with Veronica, the vivacious clerk who loves soccer. She's super-hyped about the Arezzo Wave concert, almost as excited as she was when Italy won the World Cup. I confess, I've never heard of the Wave.

She looks stunned. "It's the most famous rock concert in all of Italy... and so near to Cortona. You don't know it? I can't imagine. The best, the *very best* concert I have ever seen. The crowd went wild." She shakes her hands by her head to indicate their frenzy. (Later, I look up Arezzo Wave on the internet and she's right, it's a big deal.)

Even before I ask, Veronica says, "I have not forgotten the mirror for your powder room. I found one I think you'll like." She shows me a lovely little mirror with a wide Art Deco wood frame. It's perfect, but the price seems high. I wonder if I should ask Larry first. Being bold, I say, "Yes! I love it."

"If it is not right, you will bring it back. Pay me when you know it is perfect."

It's not heavy, so I can carry it home easily and hang it before David and Dale arrive.

This is fun — doing errands in a small Italian hilltown and interacting with people who are kind, interesting and trusting. I didn't feel so awkward today. I'm glad the walk home is flat then downhill. My fingers get numb from the weight of the bags plus a laptop over my shoulder, but there's still a bounce in my step when I reach our driveway.

In less than one-hour David and Dale will arrive at the Camucia train station. I hang the mirror with Larry's help, put the new linen hand towels by the sink, wash the cups, and do a final walk-through.

We arrive early. Of course, their train from Rome is late. A sobbing woman is standing on the platform. She looks American, but I'm not sure we should interfere. I imagine the worst: her husband left her, someone stole her luggage, her teen daughter ran away with an older Italian man. From her upset, it must be big.

Larry walks toward her and says softly, "May we help?" I join him, thinking a woman's presence may be comforting.

Through sniffles she says, "Oh, you speak English. Thank you. My daughter didn't get off the train. We were supposed to get off here, but Sarah didn't make it. I don't know what to do."

"Does she have a cell phone?" Larry asks.

The mother shakes her head.

"I'm sure she's safe," I say, trying to reassure her.

"… and scared," the mother adds.

She lifts her shoulders unknowingly and tears start again.

David and Dale's train arrives. A man on the train calls out of a window, "Your daughter got off at Terontola, she's waiting for you. She said I'd know you because you'd be crying."

The train pulls away. David and Dale wave, smiling broadly, then carry their suitcases down the stairs through the underpass.

The woman looks perplexed. "Where's Terontola? Is there a bus?"

"We'll take you," Larry offers, "We just need to collect our friends and make sure we can get all the bags in the car."

After warm and happy hugs with David and Dale, Larry explains that we need to take our new friend to Terontola.

"No, no," she refuses, "I can't impose. I'll take the next train. Or a bus… if you show me where."

Larry insists, "It's a ten-minute drive for us… and an hour wait for the next train."

Everyone fits, bags and all, but barely. For the first time all summer, I'm glad we have an SUV.

At the Terontola station, we see a young woman standing on the platform, staring up the tracks toward Cortona. It must be Sarah. I expected a child, but Sarah's an adult, totally cool and not upset at all.

Mother and daughter hug tightly. We introduce ourselves. Larry starts to explain how to catch the bus to Cortona, then looks at me and I nod.

"We'll take you. Why not? It's a short ride, but you'll have to sit on your mom's lap," he says to Sarah.

When we pile back into the car, everyone including me has something on his or her lap, either hand luggage or another person.

"How long will you stay?" Larry asks, driving toward Cortona.

"Only one night, then back to Florence," Sarah says, "We came to see Bramasole, Frances Mayes' house. Do you know about it…?"

Larry nods with a smile.

He continues to play tour guide. "It'd be a shame to come to Cortona and only see Bramasole. It's a special house in a very special town. The art museum has a treasure greater than any in the Art Institute in Chicago, and the Etruscan museum is one of the best in the world. We'll drop you at *Piazza Garibaldi*. From there it's an easy walk to Bramasole and back into town. It's also where you'll catch the bus to the train station tomorrow."

They say goodbye with effusive gratitude. We suggest a few favorite restaurants and they leave, walking toward Bramasole.

On the drive home we make small talk, bounce around the zigzag curves, park at the end of our driveway, walk through the stacks of construction materials, pass the metal gate with orange plastic fence around everything, step across the dirt clod yard, and walk into the house through the hidden door. David makes a joke about the obstacle course. Once they've deposited their bags in the sitting room where they'll sleep, we show them around, apologizing for the still-packed boxes and remaining disarray.

"Don't be silly. That's why we came — to help," Dale says. I smile, knowing Dale is organized and serious. This house will be in much better shape when she leaves.

Since it's after two o'clock and we're all starving, I put out platters of our standard *pranzo*, lunch: sliced dried meats, sweet cantaloupe, creamy *bufala mozzarella*, tiny succulent tomatoes with basil, and our own olive oil. We settle into a stimulating warm conversation, like old times. I feel happy, really happy.

Francesco arrives as we are finishing.

"Francesco! I hoped we'd see you today. Happy Birthday… a day late! Did you have a nice birthday?" I chatter with excitement and ask if he remembers David and Dale from their last visit, when we were planning the renovation, which of course he does.

Greeting them warmly, he then says, "I have a *very* nice birthday, because I make myself a gift of the end of works at Lodolina. It is a big work, so the end of works by itself is a big work. Yesterday, I spend my day preparing the papers to certify this milestone."

"Oh, that doesn't sound so happy, working on papers all day Sunday… on your birthday. But is Lodolina really finished?" I ask, a bit shocked.

"It is like the Sistine Chapel, when we declare it is finished, it is finished. Only a few details are left inside the house, nothing structural, so can be said to be finished. Of course, we still must finish the guesthouse. I am sorry to interrupt with your friends, but there are many papers Larry must sign before I give myself the gift of delivering them to the *Comune*."

I silently think of uninstalled light fixtures, guest bathtub still to be connected, library bookcases, and stone terraces that are still concrete slabs. Months of work remain on the guesthouse and then there is landscaping. The end of works for me will be when the orange fences and extra materials are gone, and workmen no longer arrive each morning.

While Larry signs the marked places on the inch-thick stack of papers, Francesco and I go over the schedule for the next ten days, including field trips to the stone quarry and the ironworker. David and Dale are enthusiastic about joining us for all of it.

"We have a small gift for you," Larry says after signing the last page, "for your birthday… and to thank you for Lodolina."

Francesco looks surprised when I hand him the carefully wrapped gift. First, he reads our note. He reads it a second time, more slowly, as if to absorb it.

He looks up through glistening eyes and puts his hand over his heart. "You make for me a big emotion," he says, his voice very low as though he can hardly speak.

A surge of emotion wells up in me, too.

"Despite all my complaining about the mess," I say softly, "it has been one of the great privileges and pleasures of my life to reclaim Lodolina with you."

Francesco kisses my cheeks, and then Larry's, and gives Larry a big American-style hug. He opens his gift, a coffee-table book of Frank Lloyd Wright homes. Mr. Wright is one of his idols, he told us when we first met, and this book includes a brief description and photo of our former home.

Francesco lingers with us for a while, savoring the camaraderie.

After we say goodbye, David and Larry walk the property. Dale and I sit in the shade on the concrete slab and chat like only girlfriends chat. It's the first time I've felt this calm since our first breakfast at *Il Falconiere* in June. Dale used to say that our friendship lowered her blood pressure. Today it has lowered mine.

"Wow, did we find trails!" Larry exclaims walking toward us. "Wild boar are everywhere."

"Your land is beautiful... tranquil," David adds, almost reverently. "I can see why you love it."

Changing the subject, he asks, "Are you girls interested in a couple of sweaty guys taking you to dinner?"

David is attentive and kind, and it's infectious to be with friends who are on vacation. Larry and I both feel more like playing with playmates like these.

After freshening up and sipping glasses of Campari over ice, we drive to Cortona for dinner at *Trattoria Toscana*, a favorite restaurant when we first came to Cortona a decade ago. As always, the evening is friendly, easy and delicious.

We only order pasta, still full from lunch. Mine is ravioli with citrus sauce, a chef's specialty. We enjoy a bottle of wine and linger over *espressi decaffinati* and *limoncelli*. No one will have trouble sleeping tonight.

Back home, I shake out a sheet to make beds on the sectional sofas in the sitting room.

"Give me those sheets," Dale protests. "David and I can make our own beds. We came to help, not to be waited on."

I exhale a happy sigh. Having friends in the house has already dissolved so much tension. The entwined roots you have with close friends seem to help them sense your needs. I'm grateful for our roots with David and Dale, and hope this week will strengthen them even more.

When I thank Dale for coming, she says, "Life is pretty much the same for us since you left Chicago. It's your life that's changed. We want to share it with you."

"Seems impossible we left Chicago only a month ago," I say. "Must confess, we've had our ups and downs. Living in construction has not been easy. But Larry and I've remained friends. Or, at least I think we have."

I glance at Larry, wondering what his reaction will be. He looks at me in the same romantic way he did when we met, with searching eyes, his intensity bordering on seductive, and he smiles that dimpled-chin smile I love.

It seems we are still friends — and more. Some things have not changed.

Defining Friendship

Tying the belt of my black silk robe securely, I tiptoe through the upstairs sitting room. Two bodies stretched out on the sofa are motionless, except for the rhythmic rise and fall of the sheets. I forgot to buy breakfast food, so can only offer toast and *marmellata*. Worse, neither Larry nor I have mastered the Pavoni, so they'll get espresso with steamed but wimpy milk. I smile, knowing our friends won't mind.

For our meager breakfast, we stand around the kitchen island. Larry, David and I are tall, so the extra-high island is comfortable for us. But petite Dale seems like Alice in Wonderland as she lifts her cup to the counter. It's pure joy to have old friends in my new kitchen.

Our conversation is easy and personal. "Did you sleep well?" "Jet-lag okay?" Larry announces he'll take two weeks off from his work while they're here. That means no more tiptoeing for me while he studies. Can I get them to stay all summer?

We take turns showering, since only our shower is hooked up, then drive to Castiglion Fiorentino to pick up Francesco. Today's field trip will be a terracotta pot maker and a stone dealer, both across the valley.

As we near Lucignano, Francesco offers to show us its old stone tower, a historically important site and his most recent renovation project.

Lucignano, called the Pearl of the *Valdichiana*, is a well-preserved medieval hilltown. The buildings, most from around 1200, survive in elliptical, concentric circles. Over 1,300 feet above sea level, it was an important lookout site, fought over by larger towns. The stone watchtower is in the very center, the oldest building of all.

Standing inside the tower, Francesco lifts his hands as though introducing us to a heavenly realm, and says, "We can see over a thousand years of history in this one space."

I look up into nothingness, searching for something interesting. It doesn't look significant at all, just a very tall stone box with wood beams, crumbling stucco walls, and tiny windows — old and in bad repair.

Francesco continues, saying the tower was built around 800 to watch for invaders. By the Middle Ages, enemies came from every direction: Siena, Arezzo, Florence and Perugia. When the village was won by Perugia, the tower was used for their military operations. During the Renaissance reign of the Medici, Lucignano was ruled by Florence and the tower was used as a granary. Then, in the 1800s, after an extended time of peace it became a theater, like many opera houses built during Italy's unification.

He adds that Lucignano still displays the Perugia coat of arms, a flying griffon, as their town flag.

Pointing toward the white, undulating protrusions from the lower walls, Francesco says, "Those curving side balconies, so modern when built, were seats added in the 1950s when the tower became a cinema. Now, fifty years later, we make the next history."

Francesco looks as if he's deciding whether or not to share his honest opinion, then adds in a whisper, "The last conversion was not so nice."

"If the *Comune* gets money," he says, "we move ahead. If not, we wait. In everything we do, we must keep important reading keys, so the building will tell its own story."

As we leave Lucignano, I notice red flags with a majestic flying griffon, the symbol of Perugia from the Middle Ages occupation. I would not have noticed or understood before Francesco's story.

The pot factory, a family-owned business, is larger than I expected. Terracotta pots in every shape and size, many made from ancient molds, are stacked on pallets in an open field covering acres. Looking across a sea of brick red, straw yellow, and sandy beige pots, I wonder how I'll ever choose. Under this searing sun, the pots radiate heat.

First, I choose two basic urns, traditional ones to flank our front door, smaller than I envisioned but larger than Francesco and Larry were thinking.

"Typical Tuscan design, so a good choice for Lodolina," Francesco agrees.

After some searching, Larry finds pots with slightly bulbous bellies and smaller openings, with three lion heads evenly spaced under thick, rounded rims.

"How about these for your lemon trees?" he asks. I nod, saying they're perfect.

Our salesperson Paola, wearing white patent knee-high boots with high heels even in this heat, disapproves.

"*No… Non è tradizionale per il limone,*" she says, shaking her head with finality.

Francesco explains, "Lemon pots have one traditional shape: smaller at the base with a wide opening for lots of water, a typical flower pot shape. They can be decorated with swags, fruit or most anything, but must be the correct shape."

We walk the entire lot. I'm ready to buy the traditional plain shape with absolutely no decoration, but Larry remains drawn to the lion pots.

Paola speaks privately to Francesco. He turns to us and says, "No one wants the lion pots. They will offer you a good price. But she won't sell them for lemons."

Dale's eyebrows rise. "Just buy the pots and put whatever you want in them. You know what I have my lemon trees in back in Chicago — nothing traditional — and they're thriving."

Paola tells Francesco these are the last four, they will not make more.

"We'll take them," I say, not sure if I'll use them for lemon trees, but I like the idea of purchasing something that is no longer made.

She nods and smiles. Everyone is sweating and miserable. There is no shade, no breeze, and no relief. I can't imagine how hot her booted legs must be.

Francesco smiles, saying, "When you decide, the builders will bring your urns and pots to you. Too big to take today, even in your very grand car."

He knows I'm not so fond of our SUV.

When we get back in the car, though we left all windows open, the seats are too hot to touch. We're running late and Francesco likes to be punctual, so we buckle up, thighs stinging through our clothes. After ten long minutes with cool air blasting, the car becomes bearable.

Francesco asks David and Larry, "How did you become such important friends? Has it been a long time?"

"David was my doctor when I was twenty-five and he was starting his practice. That was twenty-eight years ago," Larry explains. "When Vic and I got married, he became her doctor, too. But we didn't become friends until we moved to the city six years ago. Why do you ask?"

"It is unusual to have friends so warm they would come to help you move. But only six years makes you new friends, by Italian thought."

"David and Larry are opposites," I say, "but they love to discuss the topics most people avoid — politics, religion, economics — with deep respect and interest."

"We like to learn from each other," Larry says, "and to see where we agree."

David chimes in, "I love the way Larry's mind works. He's a good listener and a good thinker. Sometimes I even change my mind a little. And, together we come up with some pretty good ideas."

Francesco seems consumed by thought. Then he says, "I understand this. What I share with my important friends is values, not opinions. I do not need a friend who agrees with me but one who sharpens me. We both learn and improve in ourselves. Like you and David."

Dale and I are also very different, I think. But we're alike in the importance we place on good character, especially kindness and honesty. She is unfailingly kind and honest. I wonder what she'll say about my new life after being here a while.

We arrive at *Vaselli* at noon, precisely on time. A man rushes into the showroom and explains in rapid Italian to Francesco that he, the owner, will meet with us because the sales director, who speaks English, is on holiday. He apologizes that he doesn't speak English and offers us water, which we gratefully accept, then leads us to a large showroom of exquisitely carved travertine bowls, platters, candleholders, sinks, baths and showers.

After the display, he takes us to an enormous open lot with rows of stone slabs leaning against each other in the blazing sun, absorbing and exuding heat. From hundreds, I narrow the choice for my perfect outdoor dining table to three slabs. The owner, seeming a bit distracted, tells Francesco he should be at his mother-in-law's for lunch at one o'clock. It's one-fifteen. Francesco says we will get lunch and return in one hour.

The nearby spot Francesco knows looks quite fancy outside, clad in slabs of beige travertine with the name carved in a travertine boulder near the front door. Inside, it's not much more than a coffee bar.

"Only where travertine is abundant would this place be covered in slabs," Dale remarks as we find a table on our own.

The only waitress offers two kinds of *panini*, sandwiches: *prosciutto crudo* or *salumi*. We all order prosciutto. She brings four enormous sandwiches that overflow the plates, and puts one each in front of Dale, David, Larry and me. After waiting patiently for his for several more minutes, Francesco, the hungriest of all, goes to the front to inquire about his panino. He comes back with one, miniscule compared to ours.

When I frown, he whispers with a disappointed half-smile, "Much smaller." I cut off a chunk of mine and put it on his plate. Not a sacrifice for me, as it's more than I can eat. Francesco looks relieved.

At the next table, a group of men, likely in their fifties, talk and laugh, looking as though they intend to stay for hours.

"Is it typical for men in America to meet during the day, just to socialize?" Francesco asks. "Very common in Italy… especially at lunch. They stay some hours, then go back to work at three or four and finish around eight."

"Would never happen in the U.S," Larry explains. "Sometimes colleagues go to lunch together, but they usually take one hour and discuss work. Americans more often work through without lunch, or have it at their desk. But they also go home at five-thirty or six."

Francesco explains that in Italy men grow up together and are friends their entire lives. Part of their normal day, every day, is spending time with each other.

Larry and I often see Italian men playing chess or checkers, drinking coffee, or sitting on a park bench together. We have commented that these gatherings, and the slower pace of life we so appreciate, must reflect a higher value placed on relationships.

The men are still laughing and chatting when we leave.

Back at *Vaselli*, the owner is waiting for us with a big smile. He must not have taken too much abuse for being late to lunch with his mother-in-law.

"*Festa particolare?*" I ask, wondering if today was a special occasion. If lunch with his mother-in-law is a daily event, it must be constant stress for him to be on time or to be in trouble.

"*No, solo pranzo.*" No, he says, only lunch.

We get back to business. This time we follow him through the warehouse where massive blocks from the quarry are being cut into slabs. The equipment is gigantic and white dust like confectioner's sugar covers every surface and clouds the air.

It's the fiercest part of the day. Outside, the slabs seem hotter than ever, with narrow walkways between stacks and no shade.

The owner carries a bucket of water and a sponge to wet the parched stone, revealing the rich colors with their subtleties and striations. Most are travertine, from ivory to beige to tan, golds, even dark brown. Steam rises when water is splashed on and disappears in seconds, leaving the slab bone dry and pale again. I wish that water was trickling down my neck and back.

Larry urges me to make a decision. "This is *your* dream table, Victoria. You must decide. But we can't stand here much longer."

I narrow it to two slabs, asking to have each re-wet again and again. I want to run my hand over the stone, to see if I feel more connected to one, but they're too hot to touch.

Choosing has taken longer than anyone expected. I don't like to make these decisions on my own, but no one wants to give their opinion, not even Francesco. Everyone is drenched and ready to leave.

I finally choose a long, narrow slab of dark travertine with a wavy pattern of rich, chocolate browns and creamy taupe. The owner says it is walnut travertine and the highest quality, so I feel confirmed in my choice. Dale and Larry say they liked it best from the beginning.

"Why didn't you say so?" I ask. "Could've saved us all a lot of agony."

Back in the conference room, we have another much-needed glass of water and discuss design, delivery and price. The table will be long and narrow, the longest table I've ever had, to seat a dozen people. I imagine candles flickering on smiling faces of friends and family, stemmed crystal glasses and white plates on the dark stone, soft cool grass under foot, and Enrico Caruso crooning from windows overhead.

David asks if the granite we saw in the yard is local. The owner says it's from *Sardegna*, Sardinia. Francesco looks pained.

"I do not like so much," he says. "It is important for some clients… but I think better for tombstones. Is like making the mausoleum to use for a kitchen."

We finish the order, drive back across the valley, drop Francesco at his office, and stop at the local phone store, where David and Dale learn they cannot get Italian SIM cards without their passports. Why is everything so complicated?

At Lodolina, the scaffolding is off the guesthouse! Pierangelo and his helper are removing excess mortar with a stiff brush so each stone stands out, the final step. It's grueling work and the sun is no kinder here than in the stone yard. Both men are stripped to the waist, shiny and dripping.

Larry and David want to try the new Cortona community pool to cool down. We haven't been back to the pool since that first day, when Larry became an official resident and I did not. It would've been a welcome respite in the heat of the past few weeks, but we've stayed too busy.

"We'll drop you in town... Larry offers, knowing I need to buy breakfast groceries. Dale and I'll have to carry bags home, but at least I won't have to drive.

From Porta Colonia, a high gate in Cortona's stone walls, Dale and I work our way downhill. First, we take my sandals for repair. The repairman smiles at the teeth marks and nods his agreement: *volpe*, fox. He says my sandals will be ready *domani*, tomorrow, which surprises me, and doesn't give me a ticket, which surprises me more. He doesn't even take my name. I don't know how to ask for a receipt, so simply say, "*Grazie, arrivederci*," and hope for the best.

We cross the street to the *macelleria*, butcher shop. Fernanda, the butcheress, is taking big white sheets of paper off the trays of meat after the shop's midday break.

"That is the reddest meat I've ever seen," Dale says with admiration and a touch of concern. Dale buys Kosher meat whenever possible.

We choose a thick, lean steak on the bone and a few slices of turkey breast. Fernanda pounds the turkey slices until evenly thin, perfect for grilling.

In the hardware store, I try to say with hand gestures and halting words that I need a mop and a clothesline. It feels like a comedy routine. Dale loves to hang clothes on a line, so we'll stretch one between the olive trees on an upper terrace to make her Italian country experience complete.

The owner asks, "*Quanto lungo*? How long? I shrug. He waits for an answer.

"*Quindici metri*," I say, fifteen meters, choosing a number I can say. A bit more than fifteen yards. I'm a terrible judge of distance, but Dale agrees it should be plenty.

They only have one mop, which I don't like. Since we need it right away for Rita, I take it and will replace it when I find a better one.

I try to introduce Dale in Italian wherever we go, mentally practicing what I want to say, but freeze when I start to speak. I'm grateful for anyone we meet who speaks English, so I can be more cordial.

"Of course," Marco says when I ask if he remembers Dale from her prior visit. "She shipped many boxes to Chicago." He insists we leave our mop at the enoteca and carry only the items we need today.

"You'll get it when you come to town again," he says. I wonder how many other customers' items are waiting in his tiny office in back.

After walking down Cortona's steepest street to make reservations at *La Bucaccia*, we trudge back up and start home. It's surprisingly fast to do errands in a shopping area the size of one city block.

On the walk, Dale and I continue our chat about friendship. She tells me she read a study showing people confide in fewer friends now than in past generations.

"Why's that?" I ask.

"They didn't report the reason, only the trend. But I think we're unusual."

I thank her for our friendship, especially for supervising the movers so the buyers of our Chicago apartment could move in early. She assures me it was fun. We catch up on each other's children. David and Dale have two grown sons. Both are married and the older son has two children. I tell her about each of ours, some happier than others.

"Mothers are only as happy as their least happy child, right?" I repeat the old saying. "I worry about each one from time to time. I do feel very far away."

"You *are* far away," Dale says.

Finally, I confess what neither of us has said: I don't have one friend in Cortona other than Larry and things are not good between us.

"I could tell," she says. "I don't know how either of you live with constant chaos and workmen. It makes me crazy when I have to be home with the cable guy, and you have people around *every* day."

We descend the steepest part of the rocky trail, careful not to slip with our heavy bags.

At we turn into our driveway, Dale hesitates, and then says, "Are things okay with *you*? Your girlfriends in Chicago are worried."

I didn't expect such a direct question. Tears rim my eyes. I haven't admitted to anyone how sad and alone I feel, maybe not even to myself.

"No, I'm not okay," I whisper. I tell her I don't think Larry's happy, at least not happy with me. I admit that I'm on edge most the time making sure he's okay, and that he seems very easily irritated. It's not a good combination, I say. And I have no girlfriends, no way to get away from the house, and no one to tell. I'm afraid to drive and can't talk with most people, so I am way too dependent on him. Dale simply listens.

Then she says, "Vic, you need to stop trying to guess what Larry wants. Say what *you* want. You'll never be happy if you keep trying to make him happy. And, he won't be either. You don't need to please him all of the time. If you need a break, go back to Chicago for a while. He'll survive."

Saying what I want makes sense, but I can't imagine doing it. I tell her about the idea of calling a reset and that our interactions have improved with their visit, but I fear that, when they leave, I'll be tiptoeing around again, afraid to ask for his help or to do something wrong.

"Larry can take care of himself. You need to take care of yourself. He loves you, he married you... that independent girl with strong opinions. So *be* you."

It's a relief to have someone listen to me and provide honest, wise counsel. She's right, I've tried to fix our problems by pleasing Larry, but I've failed. Dale's advice is simple. I'm relieved that she doesn't think I'm just complaining. I feel understood. She cares about Larry too, so her comments seem balanced.

"In any relationship, friendship or in marriage, best just say what *you* want and need. Really, the rest will fall into place," she emphasizes.

At home, Dale and I can't wait to put up the clothesline before the boys get back from swimming. Funny, I feel softer-hearted toward Larry after admitting to Dale how unhappy I am.

Tying the last knot, Dale says, "Now your Tuscan home is perfect." We both stand back to admire our handiwork: a glistening white clothesline pulled taut between silvery olive trees.

Back in the kitchen, I mix a batch of granola for breakfast and put it in the oven. Dale and I sit with glasses of Campari, gazing across the valley, and continue our conversation. For the first time since we moved in, Lodolina transcends the rubble, equipment, and chaos. The situation doesn't matter.

What matters is that we're sharing life with friends who enrich, love and stretch us.

Soon the boys return, shower and join us. I have a second Campari, very unlike me.

At *Osteria La Bucaccia*, Romano remembers David and Dale and greets them like long lost friends. Dinner is superb, as always. After a shared dessert of apple *crostata*, we sip *Vin Santo* with sweet, tender, crisp and warm Agostina-made biscotti, then finish with *espressi* and, lastly, at Romano's insistence, tiny glasses of his grappa, smooth as liquid silk. When we pay the bill, David insists on adding a significant tip. Romano, who can't stand for a guest to be more generous than he is, sends us home with a bottle of wine.

My steps are light as we climb down the trail. At the rocky curve, Larry waits so I can walk with him the rest of the way, extending an arm for me to take. When I link my arm through his, his body feels strong and familiar.

I smile, reflecting on Dale's advice about simply saying what I want. I recall reading that Golda Meir, as Prime Minister of Israel, asked her directors to come to her with requests rather than complaints. It changes the dynamic from criticism to partnership.

I wonder if I will develop friendships in Cortona like mine with Dale — friends who won't always agree, but who will love and sharpen me.

A Thorough Inking

Today, Larry and I must go to Arezzo for the fingerprinting. David and Dale want to join us. Yesterday, without Francesco, we visited two ironworkers and ended our day in Sansepolcro to see paintings by Piero della Francesca, a master of the early Renaissance. Today our friends are eager to see his fresco cycle in the *Basilica di San Francesca* in Arezzo, perhaps della Francesca's most important work. So far, we haven't unpacked one box, but we've had fun.

Walking out the front door, I'm shocked to see our wild fig tree lying in the dirt. The workers must have cut it down to make it easier to build the front retaining wall. The trunk must be four inches across and the leafy branches are full of baby, unripe figs. I had watched the fruit form and was excited to make fig jam. I take photos to show Francesco and drag the tree into the olive grove where Pierangelo is on the *scavatore* creating tractor ramps.

I shake the tree at him. "*Necessario? Morire i fichi?*" Necessary? To die the figs? I don't know the word for kill.

Pierangelo looks stunned. He's probably never been confronted by an angry woman shaking a fig tree at him.

He answers gently, "*Non è necessario, ma non è morto.*" It is not necessary, but it is not dead. He looks genuinely sorry he upset me, but unconcerned about the tree.

"*Bene... grazie.*" Good, thanks, I say, my lips still tight. I turn sharply and drag the tree back to the house feeling mildly triumphant. But it's an empty victory. The tree is gone.

Larry's says he's really sorry, he knows how much I liked that fig tree and anticipated its fruit. I know I really must let it go and get on with our day, but I stew all the way to Arezzo.

At lunch in the old section of town, we sit outside and watch a number of seductively-dressed women pass by. They have low cut tops, bras meant to be seen, bare midriffs or plunging backs. Worse, their skirts don't cover much of their thighs. It's impossible not to stare and I wonder out loud if they really dress that way for work. Larry sheepishly admits the outfits look pretty good on some, but not all. He says there should be a law against women beyond a certain size or age wearing such clothing. I wonder if he considers me too large or too old.

"It should be illegal, period." Dale declares. She's a bit of a prude and the sexiness that strolled by in the last hour is beyond her tolerance.

While our friends take off to find the frescoes, we search for the finger-printer. The officer at the *Questura* points us toward "the other police station," as he calls it, several blocks away. His directions lead us to a row of unmarked, seemingly temporary buildings and we venture into the only open door. A man in a uniform looks up from his desk and asks if we need help.

Larry explains that we need to be fingerprinted and asks if this is the right place.

"*Avete foto?*" the officer asks, without saying yes or no. Do you have photos?

"We need photos?" I say in disbelief, in English.

The man nods and holds up four fingers.

Larry explains that we already have FBI fingerprints from the USA and many photos were in the package sent to Rome for our *Permesso*, which is surely enough. The man shakes his head. This is clearly non-negotiable.

I remember a booth at the train station, the type where teen girls make silly photos. So, we walk about a half-mile in the scorching sun to the station. When my photos pop out of the slot, I laugh out loud. Larry goes next. We both laugh. We look like criminals. The temperature is over a hundred degrees in the shade and hotter in the photo booth. I have no interest in going back in to try to get more flattering shots. At some point, vanity ends and sanity begins.

We hurry back to the police station, sweating at every step, enter the same open door and show the same officer our photos. He becomes friendlier and apologizes, blaming the new law on the political right. He says they've made it their cause to have all *stranieri*, foreigners, fingerprinted — with photos. He ushers us into a vault-like room with a monstrous camera. He takes another photo to put with the ones from the train station, evidently to prove the photos we gave him are truly us.

Then he squirts a glob of black ink on a big, smooth pad and runs a heavy roller back and forth. He finishes with a flourish, presses the sticky tool against Larry's right hand and slowly rolls it up and down every finger until they are thoroughly coated. Larry looks like he fell into tar, hands first. I sit on a chair against the wall, waiting, watching, and grinning.

The officer then guides each of Larry's fingers separately onto the form. He asks, "*Lavora?*" Do you work?

"*Consulente*," Larry replies.

"For a time, I work in the American Embassy," he says, now in English, trying to make a warmer connection. The officer must have thought Larry said he works in the Consulate rather than as a consultant.

Then he picks up Larry's clean left hand and traces the creases in his palm.

"You have a good life," he tells Larry.

He reads palms, too?

When Larry asks how he knows, the officer explains, "*Le sue mani sono morbidi.*" Your hands are soft.

After the officer takes Larry's fingerprints, he motions him to an adjacent room where he shows Larry how to wash the ink from his oh-so-soft hands using goop from a large tub. Then he disappears.

After several minutes, he comes back with two forms. Larry's ex-con photos are attached to the page with his fingerprints. The other form is for me.

The officer inks the fingers of my right hand, saying, "*Domani e molto importante per Lei.*" Tomorrow is very important for you, respectfully using *Lei*, the formal form of you.

I smile, realizing he read my data so knows tomorrow is my sixtieth birthday. "*Si, molto importante,*" I answer. Yes, very important. Am I really turning sixty? We chat a bit in my clumsy Italian and his okay English. He looks at my palm, but doesn't mention my lifeline. I wonder what he sees but doesn't want to say.

After inking my fingers and pressing each one onto the form, he leads me to the washing sink. I scoop a big glob of the gritty paste from the tub and work it into the ink. It smells like lye and feels like sand. It takes several washings to get the ink from between my fingers. Even then, a residue remains. My cuticles are hopeless. I'm not happy to have gray hands and black cuticles for my birthday, but I fear it's done now. He says we must personally carry our fingerprint documents back to the *Questura*.

The guard at the *Questura* door stops us. Larry explains that we were here two weeks ago to apply for our *permessi* and now we only need to turn in our fingerprints.

"We don't make the differences," the guard says. "We treat everyone equal. You must wait for your turn." He points to the line under the white plastic tent. I take a deep breath, thinking I cannot do this again.

At least fifty people are standing in the queue, slumped, overheated, and bored. The line moves slowly. It's difficult to breathe. We'll be terribly late to meet David and Dale. I hope they found Italian SIM cards by now and will call us, since we won't know their new number.

Immigrants, which includes us, are allowed inside the building six at a time. A little water and a light breeze would be welcome relief. Only those carrying their own water bottles have anything to drink. We didn't expect to need water.

After an hour, we're halfway to the door. It's almost four o'clock. Toward the front of the line, people stand jammed together as though it'll take less time if they get closer to the door. I'm drenched, parched and miserable.

Finally, we're allowed to go inside and stand in line another twenty minutes for the next open agent at window three. When it's our turn, Larry answers a few questions, gives the agent our fingerprints with photos, and confirms the data in their system. The agent checks everything carefully and nods, stamps the forms, and says we are finished. *Finished!* We are official Italian Residents, allowed to stay as long as we want? We must renew our *Permessi* in one year, she says. After the first year, we must renew it every two years.

We wait, expecting her to give us our official cards to prove our acceptance into Italy, but she tells us we must come back in two weeks to check our status.

"*Perché?!?!*" Why?!?! Larry asks, exasperated at the thought of another trip to Arezzo and hours under the tent.

She explains in slightly irritated, rapid-fire Italian that the fingerprints must be sent to Rome and only Rome can issue *Permessi*, and only if all documents, including fingerprints, are approved will they issue a card. It's the law. And with the law, whether we understand or not, we must comply.

We find David and Dale near the Basilica, our fail-safe location if they couldn't get a phone. They said they studied the Piero della Francesca cycle for over an hour, but never did find a store to buy a SIM card. Larry relays our fingerprinting drama. Dale gives me a tiny journal with a traditional paper cover decorated with interlaced flowers and peacocks.

"You can write your inking story in this," she says.

"Through the eyes of daily life, today was an ordeal," I say. "But though the eyes of a would-be author, it's a story!"

I try to press a faded fingerprint onto the first page, but the gray won't transfer.

Rejuvenated by coffees, water, and sitting in the shade, we decide to search for Giorgio Vasari's house, now a museum. Vasari, born in Arezzo, was an important Renaissance artist, author and architect. Among many famous works, he painted the dome interior in the *Duomo* in Florence and was the architect for Cortona's *Santa Maria Nuova*, the elegant Renaissance church outside the city walls. However, he's probably best known for his art history book, *Lives of the Most Eminent Painters, Sculptors and Architects*. His Arezzo home, like his book, seems overly dramatic, with Mannerist frescoes and a garden of fantasy topiary sculptures of *edera*, the same variety of ivy we plan to destroy at Lodolina.

When we stop at the phone store in Camucia on the way home, they have only two cheap mobile phones. David and Dale buy them both to use as vacation phones. I had hoped we'd buy an inexpensive phone for me, but Larry still argues that as long as we're always together, we only need one phone with one cellular plan. So far, it's been okay. We stop in Cortona to pick up the mop we left at Marco's Enoteca, buy a few more groceries, and head home to collapse.

At Lodolina, walking down the construction ramp, we're shocked to see the tall ivy hedge across the entire front lawn *gone*. What a difference! I was sad about losing the fig tree, but over-joyed at the removal of the hedge. The panorama is spectacular. But now there's nothing to protect us from the fifteen-foot drop-off. We need Luka's iron rail soon.

At the center of our concrete slab is a stack of building blocks with several old pottery shards on top, like a small display. Pierangelo must have found the pottery in the hedge and left it for us. It's speckled brown and beige, with turquoise splotches and finger-made scalloped edges. One larger piece looks like it was a pitcher. Though the workers always give us artifacts they discover, this lovely presentation feels like a peace offering for cutting down my fig tree.

David, Dale, and Larry relax on the terrace, while I go to the coat closet where we have our only phone to call my mother. I try to talk with her every Friday. There's an unfamiliar male voice on her answering machine. I hang up, dial again, and get the same automated recording. Perhaps she has a new telephone.

I reach Lara, my older daughter. She says her new relationship is going well, but she's not very chatty about this boyfriend or her job and I wonder why. She insists she'd rather talk about our Italian adventures than fall into the same conversation about how much she dislikes her job. Really, she says, she's great, but I think she says that not to worry me. I feel far away. I miss our almost-daily conversations when we lived in the same city, sharing in real time what was going on in each other's lives.

Following warm showers and more hand-scrubs, we decide to walk up the hill for dinner at the new restaurant near the swimming pool. David wants to attend a contemporary music concert at the new amphitheater. The rest of us will listen from the restaurant courtyard and decide whether or not to join him. Discordant music is David's favorite, but not ours.

We can hear musicians warming up as we climb. At the restaurant, however, the cicadas in the linden trees drown out any sounds from the nearby amphitheater. Larry, Dale, and I were hoping to judge if we should risk the concert. We agree to enjoy a leisurely dinner and join David after we finish, hoping for the best.

David devours his beefsteak *tagliata* and hurries to the amphitheater. Following delicious pasta, Larry and I both order *lampredotto* as our main course, thinking it'll be rabbit because *lampre* sounds like the word for hare, *lepre*. When the beige lumpy mass arrives, we say it isn't ours. The waiter takes it away. In a few minutes he brings the same plates back, saying shyly, "*Questa è lampredotto.*" This is *lampredotto*.

I push it around on my plate. I'm sure it's excellent *lampredotto*, but after one hesitant bite, I have no desire for a second. Thankfully, our first courses were filling and we take time for dessert, further postponing the concert. (Later I learn *lampredotto* is a traditional dish made from the fourth stomach of a cow, cooked slowly to make a thick and saucy stew, and is a local delicacy.)

David is spellbound when we join him. Though the concert is discordant beyond my comfort, the pianist is exceptional. He plays a bluesy baseline overlaid with ragtime riffs. At one point, he gets up, leans over the side of his piano and plucks the strings like a bass. Toward the end, he plays a complicated composition with both hands and his elbow. Obviously, a master. I am inspired anew to play my piano — but only after our friends are back in Chicago.

At midnight, making our way down the path with our flashlights, David and Dale suddenly belt out, "Happy Birthday to you…." Larry joins in. Moved by their expression of love, my eyes fill with happy tears.

At home, the four of us sit on the concrete slab and watch shooting stars, making out-loud wishes. Dale's is for happiness and courage for me in my new Italian life. Larry thinks she means courage to speak Italian and drive; I know she means much, much more. A really good friend knows and keeps your secrets.

Celebrating Sixty

The rooster is singing with special gusto, as though just for me. He must know today is my birthday and that I enjoy his morning summons. A squeal comes from the stream, perhaps a boar piglet. Larry is still sleeping. He usually has been up hours by now. He looks peaceful and gentle, like a little boy.

I can't wait to tell him that I had my first dream in Italian. I don't remember a thing about it except that I was speaking Italian… then someone else was speaking Italian. My sub-conscious must know more Italian than I think. Our Chicago Italian teacher, Giulia, had said, "You'll start having dreams in Italian." I wished for one then, but had forgotten her promise until today. What sweet timing.

Larry turns toward me, smiles with eyes still closed and murmurs, "Happy birthday, darling. Would my lovely wife like a cappuccino in bed?"

"If you don't mind, I'll have my coffee downstairs with you. I really want to record our finger printing and my dream before David and Dale get up." He reaches over, gently kisses my shoulder and tells me he's glad I was born.

We linger a few moments, fingers intertwined, then I get up and shoo him out so I can strip the bed. Today is Rita's second week and I want to start my new decade with clean sheets and ironed pillow cases.

With the bundle of sheets in my arms, I tiptoe through the room where our friends are sleeping. The construction dust on the stairs is so thick that my bare feet leave footprints on the wood.

"You have voice messages," Larry says as I reach the bottom. "I'll help you retrieve them whenever you want… if you need help. And, here's a birthday cappuccino."

"My messages can wait," I whisper. "I have something I want to write about first. I had my first dream in Italian."

Larry grins, sharing my pleasure over such a small but significant milestone.

"And, this is the best cappuccino you've made since we got that machine," I raise my cup appreciatively. Truly, he's made hundreds of *cappuccini* in our two decades together; few have tasted more satisfying.

"David and Dale will be pleased you've mastered the Pavoni. You should teach me, but not now," I say, opening my laptop.

I record a few quick details about yesterday's fingerprinting, last night's *lampredotto*, and my dream. I have three voice messages and over twenty emails, many for my birthday. It's such joy to have internet that I don't mind the ads.

When David and Dale come downstairs, Larry makes *cappuccini* for them. I put fruit, homemade granola and yogurt out for a help-yourself breakfast. With bowls in our laps, Dale and I sit in the wicker chairs on the front slab and chat about our hopes for the coming year. Our conversation turns to faith, a rather serious subject for early morning. I'm intrigued by her thoughts about tradition versus religion. I can hear our husbands, still standing in the kitchen, discussing God and evil. Neither of them doubts evil exists, but they have different perspectives on what can be done about it and God's role in allowing it. The boys seem oddly happy discussing evil.

Back inside, I'm greeted by a huge arrangement of fresh sunflowers on the dining room table with golden petals around black faces laced with branches of blackberries. The note expresses birthday wishes from Francesco and Rita. What a sweet surprise!

Three cabinet-makers arrive before eight o'clock to install Larry's bookshelves in the upstairs sitting room. Of course, installing bookshelves means we must move the sectional, now guest beds, and all of their belongings and the boxes.

Inside the guesthouse, plasterers are completing the walls so doors and windows can be installed next week. I want the upstairs guest room to be sky blue, because it looks out directly into the enormous horse chestnut tree and feels like a tree house. The painter brings a stick with the plaster on it to show me. I'm still in my silk robe with my hair disheveled, but the workers never act like they notice.

"Larry," I ask, "can you answer worker's questions while I get dressed?"

"Since it's your birthday, of course," he says, without a hint of irritation, "but *you* need to approve the *grassello* color. I can't do that for you." I go out to the guesthouse and ask Alessandro to make the blue a little deeper. He adds some color, dips a stick in the plaster and dries it with a hairdryer. It's perfect.

In front of the house, Pierangelo and two helpers are stabilizing a long, ancient stone wall that holds up the entire front yard. They believe the wall is at least five hundred years old. With all the construction it has started to bulge.

I hear Francesco's voice. As he enters, I do an embarrassed curtsey in my robe and thank him for the beautiful flowers. I say his message is much too gracious, even for a milestone birthday. He seems very pleased.

After a shower, I toss on clothes and hurry out to look at the bookshelves. They're beautiful, but don't fit against the irregular wall. I mention the problem to Francesco.

"Of course. Must be trimmed across the back so fit perfectly the stomach of the old wall," he reassures me. I love his characterization of the curve in the wall as a stomach. With these ancient farmhouses, they must run into this constantly.

In the *cucina*, kitchen, Francesco and I fix the exact placement over the island for three pendant lights. They'll be off center for the island, but centered in the room. Since the room is not an exact rectangle, it takes some adjusting to make them float visually and feel balanced in the space.

From the kitchen door, I look out at the front yard and am amazed at the progress this morning. Luciano is using the cut-off fig tree to brace the new low wall. Pierangelo is driving the yellow *scavatore* with three huge concrete cubes hanging from the crane. They'll be placed below the new wall, out of sight — one for electricity, one for water, and one provisional for an air conditioner, in case we decide we need it.

Pierangelo assures me again that the fig tree will grow back. Luciano says it will grow taller than Pierangelo in one year. I smile, but don't believe them.

Francesco says he needs a decision regarding the height of the iron rail so Luka can finish it before our granddaughters arrive. I tell him we want to maintain the view, so would like a rail all the way across the front yard without a wall under it. He nods, then sits in one of the wicker chairs and starts to draw.

Suddenly, a song wafts from our upstairs window: *Give me your world, I'll give you heaven.... If we just believe, the best is yet to come.*

That song became "our song" twenty years ago, on my fortieth birthday. Larry is such a romantic!

Larry calls me to the sitting room. The cabinetmakers want us to approve the placement of the bookcase before they trim the back. He wants me to make the final decision, though it's his bookcase. I agree it looks perfect.

Dale and I grab two loads of wet laundry and run up the hill, giggling like girls. We hang white bed sheets and brightly colored beach towels. Tangerine, peach, sunflower, turquoise, marine and pearl white rectangles float in the breeze like rows of sailboats off the isle of Capri. Larry comes up the hill to take photos.

I reach for his hand as we walk back. "Darling, did you decide to play our song just this morning, or have you been planning it to surprise me?"

Larry grins in my favorite chin-dimpled way, happy he has pleased me, and shrugs his shoulders without answering.

When we get back to the house, David is exercising in the sun, stripped to the waist and wearing only workout shorts and gym shoes. Since we don't have weights, he's lifting a concrete *passetto* lid. I take photos to prove he's nuts.

Ceremoniously, kitchen lights are turned on. Long cones of frosted hand-blown glass hang on thin, almost invisible wires. They look level but not straight; I adjust each one meticulously. The electrician paces. Now is the moment to make sure all is perfect or forever stay silent. I take my time.

These pendants seem intensely bright, perhaps because I've been working with one bare bulb for a fairly large room. Funny, how we become used to something, even if it's not ideal, and even a good change can seem wrong.

Every day adds a new dimension to our home. With David and Dale's help, I hope we'll find the perfect the piano placement and un-roll our antique Persian rug. That would be one room finished — except for art, accessories, and all those wardrobe boxes.

Mid-morning, we invite the workers to join us for a spontaneous birthday *pranzo*, lunch. Larry offers to go to town to pick up *panini*, if what's in our fridge is not enough. But everyone has plans, even Francesco. So, for only the four of us, Dale and I arrange platters of sliced meats and marinated vegetables, and make a grand caprese salad. For dessert, there are cheeses, melon and fresh figs from the market. Dale and I sip white wine spritzers to make our celebration more festive. The boys abstain, saying they'll wait for dinner. There's not enough room on the table for Francesco's sunflower arrangement, but I insist it stays and we set some of the food aside.

We say grace, thanking God for our children and grandchildren, the important moments of this week, Francesco and our workers, and our friendship. With deep gratitude, we toast our Maker. "The Best is Yet to Come" plays again and again. My heart's filled to bursting. I want no other song and no other life.

The *muratori*, stonemasons, are back before we finish lunch. Temperatures have climbed even higher. Dale wonders how they can lift the hot stones. They labor without talking. Dale and I feel embarrassed to sit in the shade and watch, but we do, fascinated as a perfect low stone wall rises under the cypress trees and looks as though it has been there always.

Larry drives to town to pick up Rita, another birthday gift. She tells us it's forty-four degrees in Camucia, one hundred ten degrees Fahrenheit. I make my cleaning requests in Italian, like I practiced. The construction and heat must make cleaning miserable for her, and my Italian may confuse more than communicate, but, on my birthday, I don't want to do housework.

I ask her to clean all three bathrooms, showing her the hidden powder room that I don't think she noticed last week. "*Normale*" she says to all my requests. But when she takes the supplies, she leaves the toilet brush and bucket in the laundry room. How will she give three toilets a good scrubbing without a brush or wash floors without a bucket? Perhaps she'll do it later. In Italian homes, there's a brush beside each toilet for personal use, but ours have not arrived. She must think us quite uncivilized.

Larry and Dale unpack boxes while Rita cleans and David handles phone calls regarding an unexpected situation in his office. They refuse to let me help, insisting that on my birthday I spend my time writing my stories. My fun is interrupted when the electrician wants to place bathroom pendants. But it's worth it to finally have light to apply makeup — just in time for my birthday dinner.

Rita works hard, but the grime is relentless. After she washes the stairs, they still look dirty. When I show her that a paper towel gets brown when I wipe it on a stair, she says slowly and loudly "*Pro-doo-to per eel leen-yo.*" She needs a special product for wood. I have heard that Italian women have a different product for every surface, but I have cleaned the stairs daily with a slightly damp cloth, so know that works. Looking into her bucket, I suspect the culprit is dirty mop water, but I nod and assure her I'll buy *prodotto per il legno* for next week.

I'm surprised when Rita announces she's finished after only three hours. I expected at least five. I do a quick check and find the windowsill in the kitchen covered with tiny pieces of grit. I point to it and think Rita says she can't clean it now because the floor has been cleaned. Surely, I misunderstood. I pull the vacuum out of the closet and point to the windowsill. She looks at me quizzically. I plug it in. She vacuums the windowsill and sets the vacuum in the corner. She's trying to be respectful, but doesn't seem to approve of my methods. Larry kindly takes Rita back to her bus while I dress for dinner.

I cannot find my white hand towel in our bathroom and discover it damp, dirty, and in the clothes hamper. Rita must have used it to dry something. Next week I'll set aside time to work with her. I like her and want her to work out, so I must interact with her, practicing what I want to say in Italian before she arrives.

All dressed up, we drive to Montefollonico, about an hour away. At *Ristorante La Chiusa,* we walk between beds of lavender, herbs and hydrangea to a terrace overlooking the *Val D'Orcia,* a different valley than the one we see from Cortona. A waiter greets us with frosty flutes and a bottle of chilled, sparkling Prosecco.

From the terrace, we gaze across rolling Tuscan hills, many with vineyards, toward Montelpulciano. The golden evening sun washes across the blond travertine of the *Chiesa di San Biagio,* my favorite church in Tuscany. Designed by Antonio da Sangallo the Elder, it was built starting in 1516, about the same time as *Il Palazzone,* the palace with the tower near Lodolina.

In another direction is the planned Renaissance town of Pienza. Today a UNESCO World Heritage site, this pristine hilltown with flower boxes in every window looks to me like a movie set, a little too perfect.

Dania, *La Chiusa's* owner, comes outside to greet us. She lifts her apron over her head as though she's in her own dressing room and drapes it over a chair. She's wearing a black and white flouncy skirt, sheer white blouse with a black and white polka-dot bra meant to be seen, and wild strappy shoes. On her, it all looks elegant.

In Italian, she welcomes us back to *La Chiusa.* I try to say in Italian that we first came eight years ago and have been back three times. Larry adds that a year ago we spent the weekend in one of their private rooms. We loved our grand bathroom, I note, big enough for a tub for two, a sofa and a fireplace.

Our table is ready, Dania suggests a shortcut through the kitchen, but warns it is uncomfortable with this hot weather and an open grill.

Then, flashing a smile and paraphrasing the American saying in flawless English, she says "So… if you can stand the heat, we will go this way."

She ushers us to our table, though I wanted to linger in the kitchen. *La Chiusa's* dining room is large and open, divided into cozy seating areas by antique credenzas topped with huge wildflower bouquets. Dania seats us in a private niche in front of a fireplace now filled with summer flowers.

A tiny, elderly woman adorned with perfectly coiffed hair and luminous pearls brings us bread. From prior visits, we know she also makes the tableside pasta. On our last visit, at the next table she rolled *pici,* and I decided to order it next time. Sadly, tableside pasta isn't on the menu tonight. I watch this birdlike woman gliding through the restaurant re-arranging items and delivering bread. We've also seen her carry huge trays stacked with dirty dishes, so she's strong. We guess she is Dania's mother.

Larry gives a loving toast to my birth and life, and to our marriage. It's an evening of rich food, richer wine, and richer-yet emotions.

Before dessert, I pull a card and beautifully wrapped package out of my handbag, and say "Oh, look! Someone gave me a gift."

Everyone chuckles, knowing it's the gift Dale sent before they decided to visit. I had saved it to open on my actual birthday.

"I have to confess," I say. "I peeked when it arrived. But I closed it immediately, so this is like opening it for the first time."

The pen, handcrafted walnut with turquoise inlay, is stunning. I then pull out the tiny journal Dale gave me yesterday in Arezzo and announce that I've saved both to start on this day. I ask everyone to sign my new journal with my birthday pen.

What a perfect way to enter a new decade! For a second time today, I feel like the best is *not* yet to come, the best is now.

Seaside Emergency

Awakening to another blazing day, I'm relieved the stomach pain that bothered me during the night is gone and I feel rested and honored beyond my wildest dreams by emails, calls, notes, cards and last night's birthday dinner. Today we'll drive to Pisa to see the Leaning Tower and then on to the seaside for a weekend with Lorenzo and his wife, Kaoruko, our young Florentine friends.

The ride is long. I doze, grateful for cool air. Skirting Florence, I feel queasy, more than normal for a straight, flat highway, and a hard bubble is pressing under my ribcage. Entering Pisa an hour later, everyone wants to stop for lunch since we left without breakfast. Perhaps I'll feel better with food.

We spend thirty minutes searching for a restaurant Larry and I enjoyed a few years ago. When we find it, though our Red Guide says it's open, it's closed. In need of lunch, water and a bathroom, we settle for the best-looking of the touristy places just outside the Leaning Tower wall.

One table is available in the *giardino*, the hostess says. We soon learn their garden is a small graveled area surrounded by pots of scraggly oleander on three sides and, on the fourth, a row of garbage bins. There's no shade and the tables are shiny aluminum, radiating heat. Beyond the oleander, I can see a row of kiosks offering a variety of Leaning Towers, snow-globes, tee-shirts, and aprons flaunting the private parts of Michelangelo's David. Tourists gather under their awnings, probably more for shade than for souvenirs. I watch one woman purchase a white lace parasol while we wait for menus.

Heat rises from the table. My stomach pain intensifies. The waitress brings *aqua frizzante*. I drink a huge glass, which seems to force the bubble up under my breastbone. It's the same pain I had during the night, only more severe. I breathe slowly, willing myself to relax.

David, ever the doctor, looks at me and says, "You okay?"

I hear myself say, "No." Normally, I'd insist I'm okay, not to ruin everyone's good time. But I feel disconnected and worried. I press my fingers into my sternum to show him where it hurts, adding that I feel far away.

The waitress, hovering nearby, insists we go inside for the air conditioning. We change tables. It's better. Our food arrives. My salad of lettuce, corn, black olives and mozzarella doesn't tempt me.

David asks diagnostic questions about the location and sensation of pain, the time and duration of symptoms, and personal queries about bodily functions. This isn't a nice lunch conversation, but I'm grateful for his expertise and modesty seems irrelevant. He's been our primary physician for two decades, is the best diagnostician I know and an excellent listener, to say nothing of being a dear friend. His questions are comforting.

He asks the waitress for directions to the closest pharmacy. "Be right back," he says, patting my hand.

I put my head on the cool formica table.

Dale turns to the waitress who has barely left our side. "Vanilla ice cream. Can you bring her some vanilla ice cream? David always tells me to eat vanilla ice cream when I feel nauseous."

It arrives almost instantly. I take small bites. Larry asks if he can do anything to help, but I shake my head.

By the time David returns, I feel better. He plops a tablet into a glass of water. It fizzes, making a disgusting pink liquid with a thin whitish scum. I drink it and within seconds the pain disappears. David says I surely have an ulcer or reflux, and might need an endoscopy to be sure.

Over lunch we discuss ulcers and reflux. His instruction of absolutely no alcohol doesn't thrill me since we live in Tuscany, home of Brunello and Chianti.

When I ask what causes ulcers, thinking our Italian experiment has gotten the best of me, David explains the cause is bacteria, not stress.

I eat a few bites of my salad, hoping mozzarella is as soothing as ice cream.

After lunch, all feeling revived, we enter the Leaning Tower campus through a towering stone wall and look up, stunned by the scenic panorama. Rising from manicured emerald lawns are intricately carved, glacier-white marble structures illuminated by brilliant sunlight, shimmering against a cloudless cobalt sky. It is more perfect than any postcard.

Thousands of tourists lazily meander in the *Piazza dei Miracoli,* Piazza of Miracles. Predictably, hundreds hold up the Leaning Tower while their friends snap photos. Hoping for relief from the sun, we go into the nearly empty baptistery. It feels like a furnace. Within minutes, we're all gasping for air and dripping wet, so head back outside.

"Perhaps there's a breeze," Larry teases as we leave.

Not a whiff. Nor any shade.

The line for the Leaning Tower stretches so far that Larry and David abandon their intention of climbing to the top. The tower took two hundred years to build, opened in 1350, and started leaning immediately because the underlying sand and clay subsoil on the north side is softer than on the south. Over six hundred years later, in 1990, it was closed because experts predicted it would soon collapse. The tower was stabilized and reopened in 2001. Today, every tilted, spiraling level is packed with tourists.

After a visit to the cathedral, also an oven, my armpits begin to itch. I want to scratch them, but refrain in such a public place.

At a small museum in the back, Dale and I sit on a step to wait while David and Larry study frescoes. It was too claustrophobic inside for me. The itchiness is intensifying. I'm relieved when our boys come out. We wander onto the lawn and wonder why we're the only ones enjoying the lush, cool grass. Then we see the sign: "Please don't walk on the grass" and immediately step back onto the heat-radiating gravel walkway.

I feel intolerably itchy and need a toilet. Alone, I hurry back to the bathroom at the restaurant. There, in privacy, I lift my shirt and lower my panties to look at my skin. My underarms are rosy, as is the soft skin on my inner thighs, but nothing looks as bad as it feels. Larry, Dale and David are waiting when I come out, ready to walk to the car. I don't mention the itching.

Larry lurches backward when he opens the car door.

"What's wrong," I ask.

"We forgot the garbage!" he gasps.

Sure enough, smelly refuse has been putrefying in the blistering hatchback. We open all the doors and stand outside the car, reluctant to enter. Dale points to an open bin at the end of the block. We hold our breaths, get in, roll down the windows, drive by the bin, and David tosses in three reeking bags as we pass.

Larry cranks the air conditioner on high and soon turns south onto the coastal highway toward Quercianella. I doze and wake, itchy and queasy. He exits. I can't wait to get out of this car, inhale fresh ocean air and stand on solid ground.

Quercianella is a quaint seaside village where residents of Florence and Pisa escape their cities during tourist season. Like most beach towns, white cottages are surrounded by white wood fences, palms and pines, and hot-pink geraniums tumble from pots hanging on fence posts along the sandy road — a scene that must inspire every seaside painter who visits.

We easily find our hotel. At the end of the long driveway, a lanky young man in a tee shirt and baggy calf-length shorts is pushing a baby stroller. Before we can get out of the car, Lorenzo is running toward us, stroller bouncing wildly.

His glee demonstrates part of what I so admire about our young friend: his unfettered expressiveness. We met three years ago when he was our art guide in Florence. He speaks multiple languages, was educated at the Sorbonne, teaches French literature, and is a Dante and Italian art history scholar. Yet here he is, overjoyed at the sight of us.

He hugs me as though he has waited months to see me. Larry gets a big bear hug, the kind reserved for family. Lorenzo bows gallantly when we introduce Dale, then greets David with a firm handshake. Finally, we meet his six-month old daughter, Letizia Maia, named for his mother who passed away just before we met.

The once-sumptuous hotel lobby is dark, overcrowded with garnet damask furniture and worn Persian rugs. Upstairs, Larry opens the French doors in our room and we walk out onto our terrace. Fifty yards off shore, waves crash against gigantic rocks, shooting white sea spray into the heavens. Beyond, as far as I can see, the azure Mediterranean glistens. After quickly unpacking, we all join Lorenzo for a seaside walk.

Chatting and catching up, we stroll along a long narrow walkway beside a cliff. I feel insects biting me, but don't want to ruin our walk so don't mention it. I feel bumps rising on the inside of my upper arms.

Sunbathers lounge on boulders in the shallow water; some have umbrellas with handles stuck between the rocks. Beyond, small fishing boats bob in the waves and snorkelers paddle in lazy circles.

We turn inland and climb uphill toward Lorenzo's apartment.

"I'm getting bitten. Anyone else?" I finally say.

Everyone shakes their head except Lorenzo who exclaims, "They love Letizia!"

He checks inside the stroller and says she seems fine.

Lorenzo bought the apartment years ago so his mother could spend her last months by the sea. He turns on an overhead air conditioner. I'm sure it's expensive to run and they're a young family with a baby, so I suggest we don't need it. When he insists, I stand directly under the cool air, more thankful than I want to admit. David and Lorenzo decide to play tennis in the sun. Convinced they are insane, Larry, Dale and I head back to the hotel.

Heat rises from the asphalt road. Armpits itching worse than ever, it's all I can do to keep my hands at my sides. Back in our room, I look under my shirt and am not surprised to see welts like pink nickels. I show Larry.

"Don't those itch?" he asks.

"Like crazy."

I take a tepid shower, but it brings little comfort.

After applying cortisone cream, which I always carry for mosquito bites, I lie on the bed, praying for relief. A wedding party is being set up below.

I cannot nap, so pace. When I hear David return, I show him my welts and rash. Again, he asks questions. Did I change detergents? Am I taking new medications?

"Could the rash be connected to the stomach pain?" I ask.

"Perhaps, but probably not," he says. "More likely, both are related to the heat."

I change for dinner, choosing loose white linen with as little touching my skin as possible. Makeup melts as fast as I apply it, so I give it up.

We stroll along the wharf to a fish restaurant where Lorenzo and family are waiting. Grabbing the bug spray on the entrance desk, I douse my itching feet and ankles.

Delicious seafood and warm conversation distract me, making the rash more tolerable. Letizia sleeps peacefully. When we leave hours later, the staff is cleaning the floors and turning the chairs upside down on the tables.

Back at the hotel, the wedding is in full swing, but it's too hot to close our terrace doors. I lie on top of the sheets. The itching has become unbearable and I can't sleep. It's after midnight. The wedding noise has become unbearable, too.

About one o'clock, as the party winds down, I sense that my face and tongue are swelling. I get up to look in the bathroom mirror. Both eyes are nearly closed and red welts cover my neck, torso and upper arms. I lie down again. No nightgown. No covers. Not even a sheet. I want nothing touching my skin. I feel dizzy. The walls seem to close in. I sit up to steady myself. I need to go to the bathroom again. As I find my way across the room, I stumble, forgetting there is a step up.

I also miss the step coming back and fall against the dresser. Frightened and dizzier, I crawl across the floor back to the bed. I take deep, slow breaths. It's hard to swallow. Larry is sleeping.

I feel shaky and start to cry. I stand, taking my time to get to the bathroom to drink some water, put on more cortisone, and walk back to bed running my hands along the walls and sliding my feet to find the step. The edge of my vision seems blurred. I blink, but it doesn't clear.

"Larry, Larry…" I whisper, shaking him. He opens his eyes, confused.

"I may need to go to the hospital… My tongue feels swollen and my throat is closing in. Everything's dark and I feel far away. Please ask David for help."

He tries to hold me to stop my trembling, but I motion for him to go. While he hurries across the hall, I put on my shirt and skirt, with panties but no bra. The tender skin of my torso, thighs and arms are bright rose with welts and rash. I lean against the doorway. David looks at my eyes, then the rash, and agrees we should go to the hospital, insisting they come along.

Larry hurries to the front desk to get directions to the closest hospital. I hear the woman who checked us in speaking to Larry while David and Dale help me down the stairs. The woman sounds distant. I try to stay alert.

The woman has drawn a map to the hospital and written questions the doctor may ask in both Italian and English. She tells Larry everything is well marked once we get out of Quercianella and says her daughters are waiting in their car to lead us to the *autostrada*.

Larry follows the daughters out of town and then speeds along the nearly empty *autostrada* connecting seaside villages. I watch signs pass overhead. It seems like a long trip. Larry finally slows and exits. At the first roundabout, he puts his hand on mine to reassure me, "We're almost there."

He follows the *pronto soccorso* signs, thinking it must mean emergency since *pronto* means ready. David says he's surprised the hospital is so modern. Larry drops us at the entrance and goes to park.

We walk into a large room filled with rows of dark green plastic chairs. A man and woman are slouched in the back as though they have been here all night. The reception window is closed. Near the window are two boxes containing paper strips with instructions in Italian. Larry, now with us, fills them out for me and slips them under the window.

After a couple of minutes, a male nurse comes to the door and asks, "*Che problema?*" What's the problem?

I walk to the door and show him my rash. David, by my side, says in careful English and some Italian that the rash is one problem, but they should check my heart before giving me any medication, because in the past twenty-four hours I have experienced gastric distress and chest pain, and I now feel my throat is closing in.

The nurse nods, holds up a finger to indicate we should wait, disappears, and comes back with a white metal gurney covered with a dark turquoise sheet. I lie on my back on top of the sheet and hope David is allowed to come with me. The nurse wheels me into a room nearby. David comes in without asking. Larry and Dale wait in the plastic chairs.

David explains my symptoms to the doctor. Their conversation is mostly medical terms. I feel woozy, disconnected and thankful for my friend.

The male nurse pushes my gurney into another room with painfully bright overhead lights, pulls a blue curtain around the gurney, and leaves. The doctor enters and, in halting English, asks me to tell him what happened and how I feel. I wonder where David is.

Lying flat, I start as David did, trying to speak in Italian, "*Ieri mattina,*" yesterday morning. Using mostly hand gestures, I repeat my symptoms. I show him the welts and rash. I point to my puffy eyes and lips, stick out my thickened tongue, and put both hands around my throat to demonstrate a choking sensation.

Both the doctor and male nurse are kind and concerned. The nurse sprays my wrists and ankles with something cold and positions metal clamps, then tucks something under each clamp. He unbuttons my shirt. It falls open exposing the pink, lumpy rash on my chest. He affixes suction cups attached to long tubes. I think they must be taking an electrocardiogram. They seem professional and calm. I wish I spoke better Italian or they spoke better English.

Soon, the nurse removes the appliances and gently buttons my shirt. He hangs a bag of cloudy solution on a metal stand on wheels. He places a long needle in the largest vein in my right wrist and tapes it in place.

I drift off as the fluid flows into my veins.

David is in the room when I awaken. I try to tell him that I think they did an EKG and have started a drip, but I don't know what it is. He says he informed the doctor that he is also a doctor, a nephrologist, so they will explain everything to him and he'll explain to me. The doctor shows David my EKG and tells him the name of the drip.

David puts his hand on my shoulder and says, "Your heart is perfect. The drip is for the rash."

They tell David they think I have reflux and should have the test he suggested earlier, and that I'm dehydrated and reacted to the heat.

Then the nurse wheels me through a narrow corridor, stops in a wide area with intense overhead lights, pulls the curtain around the gurney, and leaves me with the drip. I doze, then wake. I wish someone would turn off the lights. My stomach hurts again, but there's no one to tell. I lean on one elbow to relieve the pressure because lying flat makes it worse. The bag is empty. I sit up, hang my feet over the edge of the gurney and put my head in my lap. I try to lie down but the pain is worse, so stay propped on both elbows. I wonder if they have forgotten me.

A different nurse sees me resting on my elbows and asks in hand gestures if I want the head raised on the gurney. I nod. I wonder what time it is. I feel guilty that I've kept Dale, David and Larry sitting in the waiting room for so long, especially in the middle of the night. I wish the doctor would come back.

The male nurse wheels my gurney to an office where the doctor is sitting at a metal desk. He pats a low metal stool beside him. I get off, feel dizzy and hold onto the edge of the gurney for a moment before I sit. The doctor fills out forms. I wait. He explains in simple English that I should get antihistamine and reflux pills, drink plenty of water, and get a test if the stomach pain returns. I don't tell him it hurts now for fear they'll keep me. He pushes some papers toward me, saying to take them to a *farmacia*, pharmacy, *subito*, right away.

The doctor then motions for the male nurse to give me the *iniezione*. I see it on a side table. The needle is huge. The nurse indicates the shot will be in my buttock. He motions for me to stand, hold the desk with one hand and pull up my skirt with the other. I can feel my whole body tense up.

He pulls down the top edge of my panties, shakes his head and says in a low voice to the doctor, "*Molto rosso.*" Very red. The injection hurts. I grip the desk. He gently rubs my back, indicating it's done, and points to the stool. I sit down and smooth my skirt over my knees.

The doctor asks if my home is in Cortona. I say "*Sì.*"

He says I can go.

"*Adesso?*" Now, I ask? It seems sudden. He nods and smiles.

"*Il conto?*" I ask. The bill? I can't imagine it's okay to leave without paying.

They look at each other, this time with little smirks. The doctor says the hospital will send the *conto* by post. I am confused and raise my eyebrows.

The doctor says, "*Residente, giusto*? Resident, correct?

"*Sì,*" I nod.

He explains in English that I should go home and sleep without worry about the bill. He shakes my hand. I turn and shake the hand of the kind male nurse.

David, Dale and Larry greet me with long hugs. They look tired. Larry keeps his arm around me. I'm glad for his steadiness and the affection. Dale wants details. I tell them I had an EKG, a drip bag, a shot, and no bill.

David wants to see the papers. He tells them my blood work shows normal hemoglobin, which means no internal bleeding from ulcers, and normal saline, but slightly low potassium. Nothing alarming. David says the drip was a steroid and the shot was an antihistamine, both for the rash. We walk out into blinding daylight.

"What time is it?" I ask.

"Five-thirty," Larry replies without looking at his watch. I suspect they have watched the clock all night. I feel guilty and grateful.

In the daylight we see the large hospital complex. We drive back to the hotel faster than we drove to the hospital — perhaps my perception of time shifted — and agree to sleep as long as we can. Dale gives me six rose pills from her travel kit. David explains they are for reflux and I should take one now, before I go to sleep. The whole episode feels like a movie.

* * *

When I wake up, Larry is sitting in a chair by the open terrace doors, reading. The sun is bright and high.

"How do you feel, sweetheart?" he asks when he hears me stir.

"Okay, I think... better. I'm hungry."

"That's a good sign."

"What time is it?"

"About ten. David and Dale are downstairs at breakfast. I didn't want to leave you."

I shower and dress, skip makeup, and go with Larry to the terrace below. David asks how I feel and wants to see my rash. My skin is still rosy, but without welts. My stomach pain is gone. He says my eyes and lips are still puffy.

"Don't forget the reflux pills. You must take the full course," David says and repeats his instructions about a test if the pills don't work. And he reminds me that I must drink lots of water, no wine, and start taking an antihistamine right away.

"I promise. I never want to feel like that again."

The buffet of sliced meats, cheeses, breads and pastries looks tempting, but I need something easier to swallow. I ask for scrambled eggs. Everyone agrees that scrambled eggs would be perfect for them, too. David asks for a fruit plate.

A large tray arrives overflowing with artfully arranged fresh fruit, enough for all of us, followed by generous plates of steaming, soft and creamy scrambled eggs.

"I'm so sorry about all this," I say to our friends. "Did you sleep at all?"

Before they answer, since I know they couldn't have slept long, I add, "I'm *so* grateful you were here. Thank you."

"We're glad we could help. Larry's been very worried about you," Dale says.

Everyone insists they slept enough, except Dale who reminds me she never sleeps. I savor bite after bite of warm, soothing, nourishing eggs. Last night's events seem long ago.

I feel guilty that I caused everyone to lose a night's sleep and that we're getting such a late start today, but mostly I feel loved and grateful. I sense our friends are not concerned about their sleep or inconvenience, only about my well-being and are happy to help. It can be a gift to others to simply accept their gift of help, but so often we're reluctant to do so, wanting to be able to do everything ourselves or not wanting to impose. Last night I had no choice.

As we leave Quercianella, Larry pulls into a *farmacia* near the autostrada, but it's closed.

Zooming past Piombino, another seaside village Lorenzo said is particularly lovely, we pass fields of withering sunflowers. Their gold petals are twisted and translucent, as though fried in hot oil. Remembering last night, I wonder if sun-parched sunflowers experience a sense of panic.

Pink, red and white oleander fill the median until the road narrows to two lanes. Near a camping area, both sides are littered with trash. Through tall pine trees, like those I remember in Georgia, the Mediterranean ripples as if shattered glass and the tree tops create an exotic canopy of black lace.

I doze on and off, likely from residual drugs. The others decide we should go home, rather than explore seaside villages as we had planned.

Driving inland, we watch the skies darken. Lightning flashes. Before long, we drive into sheets of rain. I hope it's not this intense for long. With parched land, the run-off could damage crops, hillsides, stone walls, even roads. It feels dangerous.

The highway mysteriously ends with big barricades. In the deluge, we follow signs saying "*Raccastrada*," detour we guess. Larry turns onto a tiny asphalt road. The GPS insists we "return to the route." She's finally mute when the road becomes gravel. Eventually, it becomes blacktop again, a temporary sign says to turn right, and the GPS relocates us.

Ambulances and police vehicles with blue lights flashing surround cars and trucks off the road. It appears our detour was caused by a major accident that we just missed.

The downpour lessens to a steady pelting, then to mist. Steam rises from the pavement as Larry drives up a steep mountain road. Rivulets rush toward us. At the top is a breathtaking panorama of olive trees and vineyards, glistening in the sun. We open the windows to breathe fresh mountain air, glad the rain has stopped.

My itch is returning.

Cresting an even steeper mountain in yet another downpour, we're stuck behind a truck heading downhill on slippery asphalt. A Smart Car behind us honks incessantly, then zips out to pass us and the truck. Seeing what is ahead, the truck driver lays on his horn, jams his brakes, and skids sideways. To avoid crashing into the truck, Larry veers right onto the narrow edge of a mountain cliff and the Smart Car squeezes ahead of the truck just as a line of cars come uphill toward us. We sit, frozen and speechless. The truck driver straightens his lorry and continues downhill slowly. We wait as a dozen cars pass. Finally, a considerate driver slows and motions for Larry to pull back into traffic. We all exhale in relief.

But the weekend excitement is not over.

Our cell phone rings. Francesco says there's a surprise at *Lodolina*, but not a good surprise. He explains there has been a huge rain, totally unexpected. All should be okay, except probably there is no power. He asks if we know how to re-engage the electrical circuits. I hit the speaker button so everyone can hear. Francesco goes through what we must do to restore power, step by step.

"Please call me if you have *any* trouble," he insists. "I will come right away. By the way, without electricity for the pump, you will not have water." I tell him we know about no water, thank him for his kindness, and assure him we will be fine.

The last thirty minutes on the *superstrada* feel like hours. The itching is back and my skin's pinkish. In Cortona, Larry drives up *Via Guelfa* ignoring no-traffic signs and stops in *Piazza della Repubblica*. I jump out, run toward the blinking green cross, the signal for the pharmacy. I fear the blinking warns they're about to close, since it's two minutes before seven-thirty. I can't take this itching all night and the doctor warned to avoid a relapse.

Inside the pharmacy, I stop to catch my breath. Thankfully, there's no line. I hand the pretty pharmacist my papers. She retrieves a tube of cream and box of pills for a few euros. Prescription drugs are shockingly inexpensive in Italy. I swallow an antihistamine in the store, even without water. I wonder about pills for reflux, but they are not on my papers and I have Dale's for now.

At Lodolina, the house is pitch-black. With the tiny flashlight I now carry in my purse, Larry finds the electrical panel and goes through the process three times. Nothing. He goes outside to call Francesco because the mobile signal never works in the house and, without electricity, the house phone is dead. Francesco says Larry must reset the main breaker at the external junction box. Sure enough, when Larry re-engages that one, lights in the house blaze.

We eat leftovers and the others enjoy a glass of wine. I'm following David's no alcohol order. For the first time since leaving the hospital, I itch very little, my stomach does not hurt and I can breathe normally. When I ask if anyone minds if I go to bed, everyone insists they're ready for rest, too.

I fall asleep overwhelmed with thankfulness. Many times this weekend I felt guilty for the inconvenience I caused everyone, but looking back I feel nothing but gratitude. True friends give us no reason for feeling guilt, only for gratitude.

Time to Go

I awaken to voices and remember this is our last day with David and Dale. Sleeping in my own bed makes our bizarre seaside weekend seem long ago. A light rash reappeared overnight, but the itching is minimal.

From the top of the stairs I call, "Mornin' everyone. Sorry to sleep so late… I'll be right down."

"Take your time. We've had coffee and granola," Larry replies. I decide to go slowly.

While the shower water heats, I refill my pill container, my personal marker of time. When I count out each new seven-day regimen, I take stock of how well I lived the prior week and what I want to accomplish for the seven days to come. Last week was filled with friendship and adventure, and much less stress between Larry and me. An excellent week, despite my emergency.

I want to be aware of each week while it happens. When we live waiting for that miracle — the perfect job, perfect opportunity, perfect spouse — years can pass.

I wonder if other people have markers of time, even if not conscious. Weekends? Birthdays? A new month? Can anyone ignore time — his or her life passing?

Time is the only resource of which all humans have precisely the same daily supply. Looks, intelligence, opportunity and talent are distributed unequally, but time, the most precious of all, is given precisely equally. Spending time deliberately is more important than spending money. More money can be earned or saved, but not more time. One must invest time with presence and purpose, not let it slip away.

As the wizard-sage Gandalf proclaimed in *The Fellowship of the Ring*, "[in life] all we have to decide is what to do with the time given us."

My pillbox replenished and musings over, I lower the water temperature to avoid inflaming my rash, shower, then re-apply prescription cream. When I arrive downstairs the boys are in the living room deep in conversation and Dale is clearing breakfast dishes. Our time together has passed too quickly.

The rainstorm brought higher humidity but not cooler air. As the sun scorches and the earth bakes, I swear I can watch new jagged cracks appear in our barren front yard.

Francesco surprises us, coming to check for storm damage. Just from walking around the house and guesthouse, his shirt is drenched.

"We hope we don't always need so much of your time," I say. "Now that Larry knows how to turn the electricity back on, we should be okay. We need to be able to take care of daily life on our own."

"There could be a problem you might not see. You will care for Lodolina, but it is not yet time."

He reports everything is *va bene*, goes well, saying he inspected the hot water heater, water softener and well-pump in the technical room, plus the oven, microwave, cook top, refrigerator, lights and phone inside the house, and the outlets in the guesthouse. He asks about our computers. We tell him they're fine.

"Do you give all your clients such personalized attention?" Dale asks.

"Some clients become spoiled," he confesses. "One lady, so sweet we would do anything for her, calls when a light bulb is used up. She says to me, '*Architetto, architetto*, please come. My light is broken.'"

"What do you say to her?" I ask, stunned by such an expectation.

"We go. We change the bulb. The light is fixed. She is happy and we are happy."

"Will it work if I call and say, '*Architetto*, my light is broken'?"

Francesco doesn't miss a beat. "For her we have made three houses."

Turning to Larry, I say, "Hmm. Guess we must restore two more houses!"

I ask Francesco where the workers were in the downpour. He says all but Pierangelo left for the day, but that Pierangelo often works in the rain.

"Only without electric tools, of course. Many times, I come and see him under a yellow plastic cape, building a wall in the rain. *Anfibio*," he chuckles. Amphibian.

Francesco lingers as he says goodbye, never letting us feel his next appointment is more important than being with us, although we know he's a busy professional with many clients. Dale gets teary as she kisses his cheeks and says a last goodbye. He smiles, not quite sure what to do about her tears.

"She always cries, not to worry," I assure him.

"I am glad you know Victoria and Larry, so that I can meet and know you," Francesco says. "We had good days together."

Dale nods, wiping away more tears through her smile.

Time moves relentlessly; morning becomes afternoon. Our last lunch is delicious, but sad. Dale washes a load of laundry and hangs it on the clothesline one last time. She has a washing machine at home, but no clothesline.

My rash flares and fades, but never leaves. It's worse in the sun, so I stay in the shade. I have not had wine since our seaside dinner.

Before our last dinner in Cortona, Dale and I climb to town to shop for linen. In this heat, loose, airy linen is perfect.

"Make sure Victoria buys anything she wants… as long as it's *not* black," Larry instructs before we leave.

By the time we reach the top of the hill, Dale and I are giggling and sweating and catching our breaths, not great for my rash but medicine for my soul. I stop to apply more cream, hoping it'll soak in before I try on clothes.

The first shop has the perfect pair of black linen pants on sale. The dressing room is a stone cave in the back. A first for me, to try on clothes in a cave. I buy them despite Larry's no black orders, and feel great about it.

We find racks of colorful linen at our next stop. I try on tunic shirts and drawstring pants in lime, cherry, royal purple, marine blue and white. Dale insists everything looks great on me. I don't need so many, but buy five shirts and three pairs of pants. Dale buys two shirts.

Shopping must be good for my hives; the rash is barely visible as we hurry off to meet the boys for dinner.

We wait and wait. Both David and Larry are compulsively punctual, so we start to worry. They arrive thirty minutes late and explain that they were stuck in Terontola after buying train tickets for tomorrow's trip to the Rome airport. As they left the station, they saw an elderly woman get hit by a car. They called the police and waited to make sure everything was okay.

"Was she hurt?" Dale and I ask in unison.

"That lady's made of steel," David says. "She was thrown off her bike and stunned for a moment. She stood up, brushed off her skirt, let the driver have it, straightened her handlebars and rode off. She was furious, but not hurt. Most people would have broken bones."

Larry says they waited mostly to make sure the driver did not leave. The police took his name and license. But since the lady was gone, they do not think the guy even received a ticket.

Our dinner at *Trattoria Dardano* is bittersweet. We splurge and have a full Tuscan meal: their fantastic *bruschetta*, pasta, mixed roasted meats and sautéed spinach, wine, and dessert. Of course, Paolo makes sure we have bay leaf liquor before we say goodnight.

David and Dale may never fully grasp how their visit changed the course of our summer. Yes, they helped us unpack and settle in but, more importantly, they inspired Larry and me to reconnect. It was not what they said but how they interacted with one another — kindly and respectfully, as married individuals who value one another above all else.

I do not want these final hours to pass. I want to stop time and keep our friends here. I long to continue the joy I felt this week, and don't know how Larry and I will do together after they've left. But our time has gone; they leave at sunrise.

Creating Italian Scones

It has come too quickly, this farewell. At the station, Larry teases that we should all simply turn around and go into Cortona for another cappuccino.

When I thank them for coming, David says, "You know we didn't come just for you. We came for us. We missed you. We needed this, too."

As the train pulls away, through a grimy window I see Dale make a backward wave, more come hither than farewell. I backward wave in response, closing and opening my hand as though I'm releasing her to go back to her life in Chicago. It's when we hold loved ones with an open hand that they come back to us. Our friendship is a deep, trusting bond. I am confident they will return.

Once home, the house is too quiet. I start laundry, then decide to make scones — hoping the distraction of cooking will help my malaise. All summer the oven has only spoken German. David, who knows enough German to decipher the manual, reset it to English before they left.

"What's three-seventy-five in Centigrade?" I call to Larry, who is outside reading.

He yells back how to do the calculation.

"I want the answer, not the formula."

"You need to learn to do the conversion… Try one-ninety," he says.

I confirm the answer on the internet, which I should've done instead of asking him, set the oven for conventional baking at one-ninety-five degrees and am encouraged when it starts to heat.

Whole-wheat, lemon and walnut scones were our favorites in Chicago. I find my old recipe and start assembling Italian ingredients. This is definitely an experiment. The best whole grain flour I've found is *Pane Nero*, literally bread black, claiming *7-cereali* including *girasole e sesame*, sunflower and sesame, and five other grains I can't pronounce.

To the *Pane Nero* flour I add *crusca*, hopefully bran, some sea salt and raw sugar. I stir in melted butter, yogurt and olive oil, then taste the dough, add more salt and taste again. I pour a bit of honey over it and stir in one egg, lemon juice and zest, walnuts, and dried cranberries. I can only guess how long to bake the dark lumpy mounds. Twenty minutes should be a good start, enough time to hang freshly-washed sheets.

With scones in the oven, I walk up the hill to Dale's clothesline. It's harder to hang sheets without help and I swallow the lump in my throat, missing my friend. I recall hanging clothes with my mother. She taught me to overlap the corners, using only one clothespin so we would not run out. From the driveway hurrying back, I look up and see white squares gleaming like sheets of artic ice, all attached at the corners. Dale and Mom would approve.

The timer is beeping when I walk in. The scones smell cooked, but look raw. I turn the baking sheet around to insure they bake evenly — I don't know this oven yet — and set the timer for another ten minutes.

While the scones bake and more towels tumble in the washer, I sit outside in a wicker chair and record our last day with David and Dale. Larry sits in the chair next to me, studying silently. Andrea Bocelli wafts from the upstairs windows, crickets chirp in the hillside grass and, closer in, the tap-tapping hammers of Pierangelo and Luciano shape stones for the little wall under the *cipressi*. Life could not get sweeter. Just then, the rooster crows and perfection is improved.

The post-lady comes all the way to the house to deliver three more birthday cards. I've noticed she comes to the door when there is good mail, but leaves bills and ads in the postbox. Each card makes me teary: appreciation from Lara for my mothering and example; photos of Aiden, Amber and Chad with a chatty update on their life in Portland; and one from my mother, who has never failed to celebrate my birth. I feel far away and disconnected, but happy.

The timer buzzes again. Larry comes inside, saying the aroma has made him hungry. I break a scone open and it's nicely baked. To go with our scones, he makes us each a *macchiato*, a shot of espresso stained with a little steamed milk. It's a great word, *macchiato*, from the verb *macchiare*, to stain. I bite into crisp edges of the warm scones and know immediately that these are good.

"Ummm!" Larry's raised eyebrows make me giggle. "These are better than at home… I mean, Chicago."

He stopped himself, but it seems that Cortona may not quite be home for him either.

For the workers, I put a few scones on an Etruscan bird plate and take them outside. These are dark and funky compared to Italian breakfast breads, which are typically sweet, carefully shaped, made with white flour and white sugar, and filled with *marmellata* or honey. The guys nibble them, I think to be polite. Then they look at each other and grin. Pierangelo puts the knuckle of his bent forefinger into his cheek and turns it back and forth, the sign reserved for especially delicious foods. Others follow suit. I curtsy and smile, delighted they like my morning concoction.

Francesco and Carlo arrive, so I offer them scones. They, too, hesitate, then seem surprised when they bite into one.

Francesco says, "I am so curious about the red pieces both sweet and sour, a taste I never have before."

"Dried cranberries," I say. "I brought them from Chicago."

"What is cranberry?" he asks.

Not knowing the Italian word, I get out our English-Italian dictionary. "*Mirtilli rossi,*" I report.

"Ah, red blueberries," he says. "We do not have these in Italy."

Larry tells them that cranberries come primarily from Canada and are popular at Thanksgiving, a holiday celebrated only in America. I shake some into a bowl for sampling.

Francesco eats one, then a few more. "I like very much this flavor."

"Hope you wrote down this recipe," Larry says. "I want these again… they're exceptional."

Francesco reports that Luka and his ironworkers will come later this morning to measure the exact curve of the hill for the rail, saying that every artisan in Luka's shop is hammering our rail.

"When will it be ready?" I ask with cautious hope.

Francesco hesitates, then teases, "Maybe Tuesday, but more likely Thursday, perhaps Friday… and surely by the following Monday. But most definitely before your guests arrive."

It's become a joke between us about artisans caring more about perfection than deadlines. If we had to choose, we'd rather something be done well than on time. Of course, we would prefer both.

When we say goodbye, Francesco thanks me again for the scone and his introduction to cranberries. After a quick lunch, Larry and I drive to the outlet mall for more sheets and towels. With Ron's family arriving next week, we'll have five more bodies in our home.

It's afternoon, the hottest part of the day, and an air-conditioned car and stores will be welcome relief. We stop first in Camucia at a mattress store Francesco recommended for guesthouse beds.

Cristiano, the owner of *Dormire Sano*, which means Healthy Sleeping, is wiry, energetic and cheerful. He seems pleased to practice his quite good English on us.

"We must order immediately," he warns. "After July, nothing will be delivered until September. We do not want your family to sleep on the floor."

"We didn't bring cash. Do you take credit cards?" Larry asks.

"You pay nothing until everything is arrived and you are happy. If you were Italian, I would ask for money in advance," he teases. "But I trust anyone from Chicago… home of the Chicago Bulls. I love the Bulls!"

Walking from the showroom to his office, he talks nonstop about the Bulls. He knows players, stats and the team record, obviously a serious fan. After ordering three mattresses, and choosing pillows and mattress covers, we say goodbye like old friends.

At the outlet mall, with such unimaginative architecture it seems impossible that Italians designed it, we find a discount store for linens and buy ten bath towels, hand towels and bathmats. Sheets to fit the extra-long mattresses must be ordered, they say, but should come before the end of July. After *primo agosto*, August first, the clerk warns, nothing will be delivered until September. She promises to call when they arrive.

In another store, I'm thrilled to find stainless steel shelving for my new laundry area. The boxes are so heavy we have to drive to the loading dock to pick them up.

At home, Larry drags the boxes into the house. But when I start unpacking them, I can't find the bag of clips. Larry's certain everything is out of the car. I say we need to go back, but he says absolutely not today, maybe in a day or so. I wanted to organize my laundry space this afternoon, but, like many things this summer, it'll have to wait.

Unable to build the shelves, I decide to wash the new towels to freshen them. The cotton setting says it takes over two hours at ninety degrees Celsius — ten degrees short of boiling. I think that may be extreme, but follow instructions. While the towels tumble, I call Tedi. Saying goodbye to David and Dale has made me miss other friends even more. As we chat, I glance at the washer. My heart stops. The suds are gray. Several black items are sloshing around with our new white towels. I must have missed some of Larry's socks. I should've felt inside, since that's the only way to be sure the front-loader is empty. The LED says forty-two minutes to go. Unlike my Chicago top-loading washer, this machine locks once it starts.

Determined, I hold down the orange door release button for what seems a full minute. It finally clicks, the door swings open and water gushes out. I quickly say goodbye to Tedi, who is laughing uproariously, and yell to Larry for help. I grab my biggest kitchen bowl and pull the sopping towels into it. We use old towels to try to mop up the water, now covering the entire laundry area and moving down the hallway. The laundry is really too small for two people, so Larry goes back to his computer while I try to get the last puddles out from under the washer.

Our new towels are gray. The saleslady gave me samples packets of Vanquish, a product to keep white things white. After this cycle ends, I'll re-wash the towels with Vanquish but without the socks, and hope for the best.

Crisis handled, we decide to climb to town and stroll to Lilli's *Café Teatro*, the restaurant where we watched Italy win the World Cup only three weeks ago, and attend the *Carabinieri* concert given by amateur musicians in the police force.

An elderly man, perhaps ninety, at the next table fascinates me. He's tiny, smaller than any of his friends and when seated, his mouth is barely above his plate. As each course is served, he leans forward and spoons his food straight into his mouth in short, shoveling motions. He mops up excess sauce with a piece of bread, cleaning each dish with enthusiasm. Between courses he leans back in his chair, balances on two legs, and wipes his whole face as if to prepare for the next. He has sharp cheekbones, hollow cheeks and deep-set eyes. His owl glasses sit just under the bridge of his marvelous hooked nose, like a miniature Ichabod Crane. As the concert starts, he wipes his brow one last time, puts his napkin on the table, raises his arms and conducts the band.

At the concert, Marco's mother, Etta, sitting next to us, says her father was a carabiniere and played in the band. She has come to this concert every year since she was a child and wouldn't miss it, though her father died long ago. The emcee proudly announces he's performed this honor for several generations, and I believe him. This evening is like turning back the clock.

The *carabinieri* play surprising well and, eventually, the chairs fill and the crowd gets younger. Tonight, it's Larry who is nodding off rather than me. Following a second encore, the emcee says "*Prego… grazie e buona notte.*" People finally rise and wish their neighbors farewell until next year's concert.

Walking home, I think about *prego*. Literally, it means "*I pray,*" but in modern Italian it's used to say "please," "after you," "you're welcome," "not at all," or "don't mention it." Such a lovely word, because it puts the other person first — a spiritual word that has become a courtesy.

Lying in bed, trying to turn off my brain and fall asleep, I remember Dale waving her backward goodbye this morning. When they thanked us for a great trip, I wish I had said, "*Prego.*"

Summer Storms

Son Ron and family arrive in three days and my to-do list is endless. Larry, wearing a heart monitor strap under his tank top, leaves for his first run with Ivan, the *Il Pozzo* gallery owner. I go downstairs to put the towels in the dryer. They are still dingy after three re-washes, so I start another cycle. I'll give them one more round. Only one. Then I quit.

Ants have invaded. I noticed a few in the living room two days ago. Now they're crawling on my wood chopping block in the kitchen island. I guess it's to be expected, living in the country with churned-up earth, unscreened windows, and open doors. I add ant spray to my shopping list.

Larry's back before I know it. How did my alone time go so quickly?

"The run was great! Ivan's the *nicest* man," he says, energized by the exercise and their conversation. "A lot like me a few years ago... he's never done anything athletic in his life. Tried running one day and liked it. Now he's quit smoking and runs every day he can. He has a tough course, tougher than mine."

"Did you walk home?" I ask. Larry's not even breathing hard.

"No, I ran, but slowly. It's hot."

He showers and goes downstairs to heat Pane Nero scones and make more *cappuccini*, one for each of us.

As I join him, he looks up and smiles, "Look at you. So pretty. I do love color on you. Someday I'll sneak into your closet and take out all the black."

Larry's compliment feels double-edged. I like my black; it is elegant, anonymous and slenderizing. But I also like it when he thinks I'm pretty. My new linen shirts are uncomfortably colorful.

Francesco and Carlo arrive to review progress. Larry and I must be fast, since we have a ten o'clock appointment in Cortona with Lorenzo, our real estate agent. Francesco quickly explains that Mr. Santini will arrive at seven-fifteen tomorrow morning to install doors and windows in the guesthouse, then reviews the schedule for other trades, adding that today workers are putting up safety fences for the children.

When we walk outside to see, there are so many fences it looks like zoo for children.

"These are well-behaved girls, not rambunctious boys..." I plead. "Do we really need so many? They're so *brutto*." Ugly.

Francesco insists. "Safety is the most important thing, even more than beauty."

This morning my hives are flaring up again. I've taken the antihistamine faithfully and used my cortisone cream, but last evening I noticed my armpits itched after a glass of wine. I wonder if stress makes the rash worse. Or alcohol? David said no alcohol for my stomach, but for my rash, too?

We prepare to go but count six vehicles in the driveway. Larry runs back in the house to ask the workers to move their vans. It's always a shuffle if someone needs to leave.

In town, we call up from the piazza, as Lorenzo suggested. He leans out and says he'll come down. Standing in the piazza together, he explains a problem with our residency. Larry tells him the *Questura* says we don't need anything else.

Lorenzo explains, this time it is for our house, not us. The end of works has been filed in the *Comune*, and we are registered as residents. If, after eighteen months we are in residence when someone comes to check, no problem. If not, there is a tax. Larry reminds him that he registered for Cortona residency the day we arrived. Lorenzo says this is separate and very important.

It's easier to do whatever Lorenzo says than to explain what we already have done.

We walk together to Franco's office at the corner of the piazza to fill out more papers. Franco remembers us, probably because I was so incensed that first day when Larry was registered and I wasn't. Franco asks Lorenzo where our house is, how long we've owned it, and if it's our primary home. He then asks Larry if he knows our address, which of course Larry does. He doesn't speak to me at all. I wonder if all this bureaucracy is necessary.

Franco explains in Italian with Lorenzo translating that, after the papers are processed, we'll get a surprise visit to make sure we actually reside there. Larry says he's not sure anyone could find our home without a guide. Franco says that Lapo is our neighbor and will explain how to find us, like it's the most natural thing in the world. We're surprised Franco even knows Lapo is our neighbor. But Cortona is a small town where people have lived their entire lives.

Finally, Franco prints the form for Larry to read. It's another long Italian document. Larry reads it and signs on the bottom. Franco stamps and signs it.

"How about me? The house is in both of our names," I say. "Don't I need to sign at least?"

Larry turns to Franco and asks *"E Victoria?"* And Victoria?

"Non, solo uomini." Only men, he answers.

Here we go again. Franco grins. I can't tell if he's amused or embarrassed, but I suspect amused. Lorenzo tries to hid his smile. I act indignant, but am a bit amused myself.

Franco tears off a section of the form and hands it to Larry. *"Importante. Per dottore... andate in Camucia."*

Lorenzo explains the paper means he can go to Camucia to apply for national health care and be assigned a doctor. He says it covers me, too.

Walking back across the piazza, Larry asks Lorenzo about our road. We want to understand who actually owns it and if we might get the *Comune* to contribute to repair. Lorenzo explains there are three types. If public, the *Comune* must maintain it; if *privato*, it's up to the landowners; if *vicinali*, a neighborhood road, it's fifty-fifty *Comune* and owner. He says our architect can go to Arezzo and look up which kind of road we have, but he suspects it is private. We pay.

Lorenzo warns that before we speak with our neighbors about road improvement, we should know that we may not be warmly received. He says one of our neighbors was angry with him for selling to us without obtaining a right of refusal. Italian law requires that adjacent farmers have the option to buy at the agreed-to price. Lorenzo obtained refusals before selling to the Romans, but not before selling to us. Because it was a higher price and within a short period, new refusals seemed unnecessary.

At the *farmacia*, Larry explains that my doctor says I need a proton-pump inhibitor. The pharmacist offers branded and generic. We buy branded Prilosec, though surprised by the price. Unlike prescriptions, which are a fraction of USA costs, over-the-counter drugs are significantly more expensive in Italy.

I'm eager to take my itchy skin home, but first we must go to Francesco's office to get emails. Our internet is down again because the modem fried in the storm. When we took the old one to the *Telecom Italia* office in Arezzo for an exchange, they said it must be ordered, will take ten days to arrive at the *Telecom* office, and then we must drive back to Arezzo.

Francesco's office is sweltering and the prickly blush increases on my inner arm as we download messages and answer whatever is urgent. Francesco has good news: the Miele man wants to meet and follow us home today to check the installation of my washing machine and to make sure I know how to use it. I laugh, confessing I've used it almost daily since it was delivered.

It all seems quite complicated, this living in Italy — a second installer to approve the work of the first? I know the first guys were deliverymen and this is a licensed Miele technician, but both washer and dryer seem to work just fine.

Francesco stops with us at the outdoor furniture store to look at outdoor chairs. I point out some I like, but he shakes his head, saying they're in every café in Tuscany. We buy a dozen white plastic stackable armchairs for five euros each to have enough chairs for the kids and granddaughters. The store's internet is down so the credit card machine doesn't work. We don't have correct cash, and the owner doesn't have change, so she insists we take the plastic chairs and pay later. She's never seen us before today.

Back in the car, Francesco explains, "You will have a unique table. It must have chairs which are suitable or it will be out of balance. Certainly, you must *not* buy café chairs."

We talk about form versus function, one of Larry and my recurring design differences. I want beautiful chairs; Larry wants comfortable ones. Much easier for me to live a little with discomfort than live with unattractiveness. Larry insists function is a non-negotiable.

"The challenge," Francesco says, "is not to search for a compromise. It is to find the functional solution that is beautiful... and the beautiful solution that is functional. More difficult, but the only right way in my opinion. We do not sacrifice one for the other. In a good solution, we find both."

That's it, I think, and one reason we so value Francesco. The only improvement would be a good price. The perfect triangle of beauty, function, and value. We'll keep searching.

The Miele man meets us at the Coop grocery store and follows us to Lodolina. As we reach the access road, huge raindrops thud like stones on the car. By the time we get home, the rain has stopped, but wind is picking up and dark clouds have gathered. Another storm is approaching.

Hopping out of the car, I give my handbag to Larry and run toward the clothesline, yelling over the wind, "Gotta get the towels."

Suddenly, raindrops start again. A fierce wind almost rips the towels from my hands as I pull them off the line. Rolling them into a ball and hugging them to my body, I run toward the house. Torrents of water cascade over my head and blur my vision. My good black suede wedges, worn to look nice for our meeting with Lorenzo, are soaked and I still must cross the muddy back yard.

Workers are huddled against the back wall inside the guesthouse. Water is blowing horizontally into openings where doors and windows will be installed tomorrow. I reach the vestibule of our hidden door and knock for Larry to let me in. I knock more loudly. Then I pound. Where is he? I don't want to have to go into the downpour to another door, so I keep banging. In the deluge, I can barely hear my own fist against the door. I give up and stand there, dripping, holding the bundle of wet towels, my best shoes caked in mud. At least I'm under an eave.

Larry jerks the door open, startled to see me. He has on rain gear.

"I was coming out to look for you. I was worried. Why didn't you knock?"

"I was pounding! But no one came."

"I didn't hear you. All I could hear was rain."

Inside the kitchen, the Miele man is working. I ask, mostly by hand gestures and body language, if he can move the stacked washer-dryer next to the wall, so I can have room for shelves and a hanging rod. The technician doesn't look happy, but he moves them.

Larry stands in the kitchen doorway gazing into the valley. I join him, not wanting to miss this magnificent *tempesta*. Trees whip wildly, even the massive *cipressi* sway, and curtains of water wash across the landscape. Lightning cracks and flashes above the ridge, so bright it illuminates the kitchen. I count, one thousand one... At one thousand three the thunder rumbles. Only a couple miles away. Masses of charcoal clouds race and swirl overhead, propelled by the ferocious wind. Steam rises from the front yard, where puddles now gather.

The little wall under the cypress looks ancient in the rain.

I point. Larry smiles and nods, "The new wall. I noticed…. It's perfect."

As suddenly as the storm comes, it goes. Still in the doorway, we lean into one another's warmth and gaze at the wonder of this land. Undulating hills ripple into the valley, thick forests, silvery olive trees on steep terraces, ancient stone walls… ethereal in the mist.

The Miele man says he's finished. He sets the washing machine and dishwasher for the hardness of our water. I ask if he can make the dishwasher door close more gently, explaining, again with hand gestures, that it closes so forcefully that one time it broke two glasses. He says he must come back with parts.

As the technician leaves, the lights flicker, then go out. Larry tries to flip the circuit breakers, but power does not return. Francesco walks up the muddy construction ramp to try the main junction box, but without success. He says that power to the property must be down. He calls *Enel*. They confirm power is out, impossible to know for how long.

Sunshine returns, but not the power.

By the time Larry and I take Francesco back to his office and return home, the electricity is on. But Larry seems out of sorts. He was so tender when we were watching the storm. I'm confused.

Finally back home, the silence is too much. "Are you mad at me?" I ask when he comes into the kitchen to refill his water glass. "Do we need a reset?"

"I'm not mad at you, just the situation. I've lost another day. I fell behind when David and Dale were here, but now, when I should be working, I spent the day going to Francesco's office, looking at outdoor chairs, talking with the Miele man, and watching a storm.

"We only have a few days before the kids get here. It's important to get the house ready, too," I say softly.

"Can't you just handle it? Once the kids are here, I'll need to take more time off. I need this week to work."

I feel my blood pressure rise. He chose to take time off with David, his closest friend. Now we're preparing for his son and family to visit. All of it means extra work for me — beforehand, while they're here, and after they leave. I have not complained, but I refuse to "just handle it" to get ready for, essentially, his guests.

After simmering for a few minutes, I say, "It's not fair, Larry. I have extra work for people who are mostly your guests. You feel behind because you chose to take vacation while David was here, so you want me to do more to allow you to study now. And, we go to Francesco's for the internet primarily for you. Do you really think it's fair to expect me to 'just handle' getting ready for your son?"

"I only want the mornings, Victoria. In the afternoon, I'll help with whatever you want. In the evening, I'm totally available for questions, decisions, going out, anything you want to do. Just the mornings, *please.*"

I shake my head in dismay. On one hand, I can understand his dilemma. All summer he's only asked for one thing: mornings. And it's true, he stops every evening to have dinner and do something interesting together. But I do not want to make house decisions myself or prepare for guests, then clean up after, by myself. I am silent. I believe my point's been made.

After about thirty minutes, he comes into the kitchen and says, "I'd like to take you out tonight. You'll be cooking a lot for the next two weeks. How much time do you need to get ready?"

"Sounds fun. Fifteen minutes," I say, pleasantly surprised and feeling my irritation soften, but not erased.

"Lilli's?" he suggests and picks up the phone to reserve a table. He knows I like it when he makes reservations rather than just showing up. I had started dinner, but put the ingredients away.

Walking into *Piazza Signorelli*, we see a large temporary stage and rows of plastic chairs filling the piazza. Performers are wandering on and off the stage wearing casual shorts, jeans and tee shirts. There's space for a full orchestra.

"*Che cosa c'è stasera?*" What is it tonight, Larry asks Lilli when she seats us.

"*Un'opera,*" Lilli say, "*ma non so quale.*" An opera, but I don't know which one.

"*E libero?*" he asks. Is it free?

Lilli nods with her twinkling-eye smile.

During dinner, we're serenaded by singers warming up. After a familiar aria, we agree the opera must be *La Traviata*, one of Verdi's masterpieces. Of course, we decide to stay.

The overture starts about nine-thirty, just before dark. The set is simple: a gold silk brocade backdrop and a few pieces of furniture. We're glad to get excellent seats near the front. Late-comers wander in after the performance begins, crawling over those already seated. No one seems to react. At Chicago's Lyric Opera, doors close promptly at curtain time and late-comers must watch the entire first act on closed-circuit television in the basement, taking their seats only at intermission.

Over fifty singers and musicians seem to be in the first act. They're remarkably good, despite being young. The opera is in Italian and there are no supertitles, but we know the story. How amazing it must be to watch Verdi's operas in one's mother tongue.

During intermission, while Larry's buys gelato from Snoopy's, the backdrop becomes burgundy, blue, and white striped draperies, a clever and effective set change. Someone says the company is from Oberlin College, an American school with a famous Italian summer program.

Despite the romance of Violetta and Alfredo on stage and our best intensions to get along, it's a strained evening for me. We seem to be competing again, especially if I mention something that must be done before Ron arrives. Larry repeats that he must study before he takes more time off, as though my time is unimportant. I repeat that it's only fair that he helps.

I wish I understood this contest between men and women. It's been going on since Adam and Eve and surely will persist for all time, but I don't like it in my own marriage. A little creative tension can give life an interesting spark. But our persistent discord and feeling the other is the enemy is ruining what should be the best summer of our lives. As we walk home in the dark, I feel lonely and confused again.

Perhaps there is a lesson in the passing storm. Turbulent at the time, it replenishes the earth and washes the air. Perhaps our storm will pass, bringing a promise of good things to come. As it is, I wonder why I'm not as important as his friends, family or studies.

At home and in bed, I make lists in my head of what absolutely must be done before the kids arrive. Maybe not everything has to be perfect, but what can I not do? With my worried mind churning, sleep is elusive. At the stream at the bottom of our hill, the frogs and nightingales are conducting a nocturnal symphony. At least I'm not the only one wide awake.

Construction Countdown

Only two more days before Ron and family arrive. The morning air feels fresh, cleansed by yesterday's torrents. As the sun rises above the ridge, the last sparkles of dew evaporate into mist. Today will be another scorcher. Tomorrow, Ron's family will get on the plane and Sunday they'll land in Florence.

At Lodolina, another day of construction commences. Mr. Santini, the window-maker, arrives at seven-fifteen, as promised, which means he left his workshop before six. I'm surprised Francesco hasn't arrived, as he's always here for Mr. Santini.

In the shower I scrub my feet with a brush in preparation for pale mauve toenail polish. I put one soapy foot under the water to rinse and notice it's lighter than my other foot. I thought the Tuscan sun had tanned my sandaled feet. Could it be dirt? We've lived in construction for five weeks. I've washed my feet every morning in the shower and most nights rinsed them again in the bidet to keep our sheets clean. But the brush has revealed the truth.

Soon everything's in action with Francesco, Gabriele, Pierangelo, and the crew. Gabriele shows us his research of who owns adjacent properties, and therefore, might be willing to help pay for road upgrades. We're surprised to learn our property goes almost to the ridge, much farther than we thought.

Lights flicker. Oh, please don't go off today, I think. Power comes back on and I sigh with relief. I reset the oven clock. The dishwasher beeps, indicating the cycle is complete.

Then the electricity goes off and stays off. Francesco assures me Mr. Santini can "work by his hands" and that Pierangelo faces this all the time. They'll be fine. It's important, Francesco says, to go over the list for coming days. Sunday is August first, two days away, the day workers traditionally stop until September. My heart sinks, I have little confidence the guesthouse can be finished in two days.

Francesco assures me all will be okay. Today after Mr. Santini installs windows and doors, the plumber will hook up water and attach it to the septic tank, and the electrician will finish installing outlets and hanging light bulbs. And, he adds with a smile, they have been told to clean up their mess and remove empty boxes.

He continues, "Monday, or surely by Tuesday or Wednesday, Lukas will come with the iron rails for safety. The towel bars have arrived, but we do not know if anyone can install them before the holiday. We will try."

He says our workers have offered to continue next week, so they can be at a good stopping place. We both nod appreciatively, knowing it's a kindness from the men.

By lunchtime, chestnut doors and windows have transformed the upstairs guesthouse. It's become a little gem, a miniature of the main house. From inside, the sky-blue guest room seems perched in the branches of the enormous horse chestnut tree.

Francesco says the downstairs must be completed starting in September, after we leave for Chicago. About the time Mr. Santini finishes, the power comes back on. Naturally.

It's soon time to pick up Rita and it's up to me. I pull out of the driveway onto the access road and feel a moment of decision — I can cave into emotional instincts, fear this road and resent that I have to drive such a big vehicle. Or, I can decide that driving in Italy will not get the best of me.

I take the first curve more easily than I expect. I sit up taller, the next curve is easier. On the entire drive to town, I do not meet another car. *Grazie a Dio.*

Coming home is a little trickier. Rita, stiff as a stick under her seat belt and clinging to the door grip, becomes downright rigid as we approach the S-curve. I successfully maneuver both curves, even where bedrock is jutting into the road. She exhales and whispers "*Brava!*" then claps, beaming at me. We both laugh out loud.

For the rest of the trip, Rita doesn't turn pale or grip the armrest. Her ease makes me feel more comfortable. She teaches me some road words: *strada, corta, stretta… troppo grande macchina.* Road, short, straight… car too big. I repeat after her.

"*Grazie, Rita, grazie.*" Thank you, Rita, thank you, I say as we open our doors.

It's true, we can't always choose our circumstances, but we can choose our attitude toward them. In fact, the more difficult the circumstance, the more important it becomes to *choose* one's attitude. In the scheme of things, this access road is nothing.

At home, the mattress man has arrived. Larry has vacuumed thick construction dust off the guestroom floor. The boys carry the mattress, holding it high above the muddy back yard. Inside, Cristiano assembles the frame and they lower the mattress onto it. It looks like a floating white island in the sky-blue room. Though a loaner, the mattress seems nice and soft. Since ours didn't arrive in July, we now must wait until September.

When Larry tries to pay Cristiano, he declines, saying we should pay him only when our real mattresses arrive and we are happy. Larry insists we pay at least part. Again, Cristiano refuses. He seems determined. Larry gives up.

When Rita finishes, Larry offers to drive and then help me with errands. I'm shocked, but grateful. In town, he says he needs to get a haircut and a newspaper while I shop. With this news, Larry's offer doesn't feel as much like a gift.

"I thought you'd help me choose breakfast food and snacks. I have no idea what to buy," I say, deflated.

"You surely don't need me to follow you around in Molesini Market," he teases.

The hair on my neck bristles and I start to protest. But another argument isn't worth the upset, so I raise my eyebrows and say, "Ron is *your* son."

In the grocery store, I choose everything else, but am stuck about snacks. Marco's at the register, so I ask him. "What's the favorite Italian snack for kids?"

"Potato chips," he answers without hesitation.

Surely there's something healthier and more, well, Italian. I get non-sugared cereal, Nutella and breadsticks, and some fruity yogurts, deciding to buy more when my granddaughters can choose their own flavors.

The bags are heavy. I lug them outside to wait for Larry. He's already there, sitting on the bench.

"Did you finish early?" I ask.

"Yes, but the newsstand is out of the Wall Street Journal, so I've been waiting and wondering what took you so long."

I wonder why he couldn't come in to help, but simply glare at him, shake my head, and hand him half the bags.

"These are heavy! What did you buy?" he exclaims.

"Food for kids. I also had an idea for a dessert to try to make, so got the ingredients. Sorry the bags are so heavy," I reply with more than a hint of sarcasm.

At home, I grab a few of the bags and start to the house, but he says first he wants my help pacing off the driveway to see where our property line really is. He has the official *catasto*, property register map, with him, so it seems this request was as planned as the haircut. I want to put away the groceries and start dinner but don't want an argument, so put the bags on the ground and follow him up the driveway. As I pace, my exasperation pulses with every step.

I count two hundred eighty. He paces two hundred sixty-six. Either way, our property is almost two thirds of the driveway, much more than we originally believed, and certainly more than our neighbor has said. With good news about the property and his fresh haircut, Larry is suddenly buoyant.

"Sweetheart, let me carry those bags. They're way too heavy for you!"

Larry lights charcoal in the tiny, unstable grill while I make my fantasy peach-ricotta tart. Over dinner we discuss special places we want the kids to see. Larry kindly offers to wash dishes so I can make calls to Mom, Lara and

Amber — and again I feel grateful. I crawl into bed with a mixed sense of loneliness for loved ones and gratitude for this amazing experience and my husband's willing helpfulness.

Reflecting on today, I decide to choose my attitude and, thankfully, I can choose gratitude. It is the foundation for a happy life. As famed Austrian monk David Steindl-Rast said, "It is not joy that makes us grateful; it is gratitude that make us joyful." And gratitude can be chosen.

Reclaiming Romance

Trying not to disturb Larry, already deep in his morning study, I make my coffee then sit on the terrace with him and quietly record the events of yesterday. The little black squirrel is feasting in the cypress trees, dropping half-eaten cones onto the dirt. To me, it's as though he says, "I'm here. I'll be your friend."

Nibbled half-cones shaped like tiny apple cores clatter down the branches and bounce on the dry dirt. I pick one up to put on the mantle in the kitchen. I wonder if it would be safe for him to eat raw almonds if I left some on the low stone wall below his tree.

Despite my choice of gratitude last night, I am struggling this morning. I miss my girlfriends, my daughters, my grandson, my mom and my Chicago life where everything had its place and I had helpers. I miss my work at the church, where I could make some small difference for others.

Dale told me my friends are worried about me. When I asked what she meant, she said, "We know Larry loves having all your attention, and we think that's part of why he wanted to move. In Chicago, you had a life that was very much *your* life: girlfriends, daughters, your work. He had competition. We weren't sure what would happen in Italy, but we were afraid it might not be as good as you expected."

Why are adventures often more exciting in the imagining than in the unfolding?

I was naïve, thinking email and phone cards would keep me connected. Talking to Lara last night I realized how little I know of her daily life. I can't even meet her new friend. When she says "Jason," he feels like a stranger, because he is. Mom's best friend Joyce is in hospice. I feel separated, sad, and lonely, unable to participate in everyday life and certainly unable to help anyone, not even my own daughter and mother.

I had imagined I'd make girlfriends in Cortona before now. I think Denise is back, an acquaintance from last summer, but she's busy with houseguests. The women I met at the castle are all in their home countries.

Tomorrow Ron arrives. There will be lots of activity and Paulla will be fun to talk and cook with. She's smart and playful. I'm glad she's my daughter-in-law. But she's three decades younger than I am, so hardly a girlfriend.

I hear Pierangelo's van on the drive. I'm still in my black silk robe, writing and silently weeping.

This morning has had two bright spots: the black squirrel's visit and my first good cappuccino. When I told Marco last week that we couldn't get Italian milk to froth, he said, "Buy the blue milk. Your Pavoni is a good machine. If the problem's not the milk, then it's *you*."

So, I bought milk with a blue label, *intero*, whole milk, rather than the partially skim we use in Chicago and have been buying here. This morning, my cappuccino was the best yet. I interrupt Larry's reading to tell him about it. He feigns jealousy.

"Do you want me to make one for you? I offer.

"What I should ask for is a lesson," he says, not looking up.

In a few minutes, Larry goes in to make himself another one, but without a lesson. He's being kind today, as though he senses my sadness. I feel disconnected from him, too. No matter what I do, the comfortable partnership we enjoyed in Chicago seems out of my reach.

As Larry settles into the wicker chair, he says he doesn't want to go to market today. If I want to go, I should, but he can't afford the time. I'm baffled. I'll be stocking up to cook for the kids and can't possibly carry all the bags. When I question his choice, he says again that once the kids are here, he'll have no time to study. Neither will I, I think, and I counted on him today. Going to market alone will be drudgery and a burden, which I'll resent.

I don't know what to say, so I simply nod and go upstairs to get ready. I don't want to add an argument to my upset.

When I come downstairs, Larry announces he'll go with me. What's more, he'll take me to Francesco's office to check emails and on to Città di Castello to look for a bedroom dresser. To him, his offer is a big deal gift and concession. For me, going to market should never have been in question and I don't have time for Francesco's office or an hour journey. I take a deep breath, say thank you, and decide to make it work.

Market day lifts my mood, with the bright colors, rich smells and textures, cacophony of sounds, and gliding movements. I have grown fond of the beautiful daughter who seems to be in charge of our favorite vegetable stand, and the kind, elderly man who sits by the pots of herbs for sale. He may be her father, but seems too old. We buy bags and bags of produce, and several types of cheese at my favorite cheese vendor. Larry and I struggle to carry all the bags to the car. He questions my quantities, but, starting tomorrow, I remind him we must feed seven people three times per day or take them out.

Francesco comes down from his home above the studio wearing short blue shorts. I must have looked shocked.

"I prefer to wear shorts when I'm not working," he says shyly.

"But Italian men *never* wear shorts. Why?" I ask.

"Ugly knees" he teases. He says his shorts were issued during his military service, twenty years ago.

"Italian men don't wear shorts," he explains, "because they can't buy them. To own shorts, they must serve their country... then must not grow wider."

We finish emails and, despite knowing I should go home and finish the house, we head over the mountains to Città di Castello. Fields of sunflowers pass, some thriving but most withering. The difference must be water. I think water for plants is like love for people. With love, we thrive and blossom. Without love, we wither and die. I feel a little withered today.

Not one of the antique bedroom dressers is perfect. We take a few photos and get prices in case we change our minds, but it was mostly a wasted trip.

On the drive home, Larry and I are deep in our private thoughts. I look out the window and mentally review my plan of action once I get home. He watches the road intently. I wonder what's on his mind. I get a bit queasy with the mountain curves, so focus on the middle stripe. I'd like to talk, but hesitate to interrupt his concentration.

Finally, I say, "Can we talk? It's a long ride, we've barely spoken."

"What have I done now?" he replies.

I tell him it's not about what he did or didn't do, it's that I need his help to live here, and his compassion. I say he's been wonderful today (okay, so I exaggerate a little), but I feel I have to beg for his help and that, when I do, it irritates him. So, I'm hurt first by having to ask and then by his reaction. I explain that I didn't have time to look for furniture today, but I couldn't say so without him feeling I was ungrateful. And now that he went out of his way, I can't ask for his help to do what is left because I know he'll want to study. I feel like his study time is more important than I am.

"How can you say that?" he asks. "I willingly went to market, helped you get your emails at Francesco's, and went furniture shopping with you. We didn't find anything, but I took you without complaining. In fact, I suggested it. My summer has been consumed with house decisions and errands. Each request is reasonable, but there're so many that all my time is spent helping you, so all together, they are *not* okay. And no matter what I do, it isn't enough."

I don't know what to say. I'm tired. I'm lonely. We've had this conversation before. I stare at the fields of dying sunflowers. I can't speak without crying, so sit quietly.

Larry seems miffed. I understand his point. He did take me to market willingly. But he didn't ask if I had time to go to Francesco's or to look for dressers. He just decided, so we went. The sky hangs dark and low, ominous.

Suddenly rain pelts us. I can barely see the road. Larry must concentrate or pull over, so he drives silently. By the time we get back to Cortona, the rain has slowed, ditches are overflowing, and water gushes over stone walls along the road, but we are still not talking.

Close to home, Larry says, "I know you miss your friends and your daughters. I know you have more to do with the kids coming. But I really don't understand why you need so much help."

"It's not just the help," I say after a moment's pause. "I need you. You're my only friend here. I need you to want to do things with me. When I ask for help or companionship and you refuse, I feel rejected and lonelier. I miss you."

He continues to drive.

After a long pause, he says, "I want you to be happy here. I don't want you to be unhappy with life or with me. I'd like to make Saturday market a weekly event, together. Every week, without question. I'll drive, walk with you, carry your bags. You can count on me."

"Every week? No begging?" I am stunned.

"None. I only insist that we have fun."

"You're serious, right? Okay... Saturday morning will be our time together every week. Thank you."

After a few more seconds, he asks, "Can we have a reset?"

"Of course," I say softly. I wonder if he thinks giving me Saturday morning will make other mornings his. So important to me, it could a reasonable exchange.

Larry reaches across the wide console and squeezes my hand. "I'll help you today, too."

By the time we get to Lodolina, the rain is gentle and our tension mostly dissolved. I'm hopeful we might be in sync before the kids come, though it still baffles me that he's so quick to get irritated and I'm so quick to forgive.

At Lodolina, more orange plastic fences are everywhere and Larry has to pull back an extra safety fence to park. Mud is deep again and we make huge holes in the yard as we carry the heavy bags to the hidden door. I leave my repaired sandals outside the back door, wondering if the fox will return.

Over lunch, we chat more about plans with the kids. The rain has a soft rhythm, making Lodolina sensual and intimate. Larry does the dishes and I finish folding linens. Larry asks if I have time for a nap. Fog fills the valley and sneaks into the bedroom windows as we enjoy our last afternoon alone for two weeks. He promises to help with whatever else I need, saying I should just ask.

Late afternoon, with most tasks completed, I feel I should pay for the plastic chairs we didn't pay for yesterday. Since I also should practice driving and don't want to bother Larry, I go alone. The drive is not too bad. Embarrassingly, my credit card is refused twice and I didn't bring cash. I tell the owner I'll come back today, but she insists I return when it's convenient. "No worry, no hurry," she says in English. I drive home, uplifted by how trusting the locals are with us, kicking myself for not taking cash in the first place, and glad for the few minutes alone.

When I get home Larry is grinning like a schoolboy, "I made reservations at *Grappolo Blu* for tonight. Hope you don't mind,"

"For tonight?" I ask, thinking we should go to bed early, but how can I say no?

"I know you're worried about making everything perfect for the kids, but I'd like to take you out for a romantic dinner before they get here. Is that okay?"

He can be the most adorable man when he sets his mind to it. Marco's been telling us all summer to try *Grappolo Blu*, a fancy new restaurant only twenty minutes from Cortona.

Good to his word, Larry helps me finish, except making the guest bed. Then we dress up for our date.

At *Grappolo Blu*, the owner, Gildo, greets us at our car. His restaurant is tiny, only four tables in the elegant dining room, but he explains that next summer he will expand with a pergola across the back. Prosecco in hand, we take a leisurely tour of the gardens overlooking golden fields, green hills, and purple mountains. Cortona is in the distance, nestled against the highest hill. Gildo says it's like having our own private restaurant, since only two tables will be occupied.

He continues, "I have two restaurants in Denmark, but my wife and I wanted to move back to Italy. We've won awards and I think it will take off in the next year. In the meantime, my heart is here and my income is from Denmark."

Donatella, his wife and the chef, comes from the kitchen to greet us.

"Donatella is from *Sardegna*", he says putting his arm around her, "and I'm from Naples, so we know fish. I suggest to you our fish menu. If you prefer, we can make for you a meat menu."

We rarely get fish in this land of steak and salami. Larry looks at me and I nod.

"Fish for us!" he confirms.

Gildo and Donatella give modest bows as they leave to prepare our meal.

After first appetizers of artfully arranged miniature octopus on potato puree, a teeny patty of tuna tartar, and a funky little crustacean with shiny eyes that stare up at me, our second appetizer is a small square of the best *melanzane parmigiana* I've ever tasted, served with a warm, walnut-size ball of fried *mozzarella di bufala*. We compliment Gildo, especially on the cheese. He says he brings his cheeses from Naples.

Donatella soon arrives wearing a big smile and, balanced on her arm, two silver-domed plates. I can tell she's proud of this course as she sets one in front of each of us. Simultaneously, she lifts both domes with a flourish and describes the two ravioli: black sepia-ink ravioli with fish filling, and green spinach ravioli filled with mushroom and zucchini. Gildo pours the wine he selected to enhance the *due paste*, two pastas.

By this time, especially with irresistible rosemary focaccia and homemade paper-thin crackers Donatella calls *croccante nella bocca*, crunch in the mouth, I'm getting full.

"Would you like a break to see the cellar?" Gildo asks when he sees me puff my cheeks, the universal sign for having overeaten.

"A break? There's more? Everything's exquisite, but I can't possibly eat more."

Gildo gives me a wait-and-see look and motions us to follow.

The cellar is sophisticated yet welcoming, with a long table that seats twelve in one room and two round tables for four each in a smaller room, and walls of wine. I stand speechless, swiveling my head like a long-necked crane to take it all in.

"How many bottles?" Larry asks.

"Eight thousand." There is a pause for emphasis.

"In this region," Gildo continues, "only *Il Falconiere* has more wine, and they've been building their cellar for years."

We walk back upstairs and are soon lingering over our *secondo*, main course, of calamari stuffed with smoked cheese, served with yet a different wine.

At the perfect time, two crystal plates arrive displaying a trio of desserts: dense, nutty *semi-freddo*, like gelato with crunchy bits, plus paper-thin slices of marinated fresh pineapple topped with wild berries, and a miniature warm apple tart. Beautiful and surprisingly light, they are a sublime finish.

Despite the tension of the day, tonight we've enjoyed more than the food and wine, we've enjoyed one another. We shared how challenging the summer has been, yet agree it is beyond our highest expectations. We reinforced our hopes for the remaining weeks, agreeing to suspend personal projects while Ron and family are here. Larry promises to help cook and do the cleanup, or take everyone out — saying it's unfair for me to worry about three meals a day for so many people. I'm relieved he seems to understand. Listening and feeling listened to are essential to any enduring romance, and I'm glad tonight we took the time for listening.

By the time we finish *espressi* in sculptural white porcelain cups, softness has returned to Larry's eyes and to my heart. I love being reminded of the noble and praiseworthy in him.

When we ask for the *conto*, bill, we're shocked yet again. Not only did we have a sensational meal, with eloquent wines matched to each course, and the perfect balance between service and privacy, the bill is less than we anticipated.

Today has ended well. Life is sweeter when you're committed to finding good in your mate and your life together. Sweeter yet when you treat each other — and feel treated — with respect, patience and appreciation. And, a romantic dinner doesn't hurt.

Mouse on the Mattress

A cricket missing one of its back legs crawls up my black silk robe and onto the arm of the wicker chair, but it has trouble getting around my cappuccino cup. I lift the cup to let it pass. The black squirrel's half-eaten cones clatter down the cypress branches. Bells toll at *Chiesa Santa Margherita* and the rooster trumpets his cockle-doo, as if in harmony. Songbirds chirp, twitter and warble. In the distance I hear a vehicle driving slowly up a graveled road.

The hills washed by yesterday's downpour are a thousand shades of green, more variations than I imagined was possible. I long to linger in the tranquility of this moment, but can't. Ron and his family arrive today.

In Cortona for church, we pass two *Carabinieri*, national police, holding automatic rifles. Perhaps someone famous is arriving, or there's been trouble. Near the piazza, I hear a flute, but it stops abruptly. Then I see the flautist, wearing a black tuxedo, talking to a monk. It's a strange morning, but we have come to expect the unexpected in our town.

During church, I jot notes about my deep gratitude for what I perceive as God's gift — my passion for words. Since elementary school I have loved to write. But this summer I do so with new purpose, having so many experiences to capture every day. I think of the promise in Psalm 37 that God "gives us the desires of our hearts." Does that mean God plants the desires in our hearts, or that he fulfills them? Perhaps both.

Adding to the uniqueness of this morning, today's priest is Brother Andrea, the handsome monk who introduced himself after the concert a few weeks ago. Instead of his coarse brown robe, he's cloaked in a tunic of emerald damask lavishly embroidered with gold threads, and a golden-colored mantle over a white silk shawl. He seems equally at home in a simple monk's robe or elegant vestments. His homily is in Italian, of course, and his voice is warm and melodic. I wish I could understand his words.

Today's small congregation, perhaps one hundred and fifty, seems to lift their alleluia with extra joy. Over centuries, alleluia has become a universal expression of praise. I join in... *alleluia, alleluia, alleluia.* When the congregation repeats the Lord's Prayer in Italian, I whisper it in English. During the Eucharist I sit, listen to the music, and thank God that my faith in things I cannot see is genuine and comforting.

I'd like to greet Brother Andrea after the service, but Larry says we must hurry to the Florence airport, nearly two hours away.

We dash into the terminal barely in time as Ron, Paulla and three granddaughters, ages four, seven and nine, emerge from the secured area. Pulling huge suitcases and lugging over-stuffed carry-ons, each little girl is also wrapped in a blanket. Are they really staying only two weeks? While Larry goes with Ron to pick up their rental car, Paulla and I load bags into the back of our car. Not all will fit, even in our SUV, so we wait for Ron, Larry and the rental.

"Your hair's so long," Paulla says while we wait. "I like it."

Marianne, my Chicago stylist, would be appalled at how unstylish my typically super-short hair has become, so I'm glad for the compliment. I'd get it cut in Cortona, if I knew where to go or how to explain in Italian what I want. It may be in pigtails by the time we get home in six more weeks.

Arriving at Lodolina, we start the house tour by depositing suitcases in the guesthouse where Ron and Paulla will sleep. I gasp the moment I open the door. On the center of the bare mattress is a dead mouse. I locked the door before we left. There was no dead mouse then.

Larry tosses the still-soft carcass into the olive grove. Fortunately, its body didn't leave a mark on the mattress. I check the bathroom. Sure enough, the window is open. Evidently, the mouse was delivered though the bathroom window. I wonder what brought it in. We haven't seen cats on our property all summer.

While Larry continues the tour, I start dinner and the little girls soon join me.

Paige wants to help and, with a safely-dull paring knife, I let her dice vegetables for the pasta. Claudia begs for me to teach her a song on the piano. Sydney has fallen asleep upstairs on the sofa. Paulla joins us and slices cantaloupe to serve with prosciutto. When the aromas suggest dinner will soon be ready, Ron and Larry carry our antique walnut dining table outside onto the concrete slab.

Dinner is light, but traditional and satisfying: *melone e prosciutto*, then *pici* pasta tossed with oven-caramelized, diced red and yellow peppers, zucchini, onions, fennel, garlic, and eggplant, some toasted pine nuts, fresh basil and handfuls of grated *Reggiano Parmigiano* cheese. For dessert, we'll have the guaranteed kid-pleaser: watermelon. Tuscan watermelon is sweeter and more intense than I remember American watermelons, even from my childhood in Georgia where we grew our own. Though all three girls insisted they were not hungry, the pasta and watermelon are inhaled. We chat and giggle while evening fades into dusk and stars appear overhead. Our weary travelers are ready to retire.

The girls take quick baths in the bathtub, hooked up yesterday. Paulla and I make the upstairs sectional sofa into beds. Fortunately, it has three sections and each girl chooses a different one.

"Where's the suitcase with the pajamas?" Paulla hollers downstairs to Ron.

"Which one?" Ron says.

"The big one." Silence.

"Oh, no," he gasps, mostly under his breath. There's another long pause.

"What's wrong?" Paulla calls.

Ron runs up the stairs and looks around the room. "I must have left it at the airport. In baggage claim. Don't know how I could be so stupid."

Paige screams, "What?!?," realizing her new pink birthday bathrobe could be lost.

Paulla, whose eyes are wide in disbelief, consoles Paige and turns to Ron, whispering, "That suitcase also had all the girls' shoes, plus decorations for Paige's party and her gifts."

"Sorry... really," he rifles through travel documents looking for baggage claim tickets.

"I think I threw them away," says Paulla, heading to the trashcan.

She finds the boarding pass with baggage claim receipts. Ron remembers taking the bag off the carousel, but that's all. Larry looks on the internet for a phone number for the airport, but only finds one for Air France, not the airline they flew. Paige, exhausted and therefore even more dramatic, busts into tears again.

I find tee shirts for the girls to sleep in. Paige perks up when I hand her a new Lincoln Park Zoo shirt with a tiger face on the front. Sydney's not thrilled with my basic black. I ask if she'd rather sleep in a shirt with Tedi's picture on it, since she really likes our friend Tedi. She nods, so I dig out the shirt Tedi gave me as joke. Claudia has fallen asleep in her own shirt.

Ron is downstairs in the coat closet, where all the wires enter the house and our only phone is hooked-up, trying to reach someone at Air France to ask how to get hold of the airport or American Airlines. No one answers. After many tries, he gives up and comes back upstairs. I am as surprised as Ron that he didn't notice the suitcase was missing. Super smart and relentlessly responsible, he must have been exhausted.

While Larry and I go to the guesthouse to make the new bed, Ron tries to call one last time and Paulla tucks in the girls. Our only guest house room still doesn't have a sink with water, towel bars, or a toilet paper holder. The bidet will serve as their sink until the real one is hooked up, hopefully tomorrow. For light, there's a bare light bulb hanging in each room.

"We'll come back in to say goodnight," Ron says as Paulla opens her suitcase on the bed.

Inside the main house, Paige is still fretting. I assure her that the suitcase will be found, but it doesn't help. I tidy the room and chuckle with Larry about the lost bag, speaking softly so we don't agitate Paige's delicate equilibrium.

When Ron and Paulla come back, Larry gives them keys and a flashlight to walk more safely over the construction debris outside their door. With the girls kissed and tucked in, they head back to their room for a night of much-needed sleep.

Almost immediately, I hear a shriek, a door slam, feet running down the stairs, and a fist banging on the hidden door. Paige bolts up in her bed. I open the door.

"Something ran off with my shoe!" Paulla gulps, out of breath. "We left the door open a crack so it wouldn't lock while we were saying goodnight. When we started back, something ran out of our room. It had my shoe."

Her eyes are enormous.

Ron adds. "It was bigger than a cat, with a bushy tail. Yellowish."

"The fox!" I say. "The workers tell us we have a blonde fox. I think she chewed my sandals a couple weeks ago. Bet she also left the mouse."

"Well, she sure is bold!" Paulla declares. "She took my shoe *out of the suitcase*. It still had the price tag on it!"

"We'll look for it tomorrow. Maybe she dropped it and we can get it repaired."

Paulla is unconvinced. "Part of the strap is still in our room. It's ruined."

Ron asks if we have another key, since the door locked behind them. Larry pulls out our only extra guesthouse key and hands it to Ron, warning him not to lock this one in, since we don't have more. Ron flashes him a don't-be-such-a-dad look.

To decompress from the drama, Larry and I escape to the soft wicker chairs on the front terrace and sip *limoncello*. Though the missing suitcase is a problem, we're confident it'll be found. After midnight, I tiptoe through the sitting room to get ready for bed. The girls are barely breathing.

Larry makes one last try and is shocked when Air France answers. They say none of the airlines are able to trace a bag once it's off the plane and give him the main airport number to call tomorrow.

What a day! Something unpredictable always happens with kids — even when the kids are old enough to have kids of their own.

Larry has been kind, thoughtful and helpful for two days, which means he knows how. My hopes are raised for coming weeks. I hear him tip-toeing up the stairs as I fall into bed. Soon, he crawls in, too.

"I love having Ron and the girls here," he whispers, leaning on his elbow to face me. "Just this one day makes all the hassles of this summer worthwhile." I sense his happy grin as he reaches for my hand and kisses it.

"Goodnight, love. *Sogni d'oro*," I say, wishing him dreams of gold, as Italians say.

My hand in Larry's helps me breathe deeply. So strong is the power of human touch, a loved-one's touch, that with his warm skin pressing mine any remaining tension melts into tenderness.

Paige's Plum Pie

First thing, Ron tries to reach the airport with no answer. After a late breakfast, Ron tries again with no luck, then he, Paulla, Syd, Paige and Larry hike our property from the highest terrace down to the stream. I stay home to listen for Claudia, who's taking a morning nap, and for beeps from the washer, dryer and dishwasher, already in use.

The dryer beeps first. Unfortunately, it only means things are hot and humid, not fluffy dry. I've never thought of linen as wash and wear, but as I take my damp linen shirts and pants out of the dryer and shake them, I decide they don't look so bad. I hang damp clothes over living room chairs and the stair railing. Someday I'll have shelves and a hanging rod in the laundry space.

Claudia comes downstairs starving. I set her up with cereal and put in another load of laundry for Paulla.

Our explorers arrive with three wild plums — long purple ovals with green-tinged ends. Locals call these *coscia della monaca*, thigh of the nun. We cut them into quarters to share. Not quite ripe and puckeringly tart, the girls exclaim they're delicious.

"We want to walk to town for lunch," Larry says. "Do you and Claudia want to come?"

Claudia jumps down from her chair to grab her mom's hand, ready to go. Ron says he first must try the airport again. I say I need to finish folding laundry.

Tasks complete but still no answer at the airport, we climb uphill toward Cortona. Near the top, the neighbor everyone calls Lapo is standing by his Jeep near his *agriturismo*, a country house similar to a farm B&B. We don't think he likes us, since he wrote letters to Francesco disputing our property line and complained that Lorenzo didn't obtain his permission to sell to us. I wonder if we should wave and pass, but decide we should be neighborly no matter what.

I muster my best Italian for the introduction. "*Ciao, Lapo. Posso presentare nostra famiglia? Questi sono Sydney, Paige e Claudia... Ron, nostro figlio, e la sua moglie, Paulla.*"

The girls are blond and doe-eyed, like stair-step angels. They say, "*Ciao*" in unison, and then stumble over "*Piacere.*" Lapo seems charmed.

"*Quanti anni,*" he asks. How many years?

Larry says, "*Quattro, sette, e nove.*" Four, seven and nine.

Lapo points to something. We all turn to look, thinking he's pointing toward the valley.

"No, no..." he says. "*Volpe.*" He points to the logo on Ron's shirt — a fox!

I tell him, in my kindergarten Italian, the story of our fox who loves shoes and, we think, put a dead mouse on the mattress. He laughs and says he knows that fox. He's happy, he says, because *Casale della Torre*, his *agriturismo*, is rented through August. He invites the girls to swim when renters are not there.

"*Grazie mille, molto gentile.*" Larry thanks him, saying he's very kind.

Could a change of heart have been provoked by meeting our family? As in any culture, a sure way to shift a stranger's distrusting heart is a personal interaction with someone's family. That does depend on the family, and Ron's is courteous and charming. Italians put great value on family — the core of Italian society, revered above all.

When Larry tells Lapo we're going to Fufluns for pizza, he lights up, saying Fufluns' oil is from his olives. We promise to taste it. The girls start to shuffle from standing still so long.

After mumbling a polite *arrivederci*, the energetic angels scamper up the rest of the hill and dash through the tree-lined *Parterre*, chasing local cats and each other. We can barely keep up. Once in town, they peer into every window we pass and stop longingly at the gelateria.

"After lunch," I promise, like a good grandma.

At Fufluns, we dip chunks of bread into puddles of olive oil. Since it's not labeled, we can't tell if it's Lapo's oil, but it is very good. We order three pizzas: grilled vegetables, gorgonzola and pear, and Fufluns signature. Skinny Ron, our family's most voracious eater, declares Fufluns pizza has everything he loves — sausage, pepperoni, artichokes, tomatoes, onion, and cheese.

After lunch we stroll through town introducing our family to our favorite people and going to our favorite stores. Paige asks for more pasta "just like last night" for her birthday dinner, so we climb to the top of *Via Dardano*. The pasta store is closed. It's hard to believe I had so many bags of groceries after Saturday market and now have nothing to make for Paige's dinner. We're celebrating tonight, without the suitcase of gifts and decorations, and though her real birthday was the day they flew.

At the gelateria, Paulla warns, "NO chocolate."

I think it's a pretty extreme restriction, but she's not kidding.

"I've learned from too many bad experiences with chocolate ice cream on hot days. These are their new school clothes and I don't want stains on them," she explains.

It seems a tough position to me, especially for vacation, but I can see her point.

The girls choose fruit flavors. In the sun, the gelato melts faster than it can be eaten and ends up on everyone's shirts. Luckily, Paulla has plenty of wet wipes and the drops are not chocolate.

Larry and Ron suggest they walk home with the girls, and that Paulla and I stay to shop for dinner. I tuck cash in my pocket and we give the men our handbags, knowing our shopping bags will be heavy. At the butcher, I ask for *bistecca per tagliata per sette,* steak for seven. The butcheress cuts two slabs, each about one and a half inches thick, whacking the bone with her cleaver.

"Victoria," Paulla discreetly points to a small skinned mammal with its legs attached and eyeballs still in the sockets.

"Rabbit," I whisper. "It's popular here, but I don't plan to cook one. To me, they look like skinned cats."

Next to the rabbit are chickens with a few remaining feathers, bright red combs, and dangling yellow feet with toenails. In the same case are other small birds, I guess pigeons or guinea fowl, and a tray of dark shiny organs that look like whole calves' livers.

The sausages seem plump and lean. I ask for "*quattordici*," fourteen. The butcher counts them off, leaving them tied together. We lug bags of steak and sausages back up the street, hoping to get Paige's pasta.

The *Pasta Fresca* shop is still closed. We ask two elderly men sitting across the street "*Aperto oggi?*" Open today? "*No,*" they say, "*domani.*" Tomorrow. I know it was open when we passed it this morning. Then we see the sign: closed Monday afternoon.

"Hope risotto is okay for Paige's birthday dinner," I say to Paulla, and we turn to walk back down the hill to Molesini Market where we buy the rest of our groceries, including a dozen fruit yogurts for the girls.

Marco comes out of the enoteca to invite us to a special event August fourth, a dinner at *La Loggetta* featuring a famous vineyard. The price is good, he says, because the winery subsidizes the wine. I ask if it's appropriate for the girls and he says, "Of course," so we reserve for seven.

On the way out of town, Paulla and I stop at the produce store. We choose gorgeous ripe figs, bananas for Paige, and a kilo, over two pounds, of thin green beans plus lots of carrots for Claudia who eats "green beans, carrots and broccoli, period." Unfortunately, broccoli is out of season.

I ask for *rosmarino*. Looking in the herb bin, the owner says, *"Finito,"* shaking his head.

"Impossible! We can't make dinner without it," I say. The Tuscan preparation for grilled steak requires lots of rosemary.

In careful Italian, the shop owner explains that on the hill above the road to *Piazza Garibaldi* is a rosemary bush where I should pick what we need.

I imagine a rosemary bush well within reach. If anyone looks askance, I'll just say the veggie storeowner told me to do it. I nod and smile.

"Brava!!" he chuckles.

At the beginning of the park, halfway up a steep embankment from the road, we see a scrawny rosemary bush. It's the only one we find. Paulla gives me a boost over a low part of the wall and I crawl up the hill on all fours. Cars on the road below seem to slow down. I suspect passengers are staring at me, but don't look down. I pick plenty. It would be a shame to go home without enough after making such a spectacle of myself.

Job done, I crawl on all fours backwards down the embankment, jump off the wall, stuff the rosemary in one of our bags and we walk, heads high, through the park toward home.

Near Lapo's *agriturismo* we see him again. He stops his car, hops out, and walks toward us as if he's eager to talk. I tell him in broken Italian that we loved his oil and Fuflun's pizza. He stares at the scraggly rosemary and I confess the story. I can't tell if he doesn't understand or doesn't approve, but he doesn't react.

From his jeep, he pulls out a wicker basket overflowing with plums, many still with leaves. They're round and yellow, different than the purple plums the girls picked this morning. He gives us each one and takes one himself, biting into it. We're supposed to eat them now, I guess. Hoping they're safe without washing, I bite into mine. Paulla follows my lead. It's surprisingly sweet and juicy.

"Molto buono! Grazie." I exclaim, mouth half full.

Lapo finds a plastic bag in his car and hands it to me, gesturing that I should help myself. I take seven, one each for us. He says something about taking them to our house or picking them near our house. My Italian isn't good enough to understand. He's being warm and friendly. I wonder what we could do for him, what small gesture would cement this new relationship.

He insists on pouring the entire basket into our bag. I'm not sure what we'll do with this many and, worse, how we'll carry them home with everything else. But I'm thankful for his kindness and don't want to seem ungrateful.

I take his hand in both of mine to shake it, and then lean forward and plant a kiss on each of his cheeks. He grins. Lapo met our son and granddaughters, offered plums, we were grateful and showed appreciation. I hope we can now be good neighbors.

Nearing home, Paulla says she hopes our men have put the girls down for naps. She fantasizes we'll arrive, put away groceries, and sit on the concrete slab sipping a glass of wine with our husbands who have missed us terribly.

I tell her not to expect too much, it often leads to disappointment.

We arrive to chaos. Claudia has run into a door handle and is sobbing, with a huge bump on her head and blood drying into her hair. She won't let anyone touch her and wants only her "*Mah-ah-ah-meee.*" She immediately curls up in Paulla's arms, sniffling and trying to catch her breath.

Paige, disregarding her sister's distress and interested only in the bag of plums, asks, "Can we make a plum pie? For my birthday dinner?"

"Paigie… I'd love to make a plum pie for your birthday," I say. "But I've never eaten plum pie, let alone tried to make one."

She looks deflated, but not dissuaded.

After a moment thinking about cooking dinner for seven plus making a plum pie in the next two hours, I say enthusiastically, "Let's just eat the plums."

Frowns of disbelief shroud all three faces, even Claudia's tear-stained one. I might as well have said, "Let's go to bed without our birthday dinner." Paige, especially, looks heartbroken.

"Okay…," I say. "We'll need to make it up as we go, but we'll do our best."

The girls drag white plastic chairs into the house and place them around the kitchen island, then stand on them, poised, ready to help. Claudia has miraculously overcome her mortal injury.

I pour flour in a bowl, add a little raw sugar and salt, then chop butter into bits, crack in an egg and add a little cold water. I give Sydney a spoon.

"Stir slowly. The dough for the crust will get stiff fast. Stir only until everything is mixed into one smooth ball. Not too much... Like this..." I say, demonstrating how to hold the bowl and stir. Good thing Syd is strong for her age.

I give Paige some plums and show her how to wash one, cut it in half along the indention, and take out the pit.

"I'll cut out bad spots," Paulla offers. Wild plums are far from perfect.

Claudia awaits her job. "You'll pat the dough into the pan," I say, putting a reassuring arm around her tiny shoulders.

While the dough rests, I mix leftover ricotta cheese with eggs and sugar to make a custard filling.

Claudia starts to press the crust into a large rectangular baking sheet. The other two shove their chairs closer together, so close they nearly topple out of them, each vying to reach the pan. Six little hands make quick work of shaping the crust. I pinch a little rim to hold the filling.

I show Claudia how to spread a thin layer of peach jam on the crust, since her crust-shaping job was done by everyone.

When I nod, Paige, the birthday girl, artfully pours the custard over the jam.

Then the girls line up plums, cut side down, covering the entire top in perfect rows. I drizzle a tiny bit of honey over the plums to help them brown.

The girls admire their work with big, eager eyes.

Setting the timer for thirty minutes, I have no idea how long it should bake. The girls check on it constantly, peering through the glass window on the oven door. The aroma is intoxicating. Finally, the crust turns golden and the drizzles of honey bubble and darken. As I open the oven door, the kitchen instantly fills with the perfume of a bakery.

"Oooh," sighs Paige, "it's so pretty."

Sydney carries the steaming masterpiece to the living room to show their dad, with Paige and Claudia close behind. Paige insists I take photos.

Paige's birthday celebration delights her. Ron places citronella candles around the concrete slab, I make a nosegay of wild flowers to put in front of the birthday girl, and everyone sings "Happy Birthday to Paige" so loudly it is surely heard across the valley. The girls' *torta di prugne*, plum pie, is a culinary masterpiece, surpassing everyone's highest hopes.

When Ron announces bedtime, Claudia begs, "Gabba, would you read a story... for Paige's birthday, pleeease." Larry can't resist and reads to them from *Italian Folk Tales* by Italo Calvino. As Ron, Paulla and I clear the table and wash a mountain of pots and pans, I overhear snippets of a tale embellished with fantastic bits about an Italian princess named *Principessa Pagina* and her devious but good-hearted sisters.

Paige loved her birthday dinner despite the missing decorations and gifts. Instead, she found joy in a simple celebration with candles, a homemade plum pie, and an improvised folk tale. Perhaps we should all be more like children, experiencing life with unfettered joy, completely in the moment.

August

Finding the Suitcase, Losing the Kids

Across all of Italy, work has stopped. The tradition started in 18BC when Emperor Caesar Augustus set aside one day as an official day of rest. The month of August was later named for him, and over the centuries his day of rest, *Ferragosto*, August 15, morphed into a month-long holiday. Not everyone stops working, but not much gets done.

Last night, just before Paige's birthday celebration, Ron learned that the suitcase is in airport lost and found, tagged as abandoned. We decide to make a day of exploring Florence. I put fresh batteries in the walkie-talkies so we can talk car-to-car. Sydney and Paige want to ride with us. Claudia clings to her mom, claiming her head hurts.

To pass time on the road, I teach the older girls Italian courtesy words such as hello, my pleasure, thank you, you're welcome, and goodbye. They learn quickly. I move to colors, items in the car, then items outside the car like tree and grass. When Syd calls Claudia on the walkie-talkies and they start to giggle, I sense our Italian lesson has ended.

"Remember, walkie-talkies are not telephones," I warn, "turn them off so you don't use up the batteries." They nod, but I doubt they'll pay attention. When Sydney puts the walkie-talkie on the seat, I ask her to hand it to me. Of course, it's still on. "Syd, you *must* remember to turn this off," I scold.

"Sorry, Nana," she replies reflexively.

Finally, we pull into the airport and park both cars along a road where other cars are parked. Ron, armed with baggage claim tickets, says he won't be long. The girls play with the walkie-talkies while the rest of us wait. After a while, Claudia falls asleep.

Over an hour later, which seems like two, Ron appears grinning and pulling the suitcase. It is mammoth.

"All in?" Larry asks as Ron slams the hatch door. Larry's eager to be in Florence after so much waiting. In honor of Paige's birthday, we'll visit the Pitti Palace. Paige loves princesses and anything to do with princesses, and the Pitti Palace is where some Florentine princesses lived.

In a shop window near the palace, I spy a pink tee shirt that says *Principessa*. I slip into the store, whispering to Larry that Paige must have it. The girls follow me. Instantly, Paige clutches her pink *Principessa* shirt, declaring that pink is her favorite color and this is her favorite ever shirt. Sydney chooses an Italian soccer shirt and Claudia finds one that simply says *Firenze*, "how Italians say Florence" she informs me. The girls leave the shop overjoyed and literally skip down the sidewalk for the remaining two blocks to the Pitti.

Luca Pitti, an ambitious Florentine banker, commissioned the massive, fortress-like home in 1458. The Pitti family rivalry with the Medici was legendary. Though Cosimo di Medici (the elder) was a friend and colleague of Luca Pitti, it was rumored that Luca directed his architect to make every window bigger than those in the Medici Palace. One hundred years later, Cosimo's descendants bought the Pitti Palace as the home for ruling Florentine families, including four generations of Medici.

The girls are not so keen on visiting museum collections, so Larry takes them behind the palace to explore the extensive Boboli Gardens. When Ron, Paulla, and I arrive at our rendezvous spot, Sydney comes running down the hill yelling, "Daddy, Daddy, Gabba's telling dumb jokes again."

Larry's laughing. The girls look disgusted. I wait to hear the offense, knowing it'll be amusing, corny, and probably a pun.

Sydney, seemingly quite agitated, exclaims, "Gabba said Paige isn't really a *principessa*... she's a lion. Get it? He called Paige a liar!!"

I wonder if Sydney's standing up for her sister, trying to get Gabba in trouble, or simply vying for attention. In Gabba's defense, Paige's hair is like a lion's mane.

"Never mind," says Ron, the ultimate peacekeeper, dismissing it with an amused smirk.

We hurry over the famous *Ponte Vecchio* — by order of Hitler the only Florentine bridge German WWII forces did not destroy. Larry wants everyone to see *Basilica di Santa Croce*, the church where Michelangelo and Galileo are entombed. Since it's getting late, we race past gold shops on the bridge, through narrow streets, and across the wide piazza. Breathless, we learn the church is closed.

"Since we've come this far," I say, "how 'bout *Vivoli*, the best gelato in Florence... It's close. Anyone want gelato?"

"YES!" Paige yells, only a fraction of a second faster than her sisters.

On the way, I tell the girls the reason to go to *Vivoli* is for *cioccolato arancia,* dark chocolate with candied orange peel. *Vivoli* makes milk chocolate, hazelnut chocolate, dark chocolate, chocolate with rice, coffee chocolate, chocolate chocolate-chip, but the best is with orange peel.

"No chocolate, Nana," Claudia reminds me, looking up at her mom as I finish my enthusiastic soliloquy.

"Oops, sorry," I say.

The girls choose two fruit flavors each, but are disappointed that the cups are smaller than in Cortona, and not mounded on top. I ask for two scoops of *cioccolato arancia.*

As we stroll back to the cars, I window shop. The clothes are exquisite. Living so close to Florence, I wonder why I shop anywhere else.

When Ron starts their car it sounds funny. Larry, a former auto mechanic, listens and agrees there may be a problem. The car lurches up the exit ramp, but Larry's not sure if the problem is the car, driver, or very steep incline. Ron stops and comes back to tell us the transmission feels funny, but he thinks it'll be okay once the car warms up. It's over ninety degrees; I don't think the engine is cold. Once on the streets, he gives us a thumbs-up to indicate all is okay. We find our way out of Florence with Larry in the lead. Claudia and Paige are with us. Sydney is with her folks this time.

We lose sight of them at the roundabout near the A1 entrance, so go around several times to let them catch up. When we don't see them, we decide they must be ahead, so Larry takes his toll ticket and merges onto the A1. I try calling on the walkie-talkie, but they don't answer.

Twenty minutes south of Florence, Larry says we should go back. He's concerned they may have had car trouble, don't have a cell phone, and don't speak Italian. We take the next exit and go all the way back to the roundabout where we lost them. After circling several times, we give up again and re-enter the *autostrada*.

At the first *Autogrill*, Larry pulls into the parking lot to search for their car, just in case. I keep trying the walkie-talkie with no answer. The girls are bored, need a bathroom, and Paige insists she's starving.

Paige doesn't like anything she sees in the sandwich case, but reluctantly chooses a *panino* of *mozzarella*, *prosciutto* and a green tomato slice, agreeing to share with Claudia who declares she isn't hungry *at all*. Back in the car, Paige asks me to take off the green thing and devours her half, proclaiming *prosciutto* her new favorite food. She asks Claudia for her half.

"No. No. No." Claudia says firmly, shaking her head. Though she hasn't taken a nibble and claims to have no hunger, she protects her half, clinching it with both hands. Paige begs. Claudia refuses. I try to talk Claudia into sharing half of her half. Nothing doing. Larry and I are amused and a little exasperated. Sisters!

The sun is low in the sky as we drive south. We're concerned about Ron's car, but don't know what to do. About halfway home, Larry's phone rings.

"Hey, where are you guys?" Ron says cheerfully.

"Still on the road... and you?" I say, putting Larry's phone on speaker so he can hear.

"We're in Cortona. Didn't think I could find your house, so we're having a Campari. I'm at Marco's, using his phone. Can you meet us here?

"We're still thirty minutes away. We went back looking for you," Larry says. "We were afraid you had car trouble. Why didn't you answer our calls?"

"Didn't get any calls. Batteries must have been dead."

"Why didn't you stay with us?"

"We got ahead of you at the toll booth, but I thought you saw us, so didn't wait."

Larry shakes his head in dismay. "Okay. We'll come to town. Just don't go anywhere else without letting us know… please."

He is not happy.

I'm glad they're okay, but also annoyed we wasted so much time on the road. I do wish they had been more careful with the walkie-talkie batteries. I wish I was in Cortona sipping Campari!

By the time we park, both girls are wide-awake. We climb the steep street into town and find Ron, Paulla and Sydney in the piazza having a second drink and a snack.

"Y'all want a drink?" Ron asks.

Larry insists we go home. Ron pays their bill and all three girls go with their parents, probably sensing Larry's upset.

Even with adult children, parents act like parents when something goes awry. I feel badly for Ron. Since he was a little boy, his greatest desire has been for everyone to be happy and he still tries to make life happen that way. Today, without his knowledge, it did not go so well.

As we approach home, the roads are wet. "Looks like it rained. Hope we have power," I say jokingly, hoping to lighten Larry's mood.

Inside the house I flip the switch, fully expecting lights. Pitch black. I find a flashlight for Larry, whose is still miffed. The girls wait upstairs in the dark, perched on the edge of the sectional sofa, now their beds. Larry goes downstairs to restart the main breaker.

On top of losing the kids, I don't want a night without lights, water, or internet. I pray quietly.

Yes! Lights blaze, seeming brighter than ever after being in complete dark.

Ron drags the reclaimed suitcase into the house. The instant that bag is unzipped, Paige grabs her birthday packages and starts ripping off the paper. She "oohs" and "ahhs" with each gift. She puts on her fluffy pink birthday bathrobe and dances round and round while we sing "Happy Birthday to Pa-ige" in our most jubilant voices.

Spirits lifted, we decide to raid the refrigerator for leftovers. Claudia and Paige are thrilled to be allowed Nutella and banana sandwiches. Sydney insists on "real food" and devours most of the leftover steak. The adults are happy with a glass of wine, a few meat scraps and some cheese. Everyone enjoys another piece of Paige's plum pie.

The girls take baths, put on their newly-found pajamas and encircle Larry, tugging on his shirt and begging for another story.

As Ron, Paulla and I clean up, Larry embellishes another *Italian Folk Tale*. When *Contessa Claudina* suddenly appears on horseback, riding backward and upside down, the girls giggle like crazy.

Amazing how quickly offenses, especially unintended ones, can fade when someone looks for fun.

"Gabba, You're Not Funny Anymore"

Wearing her fancy pink robe with feathery trim and rhinestones down the front, Paige sashays down the stairs and into the living room, the first awake this morning.

"Who's that gorgeous vision in pink?" Larry asks. Paige rubs her eyes, acting half-asleep.

"Do you want a kiddie cappuccino, *Principessa Paige?*"

She nods drowsily. He's been making them kiddie cappuccini for years, steamed milk with chocolate rather than coffee.

This time he acts confused.

"You want me to put a *kitty* in your cup and stir it around?"

She pauses, then emphatically swings her head side to side. Uncombed, ultra-thick strawberry blond hair flies out, framing her head like that lion's mane. Ever the dramatic, Paige rolls her enormous caramel eyes at me, then glares at her Gabba straight on and speaks slowly and deliberately.

"No, Gab-ba... a KID cappuccino."

"You want me to put a baby *goat* in your cup?" he queries.

After another moment's exasperation, she replies matter-of-factly, "No, Gabba, just steam milk and add chocolate... in a cup... to drink."

Ron comes into the kitchen ready for breakfast and our next adventure. Today we'll explore a fort on *Lago Trasimeno*, twenty minutes south of

Cortona. While Larry makes drinks, I try to wake Sydney, but give up and take my shower.

With all three girls in the back seat of our SUV, we head to Castiglione del Lago, the biggest town on the biggest lake in central Italy. Larry tells a joke. In the rear-view mirror, I see the girls look at each other. There's a long silence.

"Gabba, you just aren't funny anymore," Sydney says flatly.

Larry looks shocked. He has adored Syd since she was born, and she's reciprocated as though he hung the moon. She has laughed at every joke, followed him around adoringly, revered his insights in countless museums, ridden tandem bikes, trained for a triathlon together, and enjoyed every moment of his attention — which he has happily lavished on her.

Not funny anymore is devastating.

After a pause with his eyes narrowed and lower lip protruding, Larry says softly, "I can't believe you said that, Syd. Take it back…"

Sydney holds her ground. "Not funny," she repeats and turns to look out the car window.

"Guess I need some new jokes," he murmurs to me, rather pathetically.

The girls blurt guffaws like it's a victory, but joy has left the car. Larry drives in silence, his lips tightly drawn. I don't know if he's pretending or is really upset, but I fear the latter. Being funny, especially in Sydney's eyes, holds enormous value for him. With the one person we believe holds us in the highest regard, any cut seems deep.

Despite his wound, Larry and I chat amicably for the rest of the drive. When we arrive at the fort's ticket office at two minutes after noon, the ticket agent says they closed at noon, an hour earlier than we expected.

Doesn't everything close at one?

"*Quando aperta?*" I ask. When open?

"*Tre ore,*" in three hours she says, covering the gift shop trinkets with cloths.

After walking every street in the medieval town of Castiglione di Lago in less than an hour, everyone sits on bench under a tree to cool off.

Larry and I decide to explore a ceramic shop nearby. I've been searching for an antique ceramic bowl for the center of our dining room table. Paige asks to come along.

"*Prego, bella,*" the owner beckons Paige to come with him. She looks at me for approval. I nod.

"You choose," he leans close and whispers to her in English, pointing to the case of tiny ceramic animals. "Any one you want."

Paige looks at me again. When I nod, she chooses a tiny pink pig. Thrilled, she tells the owner it was her birthday and she is seven and she loves pink and pigs. I'm not sure who is happier, Paige or the owner.

With two more hours to kill, we look for a place for lunch and find a restaurant with a large courtyard overlooking the lake. The hostess offers us a table in the sun near an ivy-covered stone wall. Since it's the only table available for seven, we take it. There is no breeze, the courtyard is crowded, and the stone wall radiates heat.

We sit and wait. And wait. Larry gets up to find a waiter to ask if we can have menus and water. He seems subdued, perhaps because of Syd's declaration. Water finally arrives, plus soft drinks for the girls. Wine takes another ten minutes. When the waitress finally asks if we're ready to order, the girls' choices surprise me. I ask for something I think they'll like in case they don't like what they ordered. We roast for another thirty minutes before any food appears.

My dish is a disappointment and the girls love their strange choices. I learn my lesson one more time: ask for what I want, not what I think someone else wants. It applies to more than food.

Paige names her pig Principessa Pig Tiara Pink Smith. And, no, there is no shorter version. This is an important, titled pig in every way. In honor of Principessa Pig Tiara Pink Smith, we all order outrageous, piggy-esque desserts.

The girls beg for chocolate, but Paulla shakes her head.

"You only need to throw away a couple-hundred-dollars-worth of kids' clothes before you start to hate chocolate," she insists.

Her rule seems excessively strict since we're sitting at a table rather than holding gelato cones but, as mother-in-law, I counsel but dare not override.

I feel sorry for the girls and understand why they're begging. The chocolate desserts sound divine. If I were alone with the girls, I'd give in like a good grandmother is supposed to do.

As we wait for our desserts, I notice Larry's knees are peeling, surely from scrubbing the floor before David and Dale arrived. My heart pings. He truly is a great guy. I should be more appreciative. I reach to take his hand and remind myself to express my appreciation more often. I feel sad for him because of Syd's remark. It's easier to feel softhearted for the wounded.

After too much Tuscan sun, we hurry to explore *Castello del Leone*, Castle of the Lion. I'm fascinated to learn that the castle-fortress was designed in 1245 by Brother Elia, the Franciscan who lived in Cortona and led the order after Francis died. Castles and fortresses don't seem religious or Franciscan to me, so I wonder if there is a story. Brother Elia was also the architect of the *Chiesa San Francesco* in Cortona and the grand *Basilica di San Francesco* in Assisi, both of which are churches, not fortresses.

The girls briskly walk — signs posted say *no running* — the narrow ramparts around the top and exclaim over spectacular views of Lake Trasimeno, Cortona, and beyond. The fortress has five sides and an open center, as if built around a star. A triangular tower dominates one corner and smaller towers mark others, each with the perfect vantage point to see oncoming invaders. These days, the park-like center is used for concerts, movies and community events.

By late afternoon we have resettled at home. I decide to go to Camucia again to pay for the plastic chairs, taking cash this time. Sonia, the owner, laughs, insisting it was not necessary to make a special trip only to pay. She now says the cost is forty-five euros for twelve chairs, a slight reduction. She doesn't have change for my fifty-euro bill, so calls upstairs to her mother who drops five one-euro coins from the balcony overhead.

"*Ah,*" sighs Sonia, "*piove denaro per lei.*" It rains money for you.

Back home everyone says they aren't hungry after our enormous lunch. But when I make zucchini risotto, not one rice kernel is left. Magically, we also finish off every crumb of Paige's plum pie.

Larry still seems sad that Sydney said he isn't funny anymore. She acts as though nothing is wrong and doesn't recant, though I suspect she knows her Gabba's feelings have been hurt. As we fall asleep, I reach to touch his shoulder, wanting to reconnect. He doesn't respond.

In the middle of the night I awaken to an unfamiliar noise. There's no moonlight. I listen again and hear nothing. I get up to look out the bedroom window and jump when a shadow crosses our bedroom wall. I whip around, but nothing is there. Perhaps someone is outside the bathroom window. I remember Francesco's warning about thieves. The shadow moves again. Then I laugh out loud, realizing I have been frightened by my own shadow cast by the teeny light on the thermostat.

Sometimes we jump at shadows, whether it's a light on the bedroom wall or a beloved grand-daughter's tease about not being funny anymore. Hopefully, all of tonight's shadows will have passed when morning comes.

The Skeleton Behind the Table

Yesterday Larry and I spent the day in Rome, leaving Ron and family to explore Cortona. Close friends from Chicago were coming through Rome for one day and asked if we would join them. Ron insisted we go. He had no idea how important it would be.

Over lunch, Jim gave Larry pages of jokes. Jim is a master of kids' jokes and Larry had shared his heartbreak that Sydney didn't think he was funny anymore. The boys read them aloud over pasta, *secondo*, and dessert, laughing their heads off while Kathleen and I chatted about our children, grandchildren, mutual friends, their holiday cruise and our move to Italy. I wondered how long it would take Larry to use a joke or two with Sydney, and I hoped she found them as funny as our grown-up husbands did.

In addition to being a kid-humor aficionado, Jim is an acclaimed architect who did his early study in Rome. Walking with him through winding streets, we learned new facts about the Eternal City that we thought we knew well. For example, in the Pantheon, my favorite building in Rome, Jim told us the oculus in the center of the dome not only lets in light, it's a tension ring that helps hold up the massive concrete dome. It was the largest dome in the world when it was built in 126AD and is among the largest today, nearly two thousand years later. Jim reminded us the great Roman contribution to architecture was not columns, bricks or arches, it was the invention of concrete.

At the Trevi Fountain, I was able to share a story our friends didn't know. When the fountain — perhaps the most famous in the world — was carved beginning in 1732, the artist Nicolo Salvi added an urn that still seems out of place. We've heard two versions. One is that the owner of a nearby barber shop complained one too many times that the fountain was ugly, so Salvi added the urn to block the barber's view forever. The second, related but from a different perspective, is that Salvi added the urn to block the barbershop's ugly sign from detracting from the beauty of his fountain. Maybe both are true. The urn is easy to spot because it is static, unlike the rest of Oceanus' thunderous and majestic conquering of the waters.

We bid goodbye to our friends late afternoon and headed home, turning our thoughts to a second trip to Florence with the kids. We arrived home in time to hear about their fun day in Cortona, eat a snack and fall into bed.

Like yesterday in Rome, this morning I rush to get dressed for another day of walking. I'd prefer to wear my comfortable sandals, repaired after the fox chewed the strap. However, we've been warned that Italian clerks, especially in Rome, Milan and Florence, look first at your feet. If you wear good shoes, you get good service. If not, you take your chances. I decide on prettier but less comfortable shoes for our day exploring Florence.

To my amazement, Ron and Paulla get themselves and three sleeping girls cleaned, dressed, and fed in one hour. We pile into one car for the short ride to the Camucia station. Larry translates the rules on the ticket machine and says he's pretty sure children under twelve ride for free, saying we should all play dumb if he's wrong.

Each girl begs to slide the tickets into the yellow box to stamp them. Italian trains work on a semi-honor system. A ticket is good for any day or time. Then, just before boarding, we put the ticket into the box to stamp it with the time and date. On the train, if the conductor finds us without a ticket or if our tickets are not validated, the fine is steep. Larry hands Paige the tickets to slide into the stamp machine, another birthday privilege.

We're seven in a glassed-walled compartment for eight. It's still early morning. Paige wants to sleep, so pulls up an armrest to make a bed and asks me to pull down the window shade. I'd like to sleep too, so reach for the shade. Larry frowns disapprovingly, which means he wants the shade up so he can read.

"Whoever is older should get to choose," Paige declares when I shrug, caught between pleasing my granddaughter and myself, or appeasing my husband.

"Are you younger than Gabba?" she persists. I'm sure she already knows.

"What do you think?" I whisper, trying not to bother Larry while he reads.

"Tell me, Nana. Who-is-older?"

I point to myself and silently mouth, "I am."

"How much?" she says, this time more softly.

"Twenty years." Sometimes an exaggeration is easier than the truth.

Paige rolls her eyes, feigning annoyance.

"Does that mean you always get your way? The oldest usually does," she says.

"No, it means I'm smart enough to give him his way."

"Really???" she asks, looking stupefied.

"Truth is truth," I tell her, as I glance at Larry. He looks over the top of his glasses, not charmed. We've interrupted his reading. I leave the shade open for him.

The conductor comes, punches our tickets, and doesn't mention the girls.

Larry gives up reading and starts to explain our day. First, he says, we'll visit the *Basilica di Santa Maria Novella* near the train station, to see some of Florence's most important art. We'll have lunch early since no one had breakfast and then we'll go to another church, *Santa Maria della Carmine*. He wants everyone to watch their short film, the perfect foundation for exploring Renaissance art in Florence, he says. Lastly, since it's Sunday, we'll visit the *Duomo* and attend the once-a-week English-language Mass. Then we can have gelato.

No one comments. I feel tired.

The train becomes crowded as we near Florence. Paige has to relinquish her second seat to a baby-faced man of maybe twenty. He stares at his phone.

Paige shifts in her seat and watches him. Claudia reads. Sydney writes in her journal, as do I. When we reach the station, passengers are standing like sardines in the aisles.

Larry reaches for my hand in the underground passage. He's beaming. He loves Florence and is excited to share it with his granddaughters. I smile up at him. I love Florence, too, and appreciate his warm connection.

We enter the nearby church of *Santa Maria Novella* through a small cloister shaded by a grove of ancient hemlock trees. Set into the wall beside the stone path are gravestone. In the early Renaissance, when this church was built, walking through the graveyard into the church was commonplace, symbolic of passing from death into life. It still seems appropriate today.

Inside the sanctuary, hanging high overhead near the center of the room and dominating the enormous space, is a crucifix painted by Giotto around 1300.

"Do you know what this represents?" Larry asks the girls, hovering around him.

Sydney's eager to tell everyone what she knows. "Jews killed Jesus. They nailed him to a cross and then soldiers put a sword in his side. See, there's blood spurting out... it's all over his feet." She points up at the blood.

Larry puts his arm around her shoulders and gently says, "Syd, this is important, so listen closely. Some Jews were against Jesus, but everyone there participated in killing him... Jews, Christians, Palestinians, Romans, *everyone*. People just like us. They either called for Jesus to be crucified or, maybe worse, they were quiet and didn't stand up for him. It's not right to say Jews killed Jesus."

Sydney frowns a little, tilting her head to one side as she considers this new idea. I also think she didn't like being corrected by her Gabba, even gently.

Larry points to Jesus' face, noting his long delicate nose, wavy reddish hair and warm expression of compassion. He says Giotto painted Jesus looking downward because he knew this large crucifix would hang high overhead and he wanted Jesus to be looking at the worshippers. Even his halo is slightly raised, three-dimensional, as though Jesus' head is inclined toward those below. Giotto, Larry says with admiration, is often called the Father of the Renaissance.

Today, seven hundred years later, Jesus seems to look down on me the same way — warmly, compassionately. When Larry and the girls move on, I linger one more moment under Giotto's masterful depiction and Jesus' reassuring gaze.

When I catch up, they're sitting on the steps of a chapel at the front. The church is full of tourists, but still feels reverent.

"Okay," Larry whispers, leaning toward the girls. "Let's look at *this* crucifix. It was carved a hundred years after Giotto painted the one you just saw. What's different? Look closely."

The girls are surprisingly articulate. They say he looks natural. His arms and legs are the right length, his muscles are strong, his body looks round and heavy, and his expression seems real. Without knowing it, they have identified the artistic elements that define the Renaissance, when the human ideal was elevated.

Seeing Larry as grandfather-teacher delights me. He adores these girls and they adore him. He tells them this crucifix is by Filippo Brunelleschi, who was more an architect than a sculptor. After enough, the girls stand to move on.

Near Brunelleschi's crucifix is the Tornabuoni chapel by Ghirlandaio, the Florentine master who taught the young Michelangelo how to paint frescoes. The girls ask Gabba to explain scene after scene, using the frescoes as they were meant to be used: as teaching tools. This cycle is about the life of Mary, the mother of Jesus.

Larry points to a woman in a gold dress and says she is Ludovica Tornabuoni, the daughter of Giovanni Tornabuoni, the donor. He asks the girls why an artist would paint the donor's family members into an event, the birth of Jesus' mother, that happened centuries before the family was even alive. When Sydney says to get more money, her sisters nod. Larry agrees, and explains that during the Renaissance wealthy people paid for art in churches as a way to contribute to the community, honor God, and have their families remembered through history. Seven hundred years later, Ludovica is still known because of this painting.

When Larry sees Paige fidget and shuffle, he says, "Let's go see one of my favorite paintings of all time. Then we'll have lunch." To announce that something will end soon typically extends the audience's attention span, at least a little. Toward the back of the church, we stop at a gray and pink fresco. It's one of my favorites too, a concept rather than a story. I'm curious to see the girls' reaction.

Larry stands and stares at it with reverence. Then he leans down and softly tells the girls why it's important. I think he's talking mostly to Sydney, but the other two listen attentively. They seem to want to know too.

He tells them the artist, Masaccio, was only twenty-five years old when he painted this, the first painting in the Renaissance to follow the rules for perspective. He asks if they see how all the lines get closer together toward one point. When they nod, he says Masaccio's friend Brunelleschi, the architect who carved the life-like crucifix they saw earlier, had just written guidelines for linear perspective in art, and the painter Masaccio followed his friend's rules.

Then Larry explains how this painting also breaks the rules for perspective. "See how everyone in the painting fits into the space, except God? God seems to be out of perspective, sort of floating. Do you see?"

They all nod. I hope they really do see it.

Larry pauses, then adds, "I think Masaccio wanted to say that God is everywhere — not limited by time or space. Masaccio was brilliant. He worked in Florence one hundred years after Giotto and people said he was Giotto reborn. But Masaccio took painting to a whole new level, beyond Giotto."

"What's that?" asks Claudia, eyes widening as she points to a smaller painting below, at just her level.

"Oh, I'm glad you saw that, Claudia," Larry says. "Kinda creepy, isn't it? The skeleton's banner is in Latin. It says, 'I once was what you are, and what I am you will be.' The two frescos together teach that everyone will die, but that faith in the Holy Trinity — Father, Son and Holy Spirit, all in the painting above — allows us to overcome death with life in heaven."

When they don't react, I add a side story. "That skeleton was covered up for almost four hundred years by an altar table. Can you imagine moving a table and finding that skeleton?

When still no one responds, I say, "Wanna have some fun?" Claudia looks up and smiles.

"Okay. Walk with me and watch the stair that's painted under the skeleton. Be sure to keep your eyes on it."

Claudia walks beside me and stares at the stair.

"It moves! It moves!" she exclaims, a little too loudly. Then everyone tries it. Painted in perfect perspective, the stair appears to shift position to face us no matter where we stand. Claudia walks back and forth a few more times.

Sydney asks me if they can have money to light a candle. I hand each girl a euro and am touched to see them take turns, dropping their coin into the box, then lighting their candle from a sister's flame.

I'm curious about their prayers, but prayers deserve to remain private.

As we leave, Paige asks, a little too loudly, "Why is that woman wearing a paper bag?"

I turn and see a woman in a paper poncho.

"It's to cover her shoulders," I whisper, explaining that in Italy women are modest in churches, as a sign of respect. I point to the sign near the door with symbols for no shorts, no sleeveless shirts, and no mini-skirts, and tell Paige that the ticket agent gave the lady the poncho to cover her shoulders so she could come inside."

Paige looks baffled, as bare shoulders and shorts are commonplace in churches in the heat of San Antonio, where she lives.

Outside, we rest on benches in the nearby piazza and talk about the church facade, the oldest of the great basilicas in Florence. Paige and Claudia chase pigeons while Sydney sits with the adults.

When we walk past Hotel Tornabuoni Beacci on our way to lunch, I want to say hello to Angelo, the manager who has become a friend. Larry wants to get to the restaurant before there's a line. To me, it's as important to share the people we know in Florence with the girls as it is to share the art or food. But he walks ahead and I hurry to catch up.

When we get to the restaurant, *Il Latini*, a popular restaurant that doesn't take reservations, we're shocked there's no line. Then we see the sign: *Chiuso a 15 Agosto*, closed until August 15. Who'd have imagined such an in-demand restaurant would close in the height of tourist season?

Larry suggests we go to *Santa Maria del Carmine* first and find lunch afterward.

Chiesa Santa Maria del Carmine is south of the Arno River, a hike for little legs. We head immediately to the bathroom since the girls say they can't wait. I remember it as the worst in Florence. Indeed, as we get closer, I can smell it, as odious as the vilest camp latrine. Claudia wrinkles her nose, frowns, and says she'll hold it. I warn her it'll be thirty minutes since it's time for the film to start. She says that's okay.

In the small theater we find seats and set our headphones for English. The film tells us that in 1422, when the famous Brancacci Chapel was being frescoed, Florence's artistic masters — Masaccio, Donatello, Brunelleschi — were the best the world had ever seen in their fields of painting, sculpture and architecture. In 1771, a fire consumed the church, but the revered chapel survived the flames, an event Florentines declared a miracle.

Fighting sleep since I've seen the film many times, I glance over at the girls and Ron. All are glued to the screen.

After the film, the girls say they're desperate. Shockingly, the bathroom is clean inside and smells better than outside.

Our fifteen minutes allowed in the chapel pass quickly. Many art experts consider this collection of frescoes the earliest masterwork of the Renaissance, referring to this tiny space as the Sistine Chapel of Florence, though painted nearly one hundred years earlier.

My favorite scene, if anyone can call a tragedy their favorite, is Masaccio's depiction of the expulsion of Adam and Eve from the Garden. As I stare up into their faces, I can hear Eve's anguished scream and feel Adam's shame.

Suddenly, we're ushered out. Everyone's famished, since it's nearly two. In a nearby piazza in the sunshine, we order pasta, pizzas, and salads. Probably too much food, but it matches our appetites.

Skies soon darken and the wind picks up. The umbrella shading us starts to sway. Guests try to hold down placemats and napkins as they fly off the tables. Suddenly, rain pelts everything. Grabbing belongings, we run inside. Re-seated at a table near the window, we enjoy a long leisurely lunch while a summer shower washes the piazza. Claudia, now full, naps with her head in her mother's lap and the older girls cozy up next to their dad.

The sun reappears about the time we leave, but rain persists. With simultaneous showers and sunshine, I hope for a rainbow. When we cross the Arno River, Ron wants to stop for the classic family photo with *Ponte Vecchio* in the background. Sadly, without a rainbow.

Nearing Hotel Tornabuoni again, I ask the girls, "How'd you like to meet some of my favorite people in Florence?"

Claudia and Paige say, "Yes!!" in unison.

The three of us hold hands and skip up the middle of the pedestrian-only street, leaving the others behind. Times like these I love being a grandmother more than anything on earth. One cost of our move to Italy is being unable to do the grandmother-thing. But our grandchildren live in Portland, San Diego and San Antonio, so far from Chicago that I wouldn't see them often even if we had remained. My joy makes me hold tighter to my granddaughters' hands, relishing this moment.

We skip between monumental doors that look like medieval castle doors into the hotel. I hope the people we know are working today. Angelo is the manager and Patrizia, his wife, handles administration. Gino covers the front desk. We first visited Hotel Tornabuoni Beacci 1997. In 2002 it became our home in Florence when, as Larry's fiftieth birthday gift from me, we stayed three weeks while studying art and Italian. We're still treated like family.

"*Ci sono Angelo, Patrizia o Gino oggi?*" I ask the unfamiliar lady at the front desk. Are Angelo, Patrizia and Gino here today?

"Patricia's on holiday and Gino's off today. But Angelo's here. I'll see if I can find him," she replies in flawless English to my stilted Italian.

We wait in the rooftop garden, one of the loveliest in Florence. Angelo finds us and chats with the girls like they're all princesses. He asks if he can get anything to make us more comfortable: coffee, water, a place to rest? We say we only came to say hello, which pleases him enormously. The girls are their most charming. As we leave, each girl shakes Angelo's hand and gives him a kiss on each cheek. His cherub face blushes bright pink.

Outside, Paige announces, "Angelo's adorable. He even looks like an angel!"

Larry urges us to hurry. He wants us all to explore the *Duomo* before Mass. Claudia walks with me. She's been a trooper. Her four-year-old legs take several steps to my one, but I think she's less tired than I am. I feel happy, having introduced the girls to Angelo.

Paulla wants to shop while Larry and Sydney explore the *Duomo*. Claudia and Paige ask me if they can pet the horses.

"*Quanto costa?*" I ask a carriage driver, how much, thinking a buggy ride in Florence would make a spectacular memory.

"*Cinquanta euro.*" Fifty euros, about seventy dollars.

"*Troppo,* too much," I say sadly.

The driver is most kind, showing the girls the soft part between the horse's nostrils and how to pet it. Claudia, who has a collection of over two hundred toy horses and wants a real one "more than anything," jerks her tiny hand away each time she almost touches its fuzzy nose.

When the horse snorts, whinnies and shakes its head, Claudia jumps way back.

"Did that scare you?" I ask, chuckling.

"No," she declares.

Larry and Sydney find us, announcing that the English Mass is not in the Duomo, but in the nearby Misericordia Chapel. The girls endure the service without a fuss, possibly because we promised them gelato after Mass.

On our way to the train, they find a large gelateria with dozens of flavors and beg to stop. We ask for tastes to choose. The clerk looks perturbed and the tastes are pea-sized. When I ask to try a second flavor, he insists, "*Solo uno,*" only one.

"But we're buying seven cones," I say, frowning.

The cashier, who seems to know when to break the rules, gestures to the clerk, who reluctantly serves me a miniscule taste of peach. When the grumpy clerk fills my cup, he flattens the top, though he mounds all the others. I feel punished for my second taste. The gelato is good, but I'll never visit this gelateria again.

Typically, in a foreign culture, when not treated kindly I wonder if I'm doing something wrong. But today at this grand gelateria, I'm certain the server was being rude.

On the train ride home, all-knowing Paige tells Claudia that she, Claudia, will grow up to be a woman.

"No!" Claudia says, frowning, "I'm going to stay with being a girl."

"Why?" I ask.

As though it's the most obvious truth ever, Claudia replies, "Because girls get all the fun and women get all the work." I think about my heavy handbag full of everyone's extra gear and have to agree.

The next train stop is Camucia-Cortona. As we walk from the train to our car, I say I'm too tired to lift a spatula to cook dinner. The girls ask if we can have dinner in town, jumping up and down. Do they ever tire?

"How 'bout Dardano?" Ron asks to everyone's delight, especially his.

I'm glad we can invest in the lives of our children and grandchildren, even as adults and even though we live far away. They were wonderfully engaged in Florence and I hope they will remember the art and history we discussed. I'm certain they'll remember the stinky bathroom, cherub-faced Angelo, and the fuzzy-nosed horse. Experiences are always more memorable than facts.

To share our love of Italy with our children and grandchildren, even the small stuff, is part of our dream and perhaps the most important reason for moving here. I reach to touch Larry's hand and he squeezes mine in return, sharing my joy from a memorable, happy day.

Unlikely Friends Reunite

It's been two packed days since we went to Florence. Yesterday afternoon, after exploring Siena, Sydney asked if we could go to *La Bucaccia* for dinner, saying she hasn't seen Francesca at all, and that her family has never met her. Syd and Francesca met when we brought Sydney to Cortona on vacation. The girls were only six. Despite no common language, they had formed a lovely little-girl friendship.

Last night at *La Bucaccia*, Romano seemed shocked to see Sydney, now a young lady of nine. He extended his hand in a grown-up gesture and

Sydney responded by shaking it with dignified formality. Then he enfolded her. Unprepared for such a warm embrace, she stiffened a little and turned her head to the side to breathe.

After Sydney introduced her parents and sisters, everyone courteously said hello, and Romano seated us at the large central table. Larry ordered all our favorites. Sydney and Francesca sat at one end of the table, giggling and drawing pictures, chatting in three languages: English, Italian, and the Spanish that they both had studied in elementary school. They were oblivious to the rest of us as we devoured course after course. Claudia fell asleep during our second pasta, her head in her mother's lap. Paige's chin was on the table after our first dessert, but her big eyes watched the room as Romano served warm biscotti with *Vin Santo*, and finally grappa for the adults. Romano seemed reluctant for us to leave.

Sydney and Francesca, full of energy, chattered on.

For me, the best part of the meal was not the food, though Ron declared it the best meal of his entire life, but watching Francesca and Sydney rekindle their friendship. I hope it will be an important lifetime friendship for both of them. Before we left, Sydney asked if she could come back and help serve lunch. When all the parents agreed, the girls hugged like sisters.

I fell asleep feeling grateful for God's design that humans need food to survive. So many of life's richest memories are made lingering over a meal.

* * *

It's early morning again and I'm tired, but still smiling about last night. Sitting in the wicker chair, sipping a much-needed cappuccino, I write in my journal about our dinner. The hillside is hushed and dense white fog has filled the base of the valley. Suddenly, a single crystal ray breaks over the ridge, like a beacon over a cotton lake. As the sun rises and warms the valley, the lake vaporizes into nothingness.

Today, Ron and Paulla will take the younger girls to Rome, leaving Sydney with us for two days. We have agreed that each of the girls would have a special time alone with us. Syd, impossible to awaken, is still sleeping.

Ron runs up the stairs to kiss her goodbye and comes downstairs chuckling. "She'll be out for a while," he muses.

While Sydney sleeps and Larry takes a run, I sit in my black silk robe on the front slab and enjoy my second cappuccino in luxurious solitude. The little black squirrel munches away, dropping cone remnants that look like teeny apple cores. Songbirds warble as though singing just for me. I look into the cypress tree, hoping to see a crested lark, the *lodola*, but can only hear their elaborate, happy melodies.

Two trucks rumble along the gravel road on the hill across the stream and up to the house at the end of the road. Bulldozers have started excavating a massive hole on the level below the house. For over a year, our neighbors listened to our construction, so it seems only fair that we now listen to theirs.

Back inside and reloading the dishwasher, in perpetual use since the kids arrived, I'm perplexed that nothing sparkles. Today, our glasses look cloudier than ever. When I take the tablet out for the next load, I notice the picture on the box doesn't look like a dishwasher. The claim is *Lavatrice vive di piu*. Using the dictionary, I translate: the washing machine lives longer. Suddenly I realize I've been using de-calcification tablets for a clothes washer instead of detergent for a dishwasher.

The Miele technician left a sample, which I pull out. Pictured on the front is a sparkling stemmed glass. I pour his powder into the cup and refill the *brilliante* container. I hope no permanent damage has been done to our glasses or to the innocent dishwasher.

I still have time to launder my black delicates. Standing at the washing machine, I lift my nightgown over my head and add it to the load, re-wrapping my silk robe back around my naked body. Deciphering the Italian washing machine controls yet again, I realize I've been washing all my clothes, including blacks and delicates, at ninety degrees centigrade, only ten degrees short of boiling. I search for a cooler setting or a word that looks like delicate.

What an enlightening morning! I've been decalcifying our dishes and cooking my lingerie.

As I push the flashing 'start' button, a woman's voice calls. "*Poh-stah, buon giorno, poh-stah.*" I tie my robe quickly. Uncertain it's tied securely I hold the front to keep it together. Our post-lady is dressed, coiffed, perfectly made-up, and working. I'm naked under my silk robe, have wild hair, no make-up, and flip-flops on my feet. Maintaining a sliver of dignity, I don't tell her about my nakedness, the dishwasher decalcifier, or my cooked delicates. Besides, I'd never be able to explain it in Italian.

She smiles and hands me two bills and a fat envelope. We laugh over *sempre fatture*, always bills. The fat envelope is stuffed with photos from Dale which I'll enjoy later. To show the post-lady where our new postbox has been installed, I walk with her up the dirt ramp to the driveway, still clutching the front of my robe. During our entire conversation, she does not let her gaze drop from my eyes and I wonder how much is exposed. When she turns toward her official postal car, I look down to make sure my robe is closed. It is, just barely.

By the time Larry returns, I'm dressed for the day. But Sydney is still asleep.

"Syd," he says, walking upstairs, "what time did you tell Francesca you'd be there?"

"Tehn," Sydney drawls softly, sounding like the Texas girl she is.

"Syd! It's nine-thirty. Up! Up!"

"Okay, okay." Her bare feet plod across the floor. In fifteen minutes, she's ready.

"Don't you want to eat something before you leave?" I ask.

"Still full from last night. I can get something at the restaurant," she calls cheerily as she follows Larry out the front door. "Aren't you coming, Nana?"

"Why not?" I say, grab my bag and run to catch up. I don't remember her eating one bite last night.

At Romano's insistence, Larry and I enjoy *cappuccini* at their outdoor tables. Romano offers an artful plate of homemade cheese and fresh fig marmellata. We ask him to sit with us, at least for a moment. The girls are at the next table, drawing pictures and labeling them with Italian and English words.

"*Professoressa d'italiano*," Romano says, gesturing to Francesca as he pulls up a seat, and "*Professoressa d'inglese*," motioning to Sydney. Agostina joins us, gracious as always. She shines with joy. It's her nature to be positive but it seems beyond nature. Joy must be her life choice.

The girls ignore us, engaged in their exchange.

When Larry suggests we come back in two hours, Romano holds up four fingers. "I first take the girls to the garden for vegetables for today's menu, then they help make pasta before guests come for lunch. They will have fun."

We agree, four hours. That gives us time to go to the bank in Arezzo, an errand we've been putting off since the kids arrived, and to do a few things at home.

On the way to Arezzo, I ask Larry if he thinks we're leaving Sydney too long.

"Romano's happy for a companion for Francesca," he assures me. "Syd's having a great time. This is good for all of them… and for us. I like time with just you."

Back home after our drive to Arezzo, the dishwasher is beeping. I grin when I unload it… sparkling glasses… shiny dishes… spotless flatware. Now I should re-wash everything in the cabinets to remove the cloudy film.

When I tell Larry about my dishwasher fiasco and cooked lingerie, he laughs and hugs me like I'm a little girl. It feels good. We've had a nice time alone together, even running errands.

Two o'clock approaches. He says I should pick up Sydney when I go into town to exchange my shirts, and that I should bring Francesca back to see where Sydney lives while she's in Cortona. I'm baffled. I hadn't planned to drive to town, exchange the shirts, or have a guest today. Our house is in disarray, with open suitcases and piles of clothes, sheets and blankets everywhere, unfit for even a nine-year-old guest. I don't need to exchange the shirts right away and am not comfortable driving or trying to negotiate in Italian without his help.

As I start to protest, I reconsider. I did have over an hour alone this morning while he ran and he did take me to the grocery super-store in Arezzo without complaint. I decide I can go alone. Sometimes we choose to do something, not because we want to but because it seems fair. In relationships, some voluntary give and take can be the pressure valve that keeps everything in harmony.

I negotiate the steep curves without a problem, much to my surprise. Gripping the steering wheel the entire way and praying not to meet another car, I let out a long sigh of relief when I reach town. The parking lot is jammed. I wait, then negotiate my best three-point turn and back the monster SUV into a spot abandoned by a Fiat. I have to crawl over the console and get out the passenger's side. I consider re-centering the car when I look at the SUV's angle, but both drivers can open their doors, so I leave it. Nothing like a giant car in a small car culture.

Entering through the *Bifora*, a double-arch opening in Cortona's city wall, I hurry up *Via Ghibellina*, the steepest street in town. The *Bifora*, built by Etruscans over two thousand years ago using enormous stones, is reportedly the only double-arch Etruscan portal existing in the world today. I wonder how Etruscans cut those giant stones or put them into position at the top of this hill. There are many things about my new town that remain mysteries.

With my shoulders forward for leverage as I climb, I see Sydney talking with guests sitting at an outside table. It's two thirty, so lunch is winding down.

When she sees me, I hear, "Excuse me, please. Gotta go." I suspect she was chatting rather than taking an order. Inside, Agostina greets me with kisses. I ask if I may take the girls for gelato while I run an errand. She seems to understand, but doesn't agree or disagree, so I'm not sure it's okay. Romano joins us and I ask him in English. He speaks with Agostina and they seem delighted.

"Pranzo e finito. Va bene per fare una passeggiata." Lunch is over. It is good to take a stroll, Romano says warmly.

"Aspetti," wait, he says and opens the cash register. He takes my hand, unfurls it palm up, then fills it with coins.

"Per gelato," he says, grinning.

Eight euros. I give four to each girl. It'll buy the biggest gelato of their lives.

In the town center, Sydney tries to convince me to let them go to the gelateria on their own and meet me in the piazza later. I tell her I'll leave them at the gelateria while I go to the store across the street. They can buy gelato on their own, but must stay there until I return.

They nod and giggle, as if it was worth a try. At the gelateria, I linger for a moment, watching through the window. They ask for tastes. When another family comes in, Sydney motions that they should go first. I decide the girls are happy, safe and, importantly, polite, so I quit spying and go to exchange my shirts.

Using my best Italian, I try to tell the clerk that two weeks ago I bought these shirts and want to…. Sensing my struggle, she says, "*Scambia?*" Yes, I nod, exchange. I try on several more shirts and find two I like, but nothing goes with my new dark olive linen drawstring pants.

Fearing I've been gone too long, I point to the girls and say I'll be right back. "*Mia nipote*," my granddaughter, I say proudly.

The girls are perched on stools shaped like giant cones, carefully licking three scoops each in enormous waffle cones. I examine their shirts… not a drip.

"You doin' okay?" I ask. "I need ten more minutes."

Sydney turns to me, "Take your time, Nana. We're doin' very well, thanks."

She turns back to Francesca, continuing their chat in English, Italian and Spanish. I tap her on the shoulder and point to the store across the street to make sure she knows where I am. She nods without looking up.

What a pleasure to be in a small town in Italy where nine-year-old girls can experience independence. I would never allow them unescorted out of our building in Chicago. Not because our neighborhood is unsafe or because kids are less responsible there, but because Chicago is a city. Cortona is a community.

While I was gone, the clerk found a lime green tunic that is charming with the olive pants. I don't need three more linen shirts, but in the end, it's more important to nurture a new relationship than to worry about spending a little more.

When I try to pay the difference, she tells me it's *niente*, nothing. I insist I must pay. I calculate that I owe her eighteen euros and hand her a twenty. She refuses, saying they are now on sale. She insists my Italian is *buonissimo*, very good. I laugh, flattered but knowing the truth. I finally give-in, say, "*Grazie, grazie, troppo gentile*," too kind, and leave feeling treated beyond generously and eager to shop here again.

On our walk back to *La Bucaccia*, I quietly ask Syd if she'd like for Francesca to come home with us for a visit. Sydney nods and whispers to Francesca, whose face brightens into a huge grin. I remind them we must ask Francesca's parents first.

Romano and Agostina agree as long as she's back by six. The girls jump up and down, run down the steep hill, climb into the back seat and buckle in, with me as chauffeur.

As I drive the SUV up the access road and around the sharp uphill turn, the engine grinds and wheels spin. I glance at the girls in the rear-view mirror. Francesca looks pale. At the top of the second curve, when the car bumps over the bedrock, I see Francesco put her hand over her mouth.

"*Va bene?*" I ask, it goes okay?

Francesca nods, then puts her head in her lap.

As I turn into our driveway, our car startles an old woman waddling toward our house. She scurries into the woods, swaying side to side, and peers out from behind a tree. I stop and call out, "*Buonasera!*"

I've seen the same woman gathering roadside plants. She seems harmless, in fact, quite dear. She looks up and half raises her hand in a timid greeting. Behind her is a big shiny sickle. At her feet, a bundle of greens.

She stays hidden until we pass. In the rear-view mirror, I watch her emerge from the woods, turn and walk away from us.

Francesca still has her head between her knees when I stop. Instantly, she hops out and moves her hand from her mouth in a wide arc, the universal sign for throwing up. Our road and my driving made the poor girl sick. I feel terrible, but am not surprised. We trudge over mud and rubble to get to the house. She must wonder if we are crazy.

Francesca's color returns while Sydney shows her around. The girls inspect a wall of grass seeds the ants made along the concrete slab and chat with Larry. They play the piano. Francesca is intrigued by some Mardi Gras beads from Paige's birthday decorations, so Larry gives the girls matching strands of green beads.

About five-thirty, we decide to walk to town, rather than get back in the car. As we walk down the driveway, I'm surprised to see the old woman in our olive grove hacking away. Francesca jumps up and down.

"*La mia amica!*" My friend! Francesca runs down a dirt ramp toward the woman, who looks up, shocked. Then she recognizes Francesca, grins and holds out her arms.

Francesca slips on some gravel, almost falls, and yells "*Aiutami!*" Help me!

"Stop!" I yell. Francesca freezes. I walk down the ramp, take her hand and walk with her the rest of the way. Once Francesca is on flat ground, she pulls me along faster than I want to go, eager to greet her friend.

Francesca throws her arms around the forager, who looks confused to see her young friend here. The woman is tiny and hunched over, not much taller than Francesca. She has keen dark eyes, straggly gray hair, a beaming grin, and one tooth. Her skin, leathery from the sun, makes it impossible to tell her age. Twigs and sticky seedpods decorate her blue sweater, her apron pockets are stuffed, and her huge roll of foraged plants rests beside her right foot. She squeezes Francesca close and caresses her hair.

Larry and Sydney catch up and we all look at one another in an awkward moment.

In Italian, Larry tells the woman we moved here *da Chicago*. The forager tells us she likes our house. I ask *che cose*, what things she has picked, but she either doesn't understand or doesn't want to tell me. In her bundle, I recognize Queen Anne's lace, the pink blossoms of wild sweet peas, fennel clusters, blue-star borage, and lots of mystery greens.

After we say goodbye and start up the ramp, I glance back and see her reach with the tip of the sickle and deftly roll the bundle, wider than she is, under her arm.

Foragers are common in our area. It seems anything growing along a road is available for public consumption. However, I am surprised to see her on our property.

We turn right, uphill toward the rocky trail. Francesca tells us her friend lives near their restaurant and she has known her all her life. I look back and see the gleaner emerge from our driveway and turn down the access road.

On the Roman road over Cortona's hilltop, Francesca is fast, her long, young legs accustomed to steep climbs. All that's left of the original two-thousand-year-old road are giant, thick, flat stones fitted close together, now overgrown with weeds. At the top, we pick wild blackberries for a snack. On a natural stone throne, the girls sit tall like royalty. A bowl of dog food beside the trail seems an odd thing to find in the forest. Near the end are more bowls, this time with cats nibbling away. They scatter as we approach.

Soon we arrive at the *Basilica di Santa Margherita*, the church dedicated to Cortona's patron saint. Francesca asks us if she can show Sydney something inside, takes Syd's hand and pulls her into the sanctuary.

Larry and I, giving the girls their privacy, visit our favorite side chapel with the names of the six-hundred Cortonesi lost in WWI, and a large fresco of Santa Margherita interceding on behalf of the soldiers' widows and orphans. I realize that in 1920, when the painting was unveiled, viewers would have recognized their neighbors, family and friends in the fallen soldiers' faces.

Across the sanctuary, the girls are kneeling side by side, praying together in front of the ancient wooden crucified Jesus, the one Margherita was praying before when she heard Jesus speak to her. I want to take a photo but it seems an intrusion. They rise and each light a candle, perhaps contributing their remaining gelato money. I wonder what is on their young hearts and hope it is all joy.

Outside the cathedral, the girls reclaim the long sticks they picked up on our walk. Syd ties her belongings in a plastic bag, hangs it on the end, and puts it over her shoulder like a hobo. Francesca does the same.

On our way downhill into Cortona, we hear a couple in an upstairs apartment having a ferocious argument. The girls look up, grab onto each other and giggle.

Francesca tells Sydney that she is her *"amica migliore,"* best friend.

Francesca seems to know everyone in Cortona and introduces Sydney to each person they see. Larry and I stay far enough behind to supervise without interfering. They stop to pet two pugs, a spaniel, two spotless white toy poodles, a Doberman and several mutts, all on leashes held by their owners. Sydney concludes Cortona is a dog town, adding, *"That's* cool!"

I'm glad Sydney can experience the ease with which Francesca greets everyone by name, including the dogs, and introduces her new best friend to so many of her old friends. It's the perfect demonstration of the value of living in a small town for all of one's life, even a young life. Americans rarely have this experience. I hope that Sydney grasps its uniqueness.

At *La Bucaccia*, while Sydney chats with Romano in a very grown-up way, I see Francesca in the kitchen wrapped in Agostina's arms, mom kissing her daughter's hair. I think what a tender exchange after such a short time away and then realize Francesca is crying. I approach them to make sure it's not something that happened on our trip, like my driving. Agostina explains that Francesca says Sydney is leaving tomorrow and she won't see her again. I reassure them that we're only going to Florence for the day. Sydney can come visit on Thursday. Francesca recovers instantly, a huge smile across her tear-stained face.

As we leave, Sydney respectfully asks Romano if she can help serve dinner sometime. He takes her chin in his hands and kisses her forehead. "*Bella, bella. Grazie, bella.*"

We say goodbye and Sydney promises to call. On our walk home through the *Parterre*, rain starts, then stops, then starts again and we run the rest of the way, laughing and getting soaked. At home, with the rickety grill pulled under the eve, Larry starts the charcoal.

Syd goes upstairs after dinner to get ready for bed without a word from us. She seems to know we have a big day ahead. At Syd's request, tomorrow we'll visit the famous Uffizi Gallery.

"Gaab-baaaa," she screams. "Come here *NOW*!! There's a monster scorpion in the tub."

Larry runs upstairs; I follow. Sure enough. It's over two inches long, has a hard, black shell and strong pinchers, and is flicking the stinger on its curled tail. We understand Tuscan scorpions are only deadly in August, after their venom intensifies all summer. But this *is* August. I ask Larry to get a shoe. So much for putting insects outside.

"There's never only one," Sydney insists, based on her Texas scorpion experience. She retreats to the sitting room, perches on her makeshift bed, and clutches her knees in her arms.

"I don't know if I can sleep," she whimpers, getting up to shake out the sheets and toss all the cushions aside to check underneath. I help her remake her bed, shaking the blanket as well, but she refuses to get in.

"You need to try to sleep, sweetheart," Gabba urges her. "You said you wanted to catch the early train, remember."

In ten minutes, Sydney is comatose.

I breathe a long sigh as I look at my exceptional granddaughter, recalling Francesca's tears over saying goodbye to her new best friend. Saying goodbye to Dale was sad for me. Maybe children and adults are not so different after all. At least not young girls and grown women.

I reflect on the good day this has been, not only because we've had Sydney all to ourselves, but also because things have gone so well between Larry and me. We have another day tomorrow with Syd. We'll catch a very early train and visit the Uffizi, the important art museum in Florence. It'll be a beyond-great day for Larry because he loves sharing art with others and Sydney is his favorite audience. She typically hangs on his every word and engages fully in exploring the art. I hope it'll be a day where they reunite, washing away the lingering sadness from her comment that her Gabba is not funny anymore.

In fact, this has not only been a good day, it's been a great week. Larry loves being a grandpa and has devoted this week to the girls, rising extra early to study so he can be free all day. Our tensions have eased. He's more patient and kinder; I'm less sensitive and defensive. It feels like we're helpmates again, rather than competitors.

I hope this change will persist once the kids are gone, but suspect we will struggle. Patterns are hard to break and our summer pattern has been persistent tension with one another. Other changes are likely to occur as we sort out life in our new homeland — some good, some not so good. It is always work to make a marriage work. The stresses of this summer have taken their toll but tonight I feel happy and hopeful, like the work is worth it.

"Gabba, What's Circumcision?"

Yesterday, Sydney, Larry and I took the earliest train to Florence and then stood in line for over an hour to enter the *Galleria Uffizi*. Sydney was patient beyond measure. Then we spent four more hours going through each room discussing every *Annunciazione* that Sydney and Larry could find. When Larry suggested they chose a theme, I was so relieved. Otherwise the Uffizi could have taken days, especially with these two.

Over lunch in *Piazza Signoria*, Sydney surprised us, saying, if we didn't mind, that she really wanted to take the next train home and help serve dinner at *La Bucaccia* with Francesca. Romano and Agostina were delighted and Larry offered to take me out for a relaxing dinner for two. By the time we three were back at Lodolina, and Ron, Paulla and the younger girls had returned from their two days in Rome, it was midnight.

This morning, I'm making a much-needed second cappuccino when Paulla comes in and asks if we're still going to Assisi today.

"Sure, if everyone's up for it," I reply, lifting an empty cup to offer her one. "But there's no rush. It's a half-day trip and we have nothing else planned."

Paulla nods, affirmative for the cappuccino, and says she's grateful not to rush today.

Lingering over our coffees, we chat about the chaos of Rome, especially in summer, their crazy adventure, and I tell her about Sydney's two days with us.

The drive to Assisi is uneventful. All three girls want to ride with their parents, which gives Larry and me time to talk. We chat about highlights of the kids' visit, plan our upcoming romantic holiday in Verona, and laugh that our new lawn looks like florescent emerald fur.

On our steep walk up to the famous *Basilica di San Francesco* from the parking lot, I explain to Sydney and Paige that Francis was born during the Middle Ages to a wealthy family in the town we're now visiting, Assisi. That's why he's called Francis of Assisi. As a gregarious and charming young man, Francis had a vision of Jesus telling him to rebuild his church and serve the poor. When he renounced his wealth and dedicated himself to Christian service, his father was furious. The legend is that Francis took off his fancy clothes, returned them to his father, and walked away naked.

"That's pretty cool," Paige says, as we enter the massive front doors.

In the Upper Church, encircling the entire sanctuary, are twenty-eight scenes illustrating stories from Francis' life. These unsigned frescoes are attributed to Giotto, but Larry tells the girls that art experts periodically debate who painted them and they should decide for themselves. Sydney says they look like the paintings by Giotto in the Uffizi to her. I smile, seeing Larry's delight with his young protégé.

Larry explains each story, kneeling with the girls gathered around him. One fresco shows the story I told the girls. In another, Francis gives his cloak to a poor man. In still another, he's preaching to the birds. Near the end, Francis receives the stigmata — wounds like those in Jesus's hands and feet, caused by the nails attaching Jesus to the cross.

Sydney says the perspective is bad and Larry reminds her that Giotto painted a hundred years before Brunelleschi wrote about perspective. She nods.

I want to take a photo of Larry with the girls. It's a tender scene, but photos aren't allowed in this church. Ron, Paulla and I sit in nearby pews, watching and listening.

Larry softly tells the girls that Francis challenged the Roman Catholic Church at a time when many leaders were corrupt and the Church needed reform. Unlike the Pope and Bishops who lived lavishly, Francis refused to own anything and insisted that monks in his order do the same. His teachings about simplicity, service, and love — emulating Jesus — were so powerful that tens of thousands of people listened to Francis, then more closely followed Jesus' teachings.

"*Silenzio*," a stern voice says over a loud speaker, temporarily quieting the voices of visitors. Signs throughout say this Basilica is place for prayer and worship. Every few minutes, we hear "*Silenzio… silenzio.*" There is a hush. Soon the chatter escalates. Then, again, "*Silenzio… silenzio.*"

Francis was officially canonized only two years after his death in 1226, a remarkably speedy sainthood, and the Basilica construction began almost immediately. It was finished within twenty-five years, surely a record for such a gigantic medieval structure. It remains one of the most important pilgrimage sites in the world and visitors, millions each year, are of every race, age, and, probably, most creeds.

We climb down the stairs to the Lower Church, then descend another level into the crypt. In this small room, people kneel around the stone wall encasing Francis' tomb. They kiss the railing and lay gifts against it. His burial place was kept secret for nearly six hundred years, re-discovered only in 1818. The girls are soon ready to move on.

Our final stop is a chapel in the Lower Church painted by Simone Martini, the same artist who painted an annunciation Larry and Sydney especially liked in the Uffizi. Larry sits on a pew with the girls, explaining scenes from the life of Jesus. An official approaches, calling for "*silenzio.*" He looks at Larry and the girls then nods, encouraging Larry to continue his quiet instruction.

Pointing to the fourth scene, Larry whispers to the girls, "That's the circumcision of Jesus."

Paige frowns, bolts upright and blurts loudly, "Gabba! What's *circumcision?!?*"

Larry looks at Ron, as if to say, what do you want me to do?

Ron whispers, with a lopsided grin, "It's okay… you can tell them." He turns to me, saying playfully, "Let's see what he does with this one."

Larry raises his eyebrows and half-grins at Ron, who is now choking back laughter.

Larry starts in a very low voice. "Well… boys have a part that girls don't have."

The girls nod. That much they know.

"Circumcision is when a small piece gets cuts off."

They all scrunch up their faces in disgust.

"Oh, yuk!" Paige says, again in a shockingly loud voice.

"Shhhh," Paulla warns.

Ron tries to help. "Not all of it gets cut off, just a piece they don't need."

The girls look more aghast. Paige jumps up for emphasis. I mention to Larry that this may be better discussed at home.

Over the speaker the priest reminds us, "*See-lehn-zee-o… silenzio.*"

Claudia, fighting sleep, begs to go home and insists on being carried.

Outside, big raindrops plop on the warm stone, making polka dots that instantly evaporate. We all run to the car as the drops quicken into a serious downpour.

The instant Ron buckles Claudia into her car seat, her head bobs forward and she's out. The girls ride with their parents.

By the time we merge onto the super-highway, our vision is blurred by the deluge. A red Smart Car zooms past, too fast and too close. What is most irritating about driving in Italy is not getting lost, which happens all the time and can be fun, or cars going too fast, which is typical, or even being passed in dangerous situations, also far too common. What is most irritating is being passed by a toy.

At Lodolina, fifty miles away, skies are clear. Ron and Larry carry the littlest girls inside. Paulla tries to wake Sydney, but she won't budge. Ron says he'll come back for her.

Paulla tucks the girls into bed without dinner and I make *spaghetti carbonara* for the adults. While the boys clean up, she and I sit on the front slab and sip limoncello, watch for falling stars, and giggle over Paige blurting, "Gabba, what's circumcision?"

Today's innocence captured that fleeting moment between childhood and adulthood in which Paige could ask an embarrassing question with no embarrassment whatsoever. But I wonder if she was so innocent. Sometimes kids know more than they let on, or than we adults give them credit for knowing.

The Little Sink

Birds sing and the squirrel's half-cones clatter to the ground. Still in bed, I try to pick out the song of the lark with its melodic, crystalline flutes and trills, then stretch lazily, letting this morning's cacophony of birdsongs envelope me as I ease back into the pillow for five more minutes.

Ron is unloading the dishwasher when I come downstairs. Plates gleam and glasses sparkle. Dishwasher detergent, rather than decalcifier, does make a difference. I laugh at myself.

Soon Paige swishes down the stairs, a vision of pink. She twirls into the kitchen to be admired in her birthday robe.

"Good morning beautiful, I need a hug," Ron says, pulling Paige into his arms.

"Don't touch my hair," she warns, then melts into her daddy's embrace.

She's excited to spend the whole day with Nana and Gabba, without sisters or parents. Today is Paige's special day.

After a perfunctory goodbye to her family, on their way to Pinocchio Park near Florence, she turns to me and says, "Nana, ants have taken over the bathroom."

"Are you serious... or exaggerating a little?" I wonder why she didn't divulge this problem earlier.

"Serious." Her enormous caramel eyes are sincere. I head upstairs.

Paige is not overstating. In the girls' bathroom, trails of ants are everywhere, even on the ceiling. Dirty clothes are strewn about with who-knows-what on them. I pick up each garment, shake off the ants, and put it in a plastic bag for laundry. Then I saturate the floors, walls, and ceiling with ant spray, holding my breath and trying to stay out of the mist. Outside, I spray the base of the stone walls. I close the door behind me.

After getting myself ready, I find Paige downstairs with Larry. She's sitting in a wicker chair, pretty as a picture, waiting patiently while he reads.

"You weren't kidding, Paige! Thanks for telling me. But from now on we're going to put dirty clothes in the plastic bag so they don't attract ants. Got it?"

"Did you kill them all?" she asks, without acknowledging my request.

"Maybe not every one, but zillions!" I answer.

"Good," she replies. I tell her to use our bathroom this morning.

When I ask what she wants to do on her special day, she says, "Things Sydney has never done."

Larry and I exchange a look. It must be hard to be the middle daughter.

Together we plan a day of things Sydney hasn't done. Paige is a bundle of energy, excited at each suggestion, even ones I fear could be boring.

After her favorite breakfast of pancakes with homemade syrup and a kid cappuccino, we drive to Castiglion Fiorentino to visit Francesco's studio, the art museum, and the ruins of an ancient fortress — none of which Sydney has seen.

For the entire ride, Paige charms us with chatter. She tells us what she likes to cook and all the reasons she loves pink. She complains about her sisters and how they won't let her go into their rooms. She says whatever comes to her mind, because she has no competition for our attention and no one will correct her.

At Francesco's studio, Paige is fascinated by every building model and sample of wood, tile, stone and iron. She's especially taken with the teapots Francesco designed for a German china manufacturer, asking him questions non-stop.

Castiglion Fiorentino is smaller than Cortona, but a similar walled medieval hilltown with Etruscan roots. In the city center we search for *Chiesa di San Angelo*, once a church and now the *Pinacoteca* museum. When we finally find the door, the ticket agent says they close in thirty minutes, adding that the museum is only open in the mornings. Thirty minutes may be plenty for Paige.

The collection is mostly religious art, with a few surprising treasures. I'm drawn to an enameled silver bust of a young blond girl with a jewel-encrusted crown with genuine rubies, sapphires, emeralds and pearls.

"There's your Princess, Princess Paige. She's here to greet you on your special day."

Paige's smile radiates. She gets as close to the glass case as she can without pressing her nose on it. I read the card aloud, explaining the princess is Saint Ursula, daughter of the King of Britain during the fourteenth century. She was martyred along with seven thousand virgins to save the town of Cologne.

Paige backs up, wrinkles her nose and walks to the next case.

She points to a Gothic crucifix. "That's like the Giotto one in Florence."

"Good eye, Paige," Larry says.

Soon the museum official seems to be fidgeting as if he's eager to leave, so I walk toward the door, motioning Paige to follow. It's twelve-twenty-five, almost time.

"No, no… you must stay as long as you like," he insists.

We've seen most of what's there, so we thank him and make our exit. Before lunch, we want to climb to the *fortezza* at the peak of the hill.

Not much is left of the fort. The placard says it was built in 1367 to protect townspeople from invaders from Arezzo and Florence. It became a convent two centuries later, then a prison. Now only a few precarious walls and a bell-clock-watch tower remain. Near the tower, I find a four-leaf clover for Paige, which delights her. Something, she notes, I have never done for Sydney.

Since Sydney hasn't been to Castiglion Fiorentino, we're free to choose any place we want for lunch and select a *trattoria* near the city wall, a favorite of Francesco's.

When the waitress asks about drinks, Paige says, "Coca-cola, medium." The owner, amused by this decisive little girl, answers "*Subito!*" Right away. It arrives in a Coke-bottle shaped glass nearly as big as Paige's head.

"I wonder how big the *grande* is," Paige says under her breath, obviously pleased.

She orders *ravioli* with *salsa rosa*, a tomato sauce with cream. Larry asks for *affettati misti*, assorted sliced dried meats including *prosciutto* and *salami*, and sliced tomatoes. I choose *tacchino alla griglia*, grilled turkey and *insalata verde*, a green salad. Larry and I are being careful; this has been a plumping summer.

Larry seems agitated. When I finally ask what's up, he says he's concerned that in Francesco's office he used the wrong Italian word and implied that a friend of Francesco's was ingenuous when he meant encouraging.

"Francesco acted strange," he says. "I should've been more careful and less cute."

"You can tell him what you meant instead of what you said. He'll understand. He knows you wouldn't insult anyone on purpose."

I'm glad I asked and relieved to know Larry's upset was not caused by me. It's usually better to ask than to assume, since we typically assume the worst.

Paige is staring at a TV overhead. It's a soccer match and every Italian man in the room is watching.

"Have you ever played soccer?" Larry asks.

"Yes," she mumbles between big bites.

'Did you like it?"

"Not s'much," she says, swallowing hard.

"Why?" he probes.

"Because they make us play on the hottest days. When it's cool and breezy, they say, 'We'll wait.' But on the hottest day, they say, 'Time to play soccer!' We live in San Antonio! Hot is *hot!*"

Paige consumes most of her lunch before Larry and I make dents in ours.

While Larry pays the bill, Paige and I wait outside. The elderly couple sitting near us walks out and the woman gently pinches Paige's cheeks, saying, "*Bellissima, bellissima.*"

"*Grazie,*" I say. Paige winces at the pinch, but beams at the compliment.

Nearing Cortona, Larry and Paige tell me to drop them in town so they can explore some more, saying they'll walk home. I'm quite sure they're conspiring to find gelato.

When they finally arrive at Lodolina, Paige complains that Gabba ate all her gelato. Larry says she gave him almost nothing. She then begs him to walk to Palazzone, insisting that he promised. He resists, saying he promised before she walked him all over Cortona. She insists, saying it is a matter of keeping his word.

"If you want to walk some more, you can walk in front of the car when we go to dinner," he teases.

I offer to walk with Paige to Palazzone, if he'll drive Rita to the bus when she's finished for the day. Larry says he needs to handle a few things, so can't help with Rita or Paige. That means both are up to me. I decide to take Rita so she isn't late. Paige says she wants to stay home.

As I approach the first curve on the access road, an old, turquoise jeep-like Fiat, straight from *Out of Africa*, suddenly rounds the curve and startles me. There's no room to pass and the Fiat keeps coming, so I start backing up. As I inch backward, the Fiat presses forward.

I back all the way to our driveway, over a hundred yards, where there's a space wide enough to pass. Suddenly, Larry and Paige appear from our driveway. I guess the Princess charmed him into walking to Palazzone after all.

Larry waves to the driver of the Fiat, then points to me and says, "My wife, Victoria."

I say "*Un momento*" to Rita and get out to say hello. It would be rude to drive away. The driver has a warm smile, grand presence, and is wearing an orange linen dress and funky blue jacket. When she gets out, I see she's taller than Larry. Finally, I meet Belinda, our neighbor up the hill.

"I've been wanting to come by to say hello," she says with a strong English accent. "I gave your husband a note a few days ago because your phone doesn't work. I hope you'll come next week for a drink. Lyndall, who lives at Palazzone, also wants to meet you. We'll make it a party."

"I *did* get your note and it'll be a pleasure," I say, "but right now I must take our housekeeper to catch her bus."

Turning to Larry, I ask, "Are you two walking to Palazzone?' He nods and Paige grins.

I drive faster than I'm comfortable driving down the hill and take the dirt shortcut to the lower, wider road to town.

"*Alla bus o alla tua casa?*" To the bus or to your house? I ask Rita as we get close.

"*Bus*," she says. It sounds like "boose," rhymes with "loose." She climbs down from the SUV and runs to catch her boose.

Turning onto our access road, I see Larry and Paige picking blackberries and stop to ask about their visit to Palazzone.

"We got kicked out," Paige says.

"It's beautiful inside, Vic. Just beautiful," Larry says. "It's built around a courtyard with an old well. I wanted to see the frescoes, but only caught a glimpse of the courtyard before we were told to leave."

I ask if they want a ride, but Paige quickly says they want to pick more berries.

Sadly, she comes home with a blackberry stain on her beige and pink flowered skirt. After using several products with only modest success, I pour boiling water over the remaining shadow until there's not even a hint remaining. Paige heaves a huge sigh when I show her and hugs me hard. She says it's her favorite skirt and now her mom won't be mad.

For dinner, we head up the mountain road to Portole, definitely somewhere Sydney has never been. Larry drives too fast for me and I feel queasy.

"Please, slow down. I'm getting car sick."

"Are you really sick or just afraid?" Larry asks, sounding irritated.

"Both," I answer. "What's the difference? Either way, you should be willing to slow down if I ask. Without getting irritated."

I turn around and Paige's eyes are enormous. She seems to agree. Hairpins and switchbacks are much worse in the daylight for someone prone to motion sickness, especially with a phobia of going over the edge.

He drives more slowly, for which I'm grateful, but he does not seem happy.

The restaurant at the hamlet of Portole is plain yet pleasant, with acoustic tile ceilings and florescent lights. We understand the food is great. We're the only guests, but it's early. Just inside the front door is an antique wooden bar and perched on top is a stuffed blonde fox catching a bird. The fox is barely larger than a cat. I motion to Larry, saying our shoe thief must look like that.

An energetic man introduces himself as Franco, the owner. Larry tells Franco that today is Paige's special day. She's away from her parents and two sisters, alone with her grandparents for the first time ever. Franco ushers us to a table and almost immediately a waitress brings menus and tells us today's specials. She also says that if there's something Paige would like, even if not on the menu, to ask, since she understands that today is Paige's special day. Larry translates. Paige beams.

"I would like only pasta and dessert," she proclaims.

Eventually, Paige agrees to share grilled chicken and vegetables with Larry and me, in addition to her personal pasta selections. Paige's normally good appetite is the heartiest ever, even after the ravioli lunch. She munches on my grilled *zucca*, an Italian squash that looks like pumpkin but isn't sweet, and says she likes it.

What she *loves* is her orzo, a pasta shaped like large grains of rice. Gabba wants a taste. She agrees to one bite, but then Larry won't keep his spoon out of it.

"Gabba, you're gobbling – it's *MINE*."

He looks wounded. She doesn't relent, making up names for him… "Gabba, Grabba, Grubba, Gobble."

I think it's clever; Larry feigns offence. On Larry's phone, we look up various given names. Paige means assistant. Sydney means wide field. Learning that Claudia's name means lame, Paige bangs the table with her fist and throws her head back, and laughs as though it's the funniest thing she's ever heard. Larry holds her fists, so she tries to bang her forehead on the table. The restaurant is quite full by now and I fear we're making an ugly American spectacle, so say, "Shhhh," which makes Paige laugh even harder.

With our permission, she orders two desserts, *tiramisu* and a sponge cake rolled around whipped cream, coconut and mint. Larry and I beg for a taste, but are allowed barely a morsel of either. Now I know the truth about how much gelato Larry was given earlier today. Almost nothing.

Paige scrapes the *tiramisu* plate until it looks like she licked it, though she didn't, and asks us if she please could have another serving. Since she has cleaned her plate at every meal all day, we agree. Besides, it's a grandparent's right to be indulgent — within reason, of course.

When the waitress sadly informs her that she just ate the last serving, Paige looks crushed.

Then the waitress, who we think may be Franco's daughter, brings the *tiramisu* pan from the kitchen, suggesting Paige can scrape the bottom. It has lots of left-behind *tiramisu* and Paige is thrilled.

"I don't think we'll need to wash this," the waitress teases when she picks it up, inspecting the nearly spotless pan.

"My special day is the best day ever!" Paige exclaims and tells the waitress all she did. The waitress seems interested, though I'm not sure how much English she understands. Paige's excitement alone would hold anyone's attention.

I need to go to the ladies' room. Paige says she does too.

She points inside a stall, saying, "Look, Nana, there's a big one and a little one, even in the restaurant."

When I don't respond, she persists. "What's the little one for? Is it a sink?"

"No. It's a bidet, not a sink," I reply, intending no further discussion.

"Can I wash my hands in it?"

"No, that's not what it's for."

"What *is* it for?"

"To wash your bottom, if you need to."

"Can I?"

"No."

"Why not?"

"We don't have time and you don't have a dirty bottom."

My hands washed in the big sink, I'm ready to leave. But Paige is still in the stall.

"Are you okay, Paigie?" I call softly, chuckling under my breath.

"Yes. Fine."

"I'm going out to sit with Gabba, okay?"

"Okay," she says. "Be there soon."

Larry and I wait for a long time. Just as I start to go check on Paige, she arrives with a not-so-innocent smile. I suspect she has a very clean bottom.

Ron and family return home well after eleven. Claudia and Sydney have Pinocchio noses, painted faces and are giggling uproariously. None of the girls seem tired. I'm exhausted, ready to brush my teeth and crash.

"Italians are seriously into Pinocchio," says Ron, "And there are parts of the story Americans don't tell their kids."

As Larry tucks the girls in their beds upstairs, I hear Paige telling her sisters about her special day in glowing detail. She doesn't mention the little sink.

Lights off downstairs, I drag my weary body up the stairs and into my bed, thinking how grateful I am that we can share Italy with our grandchildren. It teaches them the world is bigger than Texas or America. As they become comfortable with one new culture, I hope they'll find other cultures more approachable and interesting. Perhaps I won't have given up grand-mothering with this move to a foreign land, as I believed. Perhaps we have expanded the worlds we will explore together.

Monster Park to Maestro's Piano

We have a late start this morning and no workers. The silence seems erie, almost loud. Larry sits in a wicker chair on the front concrete slab, surveying waves of new florescent emerald grass. Randomly across the lawn, anthills have risen where the ants have collected grass seed. The cones look like green-fur party hats.

Today, Larry has two lap blankets wrapped around his body. It has gone from unbearably hot to downright chilly, unusual for August. Perhaps the day will become idyllic, but this morning is shivery.

I decide to work in the living room with my computer plugged in, as the battery is low. The moment I start typing, my screen dims. Larry says in a here-we-go-again tone, "The electricity just went out. Must be nine o'clock."

I head upstairs for a cold sponge bath, using as little water as possible and catching any extra in a bowl. Without power to the well pump we don't have any water, let alone hot water. And seven people need to get dressed.

Calling down from the top of the stairs, I say, "Larry, come look what I just killed in our bedroom. It's the biggest scorpion we've seen all summer. It was crawling up the wall above your open suitcase. We should start shaking out our shoes before we put them on." I recall something in a novel about scorpions hiding in shoes. Or in suitcases under the clothes, I think.

Without showers, lights, coffee or hairdryers, seven of us manage to get ready and out the door in record time. The girls are excited to explore the famous *Il Parco dei Mostri*, Monster Park, near Bomarzo, about two hours south on the A1.

Monster Park is an ancient forest of gargantuan, fantastical sculptures carved from natural rock formations. Prince Francesco Orsini commissioned the park in the 1560's to "vent his heart" after the death of his wife, Giulia Farnese. Prince Orsini's fantasy is officially called *Sacro Bosco*, Sacred Woods, and it's stated objective was to astonish.

We pile into two cars. Sydney and Claudia ride with us. Paige chooses her parents, saying she missed them on her special day. Three minutes into our trip, at the bottom of our S-curve, a huge insect splats against the windshield.

"Do you know the last thing that went through that bug's mind?" Larry asks Sydney and Claudia.

They know it's a joke, but don't know the answer, so try to look bored.

After a minute's silence, Larry says, "His butt."

Stifled chuckles are followed by a long pause. Then Sydney asks, "Gabba, did Mr. Jim tell you that joke?"

"Syd! What a thing to say!"

She repeats, deadpan, "Did Mr. Jim tell you that joke?"

Larry is silent. His mouth curves downward, lower lip protrudes and eyes narrow. He leans a little toward the mirror, to make sure they see his pitiful pout.

The girls giggle and I turn my head to the window, trying not to grin too broadly.

But Syd doesn't take back her question and Larry doesn't answer. In fact, it was true. It was one of the kid-jokes Jim gave Larry when we saw them in Rome.

We ride in silence. The air in the car feels heavier after Sydney dismisses Larry's joke, one he hoped would regain his status as funny. We had such a nice day with Sydney in Florence, but it seems the spell is broken again.

Barreling south on the A1, we pass more fields of faded stalks and drooping faces. There is no gold in the sunflowers this summer, color or income. I'm sad for the sunflowers, sadder for the farmers, and sadder yet for Larry who seems crestfallen.

Despite the tension, the sunny day is perfect for a road trip. Larry turns on the radio. He ignores any effort I make to connect with him. Surely, he's not that upset because the girls teased him about his joke.

Under my breath, hoping the girls can't hear, I say, "I don't understand your mood."

"I'm not in a mood."

"Then why are you ignoring me? I'm trying to connect and you're ignoring me."

"I'm just enjoying the music."

"Are you mad because we laughed at you?"

"Of course not."

I'm not so sure, but don't want to doubt his word so give up.

Finally, I whisper, "Why must I be the one to make all the effort at getting along?"

After a few more moments, he whispers, a little playfully, "Because you're the girl and that's your job."

"It's not a job I want or accept," I whisper back, looking straight ahead. By this time, I'm annoyed. This interaction seems ridiculous.

The girls start grumbling about Gabba's music and then my job becomes negotiating a truce between the grandfather, who is enjoying an opera, and the sisters who say they hate opera and can we please change the channel. When I ask what kind of music they like, Larry turns off the radio.

We approach Orvieto, about an hour into our drive.

"Tell Ron about Orvieto," Larry says.

"What do you want me to tell him?" I ask, getting out the walkie-talkies and wondering what he has in mind.

He frowns and says, "Just tell them why it's so important." I have the feeling whatever I say, it won't be what he wants them to know.

I push the walkie-talkie switch on.

"Larry wants you to look at Orvieto," I say when they answer. "It's ahead on the right."

I hold the walkie-talkie toward his face. He makes a motion that I should talk. When I don't, he leans in and says, "Orvieto is where popes would flee when they needed protection from invaders or were fed up with the Romans. It has a perfect natural fortification. Can you see it?"

"I wish we had time to stop," he adds as we pass the historical city perched above a sheer cliff, and suggests we come back, saying it's worth a full day.

I add "over and out," and that we'll see them at Monster Park.

"Over and out," comes the reply.

The girls are fussing again. I give them the evil grandmother eye which says, "cut-it-out-or-I'll-have-to-ask-your-grandfather-to-stop-and-you-don't-want-that-to-happen." They become quiet. There is too much tension in this car for me.

A driver in a white van pulls close behind our SUV and flashes his lights. Larry touches his brakes as a counter-move. It does not daunt the aggressive driver who hugs our tail even more closely and continues to flash his brights, trying to force Larry into the right lane even though Larry's going plenty fast and the right lane is full of trucks. Larry passes the entire line of lorries at a reasonable speed making it impossible for the other driver to pass at all. As Larry eases into the right lane ahead of the trucks, the white van zooms past faster than we dare calculate.

Soon after the *autostrada* drama, in unison the girls say, "There it is!!" I look up and see the sign for Bomarzo, our exit.

"There it *really* is," Claudia exclaims a couple minutes later, when she sees the sign for *Il Parco dei Mostri*, Park of the Monsters.

We drive into a weedy, nearly-empty parking lot and climb out of our cars. Claudia needs to use the toilet "right now" and I'm relieved to see one at the edge of the lot.

It's not the cleanest. There's one room with three stalls and no gender signs. The floor is covered with wet mud. No one wants to go first. Shamelessly, I say I will because I can't wait much longer. Only one stall has a door. Of course, there is no paper. With my favorite white pants down around my knees, held tightly above the wet, slimy floor, I straddle the toilet and reach my hand under the stall door to accept Paulla's gift of tissues.

When I turn on the faucet to wash my hands, water pours onto my feet. I flip it off immediately.

Claudia's still outside. "Mommy," she pleads, "There's yucky all over! Do I have to go here?"

Ron tries to reassure her, "There's no pipe under the sink, Claudia. It's just water from the sink… not what you think. It's okay, you can come in."

Paulla hands Claudia tissues, gives her the tiniest push, and adds that we don't know where there'll be another bathroom.

"You wait," I whisper to Paulla, "There'll be spotless bathrooms right by the entrance."

Everyone who needs a toilet decides to use this one. Of course, when we enter the main building, the sign on the first door beyond the ticket booth says WC. Paulla and I smile at each other, say nothing, and quickly walk toward the park.

For three hours we explore grotesque stone monsters. Most are overgrown by masses of twisted vines, dense moss and lichen, and drooping tree branches. The forest seems like it's been here since time began. While the girls climb and crawl over sea creatures, elephants, and horrific beasts with bulging eyes and massive open mouths, some leading to inner chambers, I take photos.

About two o'clock, we're famished and head back to the main building for lunch in the cafeteria. When we get there, the workers are closing the hot food bins, not at all interested in seven more customers though there's plenty of food. Larry tries to convince them to stay open, but they are unmoved. We buy soft drinks and bags of salty snacks, sit behind the building at a not-so-clean table and have a junk food lunch before our ride back to Lodolina.

This time, Paige and Claudia want to ride with us.

"So! Was that fun? Did you like Monster Park?" I ask as we drive out of the parking lot.

"YES!!" was the enthusiastic reply.

To judge how much they loved it, I ask if they'd rather have gone to a swimming pool.

"YES!!" they exclaim without hesitation. Kids are so predictable.

Now that I planted that idea, Paige begs to go to the pool when we get home. I say there's no time, but maybe we will before they leave Cortona. I suddenly feel sad, knowing we're near the end of their visit.

For tonight, Larry and I have tickets to take the older girls to a classical piano concert at *Teatro Signorelli*. It's part of the Tuscan Sun Festival and will be quite a sophisticated evening for our young ladies.

We all get dressed up. Sydney tells me she wants to ask her mother if she can wear Paulla's new scarf. I say it's too old for her and that she might get it dirty. Syd considers my warning, nods and puts on her best dress with a little jacket. She looks beautiful and appropriate for nine.

Then Paige asks her mom if she can wear the new scarf and Paulla lets her. I wish I had kept quiet, but do think both girls are too young to be wrapped like a diva in their mother's expensive new silk shawl.

Paige looks like a princess, as she probably intended. Sydney, who'd never want to be as prissy as a princess, looks lovely and a little dressing up makes her seem older and surprisingly elegant. I feel dowdy beside these beauties, though I'm wearing my best skirt and top, silk wrap, and favorite high heels. All black, of course.

"We have a box," Larry tells the girls.

Paige frowns, "Like cardboard?"

"No, we have seats in our own private room, called a box. You'll see," he assures her.

Paige turns to smile at the mirror one last time.

The plan is for all of us to go to Lilli's for dinner on *Teatro Signorelli's* terrace, the same restaurant where we watched the World Cup. Then Larry and I'll take Paige and Sydney inside to the concert. At the restaurant, Lilli offers us menus, but we ask her to bring us what is especially good tonight. She's a fabulous cook and has never disappointed us. In fact, some say she's the best cook in Cortona. But with so many great *cuoci*, it's hard to elevate only one.

Lilli first brings thinly sliced *prosciutto e melone* which Paige deems the best ever. The platter would have been plenty for seven if Paige hadn't eaten half of it. Also, as a starter, Lilli brings a plate of *pecorino* cheeses with an exotic *Vin Santo* jam she made herself. At that point I could've been satisfied for a pre-theater meal, but we all manage to eat every morsel of penne pasta with roasted yellow pepper and arugula sauce. Every plate is clean; every tummy full. Even Ron, our carnivore, says he's stuffed.

The final bell rings, so we rush inside, asking Lilli if we can pay at intermission. She waves us on. From our box we have a perfect view of the full stage. The girls sit up straight, like young royalty. Paige grins from ear to ear, then hangs way over the edge of the rail to watch people below. Sydney, a bit more reserved and lady-like, looks around the theater, studying the historical details. She asks Gabba questions which he answers, leaning toward her and speaking softly, reveling in every moment.

Cortona's opera house has not changed since the 1850s when it first opened. From the box we look up at a bright turquoise ceiling with white carved swirls and gold-gilt highlights. Vermillion silk brocade still covers the walls, and the red velvet seats and dark wood-plank floors look original. I imagine a debut of one of Verdi's masterpieces with lush costumes and bejewel audiences. The seats and floor could use an update, but I do love sitting in so much history.

Lights dim. An elderly man with snow-white hair walks onto the stage. The girls look at each other, skeptically. The stage floor is dramatically black and the shiny black piano is one of the longest I've ever seen. The maestro sits, adjusts his position, and pauses. He doesn't acknowledge the audience despite persistent applause, but keeps his head bowed. Then he lifts his hands above the keys and a hush comes over the theater.

Joaquín Achúcarro, the highly acclaimed Spanish pianist, starts with a Mozart sonata in F major. Paige shifts her weight, getting settled in. Sydney sits upright and relaxed, as if she has been attending concerts all her life. At the end of the sonata, the audience claps, not wildly but with respect.

The pianist pauses, then begins a Bach-Busoni toccata. I watch his long elegant fingers move lightning fast. His pedal foot flutters like a butterfly. I know it requires real pressure to hold or damper a note; his footwork would be challenging for a much younger man. I'm delighted we're high enough to see all his movements. With each selection, the audience becomes more fixated.

When Achúcarro finishes for an intermission, the applause is relentless. He bows deeply, bending low for an extended time. He looks at the audience with directness, then surprise when the applause continues. My hands hurt, but I cannot stop. He bows several more times, finally holds up his hands in request for silence, and leaves the stage.

After a flitter more applause, the house lights go up and the girls quickly request a bathroom. Except for early moments of skepticism, they have been spellbound.

We walk outside onto the terrace and overhear astonished gushing about the performance. Most people are speaking Italian. Several admire our dressed-up granddaughters. Syd and Paige are perfectly behaved and we're proud to be with them. We don't see other children, but I'm glad we brought ours. I hope someday all three girls will share my love of piano and learn to play.

The *maestro* begins again with Chopin, my favorite. Twenty-four preludes tumble out of the long piano as if they were etched on the soundboard. He plays the entire concert without a score.

After the last note, the audience stands instantly, as if one body, and the thunderous applause could crack the ceiling. Achúcarro accepts a bouquet of sunflowers and daisies, which seems far too modest for the concert we just witnessed.

After a seemingly endless ovation, he again raises his hands for quiet, returns to the piano and plays a fifteen-minute encore using only his left hand.

As his fingers slow… all I can think is, "Oh, please don't stop."

Everyone exits the theater in silence. People shake their heads in amazement. We are bonded, knowing we have witnessed a uniquely masterful performance.

I wonder if Sydney and Paige, who sat motionless in the box for two and a half hours, will remember this concert for as long as I will.

Once home, covers shaken out for scorpions and girls safely in bed, I pull our covers all the way back, remembering the monster over the bed this morning and the one Syd encountered on her special day. Nothing. I shake the summer blanket out, in case there's something lurking in the softness.

I drift to sleep with melodies from the concert lingering in my brain and new resolve to work harder at my piano. I also hope the concert has inspired my granddaughters to start lessons. One is never too young.

A great joy being a grandparent is seeing each grandchild become their own unique person, and to imagine you've played some small part in their dreams.

(What I didn't know that night is that Sydney will start piano lessons a few months after returning from Italy and in time will aspire to become a concert pianist. And, that Claudia will show interest because her big sister plays so well, and start to learn. Perhaps a tiny seed was planted that night when the silver-haired maestro enchanted us with his mastery and passion. There is no measure to the power of inspiration. One evening can inspire a lifetime. And, one generation can inspire generations to come.)

On the Roman Road

The days with Ron and the kids have flown. Tomorrow they return to Texas. Today we'll walk to Cortona for a last lunch in town, and this evening we'll go to the *Sagra di Bistecca*, Cortona's annual festival celebrating Chianina beef.

It's a lazy morning after last night's concert. The girls are still sleeping. Ron's been up for a while, made his own cappuccino, and is in the living room answering emails. Larry and I join him, all quietly working. When Paulla comes in from the guesthouse, her opening line gets our full attention.

"Did Ron tell you about his encounter last night?"

"Here?" I ask.

Paulla teases, "Go ahead, Ron, tell them."

Ron frowns at her, then confesses.

"I needed something out of the car, so I went out about midnight. When I got to the car, something snorted. It was right next to me! Enormous. I jumped and screamed, then ran to our room. It ran the other way, squealing all the way down the hill. I think it was more scared than I was."

"Ron was white and gasping for air," Paulla teases. "He slammed the door and had his back against it, like something might get in."

"Surely a boar," Larry chuckles.

"A big one," Ron adds to justify his fear.

Paulla is merciless, continuing to embellish how scared he was. I ask if it had tusks. Ron said he didn't stick around long enough to tell. We're all in hysterics, even Ron. Finally, swallowing laughter and with more compassion, Paulla says, "Would've scared me too," which sends us into greater fits of laughter.

Paulla can't wait tell the girls, now filing down the stairs in their pajamas, awakened by all our laughter.

After Sydney and Paige make fun of their father, re-enacting the scene and his reaction, Ron says, "Enough." He announces he wants to scramble eggs for our last breakfast and we all head to the kitchen. Larry makes kid cappuccinos, Paulla slices saltless Tuscan bread for toast and jam, and I dice peaches, nectarines, apples and white melon for *macedonia*, fruit salad. Ron's eggs, a dozen of them, are so delicious we could've eaten two dozen.

There's a prevailing sadness, but we refuse to let it ruin our last day.

I glance at emails before we head out. My mother wrote that Joyce died this morning. It seems only days ago she told me Joyce had cancer. Mom's note was matter-of-fact. Hard to know how she's taking it, but I suspect stoically on the outside with deep pain inside. She always says death is part of life, but it doesn't make each loss of a deeply-loved friend any easier.

It's times like this that I feel the farthest away. I can't even call her, since it's nighttime in Missouri.

While Larry and I are getting dressed, I tell him that Joyce died.

"I'm sorry. She was an important friend for your mother," he says. After a long pause, he gets a bit choked up and adds, "Vic, please don't die."

I feel tears come from deep inside me… tears for Mom, for Joyce's daughter, and for Larry who can be so tender with me. I know a deep loss is only possible when there has been a deep love. I'm heartbroken for my mother's loss and thankful for her long friendship with Joyce. I'll call her before we go to the *Sagra* this evening. Seven hours difference and a house full of company make finding the right time difficult.

Today we'll walk the Roman road to town, something no one but Sydney has done. On the trail the girls are delighted to find black and white striped porcupine quills, about a dozen of them. They ask if I'll carry them. We find prickly pear cactus with plump red fruit. I carefully pull one off and rub it in the grass to take off the tiny thorns. Once it's safe, I show the girls how to make lipstick with it. They all want to try. I'm dripping wet from the sun and exertion, but feel so happy.

Near the top, I find a time to walk alone with Sydney, out of hearing of others. Paulla had asked if I would have a chat with Sydney about being nicer to her sisters, a problem that is starting to emerge. Normal for Syd's age, but upsetting to the younger girls. Paige had mentioned it on her special day. I promised Paulla I would try to find a time, knowing advice is sometimes more easily accepted if it doesn't come from your mother.

"So, Syd, you're nine," I venture. "At nine you can start to think about what kind of person you want to be when you grow up."

Sydney looks ahead without replying, but doesn't walk away.

"Tell me… who do you admire?" I ask.

"Well, I like my teacher. She's smart and she lets me help her."

"Is she mean or kind?"

"Oh, she's nice… *really* nice," Syd says, nonchalantly.

"So, do you ever think about what kind of person you want to be?"

"Not really."

"Do you want to be like your teacher?"

"I guess."

"Well, you know you can *decide* if you want to be nice and kind, or if you want to be not so nice, right? Nine is a good age to start deciding if you want to be a kind person or not."

No reply. I think she's catching on faster than I anticipated and would rather not engage. I haven't asked how she wants to treat her sisters, but that's the real issue.

"Sometimes I notice you get irritated with your sisters and try to tell them what to do. Is that what your teacher'd do? Does she get irritated and criticize you, or try to help?"

"I only try to help them," Sydney insists, catching my gist immediately. "Paige never knows the right thing to do. And she does stuff that's so dumb. Claudia understands more. But she can never make up her mind."

"Syd, you are very smart. So I think you know when you're really helping, or when you're just trying to make one of them look bad or yourself look better. We all like people who make us feel good about ourselves, and we don't like people who make fun of us. I know you can be very kind, even to your sisters. It's all about choosing what kind of person you want to be, no matter what."

Pheasants fly up from the grass directly in front of us. The girls squeal and run ahead. Sydney uses the commotion to walk ahead with her dad and out of our conversation.

My grandmotherly advice may be over for today, but I am confident Sydney got my point and will think about it.

"Look, smoke from the grills," Larry stops at the crest of the hill and points down to the park where gray puffs are billowing up. To cook enough steaks for the thousands who will attend the *Sagra* this weekend, it takes a long line of enormous grills and truckloads of wood. The cooks start the fires early in the day so by evening the coals are perfect.

From the *Basilica di Santa Margherita*, we walk downhill toward Cortona. Larry stops at each of the fourteen Stations of the Cross, semi-abstract mosaics by Gino Severini, the famous twentieth century artist from Cortona. The girls stay very close to their Gabba, learning and laughing together. He must be in heaven.

In town, Ron and family say last goodbyes to Marco and to Romano's family, and we head to *Trattoria Dardano* for one final lunch. No one eats much, as we had a huge breakfast and are saving our appetites for tonight's steak feast.

Back at home, all the girls — Claudia, Paige, Sydney, Paulla and me — sit in the big leather chairs and chat, with Claudia on Paulla's lap. Ron sits on the floor, using the raised hearth as his computer stand. It feels good to *be* together.

Claudia makes a tiny stuffed animal fly over her head and I hear a soft, high-pitched story, but the words aren't audible.

"What's that?" I whisper to Paulla, not wanting to interrupt the older girls' chatter.

"Claudia's new bat," she says. "Last night, while y'all were at the concert, I went into a store to look for headbands for the girls and Claudia saw these teeny beanie babies. For some reason, she loved the bat. She found a corner, curled up to wait for me, made the bat fly over her head, and whispered imaginary stories. When I paid for the headbands, she asked for the bat. It was seven euros, so I said no. She was sad, but didn't make a fuss. The owner said she'd never seen anyone have so much fun with those animals… and gave it to Claudia as a gift."

Everyone agrees that people in Cortona have been exceptionally generous, way beyond kind, which makes me even fonder of our new hometown.

Thinking Mom should be home and awake, I try to call. The phone rings and rings. I leave a message that I'll call later this evening. I hate this distance.

For our last dinner, we walk back up the hill to the *Parterre* for the *Sagra*. At least a thousand people have arrived before us. Plastic tables are everywhere, fully occupied. We wait in a long line to buy tickets and then watch a dozen grillers flip enormous slabs of steak over red-hot coals, taking them off just as soon as they are nicely seared. We spread out, searching for a table for seven. Finally, a family gets up and Larry, Sydney, Paige and I move in. A server brings us four bottles of water, two bottles of red wine, seven rolls of plastic utensils wrapped in paper napkins, and a stack of plastic cups.

Paulla and Claudia arrive with plates of *contorni*, side dishes of Tuscan beans and sliced tomatoes, but the grillers are way behind on steaks so Ron is waiting.

Local musicians regale us with traditional Italian songs. People sing along or dance on the gravel paths. Crowds are not my favorite, but this feels like an authentic Italian festival and I'm glad we're here. It is the perfect final evening.

Paige and Claudia both need to go to the bathroom *now*, so I go with them to the new facility, made of fieldstone to look old. The line is long and moves slowly. Before each use, the next person must put a euro in the box, which triggers an automatic bathroom washdown. I'm afraid the new hygienic system will take longer than the girls can wait. I ask them if we can all go in together to save time and money.

"No," they say in unison, horrified. Seems every young lady, regardless of age, needs her privacy.

Sydney and Larry are holding our table when we return. Ron and Paulla finally arrive, loaded with seven plates of Chianina beef slabs so rare that blood drips over the edges. Not even with our voracious Ron, will we finish all this meat.

In the end, we consume all the water, wine, and every bite of beans, tomatoes and steak. The dessert is a fresh peach, rock hard and green. Since they're not yet edible, seven peaches go into my handbag for the walk home.

Ron and Sydney walk ahead and by the time we're home, Syd has showered and is in bed. Everyone must take their shower tonight, since there won't be time before they leave tomorrow morning.

After we say *buona notte* to everyone, I try again to reach Mom but she still doesn't answer. I send her another email, my heart aching.

Resting my head on my pillow, I feel forlorn. Joyce's death was a huge loss for Mom and I wish I could talk with her. I prepare myself for another loss tomorrow when Ron, Paulla and the girls leave. Perhaps sleep will ease my sorrow. Things so often seem worse at night.

Tough Goodbye

By moonlight, I look at my nightstand clock. Three-thirty. Too early to get up, even today. The kids leave at five to drive to Rome for their flight. I drift off again.

When I pull on my black silk robe an hour later, Larry is already up. I see a flashlight coming down the ramp from the guesthouse and quietly open the door.

"Morning, Ron… ready to go?" I whisper.

"Yep, car's loaded and Paulla's doing the final check."

In a startlingly loud voice, he calls, "Morning, girls. Time to wake up! You can stay in your PJ's. Car's loaded. Just brush your teeth and bring your backpacks."

No one stirs. "Com' on, com' on. Up! *Now!*"

Claudia and Paige sit up, rub their eyes, and groggily move toward the bathroom, then pick up their backpacks and stumble out the door. Thankfully, Sydney is not far behind. I check for little girl things under the sofas and hurry to the driveway for my last goodbyes. Their Fiat hatchback is stacked to the ceiling and bags are under everyone's feet except Ron's.

"You'll have to hold your own backpack," Ron replies when Paige lifts hers up to him. "You can use it for a pillow. But first… say goodbye."

Paige turns to hug me. Sydney hugs Larry. Claudia waits. I give each granddaughter a long tight hug, a kiss on each cheek, another on their forehead, and one more last hug. "I love you and will miss you," I whisper to each.

Paulla and I embrace for a long time.

"It's been a joy to be with you. I'll miss you all," I say softly, holding her hands as we part.

"Thank you for everything, especially for listening to me and for your wise advice. I'll miss you, too."

Ron gives me a strong, quick hug. "Thanks for everything. It was great." Ever the responsible dad, he's eager to get on the road.

Larry exchanges similar embraces, kisses and loving words with everyone. Claudia turns back and hugs his legs one last time, then climbs into the car. My eyes brim.

Larry and I stand in the driveway, both in bathrobes, holding hands and watching through tears as they drive away. When we can't see car lights any longer, he says, "Would you like a cappuccino... or to go back to bed?"

"Let's see if we can sleep a little more, okay?"

He puts his arm around my shoulders as we turn, walk to the house, and fall back to sleep.

After breakfast, easier for two but less fun, we walk to town. People ask where our grandchildren are since they've become such a part of our presence. We go the Post Office to pay a tax, then stop at *La Bucaccia* to relay a last goodbye from Sydney, but Francesca isn't there. Agostina says she misses Sydney. So do I.

We have lunch and dinner at home, still working on leftovers, then get dressed for another Tuscan Sun concert. Tonight, we'll go alone.

Before the concert, I reach Mom. As I expected, she says death is part of life. Of course she'll miss Joyce, she says, but she's glad they had forty years as best friends. She'll try to remember their good times — that's what counts. Though Mom is brave and positive, the sadness in her voice breaks my heart. At eighty-six, she has endured many losses, but losing Joyce is among the biggest.

Walking to town for tonight's concert, I still cannot shake the heaviness. In the *Parterre*, a few tables and chairs remain from last night's *bistecca* festival. The park feels emptier than usual, perhaps because I feel emptier. I sit on a bench to change from walking shoes to suede pumps. Perhaps if I look a little festive, I'll feel more festive.

Tonight's concert is Lang Lang, the famous pianist, Nina Kotova, a Russian cellist married to the founder of the Tuscan Sun Festival, and Dmitri Hvorostovsky, a Russian baritone. As we enter the theater, a young Asian beauty in a turquoise mermaid dress passes me. I wonder if she's someone important.

We have the same box, but tonight strangers fill the other seats.

On the black expanse, a red and gold throne-like chair commands center stage. The long black grand piano sits behind it. As the lights dim, Lang Lang and Nina Kotova enter, acknowledge the applause, and take their seats. It feels strange that Ms. Kotova sits in the position of honor on the throne, while Lang Lang is at the piano as though he accompanies her.

Nina finishes her cello repertoire with Rachmaninoff. Impeccably-performed but a little stiff, the melancholy music matches my mood.

Lang Lang and Nina take five curtain calls following their duets. The theater is sold out. I feel disconnected, yet the rest of the audience seems electrified.

Once the applause dies down, Nina's throne is removed and a youthful, white-haired idol dressed in form-fitting black shirt and trousers walks on stage and positions himself in the curve of the piano. He shifts his weight, expands his chest, and adjusts himself with small stretches and postures. He must be the Russian baritone.

"Which do you think he works on most, his voice or his body?" I murmur to Larry. "He must sing four hours a day and spend four in the gym!"

Dmitri seems to know he is strikingly handsome. Despite his early posturing that makes me suspicious of his talent, his performance is spellbinding and I applaud until my hands hurt. For a moment, as often happens when a distraction is absorbing, I am lifted out of my malaise.

During intermission, people lean out of their boxes and chat with people in other boxes and on the main floor. I imagine the era when *Teatro Signorelli* was first opened and everyone in the audience knew one another. Cortona is still a small town and tonight's glitter and camaraderie seems to harken back to an earlier epoch.

Tonight more than ever, I long to be chatting over the rail with friends. I feel isolated from loved ones except Larry. I wonder again if we made the right choice to move so far from our interesting, full life in Chicago, surrounded by friends and family. I know friends and family in the USA will remain a part of our lives as we follow this dream. We'll just fit differently than before. And I know someday we will develop friendships here. But when?

I am swept away, absorbed in the incredible piano solos by Lang Lang, which command long applause and a spellbinding encore. I almost float out of the theater.

Back at the *Parterre*, now without any trace of last night's *bistecca* festival, I take off my pretty heels and put on walking shoes for the downhill climb.

It has been a long and melancholy day. Despite the mesmerizing performances of Lang Lang, Dmitri, and Nina, tender farewells with the kids and sweet interaction with Larry, I feel detached. What I need in Cortona is to be part of something beyond Larry and me — a community of people who share everyday life and care about one another. But tonight we were at the concert alone.

Fox Tales

Another morning. The house feels empty, in striking contrast to the previous fourteen mornings when I awoke filled with anticipation of new adventures with my precious granddaughters.

Francesco and the alarm installer arrive about nine. While Max works, Francesco wants to hear all about our visit with Ron and family. We haven't seen Francesco since the day our lawn was seeded two weeks ago. I voice the usual complaints about seven mouths to feed three times a day, loads and loads of laundry and delays to get anywhere, but mostly describe our joyful times together.

Francesco laughs out loud when I tell about Paige yelling, "Gabba, what's circumcision?" and Ron's encounter with the world's largest *cinghiale*.

"Guests are a great work and a great joy," Francesco muses. "When they are gone, the joy remains, but not the work."

I remind him that tomorrow Larry and I head to Verona. The weekend package we bought at a charity auction in Chicago a year ago is about to expire. We've seen the sights in Verona several times, but have never been to an opera in the famous arena. Francesco tells us the Roman amphitheater, where the operas are held under the stars, is larger than the Coliseum in Rome.

Max finishes installing the alarm by noon. The house seems desolate after they leave. Our bags packed for Verona by evening, we leave for an *aperitivo* at Belinda's. I'm both nervous and excited to meet our neighbors.

We're first to arrive. Belinda's home is rustic, authentic. From her terrace we can see the back of Palazzone and its majestic tower, the wide Chiana Valley and mountains beyond. Five mix-matched chairs and a little table are arranged on the front terrace. I wonder who else is coming.

Offering a quick tour, Belinda says the house has electricity and water, but no heat. It's wonderfully homey inside with a gigantic fireplace, big sofas and a long wooden dining table in the main room. Upstairs rooms were added at different times, she says. Fragrant peach roses the size of saucers cling to a side wall and purple wisteria clusters hang over the front door. Belinda planted the roses, she tells us, but the wisteria was already there.

Cornelia soon arrives. She's Swiss, married to an Italian, but Alfredo can't come because he's still at work. Last is Lyndall, the *Contessa* who lives in the grand tower of Palazzone. Belinda pours cold Prosecco and offers a tray of crostini, including *fegatini*, the Tuscan chicken liver that Larry and I both like so much. Everyone is warm, friendly, without pretense, and the conversation is easy.

Our neighbors are especially curious about us and our renovation. We try to describe what we've done, insisting they must come see it.

We're all foreigners, but the others have lived here a long time. Lyndall, who is English, came to Italy as a young woman, then met the Count and stayed. That was sixty years ago. Belinda, also from England, has come for the summer and again in fall for the olive harvest for decades. Cornelia left Switzerland as a young woman looking for adventure, fell in love and stayed to raise a family. They speak multiple languages, as well as Italian and English.

Our hillside animals seem a favorite topic and I share my stories about the little black squirrel who feasts in the *cipressi* and the fox who loves shoes. Lyndall lights up. "I know that fox! She stole my shoes, too. I'm delighted she's still alive.... There were three in the litter. The mother must have been killed soon after they were born. When they were little, the three ran in a pack. Then one summer there were only two. In recent summers, I haven't seen a fox at all. I feared they all might be dead by now."

"One evening," she continues, "a couple summers ago, we were eating here, at Belinda's. A fox came up on the terrace and let us touch her. Then she darted away. That was the last time I saw her. Must be the one who ruined your shoe." Lyndall's eyes twinkle as she speaks.

I can imagine the little blond fox gingerly stepping up on Belinda's stone terrace, which looks straight out of a storybook, to sniff the humans. I tell our neighbors I've named her Imelda.

When sunset casts a coral blush on our faces, everyone reluctantly says it's time to say goodbye. I suggest they come to Lodolina for an *aperitivo* next week, after we return from Verona and before we leave for a month in Chicago. Everyone seems enthusiastic. Belinda says she's curious to try Donatella's new restaurant at the swimming pool, so maybe we could go there for dinner. It seems our neighbors have been friends for a very long time, care for one another and other neighbors, and are deeply woven into the Cortona community.

Larry and I linger with Belinda after the others have left, saying we feel fortunate to have such interesting, kind people as neighbors. Belinda agrees and adds she's happy we've moved to our hillside. I feel my heart expand with gratitude.

Instead of going home, Larry and I walk up the hill and into town for dinner at *La Loggetta*. Lara, owner and wife of the chef, seats us at the perfect table overlooking the piazza. Candles flicker, creating an aura of intimacy and romance. I feel a special kinship with Lara because she shares my daughter's name, uncommon for Italians, and we both like rubies, our mutual July birthstone.

Our *Chianti Riserva* arrives. Larry and I toast one another. I savor the *orecchiette al fumo* I've been dreaming of all day and *galletto alle diavola*, a small, flattened, grilled half-rooster. Larry says his *zuppa pomodoro*, fresh tomato soup with lots of basil, and grilled *Cinta Senese*, a special pork grown near Siena, are the best he's had all summer.

Tonight we take our time, chatting about the kids' and hoping their flight is smooth. We share dreams for our weekend in Verona and the rest of the summer, only a few more weeks. Refusing dessert, we'll have a limoncello at home, sitting on our front terrace.

On our stroll through town, we realize we don't have flashlights. We stop to chat with Ivan at his *tabaccheria* and artisan shop and I mention we forgot flashlights, confessing some fear of climbing down the rocky path in the dark.

"The path is not the problem, pigs are the problem," Ivan says. "You must take a stick and beat the bushes. Be loud. Sing. Stomp. Scare them and they will run. Just be careful not to get between a mother and her babies. If you do, she'll attack."

"Oh, that's reassuring," I say.

"I wish I had a torch to give to you," he says, truly concerned. Then, laughing, "If a pig charges, climb a tree."

With stick in hand, halfway down the trail I hear something. I stomp and beat the rocks. The sound stops. I half expect to see a pair of small, close-set eyes staring at me from above a long, hairy snout with curved white tusks.

"What are you doing?" Larry says, chuckling at my antics.

"I thought I heard something."

"You didn't hear anything."

"Yes, I did! Were you listening? Shhh… just listen."

Nothing moves, of course. Near the bottom of the path, Larry walks ahead, turns and jumps at me, making a wild, snorting sound. I freeze and stumble, nearly falling.

"Really, Vic, there's nothing here," he assures me, and walks back up to take my hand.

"That wasn't funny," I say, my heart pounding.

By the time we reach our driveway, my apprehension has subsided and I remember the sheets, still on the clothesline.

"You set up our *limoncello* and I'll get the sheets," Larry offers.

I thank him, not eager to climb in the dark to the spot where Ron encountered the *cinghiale*. While Larry gathers sheets, I put cushions on the wicker chairs, set out two stemmed glasses for limoncello, and light candles on the temporary terracotta-block table.

We linger long into the night, chatting and watching shooting stars. I've seen more shooting stars this summer than in my entire life. House lights across the valley go out one by one, leaving only sulfur-colored safety lights that stay on all night. Fog creeps in and covers the valley with a blanket of milky white. Overhead, the stars seem the brightest of the summer.

"Look, did you see that one?" Larry whispers.

I nod, in peaceful awe, and make a wish. When making a wish, one we believe could come true, we are touched by new hope — that essential emotion that spurs humans forward. A falling star, a wish, new hope for tomorrow.

Just Like Romeo and Juliet?

Sipping my coffee in silence, I long for little-girl voices asking for kiddie cappuccinos. Life has an easier rhythm without guests, but it has less, well... life. Larry, up early and finished studying, is dressed for a bike ride.

"It's the perfect morning for photos," he says. "With the orange fences and yellow *scavatore* finally gone, I should get some nice house shots from the road above."

"From that far away the yard might look solid green, without the party-hat anthills. What time do you want to leave for Verona?" I ask.

"No hurry. We just need to get there for the opera. Maybe noon?"

I nod, grateful not to rush after the relentless activity of the past two weeks.

Larry comes back exhilarated by his bike ride, pleased with his photos, and eager to get on the road. After *Pane Nero* scones and the last of the girls' pear juice, we carry our bags to the car. The drive to Verona should be three and a half hours.

While Larry drives the A1, I doze off and on, my head against the window. We hit traffic around Florence, and then breeze past Bologna on our way to Modena. I try to catch a glimpse of Modena, the home of *aceto balsamico*, balsamic vinegar. I can't see a thing from the highway and make a mental note that Modena could be a road trip for next summer.

Bologna north to Verona is as flat as an Illinois cornfield. We pass acres of sunflowers with green leaves and golden petals. Either farmers in the north can afford to irrigate or there has been more rain here. Even on vibrant plants, the sunflower faces turn down as the season is waning.

"It was hard to leave Lodolina today," I say, turning toward Larry. "I wonder if we should've stayed home and enjoyed the quiet. Soon September will be here and the workers will be back. Then we leave for Chicago."

"It's the perfect time. I love taking you away from distractions for a little holiday in Italy's most romantic town. We'll have a great time."

I hope he's right and not just trying to convince himself. Perhaps our getaway to Romeo and Juliet's town will restore some intimacy in our marriage, now that the kids are gone.

We ride in silence. Not the silence of tension when your mind is churning, but the silence of comfort. The silence when someone's words are not as important as their presence. I drift off again, relaxed and calm.

"We had a great time with the kids, didn't we?" Larry asks, rousting me out of my daze. "You were wonderful with them. I loved watching you cook with the girls."

"I think *everyone* had a great time. I'm glad we had some special time with each one, even Claudia. That was my favorite... our time alone with each granddaughter. I think Ron and Paulla had fun, too. But then, Ron *always* has fun... and makes sure everyone else has fun."

Larry nods, lost in happy memories. He seems to have relaxed, too, even driving the A1. He smiles and I wonder what moment he's just recalled.

"This'll be a great weekend, Vic. Even the drive doesn't seem so bad ... except when you were sleeping," he adds, a half-serious reminder that I failed my wifely duty of attentive companionship.

"Almost there," he says, exiting the *autostrada* for the road to our hotel.

La Magioca Relais is a pleasant surprise. It's a country villa, not grand but cozy. Dark green ivy engulfs most of the building and white roses are everywhere.

The woman at the desk asks for our passports. Larry explains that since it was only a car trip inside Italy, we didn't bring them. She says all hotels in Italy now require passports, "by law." She can't accept any other form of identification.

After an uncomfortable silence, I ask Larry, "Don't we have scans on the computer?"

"You're right! Good thinking." He turns to the woman and asks, "If you can see the passport photo and know it's us, can you just copy the number?"

"We need to photocopy the whole first page," she insists.

"What if you print them?" he asks, "I have a memory stick. We'll put the passports on it and you can make printed copies for your files."

Once she's printed our passports, she cheerfully checks us in and hands us keys.

Our room is on the top floor, like an attic with slanted ceilings and a window alcove. At least it's large and comfortable. Looking out over the back yard, I see a pool and scattered lounge chairs. More white flowers, mostly oleander and roses, create private sitting areas for guests. Not one person is in the garden.

As I turn on the shower and hang our opera attire in the bathroom to de-wrinkle, Larry says, "Let's go to town early, explore Verona and find our gate for the opera, so we know where to go. We're on our own for dinner tonight, right?"

"Unless you want to take a nap," he adds playfully. "We *are* on vacation, you know."

"If we do that, we may never wake up. Aren't you tired from driving?"

"I'm okay," he says, flashing me an exaggerated pout of disappointment.

In the car, I ask, as one of us always does, "Do you have the tickets?"

Larry gasps. That means he has them. It's an old exchange between us. One asks the other if they have the tickets, and the other acts like they forgot.

Arriving in the historic town center, my only thought is *Verona is magical.* Unlike steep Cortona, Verona is flat with cobblestone streets, Roman artifacts, and architecture spanning centuries: Romanesque, medieval, Renaissance, Gothic, Baroque, even modern. The hub of city life is *Piazza delle Erbe.* During the Roman Empire the piazza was the public forum and, for centuries, it has hosted a daily market for fruits, vegetables, and herbs — hence the name. Today, offerings also include meats, cheeses, candies, dried fruits, clothing, household goods, flowers, and souvenirs.

On one corner of the bustling piazza is a landmark brick tower, *Torre Gardello*, also called *Torre delle Ore*, tower of the hours, because of an enormous ancient clock on one of its faces.

Between *Piazze delle Erbe* and *L'Arena*, the Roman amphitheater where operas are performed, is *Via Giuseppe Massini*, one the best shopping streets in all of Italy, or so we're told. Shops are still closed for lunch when we arrive, so we stroll hand-in-hand down one side and up the other, peering into windows of Armani, Gucci, Prada, Mont Blanc, and Fendi. Pricey antique dealers and jewelry shops line side streets. Larry hopes to find a new pair of reading glasses, so we stop at every eyeglass store window, trying to see inside.

After stores reopen, Larry tries on a few sunglasses, but we learn readers, as the clerk calls them, are sold in the *farmacia*, pharmacy, not in eyeglass stores.

Unable to find glasses and uninterested in other shopping, Larry suggests we find our gate for the opera then get an early dinner, perhaps overlooking *Piazza Bra*, the piazza adjacent to the two-thousand-year-old amphitheater. As soon as I agree, he picks up his pace and I must walk quickly to keep up.

Suddenly *L'Arena di Verona* comes into view. It looks like a movie set, more majestic as we get closer. I can't wait to go inside.

Piazza Bra, in front of the arena, is strewn with pink rose petals.

"Do you think those are for us?" I ask Larry.

"What?"

"The rose petals. Do you think they're for us?"

"Sure, darling."

"I want them to be for us," I say, knowing an earlier wedding is probably the truth.

Larry stops abruptly, turns toward me, takes my face in his hands, and kisses me as if I was his bride and we were just pronounced man and wife.

"Now, my darling," he asks, tenderly holding my face, "shall we find our gate?"

I bob my head up and down and say, "I'd go anywhere with you."

We find gate sixty-one easily, then walk through three rows of arches and climb some stone steps, but can't get inside. That thrill must wait.

For dinner, our hotel clerk suggested *Trattoria Giovanni Rana* on *Piazza Bra*. At the restaurant, we're escorted to the perfect table with a view of the *L'Arena*. We share tagliatelle with Giovanni's secret ragù and, my choice, their eggplant parmesan. I want to experiment with eggplant parmesan and the menu claims theirs is world famous.

Over dinner, we reminisce about the highlights of our summer. We both treasured our time with the kids, and agree the pinnacle was Italy winning the World Cup. For me, another magical moment was my birthday lunch at Lodolina with Dale and David when we sat in plastic chairs and ate leftovers with Francesco's sunflowers as our centerpiece. Larry says he loved mornings, sitting on the terrace, studying and looking into the valley as the sun came up.

We chat about the short time we have left. I want to spend more time at Lodolina. Larry agrees. He wants to study. I want to cook and write… maybe even play my piano and work on Italian, both neglected so far. I still must learn to drive. We don't mention our stresses. This weekend is for enjoying Verona and one another.

Eventually, it's time for *Tosca*. As we stroll, I take Larry's arm, which I know he likes. He slows so our steps are in sync, looks down at me with an appreciative smile, and squeezes my arm against his firm body.

Vendors are selling blow-up cushions, drinks and souvenirs. Since my bottom is nicely padded and Larry never buys anything frivolous, I shake my head in refusal as a hawker approaches. For anyone sitting on the higher seats, which I understand are stone, a cushion could be essential.

Lights glow from inside the amphitheater, creating a heightened sense of anticipation. It's eight-thirty; curtain time is nine o'clock.

Stepping into the vast interior is unforgettable. This ancient arena is larger than I imagined, though I know it seats twenty thousand. The stage must be three times as wide as a normal one. Candles flicker across the entire stage front. Gigantic sets are in place, lifeless and in shadow. Opera-goers are everywhere, searching for their seats. It's a different universe than the street below.

Our seats are halfway forward on the first level. As I look up, the highest rows blend into the darkening sky, almost out of view. Larry tells me we're in the third section. I ask to see the tickets, but he shakes his head.

"Just stay with me, darling. Don't wander off."

He points to two seats in the center of a row and motions for me to go there. I ask the people already seated to excuse us, please, climb across, and settle in.

After about five minutes, a man with two officials claims we are in his seats. Larry shows one official our tickets. Pointing, he says our tickets are in this row, but in the side, not the center section. I say nothing, just climb back over the same people. It was a simple error, but embarrassing. Our new seats are not bad, but not as good as the wrong seats. The stage seems far away.

I ask Larry if we can buy a program for the synopsis, but he doesn't want to. We've seen *Tosca* before, but it's hard to remember each opera's plot — except that in most every opera a lover is found, then lost, and someone dies.

"Do you remember the story?" I ask.

"We can figure it out as it goes," he says. "It's more fun. Reading the synopsis ruins the suspense."

"I like to know what I'm watching, especially when I can't understand the words. I doubt we're getting English subtitles tonight," I tease, but not in jest.

With almost no overture, the singing begins.

The acoustics are astounding. It amazes me that opera singers can fill a closed opera house without microphones, but to fill a roofless amphitheater — one of the largest in the world — with full, clear sound like we are hearing is a wholly different level of voice projection.

Within minutes, the audience erupts in wild *bravos* for the tenor's first aria.

It takes concentration to understand, but, thankfully, the story does come back to me as the action unfolds and I'm drawn into the drama.

Paramedics, real ones, run quietly down our aisle as Tosca sings and weeps. They return, carrying someone in an orange sling-like stretcher. No one in the audience seems to notice except me.

A cannon booms. The audience jumps. Something bad is about to happen, then does. By the end of the first act, Tosca is convinced of her lover's infidelity and the evil police chief vows to have his way with her. Tosca runs off to confront her lover, the chief orders her followed, and then he joins a church choir in prayer.

Almost instantly, over two hundred lavishly costumed performers are on stage and forty thousand hands express thunderous appreciation. Feet stomp and booming voices roar, "*Bravo, bravissimo, braviiiisssimo.*" After numerous rounds of bows, the stadium lights come on and vendors are in the aisles, poised for intermission orders.

Sitting next to me is a lovely girl in her twenties with long black wavy hair. She's wearing all white — a spandex cropped halter-top with a low-slung leather belt and ruffled mini-skirt. Her bronzed mid-section, unusually muscular, is bare. She's with older adults, her parents I suspect, although I'm surprised anyone would dress so scantily accompanied by parents. The water boy at the end of our row cannot stop staring.

Larry wants to see the orchestra pit, so we work our way down to the front. The set is being transformed as we descend. An oversized painting leans against what looks like a cave and another painting is half off the stage. Propped against a strange edifice and growing diagonally out of the floor is a gigantic gold sword. The set does not make sense and it seems more confusing close up.

From the front, I look up at twenty thousand people. Most are standing, milling about. Especially in upper sections, viewers have spread out picnics. Aromas of salami, prosciutto and red wine waft through the air. I'm glad we had a satisfying dinner.

Larry gives me a little twirling gesture, a signal to go back. It takes a while to weave our way through the crowd in the aisle. The lights flicker, people put their food baskets away and resettle for the next two acts.

Tosca delivers a passionate aria and the audience instantly goes berserk. Opera has reached a new level of intensity for me. I'm accustomed to more formal audiences, rather than this pounding, whistling, screaming frenzy.

I look up. Stars glitter overhead like pinholes in an indigo dome. The temperature, quite hot today, has cooled. Ladies don scarves or light wraps.

The bronzed girl sitting next to us lifts her shapely arms and pulls a white beaded sweater over her white spandex halter. My cornflower blue linen tunic and silk pants seem perfect, even if not fancy or seductive.

This opera is enthralling. Tosca's lover sings another show-stopping aria. The crowd unleashes with *bravo, bravissimo* from every direction. The tenor looks at the conductor, who must have given him the nod. Someone from back stage brings him a glass of water, and then he sings the same aria again — even more brilliantly! By this time, every opera-goer is on his or her feet screaming and clapping, including me.

The orchestra begins and the audience sits, as if on cue. Tosca's tragedy is completed when she stabs the vile police chief with his own knife, watches her lover — with whom she's finally reunited — killed by a firing squad she convinced him would shoot without bullets, and leaps to her death from the wall of Castel Sant'Angelo. The lovers and opera are *finiti*.

After what seems like thirty minutes of uproar and curtain calls, we find our way out of the Roman amphitheater onto the street. Energized and exhausted, we drive to the hotel and fall euphorically into bed.

High Cost of Bargains

The next morning, as light creeps into the hotel room, I lift my head to look out the window. The view, so lovely yesterday, is now obscured by boards, as though they're preparing for construction. I hear a television in another room. I lie there, slightly disoriented, recalling Tosca's leap to her death and the wild ovation.

"Do we have to be anywhere today?" Larry asks lazily as he turns over and gently strokes my shoulder and neck.

"Not 'til afternoon. The garden tour's at four," I whisper, curling up against him and pulling his arm around me.

We take our time getting ready, enjoying the luxury of a real day off, and go downstairs for breakfast. After lingering on the terrace with a second cappuccino, we decide to go back to town to sightsee, starting with our favorite Verona church, the *Basilica di San Zeno*.

Larry is fascinated by the statue near the entry of San Zeno, a fourth-century African bishop who grins at us and holds a fishing pole. It's painted marble, carved in the twelfth century, but feels more modern. We read that San Zeno was devoted to children. In Africa, he helped with their schoolwork, taught them about faith, and was their loved and trusted counselor. He visited Verona and decided to stay, living a monastic life and serving local children. Eventually, he was elected Bishop of Verona and died here in 380.

According to legend, the secret marriage of Romeo Montague and Juliet Capulet took place in the crypt of this church where the remains of San Zeno were already buried. Though less known than some larger cathedrals, the building is one of the finest examples of Romanesque architecture in Italy. To me, it feels like being inside a living organism because every floor, wall, and column are made of Rossa Verona, a fleshy, salmon-colored local marble.

Andrea Mantegna's famous triptych hangs over the main altar. This masterpiece was stolen by Napoleon's soldiers in 1797 and taken to France. The primary paintings were returned, but not the *predella*, a row of smaller paintings below the main canvases. One, a crucifixion scene, is in the Louvre, and two others are in the museum in Tours. Copies replace the stolen pieces, so the altarpiece seems complete. I stare at it for a long time, mesmerized.

Larry says our parking ticket is about to expire, so we should go.

On the way out of the church I walk, perhaps a little too slowly, through an antique silver market in the church piazza. Larry dislikes antique markets, claiming it's all junk. I find silver-filigreed crystal glasses that would be perfect for limoncello and an oval fluted bowl. I know I'm pressing my luck simply by looking, but decide I want to buy both.

By now, Larry is pacing.

"Do you like this, sweetheart? I'd like to buy it… and the glasses." I hold the bowl toward him so he can see it, hoping he'll encourage me.

"Do we need it?"

"Need?" I ask, amused. "No one *needs* silver. But I like it and would use it."

"Come on, Vic. We'll get a ticket. I'll go to the car. If you want them, buy them. But just decide."

I don't think it's fair that we spent an hour looking for eyeglasses for him, but can't look for ten minutes at something I want. He knows we need serving pieces. Maybe not a silver bowl or those particular glasses, but they're lovely and not so expensive.

Reluctantly, I say, "*Grazie, no*" to the dealer and leave with Larry, disappointed and a tad annoyed.

Our SUV, thankfully, does not have a ticket.

I say nothing for about a mile. But I stew. As we pass over the Adige River, I speak up. Otherwise, I'll stew all day.

"I'm kicking myself for not buying that bowl."

"Do you want to go back?"

I hesitate, not sure if his question is sincere or sarcastic, as in surely you don't want to go back. After a couple seconds, I say, "Yes, I do." Adding, "Thank you."

I try to decipher his mood, but he looks straight ahead, expressionless, both hands on the wheel.

"How much are you willing to spend?" he asks after turning around.

"I don't know. The dealer said '*trenta*'."

"I heard that. I asked how much you'd spend for it."

Not wanting to start a rift when he's being nice enough to take me back, I say, "*Venti.*"

Larry finds his way back through one-way streets and pulls up to the curb. The market is closing, so I hurry.

On the way to the dealer with my fluted bowl, I pass another dealer who is slashing prices. On each item is a card with two markdowns. I pick up a tray, which was one-eighty, then one hundred, now fifty. I put it down when I see the dealer with my bowl is almost packed up.

I describe the fluted bowl to him. He remembers it, but doesn't know where it is. My hope plummets when I look at the boxes behind him.

The woman in the next booth says in English, "He'll find it. We do anything for the sale."

"I don't recall the price," I say, looking innocent and hoping for a lower one at the end of the day.

"*Trenta*," he says.

Hoping body language counts for bargaining, I wince and shift my weight,

"Too much?" the woman asks.

"*Venti?*" I ask, twenty, emboldened by the slashed prices on the table I passed.

"We will look," she says and leaves her own packing to help her colleague.

When she opens the second box, I say, "I want to go to another stand to buy something. I'll come back. If you find it, I'll pay twenty."

They continue to unwrap, so I think I must have a deal.

At the dealer with the markdowns, I find three items I really like, and buy all three for a total of one hundred euro. The dealer tells me I got an amazing deal for Sheffield.

Back at the first stall, crumpled newspapers are everywhere. I secretly hope he didn't find it, because I don't want to tell Larry I spent one hundred twenty euros on non-essential, silver-plate items we don't really need.

The dealer shakes his head. No bowl. I'm relieved, but also disappointed. I feel badly that he unwrapped all those items for me. I thank him profusely, though it's not much consolation.

I see Larry in the car watching me. He looks perturbed. I decide to charm him out of it. It won't be easy, since I bought three pieces, not one, and spent one hundred euros, not the twenty he expected.

"They couldn't find the bowl I liked," I tell him cheerfully as I buckle up, "but I found a nice silver tray and two smaller bowls, marked way down. They're Sheffield."

He starts the car and backs up to pull out.

"Do you want to see them?" I ask.

"Not while I'm driving," he replies.

I continue to justify my purchases. "The tray will be perfect for bottles of *grappa* and *digestivi*. It had been one eighty and was only fifty. I also got a bread bowl and one for my spiced nuts. They'll be beautiful in the china cabinet. And, they were steals."

"I brought you back for a bowl you said you loved. Do you love these?"

"Yes… or at least I will love them. They're more traditional. You'll see."

"Do you have the map to the garden?" he asks coolly, changing the subject.

"Yes, in the glove box." I shuffle through our papers, find the map, and start reading the directions aloud. Larry says to wait until he finds his way out of town. At the edge of town, I start again, one turn at a time. I pray we don't get lost. It will not help his mood for me to give him the wrong directions.

While he drives, I reflect on my silver purchase and become irked with myself. I wanted the fluted bowl and silver filigreed glasses. They were unusual and elegant. I argued with an already-reasonable price to appease Larry. I spent a hundred euros on items I wouldn't have chosen if they weren't bargains. I should have purchased the first items at the original price. I lost my fluted bowl over *ten* euros. I must guard against buying bargains, rather than what I really want.

Larry's steely silence intensifies my buyer's remorse. I'll enjoy using them, but right now buying cheaper, not-perfect items feels like a character flaw. And, it seems to have put a damper on our weekend.

I confess, telling Larry I wish I had not bought the three bargains, but instead had bought the fluted dish and the glasses when I first saw them.

"But it's done now," I add cheerfully. "I'm sure I'll use them and learn to love them." I expect him to be glad I learned a lesson.

"This is not the first time you've done that, Victoria," he says with parental disapproval. "We don't need a bunch of stuff you don't love and I don't want. I took you all the way back for the bowl you loved, and instead you got three things you don't love. I refuse for us to clutter Lodolina with bargains from junk markets."

It was the wrong thing to say. I cannot believe he's reprimanding me. Now I like my silver pieces more. The real lesson is that I should buy what I want without worrying about his approval. It was his disapproval that made me walk away in the first place. I do not need a lecture. I should not have confessed. I want a loving husband, not a disapproving father.

"Are you finished?" I ask. "Because I am. This lecture is over. I bought three items for our home that I wanted. It was a hundred euros, not a thousand. I'm not mad, in fact, I appreciate that you took me back and I said so. You shouldn't be mad either."

We get out of the car and start walking toward the garden. I must choose between continuing this argument or not. Hoping to resurrect the possibility of a nice evening, I put my arm through his and bump his hip with mine. It's my old method for playfully breaking the ice if things have gone awry between us. He looks at me, shakes his head with a little smile, not quite believing that he's giving in to my predictable attempt to charm him, and pulls me closer. Things seem to be okay, but I suspect we both are still a little miffed and on edge. I am.

After an hour strolling through the fantastical, exotic gardens of rare plants, we go back to the hotel to rest, read and change for dinner. Larry wants to go early to see if he can find readers at a pharmacy. The restaurant is near the shopping street, he says.

We park in a garage on the other side of the river and zigzag our way over a bridge and through narrow streets. I nearly run to match his speed to the pharmacy, where nothing he tries is perfect.

Our restaurant is the legendary *Dodici Apostoli*, Twelve Apostles. The interior looks like an old church with vaulted ceilings and frescoes. Though early, we're immediately escorted to a secluded table at the back. I open my menu. I love studying menus, while Larry typically wants to chat before launching into dinner. He frowns at me. I close the menu, being careful not to spoil our evening. We chat about what kind of wine to order. To me, since we're in Amarone territory, one of the most delicious of all Italian wines and among my favorites, the only decisions are which vineyard and vintage.

"Okay... Amarone it is," Larry agrees enthusiastically. "Instead of choosing a wine to go with dinner, tonight we'll order dinner to go with our wine." Pleased, he turns to the Amarone page of the massive wine book and studies it like I'd like to study the menu.

"This is a superb list, just superb," he murmurs to no one in particular.

I pick up my menu and open it again. If he can study the wine list, I darned-well can study my menu. While we're engaged in our individual passions, the waiter appears and pours Prosecco in the crystal flutes on our table.

"*Aqua?*"

"*Si, naturale*," Larry and I say in unison. I look up into a surprisingly stern look. Perhaps I should let him do the ordering tonight.

"Do you have questions?" the waiter asks, noticing my interest in the menu.

"Not yet," I answer sweetly.

"I haven't looked," Larry says pleasantly. "We'll need a few more minutes."

"I do have a question, but it's not about the menu," I say and point to a wall-sized painting of the last supper in the next room. "Is the restaurant named for the twelve disciples?"

"No, it's named for twelve Verona merchants who ate spaghetti and beans for lunch here every day for decades in the eighteenth century. They were such devoted friends, townspeople called them the twelve apostles."

Finally, Larry suggests we should decide on food. We agree to order three-courses, plus dessert since that's our package. After choosing a meal rich enough to go with Amarone, we know we've ordered too much and promise one another to only eat as much as we really want.

Our waiter offers to send the sommelier to help Larry select an Amarone. Larry declines, but reconsiders when he finds several he doesn't know but would like to try. The sommelier recommends one that's only six years old. Young, Larry says, for an Amarone, since most have aged over five years before they're released. A good Amarone can age decades and older ones are usually more prized. Larry decides to try it anyway.

Our wine glasses are replaced with stemmed crystal vessels big as goldfish bowls, reflecting the importance of the wine.

We are both mesmerized by the ritual of decanting the bottle. The sommelier pours a thimble-full of wine through a silver strainer into a small copper pitcher. He sniffs and tastes a drop, nods, then pours a small amount into the glass decanter, swirls it to coat the entire inside, then pours that wine into Larry's glass and then into mine, swirling to prepare the entire inside of each. With decanter and glasses rinsed with our specific Amarone, the sommelier inserts the neck of the bottle into the neck of the decanter, holds the joined necks over a candle flame, slowly pouring warmed wine into the decanter. The Amarone fans out, covering most of the inside of the decanter as it slowly fills the bowl.

The sommelier pours a taste into Larry's glass. Larry swirls to aerate and release the aroma, breathes in the rich perfume, then sips, letting the wine linger on his tongue. His face lights up and he nods appreciatively. As the decanting tools are taken away, Larry asks the sommelier to leave the bottle so he can study the label.

We toast to romance and our marriage, looking into one another's eyes. I swirl my Amarone, inhale deeply, comment on the exquisite "nose," and take my first sip.

"This should be saved for our main courses," Larry announces, putting his glass down. "It's young, so won't change as much as an old wine, but it'll be better if we give it more time to open up."

I take another teeny sip of Amarone and reluctantly lower my fishbowl, going back to Prosecco for the *antipasto* and *primo* courses.

Every course is superb and we share tastes of each exquisite dish. When the main course arrives, we eat and drink slowly, making each sip and nibble a moment of culinary pleasure. My roasted duck melts in my mouth. Despite my best intentions, I don't leave a morsel. It is definitely a celebration meal, satisfying in every way, including our conversations about *Tosca* and San Zeno.

After coffee and an *amaro*, a bitter after-dinner drink, I long to go back to our hotel and sleep. We've been dining for nearly four hours, walked most of the day, consumed an entire bottle of Amarone as well as Prosecco and dessert wines, and I'm exhausted. Larry asks for the *conto*, bill, and we're assured it was all in our package, including *servizio*. He leaves something extra, as the service has been beyond excellent.

"We need a walk," Larry says when we emerge into the midnight air.

"Hmm, I was thinking pillow," I counter, putting my arm though his. "I'm seriously tired."

"Let's just go down the shopping street again and then to the car," he says.

We start toward the shopping street, but he walks fast, gets ahead of me and turns down a side street. I rush to catch up, but lose track of where we are. It seems he's taking a longer, more complicated walk than I agreed to and I'm too tired to walk so fast.

"May I look at the map," I ask when I catch him, "to get my bearings? I want to see where we are and where the garage is."

He doesn't give me the map.

"Can I just touch it?" I tease, still a little annoyed he refused to let me look at the opera tickets last night when we sat in the wrong seats. Perhaps he thinks he's taking good care of me, but I think he prefers to be in charge.

He shoves the map into my hand. "Okay. You lead."

I'm confused. Why did my asking to look at the map provoke such a strong response?

Though after midnight, Larry wants to window shop for sunglasses. I want to go to the hotel. He tells me I'm going the wrong direction. I feel upset and disoriented. He walks ahead of me again. I thought I was supposed to be leading.

I see an interesting street parallel to the main one we've walked so many times, so I turn. I know he sees me. He continues to walk down the street he has chosen. When I don't see him where the two streets meet, I walk back up his street. He's not there. I look the other direction. He's not anywhere. Did he really walk away?

I walk all the way back to *Piazza delle Erbe*, scanning the late-night crowd and side streets for him. Perhaps he went to the intersection near the restaurant where we first turned, so I walk to that corner. No Larry. I'd telephone him, but we still only have one cell phone because he says we're always together. If I could remember the number I'd go to back to the restaurant or to a hotel and they would let me call, but I don't. I feel conspicuous and awkward, but continue to stop and look down every street.

Why would he walk away? I know he's independent and expects me to be, but he also knows I hate being abandoned. And we just had such a nice dinner.

He must have gone to the car. I walk faster. I turn right and think I'm walking toward the river, but when I get closer there is no river. I can't tell where I am on the map, so it's no help. Street markings are non-existent.

On a dark street, two men walk close behind me. I hold my keys like a weapon, but soon the men turn down another street. I pass a young couple kissing and feel sadly alone in this city of romance.

I'm relieved to see a bridge. I wait for traffic, cross the road and start across the bridge, but can't tell which bridge so can't find it on the map. I recall the garage is halfway between two bridges. There are many bridges. I feel a slight panic and walk faster. I wonder if Larry is worried about me. He and I should not be without some way to communicate. I vow to get my own phone when we get back to Cortona.

Soon, I'm in a park that I find on the map. I've gone too far. The road outside the park should take me back near the garage and I'd much rather be walking along a busy road than in this dimly lit park. I continue until I see what looks like the garage sign and, relieved, turn toward it.

Finally, I see Larry sitting on a bench near the entrance.

"Boy, am I glad to see you." I say, exhaling a deep sigh.

"Where have you been?" he asks. His tone is not warm.

"Looking for you," I say.

"Looking for me? You're the one who walked off. You turned down the street and walked to the end without ever looking back."

"Why didn't you wait for me or catch up, if you knew where I was? I went back to find you and you were gone."

"You made your point. So, I came to the car. That was twenty minutes ago."

He does not seem one bit concerned about me.

"I'm glad I found you. I was lost and getting scared."

When he doesn't reply I say, "Shall we go to the car?"

"What else would we do?" he quips, standing up and heading down the ramp. I follow.

I'm no longer frightened, just baffled and mad that he seems angry. I wish he had a little more patience with me, or concern for my welfare.

Back at the hotel, while I get ready for bed, he crawls in first and is soon asleep. I just lie there… feeling less connected than ever.

Sometime this summer we stopped touching when we sleep. For twenty years, with rare exception, we have touched toes, pressed a knee against a thigh, or let our fingers entwine. It's comforting, this connection. It makes me feel all is right with our love and, therefore, with the world.

Tonight, I miss his touch; I miss him. But I'm also angry and disappointed. How, in this beautiful, romantic city, have things gone so wrong between us?

I cannot sleep. I wish I could let go of my upset and reach out to touch him. I would feel better. It's curiously hard to stay angry when you reach to touch someone you love.

Long Road to Lodolina

Larry's not in the room when I awaken. He must be in the garden studying. I wonder if he has had breakfast or if he waited for me. The sweet aroma of baked goods fills the room from the kitchen below. The fragrance should provoke hunger, but I feel queasy and worn out. I regret that I let the sun set on my anger and feel sad our weekend isn't ending well.

In the shower, I talk to Larry in my head as if he were here. Hearing myself saying the same things over and over again, I have to laugh.

I decide to give up the inner chatter that doesn't change anything and do some self-analysis, trying to figure out what I actually want and can do:

> *I'm too old to worry about his mood or if he's happy with me. I'm too old to walk on eggshells or feel insecure in my marriage that seemed so solid before we moved. I haven't been myself this summer and I don't like it.*
>
> *I've tried saying, as a therapist once suggested, "When you do this, I feel that.... When you act irritated, I feel defensive, misunderstood, unloved." Most often he replies, "I don't want you to feel that way," then justifies his actions and I feel worse.*
>
> *I know I can't change his behavior — only my own, though it seems unfair that it's usually up to me to resolve the argument.*
>
> *The best option is simply to be who I want to be and worry less about him. We always feel more in control when we choose our own behavior, rather than reacting to someone else's.*

My tension eases, simply deciding to be myself — the *me* I'd like to be. He can choose who he wants to be. In fact, he *must* choose who he wants to be, consciously or unconsciously. I close the door behind me, head outside to greet Larry warmly and see what happens. But first, I stop at the kitchen and ask for a cappuccino. A little caffeine will go a long way.

The chef asks in Italian if I want her to bring my cappuccino to the garden beside *suo marito*.

"*Si, grazie. Nel giardino.*" Yes, thank you, in the garden... beside my husband.

Larry's in a lounge chair with his back toward the building. I walk slowly, trying to soften my heart by reminding myself how much I love this man and that he is a gift to me. As always in the morning, he's highlighting a book.

"Good morning, darling," I say softly, aware I'm interrupting.

"*Buongiorno,*" he replies without looking up. "You okay this morning?"

I cannot honestly say yes. But this isn't the time or place for a serious conversation. Besides, he seems too engaged in his study to engage in my upset.

"I've been better... you?"

"Good."

Wondering what "good" means, I sit down in the lounge chair next to him with my computer on my lap and decide to say something benign, just to connect.

"It feels weird to bring my computer to the garden, but my hand still hurts from writing so much in my journal at the opera and all that clapping. The computer's more comfortable, even if a bit un-gardeny."

"You brought it; you might as well use it," he says, not lifting his eyes from his book. It seems I should stay quiet. I sit on the foot of the lounge chair and look around, sipping my just-delivered cappuccino.

After a few moments, he looks up and says. "We can talk later about what happened last night if you want, or we don't have to. Up to you."

"Okay," I reply. "Thanks. I'd like to talk about it. Maybe later... first I'd like a nice morning with you."

The topic will be hard to avoid during our three-hour car ride to Lodolina.

He finally closes his book, looks at me and says, "How 'bout if we check out early and go to Mass at *San Zeno* before we head home? We'll still be back in time for the concert."

"Good plan," I reply, my unopened computer still in my lap. "Did you have breakfast?"

"Not yet. I waited for you," he says, with a half-smile.

He's trying to be nice. I feel exhausted, despite the caffeine, and glad we've put off any serious talk until my emotions settle.

Breakfast is bountiful. First, a basket of fresh, warm pastries, surely what I smelled earlier. Then eggs; I order scrambled and Larry orders poached. There's a fresh fruit plate, just-squeezed orange juice and another cappuccino. It's perfectly served and plenty to sustain us for the ride home.

After a poorly attended but uplifting Mass at *San Zeno*, we walk across the empty piazza. I recall the antique market. I'll eventually love the pieces I bought and forget the ones I left behind. It may take longer to forget Larry's lecture.

On the *autostrada* headed home, Larry and I first talk about the good parts of our weekend: the lovely hotel setting and gracious service, rose petals on *Piazza Bra*, the astounding *Arena*, the tenor's re-play of his aria, Tosca's grand leap, and the wine and dinner at *Dodici Apostoli*. Neither of us mentions the silver market or the ill-fated, after-dinner stroll.

Then there is silence. We're surely thinking the same thing. I wonder if we should simply stay in our nice zone. But last night's upset is like the proverbial elephant in the back seat. If our wounds are not tended and do not heal, they will fester. I wonder if I should start.

I look across at Larry. He looks at me.

"Do you want to talk about it now?" he asks. "You will not be happy with me until we do, so we might as well get it over with. I really prefer for you to be happy with me."

"Larry, I truly don't know where to start... or if I want to. Things seem okay this moment, but it wasn't a good weekend. I feel sad and not very important to you. We finally were alone on a romantic getaway. It had all the right elements, but it wasn't good for either of us. What happened?"

"All I know is it must be my fault," he remarks, a bit too quickly.

"Why do you say that?"

"When something goes wrong, it's always my fault — all my life."

"I do *not* think everything is your fault."

"Then why are you constantly on my case?"

Now I am constantly on his case? It's my fault? How did this get turned around so quickly?

"Larry, you act as though I criticize you constantly and unfairly. I did not say this weekend was your fault, nor do I think it was. I'm not criticizing, just trying to understand so we can move on and avoid a repeat. I don't want to act nice and brush stuff aside. That only drives the hurt deeper. I'm not blaming you. I see a few things I did wrong, too." I shift in my car seat.

"Like what?" he asks, with a tinge of sarcasm. Fortunately the *autostrada* is empty and he's not fighting traffic.

I collect my thoughts, making sure I don't leave anything out. I try to have a calm, level tone, but his response feels combative and I feel defensive. I don't want a rerun of confessing remorse over buying the silver, then getting a lesson on character.

I start carefully. "Well… I wish I had been more decisive about the silver… that I had bought the bowl and glasses I wanted."

I think "with or without your approval," but don't say it.

"So far, it doesn't sound like you think you did so much wrong," Larry says.

"I wasn't finished…. I wish I hadn't walked away from you last night, but I was upset. You knew I wanted to go back to the hotel after dinner, but you insisted on taking a walk and window-shopping for sunglasses. You got mad at me for wanting to look at the map. Then you insisted I take the lead. I tried, but you didn't stay with me and I lost you. When I couldn't find you, I tried to find the garage, but I really was lost… and scared. But you didn't seem concerned about me at all."

"You walked away from me to make your point," he says. "Then you were gone *twenty* minutes. What was I supposed to think?"

"That I was lost," I say. "I knew you saw me and thought you were following. Then when I thought we'd meet at an intersection, you were gone. I didn't know where you were."

"That's not true," he says. "You knew exactly where I was. You weren't scared. You just wanted to make your point."

I feel my blood pressure rise. I hate it when he tells me how I feel or think, like he knows more about my thoughts and feelings than I do — or that I'm not telling the truth. I look out the window at the passing landscape, clinching my jaw.

"Larry, I did *not* know where you were and I *was* scared," I say in a terse voice, turning to face him. "And please do *not* tell me what I think or how I feel. I am the only one who can say."

"So, what took you so long?" he asks, dismissing my recurring point about feelings.

"I told you. I got lost. Do you even care? I said I wanted to go to the hotel after dinner, but you insisted we take a walk. You knew I was tired, but you wanted to look at the stupid glasses in the windows *again*. Then you disappeared. I looked for you, but I didn't know where you were. Then I didn't know where I was. I don't even have a cell phone because you think we only need one."

"How could you be lost? You had the map. Besides, you said a walk would be nice when we left the restaurant."

"Only after you insisted, and I said a *short* walk would be nice. Your walk was much longer than you first implied."

When a huge SUV passes us going very fast, Larry grips the wheel and tightens his jaw. We sit in silence. I gaze at farmland, houses, barns, forests....

Here we are again, discussing our most difficult issues in the car. It's a private space and we're captives in it. Good and bad. I don't want to spend the next two hours arguing, or staring out the window feeling misunderstood and unloved. I want to end this and get on to more pleasant interactions, or none at all.

"What should I have done differently?" I ask.

"Nothing. You did everything perfectly. I was all my fault."

Really?

"Oh, Larry, you don't mean that. Please... just tell me what you truly mean. I think you think that I should do what you say and let you be in charge, then we wouldn't have any trouble."

"I was the one who offered to take you back for the silver!" he says. "I sat in the car and waited while you shopped. You said you were going back for one item you loved. You were gone twice as long as you said and spent five times as much as you said you'd spend on things you're not sure you like. Yet, I'm wrong for being irritated?"

I calm myself.

"Thank you for taking me back," I say. "I actually do like what I bought. Can't I change my mind?"

Another silence. We're both unwilling to let it go. We do not look at one another.

After a long pause, then more back and forth with no resolution, I say, "Larry, we're getting nowhere. You're mad. I'm hurt. You feel criticized. I feel controlled. We've blown what should've been the most romantic weekend of our summer. We're in Italy, living our dream, but we can't seem to get along unless we have guests."

When he doesn't respond, I continue. "I feel like I spend my days tip-toeing around, trying to do and be what you want me to do and be. I'm afraid to ask for help, but I need your help more than ever…. When you get mad at me over things that seem insignificant, I feel disapproved of, like you don't like the way I am. I love you. I want to be the best wife I can be. But I'm worn out… and I'm lonely."

I can feel the hard spot in my chest move into my throat. I want to punch him. I am not done. I try to sound calm, but inside I am seething.

"This summer has been much harder than we thought it'd be," I continue. "Living in chaos is rough on us both, not just you. Fitting in to a new culture is hard, even harder when I'm alone and intimidated. I feel stupid and insecure when you aren't with me, but rushed, controlled, and disapproved of when you are. We both thought this summer would be different. We've had amazing experiences, but living here has been hard."

I pause, trying not to cry. I give myself a few moments to breathe. He is silent.

I continue, in a softer voice. "The worst is that I can't tell my best friend… my *only* friend in Italy… how I feel, because he'll think I'm on his case."

I fear I'm saying too much. I take another breath, determined not to escalate or be overly dramatic.

"I am too old to live this way. I'm not a bad person and don't deserve to be treated like one. I insist that we be kind to one another, respectful and patient. I want a nicer life for us than the tension we've had this summer. I will not give up on you or lower my standards for our marriage. But I'm also done walking on eggshells, trying not to irritate you."

"Are you finished?" he asks, a bit frosty.

My eyes brim against my will. I shift in my seat and look out the window again.

We ride without talking. I wish we hadn't re-opened the argument. We had a nice breakfast, a truce even if a thin one. I should not be so sensitive about his approval. Perhaps I care too much.

"Yes, I'm finished," I finally answer, not knowing what else to say.

"Can we have a reset?" he asks. "No discussion, just a fresh start."

I pause. I must be honest. "No, I don't want a reset. A reset is a cover-up. There is no remorse or repentance, and no turning to a better place. We just restart with no apologies. I'm sorry our weekend wasn't good. I'm sorry this summer hasn't been what you hoped. I see my part in it. I'm usually independent and this summer I have been insecure and dependent. You haven't been able to do what you wanted to do. Neither have I. But a reset means no one confesses, forgives or learns. Nothing long-term changes."

We pass Bologna and Modena. We circle around Florence. After no connection for miles, Larry looks at me like he has something to say. I brace myself, not sure what to expect.

"I disappointed you in Verona and I'm sorry," he starts a bit cool. "I have not been a good husband."

This time I simply listen.

Larry continues with more warmth, "I liked being with you in Verona. It's a great town. I'm sorry I upset you, though I'm still not sure what I did. But I don't want to keep upsetting you. I don't want my wife to walk on eggshells or feel not valued. I know I can be a jerk. But what I do seems reasonable to me when I do it. I don't think I'm that bad. Am I really that bad?"

Softened by his honesty and vulnerability, I whisper, "I love you. I want you to be able to have the summer you wanted. We both love Cortona, the house and working with Francesco. Overall, this has been a remarkable summer. I just can't deal with constantly being afraid I'll irritate you. How can we make our final weeks happy?"

"We can just decide to," he says. "I promise to be more patient, helpful and available. I really will do my best. If I make you feel unimportant, just slap me."

"You don't mean that... please say only what you mean, so I can trust you."

"I love you, Victoria. I'm truly sorry for the times I've been selfish. I won't always be perfect, but I love you and will try to be better."

"Me, too. I love you and will try."

He drives for a while, seemingly deep in thought.

"One more thing," he starts again. "When I'm irritated, it doesn't mean I don't love you, it simply means I'm irritated. Love and irritation can exist at the same time. The irritation is temporary; the love is what counts. Our marriage exists within a commitment. I'm not going to stop loving you because you interrupt me, or because I don't get to do what I want."

I wait for that idea to settle into my heart, as well as in my head.

"Thank you," I say. "You're right... when you get irritated with me, I feel unloved. I know intellectually that your irritation does *not* mean I'm unloved, but that's how it feels."

Perhaps it's a girl thing, I think. When my father was upset with me, I was afraid he didn't love me. As a child, I always tried to be extra good so I wouldn't disappoint him. As a woman, I'm still afraid of disappointing important people, especially important men. I *know* Larry loves me, but there is a big difference between knowing you are loved and *feeling* loved. Sadly, for me the second seems to require constant reassurance.

Since he doesn't do the same thing — equate irritation with being unloved — perhaps he doesn't think his irritation should affect me so deeply. For him it's a moment, for me it's the entire day. I wish I knew who said "for a man, love is a chapter; for a woman, love is the whole book."

I decide to make a request. It always works better with Larry than complaining. Perhaps it seems less like criticism.

"Could you try to show more patience, even when you don't feel patient? I'm more fragile in Italy. I don't like it, but I am. I need for you to be my friend. I need some extra grace."

His face softens. "I should always give you grace," he says. "You're a gentle, kind woman, filled with grace. You deserve to be treated with patience and grace."

My eyes get watery as he takes my hand and lifts it to his lips. I'm a fortunate woman who is married to a tender and loving man. I hope he's able to do what he promised.

Finally relaxed, it's hard for me to stay awake, but I do my best in order to keep Larry company. Just before the Cortona exit, I look up, lift my chin and say, "There it is," following our tradition. Nestled against the hill, Cortona seems to beckon us. Especially today, it'll be nice to be home.

I remind myself of my new resolve to be the woman I want to be and worry less about pleasing Larry. It will be better for both of us.

An Ancient Organ and Porcini Mushroom Feast

Arriving from Verona mid-afternoon, we're home in plenty of time to freshen up for the organ concert. It's the debut an ancient organ, one of five being restored as a special project by a group of Cortonesi. Although I'm tired after the long drive, it's important to be part of a community that values its history and music. And, it could be a helpful distraction from our emotional afternoon.

Upstairs at home, a tiny iridescent green lizard is stretched out on my bedroom windowsill, as if waiting for me. It lets me get close enough to watch its lidless eyes dart back and forth, its bird-like feet poised to bolt. I know this baby reptile is not a sign of anything, but I feel a surge of pleasure that he has so little fear of me.

Downstairs, the wildlife is not so docile. In our absence, ants constructed a war camp on my kitchen island. I lift my favorite coffee cup and underneath is a dense black mass. I don't have the same tenderness toward ants as I do toward lizards. I grind hundreds, maybe thousands, of tiny beings into the counter with my bare hands, wash the area, douse it with ant spray, and wash again.

Francesco warned that with irrigation running several times a day, it's normal that ants will prefer to be inside, especially if they can find food. But I didn't imagine they could invade so quickly, or that there could be so many.

"The internet works!" Larry hollers from upstairs. It was down when we left.

"Unbelievable! Let's call the kids. You go first. I'm sweeping up a mountain of ants."

I listen as Larry dials Ron, then Angela. Ron's message says their mailbox is full. Angela answers. She's fine, but tired. Hearing her voice, I wish I spent more time talking with her, but Larry treasures their conversations and Angela rarely has time for two chats. I holler hello from downstairs and let him talk. After over twenty years we count all the kids and grandkids as ours, yet I leave it to Larry to keep up with his and I keep up with mine. Larry says it's my turn to call. In the Midwest, it's ten o'clock Sunday morning. Mom will be in church and Lara will be sleeping. For Amber it's too early, only seven. I'll make my calls later. Time differences complicate staying in touch, even with a working internet.

Nearly an hour before the concert we stop at the enoteca to ask Marco how to find the church *Santa Trinitá*, planning to first relax with a drink on *Piazza della Repubblica*.

Marco says to skip the drink, though the church is not far. "The first organ was unveiled last week and more people went than anyone expected. I know the organizers. *Trinitá* is tiny. You must go *now*."

We wind our way up narrow streets lined with stone homes joined like row houses. In one area, window boxes look as if the owners cooperated, planting red geraniums, white petunias, basil and rosemary in every box. It's one of the prettiest streets I've seen in all our years of exploring Cortona, and we've never been here. At a street marked *Via Trinitá*, we join the pilgrimage of people all walking in the same direction.

The sanctuary, a chapel more than a church, is wall-to-wall with plastic chairs, almost all taken though we're twenty minutes early. Larry sees two empty seats near the wall.

'*Liberi?*' free, he asks the nun at our end. She smiles warmly and nods. We pass in front of six women, all wearing beige habits. They must be *Clarisse*, the international women's order founded around 1200 by *Chiara*, the close friend of Saint Francis. Though the chapel is terribly hot, the sisters look joy-filled. I understand the *Clarisse* sing at Mass every morning at their convent. We've never been, but I whisper to Larry that we should go sometime. He nods.

Soon, the chapel has become a furnace. My clothes feel damp and my face and neck are dripping. Women fan themselves. I wish I had a fan. Over my shoulder, I see people standing, jammed into the vestibule. Good thing we didn't have that drink.

Without introduction, the organist arrives, sits, adjusts knobs and lifts his hands. Decibels bombard from the rafters, startling the audience. The sound is bold and harsh. Each pump of the pedals adds a wooden clunk to the melodic phrase. As I listen, I understand why organs like this are no longer made.

The organist plays strenuously and well. This is not an easy instrument. He is drenched. Two female readers make the performance a dramatic event, not simply an organ concert. I don't understand one phrase, but their voices are lush and soothing.

The enthusiastic applause is long enough to trigger an encore. I suspect most would prefer to escape into cooler evening air, but it would be un-Italian not to keep clapping until the performer provides an encore. After another virtuoso selection, the organist takes his final bow. I'm glad we came and, because of the heat, I'm glad we're leaving. We work our way to the vestibule, where some people stop to talk with friends while others try to push through to fresh air.

"Ester!" I say, delighted to see the Italian woman who was so gracious to us at the Rotary Club dinner the day we moved into Lodolina. She turns to see who spoke.

"Ah, Victoria! Larry! How nice to see you. Did you enjoy the concert?"

"Yes. I'm so glad we came," I reply. "But it doesn't seem like an easy instrument to play."

"It's a thing quite particular," Ester explains. "These old organs are difficult. They have not been played for many years. Now the restorers reclaim them one by one. But they are instruments with ancient parts. We must listen with an ear of appreciation for something quite unusual."

Larry nods, "It's a privilege to hear this organ after decades in mothballs." I wonder if Ester understands his reference to mothballs.

"The readers were quite wonderful," I add. "Beautiful voices, but I need better Italian to understand them."

We make our way outside into a soft drizzle, chatting about the suffocating heat and the number of people who couldn't get in at all. Larry tries to hold our small umbrella over the three of us.

Ester says, "Would you like to meet us this week with some friends? They speak excellent English, much better than mine. Perhaps for a pizza?" She tilts her head and her silver and pepper hair, parted in the center, frames her face in a fresh, angular way. She tucks one side behind her ear.

"Of course, that would be lovely. *Thank you!*" I say, perhaps a little too enthusiastically.

She looks at me closely, intently. I feel awkward.

"Your time in Cortona has been good for you," she says, not as a question, but a declaration. "You know the air of Cortona has curative powers," she continues. "For people who aren't well... you are not unwell, of course... they come to Cortona to enjoy the air and be restored. Yes, Cortona has been very good for you. I see you are quite renewed."

"*Grazie*," I say, feeling uplifted and a touch self-conscious.

"Truly," Esther nods with conviction. Her hair moves as she moves.

The stone streets glisten, but the rain has stopped.

We kiss both cheeks and wish each other *buona serata*, good evening. I stand a little taller because of Ester's kindness.

"That," I whisper to Larry as we stroll downhill arm-in-arm, "goes in my journal, word for word."

For dinner, we plan to go to the *Sagra di Funghi Porcini* in the *Parterre*. We loved the *Sagra di Bistecca* last week and this feast celebrates porcini, large brown mushrooms that grow in oak forests in the Tuscan hills and are prized for their distinctive flavor. We've seen porcini at the market, but they're quite expensive and I've never tried to cook them. Tonight, I hope to get some ideas.

With at least thirty people in the ticket line and every table filled, we decide to try again later.

Outside a small shop for wine and sausages on *Via Nazionale*, we stop to say hello to Gabriele, Francesco's associate and our project manager, and his Texan girlfriend Patricia, who calls herself Patrizia. Looking tanned and rested after their holiday on Ischia, they're sitting with friends, sipping Prosecco.

"I want an American hug," Patrizia says when I greet her with the traditional kiss on both cheeks. "I always think we'll see you when we're in Cortona, but I've been watching for you all summer. Today I didn't think about it and here you are!"

I'm surprised and pleased she's so friendly. They pull up chairs for us to join. Gabriele introduces Sebastian, his friend since they were six. They grew up and still live in Castiglion Fiorentino, but Sebastian spent almost three years in Atlanta. Sebastian's fiancé, Megan, is from Fort Scott, Kansas. I tell them my cousin lives in Eureka, Kansas, not far from Megan's hometown, and that I grew up in Statesboro, Georgia.

They're wonderfully animated. Though the age of our children, tonight they don't seem that much younger than Larry and me. Another good omen for life in Italy.

We chat about their vacation, our weekend in Verona, and Lodolina. Gabriele has been at the house almost daily for fifteen months, but not once during August, when the work stopped. I tell him we have grass — florescent green — and ants. He smiles, as if ants are inevitable.

"We hope to go to the *Sagra*," Larry says. "Would you join us?"

"We tried," Patrizia says, "but the line's awful so we decided to come for a drink and try again later."

After a while, Larry wants to check the line. "You may see us very soon," he says as we head back toward the *Parterre*.

The line is longer, every plastic chair at every plastic table is occupied, and people are standing, holding plates of food, waiting for tables. There must be over a thousand people eating mushrooms. Looking at the sign, I understand why. Only seventeen euros for the full meal, including wine and dessert, with porcini mushrooms in every course: fried or sautéed, then over pasta, and finally as sauce over veal. Larry knows I don't eat American veal, so suggests we go somewhere else.

When we walk back by on our way to Lilli's, Gabriele and friends are still chatting and laughing at the same table. When Larry shakes his head, saying the line is hopeless, Gabriele goes inside and returns with glasses of Prosecco for us to join them. Guess we are staying here.

Soon it's nine-thirty, we're all famished and decide to go the *Sagra* even if it means standing in line. Patrizia assures me Italian veal is not like American veal. Larry and I haven't eaten since breakfast in Verona. Thankfully, the line is short. The men buy tickets while Megan, Patrizia and I find a table near the park's edge, away from the harsh central floodlights.

Sebastian says Cortona high school students are serving tonight. Almost immediately, an adorable girl in pigtails brings paper napkins, plastic utensils, and plastic cups, and asks if we want *frizzante* or still water. An awkward, pimply boy offers red wine, one-half bottle per person. The mushroom courses begin, and as a finale, the teens bring not-so-ripe peaches for dessert, just like the *Sagra di Bistecca*. They ask if we want *caffè* or limoncello, coffee or lemon liquor. Everyone says, "*tutti e due*," both, literally all and two.

The evening is more fun with new friends, especially ones who make me feel young and energetic. When people are connected by interests and heart, age becomes irrelevant.

The evening also encourages me regarding Italian. Megan says that for months she never spoke, just concentrated, listening to what people said. Then she went on holiday to the *Cinque Terre* with her sister who spoke no Italian, so she had to use what she knew.

"It was like a switch," she recalls. "One day I wasn't saying a word. Three days later it was as if I'd spoken Italian for years." In her gentle, ultra-feminine way, Megan says it is all about necessity and courage. I pray that necessity and courage descend on me soon.

Larry has been my perfect companion tonight, attentive and affectionate. Tomorrow is another day. This week September starts, so back to daily construction. I hope we don't go back to daily discord.

Amazing how it takes so little to shift the aura of a relationship. After today's promises of greater patience and empathy, and our new tool of resets, I look forward to the rest of our summer instead of dreading it. I really do love this man and our new life. As I fall asleep, I bend my knee to touch his thigh and feel a wash of joy when he inches his leg toward mine.

I'm surprised at how awake I feel after this long, emotional day. I recall Ester saying, "Cortona has been good for you... I see you are quite renewed," and think of the powerful impact a single comment can have when made by someone you value, even if you don't know them well. Good and bad, and Ester's comment was good.

No Unfinished Business

The telephone ring mid-morning is jarring after a summer with very few calls. Larry, sitting next to me on the terrace, goes inside to answer. I strain to listen.

"*Funziona? Si, il telefono funziona, ma un momento.*... Yes, the telephone works, but just a moment...

Larry hollers from inside the coat closet, still the only live telephone jack in the house. "Victoria, have you tried the internet today?"

"Yep. No signal," I call from the terrace.

He's speaking in a very stern voice. I think he says the internet is *not* fixed, and that we must have the phone and the internet working *at the same time.*

Then he says tomorrow is *not* okay, it must be fixed today.

No, don't say that! What's one more day, if it's for sure? They've finally responded. Please don't make them mad now. Then I hear him say *domani*, tomorrow, is *va bene*, okay, if it is *sicura*, for sure. Good boy.

Larry comes back to report that *Telecom Italia* said they found the phone problem, but not the internet. Tomorrow, they promise, we will have both at the same time.

"Do you believe them?" I ask.

"No, but we can hope. Nothing else we can do. Okay if I take a run?"

"Of course," I reply. I don't say it, but I'd love some time alone.

"Before I go," he says, "I want to apologize again for being a jerk in Verona. We had a nice evening last night. Are you okay this morning? I mean with me?"

"You weren't the only jerk in Verona," I assure him again. "And, yes, I'm okay with you."

"We both know the truth," he says softly, leaning over to kiss my forehead.

"Sweetheart, you're a wonderful husband. This has been a tough summer. It's fascinating and exciting, but we expected something different and we're both stressed. When people are stressed, they're not their best."

Before leaving, he brings me a second cappuccino.

I type away, recording our breakfast in Verona, Mass at *San Zeno*, discussion on the drive home, organ concert, the kindness of Ester, and our fun at the *Sagra di Porcini* with Gabriele and his friends. I'm constantly surprised by how much happens in one day, events that would never occur in Chicago.

On the hillside across the stream, trucks are still rambling along toward the house where construction is underway. Larry and I should introduce ourselves to the new owners. We understand they're from London. After a few minutes, another backhoe clatters across the hillside. What *are* they doing?

I sit at the piano and rest my fingers on the keys. It feels strange and yet so familiar. Not only is this the first time since we moved that I have sat on its reupholstered bench, the instrument itself has been rebuilt with almost all new parts since I last played it. The keys are more responsive and the sound is surprisingly different — lively, richer, clearer and more satisfying.

Suddenly, I'm overcome with gratitude for the joy and peace I feel. I play all my old favorites, praying this tender connection with my husband will continue.

On the kitchen counter, the frozen scone Larry left for me is covered with ants. How do ants know where there is food — or find it so quickly? I blow off as many as possible, put the scone on a clean white plate and microwave it for twenty seconds. Still steaming, I lift it. On the plate are two more, wobbly but alive. I'm not afraid to eat an ant, but would rather eat as few as possible.

A car door slams. Francesco says he's come to review the construction that will start this week, a few days before the *Ferragosto* holiday officially ends. I'm still in my robe and Larry is not yet home, though it's ten o'clock. Francesco looks fresh and artsy in his marine blue shirt and lime pants. It's wonderful to see him after so long. I dress quickly while he surveys the site and we start without Larry who soon returns, smelly with sweat. After two hours walking from spot to spot with Francesco and his list, Larry goes to shower. I'm ready for another coffee, so offer to make one for Francesco. He declines, saying he must go.

Today is our last quiet morning, except Sundays, for the rest of this year. After we return from Chicago, Francesco says workers will arrive six mornings a week until Christmas.

Late afternoon, I screw up my courage to call an antique dealer I want to visit to look for dressers. Larry says he'll go with me any time, but that I must make the call for an appointment. He's forcing me to speak Italian. Practicing in my head what to say, I look up words I don't know and make sure I know how to conjugate the verbs. I dial the number. It rings twice. A woman answers.

At her "*Pronto*," I freeze.

"Do you speak English?" I blurt.

"*No, mi dispiace,*" she replies. No, I'm sorry.

I bumble on, my heart racing. She seems to understand my intent if not my words. When I hang up, I have made the appointment for tomorrow afternoon at two. I feel proud of myself. Though I did not use one complete sentence, it seems like a baby step toward living comfortably in a country where I don't speak the language.

Sitting in the soft cushions of the wicker chair and watching rainbows made by the sprinklers in the afternoon shade, I write in my journal. In these ordinary days, when I can be calm, play the piano, speak a little Italian, and write, I'm beginning to see what life on this tranquil hillside could be if Larry and I weren't living in construction or in a contest with one another.

Just a glimpse that a dream *could* come true, keeps us reaching for it.

* * *

The next morning, I awaken with the same sense of serenity. The sun peeks over the ridge with a single piercing ray. Soon, the entire sky is a golden glow. I cannot wait to start a new day.

Each day, the sunrise reminds me to whisper a prayer of thankfulness... for the gift of a new day I did not earn or create, for my husband who is still the finest man I know and wants to be a good husband despite this summer's challenges, and for our children and grandchildren who are each a treasure to me. If I begin my day with thankfulness, I feel different and my day goes better.

Francesco arrives before eight with his schedule. There's an important installation every day until we leave for Chicago, including the adjustment of the door on the dishwasher that closes with such force that three glasses have been broken. It'll take two repairmen on separate days, Francesco says, a stone man to remove the toe-kick, plus the official Miele repairman. In Chicago, the dishwasher repairman would have removed the toe-kick. Life in Italy is more complicated in so many ways.

I tell Francesco ants are now in every room except the powder room.

"You must be relentless and not let them inside your house," he says. "They come inside because of the watering of the grass. Spray the foundation every day. Otherwise they move their families and friends inside and make Lodolina *their* home. It is comfortable and dry for them, with nice food."

When I show him my ant spray, he tells me to look at the *ferramenta*, hardware store, for a stronger product with a poison symbol on front. I hate using poison, but I also hate sharing my home with ants.

In the afternoon, Larry and I spend over an hour with the antique dealer I called yesterday. Their home is a giant showroom, with almost every item for sale. I like one bedroom dresser, but the dealer said it had been her mother's, so is the only one not for sale. Their pieces are beautiful, but we don't find a dresser, dining chairs, credenza for Larry or any of the smaller things we need.

By the time we come home, the front of Lodolina has been transformed. Marcello and his assistant have worked all day laying stones on the front concrete slab. He says we must stay off until tomorrow evening. The terrace is beautiful, but I still wish it was larger.

"How about a walk?" I ask Larry before dinner. "I think the cherries are ripe and I'd like to make a compote for our dessert tonight. I need a tall, strong, handsome man to pick them."

"Let me finish this chapter," he says, not looking up. At least he didn't grimace or refuse, but I did expect some tiny reaction to my obvious flattery.

We've been watching our cherries ripen day by day. This morning they seemed red and ready. I grab a bag and the ladder, and wait for to Larry to finish reading.

Together we tramp through knee-high, crunchy-dry, flaxen-colored field grass toward the cherry trees. Larry says we need to get Oliver to mow soon because the overgrown, dry grass is surely a fire hazard. I think that means I should call Oliver. I smile. When did property management as well as the house construction and management become my responsibility?

We reach three tall, gangly wild cherry trees, with their identifiable trunk rings. To our astonishment, the branches are stripped clean. Even the ground is bare. Yesterday there were thousands of bright cherries hanging on the branches, now none. The birds must have eaten them the instant they were ripe. It's annoying, but also amusing, to compete with wild animals for fruit we believe is ours. For decades it has been theirs, as it was this year again.

Dinner is tasty and romantic, even without cherry compote. Larry asks to help with cooking, just to be together he says, and he washes the dishes.

After dinner, sharing the last bit of wine, Larry says, "I've got a new theory about ants, why they are constantly moving."

I can tell it's a joke by the funky way he holds his mouth.

"What's that?" I ask, feigning ignorance.

"They get into the coffee grounds at night and are buzzed by morning."

I shake my head at his pathetic excuse for humor, but can't hide a grin. Maybe Gabba isn't funny anymore, as Sydney declared not so long ago, but he sure is cute.

Before bed, I call Lara. I miss her. She's says she can only talk a minute. She's not supposed to take personal calls at work, but she will because I'm calling from Italy. She sounds stressed, says she's just unhappy with some things at work. I feel upset on her behalf. But no matter what I say, trying to help, it seems to be wrong and she gets more agitated. Lara's nature is to be engaging, positive and delightful. We usually laugh together. It makes me sad when she's sad. We agree to talk when she's at home, not at work. If I call at seven in the morning in Cortona, it's midnight in Chicago, a much better time for my night-owl daughter. I don't tell her, but until then, I will worry. Since a mother is never happier than her least happy child, and we have five, one usually has me on edge.

As I fall asleep, Larry holds my hand, I think to comfort me. He must know something is not quite right with Lara. Interesting how in-tune we are when there is no unfinished business between us.

Surprising Change of Heart

Morning construction sounds have a soothing familiarity after a month without them. I'm not sure how I slept so late with the grinding and scraping under my window, but it's almost nine. It will be nice to see Pierangelo, Graziano, and Luciano again after their long holiday.

To give Larry a few more minutes of quiet study, I shower and dress before going downstairs. Seeing me, he closes his computer and looks up, seeming unusually serious.

"Can we talk about how we want our day to go?" he asks without saying good morning.

"Sure," I answer without saying good morning, either. Is he mad I slept so late? This is an unpleasant way to start a new day, especially when things have been going so well.

"Just give me a minute to make a coffee, okay?" I say, deflated from my happy-morning expectation and slightly irked. I wish there was less edge in my voice.

"What's with the attitude?" he snaps. "All I did is ask if we could plan our day. If I know in advance what you want from me, I can plan around it. I thought you'd like the idea. It'd help us both. It's after nine and I've been up hours, waiting for you so I could plan my day around you."

There's plenty of edge in his voice, too.

"I showered and dressed before coming downstairs so you could read longer without interruption," I defend myself. "But I get here and you're already irritated. We were fine last night. How did I make you mad so quickly?"

"I'm not mad, I just have a lot to get done. I haven't had one good workday all summer. I'd like to schedule our time around what you need, then plan my day. Is that too much to ask? I thought you'd be glad."

"Can I just make a cappuccino first?" I ask, now unable to hide my aggravation.

He doesn't respond. I make my cappuccino and come back to the living room. This will not be fun, but there's nothing to do but endure it with as little resistance as possible.

I sit in a white leather chair and exhale slowly, reminding myself to stifle any edginess in my voice. People hear tone more loudly than words, and often it speaks more honestly. If I want a good listener, my tone must be inviting.

When he asks again about my plan for today, I tell him what I must do to be ready for company tomorrow. Friends of David's and Dale's are coming from Orvieto to see us. Larry tells me it's a to-do list, not a plan, and surely I don't need help with my own to-do list. I take another deep breath and say I need his help carrying the big packs of water bottles and would like help driving. He says I must learn to drive, and that he forbids me to carry the large packs of water bottles because I'll hurt my back. He says I should ask someone from Molesini Market to carry the water down the hill to the parking lot, or go the Coop in Camucia where I can use a grocery cart. He says he'll carry them to the house when I get home.

I calmly tell him it only seems fair that he helps me get ready for people who, essentially, he invited, and that he said he needed to go into town this morning to pay the garbage tax and get a SIM card for the new alarm system. I say if we ran errands together, it shouldn't take long.

He tells me he'll pay the tax tomorrow when we're in Cortona with our guests. I say it isn't fair or gracious to leave me with guests we barely know while he stands in line at the post office, which can take forever, to pay a tax we should've paid days ago.

The tit for tat escalates. I'm tempted to say, "Don't bother, I'll handle it," but don't because I'll resent doing it alone. Neither of us are screamers, but quiet tension can be sharper than the loudest screams, cut deeper, and last longer. After our argument, there is a heavy silence.

Something has to change. He wants to plan our days? Maybe I should try it. I always have a general schedule for my own days; why do I resist planning with Larry? Is it because it feels like control?

I suggest if he studies until eleven, we could go to town for one hour, pay the tax and get a few groceries for tomorrow. I'll do everything else to get ready and protect his afternoon to study. What's more, if he goes with me, I'll fix meals at home to save him time.

"Will you need me with Francesco this afternoon?" he asks.

"That part I can't promise. But I don't think so," I say, hoping it's true.

"By the way," he says. "Have you organized a completion plan with Francesco? We need to watch the schedule closely or things won't get finished before we go back to Chicago. And, I need a better idea of the budget."

I feel my blood pressure rise again. It seems he has been up too long this morning, thinking of what I should be doing.

"You know I have a list," I say, as unemotionally as possible. "I asked you several times to please read it to see if you have anything to add, but you say you don't have time."

Suddenly, he stands up and walks upstairs. I guess our planning session is over.

At the top, he leans over the rail and says, "By the way, we can't do it all in Cortona. We need to go to Camucia for the SIM card."

I was not ready for this. I now think it'd be easier to go alone and let him pay the tax and buy the SIM card whenever he wants.

"Never mind. I'll go on my own," I call up from my living room chair. "I really would prefer to let you stay home and study."

"No, I'm driving you," he insists. "I don't want you to carry heavy packs of water. And, I don't want you complaining that I didn't help. If you want to cook tonight, I'll take you out for lunch. I don't want you to think you're here to wait on me."

I'm not sure what to say now, but sometimes not talking at all is best. This man never fails to surprise me. I must ask him what changed his mind, but later. Could it have been my willingness to plan?

Driving down the S-curve, Larry looks into the valley and wistfully says, "This view never gets old, does it? The road is worse than ever but the hillside is beautiful. I love living here."

"You seem happy. Happier than this morning. What happened?"

"Well, I decided if I'm stuck running errands, we might as well make it fun." He smiles at me and says, "Are you willing to have fun with me?"

"Of course. Not only will I have fun, I'll *be* fun."

"Truth is, once you said I didn't have to go, I wanted to," he confesses.

I'd say "men!" but felt exactly the same way. Once he said he'd take me, I was fine going on my own.

At the phone store in Camucia, Larry gets two SIM cards, one for the new alarm system and one so I can have my own cell phone. Guess the night in Verona made him realize that two phones really are necessary. Best not to act too excited, I tell myself.

In Cortona, I get groceries while he pays the garbage tax at the post office. He carries the waters down the hill to the car and I carry the groceries. He's so congenial that I suggest we have lunch at home, though he said he'd like to take me out.

"Cortona's crowded today and I prefer the tranquility of our hillside. How about you? A little reward for your helpfulness?"

"I know how you can reward me…" he replies.

"You said you needed to study," I light-heartedly resist.

Lunch at home is the same as every other day, but it has not become boring. The cherry tomatoes, *pomodori ciliegini*, still delight me with a burst of summer in every bite, especially with creamy *mozzarella di bufala*, an abundance of *basilico* and our home-grown olive oil. With a tender, salty prosciutto and warmed onion focaccia, we feast like royalty.

While Larry studies, I set up my office. My office space is in the kitchen: one full-height cabinet. When I unpack a big box marked "office," I discover a birthday gift from Kathleen I had forgotten — a photo of four girlfriends preparing a monster salmon for a dinner party. I put the photo on a shelf with a few other favorites. With my personal work space organized, Lodolina feels more like home. I still need a desk. The kitchen table is too high for comfortable typing, but it works for now.

Today seems like another turning point. When Larry wanted to plan our day, I thought it was another way to protect his study time. But when I made a request rather than complaining of all I had to do, and said I'd go on my own, he was suddenly willing to drive and work together. I wonder if planning — which I have resisted because I fear he'll correct my plan, or I'll feel controlled and it will create an argument — might make him more willing to help.

At dinner time, I want something more interesting to cook and something nice to do for Larry. I'm bored with the pasta, grilled meat and vegetables we eat most every night.

Golden flowers are still attached to the zucchini. I understand they're delicious fried, although I've never tasted one. I look through several recipe books, then stuff them with mixed cheeses, dip in tempura batter and fry in olive oil. I put one on each plate with a slice of toasted onion focaccia, pour two glasses of crisp white wine, and take our *antipasto* outside to the new stone terrace where Larry is reading.

"Hi darling. I don't want to interrupt… but are you ready for our starter? It's warm."

He looks up and his chin gets that adorable dimpled smile I love.

"Wow… Look what you've done. That's gorgeous. What is it?"

"The zucchini still had flowers, so I fried them. See what you think."

He makes a toast to the best wife ever, saying he feels lucky. Though this has been a rough summer, he says he sees how hard I work to make life here match our dream. And, he says he hasn't been as much help as he should… or as nice as he should be. He lifts his glass and tells me he wants to be a better husband.

"Are you saying all that because I can cook?" I ask, only half teasing.

"Yes, you can cook. But you do many things well… and you take very good care of me."

I insist he eats his flower before it gets cold. I'm touched by his effusiveness and glad he sees how hard I try and that his happiness matters to me.

"Wooaaa… that's good!" Larry's expression of delight makes it worth the effort.

He raises his glass again. "Lovely *antipasto*. Lovely girl. Thank you."

"To you," I reply, lifting mine again and looking into his eyes with sincerity. The delicate white wine is a perfect complement to our *antipasto* and to our lighter mood.

We sit on the new stone terrace, enjoy dinner, and watch the evening sky take on a rosier and rosier glow. We don't see sunsets from our side of the Cortona hill, but tonight the entire sky has blushed and the clouds seem backlit by peach and fuchsia beams.

Larry suggests I call Amber while he washes dishes. Since the internet is still dead, I try to use the pre-paid card, but there's no dial tone on our landline phone. I'm thrilled when we connect on my new cell phone and the pre-paid phone card. Amber tells me about Chad's and her unproductive job searches and the cute things Aiden has done. She lets him tell me that yesterday he wore "unawaa" with no "asiden," proudly adding "yea!!" for his own potty-training success: underwear with no accident. She assures me that Lara is fine, I just called her at a bad time. She says Lara always feels terrible if she's cranky with me. I assure Amber I know children are least careful with the parent with whom they feel most safe, no matter how old they are, and thank her for her reassurance. I feel very far away.

The phone dies after only twelve minutes. An English woman's voice announces with great finality, "Your pre-paid card has expired." I knew the credit would expire faster with a cell phone, but not that fast. Without phone or internet, I can't even email Amber to tell her why our call ended so abruptly.

Despite that disappointment, I've had a great day. Larry and I seem to be on a different course. Making a daily plan may encourage the partnership I have longed for all summer. Marriage is simply better when you want to help your spouse and he wants to help you. It does not matter which comes first, the helping or the being helped. One seems to inspire the other.

As I wait for sleep to come, Larry reaches for my hand, pulls it to his lips and whispers, "I love you, Victoria. After a rough start, this has been a sweet day."

The day was sweet, but the night air smells like manure, even in the bedroom. Someone must have fertilized the old-fashioned way. Today, like most every day this summer, I've discovered something new about my hillside, my husband, and myself.

Chatting with the Rooster

This morning, Larry and I plan our day, listening to each other and making offers of help. Yesterday, in our big event of lunch with Phil and Carol, we exchanged Italian experiences and exasperations like merit badges. They have lived near Orvieto for nine years. While Larry and I confessed our struggles fitting into a different culture, living in constant construction, communicating without good Italian, and a bit of tension at home, we mostly talked about the beyond-expected, only-in-Italy experiences. They assure us living here will get better, but that it will never be easy.

It was comforting to be with people who understand first-hand. Unless someone has lived this disconnected, disorienting, other-culture adventure, it's hard to really get it. Most of our back-home friends can't imagine, as graciously as they listen to our stories. And, those we know in Cortona are mostly Italians, so can't imagine what it's like to be undone by a life they know as normal.

Today is market day and Larry says he will be my willing chauffeur, companion and carrier, but would like to be home for the afternoon. I say I'd like to experiment with eggplant parmesan for our dinner, and would love to have lunch in town if he has time.

Parking lots are jammed, as they always are on weekends. Even our secret spots are taken. If vegetables weren't so heavy, we'd give up and go home, leave the car, and walk back to town. Circling one more time toward *Piazza Garibaldi*, we notice the barrier to the *Parterre* has been removed. So, we drive up that hill and find a space on the gravel of the *Parterre*. We've never seen that barrier down in all our years visiting Cortona and wonder what's going on today.

On our way to the vegetable stand, Larry wants to stop at the *farmacia* to look at reading glasses. He likes several, but says he'll decide later. At Isa's antique shop there is a beautiful, small *crendenza* in the window. It could be exactly what Larry needs for behind his desk.

When I greet Isa with *"Come?"* short for how are you, she says she's *stanchissima e triste*, very tired and sad. *"Perche?"* Why, I ask. I think she says she has a great pain in her leg, so cannot take care of her mother who is in the hospital, and that makes her sad.

We measure the *credenza* and decide it would fit. Only one small panel in the back is not original, where *topini*, little mice, chewed holes, which could be perfect to run wires. I also measure a walnut bedroom chest with carved twisted columns on each side. Isa has exceptional antiques, but Cortona prices seem high. Both items are more than we want to spend.

We walk through *Piazza della Repubblica* and stop to say hello to Marco at the enoteca. Before buying our vegetables, Larry says he wants to talk with Arnaldo at *Pane e Vino* about planting vines on our hillside. Arnaldo, who produces his own wine near Castiglion Fiorentino, offers to come look at our land. *Molto gentile*, very kind, Larry says.

Finally, we arrive at my favorite fruit and vegetable stand. The blue-eyed Italian woman whose family owns it tells me the plum tomatoes, *pomodori roma*, are *eccellente*. Her produce stand is bursting with jewel-like colors and the sweet, earthy smell of late summer, when everything is ripe and releasing its distinctive perfume.

Today I tell her my name. She smiles and says, *"Sono Gigliola, piacere."* I'm Gigliola, a pleasure. I practice her name in my head. It's not an easy one.

Gigliola suggests some wild fennel pollen, gathered a mano, by hand, saying it is *squisito* for sauces and roasted meat. It's expensive and the pre-measured bags all hold more than I need for experimenting, so I decline. But I'll take a bag and clippers on our next walk to collect some to try. I want to understand why Tuscans prize it so.

From the *porchetta* man, we buy sandwiches. He slices meat from a piglet-sized roll of roasted, boneless pork — the head, also roasted, is poised at one end to prove its freshness. Stuffed with garlic cloves, fennel pollen, and organ chunks, and wrapped in crispy browned skin, the aroma is intoxicating. I ask for mine *"senza organi,"* hoping that means without organ meat. But with each slice the *porchetta* man chops in some organ meat. He whacks off pieces of the crispy skin and presses them onto my sandwich. I don't protest, but will take out whatever I don't want to eat.

We sit on a bench in the cathedral piazza and devour everything except the organ meat. Larry teases me that the *porchetta* man was flirting, giving me the best parts. More likely, I say, he was dumping the bad stuff on the naïve *donna americana*.

Loaded with heavy bags of vegetables, fruit and cheeses, Larry insists I carry nothing. We walk by an antique show, *Cortonantiquaria*, evidently an important annual event and perhaps what is causing today's crowds. When I suggest we look for furniture there, Larry says we'll go tomorrow, he doesn't want to drag the heavy bags through the show.

On *Via Nazionale*, we stop at Isa's shop again and tell Veronica we're interested in the *credenza*, but it's more than our budget. She says she'll ask Isa if she can do any better.

Larry wants to go for gelato, insisting it's the obvious way to top off pork sandwiches. Fortunately for our waistlines, the gelateria has an extra-long line, so we don't wait.

Just before Larry turns onto our access road, he pulls over and stops the car. He reaches out of the window and picks three wild figs from a tree that hangs into the road. I peel the riper one since I can't wash it, give half to him and eat the other half. The mouth-feel of a warm fig is like nothing else on earth. Then he stops to pick blackberries clinging to the stone wall. Our roadside dessert is much tastier than gelato.

At home, my market produce arranged on a rustic white platter is so beautiful that I take photos. Soon, the entire house has the enticing fragrance of in-season, ripe fruits. Somehow produce in American grocery stores never reaches the pinnacle of color, aroma, texture, or flavor of the fruits and vegetables we buy in Cortona's Saturday market.

Despite dark skies, we set out on foot to explore the hill across our valley. We're curious about our neighbor's construction and Larry wants to take more photos of our house from the opposite hill. I grab an umbrella. The forest is too dense to simply walk across the land, so we climb up the trail, turn right at *Viale della Rimembranza*, the road with six hundred cypress trees honoring the fallen soldiers, and go back downhill on a different road.

Larry takes photos of our house and property, with the long valley in the background. Our cypress and horse chestnut trees are among the largest in the valley.

At a chicken coop near a stone farmhouse, I walk to the fence. Three roosters and several hens are pecking the ground. One is strutting. He's enormous, has an upright red comb and looks like the boss. Must be my guy.

"Eerr-err-errdle- errrrr....," I chortle, trying to get a reaction from the big guy.

"What are you doing?" Larry asks.

"Trying to make him talk to me.... Eerr-err-errdle-err," I call again, more loudly.

"Vic, shhh! Seriously."

The big cock perks up, stands tall and jerks his head in several directions. He looks for the sound for a few seconds and then goes back to pecking. At least he was interested.

Larry looks at me in disbelief, then chuckles and shakes his head. I think he likes it when I don't mind him, especially when I'm playing.

We soon pass a grand ruin we considered buying years ago. It's still empty and as magnificent as I remember, with stunning views. Larry thinks the oldest section is about the same size and age as Lodolina. But this house, expanded over centuries, with a pig barn, ancient well, and many hectares, was a much larger project than we wanted.

I pick a cluster of sweet grapes from an abandoned vine along the road. A car approaches, so I hand a few to Larry to share the guilt.

We turn right on a dirt lane that must lead to the house with new construction. We don't go up to the house, for fear we'd be trespassing, but only as far as the excavation. It must be a swimming pool plus an enormous underground room, perhaps a garage.

A gentle rain starts. Larry opens the umbrella and we squeeze close together to huddle under it. I take his arm, telling him as I always do, "You hold the umbrella and I'll hold you." When we pass the rooster's house on the way home, a woman wearing a house dress and headscarf, and carrying a red plaid umbrella, is feeding the chickens.

She looks up. Larry and I both say, "*Buonasera.*" She walks toward us.

Across the fence, we introduce ourselves. I point across the little valley, "*Quello e nostra casa.*" That is our house.

"*Lodolina?*" she asks, surprising us that she knows the name. Perhaps the old-timers know all the houses' names.

Larry tells her in Italian, "Yes, our house. We've done lots of work. Almost finished."

"*Abbiamo translocato da Chicago,*" he adds. We have moved from Chicago.

I wonder if she's glad we brought Lodolina back to life, or if she liked it better when it was an overgrown ruin.

"*Piace vostri polli,*" I like your chickens, I say, curious if she heard me mimicking them. Maybe she clucks to them, too. My grandmother clucked to her chickens.

Light rain persists as we walk home. Another storm is brewing. Tonight's dinner will be an experiment. I've decided to make eggplant parmesan, but will bake the eggplant slices rather than frying them, as is traditional. I'll also make my first homemade tomato sauce from the plum tomatoes Gigliola said were *eccellente*.

The whole concoction takes longer than I imagined, but smells heavenly as it bakes. The skies darken while I cook and Larry studies.

Suddenly, thunder cracks and curtains of water blur the olive trees across the valley. Houses disappear. A fierce wind blows water into the doors. Rather than close them, Larry pulls our walnut table farther from the door so we can watch the storm while we eat, but not get wet. A lightning bolt illuminates the kitchen. Thunder reverberates. It's unleashed fury and incredibly romantic. Larry stands in the kitchen door, transfixed, and calls me to stand with him. I press into his protective embrace.

Back to cooking, I fry sausage and braise fennel on the cooktop. Grilling was not an option in this storm. We take our time with each course, spellbound by the storm. After repeatedly relighting candles, I give up.

Larry deems my eggplant parmesan the best ever and suggests I give cooking classes. I tell him I only cook for those I love. He requests a second, then third helping. After tonight's success, I now have the confidence to make eggplant parmesan for friends. If we had friends.

The tempest turns to drizzle. Thunder becomes distant. Leaves swirl in the air. It's late August, but feels like October. Gullies appear in the lawn.

Perhaps summer storms are a metaphor for storms in marriage that can so easily leave damaged feelings and treacherous terrain. We've had our share of storms this summer, but it seems we are in a period of calm.

The phone rings.

"We're fine," I hear Larry say, "except for the shock of hearing the phone ring. We didn't know it works. Thank you for your concern."

"That was Francesco," he says, "making sure we're okay after the storm. About the phone, he says perhaps the storm changed something in the air. He's funny."

After Larry washes dishes, he takes my face gently in his hands and gives me a long, loving kiss. His tender touch and deep love for me, even his exaggerated appreciation of my cooking, are blessings worth counting. We've had a good day: going to market together and finally sharing names with Gigliola, our walk to the opposite hillside, my chat with the rooster, a successful healthier eggplant parmesan, and a romantic dinner watching yet-another Tuscan storm.

At the end of each day, I try to remember the good things of that day. If I replay the good and leave out the bad, my life becomes about the good. How else would anyone want to live?

Unintended Cut

A rumbling tractor interrupts my sleep. I look out the window, but can't see anything in the dim light. Dense white fog fills the valley and charcoal skies look like rain — *again*. It's Sunday, so no workers. I fall back to sleep until almost eight, then slip on my robe and wander downstairs. Larry's gone; I assume for a run.

Sitting in silence on the terrace, I watch the fog creep up and over the hillside facing me like a giant white amoeba. Soon it engulfs me too, so thick I can't see through it. I hear distant rain. Suddenly I'm getting soaked. I run inside to protect my computer and realize I must get the wicker armchairs under cover. In my silk robe, clutching the back of a chair, in a half-squatted position with the heaviest part of the chair resting on my thighs, I duck walk across the terrace and around the corner to the only door wide enough to carry the chair through.

Larry's in the doorway, drenched and calling my name. He evidently came in upstairs and I couldn't hear his call over this pounding rain.

"Darling, not like a correction, but do not lift those chairs by yourself. Ever. I'd rather replace the chairs than have you injured." He's serious. I feel proud that I was able to do it, slightly irked that he wasn't more impressed, and glad he's home to help with the second one.

It's the fiercest storm of the summer. Lightning flashes and thunder cracks, sheets of water blow across the land, and the lights flicker and go off. When they don't come back on, Larry tries the circuit breakers. Nothing happens, but the storm is too fierce to go outside to the main junction box. He wets his face with water left in the pipes, enough for the shaving gel to form a lather. I brush my teeth with bottled water and put on make-up by dim natural light. As we get ready for church, the rain subsides, but the electricity stays off. Larry tries to reset the breakers at the outside junction box, with no results. Hopefully *Enel* will have restored the power before we return from church.

Walking to the car across the muddy ground, I remember I want to gather some fennel flowers on the way home, so run back to get garden clippers, a plastic bag, and the umbrella in case there's more rain. Puddles are everywhere and the sky is darkening again.

"Did you really need all that now?" Larry says when I finally reach the car.

"Yes." If I went back to get it, I need it, I think but don't say.

In town, the only parking spot we can find is in the new lot. We're curious to try the outdoor escalator. At the bottom, a white plastic chain indicates it's not working. The footpath up the hillside will be deep mud after two days of rain. We climb the stationary escalator, steeper than climbing regular stairs.

Rushing through town because we're late for church, which Larry hates, he realizes he left his phone in the car, but we go on. A handwritten sign on the door says Mass starts at eleven-thirty, a half hour later than normal.

While Larry hurries back to the car to get his phone; I buy tickets to the *Cortonantiquaria*, the antique exhibit he promised we'd go to today.

At Mass, eleven men in formal vestments walk in procession from the main door to the front altar. Two are wearing emerald green and gold damask vestments; the others have simpler white robes with emerald stoles. Larry thinks it could be the installation of new priests.

We sing *"Gloria in excelsius Dio."* I mumble through the responsive reading printed in the program. A woman reads from Paul's letter to the Ephesians — in Italian, of course. I can pick out "like Christ is the head of the church, so husband is head of the family," and then, "As Christ loved the church and gave himself for her, so the husband loves the wife and gives himself for her." A nice reminder and I hope Larry is listening. After that reading, so often misunderstood, the service is lost on me.

"La Messa è finita; andate in pace." The Mass is finished, go in peace.

The opulently dressed clergymen start to promenade out, but the presiding priest calls them back to the altar steps and arranges them with himself in the center. Several women take photos. I wish I understood what is going on.

After church, Larry and I stop at the villa where the highly-publicized antique show is underway. We hope to go for an hour now, then come back after lunch.

"Una domanda… per favore." A question, please, Larry says to the Italian attendant at the door.

Before Larry even asks his question, the attendant says in English, "Yes, you can come back if you leave. Just keep your ticket."

"The most frequently asked question?" I joke.

The attendant smiles, looks at his watch and replies. "At lunch time? Yes."

"Tell me," Larry says, "How did you know to speak English to me? I spoke Italian to you."

"At sight," the attendant says, without skipping a beat, then adds, *"Molto alto e biondo."* Very tall and blond.

"Perfect response," I chuckle.

Palazzo Vagnotti, where the show is held, was built about 1760 as a theological seminary but is now an exhibition space. Every August since 1963, the *Cortonantiquaria*, billed as one of the most prestigious antique shows in Europe, has been held here. This year's program lists one hundred and ten dealers. We're told many rare and historically significant items are displayed, but with astronomical prices.

We walk though showrooms on the ground floor, linger over a few special pieces and save the upper two floors for after lunch. Larry, still on his hunt for new reading glasses, wants to stop at the pharmacy. When we get there, the green cross is flashing, but the doors are locked. I can't figure out what that flashing green cross means. I thought it meant the pharmacy was open, but evidently not.

For lunch, we decide to try Tonino, a traditional Tuscan restaurant with spectacular views of *Lago Trasimeno*. Although Larry says he feels queasy, we share every course and he eats heartily. We agree to skip dessert, but the waiter brings a tray of tiny profiteroles, chocolate drizzled strawberries, and little chocolate cups filled with crème and decorated with candied violets, all compliments of the house. We devour every gorgeous, delicious concoction.

Back at the antique show, more crowded than earlier, the items are exquisite, especially the jewelry, but nothing is in our price range.

As we walk down the front stairs to leave, walking in are Tony and Alex, the English couple we met at the castle earlier in the summer. What a happy surprise! We knew they were in Cortona this week and the castle gang has dinner plans for Wednesday evening, but didn't expect to see them today. Though we've had little contact in two months, they feel like old friends.

"You look fabulous! Have you lost weight... or is it the tan?" Alex asks me.

They're effusive about our appearance, insisting we look happy and younger. I wonder if it's true, they're simply flattering us, or we looked that bad when we met in June. It had been a rough morning, the day the movers refused to deliver our belongings. It seems long ago.

I ask Alex if she could go antique shopping with me this week, saying that Larry says he can't take any more time to furniture shop. She says she'd love to, but they're fully occupied with meetings for their own renovation.

Chatting on the stairs, Tony asks if we'd like to see their ruin and Alex looks shocked, saying it is not presentable. Rain suddenly pours straight down in the bright sunshine, and we all rush into the palazzo. Alex looks dismayed, complaining that the excavator they hired to move trees tomorrow can't work in mud. She thinks there must be a conspiracy against them making progress on their house.

After lots of kisses and hugs, we say we'll see them Wednesday night. I love seeing friends… *Friends!* I take Larry's arm, feeling buoyant.

He says he still doesn't feel so good but, if I'd like, he'll stop at a couple of antique stores on our way out of town. Perhaps my comment to Alex that Larry can't take time for antiquing made him reconsider. Touched by his kindness, I suggest we go for gelato first, teasing that if his problem is an ulcer, gelato would be doctor's orders.

"Brilliant idea!" he says. We head to Snoopy for *menta e more*, mint and blackberry, his new favorite combo. Not exactly tummy-soothing vanilla.

Turning onto our access road, we pass an old woman foraging along the wall, but not Francesca's friend. We think she may be a neighbor because we see her frequently. Larry stops the car to greet her, introducing us both. She says her name is Maria. In Italian, Larry says we moved from Chicago and live at Lodolina. Maria lights up and begins speaking rapidly. Larry tells her he doesn't understand. "*Piano, piano,*" slowly, slowly, he says. Maria says she lives near Palazzone and knows Lodolina well. It seems everyone in our neighborhood knows Lodolina. We smile and say *buona serata*, wishing her a good afternoon.

Fifty yards into our access road, I say I'd like to collect some pollen from the wild fennel bushes growing into the road. Larry shakes his head, stops the car, and I hop out with my bag and clippers to find the perfect wild fennel plant.

Even before the clippers close, I feel the blade cut through the pad of my left middle fingertip. I can tell it didn't hit the bone, but the cut is deep. Instantly, dark red blood spurts out and runs into my hand. Instinctively, I push the flesh together and roll my thumb over it, hoping the pressure stops the flow.

I yell to Larry, waiting in the car, "I cut my finger. It's bad." He jumps out and runs to help me. When I lift my thumb, the blood gushes again.

"All I see is blood," he says.

"Does it need stitches?" I ask, suddenly queasy.

"How do I know? You need to say."

"We should find a hospital and let the doc say," I reply, feeling light-headed and far away.

When I realize we don't know where the hospital is, I wonder about the risks of not going. The blades have some rust, but I had a tetanus shot ten years ago. This much bleeding has surely washed the wound. Larry puts his arm around me, walks with me to the passenger side, opens my door and helps me in.

Buckling his seatbelt, he says, "That is one of the dumbest things you have *ever* done."

He backs the car toward the main road, since there's no place to turn around.

"We don't even have residency papers with us," he adds.

"Let's just go home," I say. "I can wash it and see how bad it is. We also need to check the electricity. Then, if I need to go to the hospital, we'll at least have our papers…."

Larry says if we should go to the hospital at all, we should go now.

I know cutting myself was dumb and that he doesn't feel well, but his comments don't feel kind or compassionate to me. He stops at the asphalt road, waiting for my decision: hospital or home.

"Larry, I don't need to be told this was dumb. I already know that. And I'm sorry you don't feel well. But you're not helping… or even being nice. My finger is bad and I don't know what to do." My voice quivers a bit.

He turns to face me. I wonder what now.

"You're right. There's a big difference between an emergency and feeling lousy. You have an emergency. If you need to go to the hospital, I'll take you gladly. So, what'll it be — home or hospital? I'll do whatever you want. Please, just decide. I'm sorry I wasn't nicer. Really, I should've been nicer."

"Home," I say, partially because I think it's what Larry wants, but also because I feel queasy and unstable, and I want to look at the cut closely before deciding.

At home, Larry flips on a light switch. No power. We left the shutters closed because they bang against the house in a storm, so the house is completely dark. I start to open shutters to let in some light. I do wish the workers would install those brackets to hold them in place.

"Victoria, stop. Rest. Please, don't make it worse or we'll be at the hospital for sure."

He finds a flashlight and goes downstairs to the electrical panel. "No good," he hollers after he tries to restart the system. With no electricity, there's no water to wash the cut.

I open one shutter on the kitchen door for some daylight, then search for the box of bandages I put in a kitchen drawer for emergencies. Larry comes to help. He gets a bottle of drinking water and helps me to the front yard. I hold my hand over the grass so I don't get blood on the new stone terrace. When I lift my thumb, blood gushes again. Larry pours water over the cut. It stings. He tries to examine it, but it's bleeding too much. I put my thumb back over it and press hard.

He gets paper towels to dry my finger, so a bandage can stick. He wraps the biggest bandage in the box tightly around my finger as I ease my thumb away. No blood. After making sure the cut is closed, Larry pours water on a fresh paper towel to clean both my hands, now covered with blood, and his own, bloody from helping me.

"Looks like a murder scene," I say, trying to be funny. "I'm good now. If it soaks through, we'll go to the hospital. If not, I'll be fine. How are you?"

"Not so great, but it's only a stomach ache. Your cut is much more serious."

He goes inside and opens shutters while I find the stomach medication David bought when we were in Pisa. I'm glad I didn't throw it away. The tablet fizzes in a glass of water, making a horrible, pale orangey-pink froth with gritty particles in the bottom. Larry drinks it, insisting it tastes like orange Fanta.

We both need to lie down. Larry, who always wants windows open even when sleeping, leaves the shutters closed for me. I prop my hand on pillows to keep it above my heart, hoping to reduce the bleeding and pain. Larry reaches to touch my shoulder.

"What if we can't get the electricity back on? Should we stay here overnight?" I ask. "With no water, the toilets won't flush and I can't make dinner — or shower for a second day."

"I think we can stay. I'll try again in a little while. You should do nothing but rest," he says. "And don't even think about making dinner."

Amazing how in the face of a health emergency, nothing else seems to matter.

Lying perfectly still is calming. When I wake up, it's past time for dinner and I'm a little hungry. Perhaps I'll serve cold eggplant parmesan by candlelight. With a flashlight, I examine my finger. Blood has seeped through the bandage, but not much. I'm relieved, as I really don't want to have to search for the hospital. Larry looks at it and offers to put on a fresh bandage for me, but I think it's best left alone.

Suddenly, he has an idea about the electricity. He runs through the circuits, one by one. Sure enough, if he leaves one circuit tripped, the main breaker will stay engaged and we have power. His theory is that in the deluge this morning, water got into an electrical line somewhere, possibly in the guesthouse. It was an *Enel* problem for a while, but now it's a Lodolina problem. At least we have power in all but one zone.

With the oven working, I put the leftover eggplant parmesan in to warm. I forgo the candles, as romance seems strange in the face of our malaise.

I go upstairs and shower, having left home this morning without one. Larry helps me with a fresh bandage and we lie in bed listening to night sounds. A donkey brays. A car traveling on a gravel road sounds like it's in our driveway. I sit up and see lights snaking through the valley. Amazing, how well sound carries up the hillside. I try to keep my hand higher than my heart, because it's starting to throb. I would take Advil, but am afraid it will thin my blood. The nightingales start their serenade. Then the frogs. The pain and earlier nap keep me awake, so I get up and take some Advil anyway. Larry says his stomach is better, but he can't sleep either.

We're a couple of quasi-invalids living in an almost-renovated house with brand-new wiring, but too often without electricity. I pray tomorrow will be a less eventful day, and feel grateful that we are safe, at home and together. After Larry's remark about my cut being stupid, he's been attentive and concerned. I think my finger will be okay without stitches. What we need to worry about now is not making deeper cuts to one another.

Larry caresses my arm and says he's sorry he wasn't nicer when I cut my finger and he's glad I'm okay. He arranges pillows to keep my hand elevated. I feel myself relax with his touch and genuine concern. When there is honest compassion, offences can melt away and healing can begin.

At least for now, a second hospital visit this summer has been avoided.

Our Hillside Family

Today promises to be another big day, but hopefully less traumatic. An electrician will repair the circuit, *Telecom Italia* assured us phone *and* internet will be operating by five o'clock, and our neighbors are coming this evening for drinks. My cut finger throbs, but I can ignore it once I get busy.

"Would you like another cappuccino?" I call out the kitchen door as the Pavoni heats. "It's my turn to do something nice for you."

"How's your finger?"

"It bled a little overnight… and it's sore. But not so bad."

"Do you need a doctor?"

"Nope, I think the worst is over. I'll look at it when I shower and then I'll know. How about that cappuccino?"

Making the *cappuccini* without touching my finger is easy and I use a tray to make carrying two cups easier. Larry looks at me seriously, like he's been thinking about something. I sit down and brace myself, wondering what it is this time.

"Victoria, I was too gruff yesterday. I did help with the bandage, so should get a few points. But I should not have said it was dumb. It was an accident and you were hurt. You didn't need me to tell you it was dumb, even if it was."

I hear as much self-defense as remorse, so am not sure what to think. There is a difference between concern for the other and justifying oneself.

"Thank you. But was that an apology… or defense?" I ask, tilting my head sweetly.

"Well, I should've been more kind. You're always kind to me…. Sorry, really."

"Thank you, darling. You're forgiven," I say, pleased that he has thought about his words and could see they were unkind. His apology makes both cuts — my finger and my feelings — somehow less painful.

Workers start to arrive. From upstairs, I hear Francesco and Gabriele talking with Larry about the electrical problem. I shower and dress quickly, inspect the wound, put on a fresh bandage, and hurry downstairs.

They both ask if I'm okay. Larry must have told them about my cut. Francesco explains where the new hospital is, in case we need it in the future.

He gives me a swatch book to choose a yellow for the stucco corner of the house and three water-colored elevations to help us choose a design for the *limonaia*. I try to concentrate on the house instead of my now-hurting finger.

Francesco lights up when I tell him our neighbors are coming this evening to see the house. "Oh, I am so curious to see what they will say. You will tell me, of course?"

As of this week, he announces, we will be free of workers, except for Pierangelo and Graziano who will come every day except Sunday for a few more months.

A few more months? I wonder when, if ever, this construction will end.

Late morning, I make spiced nuts for our gathering tonight. I can work with my right hand and four digits on my left, holding the middle finger away to keep the bandage clean. While the nuts roast, I mix chopped rosemary, butter, brown sugar and cayenne. I dump the hot, roasted almonds, hazelnuts, pecans and walnuts into the glaze and quickly stir. The only problem is eating too many before our guests arrive.

Though Rita cleaned on Friday, I want the house to feel super-fresh, so I sweep and tidy up again. Our neighbors will look at every room and we're still in disarray. Significant dust has collected under Larry's cardboard box of shoes, ignored so far. And, I don't think Rita has scrubbed the toilets. Perhaps the brush beside every toilet in Italy means cleaning is seen as a personal responsibility. I scour them all with a stiff brush, detergent and *Ace*, bleach, pronounced *ah-chay*.

At six-fifteen, ready for guests at seven but feeling a bit nervous, I decide nuts are not enough to serve with the Prosecco. I cut the tops off a dozen tiny cherry tomatoes, the ones that taste like summer, scoop out the centers and push just a bit of gorgonzola inside. They look naked on my Etruscan bird platter, so I add a sliver of basil to each tomato and big bunches to each end of the platter.

Belinda arrives first. I hear Larry greeting her at the back door. She knocked upstairs rather than walking down the ramp to the front door, the very problem we've been trying to solve.

"I'm punctual tonight," she explains as she comes downstairs with Larry trailing her. "I wanted to be here before Lyndall and the others. After all, I did the inviting."

Belinda is striking with her unusually tall, lanky frame clad in baggy white linen pants, a long sapphire silk shirt, gray-blue quilted silk jacket, marvelous Arabian necklace with a large silver disc (perhaps from her years working in the Middle East), gold-trimmed red walking shoes, and red fabric pouch hand-bag. She's not flamboyant, more like a sophisticated English explorer out on the town.

We stand in the finally level and grassy front yard, chatting and admiring the view. Belinda points to a country house barely visible in the distance and says it's an old mill where Lyndall and her husband, Count Lorenzo Passerini, lived years ago. They had many animals — gazelles and geese, stray dogs, a tame squirrel and a horse.

"Lyndall used to ride all over the valley. She was quite a horse-woman," Belinda says admiringly.

"Does she still ride?" I ask.

"Not so much, but she rode for years, especially after Lorenzo died. When he was still living, they donated *Il Palazzone* with all its valuable contents to the *Scuola Normale Superiore di Pisa*, with the right for both of them to live in the tower for life. He passed thirty years ago and Lyndall still lives there."

"Hello… Hello-oo," a man's voice signals Rennie's arrival. We all shake hands, smile and say, "*Piacere, piacere.*" Pleasure, pleasure.

Rennie seems reserved, a man small of stature with a dignified presence, curious eyes and handsome white wavy hair. I'm quite sure he introduced himself as Rainier, but Belinda said, "*Buonasera*, Rennie," so Rennie it is. He's a mystery writer from South Africa. Belinda whispers to me that his books win awards. He's working on a new one, he says, soon to be released. I ask him for the titles so I can buy them for Larry's mother, an avid mystery reader. He seems pleased.

Rennie asks if he might peek inside. Larry pours Prosecco for everyone and we take a mini-tour while we wait for Lyndall.

Stepping through the front door, Rennie looks stunned. He says it's strikingly different than when he lived here. He remembers the living and dining rooms were tiny with low ceilings and stone walls. Larry explains that to get more height, our workers lowered the floor more than a meter, jackhammering into the stone mountain beneath the house, and that we incorporated the air-passage behind the house for more interior space.

Rennie continues reminiscing, explaining that all across the back were stone mangers for cattle feed. Only cows were kept inside, with pigs and chickens in outside pens. When I tell him how unpleasant I found the kitchen, he says he remembers many wonderful meals cooked there, that his friends were excellent cooks.

He cautiously asks if he might see the upstairs. I'm amused that he's so careful. I thought inspecting the house was the purpose of our gathering.

Upstairs in the fireplace room, Rennie turns slowly and nostalgically. "I used to write in this room. I had to sit by the window to get enough light. We wrote our books in longhand in those days. My friend who rented the house did, too."

"This is now Larry's study," I explain. "His desk will be made of old chestnut beams. All the beams had to be replaced, but the good parts were saved for shelves and furniture."

Back on the front terrace, I offer nibbles, warning the nuts are spicy.

Since we don't have outdoor furniture, I put the silver bowl of nuts and the plate of stuffed tomatoes on a stack of building blocks in the center of the terrace and arrange white plastic chairs around the makeshift table. But everyone holds their snacks on napkins and stands at the front yard rail looking into the valley.

Lyndall is the last to arrive. Like last week, she seems gracious, cultured, interesting, and cheerful, a woman who'd be comfortable anywhere. I expected a *Contessa* to be more formal and aloof, but Lyndall immediately puts me at ease by her warm way of connecting. She says she's very curious about how we've transformed this house she knows so well. Once upon a time, she tells us, as if we might not know, Lorenzo owned the hillside, including our house.

"Do you recognize it?" I ask.

"Of course," she says looking up at the façade. "The outside is the same, only cleaner, with all the terrible patches fixed and stucco on the bedroom corner. That corner used to be brick. What color will you paint it?"

"Probably soft yellow," I say.

"Ah yes, the traditional color for Cortona," she nods.

I tell her that I think it'll make the house look happy. I'm pleased when she agrees.

We go back inside for Lyndall's tour.

"*Complimenti*," she says, "Truly… *complimenti*."

Rennie recalls the only way to get upstairs was by ladder. Larry says it was the same when we bought the house. When the workers put in a staircase, I wouldn't let them throw the ladder away because it's part of Lodolina's history.

Lyndall smiles, remembering. "Ah, yes, I know that ladder. The *mezzadro*, sharecropper, houses had outside staircases, since the lower floor was used for cattle. When we did up the houses for renting, first Belinda's, then yours, Renzo invented those ladder-like staircases as an alternative to spiral staircases…. Some occupants liked them. Some didn't."

Back outside, gazing into the valley, our guests share neighborhood stories. After the War, Lyndall recalls, an elderly couple always walked across our back yard to get to town. Probably they walked up from the valley and had no other means of transport. Eventually, the farmer closed the passage by putting up a large pen for his dog. The couple was upset, because, by law, it was a historical right-of-way.

"Is it still a right-of-way?" Larry asks.

"Probably, but I don't think anyone walks that far to town anymore. They all have cars or *motorini*," Lyndall assures us.

She tells us her husband gave Belinda's house and ours to her as a gift before they were married. Lodolina had been abandoned for years. She says they did it up simply and the first renters were famous, her great friend Paola Rolli, one of Fellini's casting directors, and companion Stephen Grimes, an Oscar-winning production designer. Lodolina was their weekend retreat from Rome.

Later, Rennie's friends, now living in New York City, rented the house year-round, making it their permanent home. Rennie, looking keenly nostalgic, says one of the men created many wonderful paintings in the big room upstairs.

I love learning the history of our hillside, especially of our home. Belinda recalls the winter of 1985, when an unusually long and deep freeze killed most of the olive trees. The roots remained, she says, and gave birth to our present grove.

When it's time for dinner, Larry, Belinda and I climb the steep path to the swimming pool while Lyndall and Rennie drive their cars. Belinda introduces us to Donatella, owner and chef. The restaurant has a tiny kitchen, almost no indoor seating, and a large courtyard under linden trees strung with tiny white lights. The setting feels magical.

We're the only guests. Donatella asks if we'll be okay outside since it's chilly. We brought jackets and Lyndall has a small quilt from the car, so we assure her we'll be fine.

Donatella recommends the fresh porcini mushroom soup, which sounds perfect on this cool evening. We also order beef *tagliata*, but only three portions for five of us. Belinda warned us earlier that Donatella's portions are generous. It is the best mushroom soup I've ever tasted, so I'm grateful my portion is enormous.

"Lodolina is a beautiful name for your home," Lyndall says, steering the conversation back to us. "You know *lodola* means lark, of course? They sing so sweetly… I think more are here than on any other hillside in the area. You probably hear nightingales, too. They're not so much to look at, but such a melodious song. The stream running by your house is one of the last places where the nightingales still sing. But they'll leave for winter."

"The hoopoes will soon fly south, too," Rennie says.

"Are hoopoes black and white, with orange crowns?" I ask. When he nods, I say, "I thought they were called *upupas*."

"That's the Italian name from Latin… mimics their call," he says. I suddenly realize hoopoe, pronounced hu-pu, and upupa are pretty close.

Rennie says hoopoes winter in northern Africa, then come back in May to have babies. Belinda tells us her friend has a hoopoe that builds its nest in the kitchen window every year. It smells so terrible that Belinda's friend can't open the window all summer, but she says it's worth it to watch the whole process of hatching and feeding the little ones. Seems hoopoe females and nestlings have glands that excrete a brown fluid with the odor of rotted meat. In some parts of India, Lyndall adds, the worst thing you can say about another person is that they smell like a hoopoe's nest.

My favorite of the evening's stories is about a green snake that lived under Rennie's current house. Rennie felt he and this snake had a special relationship since it would come out and sun on a wall even when he was nearby. One day, he came home and gardeners had killed the snake, proudly displaying it on a stake. Rennie was so upset he made them take it down.

I tell about my little black squirrel who visits every day and leaves cone remnants all over the ground.

We linger over desserts, not tiring of each other or hillside stories. Lyndall mentions that she's happy to see our horse chestnut tree is still green since most of the *ippocastani* in Cortona are already turning brown.

"Your chestnut is famous, important for the entire hillside," she adds.

I note she emphasizes "*your* chestnut." I like this gracious woman.

It's late, so we reluctantly say goodnight. As we pay our *conto*, Lyndall and Belinda stop to talk to a guest. Belinda introduces him as the man who organized the building of the pool, amphitheater and restaurant. When I shake his hand, I recognize him as the pharmacist who kindly helped Larry finally choose reading glasses.

We all pull our jackets tight as it has become downright cold.

After kissing Lyndall on both cheeks, Larry says tentatively, "I'm not sure if this is okay to ask... but could we see the frescoes some time?

I'm surprised he's so bold. The legendary frescos at Palazzone are rarely available for public viewing. The famous Cortona artist, Luca Signorelli, fell off his ladder in 1523 while painting a fresco of Christ's baptism in the Palazzone chapel and died soon after. We have tried several times to get in, including when Larry took Paige inside and "got kicked out," as Paige put it.

"Of course!" Lyndall exclaims, with a huge smile. "But we must wait for the school to reopen and give me their permission. I used to sneak people through an adjoining door in my apartment to look at the frescos, but they have put in a burglar alarm. I'm so afraid it will go off that I have put a cupboard in front of that door so that I don't open it accidentally."

Larry is thrilled, thanks Lyndall profusely, and says it'll be his great pleasure to wait for the appropriate time.

Climbing down the steep path toward our homes, he checks with Belinda, "I hope I wasn't too forward asking to see the paintings."

"I'm sure not," she assures him, "Lyndall would have invited you if she knew you had an interest. After all, you're part of our hillside family and those frescoes are part of our history — your history, now."

I'm delighted that we may see the inside of Palazzone after all these years, but I'm even more pleased with Belinda's comment about family. I think we passed.

Belinda takes us by a less-traveled grassy path with a view into Palazzone's courtyard from above. Lit only by moonlight, the residence's enormity is apparent — triple what we see from the road. I'm tempted to shine my flashlight into the courtyard for a better look, but refrain.

The path curves left and suddenly we're in front of Belinda's home. We say *buona notte* with more kisses and hugs. She leaves next week to go home to Oxford and will not return until the olive harvest in October. I hope to see her again before she leaves.

Back at Lodolina, Larry washes the Prosecco glasses so my finger can stay dry. We crawl into bed well past midnight, completely spent.

This has been a significant day — the day our neighbors became our friends. The sharp loneliness I've felt all summer is beginning to soften. I like each person, find them kind and interesting, and I feel accepted.

Making new friends and feeling more attached to the community is part of the long process of assimilating into a new culture. Even more painful than my fear of driving on narrow roads or being embarrassed by my Italian, has been the emptiness of feeling alone.

I'm also beginning to see the possibility that our marriage, rather than deteriorating because hidden crevices have shown up, might actually deepen and strengthen. Larry's apology this morning was heartfelt. He really did understand why I was upset and he not only apologized, he continued his kindness all day long.

"May I hold your hand?" he whispers into the dark as we lie under the covers.

"Yes, just not my cut finger. It still hurts."

"You didn't say it hurt earlier. Is it okay?"

"We had a lot going on. Just because it hurts, doesn't mean it isn't healing," I assure him. As I close my eyes, I realize that's true for a cut finger and true of life.

Castle Gang Reunites

Before dawn, I hear sprinklers. Recalling Larry's tenderness last night, I turn over and fall back to sleep feeling happy. The sun is high by the time the tapping and scraping of construction awakens me again.

"Morning, darling," I say, poking my head out the front door. "We were out late last night."

Larry nods, but doesn't look up. "You must've been tired. It's almost nine."

Francesco arrives, pleased to announce three miracles this morning. First, we can have a dedicated gas line to a built-in grill, which we feared was impossible. Second, the long-awaited carved *pietra serena* stone guesthouse sink will be delivered and installed today. I'm thrilled with that miracle — poor Ron and Paulla had to use the bidet as their only sink for the entire two weeks they were here. Lastly, for the biggest of all: Francesco met a repairman from *Telecom* on the road who informed him the phone and internet should be fixed by noon.

I tell Francesco three miracles are too much for one morning.

"But is only a miracle when it works," he cautions knowingly.

By noon, two of the three miracles have been thwarted. The little stone sink is so heavy it cannot be installed until an additional supporting wall of terracotta blocks has been built. Then, the *Telecom* repairman arrives to check the connections inside the house. The phone works, but the modem receives no signal. The repairman shrugs, looking totally dismayed, and says someone will call when they find the problem.

On top of two disappointments, I soon notice a new problem. The workers building a new wall under the horse chestnut tree are pouring concrete way too close to, maybe even on, the roots. I'm furious when I see it and tell Francesco, who immediately goes to speak with the men. He's not happy, either.

"The wall goes well," he says when he comes back, "but in the end, the tree is more important than the wall. They will put only dirt on the tree."

"And about last night?" he asks shyly.

"Oh, I almost forgot. Everyone was incredibly impressed. Lyndall kept saying, '*Complimenti, complimenti.*' She especially liked our bathroom, saying it's much nicer than those in the Palazzone."

"I am so happy!" Francesco exclaims. "Lodolina has meaning and memory for them all. It is important not to destroy the meaning or the memory when fixing the structure."

It is especially good, he says, that Contessa Passerini likes it, because it was once her house, though she did not live here. Owners are not always happy with changes.

He adds pensively, "I am pleased that your new friends can see Lodolina's history in her future life."

As he leaves, I hear Belinda's voice.

"*Buongiorno? Permesso?*" Good morning. May I come in?"

"Belinda? *Where* are you?" I ask, unable to see her.

"I'm here, at the side door," she says.

Seems no one can figure out where our front door really is.

"Come in… to the kitchen," I say, "I'm just finishing more rock cakes, as your friend called my scones. I've spoiled Larry. He now complains when we run out."

I extend my cheeks for kisses, but not a hand. One is covered in dough and the other is bandaged.

"I came to say thank you… and goodbye. I had a wonderful time last night. And thank you for the electrician you sent. He came this morning and has already installed the new outlet for my washing machine. Tenants arrive next week and now they can use the washer. So thank you for last night, my new outlet… and for moving here."

I offer her a scone if she can wait, but she says she'll have one when she returns for the olives in October. As she turns to go, she suggests renaming my scones Rockies, raises a triumphant fist, and quotes Rocky Balboa… in rapid-fire Italian.

She turns back to give me another very long hug, a seemingly un-English gesture.

Mid-afternoon, the phone rings. A woman's voice asks for "Lehwy Ahrnaldo Smeet." I hand the phone to Larry. *Telecom Italia* is sorry, but they don't know what is wrong and, therefore, don't know when it will be fixed.

Aspettiamo e vediamo, we wait and we see. Here we go again.

While it's still light, I hurry to Palazzone for one last chore before dinner. I need to select a color by tomorrow and am struggling to imagine the tiny swatch colors on a larger scale. I really like the color of Palazzone, so want to compare it to Francesco's swatch book.

Not far from the place I cut my finger, a man is stripping golden flowers from wild fennel stalks. I have a flashback of the blade slicing my flesh.

"*Buonasera*," I call to be friendly.

He looks up. "*Salve*," a more formal hello.

"*Sono Vittoria, da Lodolina*." I say.

"*Da Lodolina?*" From Lodolina? Everyone seems to know Lodolina.

When I say, "*Si*," he walks toward me, talking energetically.

"*Piano, piano. Mi dispiace ma non parlo Italiano bene*," I say. Slowly, slowly. I am sorry, but I do not speak Italian well. It's a practiced phrase, so I say it easily.

I learn he is Mario, the husband of Maria, the woman we met on the road yesterday before my incident. He says they live "*sotto Palazzone,*" below Palazzone.

Then I ask, awkwardly, pointing to the flowers in his hand, how Italians use fennel.

Mario rattles off a list: "*Porchetta. Porchetta e sugo…*" Roasted pork and gravy. He adds a dozen more: marmalade, sausage, breads, cakes, liquor and — such a surprise that I surely misunderstood — perfume for men. He must think this American woman doesn't know anything.

His apron pockets bulge with fennel flowers. I wonder if he has a pig, and if the pig can sense by the fragrance on his apron that her time has come.

He stares at me and tells me exactly how old I am. I prefer to think I look younger. I wonder if word has gotten around that the new neighbor is sixty. He tells me he is *settantotto,* seventy-eight. I would never have guessed that old. We both say, "*Ciao, piacere,*" and wave rather than shaking hands.

At Palazzone, I cautiously walk up a now-grassy, cypress-lined hill that once was a grand carriage entrance, across the lawn cautiously watching for surveillance, pull out Francesco's swatch book, and hold it up to the Palazzone stucco. I mark the closest colors, turn and hurry down the hill. I still need to dress for dinner.

Tonight we're meeting our castle friends. I want to look especially nice, but cannot find my ivory linen pants anywhere, so must wear my usual black.

On the way to town, Larry suddenly grips the steering wheel. "The steering jerked," he says, "Not good." He says he'll check the fluids tomorrow morning and call the agency. Fortunately, the contract is up soon.

This Volvo SUV has served us well, but I'll be relieved to have a smaller car so I can drive with less fear.

"What kind of car do you want next?" Larry asks, seeming to read my mind.

"Small, all-wheel drive, and automatic," I reply without hesitation.

Larry drops me at the city gate so I can get groceries while he finds a parking space. I quickly climb to *Piazza della Repubblica* and am pleased not to feel winded. It's taken all summer to develop this stamina.

Thankfully, Molesini market is still open. It's seven minutes before eight o'clock, so I grab my three items and hurry to the counter. Paolo, Marco's brother, is at the register. I don't have enough euros, so pull out my new Italian debit card. Paolo hands me the small machine for my PIN. I've never used this card and am unsure of my code. My first entry is rejected, much to my embarrassment. I try a different, similar one. It doesn't work either.

"Just pay tomorrow. It's okay," Paolo says, seeing the line forming behind me.

"I'll find Larry or go to the cash station right now," I assure him, feeling terribly self-conscious. From his expression, I think he wants me to finish and leave.

Suddenly, I think of another number and ask him if I can try one more. I enter it. Paolo remains calm while it processes.

"You are lucky," he says with a grin. "It worked!"

"Thanks for your patience," I murmur, slinking away with my bag while Paolo motions the next person forward. In Chicago no one would say pay tomorrow.

Across the *piazza*, Larry and Marco are chatting. I duck into the hair salon nearby to grab a card. I must have my hair cut soon.

In the wine shop, I tell Marco I need advice. "*Dimmi.*" Tell me, he says. I hold up the card and ask if this is where to get my haircut.

"*Si*, the best. Everyone goes there… My wife, my mother, many others. Nuccio is the *maestro*. You will go to Nuccio. Do you want me to introduce you?"

He looks out the window and sees Nuccio. "Come. I go with you now."

Marco leaves Larry in charge of the wine shop and walks across the piazza with me. When Marco tells him I want a haircut, Nuccio motions me inside. He flips pages in the appointment book and, in Italian, asks if tomorrow at noon is okay. I nod.

I expected to have more time to gear up for my first Italian haircut, but if I don't do it soon, I'll lose courage. In Chicago it would have taken weeks to get an appointment, especially a first appointment with a *maestro*.

Back at the wine shop, I tell Marco I want to have a dinner party at Lodolina for the castle gang, and ask when he could come. Marco has been beyond kind to us for ten years, and especially helpful since we bought Lodolina. I want to make absolutely sure he can come before I set the date.

Any day but Tuesday, he says, "On Tuesdays, I play soccer." We agree on this weekend.

Alex and Tony walk in, ready for dinner. After warm greetings, I ask Alex if the diggers were able to move their trees. She shakes her head as if it's hopeless, saying they worked yesterday, but not today. They need six days of good weather, which may never happen.

"The forecast is pathetic," she laments.

Soon Mike and Lynn join us and we all walk to a nearby bar where a chilled bottle of Tony's favorite sparking, *Bellavista Franciacorta Pas Operè*, awaits. We sip, chatter, and nibble on warm rosemary focaccia — Italians never serve alcohol without food. Soon the bottle is empty.

At *La Bucaccia* for dinner, Romano greets us effusively, surprised to see this group together. He knows us individually but did not realize we are friends.

Friends! I love having friends.

"The new *Cortonese*," he proclaims with a dramatic sweep of his hand and a bow, a bit of affectionate grandeur.

He seats us at the large center table. The waitress brings menus and asks if we want *acqua frizzante o naturale*. In unison, we say *tutti e due*, both. I open my menu, but when Romano starts talking about what's good tonight, we know we are in his hands.

"Bring us what you think is best," Tony says, speaking for the group. Then he adds with a mischievous smile, "But I will choose the wine."

The waitress brings a teaser of lean salami rolled into cones and stuffed with homemade ricotta and finely diced peaches. Point-to-point cones adorned with a curl of tomato skin and a sprig of parsley, they look like butterflies.

Before we pick up our forks, Romano puts a plate of warm bread on the table. He ceremoniously says, "Not good, but very, very, very good." I know immediately what he's up to. He drizzles green-gold, fragrant olive oil on the bread and turns the bottle to reveal my "*La Lodolina*, 2005" label, hand-drawn with a gold paint pen.

Everyone makes effusive compliments when they taste it.

Mike says it's quite similar to theirs, but less peppery. I'm jealous, wishing ours was more peppery. I ask when they pick, believing earlier gives more spice though opinions vary. He says they think late October is best and, besides, that's when their family can come. Our olives were not harvested until December, I say.

Alex confesses her jealousy. She had their olives picked and pressed as a surprise for Tony for Christmas. They got two bottles, at unbelievable expense, and it tasted like motor oil.

"I poured the whole lot down the drain," Tony says.

I suggest that with more regular care, their oil will surely improve.

"I fear not," Tony states with finality. "It was vile."

As six wanna-be curators of Italian properties, we chat about our experiences restoring old structures, reclaiming land, and making a hobby of this ancient work of picking olives and pressing oil. These common experiences are important bonds in what I hope will be deepening friendships. Perhaps the first shared bond is that we've all left our homelands, even if temporarily, and are trying to fit into a foreign culture. Everyone seems to have the same challenges with disorientation, driving, and language, except Alex, who is Italian and grew up with what is so stressing to everyone else.

Romano serves his best in-season dishes, including bright orange egg-shaped mushrooms, *ovoli*, so perfect that he offers them raw, thinly sliced, with only a drizzle of olive oil and pepper. Around the plate's edge, Agostina has placed drops of syrupy aged *balsamico*. The presentation is a work of art.

We chat through two pastas, served sequentially, grilled and sliced-thin beefsteak, roasted rosemary potatoes, and grilled seasonal vegetables. I savor every forkful, stopping just short of licking my plate.

Romano presents us each with three *dolci*, desserts. When I note the chocolate sauce is surprisingly spicy, he describes in great detail his education in peppers.

He pours a sweet dessert wine without asking. Not one of us resists.

Then Romano brings a magnum of grappa and pours the crystal-clear elixir into elegant grappa glasses. I sip mine slowly, feeling quite over-served.

Romano explains that this rare grappa, though high in alcohol, is uniquely smooth and flavorful.

My invitation to dinner at Lodolina is received with enthusiasm. It'll be fun, but I'm a bit uneasy cooking for this group, especially Tony. Alex says he collects and reads cookbooks like other people read novels and is an excellent chef, very particular about ingredients and precise about preparation. I insist on good ingredients, but my cooking is constant experimentation.

The moment we leave our friends to walk downhill to our car, I long to be with them again. I turn to give someone, anyone, a last wave. But they're walking up the hill and don't see me.

We crawl into bed well after midnight with my mind still in full gear, working on the menu for my dinner party... spiced nuts, *crostini* with truffle paste and melted *pecorino fresco*, another with fig *marmellata* topped with gorgonzola. Maybe eggplant parmesan.... then *Chianina tagliata* like tonight. For dessert, I'll make a tart like Paige's plum tart, but with wild figs now in season.

It has been a couple of happy days topped by an awesome evening, but I've a vague feeling there is more construction to be done by Larry and me, and not only on Lodolina.

Vittoria Nuova!

Francesco calls about ten o'clock to say he's on his way. He spoke with *Telecom Italia* and they say our internet was fixed last night. I assure him it is not.

It's almost time to leave for my haircut, but I wait for Francesco to arrive to discuss the color for the stucco. He says Palazzone's amber is too dark for our small area. In the swatch book, we find a buttery yellow with a hint of tan and peach. Francesco is right, it's better. I'm confident Larry will agree, especially since he says the color is up to me.

The internet is another story. Francesco is baffled and says he'll call *Telecom* immediately. He also informs me he'll be here every day until we go to Chicago, twelve more working days. Then he'll leave with Rita for a holiday.

"Where will you go?" I ask.

"Probably to the Amalfi coast."

"I'm so sorry. Your dream was Greece." I say.

"For most people, the Amalfi coast is not such a big problem," he says, ever-positive and smiling winsomely as he says goodbye.

Larry isn't back from his run when I must leave, so I walk to town rather than risk driving the SUV with bad steering. I set my own pace. Today the sun seems brighter and the mountains across the valley appear closer. As I near the top, Lake Trasimeno emerges from behind the far hill. I make it up the steepest part without stopping, or huffing and puffing. It feels great. Why don't I do this more often?

Near the *Parterre*, I pass the children's playground. Mothers and grandmothers sit on the park benches, chatting and watching the kids. I remember the day I wanted to paint Cortona's women. It was early June, nearly three months ago. I was upset because the *Comune* registered Larry as an official resident, but not me. Seems long ago.

Since then, I've been observing Cortona women and confirming for myself the characteristic I saw that first day. No matter what the age, how they're dressed, whether beautiful or plain, the common characteristic of Cortona women is dignity.

At *Piazza della Repubblica*, I look at my watch. It took thirty-one minutes to walk from home to the middle of town. Timing the sections: thirteen minutes to climb the hill to the blacktop road, twelve minutes to walk the kilometer-long *Parterre*, and six minutes to arrive at the piazza. A predictable walk for the future, unless I stop to chat.

I hurry to Molesini Market to get groceries before my appointment.

Marco sees me and says, "This is the big day of the new Victoria, *sì*?"

"*Sì*," I reply, a bit sheepish that he's making such a big deal of it. "But first I need charcoal and milk, and to go to the butcher. Hope I have time."

"Don't worry," he insists. "Come back to me after the *maestro*. Give me your list now. If it gets close to closing time, I will deliver your groceries to you in the salon. *Go, go*... perhaps Nuccio is ready for you now."

Standing in the salon doorway, I watch Nuccio working on a young woman with gleaming chestnut hair. He lifts her long tresses over his arm, raises them and then lets them cascade to her shoulders, making sure the lines are just right. He brushes her hair to one side and then the other. It's a gorgeous color and thick as a thoroughbred's mane.

I wonder if I should get my plain brown hair colored. Even at sixty, I have little gray, but it's definitely sprinkled through.

Nuccio sees my reflection in the mirror and comes to the door to greet me.

"*Sono un pò presto,*" I'm a bit early, I say. He takes my hand, air kisses each cheek, and says something about a few more minutes.

I say, "*Torno,*" I return, and dash out.

When it's my turn at the butcher, I ask for *agnello per scottadito*. The butcheress squints as if she doesn't understand. I add *per due*, for two, and she nods. I had failed to say how much. She takes a lamb chunk and hacks off a piece, with the bone. Then she flattens it with several whacks of a heavy metal tool. It doesn't look very meaty, so I ask for two more pieces.

I try to ask about lamb chops, pointing to my ribs to show her what I mean. I think she says that part is only used for frying. I surely misunderstood, but nod and smile. She doesn't seem to have much patience for my bad Italian. I decide to fix beefsteak for my dinner party. It is much safer, in Italian, for me to ask for *bistecca*.

Back at Nuccio's, he's finishing the chestnut mane. It's the crowning glory of an alluring Italian woman in her thirties, thin and well-dressed in a clingy sweater, distressed jeans and strappy sandals. She puts on her sunglasses before she pays the bill. I am keenly aware of my age and heft and lack of elegance in my ordinary blue jeans, black V-neck tee shirt, and bright-yellow suede tennis shoes.

A pretty young assistant motions toward the back room and points toward a chair and washbasin, saying "*Prego.*" I sit. She has spiky black hair with red and blonde streaks on top and curly tendrils down her neck. I try to tell her I like her hair. She smiles, but doesn't speak. Everyone in the salon seems to know I do not speak Italian. Sadly, my nervousness renders me even more tongue-tied, so I give up and sit quietly.

She leads me to Nuccio's chair, obviously the most important in the salon. He smiles and swirls around my shoulders a white fabric cape with *Nuccio* in black logo letters on the front.

Then he studies my face. He checks my profile in a mirror to our right. He turns the chair for another angle. He walks to the other side, and turns the chair again, staring at me straight on and then again in both mirrors. Nuccio measures the length and width of my face, assesses my neck and ears, runs his fingers through my hair, and checks the contours of my skull.

He's been nodding reassuringly until now.

"*Un problema…*," he whispers after a long moment of silence. With gestures that make his meaning clear, he informs me that my head is pointed and my face has flat sides.

I nod. I have known all my life that I had a pointed head and long face, but having a stylist, especially the *maestro*, point it out so indiscreetly seems *pointedly* unnecessary. Trying to act amused, I smile weakly and look up at Nuccio. The salon is full of clients and workers, many looking our way.

Suddenly I have a flashback of elementary school when we were lined up and instructed to walk with a book balanced on our heads to prove our good posture. My book always fell off in front of everyone, much to my youthful humiliation.

Nuccio studies me some more. He says "*Poco*," a little. I think he means he only wants to take off a little.

I stammer, even in English, "As you like…. up to you. You are the *maestro*."

He smiles like he understands. I try to explain that my last haircut was three months ago and I like it short. I confess to trimming it a bit myself, at which he gives me another half-smile and lifts my bangs to show me the bad angle.

He says, "*Ho visto*." I have seen.

Nuccio crouches down and looks at me on the same level as my head, moving his head from side to side, as though he's a sculptor and I'm a block of marble. He measures the length of my generous ears with his comb.

His assistant places his pouch of scissors on a marble-topped side table. Nuccio's side tables are Art Deco, my favorite design period, and I'm confident they're originals from the 1930's. The chairs look newer.

He sections my hair with precision and starts cutting at my neckline. He lifts a small section and cuts into it rather than across it, which is reassuring because that's how my stylist in Chicago cuts it. Then he cuts down a strand, making the finish tapered and soft, also a technique Marianne uses. I start to breathe normally. This will be a good cut. Flattering may be another issue, but technically, I'm safe.

Nuccio cuts my hair for nearly an hour. Roughing it, tussling it, smoothing it, lifting it and combing it in various directions even though it's only a couple inches long. After his observations about my pointed head and at-home trimming, we are silent.

At one point, he combs my hair forward to show me again that my bangs are shorter in the center. I did it on purpose, but Nuccio clearly does not approve, so I keep my little secret mum. I'm a bit worried about the *tondo*, round, idea he mentions. When I've gone too long between haircuts in Chicago, Marianne tells me the shape is too round and not flattering. But there's no way I'd say that to Nuccio — even if I knew the words.

I take a hard look at my face while he's cutting. The salon light is unflattering and my brow wrinkles and crow's feet look deep. My jaw sags a bit, making the straight sides of my face that Nuccio pointed out even worse because my jaw-line is full. And, my pointed head will always be pointed.

Moreover, I have five *zanzare*, mosquito, bites — two on my left check, one each on my nose, forehead and left eyebrow. Nuccio must think I have a skin disease. Every other customer is young and fit, with perfect skin and thick hair. Only Nuccio, handsome with wavy white hair that curls on the ends, is my age.

Next to me, a stylist who must be Nuccio's son is making a head of ringlets on a young lady while three of her friends watch. After he finishes, he picks six perfect petals from the sunflowers on the front desk and pins fans of gold petals amidst the ringlets. Her girlfriends clap in delight. Her father comes in, acts like he doesn't recognize her, then applauds approvingly.

Nuccio leaves me to talk with the father. It's a sweet scene. I wish I knew their story. I wish I knew them. It seems everyone else in this salon knows one another, which makes me feel even more out of place.

Nuccio re-focuses on my hair. Eventually, he trims a little more from the front. I'm glad, because I like the front shorter. I'll look more closely when I get home, but I think he cut my bangs sort of like I did.

When each strand meets his approval, he asks the girl assisting him for *"lo specchio."* She brings a hand mirror. He guides me to look at it from every angle. It's a different style than I'm used to. I cannot describe it, except it reminds me of my haircuts in the sixties… round. To Nuccio I say, *"Bene, grazie,"* and smile appreciatively.

I need to get used to it.

The bill is a fraction of what I pay in Chicago and I give Nuccio a small tip, which seems to surprise and please him. I forgot to ask Marco what the custom is, so better to err on the side of generosity. As I leave, I catch my reflection in a store window and notice I need to stand up straighter.

When I get to the enoteca, Marco exclaims, *"Ah, la nuova Vittoria!"*

"I think it's good…. What do you think?"

"He is a *maestro*, no?" Marco says, grinning ear to ear.

"Very much so. I probably got special treatment because I know you. So, thank you."

Marco nods, knowingly. I don't tell him about my pointed head. He holds up my groceries: charcoal, mozzarella, milk and fresh bread. Walking home, my bags are bulky and I feel awkwardly overloaded.

Near the end of *Via Nazionale*, the woman we met at the Rotary event the weekend we moved in and again at the organ concert is walking toward me. Ester greets me warmly, turns, and says, "I will walk with you to *l'Alberone*."

I'm not sure where she means, but am delighted to have a friend appear and want to walk with me. We chat about our health, her gardens, our matching dishwashers, and, of course, Francesco and the excellent job he's doing at Lodolina. She says they would like to have us to their home for dinner, but they spend most of the summer at their winery, *La Calonica*, and are rarely in town.

When I mention I just had a haircut, she says she likes it. I tell her I need to get used to it and work with it, but think it will be good.

"It is always the way," Ester says, confirming this universal female trait. As she walks and talks, her lovely silver-laced hair swings ever so slightly.

At an enormous tree near the middle of the *Parterre's* long gravel walkway, Ester stops.

"This is *l'Alberone*, where I must go back. *L'Alberone* means the big tree, of course. It is an important landmark, a place where friends meet. I will go now to do my shopping. Please give Larry my warm greetings."

We kiss on both cheeks. "*Ciao, cara,*" she says. Goodbye, dear one.

"*Ciao, cara,*" I respond fondly, not wanting her to leave.

I've never noticed this tree in all our walks through the *Parterre*. A bluish-boughed Atlas cedar, it's the tallest in the park, and surely the oldest. Its lower branches are cut off and the stumps look like human arms. I wonder what other things in my new world I pass but do not see. So much for my early promise to slow myself down in order to really *see*. No one is sitting on *l'Alberone's* stone benches today, but he stands waiting.

On my downhill climb, the views are as stunning as ever. A brisk wind surprises me. I should expect winds in our valley. On the ancient *catasto,* a property map of the region, our small valley is labeled *Il Mulino Vento*, the windmill.

Larry hasn't eaten lunch, though it's after two when I get home. He says he wanted to wait for me. I grin, wondering if he waited for me out of kindness or for me to fix the food. I make a huge *caprese* salad with *bufala mozzarella*, sweet cherry tomatoes and tons of basil.

Toward the end of lunch, I ask, "So, do you like my new haircut?"

"It's different for you… but, yes, I like it. You always feel better after you wash and style it yourself."

It was not an enthusiastic endorsement, but he seems preoccupied. He's had all morning to exercise and study, and I made our lunch. I wonder what's up.

When I ask, he doesn't seem to want to talk, so I chatter about how Nuccio studied my head for a long time and said I had a *problema*. He laughs, sympathetically. I tell about Nuccio's precision, Marco's curiosity, and my walk with Ester. I suggest that some afternoon we should sit under *l'Alberone*, the tree with a name.

After lunch he calls to make arrangements to switch cars. I'm impressed with his Italian, understanding some but not all of what he says. He hangs up and returns to his study.

After an hour of cool silence, I ask, "Are you mad at me? Was I gone too long?"

"No, not mad at you. Just frustrated."

"Why?"

"Because my goals for this summer are not being met."

"What goals specifically?" To me, this feels like a huge step backwards.

"You name it," he says, "study, writing, sabbatical, exercise. All of it. And it's impossible to work without the internet."

I decide to simply agree with him, sit this one out, and let him resolve his angst on his own. I typically try to fix everything, as if his happiness is up to me. But the internet problem is obviously not of my making, and it's difficult for me too.

One of the biggest lessons this summer is that I am not, can never be, responsible for Larry's happiness. It's easy to say and I know it intellectually, but not emotionally. Head knowledge and heart knowledge are often not aligned, as I've seen so often this summer when my confidence was shaken. I knew I was okay, but I didn't feel okay.

Moving to a foreign culture is typically disorienting, I have learned, making expats question what they are doing, and to doubt, not the situation, but themselves. I believe that's truer for women than for men. When men are discombobulated, they question their circumstance; when women are discombobulated, they question their competence.

Before I fix dinner, I call Mom with the new pre-paid phone card I bought today in town, despite Larry saying we didn't need to spend the five euro because the internet would soon be fixed. It's wonderful to hear her voice. Her brother Bob's surgery went well, she says, and his wife gave Lara a nice compliment about her help planning Jan's travel group trip to Chicago. Mom seems good. I call Lara to tell her about Aunt Jan's compliment and my new haircut. She tells me a funny story about work. She sounds good, too, like my always-engaging daughter. It makes me happy to hear they are happy and to be able to connect.

For the next hour, Larry is on a business call using the unwanted phone card. It's late and he's still talking, so I decide to start the fire in our rickety grill. I lugged home the charcoal, but forgot to buy charcoal starter. I try to start it with tightly wadded newspaper under the charcoal, but every time the paper flames and turns to ash. I finally give up.

After his call, Larry tries with no better luck, so goes back to his book. Though dinner would be better grilled, I sauté the lamb and zucchini. With only the *caprese* for lunch and such a full day, I'm hungry.

I start to set the table, but it's already done.

"You set the table?"

"My lovely wife deserves some help. I was too absorbed in my stuff when you got home. I complained about my summer, barely listened to your adventures, and didn't even notice your haircut. Sorry. You've made a nice meal for us, single-handedly with a hurt finger and without a grill. At least I can set the table."

Perhaps he *can* handle his issues without me jumping in and trying to solve them. In fact, he probably prefers it that way.

After dinner, Larry washes dishes and settles in with his current pleasure reading, *The Iliad*. On the piano, I play my favorite works by Beethoven, Chopin, and Cole Porter, making lots of mistakes, but enjoy the lively acoustics of our living room and the lighter touch of my rebuilt piano. Larry says he loves to hear me play.

With my Italian haircut, I feel I have achieved a deeper engagement in life here. I'd like to share that silly milestone with my husband, but he's absorbed in his reading, so I keep it to myself. It feels fine that only I know. Not being bothered by Larry's lack of attention and approval, perhaps for the first time all summer, makes me feel more independent and less vulnerable to his reactions. I feel less needy and more… well, dignified… like those *Cortonese* women I admire.

It's true, though not always easy to remember: our happiness need not be, *should* not be, dependent on another's attention or approval. It goes both ways.

September

Mice, Manual Transmission, and Messed-Up Truffles

I'm awakened by a something battering against our bedroom ceiling. At first, it looks like a huge moth, but as my eyes adjust, I see it's a tiny bird. I wonder if it's a *lodola,* a lark, the namesake of our house. It must have flown in the open window, but now wants to fly out through the roof. Not knowing how to help it, I get up and close the bedroom doors, hoping the poor little thing will be drawn to the open windows as daylight arrives.

It's early September but feels like November. From my wicker chair in the pearly dawn light, I see smoke across the valley. Someone must be burning cuttings, not allowed when dry summer field grass creates a fire hazard. I imagine trails of winter smoke rising from the chimneys of the old farmhouses, all floating the same direction. I'm eager to discover each season at Lodolina as our new life unfolds.

Larry and I both sit up straight, startled by barking unlike any bark I've heard. We stare across the stream in the direction of the sound, hoping for a clue.

"What was that?" I ask.

"How would I know? You're our nature girl."

"Definitely *not* a dog," I state the obvious.

To figure out what barked, I'd search the internet if we had one. As the sun breaks over the ridge in a single radiant beam, I go upstairs to check on the little bird, who hopefully has seen the light and flown to freedom. Indeed, the bedroom is empty.

When I come back down, Pierangelo and Luciano are working on the stone wall under the horse chestnut tree. Another van rolls into the gravel driveway. Construction is back in full swing.

I stand up, straining to see if they are pouring more concrete on the tree roots. Larry says to let Francesco handle it. But I think they are and am determined to save that tree. The workers tease me about protecting the plants and, I suspect, take me less seriously because I'm a girl. But surely, I've earned some respect after a summer of handling their construction questions. And this problem needs attention *now*.

I walk to the top of a dirt mound and look down, shocked by what I see. Graziano and Luciano look up. In child-like Italian I scold them, frowning as I speak, serious and stern. "On the roots... only dirt. No concrete, *capito?*" Understand?

Both nod. Graziano says something that sounds like an excuse. I nod like I understand, though I don't. Without smiling, I turn and walk away. They know I'll be watching. And they know I'll tell Francesco that they didn't follow his instructions.

Marco, the owner of the building company, arrives to check the work, as he does frequently. His father, who started the company years ago, is with him. The four of us stand at the iron rail, looking back at the guesthouse. In careful, slow Italian so we can understand, Marco says a new house has grown up, an offspring of the original house. What a heartwarming thought.

The workers all seem proud of their efforts here. Though I'm miffed about putting concrete on the tree roots, their work has been excellent. I don't mention the root problem to Marco.

When Francesco arrives, I hear him talking with Pierangelo. I walk around the construction fence and climb over a pile of rocks to add my two cents.

When they look up, I tell Francesco the new wall is beautiful, but they are still putting concrete too close to the roots.

Francesco turns and speaks with Pierangelo and Graziano in a serious and firm voice. When Francesco comes inside, he tells me Graziano says he understood what I said, my Italian was good, and they will put only dirt on the roots. And they want him to tell me they are sorry.

I'm certain they got the message, but I will continue to check their work.

With Larry and me, Francesco discusses the need and cost of using polarized glass for the *limonaia*.

"If not polarized, will be like a mirror. We do not want to blind your neighbors across the valley." Francesco is, as always, amusing and convincing.

Unexpectedly, the *Telecom Italia* repairman walks down the ramp and talks with Francesco. I think I hear him say *topino*, mouse. Francesco laughs out loud. He explains to us that *Telecom Italia* could not solve the mystery, so they thought to check the new underground conduit. Mice had chewed through most of the new wiring. The repairman replaced it all and would like to check if everything works in the house. He adds that we must put mouse poison inside the tube and seal the ends.

Three months with intermittent internet and it was *mice*? Why didn't *Telecom* think of that sooner?

Telecom Italia has been our biggest problem in the entire renovation. First, we paid them over one thousand euros to remove a concrete pole in our back yard, and it took a year. Then, our wireless modem fried in an electrical storm and we had to drive forty miles one way to turn it in and order a new one, and again to pick it up! Now, after months of bad service, they find the problem was mice? Surely, we are not the only customers with underground wiring.

The repairman confirms all works perfectly!

I'm eager to search for barking mammals. Google indicates the bark was most likely a roe deer. Roe deer, typically extremely timid, bark when danger arises, during mating season, or just for fun. A few times this summer we have watched small deer bounding down the hillside across from us and Oliver says he's seen deer nests in our forest. The video sounds exactly like what we heard.

We're both startled when our phone rings. Guess it works, too. It's Alex, calling to invite us to lunch and to see their project — today. We're eager to see them again and curious about their villa, but need to go to Perugia to exchange our rental car today. Larry says we can do it all in one trip. Alex warns that the restaurant closes promptly at two, so we race to get on the road.

About halfway there, I call Alex to say we're making good time, but cutting it close. Fearful we'll have trouble finding the restaurant, she says they'll meet us at the roundabout before Castiglione de Lago. The restaurant, Tony emphasizes, is punctual. He says Alex called to ask them to keep the kitchen open five minutes longer but they made no promises.

Larry's battling the SUV steering, so is afraid to drive too fast. After following Alex and Tony out of the roundabout, we get stuck behind a line of slow cars. A small car passes in a dangerous spot, upsetting Larry. Tony, just ahead of us, tries to pass on a straightaway, but a car appears over a hill and we must slow down to let Tony back in. The pokey old blue Fiat causing the backup finally turns onto a country lane.

As we zip through the village of Pozzuolo, I glimpse a grand villa on our left with a bulldozer in front. It must be Tony and Alex's. I'm queasy from the car ride over hills and around curves. Beyond Pozzuolo, vineyards and olive groves whiz by on both sides and my stomach does summersaults. We turn right, down a straight road through farmland, then turn left at a sign for *Locanda Gulliver,* arriving three minutes before two o'clock.

"Did we make it or what?" Tony exclaims as he stands and stretches.

Alex dashes up the stairs to tell the restaurant we are here. Several people are in the courtyard still eating, a good sign.

We quickly follow, but Alex meets us at the door, saying the chef has packed up the kitchen. He told her we can have cold *antipasto*, but nothing cooked.

Tony is livid. They eat here often, staff are still here, Alex called ahead, and it's one minute before two o'clock. Our waiter, obviously uncomfortable, seats us but refuses to give us menus saying the chef insists the kitchen is closed. It's as though they're doing us a favor to offer food at all. Tony begrudgingly orders sliced meats, after an argument with the woman at the front desk. Soon, the waiter brings an overflowing platter of meats, cheese and condiments. Larry and I say it's exactly what we like to eat for lunch. Tony fumes and grumbles, eating almost nothing.

Despite cold food and Tony's mood, our conversation is warm and satisfying. We share about our families, our love for Italy, how we met our spouses, why we came to Cortona, our renovation experiences, and the endless challenges of living here. Tony says, when he proposed to Alex, he promised her an Italian villa, so their project is the fulfillment of his wedding vow. So far, their building experience sounds as awful as ours is wonderful, though ours is dragging on longer than we expected.

My favorite moment of our conversation is their shock that I'm sixty, which makes me feel better about Mario guessing my age.

When we pay the bill, Tony isn't subtle about his ire. Two o'clock does seem early to close the kitchen in a culture that doesn't start lunch until one.

We go back to their villa, originally the private home of one of Mussolini's generals. It is enormous, a grand, four-story, Neo-Renaissance cube with lots of windows and carved decoration under each. Dominating the immense foyer is a cantilevered *pietra serena* stone staircase curving upward for four levels, a work of art and a late-1800s engineering feat. Ceilings are high and frescoed — most are lovely, some are curious lake creatures, including a lobster-like crustacean. Though the frescoes are the taste of another era, I am charmed by all of it.

The general's initials, GB, hang over the front door. Every room has an original chandelier, but few are worth keeping according to Alex. From a balcony on the highest floor, we see Lake Trasimeno.

As we walk the old carriageway surrounding the property, Tony tells us he hoped to sell some of the trees for lumber, but they are worthless because every tree is full of shrapnel. Seems the general's home was an Allied target. The front yard, once an exotic garden shielding the grand house from the busy road, is now a jungle. Alex explains their plans for clearing overgrowth, adding a pool, winter house, guesthouse, garage, and an underground cellar for Tony's wine.

"It's amazing," I exclaim, "elegant… and historically significant. It'll be stunning."

Larry, shocked by the magnitude of the project, especially since ours was complicated enough and a fraction of the size, says, "You know you're certifiably crazy, don't you?"

Tony and Alex look at each other with a seemingly private pact, like children looking for trouble. I think they know exactly what they have taken on.

"All of my girls love the property," Tony says dreamily. "I imagine grandchildren running through the fields and splashing in the pool. It will be a place for generations to have a safe respite. I want to give them that. And yes, we're probably crazy. A good kind of crazy."

At that, Tony laughs for the first time since the debacle at the restaurant. This must be just the kind of complicated project he loves. It may be Alex's wedding gift, but it seems to me she'll do the lion's share of the work since she's the one who speaks Italian.

We leave our new friends and hurry to Perugia, hoping to arrive before the Europcar agency closes. I'll be so relieved to have a smaller car — one I can comfortably drive.

Larry rushes into the office while I wait in the SUV. I'm thrilled when he pulls up in a tiny Fiat Panda. Thankfully, the only thing this giant Volvo and sweet little Panda have in common is their silver-gray color. I get in and fasten my seat belt, giddy with joy.

Then I see Larry shift gears.

"You rented a stick-shift?" I ask, stunned.

"You'll love it." he assures me, smiling broadly and driving toward the exit, shifting like he has a new toy.

"Stop! You have to take it back. You didn't even talk to me? You just *did* it? You knew I'd never agree. I can't drive a stick-shift. Please stop. You have to go back."

"Victoria, surely you know how. We always get manual transmissions in Italy. Have I really driven you everywhere when we've been here?"

He knows I never drive on vacation, in Italy or anywhere. We're always together and he prefers to drive.

"If so, I've spoiled you," he continues, looking amused and shifting again as he eases into traffic. "Now you will learn." He sounds just like a dad.

"No. Now you will have to drive me *everywhere*."

"Honestly, Vic, there was no choice. They don't rent small cars with automatic transmissions, and we agreed that we wanted a smaller car."

"But I thought you were going to order one in advance."

"I never said that," he replies, shifting into a higher gear and sounding irritated that I won't drop it.

"The Volvo was an automatic," I say under my breath, to prove that Italian rentals have automatics.

He picks up speed. I'm so upset I can't speak. I grit my teeth, thinking how much more difficult this will make my life. I just became secure driving at all. This feels like a massive setback.

Cruising along the *autostrada*, Larry explains the basics of operating a manual gear transmission. I listen, but only half-heartedly because I'm so mad. When I cannot focus any more, I look out the window. I truly do not want to learn.

Larry does not give up. "Victoria, if we buy a car here, it'll be a stick. You need to learn on a rental."

"I always thought we'd buy an automatic."

"You've driven a stick before," he insists.

"That was a few times thirty years ago and I *never* got the hang of it."

We drive home in silence.

After dinner with almost no conversation, Larry does the dishes — a new thing he has started recently — then uses the pre-paid card to call our granddaughter Emma for her seventh birthday. He leaves a message from only himself. I'm sad to be so far from her.

"You could've left a message from both of us," I say.

"You could've called," he retorts, going back to reading his newspaper on the newly working internet.

I want to call Mom and the girls, but the tension in my voice would worry them and the card is probably almost expired.

I decide to take my mind off my upset by making truffles for my upcoming dinner party. Cooking calms me, perhaps because I have to concentrate. Focusing on the moment is often the best anecdote for worrying about the past or the future.

I melt the butter, add cream, espresso, olive oil, cayenne pepper, brandy and Cointreau. I let it get too hot and immediately turn off the flame. After the mixture cools a little, I add chopped dark chocolate, a mixture of

Swiss and Italian. I don't know where to buy the Belgian Callebaut I use in Chicago. The chocolate melts; I stir and taste. Not quite enough spice, but delicious and silky. I sprinkle on more cayenne pepper.

As I stir in the cayenne, the oil and solids start to separate. The more I stir, the more it separates. This is not good. I get out my *Joy of Cooking* to figure out how to save it. It says separation happens when the temperature gets too high or water gets into the mix. Once chocolate breaks the temper — the bond of oil to solids — it cannot be reconstituted. I must start over, it says. It also says truffles are the easiest of chocolates to make. Not today.

This is my first ever truffle disaster and I've been making them for years. After bragging about them to the castle gang at our *La Bucaccia* dinner, I must serve them and they must be good. I'll buy more chocolate tomorrow and start over.

Larry and I haven't connected since the rental car argument. Maybe I should give up and try to drive a stick. I'm mad mostly because he didn't talk to me first. He rented it knowing I'd be upset. And, I'm seriously apprehensive about ever driving a stick safely or comfortably.

Tonight I refuse to be the one to make everything okay, so decide to go to bed early. Tomorrow I'll start anew, restoring the truffles and trying to focus on the good in my husband. I'm not sure what I'll do about the manual transmission. I fear it's unavoidable in my new Italian life.

Resurrection of Chocolate

I wake up worried about my truffles, but not about the manual transmission. The dinner is tomorrow; the car problem is bigger but will wait. The urgent so often upstages the important.

The chocolate is a hard, dull mass with a half-inch layer of separated butter on top. I'm so grateful for a working internet with advice on how to restore the mess so, with luck, I won't have to start over. I follow the instructions meticulously, scraping off the separated butter and melting it alone, dropping in chunks of the seized chocolate, then adding a few pieces of new chocolate. The glob is softer, but still dull and not fully reconstituted. Following an "if necessary" notation, I add two teaspoons of boiling water.

Like magic, glossy satin glides under my spoon. It makes no sense to me, but it worked.

"These will be just fine to serve," I say to no one in particular. "And the flavor is superb."

Sitting silently on the front terrace so I don't interrupt Larry, I record our visit to Alex and Tony's villa, the rental car disaster, and my first-ever truffle failure and restoration. Larry tells me he's reading about the Christian church's response to Islam in the eleventh and twelfth centuries.

"Did you know there was an early sect of eastern Christianity even more mystical than early western Christianity, which was much more mystical than it is today?" he asks, intrigued with this new knowledge. "It lasted for centuries. Their practice was to look inward to connect to God. They believed if someone held their breath and stared at their navel long enough, they'd see visions of Christ. Honestly. There's surely more subtlety around it... but these mystics must be the source of the expression 'staring at your navel'."

I express amusement, then we are silent again. Mid-morning, he says he wants to walk to Cortona for Saturday market, rather than drive. He knows I need lots of vegetables and meat for tomorrow nights' dinner party, but says he can carry it all. It's a beautiful day, so I decide to set aside my lingering upset and agree.

Instead of the rocky trail, today we take the grassy path past Belinda's house, the one she showed us the night of our hillside dinner.

"I like this way, though it's longer," I say nearing the top.

"The problem," Larry observes, "is that we have to pass right in front of Belinda's house. When someone's there, we invade their privacy."

"It did feel strange just now when we walked past the renter's underwear hanging on the line. I tried to look into the valley instead of toward the house."

Cortona is unusually crowded, perhaps because of the spectacular weather. At the *ferramenta*, hardware store, I find four citronella candles to put along the edge of the terrace for our party. I also need table candles that will stay lit in a breeze. Most of the store's candles are pink eggs or orange flowers and I wonder who buys them. I drop a short white candle into a flared juice glass, thinking I could make a line of them.

"*Brava!*" the blond woman behind the counter exclaims. I buy six sets.

Lastly, we need more espresso cups, like the ones I bought before. But today they're marked two-fifty rather than one euro like I paid before. Do prices really go up when *straniere*, foreigners, show interest?

Buying meat is next. I like this *macelleria*, except that the butcheress-owner makes fun of my Italian. Consequently, my brain freezes when I walk in the door.

She's hacking massive slabs with her cleaver, breaking the bones with decisive blows and pounding the pieces into thin cutlets with her flat-faced tool. She must be strong. Soon, it's my turn. I ask in awkward Italian which of the large T-bone slabs would make the best *tagliata*. She seems to understand and suggests the one with more fat.

"*D'accordo,*" I say, nodding. I agree.

"*Chianina?*" I ask. I want to make sure I'm buying the best beef in Tuscany for my dinner.

"*Si, certo,*" she says, sounding insulted that I would ask.

"*Per otto persone,*" I request, for eight people.

She cuts two thick steaks and holds them up to show me. Gorgeous, but maybe not enough. I ask for one more, "*piu basso,*" more low, since I don't know the word for thinner. It'll cook more quickly and be less rare for Alex, who likes her meat well done.

By the time I get to Gigliola's vegetable stand, they're out of figs, arugula and *rosmarino*… essential ingredients for my dinner. The in-town produce shops are more expensive, but they do have excellent, fresh products. I find all I need at Roberto's near *Piazza della Repubblica*.

Larry is anxious to move along, but next door to Molesini's enoteca is a special art exhibit — by an artist I know.

"Five minutes," I say to Larry. "It's Elizabeth. I just want to say hello."

During our first trip to Cortona, ten years ago, my friend Cynthia gave me notecards by Elizabeth Cochran. Three years ago, invited to a Women's Day dinner with complete strangers, I was seated beside an English watercolorist.

As she talked, I decided it must be Elizabeth. So, I described my cards and, of course, it was her.

She then told us a story that had us rolling in laughter. During a storm, the roof in her tiny apartment had leaked and soaked boxes of new notecards. The next day, from her balcony she had yelled at the maintenance man hoeing in the courtyard, saying he must fix the roof because it had leaked and ruined her note cards. The more insistent and loud she became, the more intently he chopped at the ground, ignoring her. Soon, residents in nearby apartments were leaning out of their windows, shocked and amused. She later realized that roof is *tetto* and nipple is *tetta*. She had been yelling at the poor man that her nipple was leaking, ruining her cards, and he must fix it right away.

Excited to see Elizabeth again, I step inside the exhibit and ask if she remembers me from Women's Day.

"Of course. I thought I recognized you in the piazza. Are you renting again?"

"Cortona's home now. We moved here in June. We love it, but we're living in construction and life in a new culture is harder than I expected…. Sorry I can't stay. My husband wants to go home. But I wanted to say hi and to tell you I've repeated your leaky roof story a dozen times."

"You won't believe it," she chuckles, "One day I saw my story on the internet, with my name but posted by someone I don't know. I'm sure it helped sell cards. None of that collection is left."

Larry motions to me to hurry. I give Elizabeth my email address so she can let me know when she has another show in Cortona.

"Please come to my opening tonight. You can meet my Cortona friends. I only have one show here each summer," she says.

Larry wants to stop in the *Parterre* on our walk home and eat the sandwiches he bought, saying it's after two and he's starving. We sit on a stone bench in the shade of *l'Alberone*. The *porchetta* is delicious. Fennel pollen permeates the meat and I now understand why it's prized. My finger is still bandaged, but no longer painful.

Back home, arms aching after helping Larry carry bags of cups, candles, meat and produce, he reads in the living room while I'm busy in the kitchen.

After about an hour, he comes in carrying a box. He says he wants to organize our CDs on the kitchen island – all three hundred of them — and keep me company. I say it's nice to have his company, but he can only use half of my workspace.

I rub the steak with garlic and rosemary and drizzle it with olive oil, make spiced nuts, and shape chocolate truffles. They are smooth and rich, like chocolate velvet.

Finally relinquishing the island to Larry to sort CD's, I dig table linens out of the bottom of a wardrobe box in the corner of the living room and iron nine eggplant-colored linen napkins, one for each guest and another to line my silver breadbasket from Verona. If it's warm enough to eat outside, we'll carry our antique dining table to the terrace, like we did with Ron and family. White plastic chairs are all we have, but they'll look okay with a white tablecloth.

Linens done, I decide to iron shirts for Larry. The last time I ironed nineteen and declared a strike. I take pleasure in doing something nice for him. He's been kinder and more supportive since our weekend in Verona — with a couple of exceptions like saying that cutting my finger was dumb and renting the manual transmission car without asking me first. After that first unkind comment, he was a hero about my finger, helpful, apologetic and concerned, and I do hope something good will come of the manual transmission.

Disagreements will happen again in our marriage; it's the normal give and take of a normal couple. After twenty-two years of knowing one another, this summer with its ups and downs is teaching us new ways to get along and to show our love.

"How's your dinner coming?" he asks. "Caught up?"

I assure him I've done everything I can do today or I wouldn't be ironing.

"What if we go to town for an old-fashioned date?" he asks, saying Marco mentioned that a movie filmed in Cortona is playing at *Teatro Signorelli* tonight. It's in Italian, but Marco was certain we'd understand the story. And, Larry offers to stop for a quick pasta, so I don't have to cook.

"Sounds great. I'd like to stop at Elizabeth's opening, too... if we have time," I say, hurrying upstairs to change out of my cooking clothes.

"Don't you want to drive?" Larry asks when I walk toward the passenger door.

"Not really, but I probably should," I mumble. "Will you be patient?"

"Will you drive well?" he teases.

"Probably not, but I'll do my best."

"Then I'll do my best to be patient."

I imagine him braced on the dashboard the whole ride, pressing his foot into the floor when I do something wrong, and instructing me on every move.

"I think you should drive this time," I say. "We're late, I'm a bit tense because of my dinner tomorrow, and we're getting along so well I don't want to risk it."

He chuckles. "How 'bout if you drive to town, I promise to be patient, and I drive home? You really do need some supervised practice."

I agree, though I don't like the sound of "supervised." Crawling into the driver's seat, my stomach is in knots and I haven't even turned the key.

"First, buckle your seat belt, then put the key in the ignition," he instructs. "Don't forget to press on the clutch *and* the brake while you turn the key."

When I don't move, he asks, "Do you want my help? Or should I just let you figure this out for yourself?"

I have flashbacks of trying to drive a friend's manual transmission car thirty years ago. I never did get the hang of it.

"Nope... instruction's good. What about the accelerator?" I pull the seatbelt strap across my chest and hook it. "Do I also need to step on it to start the car? I only have two feet."

He assures me there's enough gas in the engine to start the car.

"Okay... here we go," I sigh, mostly to myself.

Cautiously I press the clutch and brake, and then turn the key. The car starts.

"Now, keep your foot on the clutch, put the car in reverse, ease your brake foot onto the accelerator, and slowly release the emergency brake. Then back down the driveway to the turning area. Do you think you can turn it around?"

"I'll try." I focus to remember the order. That was a lot of information all at once.

Slowly, I think, do everything slowly. Make sure the clutch is in, put the gearshift in reverse, and then release the hand brake. Slowly.

The car starts backing up. When I see the edge of the driveway, I jam on the brake with my clutch foot, knowing it's a fifteen-foot drop. The car jerks and stalls.

I ask Larry to please turn the car around, because I'm afraid of going over the edge.

"Victoria, there're piles of materials on both sides. You won't go over."

"Please. If I back it up... will you turn it around?"

Larry agrees, seemingly intent on scrutinizing every detail of my actions.

"When you stop, put it in neutral, set the parking brake, and then get out. Don't forget the clutch to change gears."

I do fine backing up. Before I get out, I press on the clutch and the brake, double-check the diagram on the shift knob and jiggle the knob back and forth to make sure it's in neutral, pull up on the emergency brake, release the brake pedal... the clutch... and then my seat belt. The car is still running. My heart is racing.

Larry turns the car around easily and continues to drive toward town. He must think we've both had enough of a first try.

At *Piazza della Repubblica*, he says there isn't time for Elizabeth's reception and dinner. We inhale pasta at Fufluns, rush to the theater, and find seats just as the movie starts. The theater is less than a third full and I think we're the only foreigners. The old reels are on a cranky, noisy projector. The film keeps getting stuck. At a critical moment near the end, the film breaks. I fear we won't see the ending. But they splice it and the movie runs smoothly through the credits.

Marco was right. I understood the story even without understanding the words. It was about Gino Bartali, a famous and heroic Italian cyclist, who risked his life during World War II to save Jewish children in our area by smuggling counterfeit identity documents in the frame and handlebars of his bicycle. One battle scene was filmed on the terrace of this theater, though I doubt a real battle was fought here.

"Do you want to drive?' Larry asks on the way back to the car.

"Not at night. I don't see well enough in the dark. That okay?"

"Up to you. I think you need to say how you learn to drive. I'll just give you opportunities."

I choke back a giggle at "opportunities," but simply say, "Thanks, darling, I'd prefer if you drove this time."

Near Palazzone, we startle two black and white *istrici*, porcupines, waddling along the middle of the road. When our headlights shine on them, they pick up speed. They don't run straight, but zigzag, as though they're running with their front legs and hopping with their back legs. They seem taller, as if their legs get longer when they run. After a few yards, they hop onto the weedy shoulder, down the embankment, and into an olive grove. It's impossible not to laugh.

At home, Larry and I sit on the terrace under the night sky, sipping glasses of limoncello and making wishes on falling stars. Mine are to learn to drive a stick shift and speak Italian. Larry's is to have more time to read and write.

Larry sees a shooting star that's unusually bright and says in a hush, "When that star left its orbit, dinosaurs were finding food for their babies on earth."

"Do you want to know my truest wish?" I ask.

"Of course."

"I wish that you'd be happy with me, like right now, for the rest of my life."

"Oh, Victoria, I'm always happy with you, even when I don't show it. There are plenty of things to be unhappy about. You are not one of them."

I glance at him with an I'm-not-so-sure look and then, seeing the look in his eyes, can't help but smile. He says he loves my smile, which makes me smile again. Maybe Larry's tender moments are enough to compensate for his irritable ones and his need to instruct me, in great detail, about how to drive. He says he loves me always, even when he doesn't show it. I just wish I felt it always. Being loved and feeling loved are two different things. Right now, I feel loved.

Dancing in the Grass

It's early morning and I get up with the sun, hoping to have time to make my eggplant parmesan before church. Low gray clouds do not bode well for an outdoor dinner tonight.

Rather than launch into cooking, I take time to sip a cappuccino and listen to the dawn unfurl. Half-eaten cypress cones clatter to the ground. I can see the little squirrel sitting on his haunches inside the tree, munching away. In the olive groves, two upupa, with their black and white wings, fly from our trees to trees across the stream, whooshing, swooping and dipping. Monogamous, at least for the season, this couple seems to delight in their morning tango. Larks, sparrows and thrush sing their hearts out. It's as though they all know it's September, summer is waning, and today is important.

After finishing my cappuccino and jotting a few notes about yesterday, I make a rich tomato sauce for the eggplant. I'll finish the rest after church so it'll be fresh for tonight. I'll have a full eight hours to cook and get ready for guests after we get home. (Eventually, I learn that eggplant parmesan is best on the second day.)

At Mass, the phrases are becoming familiar, even habitual, despite still sounding foreign: *Gloria in excelsius Dio.* Glory to God in the highest. "*Le parole di Dio,*" the Word of God. *Lo Spirito Santo,* the Holy Spirit. Like the movie last night, I cannot follow the priest's words, but get the basic message. Today's topic is courage, which seems fitting. The service runs long, making me anxious. I'm eager to head home and *courageously* prepare my big dinner.

On our walk, Larry helps me pick wildflowers for a centerpiece. My arms are filled. There's fuzzy-leafed borage with bright blue star flowers, orange rose hips from wild rose bushes, *hedera* with clusters of indigo berries, *ginestra* stems that look like bear grass, and fennel with its prized mustard-yellow flowers. At home, I'll put this bundle in a bucket of water to keep it fresh and arrange just before our guests arrive.

Bees swarm around me. On most hillside walks, one or two buzz around my face and I shoo them away. A dozen trail me today. I hope my wildflower bouquet doesn't invite them to dinner.

It's two o'clock by the time I start cooking again. But six hours should be plenty of time to put together the *Parmigiana di Melanzane* and make a simple fig tart. Larry will grill the steak, already marinating, on our rickety camp grill.

I have two more near-disasters. First, my eggplant slices turn dark. Not beautifully browned as they roast, but dark like cut apples exposed too long to the air. At this rate, I'll have black eggplant parmesan. I take out a few slices and try frying them, which doesn't help. I must let the eggplant finish roasting, assemble the layers with cheeses and homemade tomato sauce, and hope no one notices the unappetizing color.

When I tell Larry that I'm worried about the eggplant, he says, "Just make it the way you did before. It was perfect." Easier said than done.

Then, my *crostata* crust melts so there's no rim to hold the custard. It was so easy and perfect when I made it with my granddaughters. I add a collar of aluminum foil, sprinkle the warm crust with chopped dark chocolate, pour in the custard, place the figs cut side down, sprinkle on some pine nuts, drizzle honey, and hope for the best.

Without a recipe, each dish is an adventure. Riskier, but more artful and fun. Larry asks if he can help, but I really need to do the cooking myself.

After resurrecting both dishes, most of my six hours are gone. I decide to let our guests help set the table, if necessary, and hurry upstairs to change.

When I come down, Larry has washed the pots and pans, tidied the kitchen, and swept the terrace. I'm thankful and impressed. We carry the dining room table outside despite gathering clouds. While I prepare appetizers, he covers the table with my favorite white tablecloth and sets it with our white outlet-mall china, then puts white plastic chairs all around. I add the juice-glass candles, purple linen napkins, and the giant bouquet of wildflowers, arranged in a colorful ceramic soup terrine. The lush grass around the terrace is emerald green, about four inches long, still awaiting its first cut. This setting is straight out of a movie.

Before making *crostini*, I pour rosemary-cayenne nuts into the silver bowl I bought in Verona. On an Etruscan bird plate, I mound chunks of *Parmigiano Reggiano*, the king of parmesan, then generously drizzle them with fifty-year old balsamic vinegar, so thick it barely drips. With nibbles on the end of the island, people will congregate there and have something to eat with their sparkling wine, while I finish cooking.

The phone rings. Lynn and Mike are walking from town and need directions. Larry tells them to wait at the top of the hill, he'll come to meet them. They arrive carrying a bottle of grappa, a basket overflowing with fresh vegetables from their garden, plus a colorful bouquet of parsley, lavender, Swiss chard, and pink and orange geraniums. So artfully arranged, I put the bouquet in a crystal vase to beautify the kitchen island.

The phone rings again. Marco says he, Alex and Tony are on their way on foot, but don't know where to turn. Larry volunteers, again, to climb up the trail and guide them down.

Giancarlo, who drove, says it's impossible to find us, but that's okay because once you get to Lodolina, you don't want to leave. He's alone; Ginny is back in Texas.

Larry offers two exceptional sparkling wines. One we brought from California; the other, Tony's favorite, they brought chilled from Marco's shop. Our guests are soon munching spiced nuts with appreciative murmurs and sipping bubbly.

While Larry gives a tour, I finish *crostini*: little toasted bread rounds swiped with a fresh garlic clove. Some are topped with gorgonzola and fig jam, others with black truffle paste and fresh pecorino cheese. A couple minutes in a hot oven improves both. When our guests come back from their tour, warm *crostini* are served.

Everyone compliments our home. My favorite comment is Marco's, who runs his hand over the *pietra serena* kitchen counter and says, "In fifty years this stone will become beautiful… after it gets it's shadows."

Surely, it won't take fifty years. I may even make some shadows tonight.

Cena, dinner, is *molto buona*, very good… thankfully. The eggplant is not as good as my earlier attempt, but by candlelight the layers do not look so dark and Marco and Tony accept a second helping. Larry grills the *Chianina* beef perfectly, cuts it into thin slices, piles it on the platter, and I drizzle it with olive oil warmed with rosemary, garlic and green peppercorns. To me, the salad of arugula, nectarine, shaved fennel and toasted pine nuts with lemon-balsamic dressing is a perfect complement to the meat. I don't think

Tony likes fruit in a salad, but you cannot please everyone. Marco doesn't eat salad, period, and asks for yet one more serving of eggplant.

The show-stopper is the *dolci*, dessert. When I remove its silver collar, the custard has cooked to the edge, but not overflowed. The figs are lime green mounds settled about halfway into the ricotta filling, shiny and firm with browned drizzles of honey and scattered toasted pine nuts. I serve generous squares with a dollop of soft whipped cream flowing down one side. The dark chocolate layer shows up only in the mouth, an intriguing surprise to everyone.

After dessert, I pile Etruscan bird plates piled with resurrected chocolate truffles and Larry offers three kinds of grappa. First, he holds up a clear one in an elegant, thin-necked bottle. "Our favorite, very smooth," he says, with modest authority.

"Girls' grappa," Marco scoffs.

The others are stronger — the second was made by Marco's cousin, the third brought by Mike and Lynn. The group affectionately deems Mike and Lynn's "guy's grappa" because it is darkest in color, which makes it the hands-down favorite. Marco's cousin's is also excellent, and everyone wants to at least sample it. Not one person touches girl's grappa, especially not the women.

Throughout dinner my wine glass is empty. I'm up and down clearing plates and serving food, so don't pay attention to how much I drink. I don't feel tipsy, though there are many happy toasts during our long evening under the indigo sky strewn with stars. I feel relaxed and happy.

Music has been wafting softly from the windows throughout dinner. An Eva Cassidy song plays and, to our surprise, Tony knows her story. "She was American, but more popular in England," he says. "Died much too young." I say my favorite phrase in all her songs is, "I see friends shaking hands saying 'how do you do?' They're really saying 'I love you'." A few minutes later when "It's a Wonderful World" graces the night air, I listen for those poignant lines and feel a sweet twinge in my chest.

Looking around the table, I realize how much I already love these friends. It's our new wonderful world and I get teary, moved by deep gratitude. When we invest in the joy of others, going a little out of our way for them as I did with dinner tonight, we feel more connected to them, whether or not they notice.

At one end of the table Giancarlo is lighting a thin cigar for Lynn, like he first did at the castle. I get up again, this time to find new candles. The first ones have burned to the base and, I fear, may crack my fancy juice glasses. Our new friends are chatting in twos and threes. This would make a touching screenplay and I could not write a better script than the conversations around our table.

Then I hear it, Patti LaBelle's crystalline voice promising "Give me the sun, I'll give you the moonlight. Love will set us free, if we just believe the best is yet to come.... Can you see what I see... on the road ahead? Do you know there's a new life there? Waiting there."

Over twenty years ago Larry and I chose this as our song, but little did we know how true it would become. Indeed... there's a new life waiting there.

"Dance?" Larry says, extending his hand. I know he put this song into the mix on purpose. It still inspires me, and so does he.

I look into his eyes, enchanted, as he stands with his boyish smile and dimpled chin, and reply, "I'd be honored..."

"Give me the world and I'll give you heaven," he softly sings along with Patti as he holds me in his arms.

Others join and we dance in the long grass, linger in the candlelight, and enjoy the company of strangers who have become as familiar as family. At some point, Marco says he really must go; he opens the store in only a few hours. Six people pile into our newly-rented, manual-transmission Panda, the two ladies on laps, and Larry drives out of our driveway toward the bumpy S-curve. I have the cleanup nearly finished when he returns.

Home is not a location, but a space filled with love. Tonight, Lodolina is home.

A Day of Contrasts

The morning after our dinner party, I was exhausted and hung over. I definitely consumed too much wine and boy's grappa. But that was almost a week ago, I've recovered and we've had several uneventful, happy construction days since then. I'm pleased our dinner was such a success and still bask in the glow of new and deepening friendships.

The dinner was also a good test of my kitchen. For all my apprehension, I seem to have managed just fine. When we first moved in, I couldn't imagine that a refrigerator eighteen inches wide and forty-two inches high would be sufficient. But fruits and vegetables are so fresh that I leave them on the counter and we make frequent trips to town. It has worked all summer, even for our big dinner.

I do struggle without a garbage disposal. Decades ago, my mother and grandmother composted, so didn't need one. Next summer, I will compost.

Despite ferocious winds this morning, workers were on the job at eight. Standing at the kitchen door, I watch an empty cement bag fly into the air and disappear over the iron rail. Whipping trees dull the construction sounds. The metal toolshed door bangs open and shut. Trash is flattened against the fence. Gusts seem to come from everywhere. In the distance a tractor rumbles, but the sound is nearly drowned out by the rush of wind. I fear our tiny olives are being ripped off their branches.

Ignoring the wind, Larry wants to run. He promises to be home and ready for Saturday market by eleven. At ten-thirty, I expect him any minute. By eleven, I'm worried. Larry is always punctual. At eleven-fifteen, I grab my new cell phone and head out to look for him.

As I open the door, dust and leaves whoosh in. A huge pile of trash has collected in the little vestibule, including a large sheet of plastic. I squeeze out, preventing more debris from blowing in.

A faint sound of men's voices lures me around the corner. I hope Larry is there, but it's Luciano and Pierangelo working on the new wall. I'm thrilled that Pierangelo is back after his holiday, greet them both and say I must go look for Larry. He's running and should've been home long ago.

I walk quickly, thinking of the dangers for runners. Drivers go fast around curvy mountain roads, unaware of runners or bikers. Roads are narrow and on one side there is often a drop-off with almost no shoulder, so runners must stay on the asphalt. If Larry has been hit, surely someone would've taken him to the hospital and called me.

Tiny pale green olives litter the ground. Hundreds, probably thousands. I can only imagine the distress of a real farmer whose harvest is destroyed in one day by Mother Nature. Nothing to be done, except hope plenty are left on the trees.

"Lar-ry! Larr-rry!" I call as I climb the trail, anxiety increasing with each step.

"Laaaar-ryyy," I persist, my voice lost in the wind.

Half running up the steepest part of the rocky path, I realize I'm still wearing flip-flops. Flip-flops aren't good for this climb, but I continue, calling Larry's name. At the top, I look left toward Cortona and right toward Torreone, still calling. When it's clear he's nowhere near, I turn and hurry back down the trail toward home.

I clutch my phone in my hand so I don't miss its ring, feeling grateful to finally have one. It's slippery with sweat. With my other hand I wipe away tears, squinting because there's dirt in the air from the wind. If he isn't home, I'll get in the car and drive his run course, though I'm not confident I know the course or can drive this stupid car.

At the place where the stream crosses our driveway, I hear something behind me. I whirl around, startling Larry. Words tumble out. "Wow! I'm glad to see you! I've been looking for you... afraid you were hurt. I even have bandages."

He slows for an instant, smiles, then runs ahead. "Tell me at home," he calls back without losing his pace or ruining his always-calculated time.

In the house, he insists he said he'd be ready by noon, that I misunderstood. So grateful he's safe, I don't argue. Maybe I was wrong about the time, but he could've acknowledged my concern instead of only insisting he was right.

"Pierangelo's here," I say. "I told him I was going to search for you and that I was worried. You should say hello."

I go with him to hurry him along, so we don't miss market. Larry asks Pierangelo about his vacation. Pierangelo says the weather was terrible, it is only good weather when he works. I laugh, pleased I can understand his Italian.

On the way to the car, Larry asks, "So, do you want to drive today?"

"Sure," I say reluctantly, then add, "Truthfully, no, but I know I need some supervised practice, as you put it. I'll drive... if it's okay with you to take the lower road."

"Up to you," he says. "You're the driver."

Feeling rushed because market soon ends, I buckle my seat belt, put my foot on the brake, and turn the key in the ignition. The car jerks forward, then dies. Larry looks straight ahead. We both roll down the windows to let in some air.

After breathing in deeply, Larry asks, "Was your foot on the clutch?"

"Does it have to be on the clutch just to start the car? I wasn't ready to shift."

This is not a good start. I turn the key again, this time with one foot on the clutch and one on the brake. I manage to turn the car around after several back and forths.

"You don't need to use the clutch unless you're going to start, change gears, or stop. It's not good to ride the clutch… wears it out. Only engage it when you need it," he instructs. Guess he could tell I had my foot on the clutch the whole time.

Driving out of the driveway seems easy. As I turn onto the access road, I wonder how long Larry's patience will hold up. He seems tense as a tightwire.

Just before the S-curve, I veer a little to the right on the same spot where Larry sometimes hits bottom. I hear a slap on his side.

"Victoria! You hit me with a branch!" he blurts.

"Roll up your window," I snap back, unnerved by his tone.

"No… *you* watch the road!" he retorts.

"At least I didn't hit bottom!!"

My ears feel hot and my heart is pounding. This is an unpleasant ride and I am not going any farther. I stop the car, feet on brake and clutch, and speak measuredly.

"I was trying not to scrape bottom on the rocks. I need to be able to use the whole road without worrying about what might come into your window. I'm going to drive to the pine tree and let you take over. You're not in the mood for this today."

"Just drive," he says, leaving his window wide open.

At the giant pine tree, where our access road meets the blacktop road to town, I decide I should keep driving or I'll never master this. Millions of drivers all over the world drive a manual transmission. They can't all be smarter than me.

Approaching the tough uphill intersection into town, Larry coaches, "Engage the clutch and the brake. Put the car in first... roll into the stop and — if you can — on through the intersection while you turn left. Watch for cars. It's steep and tricky, but you'll do fine."

I pray for no cars and follow Larry's instructions. Rolling into the stop without a car in sight, I start to turn left, just as a car speeds around the blind corner. I jam on the brake, forget the clutch, the Panda lurches and stalls.

As I restart the engine, it rolls backward. In the rear-view mirror I see a shiny new red car coming up the hill behind me.

"Emergency brake!"

I jerk the brake up with both hands.

"Okay," he starts again with his instructions. I feel like a teenager out with her dad. But I must admit I need and value his help.

With the engine running and the transmission in first, I watch for an opening in traffic, release the hand brake, and give the Panda plenty of gas while easing off the clutch. The car glides into the intersection and left onto the main road.

"That was great! Textbook. *Brava!*" Larry says. I'm exhausted, but pleased.

Our favorite parking lot is packed. While Larry puts our garbage in the dumpster, I see a car pull out and back the Panda in perfectly.

"*Brava!*" he yells, making a thumbs-up sign as he hurries back to the car and opens my door for me. I get out, a little shaky and relieved that the rest of the trip will be by foot.

First, we stop at the drycleaner, closed all of August. I leave eight pairs of pants and five shirts with the petite, dark-haired lady behind the counter. Before I ask, she brings out my ivory pants, missing all month. When she writes today's count in her book, I write it in my journal. Next time, I want to pick it all up.

Then we start our regular Saturday routine. First, we climb to the fresh pasta shop and buy our usual two meals. The cost is four euros ninety-four. Lilliana Angelica gives me too much change. I'm often given too much change in Cortona. Italians seem to live with less precision than Americans, and exact amounts aren't as important as generosity. Sometimes a small discount is given to locals, so when change is counted in my favor, I feel I'm being treated like a local.

Talking with the butcheress, Larry makes a joke in Italian about husbands only being valued to carry the bags. I buy our meat, smile, and hand the bags to Larry. If he's going to complain about having to do something, he might as well do it. He laughs. It seems we're back to having fun.

Gigliola tells me the flat, white *Saturnia* peaches are *squisita.* I ask for two and can smell their perfume as she puts them in my sack. I buy veggies for only one week, plus a pot of rosemary. I want to plant rosemary before we leave for Chicago, in only eight days.

Larry comes back from buying porchetta sandwiches with a bag of warm, freshly made sheep's milk ricotta.

In *Piazza della Repubblica,* there must be two hundred people all dressed up, probably for a wedding. The men wear suits even in the heat and most of the women have on beaded dresses and strappy shoes with stiletto heels, terrible for walking on these stone streets. The only reason I see for wearing stilettos is to look sexy, yet when women hobble on the cobblestones, to me they don't look sexy at all.

The crowd cheers as the newlyweds float down the long, wide stone stairway in front of the medieval city hall, Cortona's most famous landmark. Wedding guests shower them with confetti. In Tuscany, it's good luck to see a bride on her wedding day, and we see one most every week.

As soon as the wedding party disperses, men begin unloading metal frames and long wooden planks from a big truck. They start setting up a stage at the base of the stairway. When I ask what it's for, the worker says there's an important fashion show tonight.

Larry drives home without asking if I want to. The morning may have been enough for him, as well as for me. The car smells like roasted pork and ripe summer fruits. Just before our turnoff, he stops beside the wild fig tree and picks plump, soft figs, handing them to me two at a time.

"*Basta.* Enough. They look wonderful but I can't hold any more," I say, my lap overflowing.

Back home the wind is still strong. Inside the town walls it was hardly noticeable. As we watch the wind churn across the valley, I see countless olive trees that were swallowed by forests long ago. Their silvery leaves, turning and twisting in the wind, flicker like tinsel in the sunlight and make them easy to spot amidst the dark green forest trees. Our valley, already beautiful, would be spectacular if all the ancient olive groves were reclaimed, returning it to the glory of centuries past when olive oil production was an integral part of farm life and every hillside was terraced.

After lunch of *porchetta* sandwiches and a sweet home-grown melon Rita brought the last time she cleaned, the wind dies down. Larry suggests we hike our property to see how badly the crop has been damaged.

"We'll look for more figs," he says. "I've seen a couple trees about half way down."

Grabbing a plastic sack, I'm ready to go. I love walking our property and have been curious about making fig jam. I remember when Pierangelo cut down the fig tree in front of our house.

In the groves, tiny olives litter the ground.

"Can you imagine seeing your annual family income literally blown off the trees?" I ask. "I think half the crop is gone."

"Don't worry," Larry reassures me, "we'll still have plenty of oil. But we are fortunate we don't depend on it."

We stop to inspect a piece of stone wall covered with frilly lime-colored ferns. I've never noticed it before — a fragment of the ancient walls that once supported every terrace on our property.

"That looks more like a photo than a real wall," I say.

"The perfect illustration of history overtaken by nature," Larry observes.

Then he looks up and gasps, "Vic, look at those figs!"

The tree is loaded. Quite a few have blown off today, on the ground but still good. Larry picks figs from the tree, while I gather them from the ground.

"There's no way the wild boar or porcupines could get to any of these," he says straining to reach. "I should've brought a ladder."

As Larry hands figs to me, I put them in the bag and count. We have fifty-seven figs from two scraggly trees, plus the dozen at home. And, there are masses of unripe figs left. Imagine what these trees will produce when pruned and thriving. I show Larry that our figs and ferns are color-coordinated, exactly the same limey green.

At home, I pile the best figs on the Etruscan-bird platter. We have so many we cannot possibly eat them all, though Larry insists he'll enjoy trying. I'll need to make my *marmellata* soon. They're very ripe.

After we've eaten our fill, declaring they're the best figs we've ever tasted, we decide to take a nap. We whisper sweet-nothings to one another in Italian, giggle at our own silliness, and appreciate a lazy summer afternoon with no workers.

The wind picks up again late afternoon. We listen to debris whipping around outside, study and write, but have no internet. So much for a new underground line solving the problem. Larry says it must be wind on old wires coming into our property.

Finally, it's calm.

"Hey, Vic" Larry yells from the coat closet, "The light is solid."

Sure enough, he connects to the internet right away.

When I try to connect a minute later, it's dead again. So frustrating! At least Larry's emails were sent. Perhaps tomorrow mine will go.

Larry says he's going to demand a three-month refund from *Telecom Italia*. Says they should've found the mice long ago, since they installed our underground lines and have surely faced this before. It seems *Telecom Italia* has worn him out.

As we start to leave to go back to town, the phone rings. It's Dale. I love hearing her voice. She says she bought a phone card because reaching us by internet is impossible. She doesn't want to interrupt, only to say hello. I tell her our internet is much better since they found the mice, but not perfect. Dale says she's looking for apartments in the city, that it's time they leave the suburbs.

A new thought disquiets me, though it should have been obvious. When we get back to Chicago, things will have changed for our friends. We'll go back with a memory of when we left, but life for them is moving on too. Part of the cost of our new life is an inevitable distance from our Chicago friends.

As we walk to dinner, I tell Larry this will be a two-hill day for me. Once this morning when I was afraid that he was bleeding on a path somewhere, and now. Larry teases me that it'll be a two-hill day for him, too, and he *ran* one of them.

He stops, turns, and says, "Sorry I worried you this morning. Seriously. Sorry."

Guess it finally sunk in that I was genuinely worried. I accept his apology and we walk, fingers laced, toward the *Parterre*. It's still light, but the sun is setting earlier than it did a month ago.

In the *Parterre,* rows of plastic chairs and a huge stage fill the long park. We were told Brother Andrea, the monk we met earlier in the summer, was giving a concert this weekend, but no one seemed to know when or where. I ask a worker if this is for Brother Andrea. He nods, saying the *concerto* starts at nine-thirty. Surely, we can finish dinner in time to hear some of it.

We've heard that Andrea was a rock star in Florence before he became a Capuchin, but gave up singing when he took his vows. Then his spiritual advisor told him his voice is a gift from God and he should use it to glorify God, not hide it. Andrea started singing again, this time with teens around Cortona.

In town when we walk past Isa's antiques, I notice the credenza Larry wanted is no longer in the window. I ask Larry to wait and slip into the shop to ask about it. When I tell Larry it's sold, he seems more upset than I expect. I wish I hadn't mentioned it.

At *Pane e Vino*, Arnaldo recommends a superb wine for our dinner. We share every dish, *uno per due*, one for two. After three courses and fig and grape pie, I'm stuffed, but Larry hints about getting *gelato* on the way home.

When we turn the corner from *Piazza Signorelli* to *Piazza della Repubblica,* we see the fashion show in full swing. Every plastic chair is filled and onlookers are standing, pressed against surrounding buildings. As we work our way around the outside, "Goldfinger" blares through a raspy loudspeaker and beautiful, young, stick-thin, expressionless models zigzag down the grand stone staircase. They wear seductive evening dresses — all gold of course. I wonder how they climb down that long stairway with such grace wearing four-inch stilettos. Of course, they weigh nothing. Not one girl smiles.

We find a spot to watch the finale. The bride in a revealing, translucent, white beaded gown floats down the stairway to the traditional wedding march. Eight attendants follow in dramatic bridesmaids' dresses with see-through skirts or plunging necklines, all in avant-garde colors: indigo, melon, chartreuse, and, the *pièce de résistance*, a form-fitting masterpiece of black and white waves.

Glamorous, expressionless models line the stage for a long, standing ovation. The famous designer bounds onto the platform, full of energy and all smiles. Someone gives him an armload of sunflowers and the Mayor presents him with the key to Cortona. The spotlights, now fully powered, cast an unnatural metallic glow on the designer, officials, models and even the audience. Larry guesses this grand spectacle is being watched by over a thousand people, all crowding into this small piazza.

Walking along *Via Nazionale*, I look again in Isa's window and kick myself for not buying that credenza when Larry said it was perfect. But it was expensive and we wanted to negotiate a better price.

"We should've bought it," Larry says when he sees me looking.

I ask if he thinks it's my fault that we didn't buy it.

He says I said I would negotiate the price. Since I didn't do what I said, then yes.

He could have done the negotiations too, I think.

Then he adds, "But we'll find something better. We can look together."

I decide to drop it.

Nearing the end of *Via Nazionale*, we hear a voice… gentle, warm, melodic. Most certainly, Brother Andrea. I see the back of a man in a brown robe on stage, head lowered, crooning into a microphone. Passing the stage, I can't take my eyes off this handsome bearded monk singing about his love for *Gesù,* and whisper to Larry that I'd like to stay for the concert. We find two seats along the edge.

Brother Andrea comes forward and sits on the edge of the stage, his robe around his legs and sandaled feet dangling, and sings a tender ballad. He seems to connect individually as he looks into the crowd, as he did with me the first time we met.

Larry guesses about eight hundred people are at this event. There are nuns and monks and priests, families with toddlers and strollers, couples, and elderly men and women, and lots of teens and twenty-somethings. No matter the age, everyone seems spellbound, just as they were on the other end of town for the fashion show.

In the next song, a hip, attractive girl confesses she was going the wrong way, then found Jesus, turned and started going the right way. Many in the audience sing along, seeming to know every word.

A young man with a huge Afro joins the girl. His hair is florescent pink under the spotlights. Other performers join in, including Brother Andrea. All except Andrea wear black and all have pink halo hair.

After a series of songs, Brother Andrea introduces each performer and crew member by name. The lead female singer, a beautiful girl of barely twenty, must be famous or local, because the crowd goes wild when he introduces her.

Suddenly, dancers rush onto the stage performing interpretive dance to shockingly hard rock music. Talented, athletic and completely natural, the dancers move as though they're expressing pure joy. Muscular and grinning, they are quite a contrast to the ultra-thin, expressionless models at the fashion show.

Brother Andrea announces the final song. Larry motions and we slip out to head home. On our way down the hill, we hear the long applause and another song begin. I wish we had stayed for the encore and to express our appreciation. But we are both tired and eager to be home.

The events of today were part of what is regularly experienced and celebrated in Italy, but we've never seen anything like this array in a single day. From freshly-made pasta, to home-grown produce and warm artisan cheese, to weddings, windstorms, and abundant wild figs, from a glitzy high fashion show to a gentle monk's concert, life in Cortona seems a rich cornucopia... a cornucopia of contrasts.

Scene from Fellini

Another storm awakens us during the night. The wind and rain are deafening. Water blows in from every direction, so we get up to close windows — upstairs and down. Chilled and damp, I pull up the covers and hope to go back to sleep despite the furor outside.

By dawn, the hillside is silent and still. No rain, no wind. The larks and sparrows have begun their morning chorus and I join Larry on the terrace. We have been given a fresh new day.

Above the horizon, a thin white streak crosses the sky like a morning comet. It's a jet, perhaps carrying vacationers south toward Sicily or Malta. Dogs bark and bark into the calm silence, more than usual. We understand hunting season starts today.

Boom!... boom! A pause. *Boom!... boom!* We both jump each time.

Before long, we hear people on the hill behind our house calling to one another.

"*Aspetta*," wait, one yells.

"*Ascolta*," listen, his buddy answers.

I hear the pop, pop of shots in the distance, then the loud ka-boom of shots nearby. Cheers, hollers and clapping erupt, then silence.

"They got one!" Larry exclaims.

"Already?" I say, not sure I like this jubilation over killing. Those *cinghiale* have peacefully mated, given birth, and raised their boar babies in our forests — until this morning.

A donkey in the valley starts to bray, disturbed by the noise. No more tranquility this morning, maybe not until hunting season ends.

"I think we should put up no hunting signs," I say.

"Oh, Victoria," Larry scoffs. He seems to be enjoying the show.

Suddenly, dogs' heads appear in the tall grass below the house, pacing back and forth searching for a scent in our olive groves. Men in orange vests follow, their long guns slightly raised. They seem too close to me.

It feels like we're in a Fellini film, where real life and fantasy merge. I'm dressed in a black silk robe, sitting in a cushioned wicker armchair on the front terrace of an old Tuscan farmhouse, sipping a cappuccino and looking into a long valley, while hunters with dogs encircle our home.

Ka-boom!! Ka-boom!! Those shots were close. No cheers. I'm glad.

Oliver says boar damage this year has been terrible, so locals are anxious to thin them out. We understand that, about fifty years ago, the enormous native Tuscan *cinghiale* became scarce and hunters were concerned they might disappear. Enterprising Tuscans imported wild boar from Eastern Europe. They were smaller, had two litters each summer rather than one, and each litter had more piglets. It didn't take long for them to inter-breed and over-populate. To find food, they rummage through farmer's fields, vineyards, and irrigated lawns, plowing up roots with their hard snouts, destroying everything in their path. So far, with no landscaping, we've had no problems.

We often see *cinghiale* crossing our road when we're driving home after dark. Typically, it's a mother with about six piglets trotting behind her. The adults are nearly black, have huge bulky bodies with blunt rumps, curved tusks on long snouts, thick necks, and a shockingly dainty trot. The little ones are light brown, spotted like fawns, and trot daintily just like mom.

After the hunters move on, Larry and I give up our role as extras in the Fellini scene to get ready for church. It's warm today, as if summer has returned.

At the car, Larry asks if I want to drive. I tell him I'm all dressed up, hoping that is a meaningful reason not to. He laughs and tells me again that I need practice. I know he's right and his instructions are excellent, but his tense posture, critical reactions, and severe tone make me so nervous it's hard to concentrate.

"Did I tell you Oliver offered to teach me?" I say lightly, buckling my *passenger* seat belt. "He says wives should never learn to drive from their husbands."

Larry starts the engine and says it's a nice offer, but if I don't want my husband's help, he's sure I can learn on my own. I hope he's teasing.

Approaching the S-curves, Larry stops to drag a tree branch off the road. It must have blown down during last night's storm. More bedrock has been exposed, jutting up more than four inches. Past the limb, wheel tracks suggest someone tried to navigate the muddy road earlier. Perhaps hunters. Even with this high-clearance Panda, we scrape bottom.

"When we buy a car, it needs to be all-wheel drive," Larry says gripping the wheel and keeping the Panda in first gear. "It's good that I'm driving today. This would've been hard for you."

It's all hard for me, I think. Driving a stick shift, speaking Italian, missing family, having no girlfriends, living in construction, and trying not to irritate Larry. Learning Italian will take years, and so will making friends, but they will happen. Construction will end. Driving is the one change that would make me independent and, therefore, give Larry his study time. Larry was kind about me not driving today and is trying to do his part. Since our dinner party, we do seem back in sync. He even sets the table and washes dishes without being asked. The big remaining hurdle is depending on him to take me everywhere.

At the main road, a man wearing camouflage is standing behind his van, blocking us. He puts his gun in the back of his van and pulls into Palazzone's carriageway to let us pass.

On the road to town, we have to slow down in several places where parts of an ancient stone wall have caved in and mud and gravel have washed across the pavement. Figs hang on trees, split open from so much rain. If not picked today, they will rot.

Larry parks at the bottom of *Via Ghibelline* in a tiny spot obstructed by a tree. His driving technique and confidence allow him to put that Panda in the space as if the tree doesn't exist. I watch him and wonder if I'll ever be able to drive as skillfully.

Lights are on at *La Bucaccia* though it's early, so we go in to make a reservation for Wednesday, our last dinner there for the summer. Romano is exuberant, as always.

"*Caffè?*" he asks.

Larry declines, saying we're late for Mass.

"*Si, caffè,*" he insists, "*Mass senza caffè a molto difficile.*" Mass without coffee is very difficult.

We arrive at the *Cattedrale* caffeine-loaded and still in time to find a program. Even in the heat, every woman, regardless of age, has her shoulders covered. I wonder how many years it will be before such mores will no longer matter. It does seem an old-world sensibility, but one I quite like. An elderly man with a cane comes in, guided by his son. The sweet girl with Down's Syndrome and her mother, always together, slide into the pew in front of us. A round-faced man, I believe named Giorgio, and his spitting-image toddler son are across the aisle. Many faces have become familiar, for which I'm thankful.

During the *Alleluia,* my eyes brim with tears, reflecting on a loving God who has given us the gift of our summer in this remarkable land. This is our last Sunday and I'm nostalgic. Next Sunday we'll be in Florence boarding the plane to Paris and on to Chicago.

Today there's an amusing new attraction. A little blonde girl, about four, wearing a pink dress with a stiff white collar, is sitting in one of the choir stalls at the side of the altar and swinging her legs from the too-high seat. During the responsive reading, she walks to the podium and stands beside the priest. Realizing all eyes are on his little pink helper, the priest taps her shoulder and points back to the choir stalls. She sits back there for the rest of his homily, smoothing her dress, stretching and shuffling her feet, occasionally waving at friends and family in the congregation. When we rise to pass the peace, she runs into the congregation to find her friends and vigorously shakes their hands.

Next, the priest stands at the altar to prepare the Eucharist. His pretty pink helper moves to a chair where priests' assistants normally sit. She perches tall and stately, smooths her skirt again, and waits. The priest continues as if she's not there.

While he reads the words of consecration, holding his hands toward heaven, his pink helper jumps up to stand with him, putting her hands toward heaven, too. At one point, she leaps up, trying to reach his hand. She can't quite grab it, so continues to hold both hands high, mimicking his lead.

While he serves the Eucharist, his helper swirls and twirls, dancing behind him. A younger girl joins her and they twirl together on the steps to the altar. Congregants line up the length of the long aisle to receive the wafer. Toward the end of the Eucharist, the girl's father grabs her and whisks her out the back door. It was his first chance to get her without interrupting the service. I smile, admiring the priest's patience and focus.

There are always children and families among the congregants, but seemingly more today. I like that children are comfortable in this church. I wish my daughters had grown up being at ease in church. North American churches typically are not tolerant of the slightest misbehavior, offering Sunday School for children instead of having them stay with their parents. There's something warm and natural about worshipping as families where all ages are welcome.

Walking to the car, I reflect on the priest's pink helper and how inclusive this church community is of children. It seems like God's design. After all, who says little girls can't dance in God's house?

Larry doesn't ask if I want to drive.

Almost Over the Edge

For days, I've put off my first solo, stick-shift drive. It's Monday and workers are back after their lunch break. Stores reopen at four. We need printer ink and groceries. It's time to take the Panda out on my own and practice driving — teaching myself, as Larry put it. By now, I have the gist of the manual transmission and my clutch-brake coordination no longer feels dangerous. It'll be a long time before I shift without looking at the pattern on the knob, even though I know it's an H. It'll be even longer before I shift without thinking.

Larry smiles, wishes me luck, and says he left the Panda facing outward to make it easier for me. I'm grateful. To manage shifting will be enough without needing to turn the car around, trying to avoid workers' vans, materials still lining the driveway, and the drop-off on one side.

Walking to the car, I mentally rehearse the steps. Buckle your seat belt. Put the key in the ignition. Make sure the parking brake is engaged. Put one foot on the clutch and the other on the brake. Turn the key. Put the car in the correct gear. Push the button on the end of the parking brake lever, ready to disengage the brake. Move your right foot from the brake to the accelerator with your left foot remaining on the clutch. Ease your foot off the clutch and put gentle pressure on the accelerator as you release the parking brake.

Above all, do not panic.

Thankfully, I don't need to drive far and can take back roads. I imagine the route: back road to Euronics for printer ink, main road to the grocery store, and back road home. How hard can this be?

No more mental procrastination. I stand at the car, take a deep breath, unlock the door and get in. Just do it. Millions of people do this. You'll be fine. What's the worst that can happen?

I start the car, release the hand and foot brakes, ease off the clutch as I press the accelerator. The car crawls forward. Thankfully, the driveway seems wider in the Panda than it did in the SUV. I concentrate on the gravel in front of me.

Still in first gear, I turn onto our access road and drive toward the S-curve. The Panda is not as heavy as the SUV, so it bounces even more over bedrock and ruts. I make the first curve, breathe a sigh of relief, and start downhill.

Suddenly, a small blue car darts around the lower curve and barrels uphill toward me. I jam the brakes. The Panda lurches, stalls, and skids. The right front wheel drops slightly when the grassy edge of the road gives away. I grip the wheel and hold my breath, waiting for the car to drop since the wheel is on the edge.

The driver of the other car jumps out and runs up the hill yelling in English, "Stop!!" He holds up both arms. I sit frozen.

It's Marco, the owner of the building company. He must be thinking the Italian equivalent of "woman driver!"

He opens my door and motions for me to get out. I'm humiliated, but more relieved and grateful. My car could have slid into the olive grove five feet below. It still might.

Marco starts the car without closing the door. I stand on the other side of the gravel lane. He gives the Panda plenty of gas and slowly backs it off the edge. When the car is on solid ground, he puts it in neutral, sets the emergency brake and motions for me to get in.

I say *"Grazie"* at least a dozen times. Marco smiles and nods sympathetically.

He backs his car into a flat area off the road and waits for me to pass. As I get closer, I see his father in the passenger seat and feel even more embarrassed.

I wave sheepishly and wonder how many workers will know of my near accident by the time I get home. All of them, I suspect. He'll certainly tell Francesco, since they talk every day.

I drive the rest of the access road in first gear, riding the clutch.

At the umbrella pine, I head left onto the blacktop and shift into second, then third. I pray not to meet anyone. If I do, one of us will have to back down or uphill to a driveway where we can pass, and the driveways are far apart.

The Panda picks up speed on the narrow lane down a steep hill. I press on the brake. When it still goes too fast for my comfort, I downshift into second.

Adrenalin is pumping. "Slow down. Breathe. You are fine," I say out loud.

I make it down the hill without meeting anyone, pass the church of *San Michele Arcangelo*, my favorite neighborhood structure, and carefully ease onto the main road between Pergo and Cortona. Drivers speed on this road. I'll hold a steady pace no matter how many cars line up behind me. It's ridiculous to let some pushy driver behind me decide my speed for me.

Two cars pass and a third stays on my tail, but I do not speed up. I engage my signal and turn left onto the straight, flat road to Ossaia. I feel steadier, take another deep breath, roll down my window and look across fields of sunflowers on both sides of the road. I notice I am holding my breath again, so let out a long exhale. These sunflowers look golden and happy.

I am driving. In control. All by myself. I have made it through three intersections without stalling. Except for the one incident, I have done just fine. Actually, if our builder had not whipped around the corner and startled me, I'd have been okay on the S-curve too.

This little car is manageable. Even more important, this car is fun!

I feel exhilarated! Liberated!!! *This is freedom!*

I downshift behind a tractor. Fortunately, it turns onto a country lane so I don't need to pass. A little free-fall surprises me as I whiz over the rise above of one of the canal-ditches. I wonder if this was one of the Etruscan canals that Leonardo di Vinci re-used in his plan to drain the valley swamp centuries ago.

Joy pulses through me like an electrical surge that makes me feel lighter. I am driving and happy and free.

I recall the moment after my divorce at age twenty-five, when I realized I could handle anything that came my way: being a single mom of two young daughters, not having money, being depressed, being afraid. I had faced and survived it all. When I landed a meaningful job that gave me a new future, it was a sea-change moment. I shifted from being a victim to being the one who sets my objectives and defines my character. This seems another of those moments. After feeling so discombobulated by all the things I didn't know this summer, doubting myself, and becoming dependent on Larry, at this moment I feel like my old confident and positive self.

But it is more than regaining my self-esteem and sense of competence. This summer I have been undone, challenged, enlarged, and enriched by being immersed in another culture, expanding my perspective. The weeks ahead will be telling, but this moment I sit taller, assured and inspired.

Turning around in Ossaia, I drive the straight, blacktopped road again. At a turn off to Camucia along the canal, I settle in. I love this country road, passing a small field of tobacco, then more sunflowers. A mother, father and two children tend their small vineyard. The mother looks up as I pass.

"See how well I drive?" I holler out the window, but she goes back to her task without hearing me.

At the end of the road, I must turn left onto the busy road between Camucia and Terontola. At least the intersection is flat and there's not much traffic. I put the car into first gear, glance at the knob to make sure I got it right, watch both ways for a break in the two-direction traffic and ease onto the road. With a little speed, the Panda starts to moan and I shift to second gear. Cars, trucks and scooters pass me. I don't care. I shift into third and speed up when my sweet Panda and I are ready. At Euronics, there are easy, open parking spaces. I set the parking brake, turn off the engine, and slump with a long exhale.

Resuming normal breathing, I unfasten my seat belt and get out. Standing up, I feel wobbly at first, then taller.

Having control of this car feels familiar and good, better than any driving in the past four months. From Euronics, I drive to the grocery store without problems, pay and bag my groceries with ease, and head home on the same winding country road. I wave at the family still in their vineyard, certain my shifting is smoother.

Driving up our access road, I keep the car in first gear, slowly climb the hill and make the curves without incident. The indentation where my tire pushed the grass and dirt over the edge is obvious. I wonder how many years will pass before I stop looking at that spot.

At Lodolina, none of the workers snicker as I pass. Perhaps they don't know yet, but I feel certain Marco will tell them.

"How was it?" Larry asks when I walk into the house.

"*Excellent*. I did great!! I had one close call on the S-curve. Marco Tripponcini came around the bottom curve really fast. I panicked and stalled the car. He had to rescue me. I may never live it down, but, boy, was I thankful for his help."

"What do you mean, 'rescue you'?"

"Well, when I jammed on the brake, the car slid to the edge. The right tire sort of pushed the dirt over the edge and sunk down a little."

"Victoria! That was dangerous!"

"Probably. But it wouldn't have happened if I hadn't been startled when Marco came around the curve."

Larry looks at me skeptically, sees I am grinning, and takes me in his arms.

"I'm just glad you're safe."

"Really, I *loved* it. It felt like flying. I think I'll be fine with a stick shift... someday."

"Of course, you will. You'll learn to love it. Do you want to drive to town for dinner tonight?"

"How 'bout if we stay home? I got groceries today and we can read and go to bed early. Too bad we don't have a TV."

"I might have other ideas," Larry says.

"I need a quiet, restorative evening. Reading will be good. We'll see," I reply, amused at his predictable desire.

Today I regained my freedom, confidence, and self-respect. They seem to go hand-in-hand. We'll see what else changes, now that I have changed.

Last Walk to Town

A car door slams. The sun is already bright, warming my shoulder as I lie in bed and look out the window. When we moved to Lodolina in June, the sun rose behind the cypress trees. Three months later, the earth has shifted and the morning sunshine pours directly in, illuminating the bedroom. The sun must shine in all winter long, a farmer's wisdom about where to place his *camera di letto* and plant his *cipressi* trees.

I pull on my robe and walk downstairs. Larry, up for hours, says he has a piercing headache. We had no wine last night, so I wonder what's going on. Allergies or stress… probably stress. There is a great deal to do before we leave day after tomorrow. Workers have already started. They, too, have a list to finish today.

We're at Francesco's office at ten o'clock, the appointed time. We expect our final meeting to take an hour, but three hours later we're still choosing finishes and fixtures so progress can be made while we're in Chicago. Lastly, we sign a power of attorney, just in case.

We ask Francesco to join us for lunch, but he's eager to go with the builders to transport our stone table top from the stonecutter's to the ironworker's and talk directly with Lukas, the artisan for the table base. When we return, Francesco promises, we'll have an outdoor dining table.

Oliver is late for our evening appointment. After waiting for an hour with no call, we give up, get ready for dinner, and start to town for our final goodbyes. He pulls into the drive as we're walking out, so we reschedule for morning. I warn him tomorrow will be crazy. Our last day. He apologizes that he was delayed by a client emergency, saying with a smile that he must take care of regular clients before new ones, and promises to be on time and out of our hair quickly tomorrow. I feel surprisingly sentimental saying goodbye to him.

Dressing for dinner, Larry happily observes that his pants are a bit big. Even with the summer's excellent food and wine, his daily runs have carved off some inches. I'm not so pleased, as my pants have shrunk. Nonetheless, I do feel healthier.

On our climb to town, I almost keep up with Larry. At the top, he applauds.

"You didn't even slow down," he says. "Well done."

"I'm in better shape than when we got here," I say. "It's the hills. And determination." My heart pounds as I catch my breath.

At *La Bucaccia*, Francesca jumps into my arms. Romano yells from inside, "Victory!" Such warm greetings make Cortona feel even more like home.

Dinner is as excellent as ever, and we both eat more than we intend, despite intentions to eat less. The *gnudi*, spinach and ricotta dumplings — still my favorite dish — are especially good tonight.

After dinner, Francesca gives us a handmade wooden flower to take to Sydney. It says, "Friends Forever."

When I ask for the bill. Romano breaks into a dramatic melody of "Oh, Victoria…," arms widespread. I laugh, realizing I asked for *il canto*, the song, not *il conto*, the bill.

At least I remembered flashlights for our walk home. I'm sad, knowing this may be the last walk down this trail until next summer. When we return in October the weather may be too cold for walking. The night air already feels like fall and I pull my sweater tighter.

Near the house, after we pass the construction materials and just before he opens the construction fence gate, Larry stops. "Will you take my hand… please?" He pulls me close, takes my face in his hands and kisses me lovingly.

"Do you remember that Sunday in June when we met Francesco to inspect Lodolina? We walked up this driveway holding hands. You almost ran you were so excited. Gabriele was here… and Rita. It seems like yesterday, and yet so long ago. So much has changed."

"Really, like what?" I tease. "Our driveway's still filled with stacks of materials and the yard's a construction site."

He kisses me again and I melt into his tenderness. I don't want to count on it, but tenderness has become the norm. Yes, we have learned a great deal about fitting into a foreign culture, but we've learned even more about respect, compassion, listening, helping one another, resets, planning together, and how to be partners in a time of significant change.

I think back to our first morning in June when we began, as Larry put it, "our new life." The bumps on the access road had jolted us… physically. Since then, we've been surprised by bumps of all kinds, especially mental and emotional ones. I didn't expect to live in construction, or be afraid to drive, or feel so intimidated fitting into in our new culture — a culture I thought I knew and loved. In fact, it's almost worse when you think you know what to expect.

What I really didn't expect was that Larry and my relationship would suffer so much from our naivety. He thought life in Tuscany would be a study sabbatical. I thought it would be an extended vacation. I now know: life here never will be a vacation. It is everyday life. I suspect there will be more adjusting to come, but we'll both handle it better.

Character may not change when our situation changes, but perceptions do. And when perceptions change, behavior changes. Our perceptions about life in Italy and one another have become richer this summer and, as a result, our behavior toward one another has shifted. Understanding life from the other's view, our marriage is deeper, more conscious of the other, more playful and joy-filled. It is through overcoming struggles that we become stronger, and we have become stronger.

I know now that life in Italy will never be as easy as life in America, and that there will be many more adjustments to come. But I also know it's worth it. Grasping that reality — that life will be both exasperating and exhilarating for as long as we live in Italy — will make it easier.

On the other hand, perhaps that's why I feel more alive here — because it is *not* easy.

Now We Write for Friendship

"What's that?" Larry groans, roused from his sleep in the dark of night. Ring… ring… ring…

"Sounds like the phone." I murmur, not ready to be awakened either.

"Who would call at this hour?" he asks.

"Wrong number. Or… an emergency," I reply, feeling a rush of concern.

Larry stumbles out of bed and finds his way downstairs to the closet, yelping as he hits his toe on the stair rail. The ringing continues.

"*Pronto,*" ready, I hear as he lifts the receiver.

I hold my breath, listening hard. He hangs up without saying anything. It must be a wrong number. Or, news he needs to tell me in person.

"Who was it?" I ask when he's near.

"A fax. It'll probably ring again," he says, crawling into bed and curling up with me.

"So, this is what happens when we get a phone that works?" I ask.

I slip out of his arms to close the door. We do not need an automatic fax redial to keep waking us. We have a big day ahead.

Turning to face my little arched window with Larry's arm still draped across my waist, I gaze out at the hillside. Stars pierce the night sky and moonlight frosts the olive trees. Soon the sky will become indigo — dawn of our last day of our first summer living in Italy.

In the distance a dog barks, perhaps hoping for another hunt. I hear rustling by the stream. Could be boar, fox, deer or porcupine. The valley seems to come to life with the dawn.

"EoUUo, oUUo." Then again, "EoUUo, oUUo."

"What's that?" I whisper, hoping Larry's still awake. But he breathes heavily, making a little rustling noise with each inhale.

I try to hear it again… surely an owl. Our neighbor Lyndall says we have owls and nightingales. We've heard the nightingales, but this is my first owl. As daylight brightens, birds with different voices begin to add their songs… tweeting, whistling, warbling, trilling, and chirping. It's a symphony, as if we live in an aviary. Among other hillside songbirds, this morning I think I can pick out the exquisite song of the lark, *la lodola*.

How interesting that after almost one hundred dawns of listening to hillside wildlife, on my last morning I hear a new sound, the owl. But that's what life here has been — always something new.

I drift off. When I open my eyes again, the entire sky is coral.

I should get up. Today I must do laundry, make tomato sauce to freeze, draw designs for drawer inserts, and wrap a gift for Carlo's baby — all before Francesco arrives — plus answer emails, record yesterday in my journal, and pack for a month. The gas man will come with Gabriele at nine, the glass-wall installer at ten, then Oliver at eleven. Tomorrow we must drive away before the sun is up.

I wish we had more hours today, more days this week, more weeks in our last month at Lodolina. I am not ready to leave.

Larry is dressed and typing on his laptop when I come downstairs. I scribble my plan for today so I don't miss anything, confirm it works with his plan, and go to the kitchen to make my last Lodolina cappuccino for this summer. Larry insists on making it for me.

Workers have been here an hour when Gabriele arrives with the gas man and his father. Larry signs a contract for a year's service. The gas man apologizes that the invoice has not arrived from their company for the gas delivered in May. We agree, at his suggestion, to pay both invoices when we return in October. I'm surprised there's not more urgency about being paid, but this happens often with Italian vendors. The gas man tells us we're eligible for an eight *centesimi* per liter discount, roughly ten cents, because we live in an agricultural designation.

Then the father gives us advice, in Italian, about conserving fuel. Gabriele interprets. The gas man says it's important in life to conserve. He says we should always run the faucet on cold unless we absolutely must have hot water, because it's expensive to start the in-line water heater. In four months, we have used five hundred liters of GPL, liquid petroleum gas, half of a tank. Too much for summer, he scolds. Italians are conservative about anything that requires gas or electricity, both more expensive than in America. Fuel for cooking, he said, doesn't take much, so I should not worry. I smile, thinking Italians must place a higher value on cooking than on heating their homes.

I clean out the *frigo* and start the *odori* for a sauce of leftover tomatoes, which I'll freeze. Someday I'll have a garden and make tomato sauce stored in glass jars in our cantina for the winter, like a proper Italian *nonna*, grandmother.

Oliver arrives on time to say goodbye, deliver our bill, and discuss a budget for future work. He offers to check on Lodolina while we're away. We assure him the workers will be here every day except Sundays, but that his service could be important after the construction is complete. He promises to be easy to reach and on time, like he was today, now that we are clients.

I feel like I'm on autopilot, preparing Lodolina to be empty. Are we really leaving?

The bathroom glass walls are delivered at two o'clock. The workers told Gabriele they'd come at eleven, then changed to three, now have come before their appointment. Poor Gabriele had the appointments arranged so he could help, waited around with nothing to do, finally left, and now must hurry back. So much of our summer has been about waiting. I remember when Enza promised that Italy would teach us patience.

Four men unload wall-size frosted glass panels from a truck designed to transport glass sheets. Even so, I wonder how they got that truck up our bumpy hill without shattering them. While the walls are being installed, I transform our clothing drawers back into suitcases and find fall clothes in the wardrobe boxes in the living room. It'll be nippy in Chicago.

Francesco arrives late afternoon to say goodbye and check out the long-anticipated glass walls. I want to experience his expression when he first sees them, so rush upstairs into the bathroom and turn around before he enters.

"Looks to be perfect," he says, his whole face lighting up. "I was so worried. We measure and measure, but nothing at Lodolina is square. The first walls came in May, before you arrive, but we must send them back because they do not fit perfectly. I do not like when that happens. Now I am happy."

After inspecting the glass walls, Francesco asks if I'd like to mark the place to hang my antique sconce so the electrician can install it while we're away.

I'm thrilled. I thought the sconce would have to wait for our return.

Pulling it out of the living room fireplace where it's been stored all summer, I unwind the bubble wrap and carry it to the powder room. Francesco says we must decide the position "for forever," as wiring must be pulled through the wall. Like we did in June, we find the perfect placement, observe that the gold-leafed, antique sconce is too large and too fancy for this closet-sized toilet room, and remark that it gives the space an unexpected sense of whimsy. We laugh, agreeing we both love it, and Francesco marks the wall.

I ask him if we'll get Lodolina reports with photos every Saturday like in the past. He says there is no need; we have closed the works and made the last choices.

"Now we write for the friendship, not for the project," Francesco says, with a hint of wistfulness.

I have grown to love this man. Many people who renovate a home develop a special affection for their architect, but our experience seems to have surpassed a normal renovation.

Francesco also promises that before we return, they will prepare the area around the horse chestnut for landscaping. It will transform the entire property simply to take away the orange plastic fences.

"And the materials along the driveway?" I ask, with a hint of pleading.

"No... they must stay until the works on the guesthouse are closed. Only then we remove the equipment and materials," Francesco says firmly, but smiling. I've never told him the shock of our first day, when we saw the construction piles, or that we have become so accustomed to them now that we hardly notice.

Larry and I reluctantly say goodbye to Francesco and Gabriele. It was not long ago that we said our summer hellos. I'll never forget the ceremonial opening of the hidden door. I'll never forget so many of our times together.

"Thank you for the remarkable job creating our home. We will miss you," Larry says, with a little catch in his voice.

"But you will be back in four weeks," Francesco protests. "It is barely enough time for Pierangelo to move the dirt and for me to make a holiday with Rita. We will go to Greece, after all. We are very happy."

Turning to me, he asks, "Is there anything else on your famous Lodolina list?"

He doesn't seem to want to leave, either. I shake my head slowly.

After more kisses on both cheeks, Larry and I stand on the front terrace hand-in-hand and watch Francesco and Gabriele walk up the dirt construction ramp. I long to give them each a big American hug, but fear they would not know what to do. Italian traditions are firmly held and don't easily include real hugs.

Later in the afternoon, we drive into Cortona to finish our goodbyes, especially with Marco and Ivan, and do some last-minute gift shopping. Cortona still feels like vacation to me, but the simpler things of everyday life — morning skies, animal sounds, tempestuous storms, leisurely conversations — have become as important to me as Italy's food, wine, and art were to us on our honeymoon.

At home we finish packing and eat a quick dinner of leftovers. Suitcases packed and lists completed, despite physical exhaustion, we decide to drive back to town for one last concert in *Chiesa San Filippo Neri*. We've walked past that church with the verdigris dome dozens of times but never have been inside.

The audience, packed into every pew, soon becomes transfixed. The musical drama is about Padre Pio, a beloved Capuchin brother who was born in 1887, dies in 1968, and was canonized as a saint in 2002 by Pope John Paul II. When the concert ends, the audience applauds relentlessly, hoping for an encore.

The conductor steps forward and turns his head side to side. *"Non abbiamo preparato altro. Buona notte."* We haven't prepared anything else. Good night. To me, he was correct to end at a high point. We must do the same with our summer.

Back home, I cannot fall asleep, mulling over our experiences. Starting with the first morning, every day was filled with the unexpected. I became more aware of details. I learned that feeling uncomfortable is part of fitting in, how lonely life can be without family and friends, especially girlfriends, and how the tension between Larry and me made the loneliness worse. I discovered that it's possible, even at my age, to lose courage and self-assuredness, to become overly dependent on my husband. I've been stretched and challenged, and the difficulties have widened and deepened my perspective.

Unexpected, too, were the crevices that appeared in our marriage, some were new but some were cracks Larry and I had ignored for years. Through painful interactions and honest conversations, we have come to a new place of trust and appreciation, a stronger yet softer place, with humor and a new lightness. As I suspected that first morning, Lodolina has changed us more than we have changed it.

We are still creating our new life, and we are emerging from our first summer as different people — the same, yet stretched beyond our expectations. Oliver Wendell Holmes observed "Man's mind, stretched to a new idea, never goes back to its original dimension." I also believe man's heart, stretched by a new perspective — of the world, and of the needs and feelings of loved ones — is forever altered.

Next summer will be different. We'll be less naïve and more realistic about our dreams, but we will still dream and reach for those dreams. The construction materials and workers will be fond memories. I'll plant a garden and build a compost bin. I'll find girlfriends and take Italian lessons. We'll walk to town holding hands and linger over a cappuccino in the piazza. I'll still listen for the song of the lark, be enchanted by the nightingale, and smile when the black squirrel dines in the cypress tree.

Rewinding the Film

Rising before the sun, I take a last look from my little arched window. The ridges are outlined with a faint peach glow, but the valley is dark. With autumn approaching, the earth sleeps a little later each day.

After a last cappuccino and quick goodbye to the farmer's house we now call home, Larry locks the hidden door behind us. We wheel our suitcases past the stacks of materials and drive away under the canopy of tree branches, down the bumpy access road, and onto the asphalt road toward the *autostrada* to the Florence airport.

At the turn, I blow a kiss to the tiny roadside shrine on the high corner of the stone wall and pray for safe travels and a speedy return.

Larry watches me and says, his voice heavy with emotion, "Thank you for four wonderful months."

"Thank you too, my love." I reply softly. "So, what was the best part for you?"

"Sitting in front of the house, looking into the valley," he says without hesitating. "I miss it already."

"Me too. We've sure learned a lot this summer… *I've* learned a lot."

"*Dimmi*," he says. Tell me.

At that instant we reach the exact spot where, on the morning we arrived, he asked if I was ready for our new life.

"Well," I reply, "the biggest lesson was how much harder and more intimidating life in a different culture is than I expected. I felt awkward most of the time. It's okay to look stupid on vacation when you'll never see anyone again, but not when you live in a place. I felt more like a foreigner this summer than ever before."

We'll always be foreigners," Larry says. "We're Americans. I'm glad we're Americans. Even when we're comfortable speaking Italian and know our way around, we'll still be Americans."

"That's the one thing every expat eventually learns: no matter how engaged we become in Cortona, we will always be *stranieri*… foreigners," I nod.

"What else did you learn?" he probes.

"Hmm. Obviously, I learned to drive a stick shift… and cook new foods. I learned about how different Italian building construction is from American construction… and the impossibility of *Telecom Italia*. And how important knowing the language is to get around in a new culture… even to *understand* a culture. About life in a small town. And, I learned how much I missed everyone back home. Not the place, just the people. Especially the girls and my mom."

Teasing but not teasing, I add, "I also learned that my husband can be very difficult… and very wonderful."

When he doesn't react, I turn toward him and ask, "So, what did *you* learn?"

"That I have the best wife in the world," he answers, again without hesitation.

Suddenly, a tractor pulls onto the road in front of us and Larry has to slow to a crawl. I'm charmed by tractors on country roads. It feels like turning the clock back to a simpler time, when people grew their own food and made their own tools — a time of farmers and artisans. Locals tell us young people don't want to become farmers and artisans any more. Life on the land is too hard. I wonder how long we'll see tractors on our roads.

Larry's cell phone rings. He hands it to me to answer. It's Francesco making sure we got off okay. I tell him about the tractor and my belief that life here is changing.

"Ah, yes. We see the sunset on this kind of world," he says, and I suspect he understands much more than we ever will.

I thank him for our summer, our perfect home, all we did together, and his friendship.

For a moment, I hear only his breathing.

Then he says, his voice deeper than normal and a little wobbly, "It has been a pleasure for me, too. A rare pleasure in my career."

Larry motions for the phone, adds his thank you and a goodbye from us both, then hangs up and turns to me, saying, "I feel incredibly blessed, don't you? It was a tough summer in many ways, but the best summer of my life."

"Me too. You know, if the house had been finished when we got here, like we expected, this summer would *not* have been the same. We wouldn't have struggled as much, or learned as much… or needed each other as much," I say, watching harvested fields glide by on both sides.

"I even learned to like planning together… and the value of resets," I confess. "And I *loved* our first dinner party. Thank you for asking so many times how you could help… and for setting the table so beautifully. It was fun to work together. I felt important to you that night."

"I like helping you… I want to do more of that when we get back." Larry reaches to take my hand, kisses it, then puts it back on my lap with a gentle squeeze.

"It does seem that by the end of the summer we got back into sync," he says.

"Remember when you asked if I was ready for our new life on that first day? I was surprised. To me, we were moving to a summer house for an extended vacation, not to a new life. But we *are* forging a new life, a different life, and I'm glad to be doing it with you. Even when it was difficult, I knew you loved me. And even when we were not our best, you're still the finest man I know."

Larry, deep in thought for a moment, says, "Victoria, joy is not the opposite of pain, they exist at the same time. Love is the source of comfort within pain. It is the source of all meaningful joy."

I'm silent to let that idea sink in. "You know, for most of the summer I felt lost, like I had lost myself and maybe you. But now I feel stronger, more confident, even more than before we moved…. You may not like me becoming so independent," I tease.

Reaching to take my hand again, he kisses my palm like he did that first morning when we drove from Florence to Cortona, holding it to his lips for a long time.

While he reflects some more on the good times of our summer, I lean my head against the window and listen to this man who still surprises and enchants me.

I realize that this difficult summer, painful and lonely, may be a turning point in our marriage. If the house had been finished and our summer had been as we expected, our marriage would not be as strong as it seems now. We always learn from challenges. It is when we are pushed beyond our limits and deal with adversity that we become stronger.

When we get back to Chicago, everyone will want to know what life in Cortona is like. I don't know how to describe it, except to say that when we return it will be time to plant roses and lavender, and to pick the olives.

Our first summer will never happen again. It was the beginning of our new life and now the chapter is closing. I feel like Grover at the end of the Muppet book when he says, "Noooo, don't turn that page." Of course, Grover thinks there's a monster at the end of the book. I simply don't want the story to end.

Larry pays the toll and takes the airport exit.

Like a film being re-wound, we turn in our rental car, pull our luggage along the cracked sidewalk, and walk into the terminal. I relinquish my suitcase to the ticket agent and watch it disappear. It'll be strange to be in Chicago without a home, but good to stay with our friends Dick and Tedi. I'll make eggplant parmesan and *gnudi* for our dinners, and rock cakes with the Pane Nero flour I packed in my suitcase.

As our plane rises, I can see the terracotta roofs of Florence, this astonishing Renaissance city, my favorite in the world. I blow a kiss to the Duomo and wave, curling my fingers closed and open... the wave that begs come hither as it says farewell.

Larry puts his hand on my shoulder and I turn to smile at him through my tears. He touches my chin with his fingertips and I see that his eyes are wet, too.

"We'll be back soon," he assures me. "Will you go to market with me on the first Saturday we're home? You can buy me a cappuccino on the piazza, like you promised."

Years Later

We are year-round residents of Cortona. I've grown accustomed to the rhythm of daily Tuscan life and what felt impossible and intimidating has become normal and comfortable. We both say it's the happiest time of our lives, and we still discover new things about this place we call home and about each other.

We own a little yellow Fiat Panda 4 x 4 and I am fearless, as Larry predicted, happily maneuvering Cortona's steep, narrow stone streets, meandering though rolling hills and valleys, and charging up our access road. The manual transmission gives me more control, not less. We improved our road after six years of bumping over gullies and bedrock. The indentation where I nearly skidded over the edge, there for years, is now mostly washed away.

My Italian is improving and I have more confidence to speak, but too often suffer frozen moments when I don't understand or can't compose a phrase. Larry's Italian is good, but he is not fluent. He insists he wasn't good at all that first summer. When you become better at something, you appreciate how little you knew before.

At Lodolina, roses bloom from May to November, jasmine climbs the pergola and rosemary tumbles over walls along the stone path to the front door. Lemon trees in my non-traditional lion pots grace the back terrace. At each summer's end, I fill the house with bundles of aromatic lavender stalks and tuck sachets into my lingerie drawer, still without La Perla. My herb garden produces more basil, parsley, oregano, sage, thyme, mint, lemon verbena, chives, and borage than I can use, and in November I hang bundles of herbs to dry for winter seasonings. A small *orto*, vegetable garden, gives us zucchini, tomatoes, green beans, lettuce, kale, and strawberries. A nearby compost bin transforms our vegetable scraps into fertilizer.

The little black squirrel still feasts on cypress cones. Every few years his markings change, so I think this season's shy visitor must be a grandchild or great grandchild of my first Lodolina friend.

Reluctantly, we put screens on all the windows since my reaction to insect bites has intensified and, kissed by the Tuscan sun, my skin seems all the more succulent to them. We try to catch uninvited intruders — scorpions, crickets, daddy-long-legs, stinkbugs, and lizards — and return them to the wild.

My kitchen counters are mottled with *macchie*, stains, which I don't try to remove. Our friend Marco was right when, at our first dinner party, he said shadows would make the stone more beautiful. Not long ago, I showed Francesco a *pietra serena* threshold that was flaking and becoming rounded, thinking we should replace it. He sighed… "Ah, Lodolina becomes beautiful."

In this ancient land there's a deep appreciation for the old — for worn places, stains and patina. Living here, we've learned to value the markings of age. When ancient things are too cleaned up or made too perfect, they seem to lose their soul. I believe patina wears well on people too, that we all become more attractive as our sharp edges soften and wear away.

Larry and I linger with friends — Italians and other expats — over lunches and dinners at our long travertine table under the *ippocastano* tree. He sometimes helps me cook, usually sets the table, and washes dishes after every meal. He now loves Saturday morning, when we go to market together. Each year, I feel more respected, valued and supported. He has become better than the husband of my dreams, and he says I'm a better wife than he could have imagined.

I have good girlfriends, not one, but several. It's important since someone is always away. Each season, new people arrive and our lives are enriched in some unique way. Sadly, each season someone we treasure moves away.

Larry was invited to join the local chapter of Rotary International. He's the only foreigner. Francesco was his sponsor, and Francesco and Rita remain our good friends.

My favorite month is October, olive harvest. We rake the long branches with finger-like tools and olives bounce onto nets below. Crates of green, black and magenta fruit are stacked in Oliver's van and taken to the local mill. After a few hours, we drive home with a stainless-steel tank of our own shockingly green, fragrant, *piccante* oil. Our olive oil won first place in the local Rotary contest two different years, to the surprise and delight of our Italian friends. An olive tree expert guessed that at least one of our trees was eight hundred years old.

Sadly, our olive harvest has been decimated three years of ten, once by June hail and twice by olive fly infestations. In those years, we are reminded how fortunate we are not to be real farmers, dependent on crops for our livelihood.

Oliver and his team take care of our property year-round. He's timely, proficient, loyal, ever-helpful and my knight in shining armor if I have problems when Larry is out of town.

We now laugh at the endless challenges of living in Italy. One summer a few years ago, our well ran dry the morning that houseguests arrived. For days, we had to drive to a neighbor for showers. The Comune took nine months to grant permission for a new well. More frustrated than we with the delay, for nine months the well-digger trucked water up the hill every few days to fill our cistern.

During one dry August, desperately thirsty cinghiale broke through our electric fence and tore our irrigated lawn to smithereens — night after night. Each day we put the patches back like a puzzle and the next night the boars uprooted it up again. We eventually just let them enjoy the moist roots and Oliver re-seeded in September.

While internet speed has improved, *Telecom Italia* service still fails at the worst possible times. Our landline phone is down as I type and our mobile phones never work at home because the signal in our valley is too weak. The electrical power continues to go out during storms, or whenever *Enel* does a hillside repair.

Like other expats, we will never understand the ever-changing Italian laws and bureaucracy. Since we've chosen to live here, we do our best to follow the rules and contribute appropriately. We understand that no matter how long we live here, we will always be *stranieri*, foreigners, and feel honored to be accepted and welcomed as full-time guests.

Distance from family is still painful for me. Our kids and grandkids visit as often as possible, which is never enough. My mother came for two weeks when she was eighty-eight and I visited her several times each year, but will always regret being five thousand miles away when, at ninety-four, she took her last earthly breath.

Larry and I still have ups and downs like any normal couple, but that uniquely stressful summer taught us how to listen, be respectful and kind no matter what, care about the other's needs and dreams, overlook the small stuff, and be better partners. We talk more than ever, because we learned that real listening and sharing shifts perspective and perspective changes behavior. In fact, of all the changes in all our years in Italy, the shift in perspective that living in a new culture brings may be the biggest. And, yes, we still need an occasional "reset."

That first summer, we didn't just create a new life, we emerged as changed people — the same, yet stretched beyond our former selves. As minds can be stretched to new ideas, never returning to their original shape, so can hearts. When we gain a new, deeper appreciation of a loved one's needs, fears, and feelings, it changes our thoughts and behavior. That first summer challenged and stretched us, and we will never be the same, as individuals or as partners.

In our ten years of living here, there have been many losses — as there are in every life, in any place or culture. Several couples in this story, Italian and American, are no longer together and we were deeply saddened by each. Ron and Paulla divorced seven years after their first visit to Lodolina and Ron became a single dad, embracing custodial responsibility for his three teenage daughters. He then fell in love with Blayn, they married, and our family expanded to embrace Blayn and her three children. We remain thrilled for Ron, as he and Blayn seem perfectly matched to be lifelong partners and loving parents for all their children.

Tragically, Sydney, Ron's daughter, our granddaughter, was killed in an automobile accident on the afternoon of her eighteenth birthday. Sydney's death eclipsed any pain we have ever felt, and Larry and I clung to each other more tightly than we knew was possible. We will never be the same, neither will our family nor anyone who knew her. We are grateful for our belief that in eternity we will be reunited. Sydney's teen motto, persevere, inspires me still.

* * *

When Larry read the first half of *The Little Lark Still Sings*, all I had written at the time, I could hear him sniffling in the other room. I had been cooking and just sat down at the kitchen table that serves as my desk. He stood beside me and took both my hands in his, as if he needed my full attention. He had known what the book was about, but reading it was different.

"I have three things to say," he whispered, his voice gravelly and eyes rimmed with tears.

"First, thank you for writing such a beautiful record of our first summer at Lodolina. It will be a good book. You've told the truth, simply and with insight, true to your rules for writing."

"Second, I made our first summer more difficult for you. You were lonely, trying to fit into a new culture, and working hard to make our perfect home in a house under construction. I knew you needed my help more than ever. But I was selfish, wanting time for my own projects. I wasn't a very good husband... or a very good friend."

Then he knelt, still holding my hands, and looked up at me.

"Lastly, I am deeply sorry. Will you forgive me?"

I looked down at this remarkable man and felt my heart might burst.

Taking his searching face in my hands, I said, "Of course I forgive you. I love you."

His smile broadened and that little dimple appeared in his chin, the one that melts me. He stood, extended his hand inviting me to stand, and took me in his arms.

After a long embrace, I leaned away from him and asked a question that had troubled me all these years, "Do you think our story's too private to publish?"

Larry paused thoughtfully, then said, "Victoria, we're humans, deeply flawed like all humans. Me especially. Maybe being honest about our struggles will help someone else who is struggling. Perhaps something we learned will be useful to someone we don't even know. I'm sorry I wasn't a good husband then; I hope I'm better now and will be even better next year. It was not easy, but that summer gave us the marriage we have today. Of course you must publish your book."

My admiration for Larry, already high, took another leap, and I saw anew the competent, wise, loving man I married all those years ago. A man who is courageous and humble enough to want to grow.

* * *

Dreams do not always come true. But once in a while what happens is better than the dream.

And early each morning, in the tall cypress trees outside our bedroom window, the black squirrel munches on cypress cones and the little lark sings.

Acknowledgments

My first *grazie mille* must go to the people of Cortona, with deep gratitude for their kind and increasingly warm welcome. Open-hearted, hard-working, generous Cortonese have been welcoming strangers for centuries. Hospitality is deeply rooted in Cortonese character, and Larry and I have been fortunate recipients.

Grazie to Lorenzo Lucani for insisting that *La Lodolina* was our perfect house, even after we said no. And to Francesco Rapini for brilliantly, creatively, skillfully — and yes, ever-so-cleverly — turning a near-ruin into our beloved Tuscan home. Thank you, Francesco, even more for your friendship. Knowing you enriches our lives every day.

My deepest gratitude to Larry for asking me about my dreams on our first date and for encouraging me to reach for them ever since. Thank you for your courage, saying that I must publish our story though it reveals aspects of each of us we would rather the world didn't know. Without you, the little lark never would have hatched, taken flight, or shared her song.

Ruth Senter, author/editor and friend, worked tirelessly with me for seven years. Thank you immeasurably for teaching me to become a better writer as you guided me to make a better book. Not everyone adores working with their editor, but you were as grace-filled and encouraging as you were tough. I'm still astounded that, together, we read the entire early manuscript printed — and then again aloud!

Thank you, Mikael Melbye, portraitist/landscape-artist/opera-star/ friend, for generously offering to take a professional photo of Lodolina when you knew I was struggling — and for climbing that olive tree to get just the right angle. And for taking such a flattering photo of me.

Thank you, Barry Svigals, architect/creative-force/artist/friend, for making time in the midst of demanding projects to create our beautiful lark for the cover. She's lovely, shy but confident, and intensely alert as she opens her beak to welcome a new day.

Thank you, Cynthia Round, executive/branding-expert/friend, for introducing us to Cortona in 1997, offering to be my book-marketing partner — and forty-five years of rare friendship.

Thank you to other dear friends: Susie Russell, for inviting me to "The Art of Writing" workshop where my project became serious, and to author/ organizer Lisa Clifford for affirming my work. (We never know when a small positive comment will launch a life-changing project.) Alessandra Wood, for making sure my Italian is not embarrassingly incorrect. To girlfriends who waded through drafts and gave their honest opinions, suggestions, and support: Vicki Chamberlain, Jean Cami, Sheryl Turping, Laura Truax, Enza Valente and, especially, Lyndall Passerini, for offering historical insights. To Aziz Cami for his expert cover design advice.

Loving thanks to our children: Ron Smith for visiting that first summer with his family, Lara Mondae for her excellent graphic-design counsel, and Amber Bozman, Angela Smith, and Becky Hassett for encouraging me to tell the truth even though Larry and I might not look so good. Also to Ron's wife, Blayn, for reviewing Ron's chapters on behalf of their family.

I'm ever so grateful to Terry Whalin who said "yes" when he read my sample and persistently urged me to sign the contract and finish the book, and to my excellent team at Morgan James Publishing. They are professional, wise, skilled, and responsive. Thank you for the pleasure of working with you all.

My gratitude, lastly, to the real-life characters in this book. I hope you enjoyed reliving the memories. Without you, my dream of writing a book would not have come true.

About the Author

Victoria Smith is a former marketing executive who gave up her comfortable Chicago life for the romantic adventure of moving to Tuscany with her husband, Larry.

Typically undaunted, Victoria was one of the first women marketing executives at Procter & Gamble in the early 1970s, a senior executive with the DDB international advertising agency during the 1980s, director of volunteers at a large church in the 1990s, and single mom with two daughters for most of her career. Yet her confidence and self-esteem were rocked by the unexpected challenges of living in a foreign culture and the stresses it placed on their marriage. Determined and learning along the way, she and Larry forged a new Italian life and fell more in love than ever.

Victoria's writing is honest and vulnerable, as if a story told to a trusted friend. She reflects on whatever comes along and draws lessons to apply to herself, making them available to and relevant for most anyone. She loves people, family, architecture, nature, art, music, great stories and good poetry — and adventure. A relentless optimist, she tries to face each situation with truth and grace. Her purpose, she believes, is to bring out the best in everything — from her children and grandchildren, husband, friends, and clients, to products (for advertising), homes and the land. Mothering, marketing, and nurturing bring her great joy.

Today, Victoria and Larry are fully engaged in their hilltown community. They zip up narrow steep roads, press their own olive oil, host friends and family, cook with natural, fresh ingredients, and are inspired every day by Italy's *dolce vita*.

They return to the USA several times each year to spend time with their five children and eight grandkids in their own settings, and to stay connected to friends — most of whom happily visit them at Lodolina. They continue their work with local and global organizations, especially ScholarLeaders International, where Larry serves as president.

Please stay in touch with Victoria and her more recent Tuscan adventures by reading www.fiveminutesintuscany.com, and follow her on Instagram at victoria_smith_writer. She is currently pondering her next project and news will be posted on those sites.

CPSIA information can be obtained
at www.ICGtesting.com
Printed in the USA
JSHW041143300321
13048JS00003B/150